Integrated Security Technologies and Solutions - Volume I

Cisco Security Solutions for Advanced Threat Protection with Next Generation Firewall, Intrusion Prevention, AMP, and Content Security

Aaron Woland, CCIE® No. 20113
Vivek Santuka, CCIE® No. 17621
Mason Harris, CCIE® No. 5916
Jamie Sanbower, CCIE® No. 13637

Cisco Press
800 East 96th Street
Indianapolis, Indiana 46240 USA

Integrated Security Technologies and Solutions - Volume I

Cisco Security Solutions for Advanced Threat Protection with Next Generation Firewall, Intrusion Prevention, AMP, and Content Security

Aaron Woland, Vivek Santuka, Mason Harris, Jamie Sanbower

Published by:
Cisco Press
800 East 96th Street
Indianapolis, IN 46240 USA

01 18

Library of Congress Control Number: 2018935701

ISBN-13: 978-1-58714-706-7
ISBN-10: 1-58714-706-8

Warning and Disclaimer

This book is designed to provide information about the Next-Generation Firewall (NGFW), Next-Generation Intrusion Prevention System (NGIPS), and Advanced Malware Protection (AMP) technologies using the Cisco Firepower System. Every effort has been made to make this book as complete and as accurate as possible, but no warranty or fitness is implied.

The information is provided on an "as is" basis. The authors, Cisco Press, and Cisco Systems, Inc. shall have neither liability nor responsibility to any person or entity with respect to any loss or damages arising from the information contained in this book or from the use of the discs or programs that may accompany it.

The opinions expressed in this book belong to the author and are not necessarily those of Cisco Systems, Inc.

Trademark Acknowledgments

All terms mentioned in this book that are known to be trademarks or service marks have been appropriately capitalized. Cisco Press or Cisco Systems, Inc., cannot attest to the accuracy of this information. Use of a term in this book should not be regarded as affecting the validity of any trademark or service mark.

Special Sales

For information about buying this title in bulk quantities, or for special sales opportunities (which may include electronic versions; custom cover designs; and content particular to your business, training goals, marketing focus, or branding interests), please contact our corporate sales department at corpsales@pearsoned.com or (800) 382-3419.

For government sales inquiries, please contact governmentsales@pearsoned.com.

For questions about sales outside the U.S., please contact intlcs@pearson.com.

Feedback Information

At Cisco Press, our goal is to create in-depth technical books of the highest quality and value. Each book is crafted with care and precision, undergoing rigorous development that involves the unique expertise of members from the professional technical community.

Readers' feedback is a natural continuation of this process. If you have any comments regarding how we could improve the quality of this book, or otherwise alter it to better suit your needs, you can contact us through email at feedback@ciscopress.com. Please make sure to include the book title and ISBN in your message.

We greatly appreciate your assistance.

Editor-in-Chief: Mark Taub

Product Line Manager: Brett Bartow

Alliances Manager, Cisco Press: Arezou Gol

Executive Editor: Mary Beth Ray

Managing Editor: Sandra Schroeder

Development Editor: Ellie C. Bru

Project Editor: Mandie Frank

Copy Editor: Kitty Wilson

Technical Editor: Chad Mitchell

Editorial Assistant: Vanessa Evans

Designer: Chuti Prasertsith

Composition: codemantra

Indexer: Lisa Stumpf

Proofreader: Larry Sulky

Americas Headquarters
Cisco Systems, Inc.
San Jose, CA

Asia Pacific Headquarters
Cisco Systems (USA) Pte. Ltd.
Singapore

Europe Headquarters
Cisco Systems International BV Amsterdam,
The Netherlands

Cisco has more than 200 offices worldwide. Addresses, phone numbers, and fax numbers are listed on the Cisco Website at **www.cisco.com/go/offices.**

About the Authors

Aaron Woland, CCIE No. 20113, is a principal engineer in Cisco's Advanced Threat Security group and works with Cisco's largest customers all over the world. His primary job responsibilities include security design, solution enhancements, standards development, advanced threat solution design, endpoint security, and futures.

Aaron joined Cisco in 2005 and is currently a member of numerous security advisory boards and standards body working groups. Prior to joining Cisco, Aaron spent 12 years as a consultant and technical trainer.

Aaron is the author of both editions of *Cisco ISE for BYOD and Secure Unified Access, Cisco Next-Generation Security Solutions: All-in-one Cisco ASA FirePOWER Services, NGIPS, and AMP; CCNP Security SISAS 300-208 Official Cert Guide, CCNA Security 210-260 Complete Video Course,* and many published white papers and design guides.

Aaron is one of only five inaugural members of the Hall of Fame Elite for Distinguished Speakers at Cisco Live, and he is a security columnist for *Network World*, where he blogs on all things related to security. His many other certifications include GHIC, GCFE, GSEC, CEH, MCSE, VCP, CCSP, CCNP, and CCDP.

You can follow Aaron on Twitter: @aaronwoland.

Vivek Santuka, CCIE No. 17621 is a consulting systems engineer at Cisco and is a security consultant to some of Cisco's largest customers. He has over 13 years of experience in security, focusing on identity management and access control. Vivek is a member of multiple technical advisory groups.

Vivek holds two CCIE certifications: Security and Routing and Switching. In addition, he holds RHCE and CISSP certifications.

Vivek is author of the Cisco Press book *AAA Identity Management Security*.

You can follow Vivek on Twitter: @vsantuka.

Mason Harris, CCIE No. 5916, is a solutions architect for Cisco, focusing on cloud architectures with Cisco's largest global customers. He has more than 24 years of experience in information technology and is one the few individuals in the world who has attained five CCIE certifications. Prior to joining Cisco, he was the chief architect at cloud security startup vArmour Networks. Outside work, Mason can be found backpacking on long trails or at home with his family. A lifelong UNC Tarheels fan, he holds an undergraduate degree from UNC–Chapel Hill and a master's degree from NC State University, with a minor in Arabic.

Jamie Sanbower, CCIE No. 13637 (Routing and Switching, Security, and Wireless), is a technical solutions architect focusing on security for the Global Security Architecture Team.

Jamie has been with Cisco since 2010 and is currently a technical leader and member of numerous technical advisory groups. With over 15 years of technical experience in networking and security, Jamie has developed, designed, implemented, and operated enterprise network and security solutions for a wide variety of large clients.

Prior to joining Cisco, Jamie was the director of the cybersecurity practice at Force 3. His other certifications include CISSP, CEH, and MCSE.

About the Technical Reviewer

Chad Mitchell, CCIE No. 44090, is a Technical Solutions Architect at Cisco Systems supporting the Department of Defense and supporting agencies. In his daily role, he supports the sales teams as a technical resource for all Cisco Security products and serves as the Identity Services Engine subject matter expert for the Cisco U.S. Public Sector team. Chad has been with Cisco since 2013, supporting the DoD and other customers, as well is a contributing member to the Policy & Access Technical Advisors Group. Prior to joining Cisco, Chad spent 7 years as a deployment engineer and systems administrator implementing Cisco Security products for customers. Although his primary area of expertise is enterprise network access control with Identity Services Engine, he is well versed on all Cisco security solutions, such as ASA firewalls, Firepower NGFW/IPS/IDS, and Stealthwatch to name a few. He also has first-hand experience deploying them in customer production environments. His other certifications include: CCDA, CCNP, Network+, Security+, and many other industry certifications.

Dedications

First and foremost, this book is dedicated to my amazing best friend, fellow adventurer, and wife, Suzanne. This book would surely not exist without your continued support, encouragement, and patience, as well as the sheer number of nights you took care of absolutely everything else so I could write. Thank you for putting up with all the long nights and weekends I had to be writing and for always believing in me and supporting me. You are beyond amazing.

To Mom and Pop. You have always believed in me and supported me in absolutely everything I've ever pursued, showed pride in my accomplishments (no matter how small), encouraged me to never stop learning, and ingrained in me the value of hard work and striving for a career in a field that I love. I hope I can continue to fill your lives with pride and happiness, and if I succeed, it will still only be a fraction of what you deserve.

To my four incredible daughters, Eden, Nyah, Netanya, and Cassandra: You girls are my inspiration, pride, and joy, and you continue to make me want to be a better man. Eden, when I look at you and your accomplishments over your 19 years of life, I swell with pride. You are so intelligent, kind, and hard working. You've been rocking your first year of college, and you will make a brilliant engineer one day—or if you change your mind, I know you will be brilliant in whatever career you find yourself pursuing. (Perhaps I can convince you to follow in my footsteps.) Nyah, you are my morning star, my princess. You have the biggest heart, the kindest soul, and a brilliant mind. You excel at everything you put your mind to, and I look forward to watching you grow and using that power to change the world. Maybe you will follow in my footsteps. I can't wait to see it for myself. Natty and Cassie: You are only 16 months old as I write this, yet you have already filled all of our lives with so much joy that I cannot describe it! It is bewildering and addicting to watch you every day and see your growth, wondering what you will be like as you grow up in this limitless world.

To my brother, Dr. Bradley Woland: Thank you for being so ambitious, so driven. It forced my competitive nature to always want more. As I rambled on in the 12-minute wedding speech, you not only succeed at everything you try, you crush it! If you were a bum, I would never have pushed myself to the levels that I have. To his beautiful and brilliant wife, Claire: I am so happy that you are a member of my family now; your kindness, intelligence, and wit certainly keep my brother in check and keep us all smiling.

To my sister, Anna: If I hadn't always had to compete with you for our parents' attention and to keep my things during our "garage sales," I would probably have grown up very naive and vulnerable. You drove me to think outside the box and find new ways to accomplish the things I wanted to do. Seeing you succeed in life and in school truly had a profound effect on my life. Thank you for marrying Eddie, my brilliant brother-in-law. Eddie convinced me that I could actually have a career in this technology stuff, and without his influence, I would probably be in law enforcement or under the hood of car. I'll be seeing you on Fraser's Ridge!

To my Grandparents, Jack, Lola, Herb, and Ida: You have taught me what it means to be alive and the true definitions of courage, survival, perseverance, hard work, and never giving up.

—Aaron

To my wife and son, thank you for your unconditional love and support. All the missed gaming sessions and family time couldn't have been easy, and I appreciate you waiting for me to finish this book. It means a lot to me.

—Vivek

I would like to dedicate this book to my wife and kids. Thank you for your patience and support; it is much appreciated. And to my super wife, thanks for covering all the kid activities, meals, school pickups, homework, etc. so that I had time to finish this project. As with everything else, I couldn't do it without you!

—Mason

This book is dedicated to my better half, my soulmate, my Christianna. From CCIEs to babies, we have accomplished so much together, blowing away the status quo. You always told me I could and should write a book, and I know without your support this book would not exist. The fact of the matter is you were as much a part of the writing process as I was. Thank you for putting up with all the late nights and weekends that I was writing and you didn't complain once (except for me being ADD about writing). Your companionship and love motivate me more than you will ever know.

To my amazing kids, Cayden and Lilianna, you are my inspiration and make me want to be a better version of myself. I know you both will amaze the world the way you amaze me each and every day! You make me smile and feel loved in ways that are indescribable.

To my Mom and Dad for supporting my interests in technology from the start and certifications during grade school.

—Jamie

Acknowledgments

There are so many to acknowledge. This feels like a speech at the Academy Awards, and I'm afraid I will leave out too many people.

Vivek Santuka, for not letting me give up and get out of writing this book and for keeping us all on time and on track.

Jamie Sanbower and Mason Harris for agreeing to coauthor this beast of a book with us. You guys are amazing!

James Weathersby, for your continued support, encouragement, and guidance. Most importantly, for believing in me even though I can be difficult at times. I could not have done any of it without you.

Christopher Heffner, security architect at Cisco and my "brother from another mother," for convincing me to step up and take a swing at being an author and for twisting my arm to put "pen to paper" again.

I am honored to work with so many brilliant and talented people every day. Among those: Adam O'Donnell, Al Huger, Moses Hernandez, Steven Chimes, Andrew Benhase, Jeff Fanelli, Tim Snow, Andrew Ossipov, Mike Storm, Jason Frazier, Mo Sachedina, Eric Howard, Evgeny Mirolyubov, Matt Robertson, Brian McMahon, Ben Greenbaum, Dean De Beer, Paul Carco, Karel Simek, Naasief Edross, Eric Hulse, and Craig Williams. You guys truly amaze me—seriously.

Darrin Miller, Nancy Cam-Winget, and Jamey Heary, distinguished engineers who set the bar so incredibly high. You are truly inspirational people to look up to and aspire to be like, and I appreciate all the guidance you have given me.

Last, but not least: to all those at Pearson, especially Mary Beth Ray, Eleanor Bru, and Mandie Frank. Thank you and your team of editors for making us look so good. Apparently, it takes an army of folks to do so. I'm sorry for all the times you had to correct our English, grammar, and CapItaLizaTioN.

—Aaron

Thank you to my wonderful coauthors, Aaron, Jamie, and Mason, and our technical editor, Chad. Your efforts through professional and personal challenges are much appreciated.

To the wonderful people at Pearson—Mary Beth Ray, Eleanor Bru, Mandie Frank, and everyone else involved with this book—thank you for your tremendous work. Every time I opened an edited chapter, I couldn't help but be astonished at the attention to detail that you put into this.

Steven Bardsley and Gary McNiel, thank you for believing in me and for all the support and guidance.

Nirav Sheth, my first manager at Cisco, thank you for encouraging me to submit my first book proposal all those years ago. My professional achievements are rooted in your mentoring.

Finally, thank you to all the wonderful people I work with and learn from. There are too many to name, but you help me grow every day.

—Vivek

I am grateful to all the great teachers I've encountered over the years. Thank you for your efforts as I now know learning is a journey and not a destination. I'd also like to give a shout-out to Michael Purcell, Chad Sullivan, and Tyler Pomerhn for pushing me to be a better CCIE and Dan Zatyko for his friendship, mentorship, and leadership. Those were the good old days!

I would also like to acknowledge Eleanor Bru and the fine folks at Pearson Education and Cisco Press. You have world-class patience, and for that I am grateful.

—Mason

First and foremost, for the coauthors, Aaron, Vivek, and Mason, for creating a behemoth of a security book together.

For Chad Mitchell, a great friend and tech editor. Thanks for challenging me over the years.

To Jamey Heary for encouraging me to write this book and the entire Global Security Architecture Team at Cisco, including Jeff Fanelli, Gary Halleen, Will Young, Mike Geller, Luc Billot, and last but not least, the man who keeps the ADD security experts in line, Randy Rivera. You all are inspiring, and together we cannot be beat. Seriously the best team at Cisco.

To Alex Golovin, my first mentor, who taught me what RTFM meant and how to keep learning and growing.

Finally, to all those at Cisco Press, especially Mary Beth Ray, Eleanor Bru, and Mandie Frank. Thank you and your team of editors for producing a quality product and making the authors look good. *Volume II* awaits.

—Jamie

Contents at a Glance

Contents

Icons Used in This Book

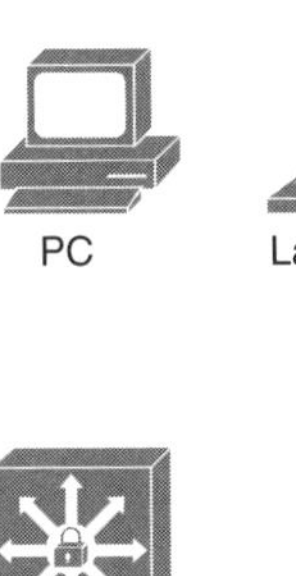

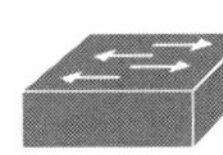

Command Syntax Conventions

The conventions used to present command syntax in this book are the same conventions used in the IOS Command Reference. The Command Reference describes these conventions as follows:

- **Boldface** indicates commands and keywords that are entered literally as shown. In actual configuration examples and output (not general command syntax), boldface indicates commands that are manually input by the user (such as a **show** command).
- *Italic* indicates arguments for which you supply actual values.
- Vertical bars (|) separate alternative, mutually exclusive elements.
- Square brackets ([ ]) indicate an optional element.
- Braces ({ }) indicate a required choice.
- Braces within brackets ([{ }]) indicate a required choice within an optional element.

Reader Services

Register your copy at www.ciscopress.com/title/9781587147067 for convenient access to downloads, updates, and corrections as they become available. To start the registration process, go to www.ciscopress.com/register and log in or create an account*. Enter the product ISBN 9781587147067 and click Submit. Once the process is complete, you will find any available bonus content under Registered Products.

*Be sure to check the box that you would like to hear from us to receive exclusive discounts on future editions of this product.

Introduction

This book is the first volume of the *Integrated Security Technologies and Solutions* set in the Cisco CCIE Professional Development Series from Cisco Press. It offers expert-level instruction in security design, deployment, integration, and support methodologies to help security professionals manage complex solutions and prepare for the CCIE Security exams.

This book is an expert-level guide for Cisco security products and solutions, with a strong focus on inter-product integration. Its aim is to help security professionals in their day-to-day jobs as well as in preparing for CCIE written and lab exams.

This volume focuses on the Security Policies and Standards, Infrastructure Security, Perimeter Security (Next-Generation Firewall, Next-Generation Intrusion Prevention Systems, Adaptive Security Appliance [ASA]), Advanced Threat Protection, and Content Security sections of the CCIE v5 blueprint.

Who Should Read This Book?

This book discusses expert-level topics on Cisco security products and solutions, with a focus on integration between these products. In particular, this volume covers NGFW, NGIPS, ASA, AMP, ESA, and WSA products. The book has been designed with the CCIE Security v5 blueprint as a reference, making it a must-have for CCIE Security candidates.

This book presents real-world deployment scenarios, configuration examples, and troubleshooting steps, so it is invaluable to any network engineer, system administrator, security engineer, or security analyst who wants to configure or manage Cisco security products and solutions.

This book is very important for channel partners and managed security service providers who want to provide technical support to their own customers.

This book is also very useful for network administrators in classified environments, such as the U.S. government, who are not allowed to share their sensitive data and want to design, configure, and troubleshoot on their own.

How This Book Is Organized

This book consists of 10 chapters divided into 3 parts.

Part I, "Hi There! This Is Network Security"

Chapter 1, "Let's Talk About Network Security"

The book begins with a discussion of the need for security and common security threats. This chapter discusses various common security standards and creating security policies for an organization. It also discusses the Cisco SAFE architecture for implementation of security policy and the benefits of an integrated security architecture.

Chapter 2, "Infrastructure Security and Segmentation"

This chapter discusses the security threats that exist in common network infrastructure and methods to mitigate them. It discusses and demonstrates recommended methods to protect the three planes of a network device, including hardening of Cisco routers and switches.

Chapter 3, "Wireless Security"

This chapter discusses security of Cisco wireless infrastructure. It describes various security risks and mitigation techniques for a wireless network. It also demonstrates configuration required for implementing risk mitigation techniques on Cisco wireless LAN controllers and access points.

Part II, "Deny IP any any"

Chapter 4, "Firewalling with the ASA"

This chapter discusses the Cisco Adaptive Security Appliance (ASA) and its use in securing the perimeter of a network. It describes and demonstrates the configuration required to implement various security mechanisms on the ASA.

Chapter 5, "Next-Gen Firewalls"

This chapter describes various aspects of the Cisco next-generation firewall Firepower Threat Defense (FTD) and the Firepower Management Center (FMC). It describes and demonstrates the configuration required to implement various security mechanisms on FTD and in the FMC.

Chapter 6, "Next-Gen Intrusion Detection and Prevention"

This chapter describes the various aspects of the Cisco next-gen IPS with FTD and FMC. It discusses IPS deployment options with FTD, signature creation, and tuning, as well as analysis and correlation of events on FMC.

Chapter 7, "IOS Firewall and Security Features"

This chapter discusses the firewall features of Cisco IOS, including Zone Based Firewall (ZBF) and address translation. It also demonstrates the configuration and verification required with these features.

Part III, "<HTML> EHLO. You have threat in content </HTML>"

Chapter 8, "Content Security and Advanced Threat Protection"

This chapter discusses the Cisco Web Security Appliance, its deployment, and key configuration options. It also discusses the Cisco Email Security Appliance and its key configuration options.

Chapter 9, "Umbrella and the Secure Internet Gateway"

This chapter discusses DNS security fundamentals, Cisco Umbrella, Cisco Security Internet Gateway, and Cisco Security Connector. It describes the security architecture of Umbrella and the configuration required to use it.

Chapter 10, "Protecting Against Advanced Malware"

This chapter discusses the Cisco Advanced Malware Protection (AMP) product family, various places and methods of deployment, and the detection mechanisms used by AMP. It also discusses Cisco Threat Grid and its integration with AMP.

Part I

Hi There! This is Network Security

Chapter 1

Let's Talk About Network Security

LO. These were the first two—and only—characters transferred between University of California, Los Angeles (UCLA) and Stanford Research Institute (SRI) when the very first ARPANET link was established between these two locations in 1969. It was an attempt to send the LOGIN command, but the system crashed. Who would have guessed that this was the birth of one of the most important tools of modern times: the Internet? Nevertheless, ARPANET continued to evolve and grow into an international network. By early 1990, especially with the invention of the World Wide Web (WWW) by Tim Berners-Lee, the Internet became an integral part of our lives. Initially ARPANET and then the Internet were designed to be government and government-body networks. The focus of early development was primarily inter-connectivity and reliability. Security was not top-of-mind for what was to be a closed network. Hence, most of the protocols the Internet is made up of do not have security built in.

As the Internet and networking in general grew in prominence, so did the opportunities for malicious actors to profit from them. Security was layered on to existing protocols by means of other protocols or security products. Adding security to these protocols would change them significantly. In addition, the cost and time needed to implement such new protocols were problematic. You don't have to look further than IPv6 to understand how difficult it is to switch to newer protocols. Even though we have run out of assignable public IPv4 addresses, the shift to IPv6 is far from over. So, we are left with adding layers of security to our networks, and malicious actors are usually a few steps ahead of us.

With the advent of the Internet of Things (IoT), cloud computing, and bring-your-own-device (BYOD) initiatives, among other advances, our networks have changed drastically in recent times. IoT and BYOD have shifted the landscape from known and controlled devices connecting to networks to unknown and uncontrolled devices. With more applications moving to the cloud, a large percentage of traffic now bypasses the corporate intranet and goes through the Internet. As the landscape changes, the threats evolve. In 2016–2017, for example, we saw a big increase in IoT device availability and usage, but we also realized that most of these devices do not have any security built into them. It didn't take long for someone to capitalize on that and create a botnet out of IoT devices. For example, the Mirai malware, which attacks IoT devices, was responsible for the biggest distributed denial-of-service (DDoS) attack yet known; the victim received close to 1 TB of traffic per second.

Cisco's chairman, John Chambers, famously said, "There are only two types of companies: those that have been hacked, and those who don't know they have been hacked." The security problems and targets are not difficult to find either. Breaking into a network is seriously lucrative. In fact, it is so profitable that Cisco's security research group, Talos, found that there is a 9-to-5 attack pattern in most cases. That is, malicious actors work the same hours as the good guys! To understand how high the stakes are for both sides, consider these two examples:

- The U.S. FBI estimates the losses attributable to the GameOver Zeus malware to be at least $100 million. More than 1 million devices were infected worldwide, and it took years and resources from 10 countries to eventually take it down.
- The CryptoLocker ransomware is estimated to have netted $27 million in ransom within two months of its release.

With critical systems such as banking, healthcare, and utilities becoming more connected, our security challenges have increased over the years. On the other hand, the malicious actors have evolved from early-day hackers whose intentions were mostly curiosity and bravado to modern-day hackers whose intentions range from financial gain to espionage and beyond. To effectively secure against these threats, it is important to understand not only what we are securing and how we are securing it but also who we are securing against.

Know Thy Enemy

To quote one of my favorite authors, Sun Tzu, "Know thy self, know thy enemy. A thousand battles, a thousand victories." This advice applies well to network security. Understanding the threat to your network is a very big part of securing it. Hence, it is important to understand who you are securing your network against. Most malicious actors who will target your network fall into one of these categories:

- **Black-hat hacker:** The term *hacker* originally meant someone who exploited the weakness of systems in the spirit of exploration and curiosity. The media now uses it as a catch-all term to describe all malicious cyber actors. They are in fact referring to *black-hat hackers*, also known as *crackers*. These are people or groups that exploit the weaknesses of a system for profit. They commonly use known exploits, social engineering attacks such as phishing, and malware such as rootkits and Trojans to get inside a network.
- **Script kiddies:** This is a derogatory term used to describe black-hat hackers who use easily available scripts and programs in their attacks. Simple denial-of-service (DoS) attacks, web server hacking using XSS, and SQL injections are favorites of script kiddies.

- **Organized criminal outfits:** Criminal organizations have recently realized the revenue potential of cyber attacks. These actors are very well organized, with a strong arsenal of attacks as well as physical presence for money laundering around the world. The most infamous example is the Business Club, which was responsible for the GameOver Zeus malware.
- **Nation-state actors:** Possibly the most sophisticated group on this list, nation-state actors are sponsored by governments. Their activities include espionage, attacks on infrastructure, and surveillance. These activities are done in the interest of the nation-state sponsoring them. Their arsenal includes undisclosed zero-days, highly sophisticated malware, and state-of-the-art social engineering tools. Stuxnet, an early example of malware targeting a physical infrastructure, is alleged to be the product of nation-state actors.
- **Hacktivists:** Internet activists, or *hacktivists*, are groups of hackers who engage in activities to promote a political agenda. Their activities are designed to gather media attention, and they are quick to claim credit for their attacks. Defacing websites, executing DDoS attacks, and leaking documents or database contents are the most common activities for this group. Anonymous and LulzSec have been two of the most notable hacktivist groups in recent times.
- **Cyber terrorists:** The primary focus of these actors is to create fear through their activities. They are usually motivated by religious or political beliefs and are associated with known terrorist outfits. They attack infrastructure, steal data such as identities of government employees, and deface websites with propaganda. Their skill levels can range from script kiddies to highly skilled black-hat hackers, but they are rarely as sophisticated as nation-state actors.
- **Insider threats:** *Insider threats* are attackers who are part of your organization. Common sources of insider threats are disgruntled employees looking to exact revenge for perceived wrongdoing. These actors may not be as skilled at attacking a network as the other groups discussed here, but because they exploit the trust and access they already have, their actions are far more damaging. For example, a network admin can easily re-configure routers and switches on his or her last day at work to bring down the whole network. Similarly, a database admin can wipe whole databases and their backups and cause massive losses for an organization. These threats are often more possible and damaging than any that originate from outside the organization.

This list of potential threats is not exhaustive, but it provides you with a good understanding of what you face. It is important to recognize that these actors and their methods evolve continuously and at a fast pace—and so should your skills and your defenses against them. Defense is what the entirety of this series focuses on, but again, it is important to understand what you are protecting. Without the combined knowledge of the adversary and the self, you will not be able to choose the best defense.

Know Thy Self

What defines a threat? Is a robber a threat to an empty bank? A robber is not a threat in this case because there is nothing to steal. It is the presence of something valuable that makes a threat credible. The value and nature of a valuable define the risk posed by a threat, the nature of the threat, and the cost of defense. Similarly, you cannot define a threat to your network until you define the assets that you have to protect, the risks to those assets, and the costs of protecting or not protecting them. This analysis of an organization's assets and risks is done when creating a security policy. Before we look at security policies, we need to define the key components of network security:

- **Threat:** A *threat* is a person or tool that can cause harm to an asset. The threat actors discussed in the preceding section or any tools such as viruses, worms, and other malware they use are collectively called a threat.
- **Vulnerability:** A weakness or flaw in an asset or environment that a threat can exploit is called a *vulnerability*. For example, failing to password-protect your computer creates a vulnerability that may allow a threat to access documents stored on it.
- **Risk:** The potential loss or damage that can result from a threat due to a vulnerability is called the *risk*. For example, if a threat shuts down your website, then the risk is the loss of revenue during and after the event.
- **Mitigation:** The measures taken to reduce a risk to an asset is called *mitigation*. All mitigation actions reduce risk and change the threat. For example, using a password to protect access to your computer mitigates the risk of unauthorized access by a threat.

The key take-away here is that a risk can never be eliminated. Mitigation will always change the vulnerability, risk, and threat to an asset. For example, a computer protected by password is vulnerable to brute-force password cracking. This can be mitigated by a stronger password, but the computer will be vulnerable to unauthorized access through the security flaws in the operating system—and so on. Generally, a risk is mitigated only to the point where the cost of mitigation does not outweigh the risk itself. At that point, a risk is accepted instead of being mitigated.

Security Policy

As organizations get more reliant on technology and connectivity, their vulnerabilities and risks increase. In addition, changes in technology bring changes in risks, too. It is difficult for an organization to keep track of its assets and risks. Organizations also have to comply with various industry regulations and legislations, failing which they can be subject to severe penalties. This is where a security policy can help. A *security policy* is a high-level document that defines the organizational security requirements, principles, and practices created by executive-level management. The policy practically defines what security means for the organization. It contains sets of rules governing the security of assets, information, and people. It is important to remember that a security policy is very high level and does not contain implementation specifics. For example, a security policy may state that encryption is required for certain information but not that it requires 3DES for encryption. This level of detail allows flexibility in adopting new technology without requiring frequent changes to the security policy. The implementation details of a security policy are left to lower-level documents, such as procedures and guidelines.

Note While a security policy is much wider in scope, the discussion in this chapter is limited to network security.

While creating a security policy is an involved and time-consuming process, it can generally be broken down into five steps:

Step 1. Identify all assets that need to be protected.

Step 2. Identify risks and threats associated with each asset.

Step 3. Identify a risk mitigation strategy for each asset.

Step 4. Document and communicate findings to all stakeholders.

Step 5. Monitor and review continuously.

Depending on the size of the organization, the security policy can be one large document that covers all aspects, or it may be several individually focused policies. Because you are preparing for a Cisco exam, it is important to understand various areas of network security that should be part of a security policy, as defined by Cisco. With the definition of each policy, this chapter maps out Cisco products that help in implementing that policy to lay the groundwork for the later chapters. Remember that not every organization will have a need for all of these policies, and a security policy will not recommend a specific product because it is a high-level document. According to Cisco, the following areas of network security should be part of a security policy:

- **Network access control (NAC):** A NAC policy defines how to control access to your network such that only the right person or device can get the right access at the right time. It also defines compliance requirements that devices should meet before access is granted. Identity Services Engine (ISE) is a Cisco product that can be used to implement this policy.
- **Antimalware:** Malware is the primary threat vector in any network, so a policy to prevent, detect, and remediate malware is one of the most important security policies that an organization should have. Cisco's Advanced Malware Protection (AMP) suite of products can be used to implement this policy.
- **Application security:** Organizations require multiple applications to run their business. These applications may contain vulnerabilities that can be exploited. An application security policy defines the security requirements of these applications.
- **Behavioral analytics:** This policy defines baselining and analytic requirements. Every network has baseline traffic patterns and user behavior. Malicious behavior can be identified by investigating deviations from the established baseline for any organization or network segment. The Stealthwatch product family from Cisco helps implement this policy.

- **Data loss prevention:** Some information in any organization is meant for internal use only. Such data being sent outside the organization can cause irreparable harm. A data loss prevention policy defines the requirements around preventing loss of such data. Various Cisco security products, such as Web Security Appliance (WSA), Email Security Appliance (ESA), Firepower Next-Generation Firewall (NGFW), and Cloudlock can be used to implement this policy.
- **Email security:** Email is the primary method of communication in and out of organizations. Email is also a primary threat vector for security breaches because it can facilitate phishing attacks as well as delivery of malware to the network. An email security policy defines acceptable use and security of email systems. Cisco ESA and Cloud Email Security combined with AMP can help implement this security policy.
- **Perimeter security:** To meet operational requirements, the trusted internal network of an organization has to interface with untrusted networks such as the Internet or networks belonging to partners and vendors. A perimeter security policy defines how the perimeter of the trusted network is protected and how access is granted across to it. The Cisco Adaptive Security Appliance (ASA) and Firepower NFGW product families can be used to implement this policy.
- **Intrusion prevention:** *Intrusion* refers to an active attempt to exploit a vulnerability or violate a policy in a network. An intrusion prevention policy defines the intrusion detection, prevention, and reporting requirements of the organization. Cisco Firepower Next-Generation IPS (NGIPS) and Firepower Next-Generation Firewall (NGFW) product families can help implement an intrusion prevention policy.
- **Mobile device security:** Mobile devices, with their increasing presence and corporate applications support, introduce credible threats in a network. A mobile device security policy defines the security posture and access control requirements for corporate and employee-owned mobile devices in the network. Cisco ISE and Meraki mobile device management product lines can help implement this policy.
- **Network segmentation:** Various segments on a network can require different security and access policies, generally based on the sensitivity of the systems and data residing in each segment. A network segmentation policy defines the requirements around segmenting different parts of the network. Cisco ISE, ASA, and Firepower NGFW, along with TrustSec, can be used to implement a network segmentation policy.
- **Security information and event management (SIEM):** Logs, events, and alarms from various security solutions in a network provide useful information. Analyzing them can help validate existing prevention solutions as well provide feedback for improvement. Events reported by security solutions should be investigated to ensure that threats have been eliminated and to assess any loss. A SIEM policy defines the requirement around collection, storage, correlation, and analysis of security information as well as security event management. Cisco security products integrate with various SIEM products to help implement this policy.

- **Remote access:** Employees, vendors, or partners often require access to applications from outside the corporate network. Branch or remote locations also need access to the corporate network or data center in order to conduct business. Using a virtual private network (VPN) is one way to provide such access. This policy defines the requirements around providing secure remote access to employees, vendors, partners, and remote locations. Cisco routers, Firepower NGFW, and ASA, along with the AnyConnect VPN client, can be used to implement this policy.

- **Web security:** Web traffic accounts for the majority of traffic in the network and is also the second biggest threat vector. A web security policy defines the requirements around acceptable web use, security of web traffic, and prevention against web-based threats. Cisco WSA, Cisco Secure Internet Gateway (SIG) (formerly known as Cloud Web Security [CWS]), and Cisco Umbrella (formerly known as OpenDNS) can be used to implement a web security policy.

- **Wireless security:** Switch ports providing access to a wired network are often protected by the physical security policies and measures employed by an organization. Because unauthorized persons will be prevented from entering a building, they will not be able to connect to the switch ports inside. Wireless network access, on the other hand, can cross physical security boundaries and hence presents a high risk. A wireless security policy defines the requirements around security and access control of the wireless network, including requirements related to wireless network access by employee-owned devices and guests. Cisco ISE can be used to implement a wireless security policy.

As you can see, defining assets, risks, and various requirements around security can be a challenging task. Even when broken down into simple steps and smaller pieces, creating a security policy is difficult. It is easier to know thy enemy than to know thy self! This is where security standards and frameworks come to the rescue.

Security Standards and Frameworks

Various government and private entities have realized that while it is increasingly important to have a security policy, creating an effective and comprehensive one is hard. Hence, they have published many standards and frameworks to help with creating and implementing security policies. You can use one or more of these frameworks as the basis of your own policy and customize as required. While there are many organizations around the world that publish and maintain such standards and frameworks, these are the two most important ones:

- **International Organization for Standardization (ISO):** ISO is an independent nongovernmental organization composed of representatives from 162 national standards organizations. ISO publishes standards that help establish quality requirements across products and services, ranging from manufacturing and technology to agriculture and healthcare. By following these standards and getting certified, organizations prove to their customers that their products, procedures, or services meet internationally accepted standards. Certification is optional. The standards can be used to simply improve quality within an organization without going through the certification process.

- **National Institute of Standards and Technology (NIST):** NIST is a measurement standards laboratory. Even though it is part of the U.S. Department of Commerce, it is a non-regulatory organization. It provides measurements and standards for technology, including cybersecurity. Much as with ISO, standards from NIST can be used to certify products and services, or they can be used simply to improve quality.

These two organizations and various others have published many security standards and frameworks. While any of them can be used to create a security policy, the two most common ones in use today—and the ones most relevant to the exam—are ISO/IEC 27001/27002 and NIST Cyber Security Framework (CSF).

ISO/IEC 27001 and 27002

ISO and the International Electrotechnical Commission (IEC) jointly publish the ISO/IEC 27000 series standards, which are collectively known as the "Information Security Management Systems (ISMS) Family of Standards." This series contains 45 individual standards related to information security. Out of these 45, 27001 and 27002 are most relevant for our discussion:

- **ISO/IEC 27001, "Information Security Management Systems—Requirements":** This standard provides the specifications for an information security management system and can be used as the framework for an organization's security policy. If an organization implements the standard and is compliant with all requirements, it can apply to be audited and certified. Certification is not mandatory, and the standard can also be used only as a reference framework for a security policy.
- **ISO/IEC 27002, "Code of Practice for Information Security Controls":** This standard outlines the best practices for implementation of a very comprehensive list of controls in information security. It is used to implement the controls identified in a security policy. The standard is based on the principles of confidentiality, integrity, and availability (CIA), which are considered cornerstones of security:
  - *Confidentiality* defines the capability to ensure that information in all its states is accessible only by authorized users. This is the most important and obvious aspect of a security system and also what most attackers aim to breach. Unauthorized access to information is the single biggest intent behind most attacks. Use of encryption and authentication are two primary ways to ensure confidentiality. For example, if data is not encrypted in transit, it can be captured on the wire using man-in-the-middle (MITM) attacks, resulting in loss of confidentiality.
  - *Integrity* defines the need to prevent unauthorized modification of information and systems in any state. Breached integrity is as bad as breached confidentiality. Encryption and authentication are also used to ensure integrity. Continuing the

previous example, during a successful MITM attack, the attacker can not only breach confidentiality but also choose to modify information in transit—which results in loss of integrity as well.

- *Availability* defines the need to prevent loss of access to information or to a system. Information should always be readily available to authorized users. DoS or the larger-scale DDoS attacks are common methods that attackers use to disrupt availability.

The latest revision of the ISO/IEC 27002 standard, published in 2013, is divided into 19 sections. The first 5 are introductory:

0. Introduction
1. Scope
2. Normative references
3. Terms and definitions
4. Structure of This Standard

The remaining 14 sections describe different security control types and their objectives:

5. Information Security Policies
6. Organization of Information Security
7. Human Resource Security
8. Asset Management
9. Access Control
10. Cryptography
11. Physical and Environmental Security
12. Operations Security
13. Communications Security
14. System Acquisition, Development and Maintenance
15. Supplier Relationships
16. Information Security Incident Management
17. Information Security Aspects of Business Continuity Management
18. Compliance

Going into detail about the sections of ISO/IEC 27002:2013 is beyond the scope of this book, as well as the CCIE exam, but it is important to map out what Cisco products and technologies can be used to implement controls described in some of the relevant sections. Table 1-1 lists relevant sections and Cisco products that can be used to implement controls specified in those sections. It is important to remember that the standard deals with a complete information security system and its management, so network security is only a part of it.

Table 1-1 *ISO/IEC 27002:2013 and Cisco Security Products*

Section	Cisco Product	Details
8. Asset Management	ISE	Section 8.1.1 lists the controls for identification of assets. The profiling feature of ISE can be used to profile assets on the network.
9. Access Control	ISE	Section 9.1.2 lists controls for access to networks and network services. ISE helps authenticate and authorize users requesting access to the network or network devices.
10. Cryptography	ASA, NGFW, routers	Section 10 lists the controls for cryptography. Various Cisco products, such as ASA, NGFW, and routers, provide encryption using different types of VPN.
12. Operations Security	AMP, ISE, Umbrella, NGFW, ESA, WSA	Section 12.2 lists the controls for protection against malware. For example, AMP provides protection against malware, and it can be integrated with NGFW, WSA, and ESA, or can be used as a standalone device in the network and on endpoints. Umbrella also prevents malware execution by preventing communication with the command and control infrastructure. Section 12.6 calls for vulnerability management. Posture validation with Cisco ISE can be used to ensure that operating systems and antimalware are updated with the latest patches and definitions.
13. Communications Security	ISE, NGFW, ASA	Section 13.1 lists controls for network security management and segregation or segmentation in particular. ISE can be used to provide segmentation with TrustSec. Segmentation can also be achieved by using NGFW and ASA with or without TrustSec.
16. Information Security Incident Management	Stealthwatch, NGFW, NGIPS	Section 16.1 lists controls for incident management. Stealthwatch, NGFW, and NGIPS generate, collect, and store event logs and analytical information that can be used to investigate incidents.

NIST Cybersecurity Framework

NIST created the Cybersecurity Framework (CSF) based on the executive order of the president titled "Improving Critical Infrastructure Cybersecurity." It is a voluntary framework developed in collaboration with private industries to provide guidance on cybersecurity risk. It helps organizations in assessing their current security profile and in determining the desired target profile.

It is important to understand that the CSF does not provide a list of specific security controls that an organization should implement. It only provides a common set of activities that an organization can use to identify and mitigate its risk. It draws on and references other standards, such as ISO 27002, for recommending controls.

The framework is divided into three parts:

- **Core:** The framework core is a set of cybersecurity activities, desired outcomes, and references applicable across the critical assets of an organization. It is organized into 5 functions: identify, protect, detect, respond, and recover. These functions are further divided into 22 categories, as shown in Table 1-2. These are further divided into 98 subcategories and references.

Table 1-2 *NIST CSF Core Functions and Categories*

Function Identifier	Function	Category Identifier	Category
ID	Identify	ID.AM	Asset Management
		ID.BE	Business Environment
		ID.GV	Governance
		ID.RA	Risk Assessment
		ID.RM	Risk Management Strategy
PR	Protect	PR.AC	Access Control
		PR.AT	Awareness and Training
		PR.DS	Data Security
		PR.IP	Information Protection
		PR.MA	Maintenance
		PR.PT	Protective Technology
DE	Detect	DE.AE	Anomalies and Events
		DE.CM	Continuous Monitoring
		DE.DP	Detection Processes

Function Identifier	Function	Category Identifier	Category
RS	Respond	RS.RP	Response Planning
		RS.CO	Communications
		RS.AN	Analysis
		RS.MI	Mitigation
		RS.IM	Improvements
RC	Recover	RC.RP	Recovery Planning
		RC.IM	Improvements
		RC.CO	Communications

- **Implementation Tiers:** The framework implementation tiers describe the degree to which an organization has implemented controls for each category of the framework core. The tiers are divided into four increasing levels: partial, risk-informed, repeatable, and adaptive. An organization has to decide the current and desired levels of implementation for each category based on risk tolerance. Increasing tier levels do not necessarily indicate maturity; the goal of the framework is not to ensure that an organization is at Tier 4 for each category.
- **Profile:** The framework comes together in the framework profiles. An organization selects the categories and subcategories that align with its business needs. Then it identifies the controls that are already in place to create the *current profile*. Next, it creates a desired state, or *target profile*. The current profile can then be used to support prioritization and measurement of progress toward the target profile, while factoring in other business needs, including cost-effectiveness and innovation. Profiles can be used to conduct self-assessments and communicate within an organization or between organizations.

Going into further details about CSF is beyond the scope of this book and the exam, but it is important to map out Cisco products and technologies that can be used in each relevant category for the framework, as shown in Table 1-3.

Table 1-3 *Cisco Security Products and NIST CSF*

CSF Function	CSF Category	Cisco Products
Identify	Asset Management	ISE, NGFW, Stealthwatch
	Risk Assessment	Cognitive Threat Analytics, NGFW
Protect	Access Control	ISE, NGFW, Umbrella
	Data Security	All Cisco Security Products
	Maintenance	ISE with AnyConnect
	Protective Tech.	ISE, NGFW

CSF Function	CSF Category	Cisco Products
Detect	Anomalies & Events	AMP, Stealthwatch, WSA/ESA, Umbrella, NGFW
	Continuous Monitoring	AMP, Stealthwatch, ESA, CTA, NGFW
Respond	Analysis	AMP, Stealthwatch, WSA, ESA, NGFW
	Mitigation	All Cisco Security Products

Regulatory Compliance

While frameworks can be used to create a security policy, an organization must also take into consideration the regulatory compliance and laws that apply to the industries and locations in which it operates. Such laws are made to protect the industry and its consumers and offer specific guidelines to ensure security of information.

Various regulatory compliance and legislative acts apply to industries around the world. An organization needs to consider them while creating its security policies. There is usually a very heavy penalty associated with failure to comply with these laws. In this section, we briefly discuss two of the most important such regulations and legislative acts.

Health Insurance Portability and Accountability Act (HIPAA)

The Health Insurance Portability and Accountability Act (HIPAA) was enacted by the U.S. Congress in August 1996. It applies to the organizations in the healthcare industry. In particular, it states that any entity that creates, receives, transmits, or maintains protected health information in electronic form must make good-faith efforts to protect the data and the computing environment from known and reasonably anticipated threats and vulnerabilities. Such entities are also required to protect the confidentiality, integrity, and availability of such electronic data.

HIPAA is technology neutral and does not define controls to allow flexibility in adopting new technology. It provides standards and in some cases implementation specifications to comply, but most often, industry standards such as ISO 27002 and NIST CSF are used to meet the requirements of the act.

Note Cisco has published a compliance guide for HIPAA security rule design and implementation. Much of the information in this section is compiled from that guide. I strongly suggest reading the guide in preparation for the CCIE exam. It can be found at http://www.cisco.com/c/en/us/td/docs/solutions/Enterprise/Compliance/HIPAA/default.html.

Penalties associated with violation of HIPAA are severe and depend on the knowledge of and actions before and during the fact. On one end of the spectrum, if the covered entity had a reasonable amount of prevention in place and could not have known or avoided the violation, the penalty ranges from $100 to $50,000. On the other end of the spectrum, if the covered entity is found willfully negligent by not having enough protection in place or allowing the violation even after having knowledge of it, the penalty ranges from $50,000 to $1,500,000—plus possible imprisonment. Ignorance of the HIPAA rules cannot be used as an excuse for violation.

While the act in its entirety is beyond the scope of this book, Table 1-4 broadly classifies and maps the security requirements to Cisco security products and technologies.

Table 1-4 *HIPAA and Cisco Security*

HIPAA Security Requirement	Cisco Security Product/Solution	Notes
Identity management and access control	Cisco ISE, ASA, NGFW	Identity management and access control to health information is a central theme in HIPAA. Cisco ISE can provide that by controlling access to the network. Further access control can be provided by ASA and NGFW.
Segmentation	Cisco ISE, TrustSec, ASA, NGFW	Segmentation of clinical and administrative information is critical to applying effective security measures. Cisco ISE along with TrustSec-enabled enforcement devices such as ASA and NGFW can provide effective segmentation.
Encryption	Various VPN solutions on ASA, NGFW, and routers	Encryption of data in transit, especially between covered entities, is a critical requirement. Various Cisco VPN solutions can be used to achieve that.
Logging, audit, and monitoring	Firepower NGFW and NGIPS with Firepower Management Center (FMC)	The act requires logging, monitoring, and audit of data access as well as intrusion attempts. Cisco NGFW and NGIPS solutions provide strong intrusion prevention along with logging, monitoring, and audit capabilities with FMC.

It is important to remember that Table 1-4 provides a generalized overview of the security requirements and corresponding Cisco security solutions. The actual design and implementation will depend on the size of the network and the organization.

Payment Card Industry Data Security Standard (PCI DSS)

The Payment Card Industry Data Security Standard (PCI DSS) is a standard for security mandated by most of the major credit card companies, including Visa, MasterCard, American Express, Discover, and JCB. This standard applies to any organization that processes, stores, or transmits credit card information. This is not a standard required by federal law but rather mandated by the credit card companies and administered by the Payment Card Industry Security Standards Council. Some states, however, directly reference either PCI DSS or an equivalent standard in their laws.

The PCI DSS standard has 6 goals, divided into 12 requirements:

- **Build and Maintain a Secure Network**
  1. Install and maintain a firewall configuration to protect cardholder data.
  2. Do not use vendor-supplied defaults for system passwords and other security parameters.
- **Protect Cardholder Data**
  3. Protect stored cardholder data.
  4. Encrypt transmission of cardholder data across open, public networks.
- **Maintain a Vulnerability Management Program**
  5. Use and regularly update antivirus software or programs.
  6. Develop and maintain secure systems and applications.
- **Implement Strong Access Control Measures**
  7. Restrict access to cardholder data by business need-to-know.
  8. Assign a unique ID to each person with computer access.
  9. Restrict physical access to cardholder data.
- **Regularly Monitor and Test Network**
  10. Track and monitor all access to network resources and cardholder data.
  11. Regularly test security systems and processes.
- **Maintain an Information Security Policy**
  12. Maintain a policy that addresses information security for employees and contractors.

You will notice that PCI DSS has fairly simple requirements, but one important point to remember is that PCI data often uses the same network infrastructure as other data in an organization. If the PCI data is not segmented, the whole network needs to be PCI DSS–compliant, which increases the cost and complexity of compliance. Hence, while the standard itself does not explicitly call for it, it is important to segment PCI data from other data. Segmentation can be achieved with traditional methods such as access lists and VLANs or with newer technologies, such as TrustSec.

Table 1-5 maps PCI DSS goals to relevant Cisco security products and technologies.

Table 1-5 *PCI DSS and Cisco Security Product/Technologies*

PCI DSS Goal	Cisco Security Products/ Technologies
Build and Maintain a Secure Network	Cisco Firepower NGFW, Firepower NGIPS, ASA
Protect Cardholder Data	Cisco VPN technologies on NGFW, ASA, and routers
Maintain a Vulnerability Management Program	Cisco AMP
Implement Strong Access Control Measures	Cisco ISE, TrustSec
Regularly Monitor and Test Networks	NGFW, NGIPS, FMC, Stealthwatch
Maintain an Information Security Policy	N/A

Security Models

So far in this chapter, we have discussed how to assess risks and create a security policy, taking into consideration regulatory requirements. Creating a security policy is just the first step in securing your organization. A security policy only indicates the requirements of the business and its management. It needs to be implemented to be of any use!

How do you effectively implement a security policy? The answer is by using security models. While it is not necessary to use a defined model, using one will make the implementation and auditing more effective and uniform. A security model helps convert requirements of a policy into a set of rules and regulations.

While an in-depth discussion is not part of the CCIE exam and this book, you should know some of the most common and widely accepted security models:

- **Bell–LaPadula Model:** This state machine model was introduced to enforce access control in government and military applications. This model is primarily focused on the confidentiality of data and controlled access to classified information.
- **Biba Model:** This lattice-based model was developed to focus on integrity of data. Data and subjects are grouped into ordered levels of integrity. The model is designed so that subjects may not write to objects in a higher level.
- **Clark–Wilson Model:** This model was developed to address integrity for commercial activities (whereas the previous two models were developed for government and military applications). The model uses a system of a three-part relationship known as a *triple,* consisting of a subject, a program, and an object. Within this relationship, a subject can only access an object through a program.

- **Lattice-Based Model:** This *mandatory access control* (MAC)–based model uses a lattice to define the levels of security for subjects and objects. A subject can only access objects that have a security level equal to or lower than its own security level.

A lot of these security models were developed a long time ago for specific use cases. Changing network and security requirements have created a need for better and simpler security models. To address this need, Cisco created the SAFE architecture and model.

Cisco SAFE

The Cisco SAFE model provides a method for analyzing threats, risks, and policies across an organization and implementing controls. It takes into account that all organizations are not the same by providing a modular structure that can be customized for any type and size of organization.

The model divides the network into logical areas called *places in the network (PINs), as* shown in Figure 1-1.

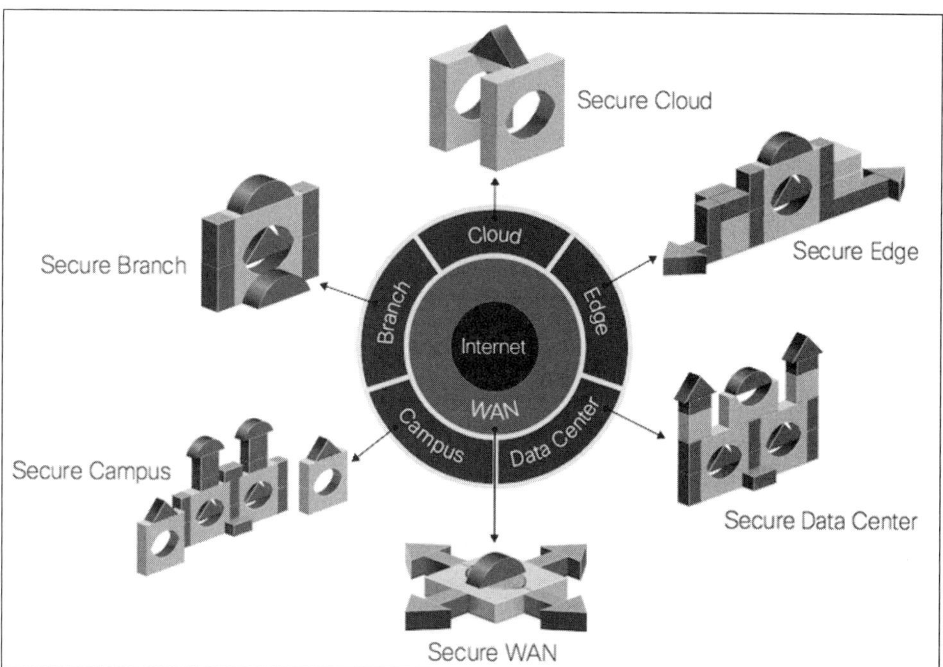

Figure 1-1 *Places in the Network, as Defined by Cisco SAFE*

Each PIN is evaluated across a set of six operational functions, called *secure domains*, as shown in in Figure 1-2.

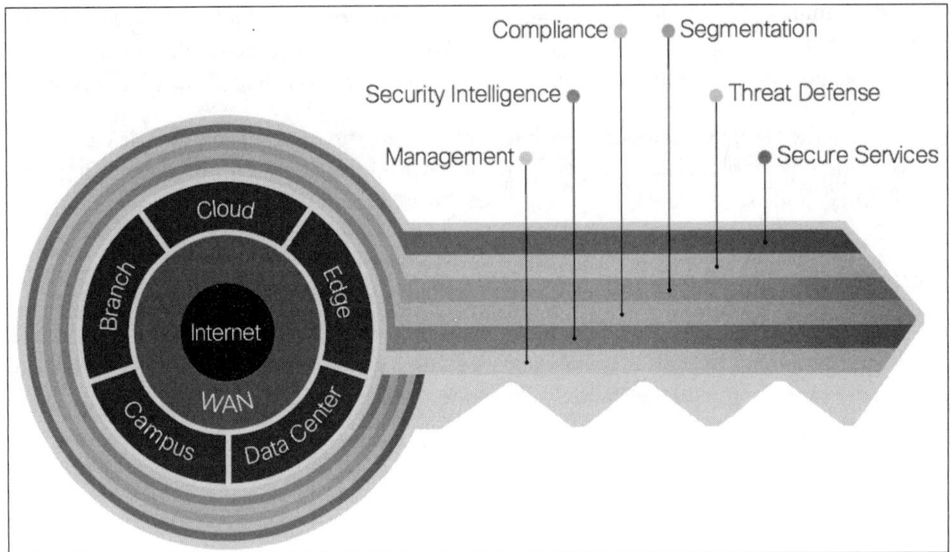

Figure 1-2 *The Key to SAFE*

Based on the PINs and security domain approach, the SAFE model defines a three-phased approach for building security in the network:

- **Capability phase:** Using business goals, security policy, risks, and threats in each PIN, justify which security capabilities are required.
- **Architecture phase:** Using the justified capabilities, arrange them in a logical architecture.
- **Design phase:** Using the architecture, create a design that is complete with a product list, configuration, services, and cost.

SAFE PINs

As mentioned earlier, the SAFE model divides the network into six logical areas, or PINs. It is not necessary for each organization to have every area, but the model is designed to be modular. You can remove PINs that do not exist in your network. Each PIN represents the infrastructure commonly deployed in these areas, such as routers, switches, firewalls, and so on.

Each of the six PINs has a typical profile and associated threats:

- **Branch:** Branches present a unique security challenge due to their smaller size and larger number of locations. Providing a level of security in branches that is comparable to the campus or data center level is cost-prohibitive. This leaves branches more vulnerable and makes them prime targets. Typical threats in branches include point-of-sale malware, wireless infrastructure exploits such as rogue access points, and exploitation of trust.

- **Campus:** Campuses contain a large number and many types of users, including employees and guests. Traditional methods of segmentation are used at the campus level, with very few internal security controls. There is often a lack of access control in the wired network within the campus. All these factors combined make campuses easy targets for phishing, malware propagation, unauthorized network access, and botnet infestation.

- **Data center:** Data centers contain the crown jewels of an organization and hence get the biggest share of the security budget. However, the data center is also the most targeted PIN. In addition, data centers contain thousands of servers, segmented by application type, data classification, and so on, using traditional manual methods. Managing and auditing these segmentations is increasingly difficult. Typical threats seen in data centers are data exfiltration, malware propagation, and advanced persistent threats.

- **Edge:** The edge is the most critical PIN in terms of business importance as well as security risk. It is the primary ingress and egress point for traffic to and from the Internet. It is very susceptible to DDoS attacks. Other threats that are common to this PIN are data exfiltration, MITM attacks, and web server vulnerability exploits.

- **Cloud:** The cloud is the new frontier, bringing high risk along with high cost savings. Security in the cloud is dictated by service-level agreements (SLAs) with the provider and requires regular audits and risk assessments. The primary threats in this PIN are DDoS and MITM attacks, loss of access, data loss, and web server vulnerabilities.

- **Wide area network:** The WAN connects other PINs, such as branch, campus, and data centers, together. In a large organization with hundreds of locations, managing security and quality of service (QoS) on the WAN is challenging. Typical threats seen in this PIN are malware propagation, exploitation of trust, unauthorized network access, and MITM attacks.

Secure Domains

The SAFE model divides the operational side of security into six secure domains. Every secure domain applies to each PIN in an organization. An evaluation of all the secure domains across each PIN provides a list of security capabilities that are required. These are the six secure domains defined by Cisco SAFE:

- **Management:** This refers to centralized management of devices and systems. Centralized management is essential for consistent security policy, vulnerability patching, security application updates, and alerting. Some of the capabilities within this domain are policy configuration, time synchronization, patch management, and logging/reporting.

- **Security intelligence:** This refers to global aggregation of emerging malware and threats to provide timely detection. A threat protection infrastructure is as good as the security intelligence it receives. The infrastructure needs to be able to dynamically enforce new policies as threats emerge and change. Some of the capabilities within this domain are threat intelligence, malware sandboxing, and posture assessment.

- **Compliance:** This refers to controls that need to exist to satisfy internal and external compliance requirements, such as those for HIPAA and PCI DSS. Some of the capabilities in this domain include virtual private networks, firewalls, and intrusion prevention systems.

- **Segmentation:** This refers to segmentation of data, devices, and users. Traditional manual segmentation uses a combination of network addressing, VLANs, and access lists. Advanced segmentation is identity-aware, dynamic, and automated.

- **Threat defense:** This refers to the ability to detect, prevent, eliminate, or contain cyber threats. Modern-day threats are evasive and persistent. Correlation of network traffic telemetry, contextual information, and reputation data is required to detect such threats. Some of the capabilities in this domain include intrusion prevention, flow and behavior analysis, antimalware systems, and application visibility controls.

- **Secure services:** This refers to technologies such as access control, VPNs, and secure email services. This domain adds security on top of services that are inherently insecure, such as email, network access, and collaboration. Some of the capabilities in this domain include email security, web application firewalls, and VPNs.

Attack Continuum

Cisco SAFE defines three phases of an attack—before, during, and after—together called the *attack continuum*:

- **Before:** In this phase of the continuum, you need to know the asset being protected and the threat against which you are defending. Establishing policies and implementing prevention to reduce risk belong in this phase.

- **During:** This phase defines the abilities and actions that are required when an attack gets through. Analysis and incident response are some of the typical activities associated with this phase.

- **After:** This phase defines the ability to detect, contain, and remediate after an attack. If an attack was successful, any lessons learned need to be incorporated into the existing security solution.

For each secure domain in every PIN, you need to define and implement capabilities such that each phase of the continuum is covered.

Figure 1-3 shows various Cisco products and solutions that work across the attack continuum.

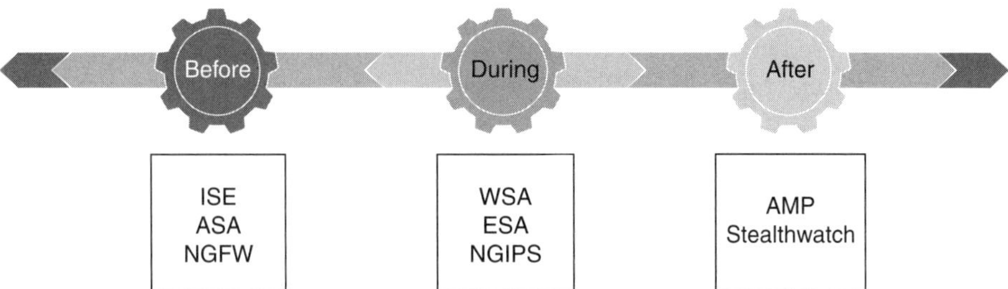

Figure 1-3 *Cisco Products and Solutions Across the Attack Continuum*

Integrating Security Solutions

The threats that current-day networks face are advanced, persistent, and evolving continuously. To protect against them, network and security solutions are becoming more complex. Complexity leads to inefficiency and increased cost. A typical large organization uses multiple security products from multiple vendors. Some organizations use up to 70 different products to secure their networks. Each of these products has different information in different management consoles. In the event of an attack, you have to look at multiple consoles and correlate information manually to even determine that you are under attack.

Most of the recent high-profile cyber attacks have had one thing in common: Security systems detected those attacks, but the event logs were lost in a flood of other logs and went undetected. Why?

To understand the complexity of incidence response, consider an example. Let's say you are looking at logs from the IPS in your organization, and you come across an attack that happened seven days ago. The only identifying information in the logs is the IP address of the internal host that was the target of the attack. To find out which host and user had that IP address from your internal DHCP range, you will need to go through the DHCP server logs—assuming that your organization stores such logs and you have access to them. From the DHCP logs, you will get a MAC address for the machine—but you will not know what user was logged on during the time of the attack. However, if your organization enforces network access control, you may be able to find that information from the access control system logs. In the absence of a network access control system, you will need to find out where the MAC address is currently connected and what that switch port is connected to. Finally, you will get a physical location of the device and, when you walk to the location, the identity of the user.

This example shows how difficult it can be to respond to and contain an attack. Now multiply the effort by the hundreds of events per day, and you begin to understand how incident response can become slow and ineffective.

To deal with the threats we face today, our security solutions need to evolve and integrate. Multiple security products and solutions contain contextual information about an event. When those products and solutions are integrated, they share this data to be correlated. Such integrations and correlation have a number of benefits:

- **Better indicators of compromise:** Not every event requires immediate remediation. In some cases, remediation may not be required at all. When security products such as IPSs analyze an event in relation to the context of the target or source, they can provide better indicators of compromise. This results in faster response to top threats. For example, consider Windows malware being downloaded by a machine running Linux. Without contextual information about the operating system, this event would be a high-severity event.
- **Event logs with contextual data:** When security products receive and store contextual data with event logs, responding to events—even days later—becomes much easier. For example, if the username is available in an event log, reaching out to the end user for remediation is easier.
- **Increased effectiveness:** With correlation of events and contextual information, the effectiveness of event detection increases drastically. Considering again the example of a Linux machine downloading Windows malware, an IPS with contextual information about the operating system can ignore that event instead of generating a false-positive event log.
- **Automated response:** When security products are integrated, they can work together to contain and remediate an event automatically. This drastically reduces the time it takes to contain the event. With a lower rate of false positives, the risk associated with automated response is also reduced. For example, consider an IPS that detects malicious activity from an internal endpoint. It can reach out to the network access control system to quarantine the endpoint.

To further understand the benefit of integration of security systems, let's revisit the previous example of tracing down the user associated with an event that is seven days old. This time, assume that the network access control system in the organization is integrated with the IPS, and it provides contextual information, including username. With this integration in place, you would have the IP address, MAC address, and username in the event log on the IPS. There would be no need to look at the DHCP server or any other logs. The time and effort taken to find the username associated with the event would be reduced to zero!

Integration of security products has begun as vendors have realized its importance. Cisco is leading this charge with multiple open standards drafts and integration between all its security products. Relevant chapters in this book and in the companion book, *Integrated Security Technologies and Solutions, Volume II*, will introduce integration technologies. For example, an entire chapter in *Volume II* is dedicated to showing how various Cisco security products integrate with each other.

Summary

In this chapter, you have learned about the threats facing today's networks and efforts required to protect against them. It all starts with identifying your assets and risks. A security policy helps in documenting risks and prevention requirements. Standards and frameworks provide help in creating a good security policy that meets the various regulations your organization may be subject to. A security model helps implement that security policy uniformly. Finally, you have learned that various security products in the organization should be integrated to provide effective security against advanced threat.

References

"GameOver Zeus Botnet Disrupted: Collaborative Effort Among International Partners," https://www.fbi.gov/news/stories/gameover-zeus-botnet-disrupted

"U.S. Leads Multi-National Action Against GameOver Zeus Botnet and Cryptolocker Ransomware, Charges Botnet Administrator," https://www.fbi.gov/news/pressrel/press-releases/u.s.-leads-multi-national-action-against-gameover-zeus-botnet-and-cryptolocker-ransomware-charges-botnet-administrator

"Security Policy Roadmap: Process for Creating Security Policies," https://www.sans.org/reading-room/whitepapers/policyissues/security-policy-roadmap-process-creating-security-policies-494

"About NIST," https://www.nist.gov/about-nist

"Framework for Improving Critical Infrastructure Cybersecurity," https://www.nist.gov/sites/default/files/documents/cyberframework/cybersecurity-framework-021214.pdf

"SAFE Overview Guide: Threats, Capabilities, and the Security Reference Architecture," http://www.cisco.com/c/dam/en/us/solutions/collateral/enterprise/design-zone-security/safe-overview-guide.pdf

Chapter 2

Infrastructure Security and Segmentation

Chapter 1, "Let's Talk About Network Security," discusses the importance of identifying and securing the assets in your network. One of the most important assets is the network itself. If your network devices are compromised, then any data flowing through it will be compromised, too. This chapter discusses the security of the network infrastructure, including the three planes: management, control, and data.

This chapter also discusses the importance of segmenting traffic within a network as well as methods for doing so. Finally, this chapter lays a foundation for traffic analysis and security integration with a discussion on NetFlow and its security benefits.

The Three Planes

Yes, this is still a book on security! We did not leave the world of security for the astral planes, and neither did we switch to the flying kind. The planes we discuss here are the three that exist on a network device: the management, control, and data planes.

Any functions related to managing a device, such as configuring it, happen in the *management plane*. Access to this plane requires use of various protocols, such as SSH, ~~Telnet~~, SNMP, and SFTP. This is the most important plane in terms of securing a device because any breach on this plane will allow access to all data flowing through the device and even the ability to reroute traffic.

In the *control plane*, the device discovers its environment and builds the foundation to do its job. For example, a router uses routing protocols in the control plane to learn about the various routes. Routes allow a router to do its primary job—route packets. A switch uses protocols such as VTP and STP to learn about various paths, and that allows it to switch traffic. If the protocols in the control plane are not secured, a malicious actor may be able to inject rogue control packets and influence the path of the packets. For example, if your routing protocols are not secure, then it is possible to inject rogue routes, causing data to flow to a different device. This technique is often used in man-in-the-middle (MITM) attacks.

The *data plane*, also called the *forwarding plane*, is where the actual data flows. When a router receives a packet to route or a switch receives a frame to switch, it does so on the data plane. Information learned in the control plane facilitates the functions of the data plane. Typically, this is where most of the network security controls are focused. Packet filtering, protocol validation, segmentation, malicious traffic detection, distributed denial-of-service (DDoS) protection, and other security measures are utilized in this plane.

In addition to the three planes, the physical security of a device itself is important. After all, the security in the software does not matter if the hardware is compromised. While it is the responsibility of the vendor—Cisco in this case—to ensure that a device is not tampered with between manufacturing and your doorstep, it is your responsibility to ensure that the devices are kept in a secure location where unauthorized access can be prevented.

The three planes and physical security can be visualized as the pyramid shown in Figure 2-1, where compromise on one layer will affect all the layers above it.

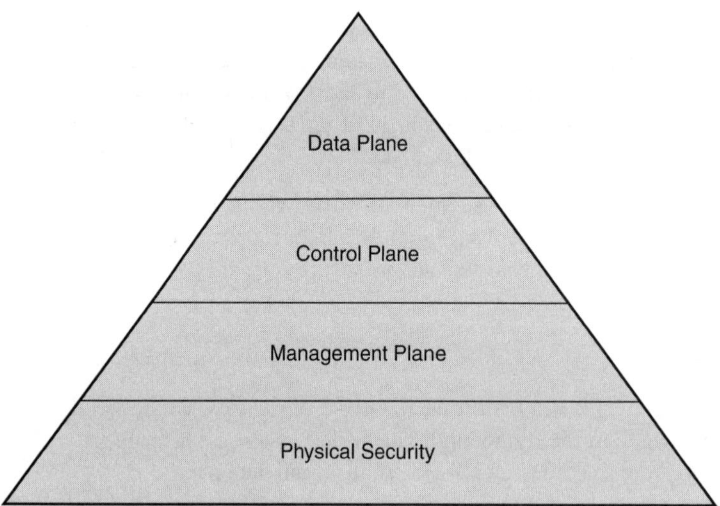

Figure 2-1 *The Pyramid of Planes*

Securing the Management Plane

Any function related to management of a device resides in the management plane. The primary means of managing Cisco routers and switches are the console and the vty. Both of these provide access to the command-line interface (CLI). In most cases, even when a GUI interface for management is available, it uses the CLI to issue commands to the device. Apart from direct access to the CLI, SNMP can be used for information gathering and change configuration.

Other noteworthy functions that reside in this plane relate to logging and time management. In this section, we discuss security of the CLI and SNMP. Before we discuss the specific topics, some of the general security practices associated with the management plane should be understood:

- **Zero trust and minimum required access:** Network devices are the backbone of your information technology infrastructure and should have very strict and restrictive access control applied. Few selected and trained individuals should have access to network devices, and their activities on devices should be authorized and logged. Centralized access control using an authentication, authorization, and accounting (AAA) server along with command authorization are highly recommended. While this chapter briefly discusses AAA, an entire chapter in *Integrated Security Technologies and Solutions, Volume II* covers it in depth.
- **Central monitoring and log collection:** Logs from network devices provide important event and performance data. They should be collected, analyzed, and correlated in a central location for preventive measures as well as incidence response. Similarly, monitoring the network devices using SNMP provides a constant view of the network security and performance while reducing the need for logging in to the device directly.
- **Secure communication:** Multiple protocols can be used to access network devices for management. The devices should be configured to use only secure protocols. For example, SSH, HTTPS, and SFTP provide encrypted transfer, whereas Telnet, HTTP, and FTP do not. Similarly, SNMP Version 3 (SNMPv3) should be used instead of earlier versions to provide secure and authenticated access.
- **Central configuration management:** Using centralized configuration management provides change versioning and archiving while also keeping your policies consistent across the network.
- **Disabling unnecessary services:** Routers and switches contain many services that listen for packets. Services that are not required on your network should be disabled to prevent the chance that they will be used to launch an attack on the device. Special attention should be paid to what Cisco calls *small servers*. These are disabled by default but can be enabled by using the **service tcp-small-servers** and **service udp-small-servers** commands.

Securing the Command Line

The Cisco IOS CLI is divided into 16 privilege levels, each of which defines what commands are available to a user. The privilege levels are divided into four categories:

- **Privilege level 0:** Includes the **disable**, **enable**, **exit**, **help**, and **logout** commands.
- **User EXEC mode:** Also called privilege level 1. By default, users log in to this mode, and it is denoted by a greater-than sign (**>**) at the end of the prompt. Commands available in this level cannot affect the device configuration.
- **Privileged EXEC mode:** Also called privilege level 15. This level can be entered by using the **enable** command in the user EXEC mode and is denoted by the hash sign (**#**) at the end of the prompt. All commands are available at this level.

- **Custom privileged modes:** Whereas level 1 provides no access to configuration, level 15 provides full access to it. In some cases, neither of these levels can fulfill the requirements of access control policies. To provide tailored access control, IOS has privilege levels 2 to 14. By default, these levels do not provide any more access than level 1 but can be configured to provide access to required commands.

Each of these privilege levels can be protected by passwords. The first level is protected by the passwords configured in the terminal lines. Different devices have different numbers of lines that can be ascertained with the **show line** command. Typically, Cisco switches and routers have 1 console line and 16 vty lines. You can configure a password to protect the lines by using the **password** command on the terminal lines as shown in Example 2-1.

Example 2-1 *Configuring Passwords on Terminal Lines*

```
R1#configure terminal
Enter configuration commands, one per line.  End with CNTL/Z.
R1(config)#line vty 0 15
R1(config-line)#password L3tm31n!
R1(config-line)#exit
R1(config)#line console 0
R1(config-line)#password L3tm31n!
R1(config-line)#
```

In addition to the password, the vty lines should be configured to use SSH instead of Telnet to allow for encrypted communication with the device. Before SSH can be enabled on the vty lines, an SSH key must be generated on the device, as shown in Example 2-2.

Example 2-2 *Generating an SSH Key*

```
R1(config)#ip domain-name cisco.com
R1(config)#crypto key generate rsa modulus 2048
```

After the SSH key is generated, the vty lines can be configured to use SSH only. To do this, use the **transport input** command, as shown in Example 2-3.

Example 2-3 *Changing the Transport Protocols on vty Lines*

```
R1(config)#line vty 0 15
R1(config-line)#transport input ssh
R1(config-line)#exit
```

vty lines can be further secured by applying an access list such that SSH sessions are accepted only from certain IP addresses or ranges. This requires an access list that contains the allowed IP addresses. That access list can be applied to vty lines using the **access-class** command, as shown in Example 2-4.

Example 2-4 *Using an ACL to Restrict Access to vty Lines*

```
R1(config)#access-list 1 permit host 192.168.1.10
R1(config)#access-list 1 permit host 192.168.1.15
R1(config)#line vty 0 15
R1(config-line)#access-class 1 in
```

The line mode provides some other commands that can be used to secure terminal access. Some of the most important ones are discussed here:

- **autocommand:** This command is used to configure the lines to execute a specific command when a remote access session is established and authenticated. The session disconnects after execution is completed. The command to be executed is specified as the argument in this case. In Example 2-5, the lines are configured to execute **show running-config** as soon as the SSH session is established. The SSH session is disconnected after the configuration is displayed.

Example 2-5 *Executing a Command on Session Establishment*

```
R1(config)#line vty 0 15
R1(config-line)#privilege level 15
R1(config-line)#autocommand show running-config
```

- **exec-timeout:** This command configures the duration, in minutes, for which an idle session will be kept alive. It is important to configure a short duration to safeguard against unauthorized access as well as to prevent all vty lines from being used up by idle sessions. Example 2-6 shows how this is configured.

Example 2-6 *Configuring the Idle Timeout*

```
R1(config)#line vty 0 15
R1(config-line)#exec-timeout 5
```

- **privilege level:** This command configures the default privilege level that the user lands into after an access session is established on the terminal lines. By default, a user starts at privilege level 1, but that can be changed to any level, including 15. In Example 2-7, the default privilege level for the console line is configured to be 15. After this, when a user connects to the console and authenticates successfully, she starts in privilege level 15 instead of 1.

Example 2-7 *Configuring the Default Privilege Level*

```
R1(config)#line con 0
R1(config-line)#privilege level 15
```

Privilege Levels

After successful authentication using the line password, a user enters privilege level 1 by default. If the user needs to access a higher level, he needs to use the **enable [level]** command and enter the **enable** password associated with that level. This password is configured using the **enable secret [level]** command. If a level is not specified with either of the commands, level 15 is assumed. Example 2-8 shows how the secrets for different levels are configured. The first example does not specify a level; hence, it is assumed to be for level 15. Example 2-9 shows how the **enable** command is used to enter different levels. Note the use of the **show privilege** command to show the level that the user is in and the **disable [level]** command to go back to a previous level. The default level for the **disable** command is 1.

Example 2-8 *Configuring* enable secret

```
R1(config)#enable secret cisco123!
R1(config)#enable secret level 5 13v315!
R1(config)#enable secret level 10 13v3110!
```

Example 2-9 *Changing IOS Levels*

```
R1>enable
Password:
R1#show privilege
Current privilege level is 15

R1#disable
R1>show privilege
Current privilege level is 1

R1>enable 5
Password:
R1#show privilege
Current privilege level is 5

R1#disable
R1>enable
Password:
R1#show privilege
Current privilege level is 15

R1#disable 10
R1#show privilege
Current privilege level is 10
```

All custom levels from 2 to 14 are no different from level 1 to start with. All configuration commands and most verification commands have a default level of 15. To populate the custom levels, you need to reduce the level of required commands from 15 to the desired level. This can be done with the **privilege** command, which has the following syntax:

privilege *mode* **level** *level command-string*

The *mode* string denotes the mode in which the command is available—such as configuration, interface, or exec. IOS has hundreds of modes. Usually the name of the mode is reflected in the command used to enter that mode.

The *level* string denotes the new level of the command. This is the custom level in which you want the command to be available.

The *command-string* option specifies the actual command that is subject to privilege level change.

As an example, if you want the **show running-config** command to be available at level 5, you need to reduce the privilege level of that command to 5, as shown in Example 2-10.

Example 2-10 *Changing Privilege Levels of Commands*

```
R1#show privilege
Current privilege level is 5

R1#show run?
% Unrecognized command

R1#enable
Password:
R1#config t
Enter configuration commands, one per line.  End with CNTL/Z.

R1(config)#privilege exec level 5 show running-config
R1(config)#exit
R1#disable 5
R1#show privilege
Current privilege level is 5

R1#show running-config
Building configuration...
```

Using custom privilege levels is an easy way to provide differentiated access based on job roles. This is particularly useful in allowing help-desk members to perform basic maintenance functions on a network device while preventing them from making changes to the overall configuration of the device. Example 2-11 shows how privilege level 10 is given the ability to shut down an interface or bring one up without allowing users in that level to make any other changes. Note the use of the mode names—**exec**, **configure**, and **interface**—with the **privilege** command. The mode name denotes the mode in which the subject command is available.

Example 2-11 *Changing Privilege Levels of Configuration Commands*

```
R1#show privilege
Current privilege level is 10
R1#configure terminal
             ^
% Invalid input detected at '^' marker.

R1#enable
Password:
R1#config t
Enter configuration commands, one per line.  End with CNTL/Z.

R1(config)#privilege exec level 10 configure terminal
R1(config)#privilege configure level 10 interface
R1(config)#privilege interface level 10 shutdown
R1(config)#exit

R1#disable 10
R1#configure terminal
Enter configuration commands, one per line.  End with CNTL/Z.
R1(config)#interface Gi0/1
R1(config-if)#shut?
shutdown
```

While using local passwords and privilege levels on the device provides the required security, it can be cumbersome to manage these on each device, and inconsistent configuration across the network is very likely. To simplify device configuration and maintain consistency, it is recommended that you use an AAA server such as Cisco Identity Services Engine (ISE). The network devices can use the Terminal Access Controller Access Control System Plus (TACACS+) protocol to authenticate users and authorize commands. Since the authorization configuration is centralized on the AAA server, policies are applied consistently across all network devices. AAA servers and their use for securing CLI access are discussed in depth in *Integrated Security Technologies and Solutions, Volume II*.

Management Plane Protection

Earlier in this chapter, we discussed the use of an access list to limit the source addresses from which remote access sessions are accepted on vty lines. While the ACL limits the source addresses, recommended best practice is to limit remote management sessions to specific trusted interfaces only.

The Management Plane Protection (MPP) feature can be used to limit remote management sessions to specific trusted interfaces only. This is very useful when a router connects a trusted network to an untrusted network such as the Internet. MPP applies to all management protocols, such as SSH, HTTPS, and SNMP. This feature is configured using the **management-interface** command in the control pane. This command can be repeated to enable the same or a different set of protocols on other interfaces. One key restriction of this feature is that it cannot be applied to an out-of-band management interface (also called a *dedicated management interface*), if the device has one. Example 2-12 shows the usage of this command.

Example 2-12 *Management Plane Protection*

```
R1(config)#control-plane host
R1(config-cp-host)#management-interface Gi0/0 allow ssh snmp https
```

CPU and Memory Thresholding

When a network device is under a denial-of-service (DoS) attack, its resources such as CPU and memory start to deplete quickly. Hence, it is important to monitor the resources on your network devices. While regular polling of devices using SNMP helps, configuring a device to send an SNMP trap when certain CPU and memory utilization thresholds have been reached is better. The CPU and Memory Threshold notification features provide this functionality.

The CPU Thresholding Notification feature can alert when CPU utilization exceeds a configured level and when the utilization drops below a configured level. The former is called a *rising notification*, and the latter is called a *falling notification*.

The syntax for the command to enable CPU thresholding notification is as follows:

```
process cpu threshold type {total|process|interrupt} rising percentage interval
seconds [falling percentage interval seconds]
```

In addition to this command, SNMP traps for CPU threshold must be enabled. Example 2-13 shows the configuration required to enable CPU thresholding notification.

Example 2-13 *CPU Thresholding Notification*

```
R1(config)#snmp-server enable traps cpu threshold
R1(config)#snmp-server host 192.168.1.25 traps version 3 priv vuser cpu
R1(config)#process cpu threshold type process rising 85 interval 60 falling
  60 interval 60
```

Similarly, memory thresholding notification can be configured to provide notification when available free memory drops below a certain level and when it rises higher than 5% of that level. In addition, you can configure the device to reserve some memory to send out critical notifications.

This is the syntax for the command to configure the notification:

```
memory free low-watermark {IO|processor} threshold
```

This is the syntax for the command to configure memory reservation:

```
memory reserve critical memory
```

In these commands, *threshold* and *memory* are specified in kilobytes. Example 2-14 shows the configuration required to enable memory threshold notification and critical memory reservation.

Example 2-14 *Memory Threshold Notification*

```
R1(config)#memory free low-watermark processor 25000
R1(config)#memory reserve critical 5000
```

Securing SNMP

SNMP is incredibly useful for monitoring network devices. It can also be used to make changes to devices remotely. This also brings with it risk of misuse and opens up an attack avenue. Hence, it is important to secure SNMP access on your network devices. There are multiple ways to do that, as discussed in the following sections, and Cisco recommends using all these methods together.

SNMP Authentication and Encryption

Three versions of SNMP can be configured on Cisco routers and switches: Versions 1, 2c, and 3. Versions 1 and 2c use simple community strings to provide read-only or read-write access. Community strings can be equated to passwords and are stored in the configuration in plaintext. Communications between the SNMP servers and clients are in plaintext and are prone to snooping.

On the other hand, SNMPv3 allows using usernames and a hash message authentication code (HMAC), and it can encrypt the traffic. SNMPv3 user details are not shown in configuration. SNMPv3 has three levels of operations:

- **noAuthNoPriv:** Uses username for authentication with no HMAC or encryption. Very similar to how Version 1 and Version 2c work.
- **authNoPriv:** Uses username with MD5 or SHA HMAC for authentication.
- **authPriv:** Uses username with HMAC for authentication and provides encryption based on DES, 3DES, or AES.

Given the security benefits, SNMPv3 should be preferred over older versions. Where SNMPv3 is not available, the community strings should be changed from the defaults. One of the most common SNMP strings is “public,” and that is typically the first string used by an attacker.

Table 2-1 lists the differences between the various versions of SNMP.

Table 2-1 *SNMP Versions and Their Security*

SNMP Version and Level	Security	Credentials Visible in Configuration?
1	Community string	Yes
2c	Community string	Yes
3 (noAuthNoPriv)	Username	Yes
3 (authNoPriv)	HMAC	No
3 (authPriv)	HMAC with encryption	No

When configuring SNMPv3, users are tied to groups and SNMP traps. All SNMP server and trap configuration is then tied to the user. The commands to create groups and users are shown here:

```
snmp-server group group-name v3 {auth|noauth|priv}
snmp-server user username group-name v3 auth {md5|sha} password [priv {3des|aes
128|aes 192|aes 256|des} encryption-key]
```

Example 2-15 shows how SNMPv3 groups and users are created and then applied to host configuration.

Example 2-15 *SNMPv3 Configuration*

```
R1(config)#snmp-server group snmpl33t v3 priv
R1(config)#snmp-server user l33t snmpl33t v3 auth sha gu3$$myPa$$ priv aes 256
  3ncrypl!
R1(config)#snmp-server host 192.168.1.25 traps version 3 priv l33t
```

SNMP with Access Lists

While authentication and encryption provide a high degree of security, SNMP access should be further restricted with an access list. Access lists can be applied to an SNMP group to limit the source address from which an SNMP read or write request will be received.

To apply an access list to a group, the previously discussed **snmp-server group** command is extended as shown here:

```
snmp-server group group-name v3 {auth|noauth|priv} access access-list
```

Example 2-16 shows how an access list is added to an SNMP group to allow SNMP queries from a known network management server only.

Example 2-16 *Adding an Access List to an SNMP Group*

```
R1(config)#access-list 1 permit 192.168.1.25
R1(config)#snmp-server group snmpl33t v3 priv access 1
```

SNMP Views

The SNMP server on Cisco devices allows access to the whole MIB tree by default. Using authentication, encryption, and IP-based access restriction provides good security, but it can be further enhanced by restricting the MIBs that can be accessed. SNMP views provide the ability to define what MIBs an SNMP group has access to. A view is a list of MIBs that are included or excluded. The following command creates a view:

```
snmp-server view view-name mib-name-or-oid {included|excluded}
```

After a view is created, you can apply it to the SNMP group by extending the previously discussed **snmp-server group** command as shown here:

```
snmp-server group group-name v3 {auth|noauth|priv} [read view-name]
[write view-name] [access access-list]
```

Example 2-17 shows how to configure a view and apply it to an SNMP group with an access list.

Example 2-17 *Adding a View to an SNMP Group*

```
R1(config)#access-list 1 permit 192.168.1.25
R1(config)#snmp-server view limited system included
R1(config)#snmp-server group snmpl33t v3 priv read limited write limited access 1
```

Securing the Control Plane

The control plane is where a Cisco switch or router learns about its environment, using various protocols to talk to neighboring devices. The protocols operating on the control plane of a router are different from those of a switch. Therefore, the types of attacks and the intended results are also different, but they can be generalized into two broad sets:

- **Overwhelming the control plane:** This is a DoS attack in which an attempt is made to overwhelm the CPU by sending a large number of control packets. When the CPU is busy handling this flood, it isn't able to process normal traffic.
- **Corrupting control plane data:** In this type of attack, malicious control plane protocol packets are used to inject rogue information to affect the actual flow of data. Typically, STP, VTP, and routing protocols are used in the control plane to create routing tables, forwarding tables, and other tables. An attacker managing to inject incorrect information in these tables can result in a DoS attack or, worse, the data can be redirected to a rogue device for a MITM attack.

There are two ways to protect the control plane. The first is to secure each protocol used on this plane, and the second is to police the traffic arriving at it. While the mechanisms used to secure various protocols differ, policing the traffic is done using a feature called Control Plane Policing (CoPP). The next section discusses CoPP, and the two sections after that discuss the security of the protocols most commonly used at this plane on switches and routers.

Control Plane Policing (CoPP)

The CoPP feature on a Cisco device does exactly what it sounds like: It polices the traffic coming to the control plane. For this purpose, the control plane is treated as a logical source and destination, with its own inbound and outbound interfaces. Only traffic that is destined for the control plane is policed as part of this feature. This is in addition to any policing, filtering, or any other processing done at the interface where the packet was received by the device.

Examples of packets that get routed to the control plane are routing protocol packets, STP and VTP packets, and packets destined to any of the IP addresses of the device, including those of management plane protocols.

CoPP is configured almost the same way as quality of service (QoS) on any interface, with the difference being that the service policy is applied to the control plane. A detailed discussion of QoS is beyond the scope of this book, but as a refresher, the Modular QoS CLI (MQC) is used to configure QoS, which can be divided into three steps:

Step 1. **Defining the traffic:** In the first step, the interesting traffic is defined in a class map. A common method of defining interesting traffic is to create an access list and reference it in a class map, as shown in Example 2-18. This example creates a class map for all BGP and SSH traffic.

Example 2-18 *Defining a Class Map for QoS*

```
R1(config)#access-list 100 permit tcp any any eq bgp
R1(config)#access-list 100 permit tcp any any eq ssh
R1(config)#class-map copp_class
R1(config-cmap)#match access-group 100
```

Step 2. **Defining a service policy:** In this step, the actual QoS policy and associated actions are defined in a policy map. For CoPP, **police** is the only valid QoS option. Example 2-19 shows a policing policy applied to the CoPP class map created in the previous example. In this example, the QoS policy is configured to police all BGP and SSH traffic to 300 kbps and to drop any traffic that exceeds this rate.

Example 2-19 *Defining a Service Policy*

```
R1(config)#policy-map copp_policy
R1(config-pmap)#class copp_class
R1(config-pmap-c)#police 300000 conform-action transmit exceed-action drop
```

Step 3. **Applying the service policy:** The last step is to apply the service policy to the correct interface. Normally, the policy is applied to an interface, but in the case of CoPP, it is applied in the control plane configuration mode, as shown in Example 2-20.

Example 2-20 *Applying CoPP Service Policy*

```
R1(config)#control-plane
R1(config-cp)#service-policy input copp_policy
```

Securing Layer 2 Control Plane Protocols

A Layer 2 network can be very complex and requires various protocols to run efficiently. Of these protocols, Spanning Tree Protocol (STP) and VLAN Trunking Protocol (VTP) are the most important. While an in-depth discussion of STP and VTP is beyond the scope of this book, this section examines the core functioning of the protocols, their inherent weaknesses, and how to secure them.

Securing Spanning Tree Protocol (STP)

While redundant links are a necessity for a Layer 2 network, they can cause broadcast frames to loop around the network. Since Ethernet frames do not have a time to live (TTL), the frames can loop forever and eventually bring down the network. STP was created to resolve this by allowing redundant links to be in a blocked state until they are needed.

To understand the inherent weakness in STP, it is important to know how it works. STP forms a tree-like topology with the root bridge at the base. The root bridge is elected based on data shared in bridge protocol data units (BPDUs). BPDU frames are sent to well-known multicast addresses and contain, among other information, the switch's MAC address and a user-defined priority value. A combination of these values is called the bridge ID, and the switch with the lowest ID is elected the root bridge.

After a root bridge is elected, each switch in the domain finds the interface that leads to the best path toward the root bridge and designates it as the root port, while redundant links are placed in a blocked mode. All active interfaces on a switch will be in either forwarding mode or blocked mode at the end. This process is called *convergence*. Figure 2-2 shows a topology after normal STP convergence. In this figure, traffic from

WS-1 to WS-2 will take the path from SW-A to the root bridge, SW-B, on the way to SW-D. Notice that the path between SW-A and SW-C is blocked because it is redundant to the path between SW-A and SW-B.

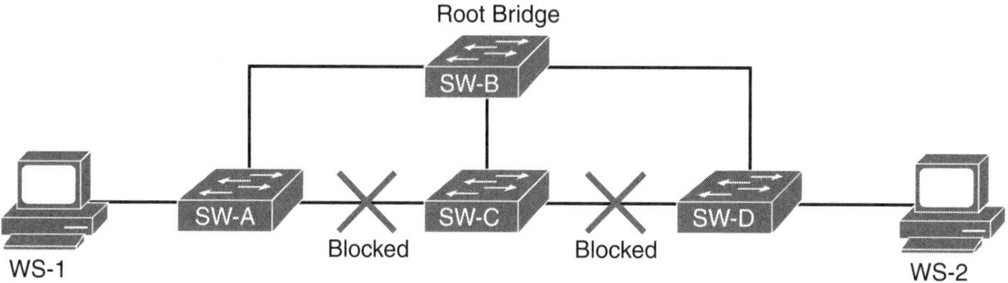

Figure 2-2 *Network During Normal STP Operations*

Changes to topology, addition of new switches, and other similar events can cause a new root bridge to be elected and the STP domain to go through convergence. The time it takes to finish the process is significant, and no traffic is forwarded during that time.

> **Note** The original STP was defined in the IEEE 802.1d standard and had a high convergence time. IEEE 802.1w was later introduced as Rapid STP, which has a much lower convergence time.

In addition to the forwarding disruption during convergence, STP has absolutely no security built into it. BPDUs are exchanged in plaintext, and there is no authentication mechanism. A switch trusts and uses whatever BPDU frames it receives. Given this information, it is easy to understand that STP can be exploited in multiple ways:

- DoS attacks: By sending out crafted BPDUs, it is not difficult to assume a root bridge role in the STP domain, thereby causing a significant part of traffic to be switched to a rogue machine instead of the actual destinations. Even if the root bridge role is not assumed, sending out BPDUs with topology change notifications in short intervals can cause traffic disruption by forcing convergence repeatedly.
- MITM attacks: In certain cases, a rogue device can advertise a low bridge ID and become the root bridge. This causes a significant part of traffic to be switched toward it, where it can be copied, modified, and forwarded to the actual destination. To illustrate this, Figure 2-3 shows what happens when a malicious user is able to form a trunk to SW-A and SW-C, in the previous example, and become the root bridge by advertising a lower bridge ID. Now the path between SW-A and SW-B is also blocked. All traffic between WS-1 and WS-2 will now flow through the malicious root bridge WS-R, where it can be intercepted and modified before being forwarded on.

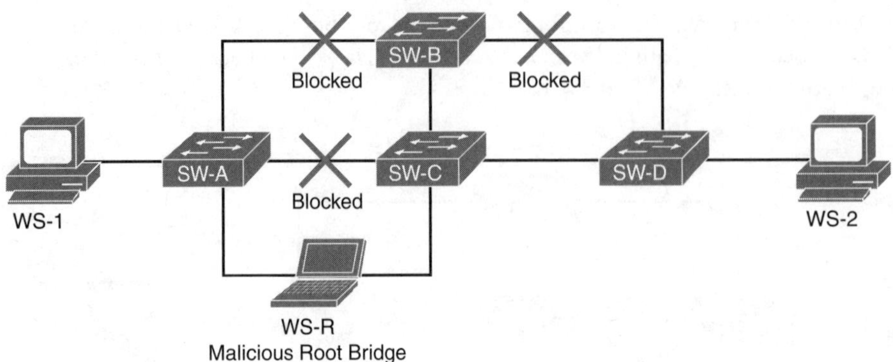

Figure 2-3 *Network After a MITM Attack with STP*

STP itself does not have any security mechanism, but three methods can be used to mitigate the risk on Cisco switches:

- **Disabling Dynamic Trunking Protocol (DTP):** Cisco switches use a proprietary protocol, DTP, to automatically negotiate trunking between two switches. It is enabled on all interfaces by default and can be easily exploited to create unauthorized trunk links. Trunk links are special because they can send traffic on multiple VLANs. Hence, DTP should be disabled on all interfaces, and trunking should be configured manually where required. To disable DTP use the **switchport nonegotiate** command on all interfaces. In addition, all interfaces where trunking is not required should be configured to be in the access mode with the command **switchport mode access**. Example 2-21 shows the configuration required on interfaces to disable DTP and manually configure it to be in the access mode.

Example 2-21 *Disabling DTP and Trunking on an Interface*

```
SW1(config)#interface Gi0/5
SW1(config-if)#switchport mode access
SW1(config-if)#switchport nonegotiate
```

Note Disabling DTP on interfaces and statically configuring non-trunk interfaces as access ports are the most important security measures that you can take for your Layer 2 network. These measures alone mitigate risks associated with various protocols, such as LACP, VTP, and STP.

- **Enabling BPDU Guard:** BPDUs are generated and consumed by network switches. They should never be accepted on interfaces that do not connect other switches. Unfortunately, by default, a switch consumes BPDUs received on any interface, including those that connect to end-user devices such as workstations and printers. This can be prevented with a security feature called BDPU Guard. Where enabled, it shuts down an interface if BPDUs are received on it. BPDU Guard can be configured globally or on a per-interface basis. When configured globally, it is only enabled on ports configured as PortFast edge (or simply PortFast on older switch codes). Example 2-22 shows how BDPU Guard is enabled globally while Example 2-23 shows how it is enabled on a per-interface basis.

Example 2-22 *Enabling BPDU Guard Globally*

```
SW1(config)#interface Gi0/5
SW1(config-if)#spanning-tree portfast edge
SW1(config-if)#exit
SW1(config)#spanning-tree portfast edge bpduguard default
```

Example 2-23 *Enabling BPDU Guard on a Per-Interface Basis*

```
SW1(config)#interface Gi0/5
SW1(config-if)#spanning-tree portfast edge
SW1(config-if)#spanning-tree bpduguard enable
```

> **Note** In older switch codes, the **edge** keyword in PortFast commands is not used. Remove the **edge** keyword from the commands if you are practicing on older codes. Be sure of the proper command based on the IOS versions published in the CCIE blueprint.

- **Enabling BPDU Filter:** Whereas BPDU Guard is applied to incoming frames, BPDU Filter prevents BPDUs from being sent and received on an interface. This is useful in preventing users from gathering information about the network while also blocking unauthorized BPDUs. Much like BDPU Guard, this feature can be enabled globally on all PortFast-enabled interfaces or on a per-interface basis. Example 2-24 shows the global configuration, and Example 2-25 shows how BPDU Filter is enabled on a per-interface basis.

Example 2-24 *Enabling BPDU Filter Globally*

```
SW1(config)#interface Gi0/5
SW1(config-if)#spanning-tree portfast edge
SW1(config-if)#exit
SW1(config)#spanning-tree portfast edge bpdufilter default
```

Example 2-25 *Enabling BPDU Filter on a Per-Interface Basis*

```
SW1(config)#interface Gi0/5
SW1(config-if)#spanning-tree portfast edge
SW1(config-if)#spanning-tree bpdufilter enable
```

Securing VLAN Trunking Protocol (VTP)

Using VLANs for segmentation of traffic is a common method for optimizing a network and security. For VLANs to work properly, they should be created consistently across the network. Incorrect VLAN configuration can result in undesired results, such as connectivity problems. VTP can be used to create and maintain a consistent VLAN database. When VTP is implemented, the switches participate as a server or a client. VLANs are created and modified on the VTP server, and replicated to VTP clients. All switches configured as VTP clients create and modify VLANs locally based on the received data. A VTP client does not allow manual local changes to the VLAN database.

Before looking at the security implications of VTP, it is important to understand some key definitions:

- **VTP domain:** A VTP domain is a logical grouping of switches that share a VLAN database. The domain name in a VTP update should match the domain configured on the switch. The update will be dropped if the domain names do not match.
- **VTP server:** A switch can operate in three VTP modes: server, client, and transparent. The server is the single source of truth, and all changes are made to it. Each change is replicated on the clients through an update sent by the server.
- **VTP client:** Most switches participate as VTP clients. When they receive an update, they verify the domain name and make changes to the local VLAN database.
- **VTP transparent:** A switch in the VTP transparent mode does not participate in a VTP domain but forwards all updates out its trunk interface. A switch in this mode maintains its own VLAN database and allows local manual changes.
- **Revision number:** The VTP revision number allows you to maintain version information of the VLAN database. A client does not use an update unless it has a higher revision number than that of the current local database.
- **VTP version:** VTP has three versions: 1, 2, and 3. While Versions 1 and 2 are fairly similar, Version 3 adds the ability to hide VTP passwords in configuration and to disable VTP on an interface, among other functions.
- **VTP password:** An optional pre-shared key is used to generate an MD5 HMAC in the update packets. The HMAC is used to authenticate VTP updates from a server to prevent unauthorized updates.

When a client receives a VTP update, it matches the domain and revision number and updates the local VLAN database. Because VTP traffic is sent to a specific multicast address, it is not difficult to capture these packets and glean the correct domain and latest revision number. With this information, a malicious user can inject rogue VTP updates with the correct domain and higher revision numbers. A simple act of sending an update with most VLANs removed causes a DoS attack on the Layer 2 network.

Fortunately, VTP provides several methods to safeguard against unauthorized updates:

- **Using VTP passwords:** While VTP passwords are optional, they should always be used. Without the pre-shared key, rogue updates do not have the correct HMAC, and the updates are dropped.
- **Disabling DTP:** VTP updates are only sent to and received from trunk ports. As mentioned in the previous section, disabling DTP prevents a rogue device from establishing a trunk link. This prevents VTP updates from being received from unauthorized devices.
- **Selectively enabling VTP:** VTP is enabled on all interfaces by default, and updates are sent out on and received from all trunk interfaces. VTP should be enabled only on the interfaces that connect toward the VTP server.

Example 2-26 shows the configuration required to secure VTP on a client.

Example 2-26 *Securing VTP on a Client*

```
SW1(config)#vtp mode client
SW1(config)#vtp domain S3cur3MyVTP
SW1(config)#vtp password Str0nGP@$$w0rD
SW1(config)#interface range Gi0/2-48
SW1(config-if-range)#switchport mode access
SW1(config-if-range)#switchport nonegotiate
SW1(config-if-range)#no vtp
```

In this section, we have covered multiple methods of securing the Layer 2 control plane. To summarize the section, Example 2-27 shows what a secure Layer 2 access port configuration should start with. It is by no means complete, and we will continue to build on it in later sections and chapters.

Example 2-27 *Secure Access Port Configuration*

```
SW1(config)#interface Gi0/5
SW1(config-if)#switchport mode access
SW1(config-if)#switchport nonegotiate
SW1(config-if)#switchport access vlan 10
SW1(config-if)#spanning-tree portfast edge
SW1(config-if)#spanning-tree bpdufilter enable
SW1(config-if)#spanning-tree bpduguard enable
SW1(config-if)#no vtp
```

Securing Layer 3 Control Plane Protocols

Earlier in this chapter, we discussed methods for general control plane security, including CoPP. Along with securing the control plane of the device, it is also important to secure the protocols used there. Layer 3 is where a router uses routing protocols such as BGP, EIGRP, and OSPF to learn about the network and create its routing table. If the routing protocol is compromised, the routing table can be changed to drop traffic for a DoS attack or route traffic toward a malicious endpoint for a MITM attack. The good news is that routing protocols have built-in mechanisms to secure routing protocols. This section looks at ways to secure some of the most commonly used routing protocols.

Securing Border Gateway Protocol (BGP)

BGP is the routing protocol of the Internet. A compromised BGP peering session can result in significant problems. The two major threats to BGP come from injection or manipulation of routes and CPU exhaustion attacks in the form of malicious BGP packets.

To protect against BGP peering hijacking and unauthorized route updates, you can use an MD5-based neighbor authentication mechanism with pre-shared keys. You enable authentication with the **neighbor** *neighbor-address* **password** *password* command in BGP configuration mode. Example 2-28 shows how BGP peering with authentication is enabled.

Example 2-28 *Enabling Authentication with BGP Peering*

```
R1(config)#router bgp 70000
R1(config)#neighbor 72.163.4.161 remote-as 70001
R1(config)#neighbor 72.163.4.161 password 1s1tS3cur3!
```

The second threat to BGP comes from CPU exhaustion attacks, which can be executed by sending large numbers of crafted packets. This is particularly concerning with external BGP (eBGP), where a router peers with another autonomous system (AS). With external peering, such as with your ISP, you are open to attacks from public networks such as the Internet. For example, an attacker could send large numbers of TCP SYN packets to a BGP router in hopes of overwhelming the BGP process. To prevent this, you can limit the acceptable hop count for a BGP packet by using the TTL Security feature. This is configured in the BGP configuration mode using the command **neighbor** *neighbor-address* **ttl-security hops** *maximum-hop-count*.

Note Cisco routers set a TTL of 1 for eBGP peers by default. The **neighbor ebgp-multihop** command was traditionally used to set a higher TTL value. The eBGP multihop feature expects the TTL to be 1 when the packet is received at the destination. This is fairly easy to spoof if the attacker knows how many hops exist to the target device. The TTL security feature is more secure because the TTL value is set to 255 by the source, and the receiving router checks the remaining value against the configured hop count. This truly limits the radius within which a valid BGP packet can originate. The eBGP multihop and TTL security features cannot be configured at the same time. If you have the eBGP multihop feature configured, you need to remove it before using the TTL security feature.

Example 2-29 shows how TTL security is configured for an eBGP peer. In this example, the hop count is set to 2. With this configuration, any eBGP packets with a TTL value lower than 253 will be discarded. (The number 253 is derived by deducting the configured hop count from 255, the maximum IP TTL value.)

Example 2-29 *Configuring TTL Security with eBGP*

```
R1(config)#router bgp 70000
R1(config)#neighbor 72.163.4.161 remote-as 70001
R1(config)#neighbor 72.163.4.161 password 1s1tS3cur3!
R1(config)#neighbor 72.163.4.161 ttl-security hops 2
```

Securing RIPv2 and EIGRP

Routing Information Protocol Version 2 (RIPv2) and Enhanced Interior Gateway Routing Protocol (EIGRP) both support using an MD5 hash based on pre-shared keys for authentication; in addition, they have similar methods for configuration.

For both of these protocols, authentication is configured on a per-interface basis using keychains. A *keychain* is a repository of pre-shared keys configured on IOS. Example 2-30 shows how to create a keychain.

Example 2-30 *Creating a Keychain in IOS*

```
R1(config)#key chain myRoutingKey
R1(config-keychain)#key 1
R1(config-keychain-key)#key-string MyS3cur3R0ut1ngK3y
R1(config-keychain-key)#exit
```

A keychain can be used to configure authentication for RIPv2 on a per-interface basis, using the **ip rip authentication** command, as shown in Example 2-31. RIPv2 supports both plaintext and MD5-based authentication. The **ip rip authentication mode md5** command is used to enable MD5-based authentication. Once it is configured, all RIPv2 updates out that interface contain the MD5 hash, and all updates received require the hash, too. Every interface that participates in RIPv2 needs this configured for authentication to be consistent across the network.

Example 2-31 *Configuring Authentication for RIPv2*

```
R1(config)#interface Gi1
R1(config-if)#ip rip authentication key-chain myRoutingKey
R1(config-if)#ip rip authentication mode md5
```

Much as with RIPv2, authentication for EIGRP can be configured on a per-interface basis using the keychain, as shown in Example 2-32. The command needed to enable authentication for EIGRP is **ip authentication key-chain eigrp** *AS-number keychain-name.*

The command to enable MD5-based authentication is **ip authentication mode eigrp** *AS-number* **md5**.

Example 2-32 *Configuring Authentication for EIGRP*

```
R1(config)#interface Gi1
R1(config-if)#ip authentication key-chain eigrp 10 myRoutingKey
R1(config-if)#ip authentication mode eigrp 10 md5
```

Note EIGRP for IPv6 can also be configured for authentication, using the same commands discussed previously, except with **ipv6** replacing **ip** at the beginning.

Securing OSPF

Open Shortest Path First (OSPF) also supports plaintext or MD5-based authentication. The pre-shared key is configured on a per-interface basis, and authentication itself can be configured under OSPF configuration for the whole area or on the interface for a segment. The pre-shared key for MD5 authentication is configured using the **ip ospf message-digest-key** command, as shown in Example 2-33.

Example 2-33 *Configuring OSPF A Pre-shared Key for MD5*

```
R1(config)#Interface Gi1
R1(config-if)#ip ospf message-digest-key 1 md5 MyS3cur3R0ut1ngK3y
```

After the key is configured, authentication can be enabled on a per-interface basis, using the **ip ospf authentication message-digest** command, as shown in Example 2-34. The authentication can also be enabled for the whole OSPF area by using the **area** *area-number* **authentication message-digest** command in the OSPF configuration mode, as shown in Example 2-35.

Example 2-34 *Configuring OSPF Authentication on the Interface*

```
R1(config)#Interface Gi1
R1(config-if)#ip ospf message-digest-key 1 md5 MyS3cur3R0ut1ngK3y
R1(config-if)#ip ospf authentication message-digest
```

Example 2-35 *Configuring OSPF Authentication for the Area*

```
R1(config)#router ospf 1
R1(config-router)#area 1 authentication message-digest
```

OSPFv3 or OSPF for IPv6 does not have an authentication mechanism of its own but uses IPsec to secure communication between OSPF peers. IPsec for OSPFv3 does not require crypto commands like normal IPsec on IOS. It uses a single command on the interface or under the OSPF configuration mode for the whole area. The command to enable OSPFv3 authentication on the interface is **ipv6 ospf authentication ipsec spi** *spi-number* **{md5|sha1}** *key*, as shown in Example 2-36.

In the previous command, *spi-number* is similar to a key ID in a chain but must match on both peers, while the key is written in hexadecimal.

Example 2-36 *Enabling Authentication for OSPFv3 on an Interface*

```
R1(config)#interface Gi1
R1(config-if)#ipv6 ospf authentication ipsec spi 300 md5 9b635903a7f9e11843aad6b-
  20de9e2d2
```

The command to enable authentication for an OSPFv3 area is very similar, as shown in Example 2-37, but is applied in the OSPF configuration mode.

Example 2-37 *Enabling Authentication for OSPFv3 on an Interface*

```
R1(config)#ipv6 router ospf 1
R1(config-rtr)#area 1 authentication ipsec spi 500 md5 9b635903a7f9e11843aad6b-
  20de9e2d2
```

Securing the Data Plane

The purpose of a network is to move data from its source to its destination. Network devices are geared toward that one function alone, and the data plane is where it is executed. Hence, it should not be surprising that most attacks are targeted toward this plane, and most security is also implemented here.

The difference between the data plane of a Layer 2 device and that of a Layer 3 device is far more distinct than in any other plane. The security objectives, challenges, and solutions are very different between those two layers.

Layer 2 security is primarily focused on unauthorized or spoofed access, segmentation, and resource protection. On the other hand, Layer 3 security is primarily focused on the data itself and ensuring that the right kind from the right source is allowed. Even with the differences, some general security considerations apply to the data plane of both layers:

- **Zero trust and minimum required access:** This principle applies to the data plane also. No traffic or its source should be trusted, and each device should be given the minimum required access. Access control and segmentation of traffic play a crucial role in this.

- **Protocol validation:** Most of the common protocols used in the data plane have absolutely no security built in. They are usually easy to spoof and exploit. In fact, some of the most effective attacks are executed by exploiting transport protocols. Measures should be taken to prevent attacks using these protocols.
- **Audit trail collection:** Cisco devices provide various methods to generate and export audit trails in the form of logs. Common examples of these are access lists with logging and NetFlow. These should be enabled, exported to central collectors, and analyzed for incidence response and policy correction.

Security at the Layer 2 Data Plane

The data plane on a switch is focused on switching frames in the local network segment. To accomplish this, it needs to know where a given MAC address is located and, sometimes, what IP address it is mapped to. To keep track of these two important details, a switch uses some protocols and tables, such as the CAM and ARP tables. The next few sections discuss the inherent vulnerabilities in the switching mechanism and the security features used to protect them.

The CAM Table and Port Security

The content addressable memory (CAM) table is a list of all MAC addresses known to the switch, along with their physical location and VLAN ID. When an endpoint sends a frame, its MAC address, source interface, and VLAN ID are recorded in the CAM table. The switch searches this table to find the location of a MAC address when it needs to deliver a frame. If the destination MAC address is not found in the CAM table, the frame is flooded out all interfaces except the one where the frame was received.

The process of learning a MAC address and its location has no security built into it. Anyone can send a frame with a spoofed source MAC address to cause the switch to update its CAM table. This can be used for a MITM attack such that frames are switched to the spoofed location instead of the intended destination. The traffic continues to flow to the attacking host until the original endpoint sends a frame, causing the switch to update the CAM table again. This is called a *MAC spoofing attack*.

Another problem with the CAM table is its limited size. An attacker can send hundreds of thousands of frames with difference source MAC addresses within a short period of time. This causes the switch to add these spoofed MAC addresses in the CAM table. Once the CAM table has reached its limits, it stops learning new MAC addresses and starts flooding frames with unknown MAC addresses out all its interfaces. This can cause severe degradation of the network to the point of a DoS situation. This attack is called *CAM flooding*. Each switch has a different CAM table size limit. The size of the CAM table on a Cisco IOS switch can be found by using the **show mac address-table count** command, as shown in Example 2-38.

Example 2-38 *MAC Address Table Limit*

```
SW1#sh mac address-table count

Mac Entries for Vlan 1:
---------------------------
Dynamic Address Count  : 17
Static  Address Count  : 37
Total Mac Addresses    : 54
Total Mac Address Space Available: 16303
```

CAM table attacks can be prevented with the port security feature in Cisco switches. With port security, an interface can be configured to learn only a limited number of MAC addresses. The addresses an interface can learn can be dynamic, static, or a combination of these. Port security can be enabled on an interface with the **switchport port-security** command.

The following MAC address learning restrictions can be configured with port security:

- **Static Secure MAC Addresses:** With this option, an interface is configured to learn only the manually configured MAC addresses. This option limits the devices that can connect to a given interface and is best used for static devices such as printers, cameras, servers, and other devices that do not change locations. This also prevents MAC spoofing by preventing the configured MAC address from connecting to another switch port. Static secure MAC addresses can be configured on an interface with the **switchport port-security mac-address** *mac-address* command.
- **Dynamic Secure Addresses:** This option configures the maximum addresses that an interface will learn. The addresses are learned dynamically as devices connect to the interface. This option can be used to prevent CAM flooding attacks and the addition of unauthorized switches or hubs. The number of maximum allowed addresses can be configured on an interface with the **switchport port-security maximum** *number* command.
- **Sticky Secure MAC Addresses:** Configuring each interface to allow a static MAC address is administratively prohibitive and restrictive to users. The Sticky Secure MAC Addresses for port security solves this by dynamically learning the MAC addresses that connect to it and storing them in the configuration as static. Sticky secure learning can be enabled on an interface with the **switchport port-security mac-address sticky** command.

Note When sticky secure addressing is enabled, all addresses already learned on the interface are also stored in the running configuration. Sticky addresses are stored only in the running configuration and not the startup configuration. A reboot of the switch removes all sticky addresses unless the running configuration is saved as the startup configuration.

The three options can be combined to meet different requirements. For example, an interface can be configured to learn a maximum of two addresses, while one is statically defined, as shown in Example 2-39. Such a configuration allows the interface to learn one dynamic address along with the statically configured one.

Example 2-39 *Port Security with Static and Dynamic Address Learning*

```
SW1(config)#interface Gi0/5
SW1(config-if)#switchport port-security mac-address 1001.1001.1001
SW1(config-if)#switchport port-security maximum 2
```

Example 2-40 shows another combination in which an interface is configured for a maximum of three addresses with sticky learning enabled. This means the switch will learn and save the MAC addresses of the first three devices that connect to it. After that, only those three devices will be able to connect to that interface.

Example 2-40 *Three Sticky Secure Addresses*

```
SW1(config)#interface Gi0/9
SW1(config-if)#switchport port-security maximum 3
SW1(config-if)#switchport port-security mac-address sticky
```

Port security defines three actions that can be taken when a violation occurs. An interface can be configured to take one of these actions:

- **Protect:** When the number of secure MAC addresses exceeds the maximum allowed limit on an interface, packets with unknown source addresses are dropped silently. The switch continues to drop frames until a sufficient number of addresses have been removed or the maximum number of allowed addresses has been increased in the configuration. The switch does not generate any alerts or logs in this mode. This mode can be enabled on an interface with the **switchport port-security violation protect** command.
- **Restrict:** Like the Protect mode, this mode also drops frames, but it generates alerts in the form of SNMP traps and syslog, and it also increases the violation counter for that interface. This mode can be enabled on an interface with the **switchport port-security violation restrict** command.
- **Shutdown:** An interface in this mode enters an error-disabled status and shuts down as soon as a port security violation occurs. An interface can be brought out of this state with the **errdisable recovery cause psecure-violation** command in the global configuration mode or with the **shutdown** command followed by the **no shutdown command** on the interface. While this mode is the default, it can be reenabled on an interface with the **switchport port-security violation shutdown** command.

With dynamic secure addressing, it is important to allow the learned addresses to age out of the CAM table. Without proper aging, new devices will not be able to connect on the interface. The aging timer can be configured with the **switchport port-security aging time** *minutes* command.

The aging timer can be configured to be absolute so that it starts as soon as the address is learned, or it can be configured to start when a period of inactivity begins. The type of timer can be configured with the **switchport port-security aging type** {**absolute**| **inactivity**} command.

Example 2-41 shows an interface configured to learn four addresses, out of which one is configured statically and three can be learned dynamically. The interface is also configured to remove the dynamically learned addresses after 10 minutes of inactivity.

Example 2-41 *Port Security Aging*

```
SW1(config)#interface Gi0/9
SW1(config-if)#switchport port-security
SW1(config-if)#switchport port-security mac-address 1001.1001.1001
SW1(config-if)#switchport port-security aging time 10
SW1(config-if)#switchport port-security aging type inactivity
```

Port security configuration of an interface can be verified with the **show port-security interface** *interface* command, as shown in Example 2-42.

Example 2-42 *Verifying Port Security Configuration*

```
SW1#show port-security int Gi0/9
Port Security              : Enabled
Port Status                : Secure-down
Violation Mode             : Shutdown
Aging Time                 : 10 mins
Aging Type                 : Inactivity
SecureStatic Address Aging : Disabled
Maximum MAC Addresses      : 3
Total MAC Addresses        : 1
Configured MAC Addresses   : 1
Sticky MAC Addresses       : 0
Last Source Address:Vlan   : 1001.1001.1001:1
Security Violation Count   : 0
```

Note A more scalable method for preventing MAC spoofing and CAM table attacks is to use port authentication with 802.1x. Port authentication, 802.1x, and related technologies are discussed in *Integrated Security Technologies and Solutions, Volume II.*

DHCP Snooping

One of the key protocols in modern networks is Dynamic Host Configuration Protocol (DHCP). It provides IP addressing, default gateway, and other information to endpoints as they connect to the network and enables them to communicate. When an endpoint connects, it broadcasts a DHCP request, and any DHCP server in the network can respond to it. That is where the problem with DHCP lies. As you can imagine, the DHCP communication has no security built into it. Any host can claim to be a DHCP server and respond to requests, while any endpoint can forge DHCP requests to get an address assigned. This situation can be exploited to carry two attacks:

- **DHCP spoofing MITM:** An attacker can set up a rogue DHCP server to respond to DHCP requests. This DHCP server responds to requests with its own IP address as the default gateway. This causes the victims to send their traffic through the rogue gateway, where it can be read, stored, and modified before being sent to the real gateway, resulting in a MITM attack.
- **DHCP starvation DoS:** Because a DHCP server responds to any client request, it is trivial to forge thousands of DHCP requests with different MAC addresses and cause the server to exhaust its address pool. When the pool is exhausted, legitimate clients do not receive IP addresses, resulting in a DoS situation. This attack is often a precursor to a DHCP spoofing MITM attack, just described. If the legitimate DHCP pool is exhausted, a larger number of endpoints receive IP addresses from the rogue DHCP server.

While a DHCP starvation attack can be prevented with port security, as described earlier, mitigating DHCP spoofing attacks requires the use of DHCP snooping on Cisco switches.

DHCP snooping is a security feature that acts as a filtering mechanism between DHCP servers and clients. It works by defining trusted and untrusted interfaces. Trusted interfaces are those from which DHCP server messages can be expected, while all other interfaces are untrusted. This prevents rogue DHCP servers from responding to requests.

Note DHCP servers are usually a few hops away from the endpoints. All uplink interfaces, including redundant links, should be configured with DHCP snooping trusted.

In addition to filtering rogue DHCP server packets, DHCP snooping also builds a database of clients connected to untrusted interfaces, along with the IP address, MAC address, and VLAN ID of each one. When a DHCP packet is received from an untrusted interface, its content is validated against the database. This prevents spoofed DHCP requests from being sent out.

Note The DHCP snooping database is also used by other security features, such as Dynamic ARP Inspection (DAI) and IP Source Guard. These functions are discussed later in this chapter.

Finally, DHCP snooping has a rate-limiting function that limits the number of DHCP packets allowed on an untrusted interface. This helps prevent starvation attacks against the DHCP server.

DHCP snooping configuration can be broken down into four steps:

Step 1. Enable DHCP snooping on VLANs that require it with the **ip dhcp snooping vlan** *vlan-id* command. Multiple VLANs can be specified, separated by commas, or a range of VLANs can be specified by using a dash.

Step 2. Configure trusted interfaces from which DHCP server messages are expected with the **ip dhcp snooping trust** command. All interfaces are untrusted by default.

Step 3. Configure DHCP rate limiting on untrusted interfaces with the **ip dhcp limit rate** *limit* command.

Step 4. Enable DHCP snooping globally with the **ip dhcp snooping** command.

Example 2-43 shows DHCP snooping configuration on a switch. In this example, interface GigabitEthernet0/10 is the trunk interface toward the DHCP server, and interfaces GigabitEthernet0/1 to 9 are access ports for endpoints. Interface Gi0/10 is configured as trusted, while others have rate limits applied to them.

Example 2-43 *Configuring DHCP Snooping*

```
SW1(config)#ip dhcp snooping vlan 1,4
SW1(config)#interface Gi0/10
SW1(config-if)#ip dhcp snooping trust
SW1(config-if)#exit
SW1(config)#interface range Gi0/1-9
SW1(config-if-range)#ip dhcp snooping limit rate 5
SW1(config-if)#exit
SW1(config)#ip dhcp snooping
```

DHCP snooping can be verified with the **show ip dhcp snooping** command, as shown in Example 2-44.

Example 2-44 *Verifying DHCP Snooping*

```
SW1#show ip dhcp snooping
Switch DHCP snooping is enabled
DHCP snooping is configured on following VLANs:
1,4
DHCP snooping is operational on following VLANs:
1
– removed for brevity -
DHCP snooping trust/rate is configured on the following Interfaces:

Interface                  Trusted    Allow option    Rate limit (pps)
-----------------------    --------   ------------    ----------------
GigabitEthernet0/1         no         no              5
– remove for brevity –
GigabitEthernet0/10        yes        yes             unlimited
```

The ARP Table and Dynamic ARP Inspection (DAI)

While forcing an association change in the CAM table by spoofing the source MAC address is effective, it is not very practical. The device that actually owns the MAC address may send a frame any time and update the table. ARP poisoning, on the other hand, is easier to execute and lasts a longer time.

With ARP poisoning, the ARP table of a router, switch, or target host is changed to map an IP address to the MAC address of a different host. This causes IP packets to be switched to a rogue device instead of the intended destination.

Two methods can be used to poison the ARP table. The first involves using a forged ARP response to a broadcasted query. The second involves using a Gratuitous ARP (GARP) packet to announce a false IP-to-MAC address mapping. The new mapping announced with the GARP packet overwrites the existing one and causes the packets to be delivered to the newly mapped MAC address.

ARP poisoning attacks can be prevented with the DAI security feature of a Cisco switch. When this feature is enabled, the switch checks all ARP packets against the DHCP snooping database to validate mappings being announced. If a mapping does not match the information in the database, it is dropped. Just as with DHCP snooping, interfaces can be configured as trusted or untrusted for DAI. Only ARP packets from untrusted interfaces are inspected. If the network segment contains hosts that do not use DHCP, an ARP access list must be configured for DAI to use.

Note All upstream links to other switches and routers should be configured as trusted. If these links are not configured as trusted, DAI breaks the Proxy ARP functionality.

DAI can be enabled for a VLAN with the **ip arp inspection vlan** *vlan-ID* command. *VLAN-ID* can be a single VLAN, a comma-separated list, or a range.

An ARP access list is created using the **arp access-list** *acl-name* command. Within the access list, individual entries are defined using the **permit ip host** *ip-address* **mac host** *mac-address* command. The access list can be applied to a VLAN with the **ip arp inspection filter** *filter-name* **vlan** *vlan-ID* command.

Example 2-45 shows DAI configuration on a switch. In this example, DAI is enabled on VLAN 1, an ARP inspection access list is applied for a static IP address, and Gi0/10 uplink is configured as a trusted interface.

Example 2-45 *Configuring Dynamic ARP Inspection*

```
SW1(config)#ip arp inspection vlan 1
SW1(config)#arp access-list static-map
SW1(config-arp-nacl)#permit ip host 192.168.1.24 mac host 1001.1001.1001
SW1(config-arp-nacl)#exit
SW1(config)#ip arp inspection filter static-map vlan 1
SW1(config)#interface Gi0/10
SW1(config-if)#ip arp inspection trust
```

DAI configuration and operation can be verified with the **show ip arp inspection** command, as shown in Example 2-46.

Example 2-46 *Verifying Dynamic ARP Inspection*

```
SW1#show ip arp inspection
—removed for brevity—
 Vlan     Configuration    Operation   ACL Match          Static ACL
 ----     -------------    ---------   ---------          -----------
    1     Enabled          Active      static-map           No

 Vlan     ACL Logging      DHCP Logging      Probe Logging
 ----     -----------      ------------      -------------
    1     Deny             Deny              Off

 Vlan     Forwarded        Dropped     DHCP Drops      ACL Drops
 ----     ---------        -------     ----------      ---------
    1            19              6              6              0
—removed for brevity—
```

Segmentation

Flat networks provide a high degree of flexibility because all resources and users are connected to the same network and can access anything. With the increasing popularity of wireless networks, accessing networks is even easier. The operational and administrative ease make flat networks very popular. You are probably wondering why we are talking about segmentation. Flat networks are not secure! With a flat network, anybody who has access can try to move laterally and may compromise the whole network. In fact, most worms do this.

The most common form of network architecture places critical assets in a central location such as a data center and segments that off while the rest of the network is kept flat. The problem with this approach is that it does not take into consideration the potential to escalate privilege with a lateral attack.

With the increasing numbers and types of devices, such as the IoT and mobile, it is more important than ever before to segment traffic even at the access layer. Such segmentation provides a few key benefits:

- **Network performance:** Segmentation divides broadcast domains and improves network performance. A very large and flat network has degraded performance due to the number of broadcast packets.
- **Reduced area of attack:** When an endpoint is compromised, an attacker or an agent such as a worm attempts to move laterally to compromise other endpoints. Segmentation limits the number of devices that can be targeted.
- **Compliance:** Certain standards, such as the Payment Card Industry Data Security Standard (PCI DSS), require relevant traffic to be kept separate. Segmentation helps achieve that while using the same physical infrastructure.
- **Secure mobility and guest access:** Users are increasingly mobile within and outside offices. On the other hand, visitors and employees require Internet access for their devices. Segmentation allows traffic from guests, non-corporate devices and remote users to be kept separate from normal business traffic.
- **Monitoring and analytics:** The difficulty involved in monitoring and analyzing traffic increases with the size of the network. With segmentation of traffic, monitoring can also be divided into smaller pieces while also adding context to analytics.

Segmentation at the Layer 2 data plane can be achieved with either VLANs or Cisco TrustSec. VLANs work by placing endpoints into logical broadcast domains, while TrustSec works by tagging traffic with scalable (formerly security) group tags (SGTs). TrustSec and SGTs are covered in detail in *Integrated Security Technologies and Solutions, Volume II.* While configuring and managing VLANs is beyond the scope of this book, this section looks at private VLANs (PVLANs).

Typically, devices within a VLAN belong to the same broadcast domain and can communicate directly without going through a Layer 3 device. Each VLAN is assigned a separate IP subnet, and inter-VLAN traffic is routed through a Layer 3 device. In a multitenant environment or segments with few devices, using multiple VLANs and subnets is not always feasible. In such situations, PVLANs can be used to provide segmentation within a VLAN.

PVLANs treat the existing VLAN domain as the *primary VLAN* and then create subdomains called *secondary VLANs*. Traffic within the secondary VLANs is kept separate and has to be routed by a Layer 3 device to reach another secondary VLAN. The traffic between secondary VLANs can be filtered at Layer 3 to provide additional security. PVLANs work by assigning switch ports into three types:

- **Promiscuous ports:** These ports are part of the primary VLAN and can communicate with all other ports in that VLAN, including all ports in secondary VLANs. These ports generally connect to the VLAN gateway to allow traffic to be routed between different secondary VLANs and other primary VLANs.
- **Isolated ports:** These ports are part of a secondary isolated VLAN. PVLANs block all traffic to isolated ports except traffic from promiscuous ports. Similarly, traffic received from an isolated port is forwarded only to promiscuous ports. Isolated ports provide an absolute separation for the hosts connected to them.
- **Community ports:** These ports are part of a secondary community VLAN. Community ports communicate with other ports in the same community VLAN and with promiscuous ports. These interfaces are isolated at Layer 2 from all other interfaces in other communities and from isolated ports within their private VLAN.

A PVLAN can work across multiple switches, and VTPv3 can be used to carry PVLAN information across the domain. Configuring PVLAN can be broken down into four steps:

Step 1. **Defining the secondary VLANs:** Each secondary VLAN should be configured as required. The **private-vlan** {**community**|**isolated**} command is used in VLAN configuration mode for this.

Step 2. **Defining the primary VLAN:** The primary VLAN is configured for the PVLAN, and the secondary VLANs are associated with it. A VLAN can be declared primary with the **private-vlan primary** command in VLAN configuration mode. Secondary VLAN associations are also declared in that mode, using the **private-vlan association** *vlan-ID* command. Multiple VLANs can be specified as a comma-separated list.

Step 3. **Configuring a promiscuous port:** A switch interface can be configured as a promiscuous port with the **switchport mode private-vlan promiscuous** command. The PVLANs should then be mapped to the interface with the **switchport private-vlan mapping** *primary-vlan-ID*, *secondary-vlan-list* command, where *secondary-vlan-list* is a comma-separated list of all secondary VLANs of that PVLAN.

Step 4. **Configuring member ports:** The PVLAN can be enabled on each participating interface with the **switchport mode private-vlan host** command. The primary and secondary VLANs can be mapped to the interface with the **switchport private-vlan host-association** *primary-vlan-ID secondary-vlan-ID* command.

Example 2-47 shows the configuration of private VLANs with interface Gi0/10 configured as the promiscuous port in primary VLAN 10, interface Gi0/11 configured as an isolated port in secondary VLAN 20, and interface Gi0/12 configured as a community port in secondary VLAN 30.

Example 2-47 *Configuring Private VLANs*

```
SW1(config)#vlan 20
SW1(config-vlan)#private-vlan isolated
SW1(config-vlan)#exit
SW1(config)#vlan 30
SW1(config-vlan)#private-vlan community
SW1(config-vlan)#exit
SW1(config)#vlan 10
SW1(config-vlan)#private-vlan primary
SW1(config-vlan)#private-vlan association 20,30
SW1(config-vlan)#exit
SW1(config)#interface Gi0/10
SW1(config-if)#switchport mode private-vlan promiscuous
SW1(config-if)#switchport private-vlan mapping 10 20,30
SW1(config-if)#exit
SW1(config)#interface Gi0/11
SW1(config-if)#switchport mode private-vlan host
SW1(config-if)#switchport private-vlan host-association 10 20
SW1(config-if)#exit
SW1(config)#interface Gi0/12
SW1(config-if)#switchport mode private-vlan host
SW1(config-if)#switchport private-vlan host-association 10 30
```

Attacks Against Segmentation

VLANs and PVLANs are both subject to some attacks. The primary motivation behind the attacks is to send traffic outside the segment that the attacker belongs to without going through a Layer 3 device and any filtering configured there. Whereas VLANs are subject to *VLAN hopping attacks*, PVLANs are suspect to the unimaginatively named *private VLAN attacks*.

In a VLAN hopping attack, two methods can be used to send traffic outside the VLAN without going through a router:

- **Basic VLAN hopping:** To execute a basic VLAN hopping attack, the attacker establishes a trunk link with the switch and is then able to tag frames with any VLAN. As mentioned earlier, Cisco switch interfaces have DTP enabled by default, which allows trunk negotiation on any interface if not disabled.

- **Double tagging:** In this type of attack, the attacker sends a frame with two 802.1q tags. The first tag specifies a VLAN that the attacker's host actually belongs to, and the second frame specifies a VLAN of the destination host. This attack attempts to exploit the fact that most trunks have their native VLANs set to the same one as the hosts, and they allow frames in native VLANs to be sent without any VLAN tags. This results in the first tag being stripped at the source switch and being delivered across a trunk to the destination switch, where the second tag is read and the frame is delivered to the destination.

Basic VLAN hopping attacks can easily be mitigated by disabling DTP negotiation on interfaces and by configuring non-trunk interfaces in access mode.

Double tagging attacks can be mitigated by either configuring the native VLAN on trunk links to be an unused VLAN or by forcing trunks to tag frames in native VLANs also. The native VLAN of a trunk interface can be changed with the **switchport trunk native vlan** *vlan-ID* command, and native VLAN tagging can be enabled with the **vlan dot1q tag native** global configuration command.

In a PVLAN attack, the attacker attempts to send a packet to a host in another isolated or community VLAN. This is done by sending a crafted IP packet with the following:

- Real source MAC and IP addresses
- A real destination IP address
- The destination MAC address of the gateway router instead of the destination host

Because the destination MAC address belongs to the gateway router connected to a promiscuous port, the switch delivers it. Because the router only looks at the destination IP address, it routes the packet to the destination. This results in the packet being delivered outside the PVLAN's secondary VLAN.

PVLAN attacks can be mitigated by applying an ACL on the router interface, connected to the promiscuous port, to drop packets that originate from and are destined to the same IP subnet.

Traffic Filtering at Layer 2

While filtering and access lists are generally associated with routers and firewalls, they can also be applied at Layer 2 interfaces and to VLANs to provide granular security. The following are some of the benefits of using access lists at Layer 2:

- **Contextual filtering:** Filtering at Layer 3 is generally based on subnets of the source traffic. A subnet can have multiple types of devices, such as IP phones, workstations, printers, and such. This context of the device is lost when filtering is done at that level. On the other hand, the context of the device is known at the switch interface it connects to, and filtering can be designed based on that. For example, an IP phone only needs to communicate with a certain set of services, so filtering can be applied to drop traffic destined to any other service.

- **Containing lateral attacks:** In most cases, devices in a subnet do not need to communicate with each other. Most services are centrally located, and there is little need for endpoints in a subnet to communicate with each other. For example, in many cases workstation-to-workstation or printer-to-printer communication is not required. Restricting intra-subnet communication with Layer 2 ACLs reduces the chance for lateral movement from a compromised host.
- **Reduced load on Layer 3:** When filtering is applied right at source, the rest of the network has to do less. This improves network performance and simplifies configuration

Filtering on a Cisco switch can be configured with port access control lists (PACLs) or VLAN access control lists (VACLs).

PACLs are standard, extended, or named IP ACLs, and named MAC address ACLs applied to a switch interface. The syntax for creating PACLs is the same as the syntax for creating ACLs on any Cisco IOS router.

Note Cisco IOS router ACLs are covered in depth later in this chapter.

When the PACL is applied, it filters incoming traffic on an interface. A few restrictions apply to PACL:

- Log, reflect, and evaluate keywords cannot be used.
- Physical and logical link protocols such as CDP, STP, DTP, and VTP cannot be filtered with a PACL.
- Ingress traffic is evaluated against PACLs before any other ACLs, such as a VACL.
- PACLs take up Ternary Content-Addressable Memory (TCAM) space and should be kept as small as possible. Generally, 20 to 30 Access Control Entries (ACEs) per PACL is an acceptable value.

Note Another form of PACL is a downloadable ACL (DACL), which can be downloaded during 802.1x or MAB authentication from a RADIUS server. The content of the DACL is received from the RADIUS server and applied on the interface. The DACL overwrites any PACL configured on the interface. DACLs are covered in *Integrated Security Technologies and Solutions, Volume II.*

A PACL is applied to an interface with the **ip access-group** *access-list* **in** command. Example 2-48 shows a PACL applied to interface Gi0/5 to block RDP and Telnet traffic.

Example 2-48 *Applying a PACL*

```
SW1(config)#ip access-list extended pacl-5
SW1(config-ext-nacl)#deny tcp any any eq 3389
SW1(config-ext-nacl)#deny udp any any eq 3389
SW1(config-ext-nacl)#deny tcp any any eq 23
SW1(config-ext-nacl)#permit ip any any
SW1(config-ext-nacl)#exit
SW1(config)#int Gi0/5
SW1(config-if)#ip access-group pacl-5 in
```

A PACL can be further augmented with the IP Source Guard (IPSG) feature, which uses information from DHCP snooping to dynamically configure a port such that traffic is allowed only if it is sourced from an IP address bound to the interface. This is an effective method for blocking traffic with spoofed IP addresses. IPSG can be enabled with the **ip verify source** command on the interface and verified with the **show ip verify source** exec mode command. Example 2-49 shows IPSG enabled on the Gi0/9 interface, and only packets with source IP address 192.168.1.10 will be allowed out.

Example 2-49 *Verifying IP Source Guard*

```
SW1#show ip verify source
Interface  Filter-type  Filter-mode  IP-address    Mac-address  Vlan  Log
---------  -----------  -----------  ----------    -----------  ----  ---
Gi0/9      ip           active      192.168.1.10               1     disabled
```

The second method for filtering traffic at Layer 2 is to use VACLs. VACLs filter traffic that enters the VLAN from any source, including hosts in the VLAN. This makes it an effective tool for filtering traffic between hosts in the same VLAN as well as traffic being received from outside.

VACLs are configured using a VLAN access map. An access map is a series of **match** and **action** sets that define interesting traffic and action to be taken on them. Interesting traffic is defined by matching an IPv4, IPv6, or MAC access list. For each set of matched traffic, two actions can be defined: **forward** or **drop**. Optionally, the **log** keyword can be used with the **drop** action.

Access maps are defined with the **vlan access-map** *name sequence* command. Each map can have multiple sequences, with each sequence defining a **match** and **action** set. The access map can be applied to VLANs with the **vlan filter** *map-name* **vlan-list** *vlan-list* command, where *vlan-list* can be a single VLAN, a range of VLANs, or multiple VLANs as a comma-separated list.

Example 2-50 shows a VLAN access map applied for VLAN 1 to drop RDP and Telnet traffic. Note that the named ACLs, **rdp-traffic** and **telnet-traffic**, include a **permit** statement for the interesting traffic. Interesting traffic is always defined with a **permit** statement in the ACL so that it matches a VACL sequence. The VACL itself, though, is configured to drop the matched traffic.

Example 2-50 *Creating and Applying a VACL*

```
SW1(config)#ip access-list extended rdp-traffic
SW1(config-ext-nacl)#permit tcp any any eq 3389
SW1(config-ext-nacl)#permit udp any any eq 3389
SW1(config-ext-nacl)#exit

SW1(config)#ip access-list extended telnet-traffic
SW1(config-ext-nacl)#permit tcp any any eq 23
SW1(config-ext-nacl)#exit

SW1(config)#ip access-list extended other-traffic
SW1(config-ext-nacl)#permit ip any any
SW1(config-ext-nacl)#exit

SW1(config)#vlan access-map vacl1 10
SW1(config-access-map)#match ip address rdp-traffic
SW1(config-access-map)#action drop log
SW1(config-access-map)#exit

SW1(config)#vlan access-map vacl1 20
SW1(config-access-map)#match ip address telnet-traffic
SW1(config-access-map)#action drop log
SW1(config-access-map)#exit

SW1(config)#vlan access-map vacl1 30
SW1(config-access-map)#match ip address other-traffic
SW1(config-access-map)#action forward

SW1(config)#vlan filter vacl1 vlan-list 1
```

Security at the Layer 3 Data Plane

The data plane of a Layer 3 device uses information learned from the control plane protocols to route traffic between subnets. It uses the IP headers to determine where the intended destination is and routes the packet to the next hop. Given that a router works on a subnet level, it is easy to apply broad controls such as filtering and QoS. This section looks at some of the most common security features applied at the data layer of a Layer 3 device.

Traffic Filtering at Layer 3

The primary method of filtering traffic at Layer 3 is using access control lists (ACLs). ACLs are the Swiss Army knife of security with various uses. From broad traffic filtering based on source or destination address to granular filtering based on ports, protocol characteristics, or time, ACLs can be used in various ways. As mentioned before, they are even used to classify traffic for other security and non-security features.

ACLs are sequential lists of **permit** or **deny** statements, called access control entries (ACEs), that packets are evaluated against until the first match. When a packet matches an ACE, the specified action is taken. Using ACLs consists of two steps:

Step 1. **Creating ACLs:** The first step in using ACLs is to create them. The type of ACL and its content determine the steps required to create it. While there are many variations of access lists, sometimes based on their usage, the five most common types—standard, extended, named, time-based, and reflexive—are discussed in the following sections.

Step 2. **Applying ACLs:** ACLs need to be applied to interfaces, in the path of traffic, before they can be used. In addition to the interface, the direction in which the ACL needs to be applied has to be specified. Cisco routers allow one ACL per interface per direction.

Note The interface and direction for an ACL are subjective because the ACL will have the same effect when applied in the inbound direction of the ingress interface as when applied to the outbound direction of the egress interface. The difference is that outbound traffic on the egress interface has been processed by the router, while the inbound traffic on the ingress interface has not. There is no right or wrong way to apply an ACL, as long as it has the desired result, but generally inbound ACLs are preferred to prevent unnecessary processing of traffic that will eventually be dropped.

Before looking into specific ACL types, it is important to know that ACLs on Cisco routers use something called inverse masks or wildcard masks instead of subnet masks to define source and destination traffic. As the name implies, an inverse mask is an inversed subnet mask. When broken down into binary numbers, each 0 bit in an inverse mask indicates that the corresponding address bit has to match exactly, while a 1 indicates that the corresponding address bit can be anything. For example, an IP address of 10.1.2.0 with an inverse mask of 0.0.0.255 means all bits of the first three octets must match exactly, while all bits of the last octet can be anything. Any IP address from 10.1.2.0 to 10.1.2.255 will match such an inverse mask.

An easy way to determine the inverse mask for a given subnet mask is to subtract it from 255.255.255.255. Example 2-51 shows a few examples of this.

Example 2-51 *Finding the Inverse Mask from a Subnet Mask*

```
255.255.255.255 - 255.255.255.0 = 0.0.0.255
255.255.255.255 - 255.255.255.128 = 0.0.0.127
255.255.255.255 - 255.255.240.0 = 0.0.15.255
255.255.255.255 - 255.128.0.0 = 0.127.255.255
```

One important thing to remember about ACLs is that each of them has an implicit deny at the end. Traffic that is not permitted by any ACE in the ACL will be denied by the implicit deny at the end.

Standard ACLs

Standard ACLs are the simplest form of ACLs, and they filter based on only the source IP address of a packet. These ACLs can be numbered between 1 and 99 or 1300 and 1999. The source address can be a single host address, a subnet defined with an inverse mask, or simply all hosts defined with the **any** keyword. The syntax for creating a standard ACL is as follows:

access-list *access-list-number* {**permit**|**deny**}{**host** *source*|*source inverse-mask*|**any**} [**log**]

The optional **log** keyword at the end of the command causes the router to generate a syslog every time a packet matches that ACL. The log message includes the ACL number, the action taken on the packet, the source IP address of the packet, and the number of matches from a source within a five-minute period. The **log** keyword should be used sparingly to reduce CPU load. Typically, this keyword is used on ACEs that deny certain traffic to monitor for suspicious activity.

The **access-list** command can be repeated with the same *access-list-number* as often as required to add more ACEs in the ACL. Each subsequent command adds the new ACE at the end of the existing list. The order of the ACEs in an ACL is important because the ACL will be evaluated from the top, and the first match will be applied to a given packet. So, if there is a **deny** statement before a **permit** statement for the same source, the packet will be dropped.

The access list can be applied to an interface with the **ip access-group** *access-list-number* {**in**|**out**} command. The **in** and **out** keywords indicate the direction in which the access list is applied.

Example 2-52 shows how an access list is created and applied to deny traffic from the 10.1.1.0/24 subnet and from host 10.2.1.1, while all other traffic is permitted coming into interface Gi1. In the example, note the last ACE that explicitly permits all traffic. If this ACE is not added, all traffic will be dropped because of the implicit deny.

Example 2-52 *Creating and Applying a Standard ACL*

```
Router(config)#access-list 10 deny 10.1.1.0 0.0.0.255
Router(config)#access-list 10 deny host 10.2.1.1
Router(config)#access-list 10 permit any
Router(config)#interface Gi1
Router(config-if)#ip access-group 10 in
```

Extended ACLs

While standard ACLs are simple, they have limited functionality because they can only filter based on the source address. Most security policies require more granular filtering based on various fields, such as source address, destination address, protocols, and ports. Extended ACLs can be used for such filtering requirements.

Extended ACLs are created and applied in the same way as standard ACLs and follow similar rules of sequential ACEs and implicit deny. The difference begins with the ACL numbers: Extended ACLs are numbered from 100 to 199 and 2000 to 2699. The syntax of extended ACLs is also different, as shown here:

```
access-list access-list-number {deny|permit} protocol source destination
[protocol-options] [log|log-input]
```

As with standard ACLs, *source* and *destination* can be defined as a single host with the **host** keyword or a subnet with inverse mask or as all hosts with the **any** keyword.

The optional *protocol-options* part of the command differs based on the protocol specified in the ACE. For example, when TCP or UDP protocols are defined, **eq**, **lt**, and **gt** (equal to, less than, and greater than) keywords are available to specify ports to be matched. In addition to ports, various bits in the TCP headers, such as SYN and ACK, can also be matched with available keywords.

Example 2-53 shows access list 101 created and applied to block all Telnet and RDP traffic coming into interface Gi1. In addition, the access list blocks all communication between hosts 10.1.1.1 and 10.2.1.1. Note the use of the **eq** keyword with TCP in the first two lines to deny Telnet and RDP traffic.

Example 2-53 *Creating and Applying Extended ACLs*

```
Router(config)#access-list 101 deny tcp any any eq 23
Router(config)#access-list 101 deny tcp any any eq 3389
Router(config)#access-list 101 deny ip host 10.1.1.1 host 10.2.1.1
Router(config)#access-list 101 permit ip any any
Router(config)#interface Gi1
Router(config-if)#ip access-group 101 in
```

Named ACLs

During the course of normal operations, it is not uncommon to see tens or hundreds of ACLs created on a device. Eventually, when ACLs are identified with numbers only, it becomes difficult to keep track of the reason an ACL was created. To make administering ACLs easy, you can give them names instead of numbers; in this case, they are called named ACLs. Both standard and extended ACLs can be created as named ACLs, and all the previous discussed rules apply. The difference is in the commands used to create the ACL. Named ACLs are created using the **ip access-list** command, shown here:

```
ip access-list {standard|extended} name
```

This command creates an ACL and brings you to the **nacl** prompt, denoted **config-std-nacl** for a standard ACL or **config-ext-nacl** for an extended ACL. At this prompt, you can add ACEs as usual, starting with a **permit** or **deny** command. The rest of the command follows the syntax discussed earlier for standard and extended ACLs.

The command to apply a named ACL is the same command that is used to apply the standard and extended ACLs except that a name is used instead of a number in the **ip access-group** command, as shown here:

```
ip access-group name {in|out}
```

To illustrate the differences and similarities between creating numbered and named ACLs, Example 2-54 re-creates the standard ACL from Example 2-52 as a named ACL, and Example 2-55 does the same for the extended ACL shown in Example 2-53.

Example 2-54 *Creating and Applying Standard Named ACLs*

```
Router(config)#ip access-list standard bad-hosts
Router(config-std-nacl)#deny 10.1.1.0 0.0.0.255
Router(config-std-nacl)#deny host 10.2.1.1
Router(config-std-nacl)#permit any
Router(config-std-nacl)#exit
Router(config)#interface Gi1
Router(config-if)#ip access-group bad-hosts in
```

Example 2-55 *Creating and Applying Extended Named ACLs*

```
Router(config)#ip access-list extended bad-traffic
Router(config-ext-nacl)#deny tcp any any eq 23
Router(config-ext-nacl)#deny tcp any any eq 3389
Router(config-ext-nacl)#deny ip host 10.1.1.1 host 10.2.1.1
Router(config-ext-nacl)#permit ip any any
Router(config-ext-nacl)#exit
Router(config)#interface Gi1
Router(config-if)#ip access-group bad-traffic in
```

Time Based ACLs

ACEs in an extended ACL can be configured to be enforced during certain times only. To do this, you specify a time range at the end of an ACE with the **time-range** *time-range-name* command. *time-range-name* references an object in IOS that defines a time period. The object can be created with the **time-range** *name* global configuration command. Within the object, a time period is defined as recurring or absolute. A recurring, or periodic, range starts and ends at the same time on certain days of the week, while an absolute range starts and ends at a specific date and time.

A recurring, or periodic, range can be defined with the **periodic** {*day-of-the-week*|**daily**|**weekdays**|**weekends**} *start-time* **to** *end-time* command. *start-time* and *end-time* are defined in *hh:mm* format.

An absolute range can be defined with the **absolute** {**start**|**end**} *hh:mm day month year* command. The *month* option is specified with the first three letters of a month.

In Example 2-56, two time ranges are created. The first range, called *daily*, is a periodic range that starts at 00:00 hours and ends at 02:00 hours. The second range is an absolute range that begins on December 1 at 00:00 hours and ends on December 31 at 21:59 hours.

Example 2-56 *Recurring Time Range*

```
Router(config)#time-range daily
Router(config-time-range)#periodic daily 00:00 to 02:00
Router(config-time-range)#exit
Router(config)#time-range december
Router(config-time-range)#absolute start 00:00 01 December 2017 end 21:59
  31 December 2017
Router(config-time-range)#exit
```

Example 2-57 shows the ACL from Example 2-50 modified to allow RDP traffic every day between midnight and 2:00 a.m. It uses the recurring time range shown in Example 2-53 to accomplish this. Note how the second ACE in the example is changed from **deny** to **permit** with the time range, while a new line is added below it to deny RDP traffic during other times. If the new line is not added, RDP traffic is permitted by the **permit ip any any** ACE at all times.

Example 2-57 *Using a Time Range in an ACL*

```
Router(config)#access-list 101 deny tcp any any eq 23
Router(config)#access-list 101 permit tcp any any eq 3389 time-range daily
Router(config)#access-list 101 deny tcp any any eq 3389
Router(config)#access-list 101 deny ip host 10.1.1.1 host 10.2.1.1
Router(config)#access-list 101 permit ip any any
Router(config)#interface Gi1
Router(config-if)#ip access-group 101 in
```

Reflexive ACLs

It is difficult to keep track of all traffic that should be allowed between various networks connected to a router. This is especially true when one of those segments is a public network, such as the Internet or an untrusted network. For example, when a router connects to the Internet, traffic in response to queries sent from inside is expected and should be allowed, whereas any other traffic not in response to an explicit query should not be allowed.

Extended ACLs in IOS allow tracking of sessions in one direction while allowing return traffic in the other. This is done by marking each ACE that needs session tracking in an outbound ACL with the **reflect** keyword. Every time a new session matching that ACE is encountered, a reflexive ACE entry is created in an inbound ACL that is marked with the **evaluate** keyword.

Each reflexive ACE is a temporary entry in the inbound ACL that matches the IP address pair, protocol, and port pair of the original outbound session that triggered the reflect. The temporary ACE is removed after the original session ends. The end of a session is determined by TCP packets with FIN or RST bits set or when a certain configurable time has passed without any packets seen for that session. The latter option is always used for non-TCP sessions.

To further understand how reflexive ACLs work, consider the network diagram shown in Figure 2-4. The figure shows router R1 connected to the internal network 10.1.1.0/24 on interface Gi1 and to the Internet on interface Gi3. On Interface Gi3, an outbound ACL called **allow-out** and an inbound ACL called **allow-in** are configured. The contents of the two ACLs are shown in Example 2-58.

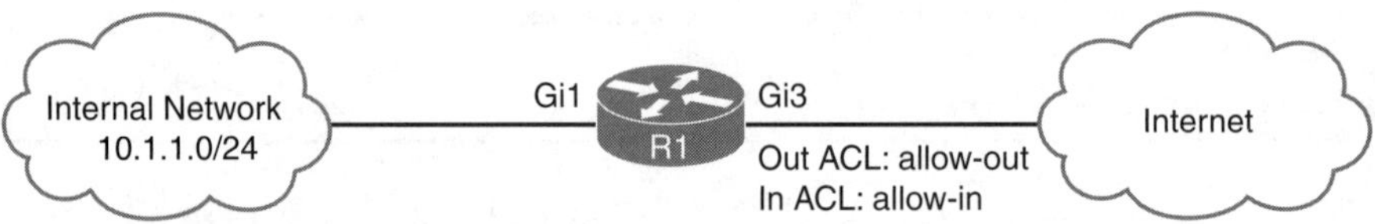

Figure 2-4 *Reflexive ACL*

Example 2-58 *Initial Configuration for a Reflexive ACL*

```
R1#show running-config
—removed for brevity—
ip access-list extended allow-in
 permit tcp any eq www any
 permit tcp any eq 443 any
 deny   ip any any
ip access-list extended allow-out
 permit tcp any any eq www
 permit tcp any any eq 443
 deny   ip any any
```

```
!
interface GigabitEthernet3
 ip address dhcp
 ip nat outside
 ip access-group allow-in in
 ip access-group allow-out out
 negotiation auto
—removed for brevity—
```

Notice that the inbound ACL allows all traffic sourced from ports 80 and 443. While this permits responses from web servers, it also permits an attacker to reach any inside destination with a packet sourced from port 80 or 443. Hence, this is not a very secure or desirable configuration.

With reflexive ACL, the router in Figure 2-4 can be configured such that all web traffic going out of Gi3 will be evaluated, and a reflexive ACE will be created in the **allow-in** ACL to allow only return traffic to come in from the Internet.

To configure this, the two ACLs on R1 are changed as shown in Example 2-59. Notice that the **allow-in** ACL contains a single **evaluate** command pointing to the reflected ACL **racl**. IOS creates temporary ACEs in the **allow-in** ACL as sessions, matching the two permit statements in the **allow-out** ACL, and exits the Gi3 interface toward the Internet.

Example 2-59 *Configuring Reflexive ACL*

```
R1#show running-config
—removed for brevity—
ip access-list extended allow-in
 evaluate racl
ip access-list extended allow-out
 permit tcp any any eq www reflect racl
 permit tcp any any eq 443 reflect racl
!
interface GigabitEthernet3
 ip address dhcp
 ip nat outside
 ip access-group allow-in in
 ip access-group allow-out out
 negotiation auto
—removed for brevity—
```

Note You may have figured that a similar result can be achieved by using the **established** keyword in an inbound ACL. While that is partially true, reflexive ACLs provide better security because each reflected ACE contains the exact source address, destination address, and port information. Another thing to note is that similar stateful functions are provided by IOS zone-based firewall (ZBFW) and all other firewalls. IOS ZBFW is covered in Chapter 7, "IOS Firewall and Security Features."

Unicast Reverse Path Forwarding

One of the key uses of traffic filtering is to prevent traffic with spoofed sources. While ACLs can be used to do this, creating and maintaining ACLs for this purpose can be cumbersome. IOS provides a nifty security feature called Unicast Reverse Path Forwarding (URPF) to simplify detection of spoofed IP packets.

When Unicast RPF is enabled on an interface, the router examines all packets received on that interface to see if the packet was received at an interface that is the best return path back to the source of the packet. In other words, it does a reverse lookup, or a "look back," on each packet to see if the source of the packet appears in its forwarding table and is connected to the same interface where the packet was received.

If the router determines that the source of the packet cannot be reached through the interface where the packet was received, it drops the packet.

Note IOS uses its Cisco Express Forwarding (CEF) forwarding information base (FIB) to look up source addresses for URPF. CEF must be enabled on the device before URPF is enabled.

URPF can be used in any "single-homed" environment, where there is essentially only one access point out of the network (that is, one upstream connection). Networks having one access point offer the best example of symmetric routing, which means the interface where a packet enters the network is also the best return path to the source of the IP packet. URPF is best used at the network perimeter for Internet or other untrusted networks or in ISP environments for customer network terminations.

Note URPF can be used in multihomed environments as long as the costs of all paths are the same because multiple equal-cost paths are considered in URPF lookups.

URPF can be configured on an interface with the **ip verify unicast reverse-path** command and can be verified with the **show ip interface** *interface* command.

Network Based Application Recognition (NBAR)

While filtering traffic with IP access lists is a good security practice, it has its shortcomings. Lot of applications and protocols, such as Real Time Protocol (RTP), use dynamic port ranges and are difficult to block with ACLs. For a better security posture, it is important to understand and limit traffic based on applications and protocols. This is where the Network Based Application Recognition (NBAR) feature of IOS helps.

NBAR is a classification engine that recognizes and classifies a wide variety of protocols and applications, including web-based and other difficult-to-classify applications and protocols that use dynamic TCP/UDP port assignments.

As traffic flows through interfaces configured for NBAR discovery, it recognizes and classifies protocols or applications that the packets belong to. The router can be configured to apply QoS policies based on the NBAR classifications, including dropping packets belonging to unwanted applications and protocols. The following are some of the key uses of NBAR:

- **Classification by HTTP header:** NBAR can be used to classify traffic based on HTTP header information, including URL, host, MIME, and user agent. This classification can be used to filter traffic going to known malicious sites or coming from unknown clients.
- **Classification of peer-to-peer (P2P) file-sharing traffic:** NBAR can be used to identify and block traffic belonging to P2P file-sharing applications such as BitTorrent to prevent data loss.
- **Classification of real-time traffic:** NBAR can be used to classify and filter or rate limit RTP or Real Time Streaming Protocol (RTSP) to prevent misuse of network resources.

NBAR uses its Protocol Discovery function to classify traffic. With Protocol Discovery, you can discover any protocol or application traffic that is supported by NBAR and obtain statistics that are associated with that protocol. Protocol Discovery maintains the following per-protocol statistics for enabled interfaces:

- Total number of input packets and bytes
- Total number of output packets and bytes
- Input bit rates
- Output bit rates

To use NBAR in QoS policies, Protocol Discovery needs to be enabled on router interfaces with the **ip nbar protocol-discovery** command. The collected data from Protocol Discovery can be verified with the **show ip nbar protocol-discovery interface** *interface* command.

While an in-depth discussion on QoS is beyond the scope of this book, as a quick refresher, QoS is configured using the Modular QoS CLI (MQC). Earlier in this chapter, you saw MQC used to configure CoPP. The MQC is a CLI that allows you to define traffic classes (class maps), create and configure traffic policies (policy maps), and attach the traffic policies to interfaces. Using MQC to configure NBAR consists of the following steps:

Step 1. **Defining a traffic class with a class map:** Class maps are created using the **class-map** *name* command and contain a **match protocol** statement to classify traffic using NBAR. Hundreds of applications and protocols are available, with numerous sub-options to create granular classification.

Step 2. **Defining a traffic policy:** A traffic policy or policy map defines what action to take on defined traffic classes. Policy maps are created using the **policy-map** *name* command. Within a policy map, multiple class maps can be associated with actions such as **drop**, **police**, and **shape**.

Step 3. **Attaching the traffic policy to an interface:** A traffic policy or policy map needs to be attached to an interface in order to be effective. This can be done using the **service-policy** {**input**|**output**} *policy-map-name* command.

Example 2-60 shows how NBAR is used with MQC to classify and drop P2P file-sharing traffic. This example is based on the network shown in Figure 2-4. Interface Gi1 on R1 is configured for NBAR Protocol Discovery, and a policy map is applied to that interface to drop P2P file-sharing traffic.

Example 2-60 *Configuring NBAR to Drop P2P File-Sharing Traffic*

```
R1(config)#interface Gi1
R1(config-if)#ip nbar protocol-discovery
R1(config-if)#exit
R1(config)#class-map p2p-traffic
R1(config-cmap)#match protocol bittorrent
R1(config-cmap)#match protocol fasttrack
R1(config-cmap)#match protocol gnutella
R1(config-cmap)#match protocol kazaa2
R1(config-cmap)#exit
R1(config)#policy-map drop-p2p
R1(config-pmap)#class p2p-traffic
R1(config-pmap-c)#drop
R1(config-pmap-c)#exit
R1(config-pmap)#exit
R1(config)#interface Gi1
R1(config-if)#service-policy output drop-p2p
R1(config-if)#service-policy input drop-p2p
```

Note On some routers, the **drop** action may not be available inside the policy map. You can use a police action to drop traffic by using the command **police cir 8000 conform-action drop exceed-action drop violate-action drop**.

TCP Intercept

TCP Intercept is an important security feature on Cisco routers that is used to protect TCP servers from SYN-flooding attacks. A SYN-flooding attack occurs when a hacker floods a server with requests for TCP connections sourced from spoofed addresses. Because these messages come from spoofed or unavailable addresses, the connections do not get established, and the server is forced to keep them open for a while. The resulting volume of unresolved open connections eventually overwhelms the server and can cause it to deny service to valid requests.

The TCP Intercept feature protects the servers, such as web servers, in a network from such SYN-flooding attacks. It does so by intercepting and validating TCP connection requests. In intercept mode, the router intercepts TCP synchronization (SYN) packets from clients to servers. It establishes a connection with the client on behalf of the destination server, and if that connection is successful, it establishes a connection with the server on behalf of the client and knits the two half-connections together transparently.

With the router intercepting all TCP connection requests, a SYN-flooding attack never reaches the servers itself. To protect itself from being overwhelmed in case of an attack, the router uses aggressive timeouts of half-open or embryonic connections.

Another way to protect the server and the router both is to use TCP Intercept in *watch* mode. In this mode, the router does not intercept TCP connections but passively watches each connection request. If the request is not completed within a configured time interval, the router intervenes and terminates the connection.

Before configuring TCP Intercept, an extended access list containing a list of servers to protect needs to be defined. You can choose to allow the whole inside network to be protected, but that may cause the router to be overwhelmed. It is recommended that you define the critical servers that require the protection.

After defining the access list, TCP Intercept can be enabled with the **ip tcp intercept list** *access-list* global configuration command. The TCP Intercept mode can be configured with the **ip tcp intercept mode** {**intercept**|**watch**} command. Example 2-61 shows how TCP Intercept is enabled to protect three servers in watch mode.

Example 2-61 *Configuring TCP Intercept*

```
R1(config)#access-list 105 permit tcp any host 10.1.1.10
R1(config)#access-list 105 permit tcp any host 10.1.1.11
R1(config)#access-list 105 permit tcp any host 10.1.1.12
R1(config)#ip tcp intercept list 105
R1(config)#ip tcp intercept watch
```

Visibility with NetFlow

Chapter 1 discusses the importance of visibility of assets that you are trying to secure. To effectively design and improve security, though, it is important to have visibility of your entire network. With continuous visibility, you can monitor for anomalous behavior that indicates new attacks and also monitor the effectiveness of your existing policies.

Visibility, as I like to put it, is a two-sided coin. On one side is the visibility of what and who is accessing your network and resources, while on the other side is visibility of what they are doing after being granted access.

The first side of the coin—visibility of what and who—is gathered by access control on every entry point of the network. Access control and visibility related to it are covered in *Integrated Security Technologies and Solutions, Volume II.*

The second side of the coin—visibility of what everyone is doing on the network—can be gathered from multiple sources. Some of it comes from various security devices in the network, such as firewalls and IPS devices, but those are reliant on traffic passing through them. A significant portion of network traffic stays internal and never passes through firewalls or IPS devices. Hence, the most important place to get visibility data is from the network itself—from the switches and routers.

The Cisco IOS application NetFlow helps in gathering this data from the network. It provides statistics on packets flowing through the network devices. Each packet that is forwarded within a router or switch is examined for a set of attributes. These attributes combined become the fingerprint of the packet and determine whether the packet is unique or similar to other packets. In most cases, these are the attributes NetFlow uses to create the fingerprint:

- IP source address
- IP destination address
- Source port
- Destination port
- Layer 3 protocol type
- Class of service
- Router or switch interface

All packets with the same fingerprint are classified as a single flow, and then packets and bytes are tallied. The details of the flow are then exported to NetFlow collectors for analysis and storage.

Because a flow record is unidirectional, some products, such as Cisco Stealthwatch, further combine multiple flows to create a complete bidirectional flow record. An analysis of such unidirectional or bidirectional flows provides a baseline of the network traffic, and any anomaly can immediately be detected. In addition to behavior-based anomalies, transactional anomalies can be immediately detected. For example, if you see 5 GB of traffic being sent as ICMP packets, it immediately indicates a covert attempt to transfer data.

Note At the time this book was published, the Cisco Stealthwatch product family was not part of the CCIE blueprint. Hence, that product family is not discussed in this series.

The configuration of NetFlow can be divided into two general steps:

Step 1. **Enabling NetFlow:** NetFlow collection needs to be enabled on a per-interface and direction basis. The **ip flow** {**ingress**|**egress**} command is used to enable collection.

Step 2. **Defining the export destination:** Define the destination IP address and port where the export flow data needs to be sent. The **ip flow-export destination** *ip-address port* command is used to define the export destination.

NetFlow collection can be verified with the **show ip cache flow** command. Example 2-62 shows how NetFlow is enabled on a router interface and a destination is configured to export the flows to.

Example 2-62 *Enabling NetFlow*

```
R1(config)#interface Gi1
R1(config-if)#ip flow ingress
R1(config-if)#exit
R1(config)#ip flow-export destination 192.168.1.20 2055
```

Note Support for NetFlow varies by hardware and software on Cisco routers and switches. Even commands needed to enable flow collection and export can vary. Some devices support Flexible NetFlow with Version 9, while some support sampled collection only.

Summary

Securing network devices is key to securing your data and assets. If the infrastructure is compromised, the rest of the network will be easily compromised, too.

This chapter discusses security for each of the three planes of a network device. Various common attacks are discussed at each plane of Layer 2 and Layer 3 devices.

A large part of this chapter is dedicated to data plane security because that is where the majority of attacks are focused. For the CCIE exam, you are expected to understand these attacks as well as methods to mitigate them.

This chapter also lays the foundation that is required to understand operations of various security devices and solutions discussed throughout the rest of the series. Some of the attacks discussed here are revisited in other chapters, along with other methods to mitigate them.

Finally, this chapter focuses on the security of the wired network infrastructure only. Chapter 3, "Wireless Security," extends the discussion to wireless networks.

References

"Cisco Guide to Harden Cisco IOS Devices," http://www.cisco.com/c/en/us/support/docs/ip/access-lists/13608-21.html

"Catalyst 3560 Software Configuration Guide, Release 12.2(52)SE: Configuring Private VLANs," https://www.cisco.com/c/en/us/td/docs/switches/lan/catalyst3560/software/release/12-2_52_se/configuration/guide/3560scg/swpvlan.html

"Cisco IOS Security Configuration Guide, Release 12.2: Configuring Unicast Reverse Path Forwarding," https://www.cisco.com/c/en/us/td/docs/ios/12_2/security/configuration/guide/fsecur_c/scfrpf.html

Chapter 3

Wireless Security

This chapter provides details about wireless security that a security professional needs to understand. This chapter explores the history, standards, and basics of wireless, along with advanced topics related to securing wireless LANs. You will learn how to connect a wireless access point (WAP) to a wireless LAN controller (WLC) and how to secure the wireless data plane and management plane for unified deployments.

What Is Wireless?

Today it is hard to think about what it was like to be tethered to a desk by an Ethernet cable. Wireless communication in businesses and homes is now pervasive and critical to productivity and our daily lives. Wireless communication at a basic level is the ability to communicate between computers without wires, and it typically involves wireless access points (APs) and stations (STA).

Wireless Standards

Since 1997, the Institute of Electrical and Electronics Engineers (IEEE) has been defining 802.11 standards for what we know today as the wireless local area network (WLAN). You might also use the term Wi-Fi, which comes from the Wi-Fi Alliance, the organization responsible for ensuring its members follow the IEEE standards and certifying products to ensure interoperability. Thanks to this standardization, when you buy a WAP from one company and a wireless adapter or interface from another company, they can actually work together.

802.11 Standards

Over the years, 802.11 has advanced a lot. Most users and organizations purchase the latest and greatest WAP, and they get better performance, reliability, and coverage.

The IEEE and Wi-Fi Alliance have been relentlessly improving the way wireless stations communicate with access points to achieve these results. One way we have gained additional speed is by increasing the bandwidth. You can equate increasing bandwidth to adding additional lanes on a highway. The other primary method of increasing speeds is by increasing the number of antennas being used simultaneously. Using multiple antennas, or multiple-input, multiple-output (MIMO) technology, is the equivalent of adding multiple roads between the source and destination. Table 3-1 provides a summary of the standards changes over the years since the 802.11 standards were introduced in 1997.

Table 3-1 *802.11 Standards*

Standard	Year	Band	Bandwidth	Speed
802.11	1997	2.4 GHz	22 MHz	2 Mbps
802.11a	1999	5 GHz	20 MHz	54 Mbps
802.11b	1999	2.4 GHz	22 MHz	11 Mbps
802.11g	2003	2.4 GHz	20 MHz	54 Mbps
802.11n	2009	2.4 and 5 GHz	Up to 40 MHz	Up to 300 Mbps
802.11ac Wave 1	2013	2.4 and 5 GHz	Up to 80 MHz	Up to 1.3 Gbps
802.11ac Wave 2	2016	2.4 and 5 GHz	Up to 160 MHz	Up to 2.3 Gbps

802.11 MAC Frame Formats

802.11 is a little more advanced at the MAC layer than the 802.3 Ethernet specification. Understanding the different frames will help you understand how to secure WLANs.

Figure 3-1 illustrates the 802.11 MAC frame format, including the control frame information.

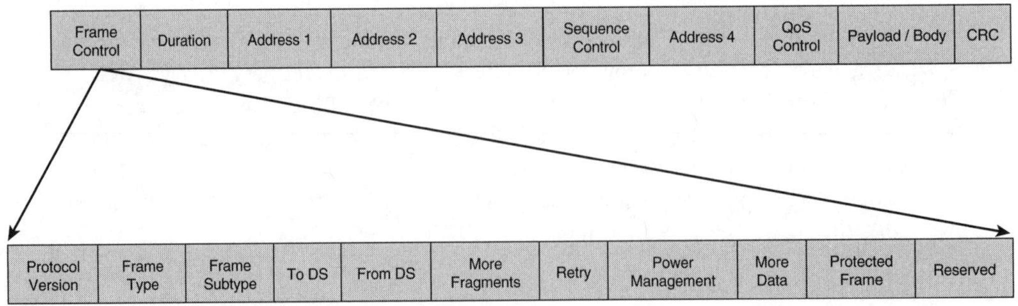

Figure 3-1 *802.11 Frame Format*

There are three types of frames defined in the standard:

- **Control frame:** This type of frame sets up data exchanges and facilitates the data frames.
- **Management frame:** This type of frame facilitates WLAN connectivity, authentication, and status.
- **Data frame:** This type of frame handles station data between the transmitter and receiver.

Association and Authentication

Two things must take place for a station to be connected and forward data: association and authentication. Figure 3-2 illustrates a station and WAP exchanging a series of management frames in order to get to an authenticated and associated state.

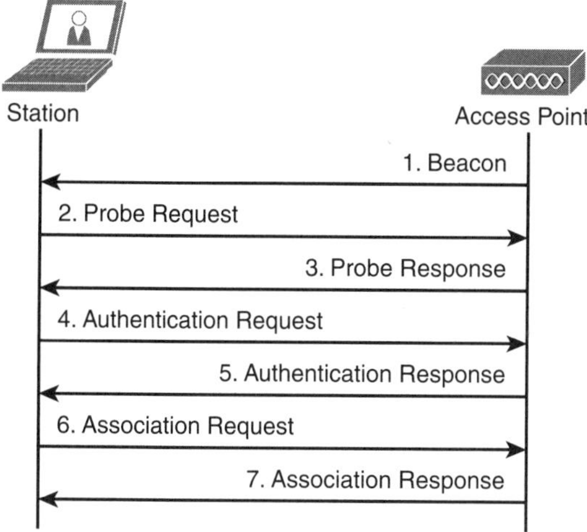

Figure 3-2 *Station and WAP Connection Process*

The following steps are involved in the association and authentication process:

Step 1. Beacon frames are transmitted periodically to announce the presence of a WLAN and contain all information about one or more Service Set Identifiers (SSIDs), data rates, channels, security ciphers, key management, and so on.

Step 2. The STA sends a probe request.

Step 3. The AP sends a probe response to the STA.

Step 4. The STA sends an authentication request frame to the AP. (Note that this assumes Open Authentication.)

Step 5. The AP send an authentication response frame to the STA.

Step 6. The STA sends an association request to the AP with security.

Step 7. The AP send an association response frame to the STA.

Note Do not confuse wireless authentication with 802.1X authentication. 802.1X comes after the full 802.11 association and authentication between the AP and STA.

Autonomous Versus Controller-Based WLANs

Early wireless deployments all had individual APs with stations or clients directly connected. Such APs are called autonomous APs because they act independently of each other. Organizations very quickly ran into issues trying to manage tens or hundreds of autonomous APs. The wireless LAN controller was created to address the management, scalability, and reliability issues previously seen with autonomous APs. With controller-based architectures, you can build a WLAN with hundreds or thousands of APs and still centrally administer, operate, and troubleshoot. Today, the only autonomous APs that are being deployed are typically for point-to-point or point-to-multiple bridges. Therefore, this chapter focuses on and assumes a controller-based deployment.

WLC Fundamentals

WLCs support centralized management functions to deliver the following:

- WLAN management for centrally creating SSIDs and associated settings
- Radio resource management (RRM), which includes the following:
  - Transmit power control (TPC), which sets the transmit power of each AP to maximize the coverage and minimize co-channel interference
  - Dynamic channel assignment (DCA), which evaluates and dynamically manages channel assignments
  - Coverage hole detection (CHD), which detects coverage holes and mitigates them
- Mobility management for managing roaming between APs and controllers
- Access point configuration
- Security settings and wireless intrusion prevention system (wIPS) capabilities
- Network-wide quality of service (QoS) for voice and video
- Operations and troubleshooting

Note For more information about configuring, designing, and deploying WLCs, read *Controller-Based Wireless LAN Fundamentals: An End-to-End Reference Guide to Design, Deploy, Manage, and Secure 802.11 Wireless Networks* by Jeff Smith, Jake Woodhams, and Robert Marg (Cisco Press).

CAPWAP Overview

Control and Provisioning of Wireless Access Points (CAPWAP) is a standard protocol that enables a WLC to manage APs. CAPWAP is based on the Lightweight Access Point Protocol (LWAPP) that was originally designed and used by Cisco. CAPWAP is defined in the following Internet Engineering Task Force (IETF) Requests for Comments (RFCs):

- RFC 4564 defines the objectives for the CAPWAP protocol.
- RFC 5418 covers threat analysis for IEEE 802.11 deployments.
- RFC 5415 defines the CAPWAP protocol specifications.

CAPWAP carries control and data traffic between the AP and the WLC. The control plane is Datagram Transport Layer Security (DTLS)–encrypted and uses UDP port 5246. The data plane is optionally DTLS encrypted and uses UDP port 5247. The CAPWAP state machine, which is used for managing the connection between AP and controller, is shown in Figure 3-3.

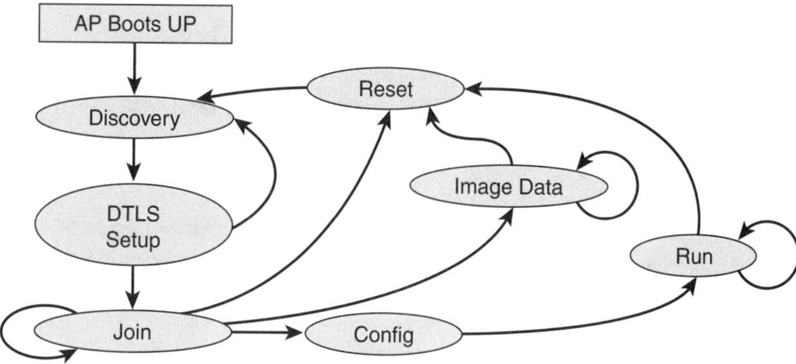

Figure 3-3 *CAPWAP State Machine*

Access Point Discovery Process

Making sure access points join up to a WLC is an important step in any deployment. Understanding the details of this process is critical in troubleshooting connection problems. In local AP mode (discussed in the next section), if the AP loses its connection or cannot connect to the WLC, then no SSIDs will be active, and traffic will not be forwarded by the AP until it can successfully connect.

After an AP gets an IP address using DHCP or uses a previously assigned static IP address, the AP uses one of the following methods to connect to a WLC.

- **Layer 3 CAPWAP discovery:** This feature can be enabled on different subnets from the access point and uses either broadcast IPv4 or IPv6 addresses and UDP packets. Any WLC that is Layer 2 adjacent to the AP will respond to the request.

- **CAPWAP multicast discovery:** Broadcast does not exist in IPv6 addresses. An access point sends a CAPWAP discovery message to all of the controller's multicast addresses (FF01::18C). The controller receives the IPv6 discovery request from the AP only if it is in the same Layer 2 segment and sends back the IPv6 discovery response.
- **Locally stored controller IPv4 or IPv6 address discovery:** If the access point was previously associated to a controller, the IPv4 or IPv6 addresses of the primary, secondary, and tertiary controllers are stored in the access point's nonvolatile memory. This process of storing controller IPv4 or IPv6 addresses on an access point for later deployment is called *priming the access point*.
- **DHCP server discovery using option 43:** DHCP option 43 provides controller IPv4 addresses to the access points. Cisco switches support a DHCP server option that is typically used for this capability.
- **DHCP server discovery using option 52:** DHCP option 52 allows an AP to discover the IPv6 address of the controller to which it connects. As part of the DHCPv6 messages, the DHCP server provides the controller's management with an IPv6 address.
- **DNS discovery:** The AP can discover controllers through your DNS server. You must configure your DNS server to return controller IPv4 and IPv6 addresses in response to **CISCO-LWAPP-CONTROLLER.***localdomain* or **CISCO-CAPWAP-CONTROLLER.***localdomain*, where *localdomain* is the access point domain name.

It is recommended for predictability and stability that you manually insert the primary, secondary, and tertiary controllers into Wireless > Access Points > All APs > Details for *AP Name* > High Availability, as shown in Figure 3-4. This is recommended regardless of the discovery method the AP uses.

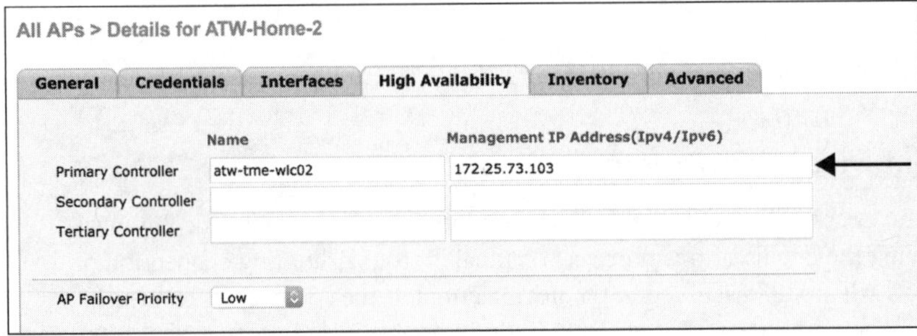

Figure 3-4 *Manual WLC Definition*

You may also define backup WLCs for all APs by going to Wireless > Access Points > Global Configuration, as shown in Figure 3-5. You can configure primary and secondary backup controllers for all access points (which are used if primary, secondary, or tertiary controllers are not responsive) in this order: primary, secondary, tertiary, primary backup, and secondary backup.

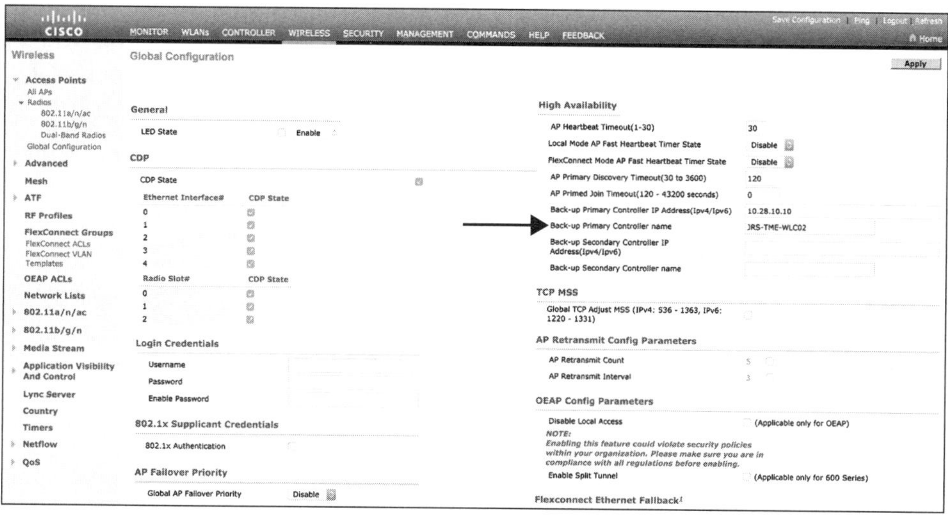

Figure 3-5 *WLC Primary and Secondary Definitions for all APs*

AP Modes

Access points can run in different operating modes. The following are the options to specify the operating modes of access points:

- **Local:** This is the default (unless you are running a flex controller) and most commonly deployed mode. The AP uses its CAPWAP tunnel for data forwarding and management (authentication, roaming, and so on). All client traffic is centrally switched by the controller, meaning the controller forwards the traffic from its data interfaces. Lightweight Access Points (LAPs) are sometimes referred to as "dumb" APs, primarily due to the fact that they do very little thinking on their own when in local mode.

- **FlexConnect:** This mode is typical for branch and remote office deployments. It allows for central (at the WLC) or local (at the AP) switched traffic. More details can be found in the next session, "FlexConnect Access Points."

- **Bridge:** This mode is for using the AP to connect to a root AP.

- **SE-Connect:** This mode allows you to connect to a spectrum expert, and it allows the access point to perform spectrum intelligence.

- **Monitor:** This mode is the monitor-only mode.

- **Sniffer:** The access point starts sniffing the air on a given channel. It captures and forwards all the packets from the clients on that channel to a remote machine that runs Airopeek or Wireshark (packet analyzers for IEEE 802.11 wireless LANs). It includes information on the time stamp, signal strength, packet size, and so on.

- **Rogue Detector:** This mode monitors the rogue APs on the wire. It does not transmit or receive frames over the air or contain rogue APs.

Access points also have an option to configure the AP submode:

- **wIPS:** The AP is in local, FlexConnect, or monitor mode, and the wIPS submode is configured on the access point.
- **None:** The AP is in local or FlexConnect mode, and the wIPS submode is not configured on the AP.

FlexConnect Access Points

FlexConnect (previously known as Hybrid Remote Edge Access Point [H-REAP]) is a wireless solution that can switch client data traffic locally and perform client authentication locally when the connection to the controller is lost. When a client is connected to the controller, it can also send traffic back to the controller. In connected mode, the FlexConnect access point can also perform local authentication.

Locally switched WLANs map wireless user traffic to VLANs to an adjacent switch by using 802.1Q trunking. If desired, one or more WLANs can be mapped to the same local 802.1Q VLAN. All AP control/management-related traffic is sent to the centralized WLC separately using CAPWAP.

Central switched WLANs use CAPWAP to tunnel both the wireless user traffic and all control traffic to the centralized WLC, where the user traffic is mapped to a dynamic interface/VLAN on the WLC. This is the normal CAPWAP mode of operation.

On FlexConnect access points, two types of WLANs can be configured:

- **Connected mode:** The WLC is reachable. In this mode, the FlexConnect AP has CAPWAP connectivity with its WLC.
- **Standalone mode:** The WLC is unreachable. The FlexConnect AP has lost or failed to establish CAPWAP connectivity with its WLC.

You can have one WLAN that is centrally switched (for example, for a guest) and still have a locally switched WLAN (for example, for an employee). When the FlexConnect AP goes into standalone mode, the locally switched WLAN still functions, and the centrally switched WLAN fails.

FlexConnect groups allow you to group together APs in a branch or remote office that share common configuration items, such as the following:

- Local/backup RADIUS servers' IP/keys
- Local user and EAP authentication
- Image upgrade
- ACL mappings, including AAA VLAN-ACL mappings and WLAN-ACL mappings
- Central DHCP settings
- WLAN-VLAN mappings, which allows override of the WLAN VLAN/interface for the group
- WLAN-AVC mappings

Figure 3-6 illustrates some of the options configurable for FlexConnect groups.

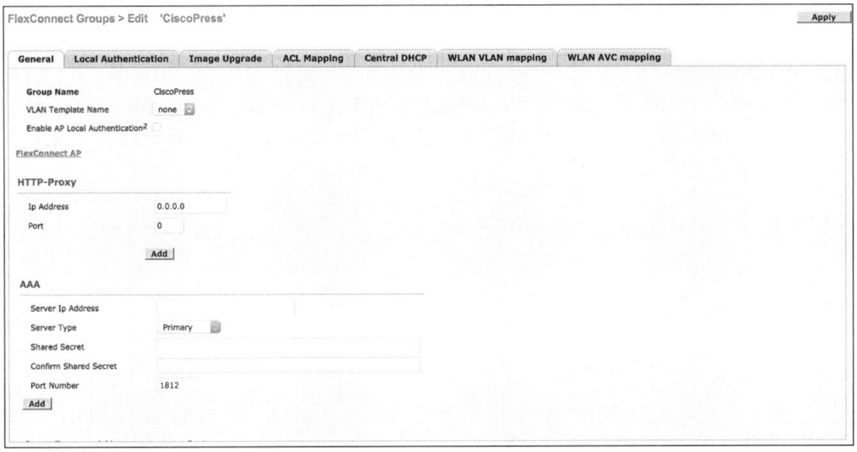

Figure 3-6 *FlexConnect Groups*

FlexConnect ACLs allow for filtering of traffic on FlexConnect APs and groups. The same configuration options exist for FlexConnect ACLs as for regular ACLs.

Guest Anchor Controllers

It is common for a wireless deployment to have a dedicated guest SSID to allow for visitors, contractors, or guests to connect to the Internet. One challenge is that typically an organization does not want to terminate guest users on the inside of its network. You can use anchor controllers to create a tunnel from the WLC in the core or campus of your network to an isolated network, such as a demilitarized zone (DMZ), as illustrated in Figure 3-7. The WLC uses Ethernet over IP (EoIP) tunnels to logically segment and transport the guest traffic between remote/foreign and anchor controllers. The original guest's Ethernet frame is maintained across CAPWAP and EoIP tunnels. Other traffic on other SSIDs (employees, for example) is still locally bridged at the remote controller on the corresponding VLAN. Security features such as web authentication and ACLs are applied to the session at the anchor controller.

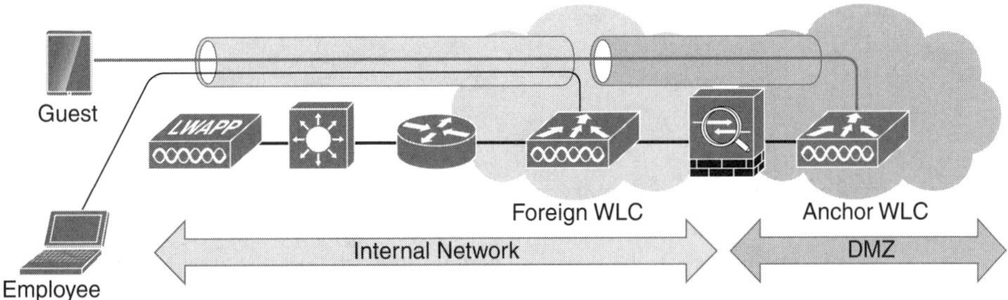

Figure 3-7 *Guest Anchor Controller*

When building a connection from a foreign controller to an anchor controller, IP port 97 for EoIP packets and UDP port 16666 for mobility control and new mobility data must be opened bidirectionally on any firewalls or packet filtering devices.

To create a guest anchor controller, perform the following steps:

Step 1. Go to Controller > General > Default Mobility Domain Name and RF Group Name and ensure that the anchor and foreign WLC are in different mobility groups (see Figure 3-8).

General

Name	ATW-TME-WLC02	
802.3x Flow Control Mode	Disabled	
LAG Mode on next reboot	Disabled	(LAG Mode is currently disabled).
Broadcast Forwarding	Enabled	
AP Multicast Mode 1	Multicast 228.10.11.13	Multicast Group Address
AP IPv6 Multicast Mode 1	Unicast	
AP Fallback	Enabled	
CAPWAP Preferred Mode	ipv4	
Fast SSID change	Disabled	
Link Local Bridging	Disabled	
Default Mobility Domain Name	securitydemo.net	
RF Group Name	securitydemo.net	
User Idle Timeout (seconds)	300	
ARP Timeout (seconds)	300	
Web Radius Authentication	PAP	
Operating Environment	Commercial (0 to 40 C)	
Internal Temp Alarm Limits	0 to 65 C	
WebAuth Proxy Redirection Mode	Disabled	
WebAuth Proxy Redirection Port	0	
Global IPv6 Config	Enabled	
Web Color Theme	Default	
HA SKU secondary unit	Disabled	
Nas-Id	ATW-TME-WLC02	
HTTP Profiling Port	80	
DNS Server IP	10.1.100.103	
HTTP-Proxy Ip Address	0.0.0.0	Port 80

Figure 3-8 *Mobility Group Configuration*

Step 2. Go to Controller > Mobility Management > Mobility Groups > New and add the anchor controller to the foreign controller and add the foreign controller to the anchor controller mobility group members (see Figures 3-9 and 3-10).

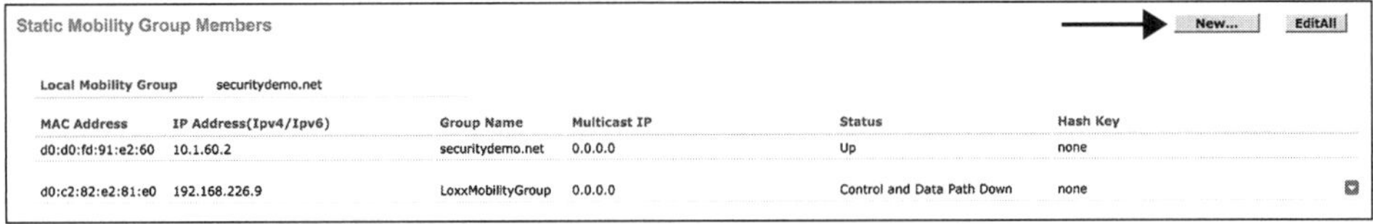

Static Mobility Group Members
New...
EditAll
Local Mobility Group securitydemo.net
MAC Address IP Address(Ipv4/Ipv6) Group Name Multicast IP Status Hash Key
d0:d0:fd:91:e2:60 10.1.60.2 securitydemo.net 0.0.0.0 Up none
d0:c2:82:e2:81:e0 192.168.226.9 LoxxMobilityGroup 0.0.0.0 Control and Data Path Down none

Figure 3-9 *Adding a Mobility Group Member*

Mobility Group Member > New

Member IP Address(Ipv4/Ipv6) 10.28.1.28

Member MAC Address 00:11:22:33:44:55

Group Name anchor.securitydemo.net

Hash none

1. Hash is not supported for IPv6 members

Figure 3-10 *Configuring a Mobility Group Member*

Step 3. Go to Controller > Interfaces > New and add a VLAN on the anchor controller for guest users.

Step 4. Go to WLANs > Mobility Anchors > New and configure the WLAN on the anchor WLC's mobility anchor to be local. Figures 3-11 and 3-12 show where to add the local mapping on the anchor WLC.

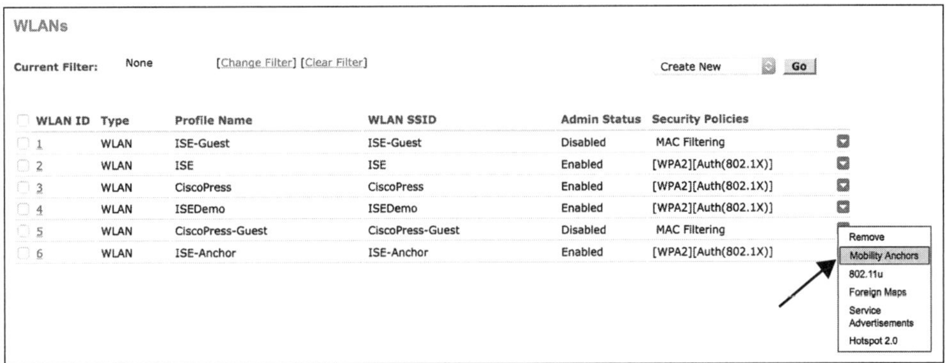

Figure 3-11 *Configuring a Mobility Anchor on the WLAN*

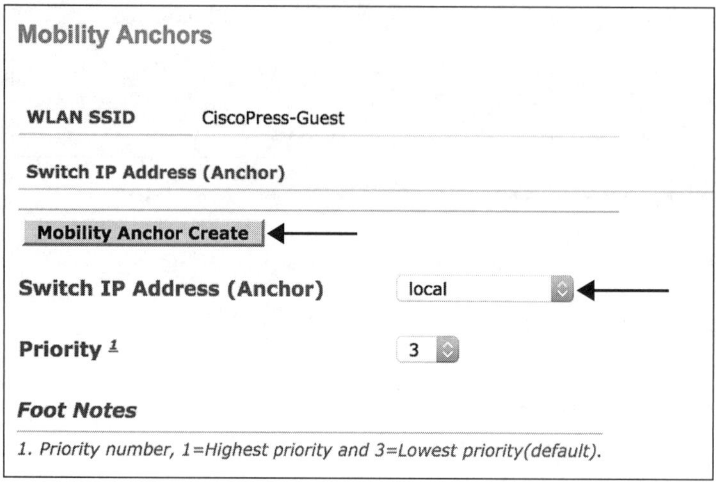

Figure 3-12 *Mobility Anchor Create on the Anchor Controller*

Step 5. Add the anchor controller's IP to the foreign controllers as shown in Figure 3-13.

Mobility Anchors

< Back

WLAN SSID CiscoPress-Guest

Switch IP Address (Anchor)	Data Path	Control Path	Priority
local	up	up	0
10.28.1.28	down	down	1

Mobility Anchor Create

Switch IP Address (Anchor) 192.168.226.9

Priority 1 3

Foot Notes

1. Priority number, 1=Highest priority and 3=Lowest priority(default).

Figure 3-13 *Mobility Anchor Created on the Foreign Controller*

One guest anchor controller can terminate up to 71 EoIP tunnels from internal WLAN controllers. This capacity is the same across models of the Cisco WLC except the 2504. The 2504 controller can terminate up to 15 EoIP tunnels. More than one guest anchor controller can be configured if additional tunnels are required. EoIP tunnels are counted per WLAN controller, independently of the number of tunneled WLANs or SSIDs in each EoIP.

Wireless Security Overview

As adoption of wireless became popular, security concerns were immediately raised. Wireless needed to address who or what can use a WLAN (authentication), and it needed to be able to provide privacy and integrity for wireless data (encryption).

WEP

The initial attempt to address wireless security and data privacy was Wired Equivalent Privacy (WEP). WEP is based on the RC4 symmetric stream cipher. (For more information on stream versus block ciphers, see *Integrated Security Technologies and Solutions, Volume II*.) A symmetric encryption assumes the same WEP keys on both sides, either 40 or 104 bits in length and statically configured on the client and WAP. Symmetric encryption was chosen because of the low computational power required. WEP uses a 24-bit initialization vector (IV), which is concatenated to the key before being processed by the RC4 cipher. WEP only encrypts the data/payload and the integrity check value (ICV). WEP can use open or shared-key authentication. The default is open. Shared-key authentication is a standard challenge-and-response mechanism that makes use of WEP and a shared secret key to provide authentication. Upon encrypting the challenge text with WEP using the shared secret key, the authenticating client returns the encrypted challenge text to the access point for verification. Authentication succeeds if the access point decrypts the same challenge text. Shared-key authentication is used only with WEP.

WEP was found to be insecure because of its relatively short IVs and static keys. The RC4 encryption algorithm has nothing to do with the major flaws. By having a 24-bit IV, WEP eventually uses the same IV for different data packets. For a large busy network, this reoccurrence of IVs can happen very quickly, resulting in the transmission of frames having keystreams that are too similar. If a malicious person collects enough frames based on the same IV, the individual can determine the keystream or the shared secret key. This, of course, leads to the hacker decrypting any of the 802.11 frames.

Wi-Fi Protected Access (WPA)

After the serious weaknesses were found in WEP, the Wi-Fi Alliance released Wi-Fi Protected Access (WPA) in 2003. Some people refer to WPA as the draft IEEE 802.11i standard because the Wi-Fi Alliance released WPA as an interim measure to address the vulnerabilities in WEP. WPA still uses RC4 as its cipher, which meant it could be used on existing wireless adapters without changing the hardware. APs did have to be replaced because of the additional computational requirements of WPA. WPA uses the Temporal Key Integrity Protocol (TKIP) encryption algorithm. TKIP uses a dynamically generated 128-bit key for each packet and rekeying, meaning that it prevents the types of attacks that targeted WEP. Using a 48-bit initialization vector, TKIP doubles the 24-bit IV used by WEP. Also, TKIP specifically uses three additional security features to address the weaknesses in WEP:

- **Key mixing function:** TKIP combines the secret root key with the IV before passing it on to RC4.
- **Sequence counter:** TKIP uses this counter to protect against replay attacks, in which valid data transmission is repeated maliciously.
- **Message integrity check (MIC):** A 64-bit MIC is able to protect both the data payload and the header of the packet.

Even with the additional levels of security it provides over WEP, WPA is considered obsolete and superseded by WPA2.

Wi-Fi Protected Access 2 (WPA2)

WPA2 is the latest ratified version of Wi-Fi security. WPA2 is the Wi-Fi Alliance's interoperable implementation of the ratified IEEE 802.11i standard. WPA2 uses the Advanced Encryption Standard (AES) encryption algorithm with the use of counter mode with Cipher Block Chaining Message Authentication Code Protocol (CCMP). AES counter mode is a block cipher that encrypts 128-bit blocks of data at a time with a 128-bit encryption key. The CCMP algorithm produces a MIC that provides data origin authentication and data integrity for the wireless frame.

Note CCMP is also referred to as CBC-MAC.

WPA2 offers a higher level of security than WPA because AES offers stronger encryption than RC4, and CCMP is superior to TKIP. WPA2 creates fresh session keys on every association. The encryption keys that are used for each client on the network are unique and specific to that client. Ultimately, every packet that is sent over the air is encrypted with a unique key. Cisco recommends that customers transition to WPA2 as soon as possible.

WPA Personal Versus WPA Enterprise

Authentication and key management (AKM) offers the option to have Pre-Shared Key (PSK) or 802.1X. PSK, also referred to as personal, is typically used for networks that do not support 802.1X. Most wireless deployments in homes are personal or PSK to remove the requirement to have usernames and passwords and the certificate requirements of 802.1X. In enterprises, PSK is still used today for some devices, such as wireless printers or cameras, that can only support PSK. PSK is also used for some guest networks to provide a level of encryption for the guests but not an overly complicated authentication scheme.

Enterprise authentication, or 802.1X, is the de facto standard for almost all businesses and organizations. 802.1X allows for individual user visibility (for example, John Smith is connected to AP2 on the Employee SSID) and mutual authentication through authentication type, such as Extensible Authentication Protocol Transport Layer Security (EAP-TLS). RADIUS is a networking protocol that provides centralized authentication, authorization, and accounting (AAA) and is responsible for determining whether a user or device is authorized to connect to the WLAN. Authentication and validation of the RADIUS server is helpful in preventing attacks such as evil twin attacks. In this type of attack, a rogue Wi-Fi access point that appears to be legitimate because it mirrors the enterprise SSID is set up to sniff wireless traffic or steal credentials.

Note 802.1X, EAP, authentication, and RADIUS are all discussed in detail in *Integrated Security Technologies and Solutions, Volume II.*

The WLC allows you to configure either PSK or 802.1X for each WLAN or SSID, as shown in Figure 3-14.

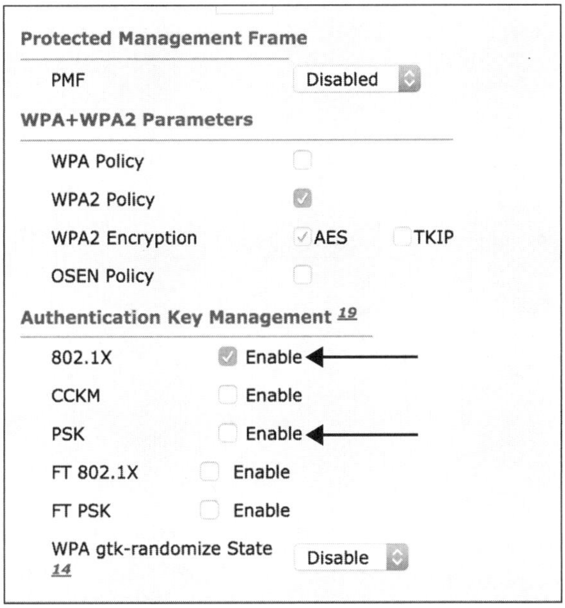

Figure 3-14 *Configuring PSK Versus 802.1X*

Roaming

In most deployments, multiple access points are deployed, and clients expect to be able to move freely between them without reauthenticating every time. Cisco introduced Cisco Centralized Key Management (CCKM) in pre-802.11i to address the industry needs for roaming. CCKM is most widely implemented in voice over WLAN (VoWLAN) devices. To work across WLCs, WLCs must be in the same mobility group. CCKM is standardized in 802.11r Fast Transition (FT). It is recommended that you have a new unique WLAN that uses FT to keep legacy client support (for example, one SSID for FT clients and one SSID for legacy clients).

802.11r is the IEEE standard for fast roaming. FT introduced a new concept of roaming where the handshake with the new AP is done even before the client roams to the target AP. The initial handshake allows the client and APs to do Pairwise Transient Key (PTK) calculation in advance, thus reducing roaming time. The pre-created PTK keys are applied to the client and AP when the client does the re-association request/response exchange with the new target AP. 802.11r provides two ways of roaming:

- **Over-the-air:** With this type of roaming, the client communicates directly with the target AP using IEEE 802.11 authentication with the FT authentication algorithm.
- **Over-the-DS (distribution system):** With this type of roaming, the client communicates with the target AP through the current AP. The communication between the client and the target AP is carried in FT action frames between the client and the current AP and is then sent through the controller.

Roaming is configured per WLAN in the Fast Transition section, as shown in Figure 3-15.

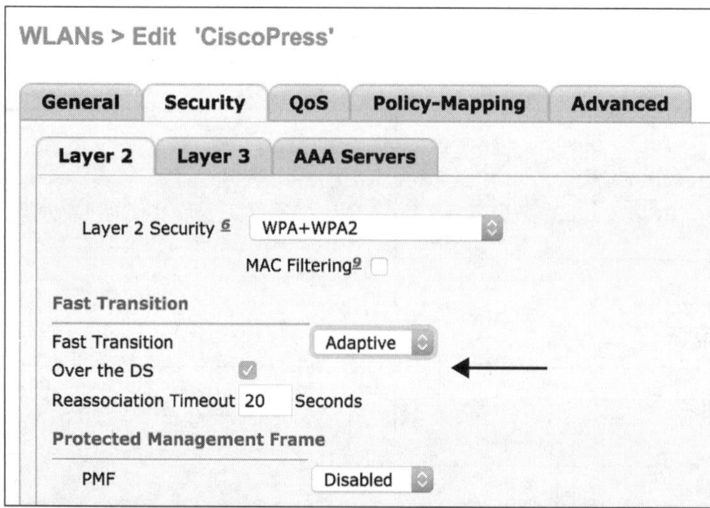

Figure 3-15 *Roaming Configuration with Fast Transition*

You also need to use FT 802.1X or FT PSK in the Authentication Key Management section for the Layer 2 security in order for FT to work correctly.

Securing the WLAN

Let's start to put the pieces together to create a new WLAN following best-practice recommendations for an enterprise SSID built for employees. People often fail to carefully consider the WLAN ID they chose. If you chose an ID greater than 16, the SSID will *not* belong to the default AP group. AP groups allow you to selectively publish different WLANs to different APs. By default, all access points are put into the default AP group. This means if you want your newly created WLAN to be published to all APs in the default AP group, it needs an ID less than 17.

To create a new WLAN go to WLANs > Create New > Go. Then, as shown in Figure 3-16, select the type (typically WLAN), create a profile name, add an SSID name, and select the ID.

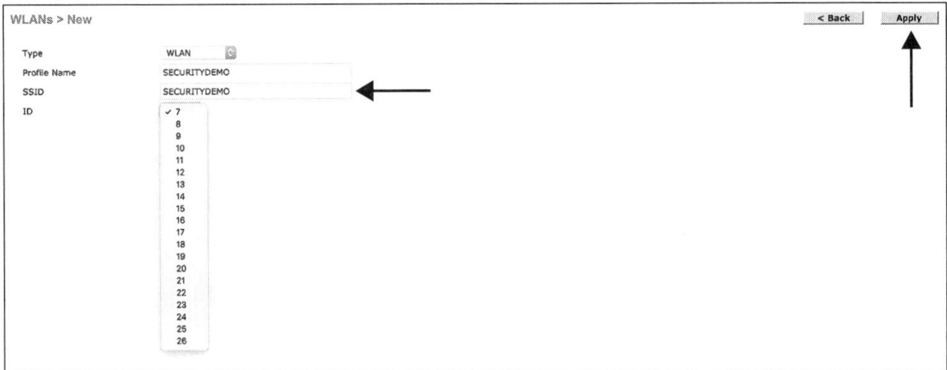

Figure 3-16 *New SSID*

After clicking Apply to create the new WLAN, the next step is to choose an interface to put the clients on after connection is made to the WLAN. Figure 3-17 illustrates selecting the employee interface.

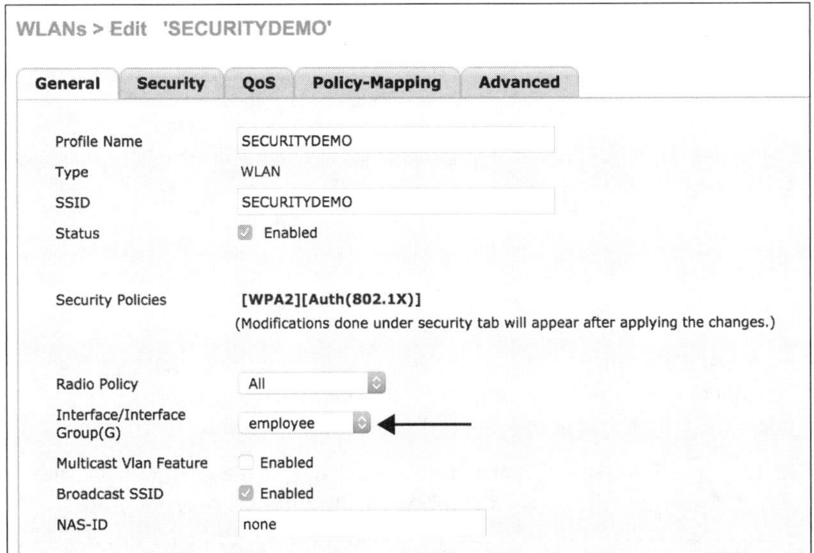

Figure 3-17 *Selecting an Interface for a WLAN*

When Security is selected, the default settings already have WPA2 with AES for encryption and 802.1X for AKM. These are the recommended options for Layer 2 security. The next step is to reference the correct RADIUS servers on the AAA Servers page, which is shown in Figure 3-18.

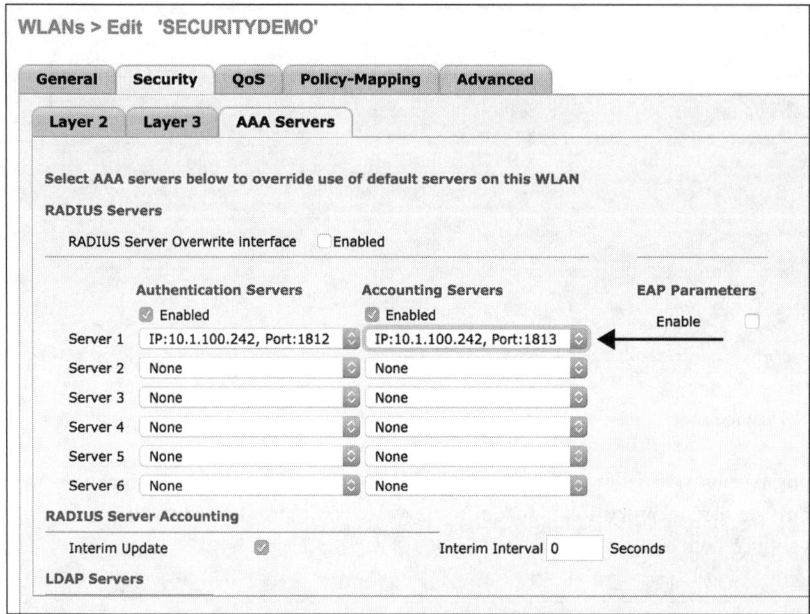

Figure 3-18 *Select RADIUS Authentication and Accounting Servers*

> **Note** For a detailed explanation of and configuration options for RADIUS, see *Integrated Security Technologies and Solutions, Volume II.*

The advanced options of the WLAN offer a lot of individual configuration items. Following is a list of the most import ones for securing a WLAN:

- **Allow AAA Override:** Allows the VLAN, QoS, and ACLs to be assigned by the RADIUS server and override the settings on the WLAN. The recommendation is for this setting to be enabled for deployments that integrate with ISE.
- **Override Interface ACL:** This option allows you to override the interface ACL and apply an ACL that is specific to the WLAN. Normally, this feature is not used.
- **URL ACL:** This option allows you to apply a URL ACL to the WLAN. This allows organizations to develop a blacklist of URLs for the WLAN and apply it before reaching the network.
- **P2P Blocking Action:** Selecting Drop causes the Cisco WLC to discard the P2P packets. This is very useful where you want to isolate all traffic between users on the WLAN. Selecting Forward-UpStream causes the packets to be forwarded on the upstream VLAN. The device above the Cisco WLC decides what action to take regarding the packet. If you have a router with ACLs or a firewall, the external device now can control what types of traffic can be forwarded between clients. For example, you might want to allow Jabber messages and voice but not MS-RPC traffic between wireless users.

- **Client Exclusion:** This option allows you to enable or disable the timeout for disabled client machines. Client machines are disabled by their MAC address. This option is normally enabled. For more information, review the "Client Exclusion" section, later in this chapter.
- **DHCP Addr. Assignment:** This option requires all WLAN clients to obtain IP addresses from the DHCP server. This prevents clients from assigning their own static IP addresses.
- **MFP Client Protection:** The default, Optional, is normally left selected because MFP on the client requires Cisco Compatible Extensions (CCX) to be supported on the client. For more information, review the "Management Frame Protection" section, later in this chapter.
- **NAC State:** ISE NAC is the recommended setting for deployments with ISE.
- **RADIUS Client Profiling:** This allows the WLC to send up RADIUS accounting information about the client for ISE to profile the connected clients. If you are using ISE, this is normally enabled.
- **Local Client Profiling:** This allows the WLC to learn what type of device is connecting to the WLAN. Normally, you should enable both DHCP and HTTP profiling, regardless of whether or not RADIUS profiling is enabled.
- **FlexConnect:** If you are doing a FlexConnect deployment, you need to review and configure this set of options, which includes everything from local switching and authentication to DHCP processing.

Figure 3-19 illustrates some of these advanced settings.

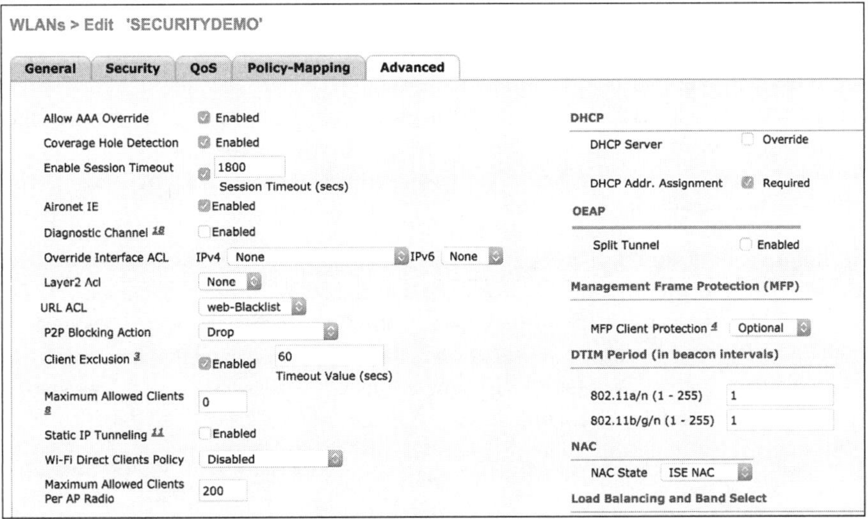

Figure 3-19 *Advanced WLAN Settings*

Configuring Wireless Protection Policies

Wireless is a medium for communication and is great for productivity, but it introduces challenges that do not exist on wired networks. The simple fact that malicious individuals can see wireless signals from their car in the parking lot opens up wireless to a slew of different threats and risk. In order to address the threats, Cisco and the rest of the industry have added useful features to minimize the risks of wireless deployments. Some of the most desirable features are configured under Security > Wireless Protection Policies. This section reviews these features and the benefits each of them brings.

Rogue AP Detection

Rogue AP detection is all about identifying any device that is sharing your spectrum but is not managed by you. A majority of rogues are set up by insiders, who can run to the store and get an AP inexpensively so that they can have the convenience of controlling their own AP. These users are ignorant of the risks involved with this behavior. A rogue AP becomes dangerous to an organization when it is set up to use the same SSID as your network, when it is detected to be on the wired network, or when it is set up by an outsider, most of the time with malicious intent.

How does any organization deal with the rogue AP threat? By detecting, classifying, and mitigating rogue APs.

Detecting Rogue APs

A WLC can tell APs to listen for non-infrastructure access points, clients, and ad hoc networks. Radio resource management (RRM) scanning is used to detect the presence of rogue devices. RRM can use two types of scanning:

- **Off-channel scanning:** This operation, performed by local mode and FlexConnect (in connected mode) APs, uses a time-slicing technique that allows client service and channel scanning using the same radio. By going off channel for a period of 50 milliseconds every 16 seconds, the AP, by default, spends only a small percentage of its time not serving clients.

- **Monitor mode scanning:** This operation, which is performed by monitor mode and adaptive wIPS monitor mode APs, uses 100% of the radio's time for scanning all channels in each respective frequency band. This allows for greater speed of detection and enables more time to be spent on each individual channel. Monitor mode APs are also far superior at detecting rogue clients as they have a more comprehensive view of the activity occurring in each channel.

Any AP not broadcasting the same RF group name or part of the same mobility group is considered a rogue.

Another way to detect rogue APs is to use Rogue Location Discovery Protocol (RLDP). Rogue detectors are used to identify whether a rogue device is connected to the wired network. An AP connects to a rogue AP as a client and sends a packet to the controller's IP address. This works only with open rogue access points. Figure 3-20 shows the options for selecting which APs can use RLDP.

> **Note** If AllAps is selected, the AP removes all client sessions and shuts down its radio prior to performing RLDP. For this reason, most organizations choose to only use monitor mode APs.

Rogue Policies

Rogue Detection Security Level	Low / High / Critical / Custom
Rogue Location Discovery Protocol	MonitorModeAps / ✓ AllAps / Disable
Expiration Timeout for Rogue AP and Rogue Client entries	
Validate rogue clients against AAA	Enabled
Validate rogue AP against AAA	Enabled
Polling Interval	0 Seconds
Validate rogue clients against MSE	Enabled
Detect and report Ad-Hoc Networks	Enabled
Rogue Detection Report Interval (10 to 300 Sec)	10
Rogue Detection Minimum RSSI (-70 to -128)	-90
Rogue Detection Transient Interval (0, 120 to 1800 Sec)	0
Rogue Client Threshold (0 to disable, 1 to 256)	0
Rogue containment automatic rate selection	Enabled

Auto Contain

Auto Containment Level	1
Auto Containment only for Monitor mode APs	Enabled
Auto Containment on FlexConnect Standalone	Enabled
Rogue on Wire	Enabled
Using our SSID	Enabled
Valid client on Rogue AP	Enabled
AdHoc Rogue AP	Enabled

Figure 3-20 *RLDP Access Point Selection*

An organization can make an AP operate as a rogue detector full time by selecting Rogue Detector as the AP mode and placing it on a trunk port so that it can hear all wired-side connected VLANs. It proceeds to find the clients on the wired subnet on all the VLANs. The rogue detector AP listens for Address Resolution Protocol (ARP) packets in order to determine the Layer 2 addresses of identified rogue clients or rogue APs sent by the controller. If a Layer 2 address that matches is found, the controller generates an alarm that identifies the rogue AP or client as a threat.

Classifying Rogue APs

Classification can be based on threat severity and mitigation action. For example, if a rogue AP has a foreign SSID, is not on your network, is secured, and has a weak RSSI (indicating a distant location), then it probably is a neighboring business's AP and not something to be concerned about. Classification allows you to customize the rogue rules and should be tailored to the customer risk model.

To create a rogue rule, go to Security > Wireless Protection Policies > Rogue Policies > Rogue Rules > Add Rule. For example, Figures 3-21 and 3-22 illustrate the creation of a rogue rule for a friendly classification for a coffee shop SSID and RSSI minimum of −80 dBm.

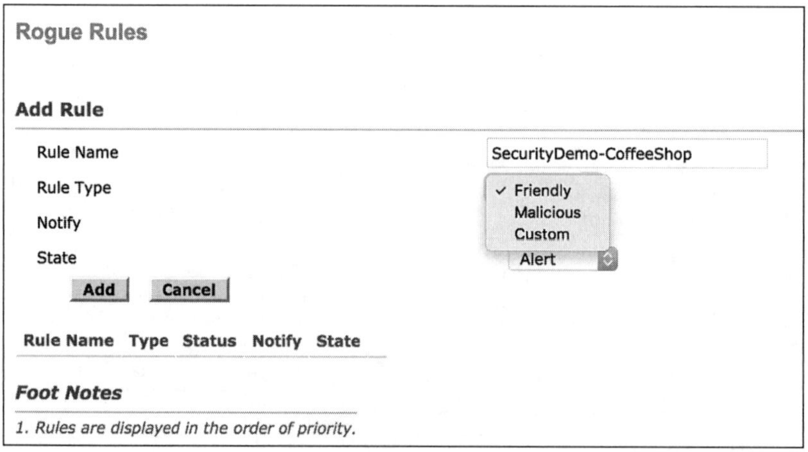

Figure 3-21 *Adding a New Rogue Rule*

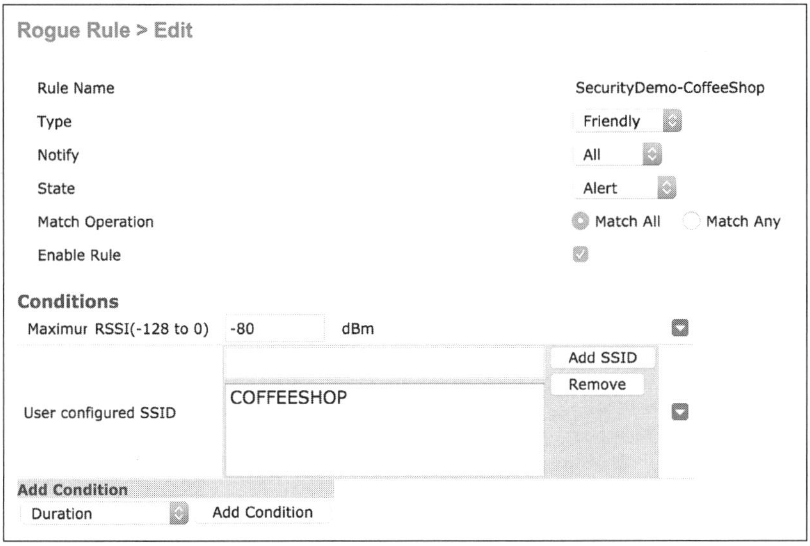

Rogue Rule > Edit

Rule Name SecurityDemo-CoffeeShop
Type Friendly
Notify All
State Alert
Match Operation Match All Match Any
Enable Rule

Conditions
Maximur RSSI(-128 to 0) -80 dBm
Add SSID
Remove
User configured SSID COFFEESHOP
Add Condition
Duration Add Condition

Figure 3-22 *Friendly Rogue Rule with SSID and RSSI Criteria*

Another popular rule looks for rogue APs that are impersonating your SSID. Figure 3-23 shows a rule that matches a managed SSID (that is, an SSID that is added to the controller) and has a minimum RSSI of –70 dBm.

Figure 3-23 *Malicious Rogue Rule with Managed SSID and RSSI Criteria*

You can manually classify SSIDs as friendly by adding the MAC address of the AP to Security > Wireless Protection Policies > Rogue Policies > Friendly Rogue.

By default, all access points are unclassified unless you create rules, manually set the MAC address to friendly, or manually classify them under Monitor > Rogues > Unclassified Rogue APs. Figure 3-24 shows how an unclassified AP can be manually classified as friendly or malicious.

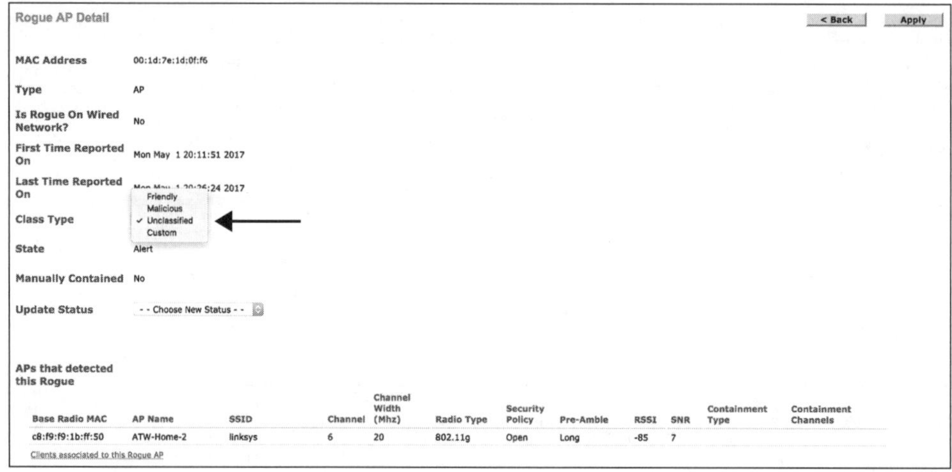

Figure 3-24 *Manually Classify a Rogue AP*

Mitigating Rogue APs

Mitigation can be done by physically sending someone to find and remove a rogue, manually shutting down switch ports, or implementing wireless containment. A valid AP can contain a rogue AP and clients by sending de-authentication packets to the rogue clients and AP. An organization can employ local, monitor mode, or FlexConnect APs to perform this function, but there can be an impact on client performance on managed APs. Use auto containment to nullify the most alarming threats.

Warning Improperly used containment can have legal consequences, depending on the country and local laws. Pay attention when the WLC presents the warning "Using this feature may have legal consequences. Do you want to continue?"

When configuring containment (in Security > Wireless Protection Policies > Rogue Policies > General), you must set a rogue detection security level to support containment:

- **Low:** Basic rogue detection for small-scale deployments. *Auto containment is not supported for this security level.*
- **High:** Basic rogue detection and auto containment for medium-scale or less-critical deployments. RLDP is disabled for this security level.

- **Critical:** Basic rogue detection, auto containment, and RLDP for highly critical deployments.
- **Custom:** Customized rogue policy parameters.

The Auto Contain section of the Rogue Policies page gives options on the types of events/rogues that warrant auto containment. The Auto Containment Level setting allows an administrator to configure how many APs will be used for auto containment; if Auto is selected, the ASA dynamically determines the appropriate number of APs to use. Rogue on Wire, Using Our SSID, Valid Client on Rogue AP, and AdHoc Rogue AP are all configurable items for enabling auto containment. Figure 3-25 illustrates a sample configuration that uses monitor mode APs to provide auto containment of some of the event types.

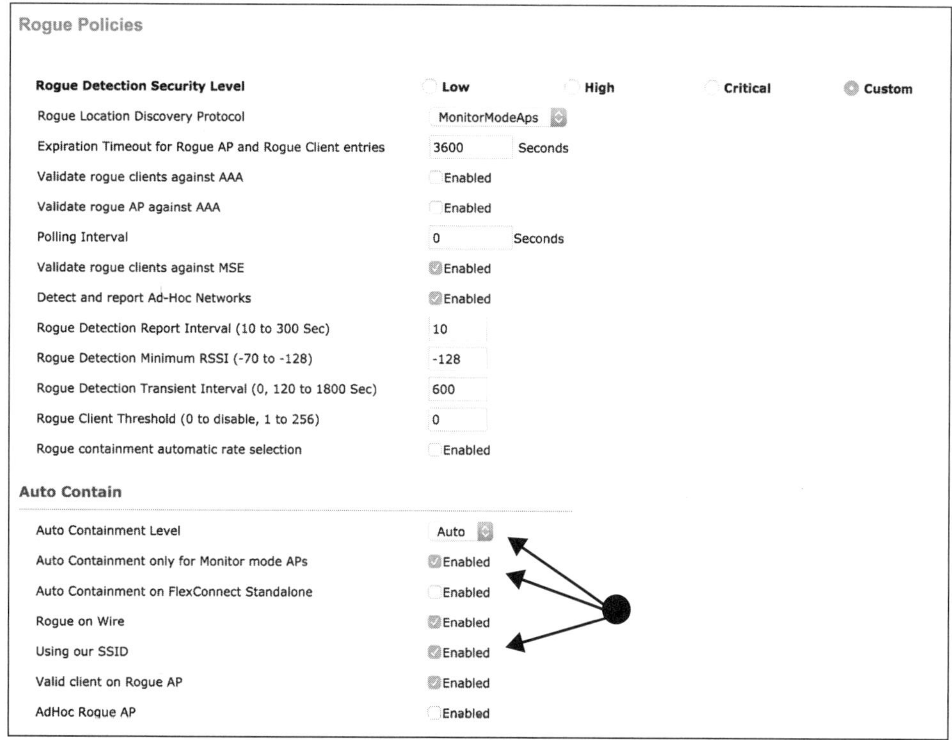

Figure 3-25 *General Rogue Policy and Containment Configuration*

If a malicious SSID or criterion is known in advance, a rule can be specified to match and contain it, as illustrated in Figure 3-26.

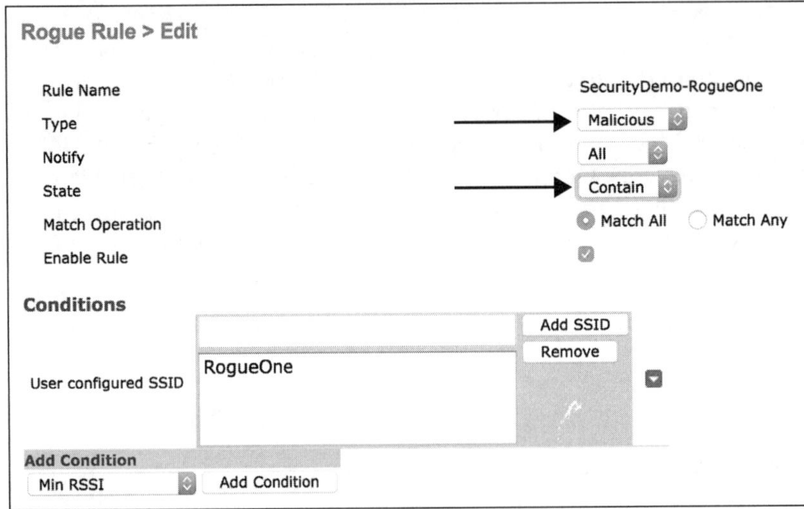

Figure 3-26 *Malicious Rogue Rule with SSID Criteria*

Also, you can manually contain an AP the same way you would manually classify rogue APs.

Wireless Threat Detection and Mitigation

Most organizations have deployed some type of intrusion detection or prevention on their wired networks, but many of them do not realize that there are threats that focus on 802.11 that otherwise are not visible or available to a wired network IDS/IPS. The next sections describe the capabilities of both wireless IDSs and IPSs in a Cisco Unified Wireless deployment.

Wireless Intrusion Detection Systems

The WLC performs IDS analysis using information obtained from all the connected APs, and it reports detected attacks to WLC. The wireless IDS analysis is complementary to any analysis that can otherwise be performed by a wired network IDS/IPS. The wireless IDS signature files used by the WLC are included in WLC software releases; however, they can be updated independently using a separate signature file. By default, 17 standard signatures come with a WLC.

The list of default signatures is illustrated in Figure 3-27 and can be found by going to Security > Wireless Protection Policies > Standard Signatures.

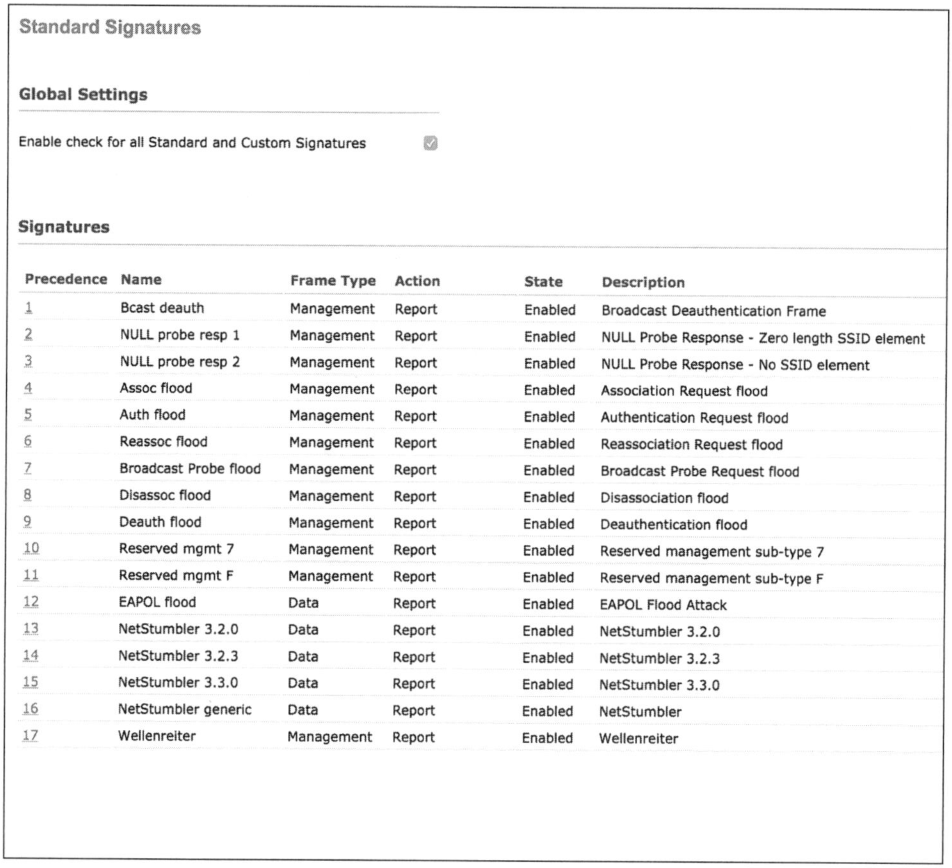

Standard Signatures

Global Settings

Enable check for all Standard and Custom Signatures ☑

Signatures

Precedence	Name	Frame Type	Action	State	Description
1	Bcast deauth	Management	Report	Enabled	Broadcast Deauthentication Frame
2	NULL probe resp 1	Management	Report	Enabled	NULL Probe Response - Zero length SSID element
3	NULL probe resp 2	Management	Report	Enabled	NULL Probe Response - No SSID element
4	Assoc flood	Management	Report	Enabled	Association Request flood
5	Auth flood	Management	Report	Enabled	Authentication Request flood
6	Reassoc flood	Management	Report	Enabled	Reassociation Request flood
7	Broadcast Probe flood	Management	Report	Enabled	Broadcast Probe Request flood
8	Disassoc flood	Management	Report	Enabled	Disassociation flood
9	Deauth flood	Management	Report	Enabled	Deauthentication flood
10	Reserved mgmt 7	Management	Report	Enabled	Reserved management sub-type 7
11	Reserved mgmt F	Management	Report	Enabled	Reserved management sub-type F
12	EAPOL flood	Data	Report	Enabled	EAPOL Flood Attack
13	NetStumbler 3.2.0	Data	Report	Enabled	NetStumbler 3.2.0
14	NetStumbler 3.2.3	Data	Report	Enabled	NetStumbler 3.2.3
15	NetStumbler 3.3.0	Data	Report	Enabled	NetStumbler 3.3.0
16	NetStumbler generic	Data	Report	Enabled	NetStumbler
17	Wellenreiter	Management	Report	Enabled	Wellenreiter

Figure 3-27 *Wireless IDS Signatures*

When the ID of a signature is clicked, the details of the signature, including frequency and data pattern to match, are shown. Figure 3-28 shows the NetStumbler generic signature as an example.

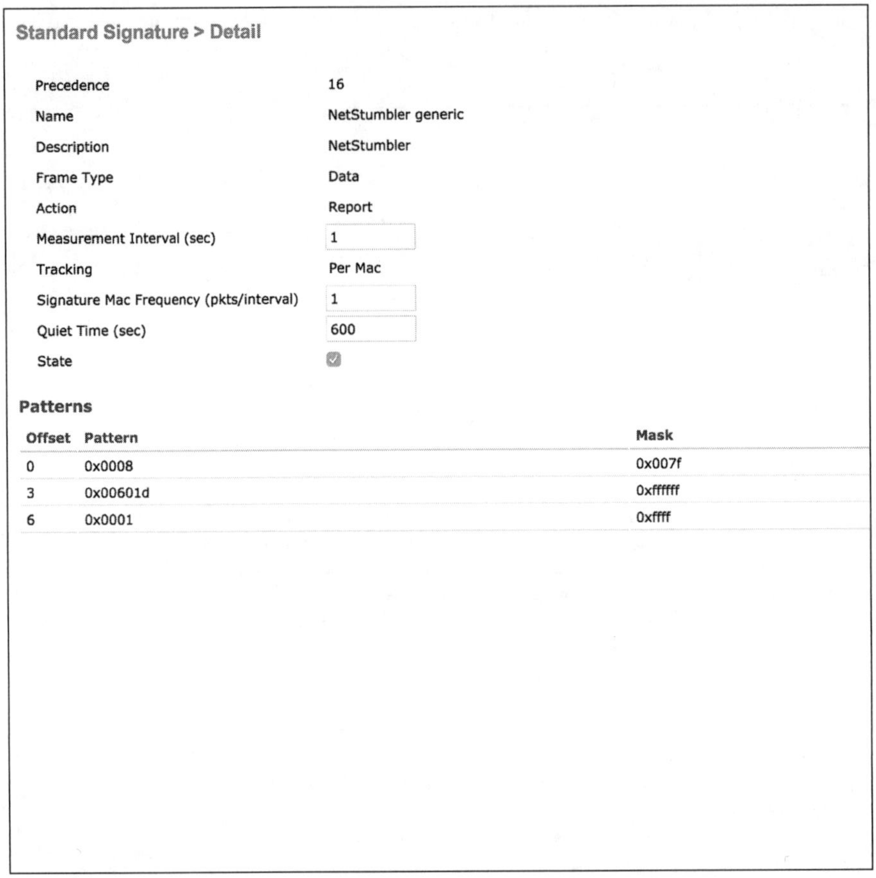

Standard Signature > Detail

Precedence	16
Name	NetStumbler generic
Description	NetStumbler
Frame Type	Data
Action	Report
Measurement Interval (sec)	1
Tracking	Per Mac
Signature Mac Frequency (pkts/interval)	1
Quiet Time (sec)	600
State	☑

Patterns

Offset	Pattern	Mask
0	0x0008	0x007f
3	0x00601d	0xffffff
6	0x0001	0xffff

Figure 3-28 *NetStumbler Generic Signature Detail*

Custom signatures are displayed in the Custom Signatures window. You can configure custom IDS signatures or bit-pattern matching rules to identify various types of attacks in incoming 802.11 packets by uploading them to the controller. You do this at Commands > Download File by selecting Signature File and specifying the transfer method and filename. Example 3-1 shows an example of a signature in text format that could be uploaded as a custom signature.

Example 3-1 *Signature in Text Format*

```
Name = "NetStumbler generic", Ver = 0, Preced= 16, FrmType = data, Pattern =
0:0x0108:0x03FF, Pattern = 27:0x00601d:0xFFFFFF, Pattern = 30:0x0001:0xFFFF, Freq
  = 1, Quiet = 600, Action = report, Desc="NetStumbler"
```

To see if an IDS signature is alerting, you can go to Security > Wireless Protection Policies > Signature Events Summary, as shown in Figure 3-29.

Signature Events Summary

Signature Type	Precedence	Signature Name	# Events
Standard	2	NULL probe resp 1	1

Figure 3-29 *Signature Events Summary*

Wireless Intrusion Prevention Systems

The one problem with an IDS is that it cannot block traffic; it can only alarm. Enter Cisco's adaptive Wireless Intrusion Prevention System (wIPS). With extended signature support and protection against more than 100 different threat conditions, wIPS is an important part of any mission-critical wireless deployment. In order to provide wIPS, a WLC must integrate with Cisco's Mobility Services Engine (MSE) and Cisco's Prime Infrastructure (PI) solutions. Figure 3-30 illustrates the communication that takes place between the different solutions.

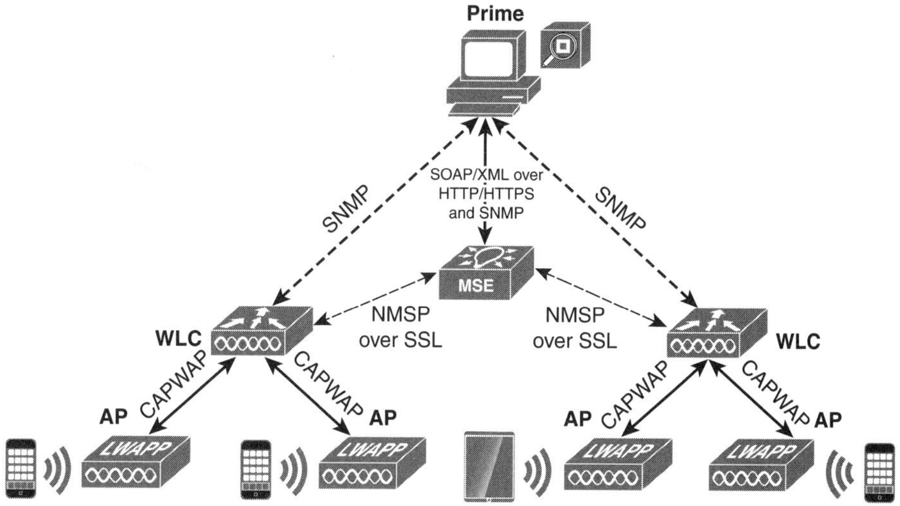

Figure 3-30 *Adaptive Wireless Intrusion Prevention System*

The following important protocols are needed for the adaptive wIPS architecture to function:

- **Network Mobility Services Protocol (NMSP):** This protocol is used for communication between WLCs and the MSE. In the case of a wIPS deployment, this protocol provides a pathway for alarm information to be aggregated from controllers to the MSE and for wIPS configuration information to be pushed to the controller. This protocol is encrypted.

- **Simple Object Access Protocol (SOAP/XML):** This protocol provides a method of communication between the MSE and PI. This protocol is used to distribute configuration parameters to the wIPS service running on the MSE.
- **Simple Network Management Protocol (SNMP):** This protocol is used to forward wIPS alarm information from the MSE to the PI. It is also utilized to communicate rogue access point information from a WLC to the PI.

In order to configure adaptive wIPS, a profile must be configured on PI and pushed to the controllers and MSE. Figure 3-31 shows the details of a wIPS profile on PI.

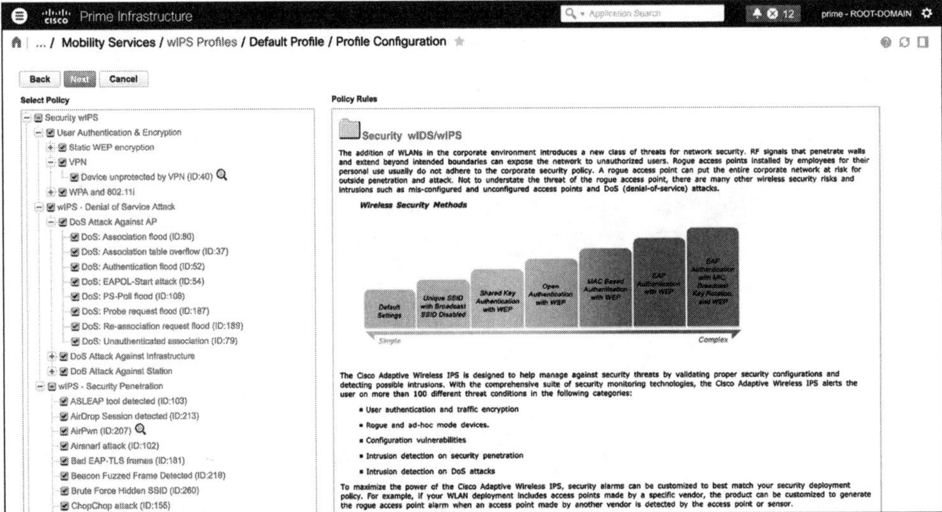

Figure 3-31 *Prime Infrastructure wIPS Profile Configuration*

An adaptive wIPS solution has several enhancements over the WLC's wIDS solution. First, it provides additional threat identification and protection:

- **Customizable severities:** Severity of alarms is set based on the security threat level and operation impact on a wireless production network. For example, most DoS attacks may have an operational impact on the wireless infrastructure. Thus, their severity is set to Critical by default.
- **Capture attack forensics:** A toggle-based packet capture facility provides the ability to log and retrieve a set of wireless frames. This feature is enabled on a per-attack basis from within the wIPS profile configuration of PI.
- **Location integration:** With MSE location, administrators can easily find an attacker on the floorplan.
- **Consolidation of alerts:** PI can provide a unified view of security alerts from multiple controllers and MSE.

Access points are responsible for detecting threats with signatures. The following options exist to provide wIPS capabilities for enterprise deployments:

- **Enhanced local mode (ELM):** This mode allows local or FlexConnect APs to run an AP submode of a wIPS and operates effectively for on-channel (the channel the AP is currently servicing clients on) attacks, without any compromise to performance in terms of data, voice, and video clients and services. ELM does scan for off-channel (other channels the AP is not servicing clients on) attacks, but it is considered best effort.
- **Dedicated monitor mode APs:** This allows for 100% channel scanning but requires an organization to deploy an overlay network to passively listen for threats.
- **Wireless Security and Spectrum Intelligence (WSSI) module:** For organizations running 3600/3700 series APs, instead of deploying extra APs and creating an overlay network, the WSSI module allows you to install a module into the local/FlexConnect AP, whose sole responsibility is to scan all channels for threats and spectrum intelligence.
- **2800/3800 series access points:** These newer APs contain a flexible radio architecture. In a sense, the AP is a tri-band radio as it contains a dedicated 5 GHz radio to serve clients and another flexible radio (known as an XOR radio) that can be assigned the wIPS function within the network.

Non-802.11 Attacks and Interference

While normally not thought of as a security feature, Cisco CleanAir technology is an effective tool for monitoring and managing your network's RF conditions. The following are some of the threats that can be addressed using CleanAir:

- Non-Wi-Fi transmitter or RF jammer detection and location
- Non-Wi-Fi bridge detection and location
- Non-Wi-Fi access point detection and location
- Layer 1 DoS attack location and detection (Bluetooth, microwave, and so on)

Client Exclusion

At a basic level, client exclusion is a set of rules that a WLC uses to evaluate whether clients are misbehaving when connecting or while connected to the WLAN. By default, each WLAN automatically excludes for 60 seconds clients that match any of the following rules:

- **Excessive 802.11 association failures:** Clients are excluded on the sixth 802.11 association attempt after five consecutive failures.
- **Excessive 802.11 authentication failures:** Clients are excluded on the sixth 802.11 authentication attempt after five consecutive failures.

- **Excessive 802.11X authentication failures:** Clients are excluded on the fourth 802.1X authentication attempt after three consecutive failures.
- **IP theft or reuse:** Clients are excluded if the IP address is already assigned to another device.
- **Excessive web authentication failures:** Clients are excluded on the fourth web authentication attempt after three consecutive failures.

Client exclusion can be configured at Security > Wireless Protection Policies > Client Exclusion Policies (see Figure 3-32).

Client Exclusion Policies

Excessive 802.11 Association Failures	☑	
Excessive 802.11 Authentication Failures	☑	
Excessive 802.1X Authentication Failures	☑	
Maximum 802.1x-AAA Failure Attempts	3	(1 - 10)
IP Theft or IP Reuse	☑	
Excessive Web Authentication Failures	☑	

Figure 3-32 *Client Exclusion Policies*

After the default 60 seconds, clients are able to try to connect again. If the timer is severely increased or a timeout setting of 0 is used, indicating that administrative control is required to reenable the client, then sometimes the users will call the helpdesk to be manually removed from the excluded list. To remove the client from the exclusion list manually, go to Monitor > Clients and click the blue drop-down for the client and then click Remove.

Management Frame Protection

Management frames facilitate connectivity and status but can also be used by malicious users for attacks. One popular attack is a de-authentication attack, where the attacker sends disassociate packets to one or more clients that are currently associated with a particular access point. This allows the attacker to uncover hidden SSIDs, attempt to get the client to connect to a rogue AP, or capture WPA/WPA2 handshakes. The only way to protect against this type of attack is to use management frame protection (MFP).

MFP provides security for the otherwise unprotected and unencrypted 802.11 management messages passed between access points and clients.

The MIC component of MFP ensures that a frame has not been tampered with, and the digital signature component ensures that the MIC could have only been produced by a valid member of the WLAN domain.

Infrastructure MFP

Infrastructure MFP protects management frames by adding the message integrity check information element (MIC-IE) to the frames emitted by APs (and not those emitted by clients), which are then validated by other APs in the network. Infrastructure MFP uses a cryptographically hashed digital signature mechanism to insert the MIC into 802.11 management frames. This allows for identification of legitimate members of a WLAN deployment, as well as rogue infrastructure devices and spoofed frames through their lack of valid MICs. When enabled, infrastructure MFP provides management frame protection, management frame validation, and event reporting. When an AP that is configured to validate MFP frames receives a frame with an invalid MIC, it reports it to the WLC.

Infrastructure MFP is configured under AP Authentication Policy, found at Security > Wireless Protection Policies > AP Authentication (see Figure 3-33).

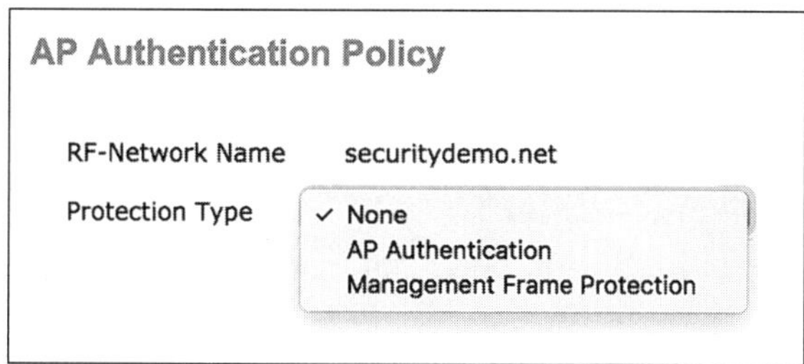

Figure 3-33 *AP Authentication Policy*

When you enable the AP authentication feature, the access points sending RRM neighbor packets with different RF network names are reported as rogues.

When you enable infrastructure MFP, it is enabled globally for the Cisco WLC. You can enable or disable infrastructure MFP validation for a particular access point or protection for a particular WLAN if MFP is enabled globally for the Cisco WLC.

> **Note** This setting does not affect client MFP, which is configured per WLAN.

Client MFP

Client MFP shields authenticated clients from spoofed frames, which prevents many of the common attacks against wireless LANs. Cisco client MFP requires a client to have Cisco Compatible Extensions v5 (CCXv5) in order to negotiate a signature process with the AP. CCXv5 allows the clients to learn the mobility group MFP key before they can detect and reject invalid frames.

Client MFP encrypts management frames that are sent between APs and CCXv5 clients so that both the AP and the client can take preventive action by dropping spoofed class 3 management frames (that is, management frames passed between an AP and a client that is authenticated and associated). Client MFP leverages the security mechanism defined by IEEE 802.11i to protect the following types of class 3 unicast management frames: disassociation frames, deauthentication frames, and QoS WMM actions.

Client MFP supplements infrastructure MFP rather than replacing it because infrastructure MFP continues to detect and report invalid unicast frames sent to clients that are not client-MFP capable as well as invalid class 1 and class 2 management frames. Infrastructure MFP is applied only to management frames that are not protected by client MFP. If you require a non-CCXv5 client to associate a WLAN, client MFP should be configured as disabled or optional.

By default, client MFP is optional for a WLAN, but you can set it to Disabled or Required in the WLAN configuration, found at WLAN > *SSID Name* Edit > Advanced (see Figure 3-34).

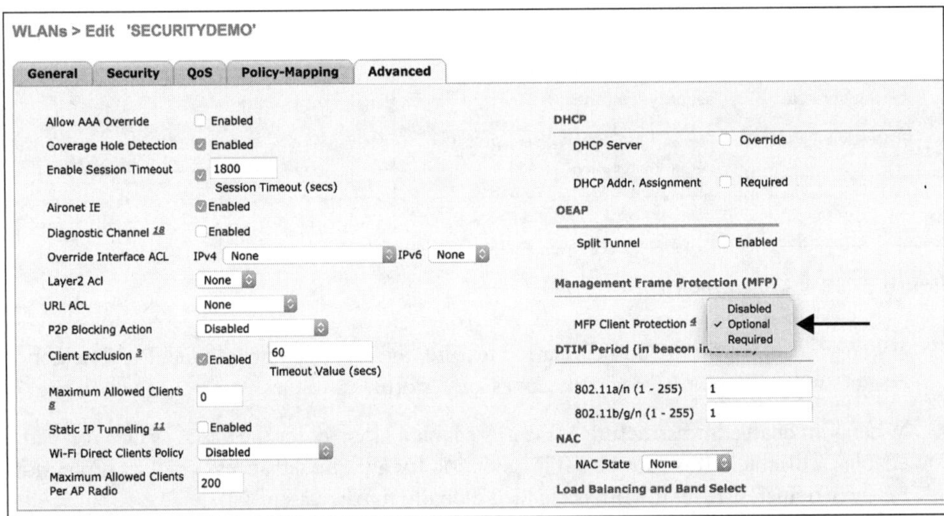

Figure 3-34 *Client MFP Configuration*

> **Note** Most commercial devices, such as iOS and Android, do not natively support CCXv5. If MFP is required, be aware that some clients may not be allowed to connect.

Protected Management Frames

Cisco Client MFP was used as a basis for IEEE 802.11w Protected Management Frames (PMF) development. 802.11w was ratified in 2009. One of the main drivers for standardizing PMF was to ensure pervasive client support. Today, most operating systems already support 802.11w. Technically, on Cisco controllers, you can enable both PMF and MFP.

The 802.11w protocol applies only to a set of robust management frames that are protected by the PMF service. These include disassociation, deauthentication, and robust action frames. Client protection is achieved by the AP through the addition of cryptographic protection for deauthentication and disassociation frames, thus preventing spoofing of a client in an attack.

PMF configuration is done at WLAN > *SSID Name* > Edit > Security > Layer 2:

Step 1. Enable PMF by changing PMF from Disabled to Optional or Required (see Figure 3-35).

Step 2. Change the Authentication Key Management setting from PSK or 802.1X to PMF PSK or PMF 802.1X (see Figure 3-36).

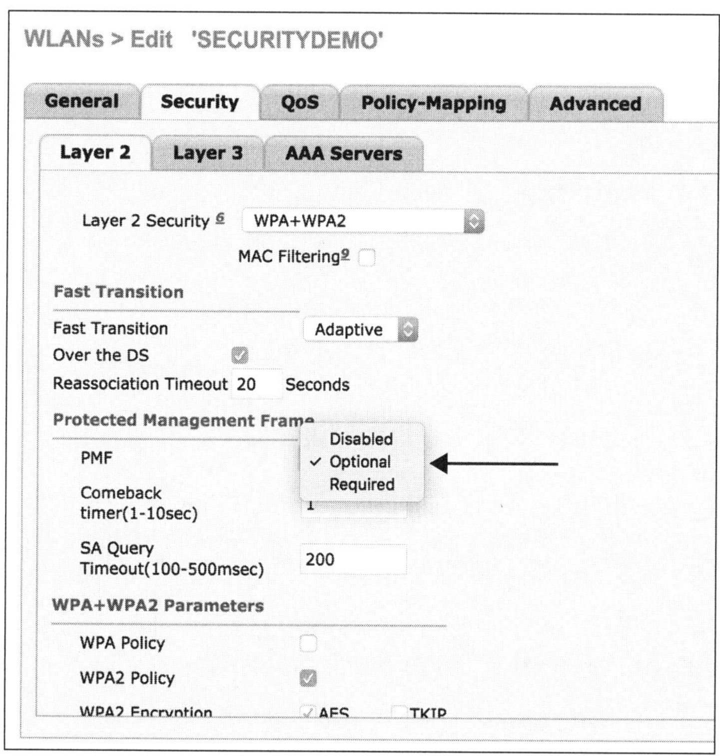

Figure 3-35 *Enable PMF on the WLAN*

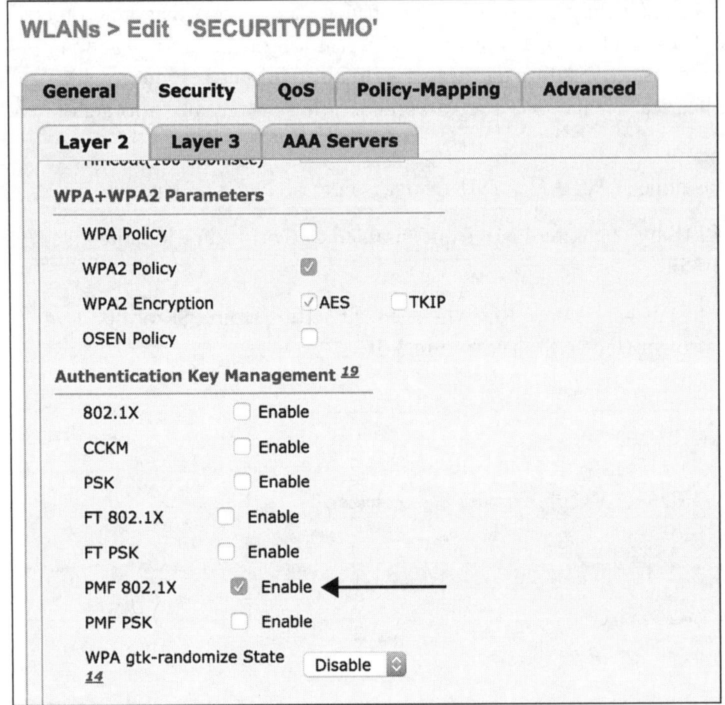

Figure 3-36 *Enable PMF on Authentication Key Management*

> **Note** Infrastructure MFP cannot be replaced with 802.11w. In infrastructure MFP, the APs sign their beacons and other broadcast management frames. Other APs can detect unsigned broadcast management frames and report rogues to the WLC. This mode does not exist with 802.11w.

Management and Control Plane Protection

The goal of this section is to help with the security interaction between WLCs and APs and the network where they are connected. While not normally a focal point of securing wireless, the management and control plane is an important part of providing a secure wireless solution.

Management Authentication

Authentication can be performed using a local database, RADIUS, or TACACS+ server protected with a username and password. The priority for the different databases is configured at Security > Priority Order > Management User (see Figure 3-37). In cases where multiple databases are configured, an organization can dictate the priority order for the back-end databases.

Priority Order > Management User

Authentication

Not Used		Order Used for Authentication	
RADIUS	>	LOCAL	Up
	<	TACACS+	Down

If LOCAL is selected as second priority then user will be authenticated against LOCAL only if first priority is unreachable.

Figure 3-37 *Management Authentication Priority*

Authentication and authorization services are tied to each other. For example, if authentication is performed using RADIUS or a local database, then authorization is not performed with TACACS+. Rather, authorization would use the permissions associated for the user in the local or RADIUS database, such as read-only or read/write, whereas when authentication is performed with TACACS+, authorization is tied to TACACS+.

To add a new RADIUS authentication server, go to Security > AAA > RADIUS > Authentication > New and add the IP address and shared secret and ensure that Management is checked. If the server will be used only for management authentication, ensure that the Network User check box is not selected.

To add a new TACACS+ authentication server, go to Security > AAA > TACACS > Authentication > New and add the IP address and shared secret. Figure 3-38 illustrates a new TACACS+ authentication server being added in a WLC.

TACACS+ Authentication Servers > New

Server Index (Priority)	2
Server IP Address(Ipv4/Ipv6)	10.28.1.28
Shared Secret Format	ASCII
Shared Secret	••••••••
Confirm Shared Secret	••••••••
Port Number	49
Server Status	Enabled
Server Timeout	5 seconds

Figure 3-38 *New TACACS+ Authentication Server*

Authorization that is specific to TACACS+ deployment is task-based rather than per-command-based. The tasks are mapped to various tabs that correspond to the seven menu bar items that are currently on the web GUI:

- Monitor
- WLANs
- Controller
- Wireless
- Security
- Management
- Command

This mapping is based on the fact that most customers use the web interface rather than the CLI to configure a controller. An additional role for lobby admin management is available for those who need to have lobby admin privileges only. In order for basic management authentication via TACACS+ to succeed, you must configure authentication and authorization servers on the WLC. Accounting configuration is optional. Figure 3-39 illustrates adding a new TACACS+ authorization server in the WLC. The IP address and shared secret must match the authentication server information.

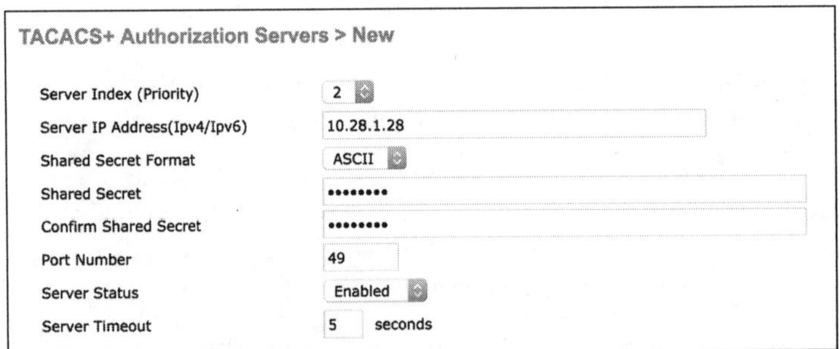

Figure 3-39 *New TACACS+ Authorization Server*

Accounting occurs whenever a particular user-initiated action is performed successfully. The attributes changed are logged in the TACACS+ accounting server, along with the user ID, the remote host where the user is logged in, date and time, authorization level, and what action was performed and the values provided.

To add a new RADIUS accounting server, go to Security > AAA > RADIUS > Accounting > New and add the IP address and shared secret (the same as the authentication shared secret); also, if the server will only be used for management authentication, ensure that the Network User check box is not selected.

To add a new TACACS+ accounting server, go to Security > AAA > TACACS > Accounting > New and add the IP address and shared secret. Figure 3-40 illustrates adding a new TACACS accounting server in the WLC.

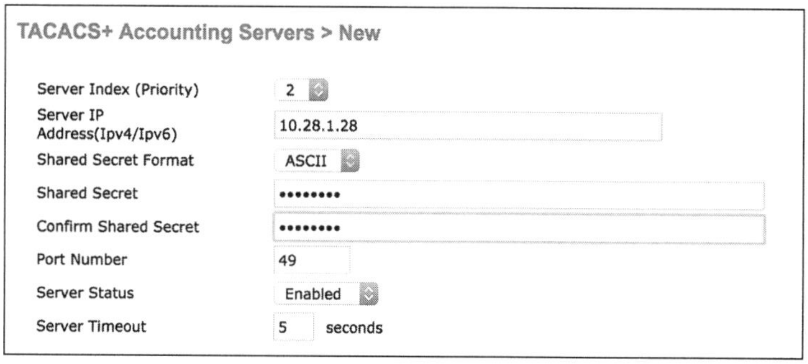

Figure 3-40 *New TACACS+ Accounting Server*

> **Note** Detailed configuration information of the RADIUS and TACACS servers is provided in *Integrated Security Technologies and Solutions, Volume* II.

Management Protocols and Access

After enabling external authentication for the WLC, it is important to lock down the management protocols that are allowed on the WLC.

Figure 3-41 shows how HTTP can and should be disabled on the Management > HTTP-HTTPS page.

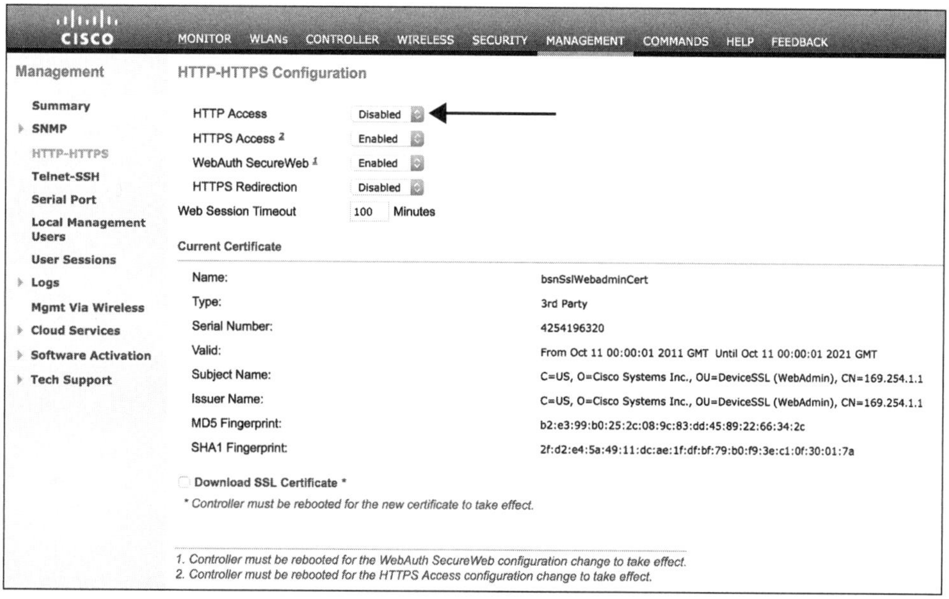

Figure 3-41 *HTTP-HTTPS Configuration*

Telnet is another protocol that is risky to use for management access. Figure 3-42 shows how *Telnet* can and should be disabled on the Management > Telnet-SSH page.

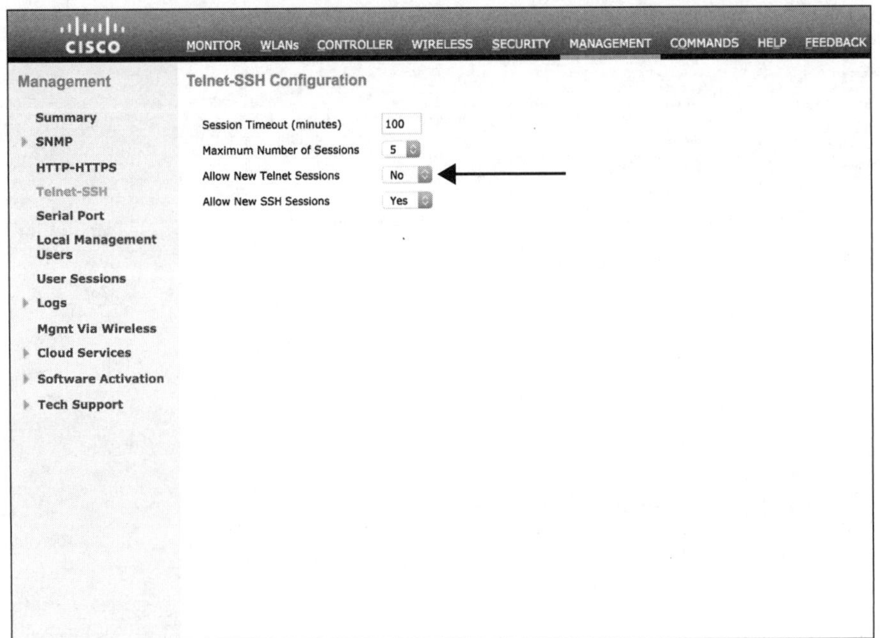

Figure 3-42 *Telnet-SSH Configuration*

The management over wireless feature allows you to monitor and configure local controllers using a wireless client. In most cases, wireless users should not be allowed to log in to the WLC. To disable management over wireless, go to Management > Management Via Wireless page and uncheck the box, as shown in Figure 3-43.

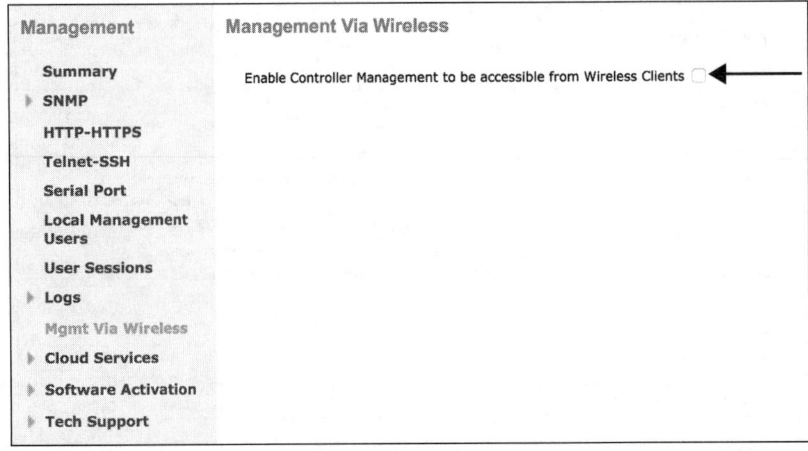

Figure 3-43 *Management Via Wireless*

CPU ACLs

A CPU ACL controls requests from specific networks/clients to the controller directly. A CPU ACL actually filters traffic that is destined to one of the WLC IP addresses, meaning it is applied on all interfaces but does not filter all types of traffic—only traffic that is destined to the WLC itself.

> **Tip** It is very easy to block yourself from accessing the WLC if you are not careful. If you lock yourself out, log in via the console and remove the ACL that is applied to the controller CPU and then enter the **config acl cpu none** command. To see if the ACL is applied to the controller CPU, enter the **show acl cpu** command.

The safest way to create a CPU ACL is to explicitly deny traffic and/or networks that are not supposed to communicate with the WLC and explicitly allow all other traffic. The following is a logical example (not a real configuration example):

```
deny tcp [CLIENT NETWORKS] [WLC mgmt IP] eq 443
deny tcp [CLIENT NETWORKS] [WLC mgmt IP] eq 22
permit ip any any
```

To apply the created ACL for IPv4 or IPv6, go to Security > Access Control Lists > CPU Access Control Lists, select Enable CUP ACL, and select the ACL to apply. Figure 3-44 illustrates setting an IPv4 ACL.

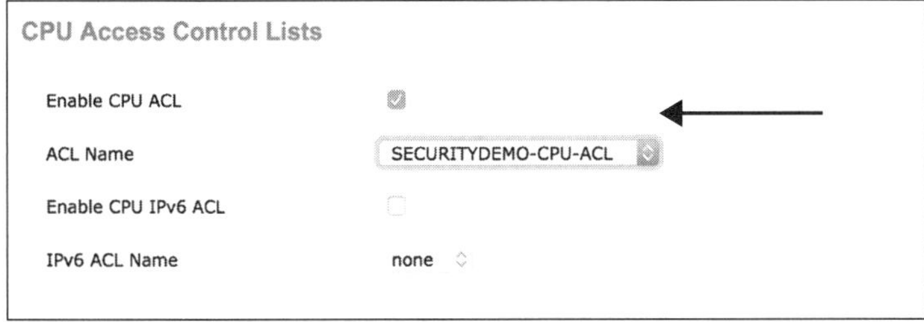

Figure 3-44 *CPU ACL*

Access Point Protection

The same best practices for securing the WLC apply to APs as well.

By going to Wireless > Access Points > Global Configuration, you can configure the following to help secure the APs (see Figure 3-45):

- **Login credentials:** You can set the username and password to log in directly to an AP through Telnet or SSH.
- **802.1X supplicant credentials:** You can set the username and password the AP will use to perform EAP-FAST 802.1X login on the wired interface.
- **Global Telnet SSH:** You can turn on/off Telnet and SSH login directly to the AP.

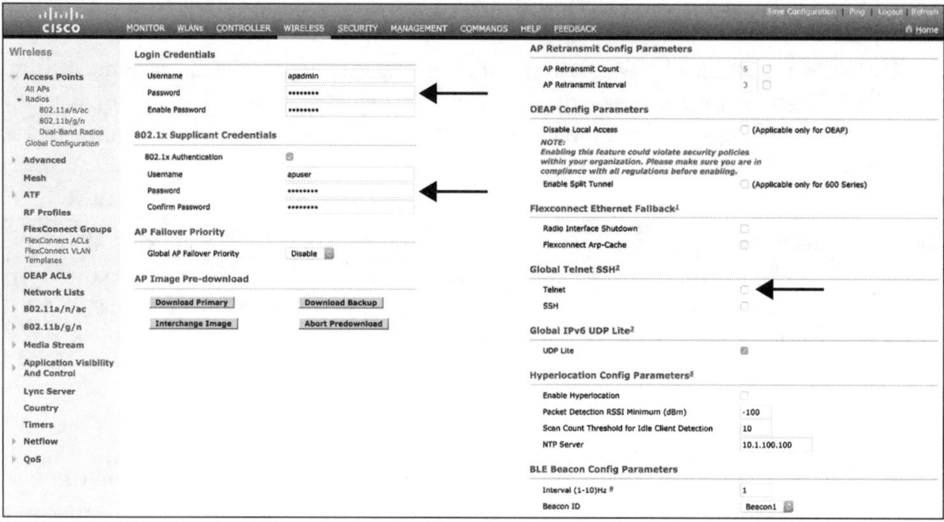

Figure 3-45 *Access Point Global Configuration*

Integrating a WLC with Other Security Solutions

A WLC, along with its inherent protections like wIDS and rogue detection, also integrates with other solutions to provide additional security coverage, the primary goal being to secure all connections and the users of wireless.

WLC and ISE

Identity Services Engine (ISE), described in detail in *Integrated Security Technologies and Solutions, Volume II*, can be used as a RADIUS or TACACS authentication source with a WLC. This enables both 802.1X authentication and guest access through Central Web Authentication (CWA). The WLC can also use Cisco TrustSec to allow for segmentation and integration with other security enforcement points in the network. Starting in the WLC 8.4 release, TrustSec native tagging and Security Group Access Control Lists (SGACL) are supported. This means the WLC or an AP could be used to tag wireless clients' network traffic with an SGT when bridging from wireless to wired. Instead of using an upstream switch/router for enforcement, the wireless traffic can be enforced directly on the WLC or APs. The WLC or AP can also download an SGACL from ISE. In order to configure TrustSec support, the RADIUS servers must be configured with PAC provisioning, and you must go to Security > TrustSec > General to enable CTS and configure the device ID and password. After configuration, TrustSec environment data is downloaded from ISE, and the security group name table is downloaded onto the WLC.

The WLC can also use SGT Exchange Protocol (SXP) to propagate the security group tags (SGTs) assigned to users across network devices that do not have hardware support for Cisco TrustSec. The SXP sends SGT information to the TrustSec-enabled devices or ISE so devices have the appropriate IP-to-SGT mappings. The WLC can send mappings for IPv4 and IPv6 clients. From WLC release 8.3, the SXP on the Cisco WLC is supported for both centrally and locally switched networks. Also, IP-to-SGT mapping can be done on the WLANs for clients that are not authenticated by Cisco ISE. The Cisco WLC is always in SXP Speaker mode, meaning it sends the mappings. SXP can be configured under Security > TrustSec > SXP Config. For locally switched WLANs in local or FlexConnect mode APs, SXP can be configured by going to Wireless > Access Points > All APs > Trusted Security.

WLC and Stealthwatch

The WLC uses NetFlow to integrate with Cisco Stealthwatch. NetFlow is a record that contains the important details about network transactions: information about when the conversation occurred, the duration of the session, and what ports and protocols were used. Stealthwatch can provide visibility of traffic across the wireless network. Its flow-based analytics can see stealthy attacks, such as data exfiltration, data hoarding, and reconnaissance attacks. Stealthwatch allows your existing network to be used as a security sensor and enforcer to dramatically improve threat defense.

WLC release 8.2 introduced the enhanced NetFlow records exporter. NetFlow v9 sends 17 different data records, as defined in RFC 3954, to external third-party NetFlow collectors such as Stealthwatch.

To configure NetFlow, go to Wireless > NetFlow and create an exporter and a monitor. Then under WLAN > Edit > QoS, select the NetFlow monitor.

Figure 3-46 illustrates how the WLC can send NetFlow to Stealthwatch and Stealthwatch can use ISE to quarantine wireless users.

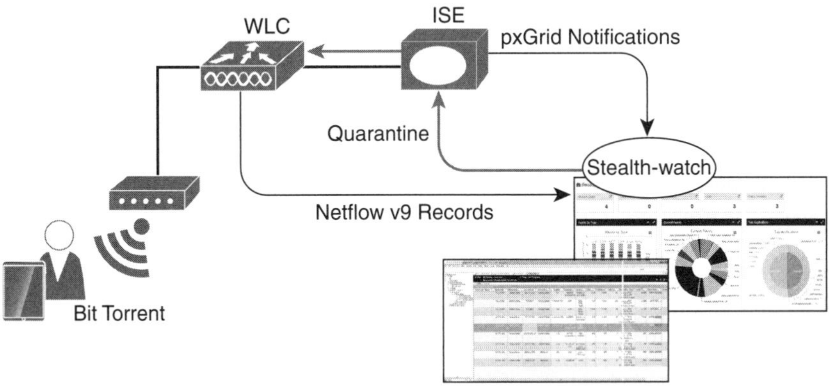

Figure 3-46 *Integration with ISE and Stealthwatch*

WLC and Umbrella

One security integration that was added in WLC version 8.4 is integration with Cisco Umbrella, formerly known as OpenDNS Umbrella. This integration provides administrators a seamless way to redirect DNS requests to Umbrella. A DNS request always precedes a web request. A WLC intercepts wireless users' DNS requests from the client and redirects the query to Umbrella servers in the cloud (208.67.222.222, 208.67.220.220).

Umbrella servers resolve the DNS query and enforce preconfigured security filtering rules on a per-identity basis to mark the domain as either malicious (and return a blocked page to the client) or safe (and return the resolved IP address to the client). In order to set up the integration, an administrator must obtain an API token for device registration from the Umbrella dashboard and apply the token on the WLC under Security > OpenDNS > General. This registers the device to the OpenDNS account. After registration, profiles should be added to the same page. These profiles then show up in the Umbrella console for customized policies. There are two deployment options on the WLC to redirect wireless clients to Umbrella with the appropriate profile mapping:

- **Local policies:** Allows administrators to customize Umbrella policies based on user roles. In essence, a user is assigned a role via RADIUS authentication from ISE, and a local policy configuration can map that role to an Umbrella profile on the WLC. This allows administrators to customize policies for different user roles in their organization; for example, employees, contractors, and guests can all have different policies.
- **Per WLAN/AP group:** Administrators can statically map an entire WLAN or AP group to an Umbrella profile.

Along with the profile mappings, there are three Umbrella modes that can be used, depending on the deployment:

- **Force mode:** This mode, enabled by default, is enforced per WLAN and forces all DNS traffic to query Umbrella.
- **Ignore mode:** WLC honors the DNS server used by the client; it could be an Umbrella server or an enterprise/external DNS server.
- **Copy mode:** All Internet-bound DNS traffic is forwarded to an Umbrella cloud without any policy options (no blocking/redirection).

For detailed information on Umbrella, see Chapter 9.

Summary

In this chapter, you learned about deploying and securing a Cisco Unified Wireless deployment with a wireless LAN controller and access points. You examined the 802.11 standards and how they are applied in the solution and how each of them provides additional security. You found out all the ways to identify threats and risk by deploying wireless and the solutions to minimize or mitigate them.

References

"IEEE 802.11", https://en.wikipedia.org/wiki/IEEE_802.11

"Wireless TrustSec Deployment Guide," https://www.cisco.com/c/en/us/td/docs/wireless/controller/technotes/8-4/b_wireless_trustsec_deployment_guide.pdf

"Cisco Umbrella WLAN Integration Guide", https://www.cisco.com/c/en/us/td/docs/wireless/controller/technotes/8-4/b_cisco_umbrella_wlan_integration_guide.html

Part II

Deny IP any any

Chapter 4

Firewalling with the ASA

ASA Fundamentals

The Adaptive Security Appliance (ASA) is Cisco's firewall that was introduced in 2005 as the successor to the venerable PIX firewall. While it retains many components from the PIX, the ASA has evolved into a more Cisco IOS–like device, with some spillover from Cisco's routing products. In recent years, the number of ASA features has increased exponentially. Understanding these features and how they are used is mandatory for any CCIE candidate.

Given the various options for deployment, the initial configuration of the ASA requires a bit of advanced planning. An ASA can be deployed in various forwarding modes with or without virtualization (contexts). Interfaces are given security values, which determine whether they require permitting access control entries. Having an understanding of packet flows and access policies will make this process easier.

It is a well known fact in CCIE lab preparation that maximizing hands-on time with the gear increases the chances of successfully passing the exam. The CCIE lab rewards candidates who can quickly configure, diagnose, and troubleshoot complex technologies.

Where do you find gear to practice on? There are many online virtual labs available, as well as training classes, but in our experience, there is no substitute for actually building a lab that is dedicated to CCIE preparation. Years ago, this meant investing several thousands of dollars in equipment for an adequate physical lab environment plus powering and cooling a rack of gear.

Virtualization has changed this model considerably. It is now possible to virtualize nearly all of the lab components for a much more cost-effective lab setup. Likewise, the CCIE lab has evolved over time as well, with the current blueprint consisting of a mix of physical and virtual devices. A successful candidate understands how to configure and troubleshoot both virtual and physical devices.

Note This chapter uses a virtualized ASA for all sample configurations except where noted.

The virtual ASA is included in Cisco's virtualization platform, which is available for purchase. For more information on Cisco's Virtual Internet Routing Lab (VIRL), see https://learningnetworkstore.cisco.com/virtual-internet-routing-lab-virl/cisco-personal-edition-pe-20-nodes-virl-20.

Setting Up a Lab Virtual ASA (ASAv)

In order to download the ASA virtual firewall, a valid Cisco.com login is required. The ASAv is supported in multiple environments, including (at the time this book was published) VMware, KVM, Microsoft Azure Cloud, AWS Cloud, and Microsoft Hyper-V. During the install, a pre-deployment configuration process gathers details for basic connectivity, including ASA Device Manager (ASDM) and Secure Shell (SSH) support, to get the ASAv bootstrapped.

Note At the time this book was published, ASAv was not supported on VMware vSphere 6.5. Please check the release notes prior to installation.

The following are some important items for initial configuration:

- Configuring the interface
- Setting up the ASDM
- Configuring zones and security levels
- Determining the firewall mode (routed or transparent)

When the base configuration is complete, more advanced features can be considered, including the following:

- ASA high availability
- Routing protocols
- Network Address Translation (NAT)
- Application visibility
- The Identity Firewall

This chapter examines how to perform an initial setup of the ASA, how traffic moves through the ASA, and some of the more advanced features, such as high availability options, application visibility, and Identity Firewall.

Best practices and recommended deployment options are included in each section.

ASA Initial Configuration

Basic bootstrapping for both physical and virtual ASAs are performed via the console connection. The ASAv has an additional option of using a zero-day configuration file for initial configuration. This is helpful when deploying large numbers of virtual ASAs. For more information on setting up a zero-day configuration file, see the *ASA Configuration Guide* for your ASA release.

Getting Connected

When the ASA has some minimal IP address and routing information configured, it is possible to use an in-band management protocol such as SSH or Telnet. For reasons that should be obvious, SSH is preferred. At a minimum, a management interface (M0/0) is set up and, optionally, access to the ASDM may be set up.

Management interfaces by default are stub networks that do not pass transit traffic and are configured with the **management-only** command. You can use any interface for management by designating it as **management-only**. Removing the command from an interface allows it to pass transit traffic.

Configuring SSH access to the ASA is fairly straightforward. It involves the following steps:

Step 1. Enable SSH and permit subnets and interface access by using the **ssh** command. For example, to allow only SSH connections to the interface named **mgmt** and sourced from the 10.1.1.x/24 management subnet, use **ssh 10.1.1.0 mgmt**.

Step 2. Define at least one user account with a password by using the command **username johnd password letmein**.

Step 3. Tell the ASA to look in the local database for SSH connections by using the command **aaa authentication ssh console** LOCAL.

Step 4. Verify that an RSA public key has been set by using the command **show crypto key mypubkey rsa**.

Tip Console connections are preferred as they show out-of-band changes.

ASA Device Manager

ASDM is the ASA GUI manager. Newer ASAs come preconfigured with default network settings that already have ASDM enabled. ASDM contains many useful configuration wizards, an embedded event console, and a graphical packet debugging utility. Given that the majority of focus on the CCIE lab is hands-on expertise, this book focuses on command-line examples. However, for study purposes, ASDM can be a useful tool. Our recommendation is to enable the check box Preview Commands Before Sending Them to the Device, which you reach by selecting Tools > Preferences and selecting the General tab (see Figure 4-1). This provides an easy way to see how configuration changes in the ASDM GUI map to the CLI commands.

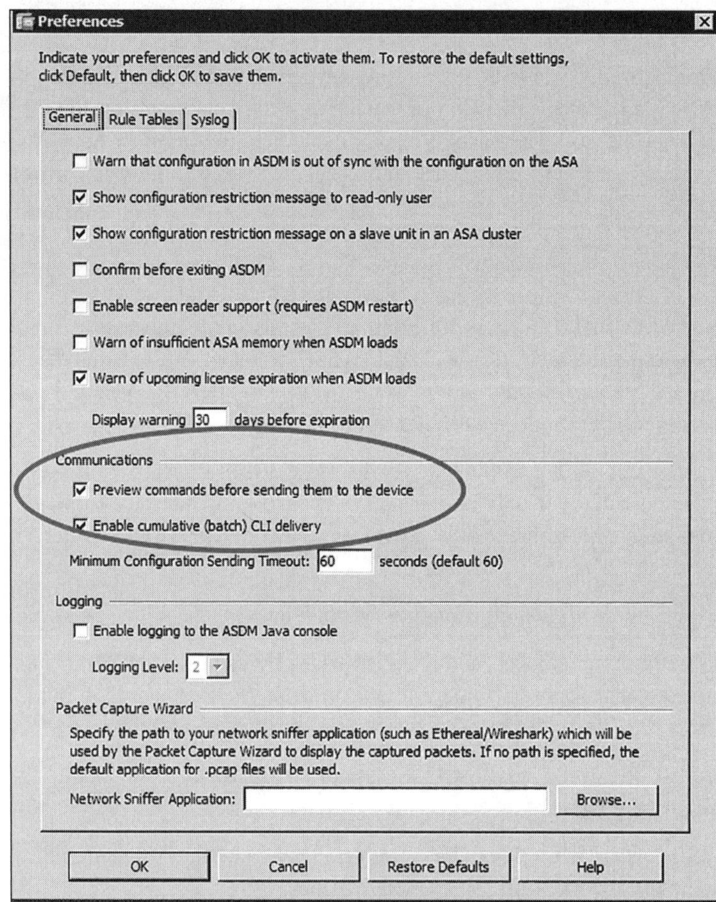

Figure 4-1 *ASDM Preferences Pane Configuration*

By default, ASA appliances have the management address set to 192.168.1.1, but sometimes it is necessary to alter the default configuration. Example 4-1 shows the setup of an interface configured for management with IP address 172.16.1.1. ASDM is enabled via the **http server enable** global command.

Example 4-1 *Enabling ASDM for ASA Management*

```
asa(config)# http server enable
asa(config)# http 172.16.1.0 255.255.255.0 management
asa(config)# interface management 0/0
asa(config-if)# nameif management
asa(config-if)# security-level 100
asa(config-if)# no shutdown
asa(config-if)# ip address 172.16.1.1 255.255.255.0
```

Enabling ASDM has five requirements, at a minimum:

- A binary image (for example, asdm-791.bin) must be present in ASA flash memory.
- There must be a configuration line in the ASA that points to the image.
- At least one user account must be configured as this is required for logging in to the ASA.
- The **http server enable** command must be enabled.
- Access to the HTTP server (ASDM) must be allowed from at least one interface.

ASA Security Levels

Data plane interfaces can be configured and addressed with some consideration for security levels and zones.

Setting up an ASA interface is fairly straightforward. Once in the configuration shell, the physical interface is enabled, addressed (IPv4, IPv6, or both), and given a description via the **nameif** command, which, as it sounds like it would do, "names" the interface. This is important as this name is referenced by the ASA policy engine for configuration and allows the interface to be associated with a security level.

Security levels must be assigned in the range of 0 to 100, where 0 is least trusted and 100 is most trusted. The ASA uses security levels to determine if traffic is checked against access control entries. Traffic from higher-number interfaces to lower-number interfaces is passed without access list checking by default. Interfaces with the same security level by default do not pass traffic. The ASA policy engine by default always allows traffic to pass from a higher security interface to a lower security interface without an explicit permit condition.

In order to simplify configuration and troubleshooting, sometimes it is necessary to allow traffic on the ASA to pass between two interfaces with the same security level. The **same-security-traffic permit inter-interface** command overrides the default behavior and allows traffic to pass without an access list.

The ASA by default does not allow traffic to exit and then enter an interface (that is, "hairpin" traffic). The **same-security-traffic permit intra-interface** overrides this action.

Some **nameif** command options have default security levels assigned to them. For example, **outside** is always assigned 0, and **inside** is assigned 100. Of course, these defaults can be changed as needed. They are in place only to help speed up the initial configuration process.

ASA Security Zones

The ASA historically only allowed access policy based on interfaces. The challenge to this method is that as the number of interfaces increases, so does configuration complexity. ASA 9.3(2) began to allow interfaces to be grouped into traffic zones. Interfaces with a similar purpose are placed in the same zone, and policies are applied to the zones instead of each specific interface. This is helpful when the ASA has a large number of physical interfaces because zone-based policy is easier to troubleshoot and configure. Zones may also assist when asymmetric flows are present or when there is a need for equal-cost load balancing to a destination connected to multiple interfaces on the same ASA. Example 4-2 shows a simple ASA security zone configuration.

Example 4-2 *Configuring ASA Traffic Zones*

```
asa(config)# zone outside
asa(config)# zone inside
asa(config)# interface gigabit 0/0
asa(config-if)# zone-member outside
asa(config-if)# interface gigabit 0/1
asa(config-if)# zone-member inside
```

ASA Routed and Transparent Mode

The ASA supports two modes of operation: routed mode and transparent mode. In routed mode, the ASA acts like a routed hop in the network path, with each interface in a different subnet. In transparent mode, the ASA is inserted at Layer 2, which allows it to function as a "bump in the wire." In this mode, the ASA inspects and bridges traffic between two or more VLANs.

Routed mode is typically deployed at the network edge, where the ASA is inspecting traffic. A common example of this would be an ASA deployed at the boundary of a trusted network and an untrusted network (such as the Internet). This is the most common deployment mode used with the ASA today. It also supports VPN termination and is the default mode for new installs.

Transparent mode is more commonly found in the data center, where there is less tolerance for changing subnets and Layer 2 domains. In this model, the ASA in transparent mode is typically deployed between the host and the gateway. The benefit is that the network does not require a major configuration change, and the ASA can be deployed more quickly and with less operational overhead than in routed mode. A transparent mode ASA can also pass non-IP traffic, which may be helpful in certain scenarios.

Determining the firewall mode is an important part of the initial configuration process because changing it clears the running configuration. Because of this, it is recommended that you use the console for the initial configuration.

ASA Routed Mode

As mentioned earlier in this chapter, routed mode (also known as Layer 3 mode) is the default and most common deployment mode for the ASA. This is due to the firewall's traditional placement at the network edge in order to provide access control for traffic entering or leaving the network.

A newly installed ASAv confirms that ASA routed mode is indeed the default:

```
asav# show firewall
Firewall mode: Router
```

A routed mode ASA has interfaces in different subnets and routes packets that pass access control policy through the firewall. An ASA in routed mode could act as a default gateway for hosts and provide DHCP services and/or could exchange routing protocols with another Layer 3 device. Figure 4-2 shows a typical Layer 3 configuration with NAT.

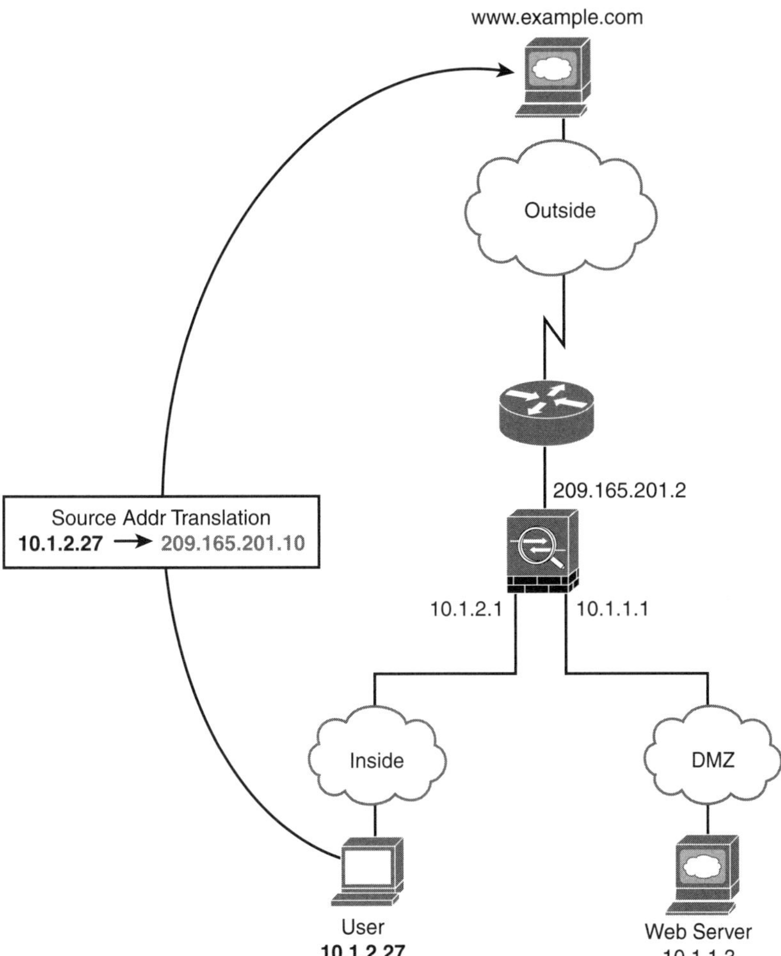

Figure 4-2 *Routed Mode ASA*

Transparent Mode

Transparent mode (also known as Layer 2 mode) offers a unique to way to insert an ASA at Layer 2, but you need to understand the nuances of this mode of operation. This mode introduces the concept of bridge groups and a Bridge Virtual Interface (BVI). It should be no surprise that routed mode uses Layer 3 addresses and routing, while transparent mode uses Layer 2 addresses to move traffic into and out of the ASA.

A bridge group is a group of two or more interfaces where the ASA bridges traffic. Traffic moving from one interface to another is controlled using access control lists. Each bridge group has only one BVI, and it must be in the same subnet as the bridge group member interfaces. The BVI address is used for sourcing frames from the bridge group. Traffic in a bridge group is isolated from other bridge groups.

Note Because the BVI requires a valid address in the subnet, it is not possible to use /30 network masks as at least three host addresses are required when the BVI address is added.

An ASA in transparent mode actually bridges between two broadcast domains (VLANs). Unlike devices from other firewall vendors, where both interfaces reside in the same VLAN, an ASA in transparent mode has interfaces in different VLANs. These interfaces, however, are mapped to each other as being part of the *same* bridge group. Understanding the details of how this works with Layer 2 protocols like ARP is critical to passing the CCIE exam.

Figure 4-3 shows a simple configuration of two bridge groups, 1 and 2. Note that the subnets are the same on the two sides of the ASA.

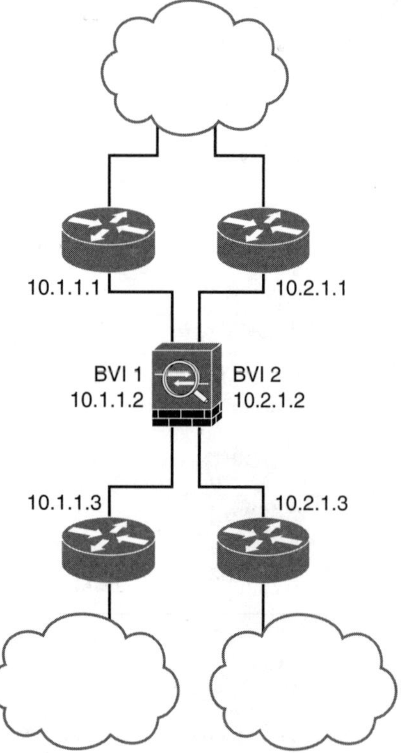

Figure 4-3 *Transparent Mode ASA*

The BVI interface allows flexibility for an ASA in transparent mode. For example, it is possible for the ASA to act as a DHCPv4 server and perform NAT in this mode of operation.

In addition, consider the following:

- As in routed mode, an access rule is not required for traffic sourced from a lower security level and passing to a higher security level. This traffic is allowed by default.
- ARP traffic is allowed through the bridge group in both directions without an access rule. ARP traffic can be controlled by ARP inspection.
- IPv6 neighbor discovery and router solicitation packets can be passed using access rules.
- Broadcast and multicast traffic can be passed using access rules.
- Using EtherType rules, AppleTalk, IPX, BPDUs, and MPLS can be allowed.
- Dynamic routing protocols and VPN traffic can be passed *through* the ASA in Layer 2 mode.

This last item is important to note as the ASA does not actually participate in the VPN traffic or routing protocol. Instead, it allows the traffic to pass between two other entities. For example, it is a common deployment in the data center to place a transparent mode ASA between two routers. The routers are peered to each other, but the ASA is still providing stateful inspection and access control of traffic.

BPDUs are passed by default to prevent spanning-tree loops. However, when using failover, it may be beneficial to block BPDUs via an EtherType rule in order to minimize switch ports from going into a blocking state. More details on that can be found later in this chapter, in the section "ASA High Availability Options."

Unsupported features in transparent mode include DHCP relay and remote access VPN termination.

Transparent Mode Configuration

Configuring an ASA in transparent mode is simple, as shown here:

```
asa(config)# firewall transparent
```

Keep in mind that when you do this, the ASA erases its running configuration, so it is important to either have a backup configuration or make this the first command in the initial configuration.

ASA Multiple-Context Mode

Years ago, service providers began offering managed services for their customers. They commonly deployed network devices and then had multiple customers connect to those devices as this saved them money and critical rack space. In this model, each customer did not require new gear.

ASA multiple context (also known as multi-context) mode allows an ASA to be virtually split into multiple logical firewalls, each having a unique access control policy and networking addressing, with individualized management. Enterprise customers benefit from this mode as it allows multiple smaller firewalls to be collapsed into one larger physical ASA. Think of a company with different divisions or a university with different departments; both of these situations provide opportunities for deploying a virtualized ASA, with each department or unit managing only its own virtual firewall.

ASA multiple context mode allows a myriad of ASA deployment options, especially when considering that some contexts could be routed and some could be transparent for the ultimate in flexibility (as discussed later in this chapter).

> **Note** Given that it's already a virtual appliance, the virtual ASA unfortunately doesn't support multi-context mode. An ASAv could be deployed similarly to a multi-context ASA except that it uses multiple virtual firewalls in the cloud or on a hypervisor to achieve what the physical ASA does in the chassis.

Multiple Context Configuration Basics

A multi-context mode ASA allows for creative deployment options, and understanding how it works will help a CCIE candidate.

First, let's cover the basics. Cisco calls each virtualized ASA a "context." Contexts are licensed features that show up in the standard **show version** ASA command under "Security Contexts".

There are two required contexts: the system context and the admin context. The system context is where basic settings such as context names, configuration file URL, and context-to-interface mappings are found. The admin context is like any other context with one exception: It provides root access to all contexts on the physical ASA host.

Physical interfaces are assigned to contexts via the **allocate-interface** command. It is common to use trunks with sub-interfaces in order to logically carve out more network interfaces as the number of contexts grows.

Using the **show context** command is a quick way to see contexts and what interfaces are mapped to each, as shown in Example 4-3.

Example 4-3 *Multi-Context Mode ASA*

```
asa# show context

Context Name       Interfaces                   URL
*admin             GigabitEthernet0/1.100       disk0:/admin.cfg
                   GigabitEthernet0/1.101
sales              GigabitEthernet0/1.200       disk0:/sales.cfg
                   GigabitEthernet0/1.201
marketing          GigabitEthernet0/1.300       disk0:/marketing.cfg
                   GigabitEthernet0/1.301
Total active Security Contexts: 3
```

Despite the number of contexts, each ASA contains a finite amount of CPU, memory, and other resources. Without any governance, it is possible for one context to consume most of the resources of a physical ASA. Therefore, Cisco provides features that can limit the amount of resources a context can consume. While memory and CPU cannot be limited, it is possible to limit resources that consume memory and CPU in order to protect other contexts from resource starvation. For example, you can limit the number of active connections, application inspections per second, routing table entries, and similar resources for each context by creating a resource class and specifying which resources are being managed.

Each context uses the resource limits set by the class. To use the settings of a class, assign the context to the class when you define the context. All contexts belong to a default class if they are not assigned to another class. A resource class can be assigned to only one context, which allows the ASA to set the maximum limit. Note that this does not "reserve" the resources for a context but is set as a maximum limit that will not be exceeded.

All contexts are assigned to the default class if they are not explicitly defined to a resource class. For most resources, the default class provides unlimited access to resources for all contexts, except for the following limits:

- **Telnet sessions:** 5 sessions
- **SSH sessions:** 5 sessions
- **IPsec sessions:** 5 sessions
- **MAC addresses:** 65,535 entries

At the command line, changing from one context to another requires the **changeto context** command. The prompt changes accordingly, as shown below:

```
asa# changeto context sales
asa/sales#
```

Tip Use a command alias to make this easier.

Occasionally, it may become necessary to reload a context. Unlike the Cisco Nexus switches, the ASA doesn't support this functionality outwardly. However, it is possible to effectively reload a context by clearing the running configuration and then importing the startup configuration. It is also possible to have a multi-context mode ASA in which some modes are routed and some are transparent. This *mixed mode* allows for even greater deployment flexibility in a multi-context ASA design. However, not all features in single-context mode are available in mixed multi-context mode.

Understanding the ASA Classifier

When traffic enters a multi-context mode ASA, it must be "classified" in order to determine to which context to send the packet. If each physical interface maps to a context (that is, there are no "shared" interfaces), this usually does not present an issue as the ASA simply sends the packets to the allocated interface(s) for that context. For example, transparent firewall mode requires unique interfaces; they cannot be shared in this mode.

The situation becomes more challenging when interfaces are shared between contexts as the ASA then uses the MAC address to determine where to send the packets. In this case, it is important that each MAC address be unique on each logical interface. This can easily be overridden with manual configuration of unique MAC addresses, but understanding how this works is critical for a CCIE candidate.

If unique MAC addresses are not configured, the classifier performs a destination IP address lookup. For this to work properly, the ASA must have knowledge of the subnets located behind each context, and the ASA relies on the NAT configuration to determine this information. Because each NAT deployment is unique in scope, this can lead to issues if not thought out in advance; therefore, the best practice recommendation is to use unique MAC addresses, which is why this has been the default mechanism since the 8.5 release. Unique MAC addresses are generated using the last 2 bytes of the interface, which can be changed to a custom prefix, if needed.

ASA High Availability Options

Since the earliest days, firewalls have offered various techniques to provide high availability. The oldest and most common is the Active/Standby (A/S) model, where, as the name implies, one firewall unit is active and the other is passive, or standing by. A newer method is the Active/Active (A/A) model, which seeks to improve on weaknesses of the older A/S model. And finally, there is the concept of ASA clustering, which is an N+1 model and achieves both HA and throughput aggregation. Let's explore each in more detail.

ASA Active/Standby Failover

ASA failover is built on the A/S model. It has been the most commonly deployed high-availability option since the release of the platform in 2005. The primary ASA does all the work, and the standby unit basically waits to come into service only if there is an issue with the primary unit. It also supports a stateful failover mechanism such that state-based traffic flows are minimally impacted during a failover event.

For this mode, several requirements must be met:

- The hardware footprint of the two units (RAM, physical interfaces, and model) must match.
- Both units must be in the same firewall mode (routed or transparent).
- Both units must be in the same context mode (single or multi-context).
- Because failover is a licensed feature, each ASA must have proper licensing.
- The two units must be connected via a physical interface known as the *failover link*.
- Optionally, a stateful failover link can be connected if stateful failover is required.

Both units could optionally share the failover and stateful link on the same connection to maximize interface efficiency. It is a best practice to connect the two units directly. It is a supported configuration to connect both units using a switch—but only if it is a different switch than the one connecting to the data interfaces. This minimizes the failure domain if one of the switches has issues.

Note Cisco has very specific recommendations on which scenarios are supported and which are not, with many variations on each. For a much deeper discussion on these scenarios and their specifics, see the *ASA Configuration Guide*: https://www.cisco.com/c/en/us/td/docs/security/asa/asa97/configuration/general/asa-97-general-config/ha-failover.pdf.

Today the granularity to which the A/S ASA monitors the active unit's health is significant. Timers can be minimized for a more aggressive failover condition, as can the interface monitoring and health tests. For example, if the ASAs each have six physical interfaces, a failover condition could be that a minimum of two interfaces must fail before a failover is initiated. Details and scenario examples are available in the *ASA Configuration Guide* for each specific code release of the ASA.

A significant benefit of ASA A/S failover is that the active unit replicates the configuration to the standby unit. In fact, when failover occurs, the standby unit effectively assumes the addressing and configuration of the active unit in order to minimize downtime. With newer versions of ASA code, it is possible to execute commands on just the primary or just the standby unit for statistics and network monitoring tools.

Here's a short summary of the benefits of ASA A/S failover:

- It is the most commonly deployed method for ASA high availability.
- It allows for configuration synchronization from the active unit to the standby unit.
- It allows for stateful failover.
- It allows granular control over the conditions that could lead to a failover event.

The biggest downside to the A/S model is that it can be deployed only in pairs, and one unit is essentially doing nothing as long as the active unit is working properly. Having two units doubles the amount of rack space, power, and cooling required for every single firewall deployed. It also doubles the cost of the investment in hardware.

Tip You can change the ASA prompt to reflect active versus standby members in a high-availability pair by using the **prompt hostname state priority** command.

ASA Active/Standby Failover Configuration

When configuring ASA failover, start with the ASA that you want to be the primary. Remember that the ASA will require at least one network interface dedicated to the standby unit. Optimally the two ASAs will be cabled directly together, but Cisco supports ASA failover under specific conditions. Please reference the *ASA Configuration Guide* for details on what is supported.

The following is a sample configuration on the ASA primary unit for Active/Standby high availability.

Use the following command to make this ASA the primary unit at startup:

```
failover lan unit primary
```

Use the following command to designate a dedicated interface for failover:

```
failover lan interface failover GigabitEthernet0/4
```

This is the interface where heartbeats are exchanged between units and, optionally, state information.

Failover traffic by default communicates in plaintext. Using a key allows the traffic to be encrypted:

```
failover key {key}
```

Tell the ASA to use this interface for passing state information between units:

```
failover link failover GigabitEthernet0/4
```

Assign active and standby addresses to the failover link:

```
failover interface ip failover 10.10.99.1 255.255.255.252 standby 10.10.99.2
```

Note that failover is not active until the **failover** command is applied:

```
failover
```

Assuming that the standby unit is using the same failover interface (g0/4), the configuration on that unit is exactly the same except that it is designated as the standby unit in the **failover lan unit** command.

After waiting for the two units to handshake and sync configuration, you can verify that failover has been configured correctly by using the **show failover** command, as shown in Example 4-4.

Example 4-4 *Verifying ASA Active/Standby Failover Configuration*

```
asa/pri/act# sh failover
Failover On
Failover unit Primary
Failover LAN Interface: failover GigabitEthernet0/4 (up)
Reconnect timeout 0:00:00
Unit Poll frequency 1 seconds, holdtime 15 seconds
Interface Poll frequency 5 seconds, holdtime 25 seconds
Interface Policy 1
Monitored Interfaces 1 of 516 maximum
MAC Address Move Notification Interval not set
failover replication http
Version: Ours 9.4(4)5, Mate 9.4(4)5
Last Failover at: 18:13:58 EST Dec 8 2017
```

```
        This host: Primary - Active
                Active time: 5087761 (sec)
                slot 0: asa hw/sw rev (1.0/9.4(4)5) status (Up Sys)
                  Interface outside (192.168.1.5): Normal (Not-Monitored)
                  Interface outside2 (10.1.1.1): Normal (Not-Monitored)
                  Interface dmz (10.1.2.1): Link Down (Not-Monitored)
Other host: Secondary - Standby Ready
                Active time: 0 (sec)
                slot 0: asa hw/sw rev (1.0/9.4(4)5) status (Up Sys)
                  RTP-DMZ Interface outside (192.168.1.6): Normal (Not-Monitored)
                  RTP-DMZ Interface outside2 (10.1.1.2): Normal (Not-Monitored)
                  RTP-DMZ Interface dmz (10.1.2.2): Normal (Not-Monitored)
```

ASA Active/Active Failover

Active/Active failover was introduced on the ASA to improve upon the legacy A/S model. As the name implies, both units are active, which is an improvement over the A/S model discussed previously.

However, A/A can be deployed only in pairs and requires the use of ASA multiple context mode. In fact, the ASA A/A model still uses A/S, but with ASA virtualization, it provides for two logical A/S failover pairs in two physical ASAs. Given that multiple context mode, like A/S failover, is a licensed feature, care must be taken to ensure proper feature licensing to make this work.

From a feature standpoint, A/A failover is nearly the same as A/S failover. Remember that calling it A/A is really a bit of marketing because it really is two A/S pairs running in multi-context mode. Figure 4-4 shows an example of A/A failover.

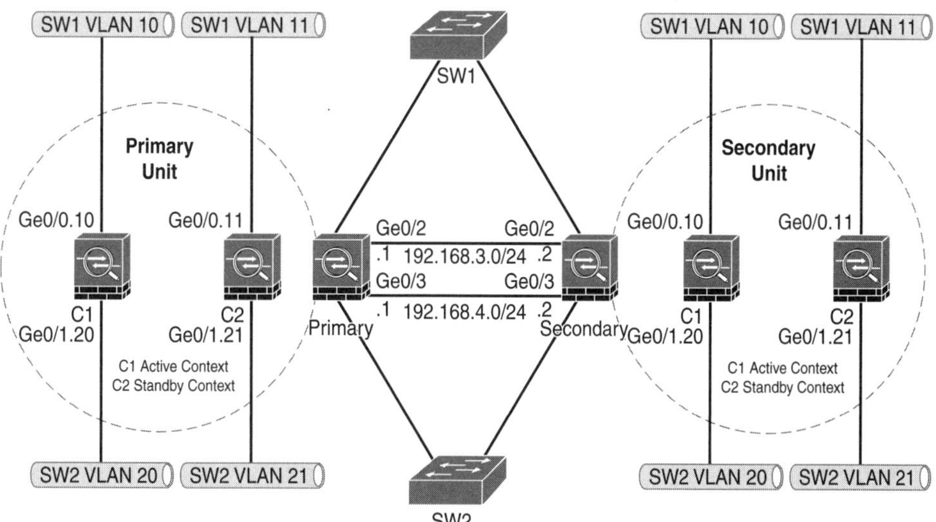

Figure 4-4 *ASA Active/Active Failover*

There is one more shortcoming that a good CCIE candidate has likely noticed: A/A mode does not really increase the amount of available ASA throughput. It is a common mistake to think that two ASAs would allow for double the amount of data plane throughput. They do provide double the throughput until one of the ASA failover units fails, and then the available throughput is cut in half. Here's the problem: If the network throughput minimum requirements were based on the double number, then half the packets will be dropped during a physical ASA failover!

Note An ASA in Active/Active failover can only fail over as a hardware unit. Individual contexts cannot fail over separately.

ASA Active/Active Failover Configuration

A/A failover requires multiple context mode to be enabled. The security contexts are then divided into failover groups. A *failover group* is a logical group of one or more contexts with a maximum of two groups allowed. The admin context is always a member of failover group 1. Unassigned contexts by default appear in this group as well. From this point, the configuration is nearly identical to the configuration of Active/Standby with some differences.

Active/Active failover generates virtual MAC addresses for the interfaces in each failover group. Best practice is to manually assign these addresses because different ASAs can auto-generate duplicate virtual addresses and cause connectivity problems.

The same configuration shown earlier, in the section "ASA Active/Standby Failover," is used again in Example 4-5 for clarity.

Example 4-5 *ASA Stateful Failover Configuration*

```
failover lan unit primary
failover lan interface failover GigabitEthernet0/4
failover key {key}
failover link failover GigabitEthernet0/4
failover interface ip failover 10.10.99.1 255.255.255.252 standby 10.10.99.2
```

And now you create the failover groups, placing the admin context in failover group 1, as shown in Example 4-6.

Example 4-6 *ASA Failover Group Configuration*

```
failover group 1
  primary
  preempt
failover group 2
  secondary
  preempt
context admin
  join-failover-group 1
```

Handling Asymmetric Traffic

In some cases, ASAs configured for A/A failover may receive asymmetric traffic. The A/S model avoids this completely because only one path is active at any given time (the standby never passes traffic). By default, asymmetric traffic is dropped by the stateful inspection engine on the firewall. To mitigate this, the ASA supports sending the asymmetric traffic back to the source ASA. The ASA allows for interfaces to be defined as part of an ASR group. The **asr-group** command is placed under the interface configuration as shown in Example 4-7. Note that it is defined only on interfaces where asymmetric traffic might appear. Figure 4-5 shows how asr-groups forward asymmetric traffic on the Active/Active ASA pair.

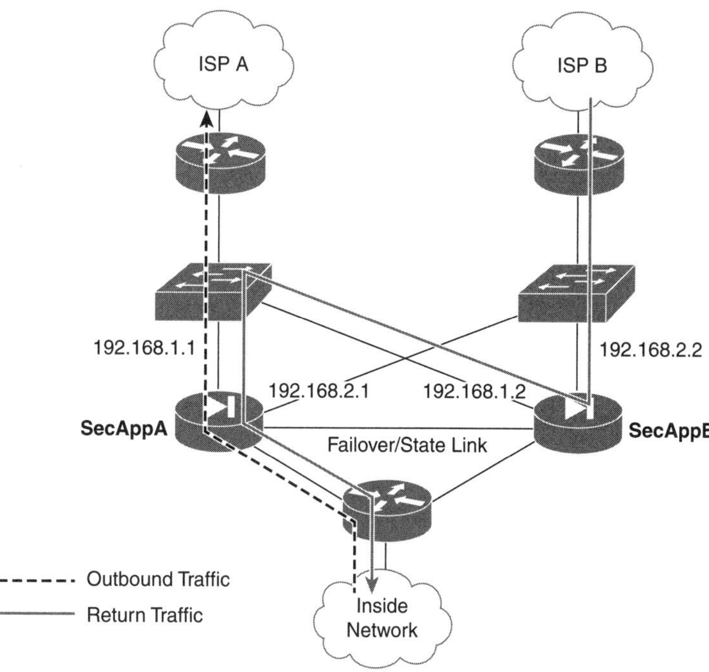

Figure 4-5 *Asymmetric Flow on an Active/Active ASA Pair*

Example 4-7 *Configuring an ASR Group*

```
Context ISP-1
interface GigabitEthernet0/0
  nameif outsideISP-A
  security-level 0
  ip address 192.168.1.1 255.255.255.0 standby 192.168.1.2
  asr-group 1
Context ISP-2
interface GigabitEthernet0/0
  nameif outsideISP-B
  security-level 0
  ip address 192.168.2.1 255.255.255.0 standby 192.168.2.2
  asr-group 1
```

ASA Clustering

ASA clustering is a feature that allows for multiple ASA physical firewalls to be combined together in order to provide a scalable way to increase available firewall throughput. Historically customers were forced to buy bigger and more powerful firewalls as their throughput requirements increased. ASA clustering allows for more firewalls to be added over time, which provides investment protection.

ASA clustering also provides a new mechanism for high availability. This is an improvement over the A/S and A/A pair limitation as clustering supports up to 16 members providing N+1 redundancy. However, not every ASA feature is supported when clustering is enabled, so design requirements must be carefully considered. ASA clustering is a licensed feature that must be enabled before configuration.

Similar to A/S and A/A, clustering automatically replicates the configuration across cluster members. In addition, much as with the failover and stateful failover link required in A/S and A/A, clustering requires the configuration of a cluster control link (CCL). This link acts as both a control plane and a data plane for cluster operations. Member unit health checks and state table replication both happen across the CCL. Given its role in cluster operations, the CCL must be protected with redundancy mechanisms because losing the CCL causes an immediate evacuation of the member unit from the cluster.

Note Cisco recommends that the CCL sizing be equal to the maximum aggregate throughput of the combined data plane. For example, if an ASA has two 10 GB interfaces in a port channel, it is recommended that the CCL also be sized as two 10 GB interfaces via a port channel.

Best practice is to use Link Aggregation Control Protocol (LACP) to dynamically configure port channels for the CCL, with each link connecting to a different switch. This extends the potential failure domains across the two switches and avoids dependency on a single interface link failure. This configuration is shown in Figure 4-6. Each ASA cluster member has one "leg" to each switch, and each one is placed in a port channel. The port channel provides bandwidth aggregation, link redundancy, and load-balancing capabilities by default. The recommended best practice is to also use port channels for the CCL as it must match the aggregate data plane bandwidth. In addition to link bandwidth aggregation, the port channel provides fault tolerance, which is critical due to the role of the CCL.

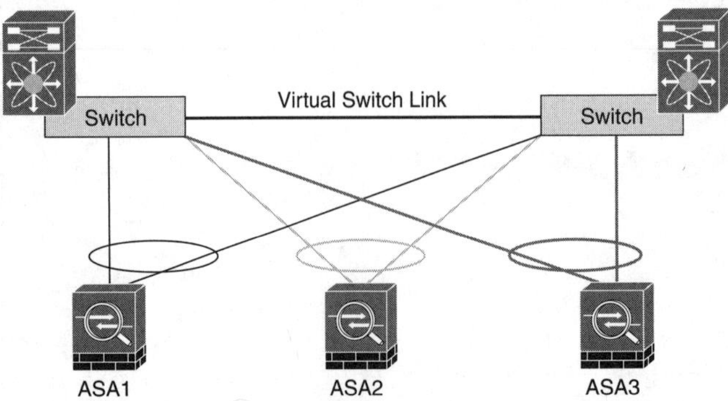

Figure 4-6 *ASA Clustering Operation*

Clustering Performance

Due to the overhead required by the ASA clustering control plane, a cluster will likely not achieve the maximum combined throughput of the individual ASA units. Many factors affect the actual overhead, including size of cluster, asymmetric flow reassembly and health of individual units. For design purposes, Cisco has created benchmarks that allow a reasonable ASA cluster throughput calculation:

- 70% of the combined throughput
- 60% of the maximum connections
- 50% of connections per second

For example, an ASA 5585-X with SSP-40 can pass approximately 10 Gbps of stateful firewall traffic (multiprotocol) by itself. A cluster of eight units would yield a total available throughput of approximately 56 Gbps (8 × 10 × .70).

Requirements for ASA Clustering

Clustering has a very specific set of prerequisite requirements:

- All units in a cluster must be the same hardware model with the same DRAM. Flash memory can vary.
- All units in a cluster must be on the same major software release. Hitless upgrade is supported across minor releases.
- All units in a cluster must be in the same firewall mode (routed or transparent).
- All units in a cluster share the same cluster ID, encryption, and 10 Gbps I/O license information (5585-x only).

Clustering requires the use of custom extensions to the LACP that Cisco created in the switches as cLACP. This allows the ASA firewalls in the cluster to be treated as one logical firewall by the switching fabric, allowing them to negotiate port channels for the data plane. This in turn allows for scalability and redundancy in the data center fabric as clustering is not intended for use at the network edge.

Operational Modes

Understanding how an ASA cluster processes connections is critical for deployment. To begin, there are three possible roles for each cluster member: owner, director, or forwarder. These roles are for every connection traversing the firewall. It is not uncommon in a data center with significant traffic load for every cluster member to be in all three roles simultaneously. Let's examine the differences:

- **Owner:** The owner role is the first unit to receive the connection request. There is only one owner per connection, and the owner maintains the state of the connection.
- **Director:** The director processes lookup requests from forwarders and acts as a backup in case the owner fails. Every connection has an owner and a director. The director is derived from a hash from the source and destination IP address and TCP ports.

- **Forwarder:** In the case of asymmetric traffic flows, the forwarder forwards packets to the owner. A forwarder queries a director to find the owner, and this traffic is back-hauled across the CCL. For network forwarding efficiency, it is critical that asymmetry be avoided if possible because these flows eat up valuable bandwidth in the CCL.

Figure 4-7 shows a typical new connection forming in an ASA cluster.

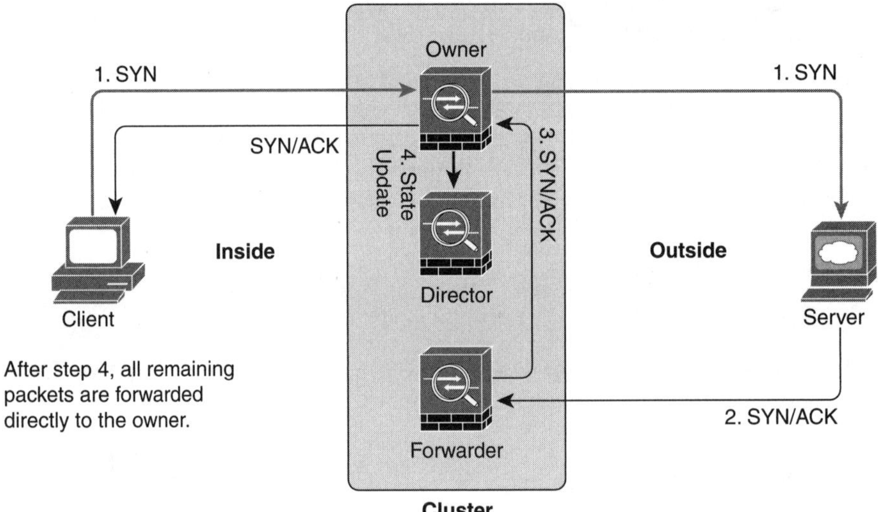

Figure 4-7 *ASA Cluster Control Plane Operation with Asymmetric Traffic*

ASA Clustering Data Plane

As noted earlier, scalable firewall throughput is a main reason for enabling the ASA clustering feature. Because the ASA cluster acts as one logical firewall entity, how it connects to the switch fabric is vital.

The best practice for configuring the data plane interfaces in an ASA cluster is to use the Spanned EtherChannel method. This provides the benefit of link aggregation and link redundancy for all the link interfaces in the port channel. The switches terminating the port channel allow for different means to load-balance traffic through the ASA cluster. The recommended practice is to use either **source-dest-ip** or **source-dest-ip-port** load-balancing algorithms in order to minimize the potential for asymmetric flows. Asymmetric flows degrades the overall capacity of the cluster as each flow has to be forwarded across the CCL.

Figure 4-8 shows a typical Spanned EtherChannel configuration.

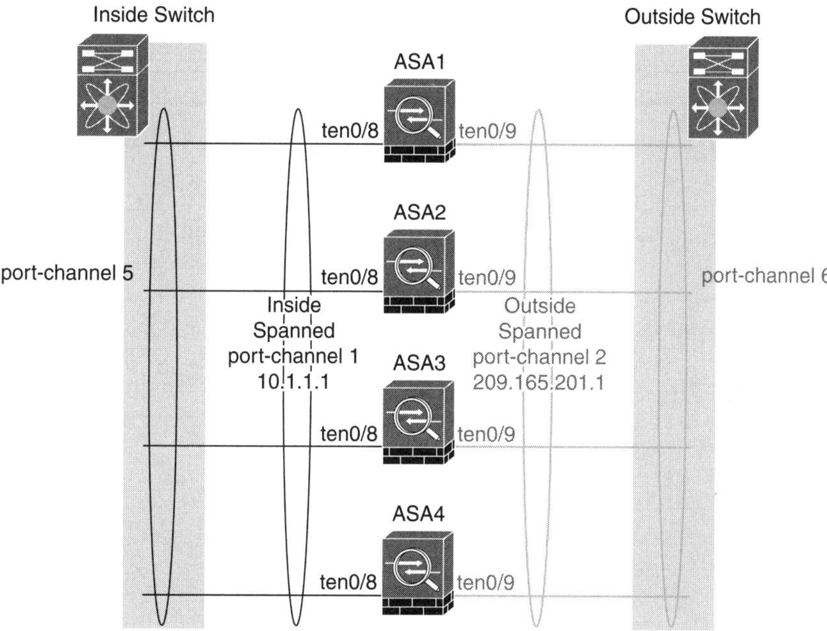

Figure 4-8 *ASA Cluster of Spanned Port Channels*

> **Note** As noted earlier, some ASA features are not supported with clustering. In addition, some features may work in a distributed fashion on each cluster member, while others work only centrally on a single cluster member at a time. See the *ASA Configuration Guide* for your software release for more details.

ASA Clustering Data Plane Configuration

If the hardware and software requirements are met, an ASA clustering configuration requires only a few commands. Because most ASA cluster deployments use the spanned port-channel method, make sure the port channels are up and that LACP is configured properly.

To begin, you need to tell each ASA in the cluster that you are using Spanned EtherChannel mode. This is by far the most common deployment as it takes advantage of the integrated load sharing in port channels combined with link aggregation and redundancy. This is performed as a global command and may require a reboot, so it should be configured first, in global configuration mode, as shown in Example 4-8.

Example 4-8 *ASA Spanned Port-Channel Configuration*

```
cluster interface-mode spanned
Cluster interface-mode has been changed to 'spanned' mode successfully. Please
complete interface and routing configuration before enabling clustering.
```

In Example 4-9, g0/0 and g0/1 are configured in port-channel 1, and g0/2 and g0/3 are configured for port-channel 2. Port-channel 1 will act as the ASA inside interface, and port-channel 2 will act as the outside interface. The **active** mode designates that these interfaces will actively use LACP to establish the port channel. Active mode LACP is recommended for ASA port channels.

Example 4-9 *ASA Port-Channel Configuration*

```
interface GigabitEthernet0/0
 channel-group 1 mode active vss-id 1
!
interface GigabitEthernet0/1
 channel-group 1 mode active vss-id 1
!
interface GigabitEthernet0/2
 channel-group 2 mode active vss-id 2
!
interface GigabitEthernet0/3
 channel-group 2 mode active vss-id 2
```

When your port channels are up and valid, it's time to layer in the ASA clustering configuration. You need to make sure that your load-balancing method is set correctly. As noted in the previous section, Spanned EtherChannel mode is the most common configuration option. Both port channels in Example 4-10 are spanned.

Example 4-10 *ASA Spanned Port-Channel Configuration*

```
interface Port-channel1
 lacp max-bundle 8
 port-channel span-cluster vss-load-balance
!
interface Port-channel2
 lacp max-bundle 8
 port-channel span-cluster vss-load-balance
```

Now that your data plane interfaces are up and port-channeled, you can insert the clustering commands. First, you need to name the cluster. Any name works, as long as it matches on all cluster members. Here's an example:

```
cluster group CCIE
```

Next, you need to give the local cluster member a unique name so it can be easily identified in the cluster and for troubleshooting:

```
local-unit 5525-1
```

Next, you have to define the cluster control interface (also called the cluster control link [CCL]). This is the interface, discussed previously, that is used for intra-cluster communication, asymmetric traffic forwarding, and other miscellaneous control plane functions for the cluster. Best practice is to use another port channel, but this is not required. In the lab for this book, we are using port-channel 3 as the cluster control interface. The address needs to be unique as all cluster members will communicate using this address. Here is an example:

```
cluster-interface Port-channel3 ip 99.99.99.1 255.255.255.0
```

Finally, you have to give this cluster member a priority to break ties during the election process. Lower numbers are higher priority. Here is an example:

```
priority 10
```

And when everything else looks good, you enable clustering:

```
enable
```

ASA Clustering Troubleshooting

Most of the issues around ASA clustering fall into two areas: physical interface configuration and the cluster control plane. Ensure that physical interfaces are cabled properly and that port channels, when used, are up. Clustering relies on a stable data plane in order to manage traffic flow, load-balancing, and intra-cluster communication. In addition to information learned with the basic **show interface** command, the output from **show port-channel brief** is helpful for a quick sanity check.

The cluster control plane is used by all cluster members to communicate everything from cluster health, to reachability, to flow ownership. Therefore, making sure the cluster connection is up and that all units are able to communicate with each other over the network is important. There are many reasons cluster members may be unable to join the cluster. Example 4-11 shows the output of the **show cluster info** command from a properly working ASA cluster with two members, 5525-1 and 5525-2.

Example 4-11 *Verifying ASA Cluster Health*

```
ASA5525-1/master# show cluster info
Cluster CCIE: On
    Interface mode: spanned
    This is "5525-1" in state MASTER
        ID        : 0
        Version   : 9.4(4.5)
        Serial No.: FEH199XXXX
```

```
        CCL IP     : 99.99.99.1
        CCL MAC    : c067.af03.2dee
        Last join : 09:20:04 EST Dec 11 2017
        Last leave: 09:14:16 EST Dec 11 2017
Other members in the cluster:
Unit "5525-2" in state SLAVE
        ID         : 1
        Version    : 9.4(4.5)
        Serial No.: FDH199XXXX
        CCL IP     : 99.99.99.2
        CCL MAC    : c067.af03.2cee
        Last join : 09:21:04 EST Dec 11 2017
        Last leave: 09:15:16 EST Dec 11 2017
```

Other useful **show** commands are as follows:

```
show cluster info [health]

show asp cluster counter

show conn
```

ASA clustering has a fairly robust set of debugging commands. On a production network, you should use these commands with discretion. Some of the most useful commands are **debug cluster ccp** for troubleshooting the cluster control plane and **debug cluster datapath** for troubleshooting data plane issues.

Enabling Routing Protocol Support on the ASA

At a basic networking level, an ASA in routed mode acts like a router. It contains a routing table and supports dynamic routing protocols and may be used as a gateway in deployment. The ASA has evolved to be more router-friendly, but it has not always been this way. Customers today require that a firewall be both a security device and a networking device, and this section examines some of those features.

The most important criterion for moving traffic through an ASA is determining the egress interface followed by the next-hop selection. NAT changes this behavior on the ASA somewhat (and is examined in more detail in the next section).

The ASA supports equal-cost multipath (ECMP) routing with up to eight equal-cost static or dynamic routes per interface. The hashing algorithm uses the source and destination IP address to determine which interface to use. The ASA also supports policy-based routing (PBR), which allows an override of the routing table based on specific criteria. PBR is used when certain defined conditions are met, causing the ASA to forward traffic to a specific destination. Like IOS, PBR on the ASA is configured via route maps and is a powerful tool in scenarios where the general routing table is not sufficient.

More recently, the ASA has added support for Bidirectional Forwarding Detection (BFD). This feature is used as a failure detection method that allows fast failover for routing protocols. It originated in the data center, where downtime can be costly, and it works on the principle that peers exchange control information that advertises their reachability. It vastly improves the timers and heartbeat mechanisms built into the routing protocols and is considered a complementary feature.

As of the 9.6 release, the ASA supports the following routing protocols as well as static and multicast routing:

- BGP
- OSPF
- IS-IS
- EIGRP

These protocols have been around for many years, and their usage is well known in the networking industry; this book therefore does not discuss them in detail. Their configuration on the ASA, in many cases, is very similar to configuration in IOS. It is important to consider the application of the routing protocol and how it integrates into the networking fabric. As mentioned earlier, the ASA today is both a security device and a network device and should be treated accordingly. It should be noted that all these routing protocols are supported only in ASA routed mode.

BGP is the standard for both Internet routing and enterprise networks. It is very powerful in that it has the ability to carry metadata (tags) in the routing updates. BGP Multipath makes it attractive for networks where equal-cost prefixes point to the same destination prefix. The ASA version, while not as robust as its Cisco router counterpart, still provides a strong capability to standardize on a single routing protocol for both enterprise and service providers. It supports both IPv4 and IPv6, making it well suited for dual-stack environments.

OSPF has become a dominant IGP in the past 15 years due to its multivendor interoperability. OSPF and BGP both support the Nonstop Forwarding (NSF) feature, which allows the data path to still function even while routing protocol peering information is being restored. The ASA is flexible in that it supports most of the necessary OSPF features, including supporting two process IDs running concurrently. The ASA supports OSPFv1, OSPFv2, and OSPFv3. Notably, OSPFv2 does not support IPv6, but OSPFv3 does.

IS-IS has been most popular in the service provider world but has seen a recent resurgence in enterprise networks. Like most other link-state routing protocols, it requires some planning to come up with the best network design.

EIGRP is arguably the easiest routing protocol on this list to get up and running as it requires very little planning and handles the neighboring process automatically. Its popularity stems from its deployment simplicity. Unfortunately, it does not support IPv6, which may limit its popularity for dual-stack networks.

Firewalls have traditionally faced challenges with multicast traffic. It is common in a network with large amounts of multicast traffic to deploy the ASA in transparent mode to minimize disruption because the ASA in this mode does not actively route the multicast packets. However, for the adventurous, the ASA supports stub multicast routing and PIM multicast routing—but only one at a time. Multicast routing is supported only in single-context mode, and if the ASAs are clustered, only the primary unit participates in the multicast routing process.

ASA Routing Protocol Configuration

Configuration of ASA routing protocols is very similar to configuration in IOS devices. It involves defining the routing protocol and process and any networks to be advertised, followed by any options. Example 4-12 shows a sample EIGRP configuration on an ASA followed by a listing of its neighbors:

Example 4-12 *ASA EIGRP Configuration*

```
router eigrp 150
 network 10.1.1.0 255.255.255.0
 network 10.254.254.0 255.255.255.255
 passive-interface default
 no passive-interface inside

asa(config)# show eigrp neighbors
EIGRP-IPv4 Neighbors for AS(150)
H   Address                 Interface       Hold Uptime   SRTT   RTO   Q   Seq
                                            (sec)         (ms)        Cnt  Num
2   10.9.0.2                inside           13      3d19h 1      200   0   275156

1   10.9.0.13               inside           13      3d19h 1      200   0   54719

0   10.9.0.1                inside           11      3d19h 5      200   0   19741
```

ASA Routing Protocol Troubleshooting

ASA routing protocol configuration troubleshooting is identical to IOS troubleshooting. Ensuring that adjacencies are formed and links are properly configured are good starting points. In most cases, the ASA routing protocol commands are not as advanced as on IOS devices.

Debugging EIGRP is limited to a few commands, as shown in Example 4-13. **debug eigrp neighbors** is useful for troubleshooting the neighbor EIGRP peering process, and **debug eigrp packets** shows adjacency information and advertisement update–related information.

Example 4-13 *Debugging EIGRP*

```
asa(config)# debug eigrp ?
exec mode commands/options:
  fsm        EIGRP Dual Finite State Machine events/actions
  neighbors  EIGRP neighbors
  packets    EIGRP packets
  transmit   EIGRP transmission events
```

ASA Clustering Best Practices

Checking the health of a cluster involves understanding what is happening at a cluster level as well as for each individual cluster member. Because the cluster member slaves replicate their configuration from the master, it can be confusing to troubleshoot and maintain individual ASAs. As mentioned earlier in this chapter, best practice is to change the prompt to make it easy to know the name and state of the member to which the console is attached, as follows:

```
prompt cluster-unit state
```

Optionally, if this is a multi-context cluster, add the **context** keyword:

```
prompt cluster-unit context state
```

During the CCIE lab exam, time must be used as efficiently as possible. Using command aliases on the ASA helps you save time and keystrokes. ASA clustering allows for commands to be sent to all cluster members simultaneously via the **cluster exec** command. This is useful when you're saving a configuration or doing other similar tasks that need to be sent to the cluster as a whole. For example, you can use **ce** in order to reference the command **cluster exec**, which saves keystrokes:

```
command-alias exec ce cluster exec
```

It is best practice during the lab exam to set other common commands using **command-alias** in the same fashion.

Traffic with the ASA

All modern firewalls, including the ASA, provide some level of address translation capability. The ASA's features have evolved over time to become more IOS-like in their command structure as the use cases for translation continue to grow.

Network Address Translation (NAT)

In the early days of the Internet there was no need for NAT as there were more IPv4 addresses than there were hosts. But as the Internet grew, so did the need to come up with methods to conserve the address space to accommodate the growth. Like most other features, ASA NAT evolved to be more granular in order to fit more extreme use cases. Today NAT is more than just a security mechanism. It has become a common tool for fixing overlapping address spaces and connecting dissimilar networks together. NAT is supported in both routed and transparent mode on the ASA, which makes it nearly universal in its application. This section examines different types of NAT and the ways it is configured.

ASA 8.3+ NAT Configuration Changes

Note that the ASA NAT configuration changed significantly in the 8.3 release. Cisco reworked the ASA to make NAT easier to configure and troubleshoot. Candidates familiar with older versions of the ASA need to understand the differences between older and newer versions as they are significant. The biggest change is that IP addresses referenced in ACL configuration (in 8.3 and newer) now use the real IP address, whereas older versions of code referenced the global (translated) IP address. Cisco has detailed documentation on its website highlighting more differences between the old and new configuration methods: https://www.cisco.com/c/en/us/td/docs/security/asa/asa83/upgrading/migrating.html

A CCIE candidate needs to have a strong understanding of the various ways NAT is configured on the ASA. In concept NAT is fairly simple; after all, you are exposed to it every day as you surf the Internet. However, ASA NAT configuration has some nuances that can only be absorbed by thoroughly exploring the vast configuration options offered. This section introduces NAT using the Cisco nomenclature.

NAT Terminology

Cisco uses specific terminology to explain NAT configuration:

- A *real address* is an address prior to translation. Typically this is the inside, or private side, network.
- A *mapped address* is an address that a real address is translated to. Typically this would be the outside or untrusted network.
- *Bidirectional initiation* indicates that NAT applies to both directions: traffic to the host and from the host.
- *Source and destination NAT* compares both source and destination to NAT rules. One or both can be translated or not.

Types of NAT

Cisco has defined specific applications of NAT:

- **Dynamic NAT:** Real addresses are translated to mapped addresses (many-to-many), which is commonly used for Internet access, as an example.
- **Dynamic Port Address Translation (PAT):** Real addresses are translated to a single mapped address (many-to-one). Often in the egress interface address, ports are used to differentiate between real hosts.

- **Static NAT:** This is a static (one-to-one) mapping between a real address and a mapped address. This mapping will always translate bidirectionally and is common for mail servers, web servers, and so on.
- **Identity NAT:** This is a unique application of NAT in which a real address is translated to itself. This is a common way to exempt certain hosts from NAT translation.

Applying NAT

Like many other features on the ASA, NAT has evolved to meet the needs of a variety of uses and deployment scenarios. The vast majority of NAT configurations are covered by network object NAT. This is the easiest way to configure NAT on the ASA because it is defined at the same time as the network object. A network object can be a single IP host, a range, or a whole subnet. These objects can then be referenced in network groups to simplify policy creation on the ASA. Because NAT is configured at the object level, it offers easy differentiation between hosts that require NAT and those that don't.

NAT and IPv6

The ASA has a long history of robust features with IPv6. Accordingly, NAT features have evolved to incorporate IPv6. The ASA can translate between IPv4 and IPv6 (NAT46), IPv6 and IPv4 (NAT64), and IPv6 and IPv6 (NAT66) at the same time. The recommended best practice for NAT46 and NAT66 is to use static NAT due to the large amount of available IPv6 address space. Dynamic PAT is recommended for NAT64 because the IPv4 mapped address space is often more constrained.

Dynamic NAT

Dynamic NAT is the most common and easiest NAT configuration on the ASA. It translates real addresses to mapped addresses where the mapped address pool is typically smaller than the real address pool. Addresses are translated on a first-come, first-served basis from the mapped pool. A NAT translation exists only for the duration of the connection, and there is no guarantee that a given host will receive the same mapped address. Dynamic NAT usage is very common for allowing hosts to communicate on the Internet.

Figure 4-9 illustrates basic dynamic NAT.

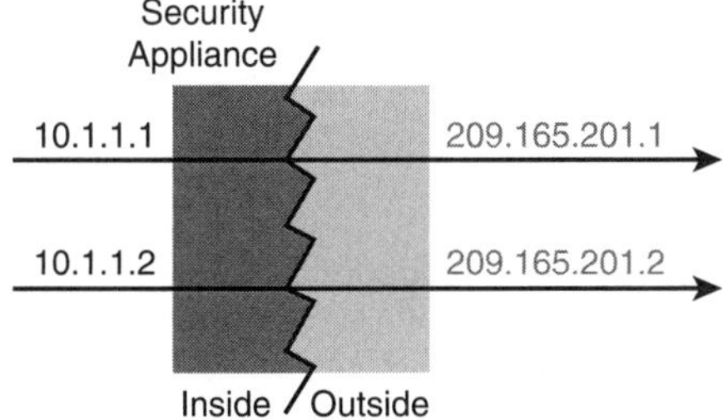

Figure 4-9 *Dynamic NAT*

Dynamic NAT has some limitations. Most obvious is that the mapped pool can run out of addresses if there are more real hosts than mapped addresses. New real host connections would not be allowed. Dynamic PAT, covered in the next section, is often used in conjunction to assist where hosts may overload a dynamic pool.

Another downside to dynamic NAT is that it may consume a larger number of mapped addresses. Some networks may not have the address space to dedicate for this function.

Dynamic PAT

Dynamic PAT is similar to dynamic NAT except that only a single mapped address is used for translation. This allows multiple real hosts to communicate with translation while minimizing the number of mapped addresses that are in use. It also serves as a method to protect the network from exhausting mapped address space when used in conjunction with dynamic NAT.

Real hosts are tracked via port numbers. If possible, the actual source port number is used; otherwise, a unique port number is assigned to a connection (see Figure 4-10).

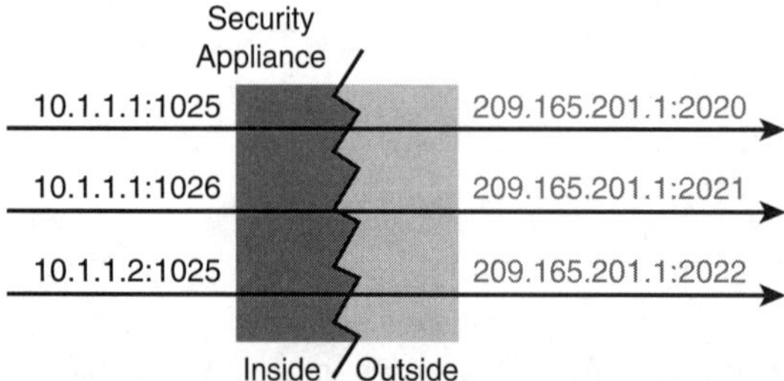

Figure 4-10 *Dynamic PAT (NAT Overload)*

Like dynamic NAT, dynamic PAT has some drawbacks:

- Some multimedia applications and protocols don't work with PAT if their control plane is different than the data plane.
- When dynamic PAT is used, network traffic analytics show a large amount of traffic from a single address. This might affect thresholds for network packet dispersion.

Static NAT

Static NAT is used when continuous bidirectional address mapping is required for a host. Unlike dynamic NAT, which pools mapped addresses, static NAT creates a one-to-one relationship for the host. Static NAT is commonly used when specific hosts need to be reachable from outside the network.

Static NAT operation is outlined in Figure 4-11. Note the directions of the arrows.

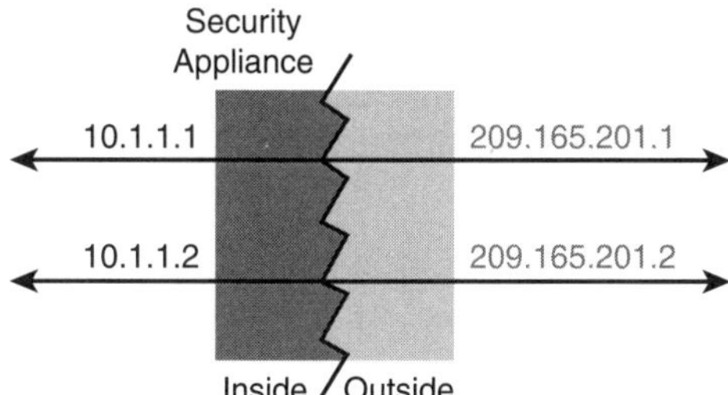

Figure 4-11 *Static NAT*

Static NAT can also statically map ports as well as addresses. This provides more flexibility when a variety of network services are offered (see Figure 4-12).

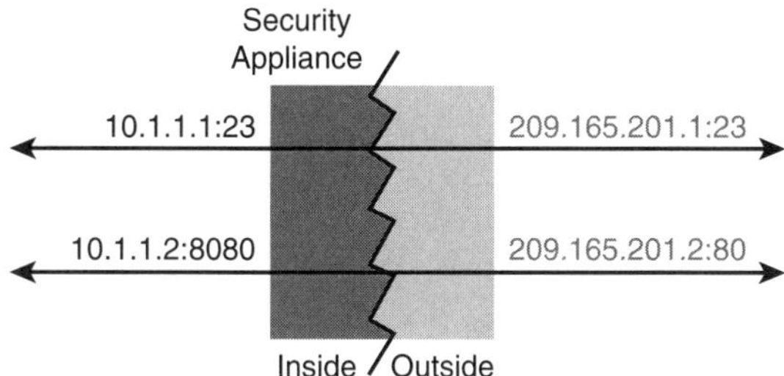

Figure 4-12 *Static NAT with Port Mapping*

It is also possible to use static NAT for a one-to-many mapping where a single real address maps to multiple mapped addresses. This is common in deployments where a load balancer is managing connectivity to a server farm. The load balancer is the single real IP address that is known by multiple mapped addresses. In this case, only the first mapped address is used for outbound traffic, but the additional mapped addresses are used for inbound traffic (see Figure 4-13).

Identity NAT

Identity NAT is a specialized mapping option in which a host maps an address to itself. It is typically used to exclude a specific host from translation when a large range of hosts are part of a NAT rule. It is also required for remote access VPN when host client traffic needs to be exempt from NAT. Identity NAT is shown in Figure 4-14.

Host

Undo Translation
209.165.201.3 → 10.1.2.27

Outside

Undo Translation
209.165.201.5 → 10.1.2.27

Inside

Undo Translation
209.165.201.4 → 10.1.2.27

Load Balancer
10.1.2.27

Web Servers

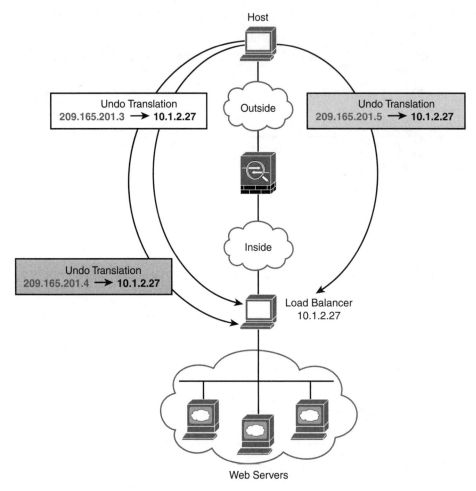

Figure 4-13 *Static NAT Mapped to Different Addresses*

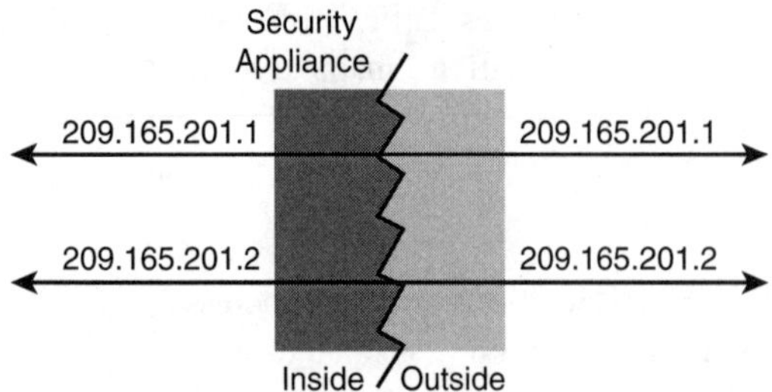

Figure 4-14 *Identity NAT*

Identity NAT Configuration

Cisco recommends using auto-NAT via network object configuration for most NAT configurations. Manual NAT, such as identity NAT outlined previously, should be used only when necessary. There are differing opinions on which form is easier to configure, but a CCIE candidate should have a good working knowledge of both.

Let's begin with a simple auto-NAT configuration that is performing dynamic PAT on the outside interface for the internal network. This is similar to the majority of firewall NAT configurations used in the world today. Here are the steps required to configure dynamic PAT on the ASA:

Step 1. Create a network object that defines the local inside network. In this example, it is 10.1.1.0/24, called **INSIDE-NET**:

```
object network INSIDE-NET
 subnet 10.1.1.0 255.255.255.0
```

The best practice of using network objects on the ASA allows for policies that are easier to understand, which is helpful when troubleshooting.

Step 2. Define a NAT policy under the network object:

```
nat (inside,outside) dynamic interface
```

This tells the ASA to dynamically translate any traffic from the inside network (defined in the network object) destined for the outside interface. NAT uses the outside interface of the ASA, which conserves the global address space.

An option is to use the **any** keyword in the NAT statement to allow greater flexibility if the ASA has multiple egress interfaces:

```
nat (inside,any) dynamic interface
```

Without it, each egress interface would have to be defined, adding more complexity to the configuration.

Note The ordering of the NAT configuration commands could confuse some candidates as the ASA will take all the commands as ordered here. However, the commands are actually placed in the ASA configuration in different sections. The address configuration is placed within the network objects section, while the NAT configuration is placed in the respective NAT section. Candidates should familiarize themselves with where the commands are entered in the configuration.

Another common deployment option is to build a static NAT translation for a web server on a DMZ for outside (untrusted) access. Much as in the preceding steps, you create the network object and then apply the NAT statement. In this example, the object is a host called **WEB-SERVER**, and its global address is 10.100.100.15. There is also an interface with a **nameif** called **dmz** already defined:

```
object network WEB-SERVER
 host 10.1.1.15
 nat (dmz,outside) static 10.100.100.15
```

What if there is a pool of real (global) addresses from which to pull dynamically? In familiar fashion, create the network pool object and then map the dynamic NAT statement:

```
object network NAT-POOL
 range 10.100.100.100 10.100.100.125
object network INSIDE-NET
 subnet 10.1.1.0 255.255.255.0
 nat (inside,outside) dynamic NAT-POOL
```

The pool is using a portion of the global address defined as 10.100.100.100 through 10.100.100.125. This example uses the **INSIDE-NET** object from earlier. The NAT policy is applied under the **inside** network object group configuration.

Identity NAT is an option when a host gets translated to its originating (real) source address. Using the web host from earlier, this sample configuration translates the server's address to itself:

```
object network WEB-SERVER
 host 10.1.1.15
 nat (dmz,outside) static WEB-SERVER no-proxy-arp route-lookup
```

In some cases, more granular control is required. Twice NAT (also called manual NAT) is an option that identifies the source and destination addresses in a single rule. For example, when accessing ISP A, host A presents one address, and when accessing ISP B, host A is translated into a different address. It is important to remember that in Twice NAT, the rules are bidirectional, so source and destination are temporal. Using the subnet from earlier in this example, this configuration allows web hosts for the specified network to be translated into different addresses based on the traffic destination.

Twice NAT is a more advanced option that allows greater flexibility than network object NAT in that both the source *and* the destination addresses are identified in a single rule. A typical use case for twice NAT is a scenario where a host communicates with two different company divisions that have different IP subnets. Twice NAT translates the addresses based on the destination address, which network object NAT can't easily accommodate. Here is a simple configuration for twice NAT:

```
object network WEB-NET
 subnet 10.1.1.0
 nat (inside,dmz-1) source dynamic WEB-NET interface
 nat (inside,dmz-2) source dynamic WEB-NET interface
```

Finally, another keyword is used in some scenarios, where ordering of the NAT statements (as in the CCIE lab exam) is critical. The **after-auto** keyword is used in the manual NAT statements to push the NAT statements *below* the network object section of the NAT rules. Remember that, by default, manual NAT rules appear at the top of the NAT table. Using **after-auto** in the NAT statement, as its name implies, pushes that specific NAT configuration to the bottom section of the table as seen here:

```
 nat (inside,dmz-1) after-auto source dynamic WEB-NET interface
 nat (inside,dmz-2) after-auto source dynamic WEB-NET interface
```

It's important to check the order of the NAT statements to verify it is as intended. In certain cases, the ASA does not overwrite the old NAT statement, and it must be deleted manually; otherwise, it will never be checked.

NAT and IPv6

When hosts on IPv4-only networks need to talk to hosts on IPv6-only networks, address translation must occur. NAT46 describes the translation of IPv4 addresses into the IPv6 address space, while NAT64 describes the translation from IPv6 to IPv4. On the other hand, NAT66 translates IPv6 addresses into IPv6 addresses. Fortunately, the ASA can do both IPv4 and IPv6 NAT at the same time. The IPv6 configuration steps are nearly identical to those for IPv4 NAT.

It is common with NAT64 to use dynamic PAT due to the relatively small IPv4 address space compared to IPv6. For the same reasons, it is not recommended that you use dynamic PAT with NAT46; therefore, the ASA supports only static mappings into the IPv6 space.

Let's look at a configuration example that has two networks: Host A on the inside speaks only IPv4, while Host B on the extranet interface has only an IPv6 address (see Figure 4-15). Configuring dual-stack NAT on the ASA allows them to communicate.

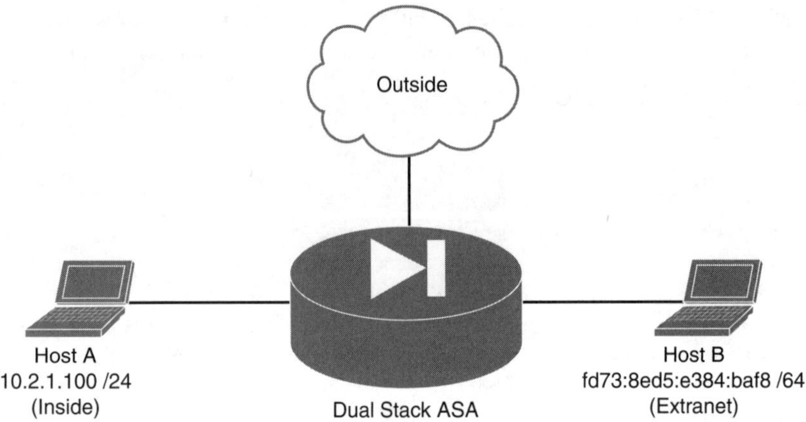

Figure 4-15 *NAT and IPv6*

You need to configure both NAT46 and NAT64 on the ASA for the two hosts to pass traffic. Follow these steps:

Step 1. Create network objects for the IPv4 and IPv6 networks:

```
object network INSIDE_V4
 subnet 10.2.1.0 255.255.255.0
object network EXTRANET_V6
 subnet fd73:8ed5:e384:baf8::/64
```

Step 2. Define a NAT64 policy under the network object to allow the ASA to use dynamic PAT on any traffic from the IPv6 extranet using the inside interface of the ASA:

```
 nat (extranet,inside) dynamic interface
```

Step 3. Add the following additional NAT46 statement for traffic going from the inside to the extranet:

```
object network INSIDE_V4
 nat (inside,extranet) static fd73:8ed5:e384:baf8::/64 dns
```

Because you can't use dynamic PAT, you must use static NAT with the IPv6 network. You do this inside the network object. The **dns** keyword allows any IPv6 DNS addresses to be converted as well.

NAT66

There are times when it might be necessary to translate IPv6 addresses. Due to the extremely large IPv6 address space, this scenario is unlikely but, if needed, the ASA can be configured in such a way. In fact, the configuration is exactly the same as for static IPv4 NAT. Let's walk through an example:

Step 1. Create the IPv6 **network** object:

```
object network NET1_V6
 subnet fd73:8ed5:e384:baf8::/64
```

Step 2. Apply the static NAT statement:

```
 nat (inside,extranet) static fd73:8ed5:e384:baa9::/64
```

ASA NAT Troubleshooting

Troubleshooting Cisco ASA NAT requires an understanding of the order in which the NAT rules are applied and the logic used within. The NAT table is made of up of three sections, with a general rule that static NAT translations should be placed before dynamic translations. NAT rules are applied in this order:

- Twice NAT (manual NAT) rules are processed first, based on the order of configuration. By default, they are placed in the first part of the NAT rules table.
- Network object NAT rules are placed in the middle part of the NAT rules table. Static rules are processed first, followed by dynamic rules.
- The most general (least-specific) twice NAT rules are at the bottom of the rules table. Proper ordering is essential to make sure the proper NAT logic is being applied.

To verify that the rules are in the proper order, use the **show run nat** command to list the NAT configuration. Note how the static NAT is placed above the dynamic NAT in the short config example shown in Example 4-14.

Example 4-14 show run nat *Command*

```
asa# sh run nat
nat (inside,outside) source static any any destination static NETWORK_
OBJ_10.3.1.0_25 NETWORK_OBJ_10.3.1.0_25 no-proxy-arp route-lookup
!
object network INSIDE-NET
 nat (any,outside) dynamic interface
```

The **show nat detail** command is most helpful for understanding how the ASA is viewing the NAT configuration. It also shows each NAT numbered section to eliminate confusion over the order of rule processing, as shown in Example 4-15.

Example 4-15 *Output from* **show nat detail**

```
asa# show nat detail
Manual NAT Policies (Section 1)
1 (inside) to (outside) source static any any destination static NETWORK_
OBJ_10.3.1.0_25 NETWORK_OBJ_10.3.1.0_25 no-proxy-arp route-lookup
    translate_hits = 15631, untranslate_hits = 16354
    Source - Origin: 0.0.0.0/0, Translated: 0.0.0.0/0
    Destination - Origin: 10.3.1.0/25, Translated: 10.3.1.0/25

Auto NAT Policies (Section 2)
1 (any) to (outside) source dynamic INSIDE-NET interface
    translate_hits = 18160, untranslate_hits = 28
    Source - Origin: 10.2.1.0/24, Translated: 192.168.1.250/24
```

If more NAT validation is required, you can enable the command-line Packet Tracer utility for a detailed analysis of the complete order of operation in the ASA. (For more on the ASA Packet Tracer, see the "Troubleshooting the ASA" section, later in this chapter.)

Example 4-16 shows the output from the **packet-tracer** command.

Example 4-16 *Packet Tracer for NAT Troubleshooting*

```
asa# packet-tracer input inside tcp 10.2.1.10 53 8.8.8.8 53

Phase: 1
Type: ACCESS-LIST
Subtype:
Result: ALLOW
Config:
Implicit Rule
Additional Information:
MAC Access list

Phase: 2
Type: ROUTE-LOOKUP
Subtype: Resolve Egress Interface
Result: ALLOW
Config:
Additional Information:
found next-hop <deleted> using egress ifc  outside

Phase: 3
Type: NAT
Subtype:
```

```
Result: ALLOW
Config:
object network SAE-Mgmt-Net
 nat (any,outside) dynamic interface
Additional Information:
Dynamic translate 10.2.1.10/53 to <deleted>/53

Phase: 4
Type: NAT
Subtype: per-session
Result: ALLOW
Config:
Additional Information:

Phase: 5
Type: IP-OPTIONS
Subtype:
Result: ALLOW
Config:
Additional Information:

Phase: 6
Type: NAT
Subtype: per-session
Result: ALLOW
Config:
Additional Information:

Phase: 7
Type: IP-OPTIONS
Subtype:
Result: ALLOW
Config:
Additional Information:

Phase: 8
Type: FLOW-CREATION
Subtype:
Result: ALLOW
Config:
Additional Information:
New flow created with id 36725, packet dispatched to next module
```

```
Result:
input-interface: inside
input-status: up
input-line-status: up
output-interface: outside
output-status: up
output-line-status: up
Action: allow
```

The **show xlate** command is also useful in troubleshooting NAT. Example 4-17 shows the translation details for an ASA doing PAT on the outside interface.

Example 4-17 *Output from* **show xlate**

```
asa(config)# sh xlate
3 in use, 896 most used
Flags: D - DNS, e - extended, I - identity, i - dynamic, r - portmap,
       s - static, T - twice, N - net-to-net
NAT from inside:0.0.0.0/0 to outside:0.0.0.0/0
    flags sIT idle 3:16:39 timeout 0:00:00
NAT from outside:10.3.1.0/25 to inside:10.3.1.0/25
    flags sIT idle 3:16:39 timeout 0:00:00

TCP PAT from any:10.2.1.5/49687 to outside:172.16.1.100/49687 flags ri idle 27:57:45
timeout 0:00:30
```

Service Policies and Application Inspection

Using service policies on the ASA is a flexible way to configure ASA features. Service policies utilize the Modular Policy Framework (MPF), which defines actions or rules and their usage for applying advanced features. The MPF is used for a variety of ASA features, such as defining traffic to be redirected to a service module or applying predefined conditions to a specified traffic class. Service policies can be applied per interface or globally to all interfaces and make up the basic configuration for application inspection.

Each service policy is composed of the following elements:

- A service policy map, which is the ordered set of rules and is named on the **service-policy** command
- Rules, each of which is a **class** command within the service policy map and the commands associated with the **class** command
- The **class** command, which defines the traffic-matching criteria for the rule

Service policies can apply traffic both bidirectionally and unidirectionally. The specific direction depends on the enabled inspection feature. Policies can also apply to management traffic only or to traffic that is transiting the firewall. For example, quality-of-service (QoS) priority queuing applies only to traffic in one direction, depending on configuration parameters. Refer to the *ASA Configuration Guide* for specific features and how they are supported.

Service policies applied to an interface override a global service policy. The ASA has one built-in global service policy as part of the initial configuration. By default, it has some application inspections enabled for general ASA functionality. The features in the default global service policy can be modified or the policy can be disabled and a new global service policy created. Only one service policy may be applied to an interface at any time, but multiple service policies can exist in the configuration. The default global policy contains a special class called the *default class* that is used to match the default ports for all inspections.

Like other ASA features, service policies operate in a top-down first-match process. In most cases, once a match is found, the defined action is taken. There are some exceptions to this logic, depending on the protocol and the matching logic.

Service Policy Configuration

Let's walk through configuration of a service policy that matches on all TCP traffic and sets the TCP idle timeout to 5 minutes:

Step 1. Define a class map:

```
asa(config)# access-list ALL_TCP permit tcp any any
asa(config-cmap)# class-map ALL_TCP_CMAP
asa(config-cmap)# description "This class-map matches all TCP traffic"
asa(config-cmap)# match access-list ALL_TCP
```

Class maps can be reused in different policy maps and contain match statements that can point to an access list, a single port, or a range or any traffic (with the **any** keyword).

Step 2. Create a policy map that includes at least one class map. In this example, the policy map is called **MY-TEST-POLICY**:

```
asa(config)# policy-map MY-TEST-POLICY
asa(config-pmap)# class ALL_TCP
```

Step 3. Define the action to take on matched traffic. This is typically via the **set** command in the policy map:

```
asa(config-pmap-c)# set connection timeout idle 0:5:0
```

In order to actually inspect traffic, the policy map has to be applied either globally or to an interface. Here it is inspecting traffic on the outside interface.

Step 4. Apply the policy map as a global policy or specify an interface. Here you apply the policy map to traffic on the outside interface:

```
asa(config)# service-policy MY-TEST-POLICY interface outside
```

IPv6 service policies are supported for most features and can be combined with other inspections—with some caveats. It is possible for a packet to match both IPv4 and IPv6 inspections, and therefore actions for both would be valid.

Application Inspection

As noted earlier, the ASA contains built-in default application inspection engines. These engines can be viewed in the running configuration using the **show running-config all** command. Inspection engines are required for services that open secondary channels on dynamically assigned ports, which is common with many multimedia protocols. In order to properly inspect these types of traffic, the ASA engages the application inspection engines.

Inspection engines use a construct called an *inspection policy map* to define the criteria for the inspection type. These maps can be edited, disabled, or removed altogether, depending on the use case with service policies and the MPF. It is a common practice to edit the default global policy to customize the application inspection deployment. This special default policy includes the **inspection_default** class map, which includes default ports for all inspection types. The **inspection_default** class map is a reserved name on the ASA and is linked to the special command **match default-inspection-traffic** that is used to match the default ports in the default class map.

If nonstandard ports need to be inspected, a new class map should be created and applied to the default policy. Note that matching criteria that use the wildcard **any** could negatively impact ASA performance and should be used with care.

Sometimes it may be necessary to configure the ASA application inspection to search text strings. For example, a basic URL filtering policy could be configured to look for a specific string inside an HTTP packet. In order to accomplish this inspection, regular expressions must be used. Specific regular expressions can be defined as part of a class map and thus included in a policy map.

Commonly Used Application Inspection Engines

The ASA has a comprehensive feature set for inspecting common applications (FTP, DNS, HTTP, and so on) as well as voice and video protocols. Over the years, Cisco has added modules to the ASA that allow the firewall to offload the CPU-intensive operations of application inspection to specialized hardware. While HTTP inspection does not require these modules, the modules do allow the ASA to deliver next-generation firewall capabilities. The process for redirecting traffic to a dedicated module on the ASA uses the same MPF and policy map commands discussed previously.

Note If a hardware module is present, the two types of HTTP inspection are not compatible and should not be used together. The Firepower next-generation capabilities of the ASA are discussed in Chapter 5, "Next-Gen Firewalls."

Basic (non-module) HTTP inspection on the ASA is useful for protecting against some specific HTTP exploits and maintaining protocol conformance. For example, a basic HTTP inspection policy map can scan HTTP headers and body because these are presented in plaintext.

Example 4-18 shows a basic HTTP inspection policy that allows and logs an HTTP connection attempting to access www\.xyz.com/.*.asp with an HTTP **GET** or **PUT**.

Example 4-18 *ASA HTTP Inspection Configuration Example*

```
asa(config)# regex url1 "www\.xyz.com/.*\.asp"
asa(config)# regex get "GET"
asa(config)# regex put "PUT"

asa(config)# class-map type regex match-any url_to_log
asa(config-cmap)# match regex url1
asa(config-cmap)# exit

asa(config)# class-map type regex match-any methods_to_log
asa(config-cmap)# match regex get
asa(config-cmap)# match regex put
asa(config-cmap)# exit

asa(config)# class-map type inspect http http_url_policy
asa(config-cmap)# match request uri regex class url_to_log
asa(config-cmap)# match request method regex class methods_to_log
asa(config-cmap)# exit

asa(config)# policy-map type inspect http http_policy
asa(config-pmap)# class http_url_policy
asa(config-pmap-c)# log
```

ASA Advanced Features

Over the years, the ASA has become more than just a packet-filtering firewall. It has adopted many of the IOS routing features in order to provide a more consistent offering in the Cisco portfolio. In addition, it allows a policy to be built with users and groups defined externally. This section examines some of the more advanced ASA features.

Identity Firewall

As part of its continuing evolution, the ASA firewall has a feature set that provides access controls to users and groups. Cisco calls this feature set Identity Firewall. It works through an integration with Microsoft Active Directory (AD) to gather user identity and IP address information that can be used in ASA policy. This has the advantage of decoupling network topology from security policy. Today's users are mobile, and a robust security policy takes that into account.

Identity Firewall consists of three components:

- ASA
- Microsoft AD
- The AD agent running on a Windows server (2003, 2008, or 2008 R2)

The ASA uses LDAP queries to the AD server for user and group information. The ASA uses RADIUS to query the AD agent for IP user database information. No active authentication is required of the client because the ASA is able to gather this information from the AD server and agent. This is illustrated in Figure 4-16.

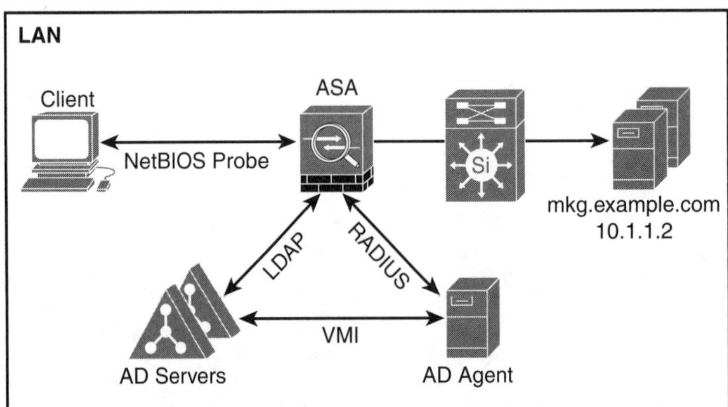

Figure 4-16 *ASA-to-AD Communication*

The ASA can be configured to communicate to multiple AD servers for redundancy. Likewise, multiple AD agents can be deployed to eliminate a single point dependency.

Identity Firewall Configuration

As noted earlier in this chapter, the ASA needs to be configured with AD server information and the AD agent. For proper operation, the ASA needs to bind to the correct directory name (DN) information in Active Directory. The configuration steps are shown here:

Step 1. Configure the ASA to speak LDAP, bind to DN, and provide authentication credentials to query the LDAP directory, as shown in Example 4-19.

Example 4-19 *ASA LDAP Active Directory Configuration*

```
asa(config)# aaa-server adserver protocol ldap
asa(config-aaa-server-group)# aaa-server adserver (interface) host <ip address>
asa(config-aaa-server-host)# ldap-base-dn DC=SAMPLE,DC=com
asa(config-aaa-server-host)# ldap-scope subtree
asa(config-aaa-server-host)# ldap-login-password <password>
asa(config-aaa-server-host)# ldap-login-dn cn=user1,DC-SAMPLE,DC=com
asa(config-aaa-server-host)# server-type microsoft
asa(config-aaa-server-host)# ldap-group-base-dn OU=Sample Groups,DC=SAMPLE,DC=com
asa(config-aaa-server-host)# ldap-over-ssl enable
asa(config-aaa-server-host)# server-port 389
```

Step 2. Configure the ASA to communicate using RADIUS to the AD agent, as shown in Example 4-20.

Example 4-20 *ASA RADIUS-to-AD Agent Configuration*

```
asa(config)# aaa-server adagent protocol radius
asa(config-aaa-server-group)# ad-agent-mode
asa(config-aaa-server-group)# exit
asa(config)# aaa-server adagent (interface) host <ip address>
asa(config-aaa-server-host)# key <key>
asa(config-aaa-server-host)# exit
asa(config)# user-identity ad-agent aaa-server adagent
```

Step 3. Optionally test the AD agent communication with the ASA to verify proper configuration:

```
asa(config-aaa-server-host)# test aaa-server ad-agent adagent
```

Step 4. Enable the Identity Firewall feature on the ASA:

```
asa(config)# user-identity enable
```

Once the Identity Firewall feature is enabled, the ASA can apply user- and group-based policy decisions through the use of extended ACLs. Example 4-21 shows a simple Identity Firewall–based ACL.

Example 4-21 *ASA Group-Based Access List*

```
access-list 100 ex permit ip user ACME\Group1 any any
access-list 100 ex deny ip user ACME\Group2 any any
access-list 100 ex deny any any
access-group 100 in interface inside
```

Security Group Tags (SGTs)

Mobile users and virtualized workload mobility have created challenges for security policies based on static mechanisms such as IP addresses. Cisco created an architecture called TrustSec that combines user and group identity information with a centralized access control policy. An SGT is a 16-bit number passed as metadata between Cisco devices. The ASA supports the capability to be part of a TrustSec network, where access decisions are based upon this SGT metadata.

Note For more information on Cisco TrustSec, see http://www.cisco.com/c/en/us/solutions/enterprise-networks/trustsec/index.html.

Three components make up the ASA configuration in TrustSec:

- The ASA
- The Identity Services Engine (ISE)
- The SGT Exchange Protocol (SXP)

The ASA creates a secure channel via RADIUS with ISE in order to download the TrustSec environment data. This security group table contains the SGT-to-group name mappings. SXP is the method by which the IP-SGT bindings are communicated to and from the ASA. It was developed as a control plane to extend the TrustSec network to devices that don't natively support hardware tagging. SXP is not required, however, as the IP-SGT bindings can optionally be manually configured. For scalability reasons, SXP is recommended for larger networks. ASA has supported SXPv3 since the 9.6 release and is backward-compatible with other SXP versions.

Note Security Exchange Protocol (SXP) is now an IETF standard; see https://tools.ietf.org/html/draft-smith-kandula-sxp-00.

TrustSec Configuration

Much as with Identity Firewall, the ASA requires some initial configuration steps, as outlined here:

Step 1. Configure the ASA to speak RADIUS to the ISE server and configure it to work with TrustSec:

```
asa(config)# aaa-server ISEserver protocol radius
asa(config-aaa-server-group)# aaa-server ISEserver {interface} host
{address}
asa(config)# cts server-group ISEserver
```

Step 2. Create the trusted relationship with ISE by importing a PAC file from ISE onto the ASA:

```
asa(config)# cts import-pac path password password
```

Step 3. Enable SXP on the ASA and connect to a peer so that ASA is configured to receive updates from the peer:

```
asa(config)# cts sxp connection peer peer password default mode local
listener
```

When the ASA is configured to receive IP-SGT binding information, access control policies may be enabled to utilize the security group information contained within the tags. Any feature that uses extended ACLs (unless otherwise unsupported) can take advantage of these mappings. To verify that SXP is working properly, the best practice is to refresh the environment data received from ISE via the **show cts environment-data** command on the ASA. Example 4-22 shows sample output from this command.

Example 4-22 *ASA SXP Operation Verification*

```
asa(config)# show cts environment-data

CTS Environment Data
Status:                      Active
Last download attempt:       Successful
Environment Data Lifetime:   86400 secs
Last update time:            05:05:16 UTC Apr 14 2017
Env-data expires in:         0:23:56:15 (dd:hr:mm:sec)
Env-data refreshes in:       0:23:46:15 (dd:hr:mm:sec)
```

You are now ready to create an ACL on the ASA that filters traffic based on the security group information. In this example, only ICMP traffic from security-group 3 to security-group 2 is allowed:

```
access-list ICMP_ONLY extended permit icmp security-group tag 3 any security-group
2 any
access-group ICMP_ONLY in interface inside
```

An alternative option is to use the actual group names in the ACL instead of the tag numbers, as shown previously. Assume that security-group 3 maps to a group called **SALES**, and security-group 2 represents a group called **ENGINEERING**:

```
access-list ICMP_ONLY extended permit icmp security-group name SALES any security-
group name ENGINEERING any access-group inside in interface inside
```

TrustSec builds on Identity Firewall as it allows for a centralized access control policy on ISE to be applied in a distributed manner throughout the Cisco network. The ASA can enforce these policies, which provides a more scalable policy than is available by replicating ACLs on every perimeter network device.

Advanced Firewall Tuning

Given its role in the network, the firewall is both a device for enforcing policy and a means of protecting services from external exploitation. This section explores both types of features on the ASA and how they are configured.

A common configuration on an Internet-facing ASA is to protect externally reachable servers from exploitation. Most of the features needed for this protection are enabled by default and can be configured to be much more aggressive.

Every time a new connection is created in the ASA, several settings can be configured. The default settings for maximum connection limits, timeouts, and TCP normalization are appropriate for the majority of deployments. For example, the ASA by default randomizes the ISN of TCP sequence numbers for connections. This makes it more difficult for an attacker to predict the next ISN for a new connection in order to hijack the session. This can be disabled per traffic class, if necessary, through the MPF.

TCP Intercept is a feature that protects hosts from denial-of-service (DoS) attacks. These attacks attempt to overwhelm a device with TCP SYN traffic that often is generated from spoofed IP addresses. If the DoS traffic rate is high enough, the target host is not able to respond to legitimate connection requests.

By design, the ASA responds on behalf of hosts and responds to the initial TCP SYN for a new connection with an appropriate SYN ACK. When the three-way handshake is complete, the ASA completes the connection and allows traffic to pass to the internal host. This process is called *TCP Intercept*, and these half-completed connections are known as *embryonic connections*.

Advanced Firewall Configuration

Sometimes default protection limits are not enough for high-value servers, which need more robust controls on inbound connections. The ASA uses a policy map to set these limits, as shown in this example, assuming two web servers, 10.1.1.5 and 10.1.1.6:

Step 1. Create an access list and define the class map and match criteria:

```
asa(config)# access-list SERVERS extended permit tcp any host 10.1.1.5
eq http
asa(config)# access-list SERVERS extended permit tcp any host 10.1.1.6
eq http
asa(config)# class-map protected-servers
asa(config-cmap)# match access-list SERVERS
```

Step 2. Define the policy map and apply the class to it:

```
asa(config)# policy-map DOS_policy
asa(config-pmap)# class protected-servers
```

Step 3. Set the embryonic connection limits to a maximum of 100, limited to 50 per client:

```
asa(config-pmap-c)# set connection embryonic-conn-max 100
asa(config-pmap-c)# set connection per-client-embryonic-max 50
```

Step 4. Apply the service policy to the outside interface:

```
asa(config)# service-policy DOS_policy in interface outside
```

TCP State Bypass

In some cases, it may be necessary to turn off ASA state checking when asymmetric traffic flows are present. Asymmetric flows can occur when connections are created through one firewall but return through a different firewall, as shown in Figure 4-17.

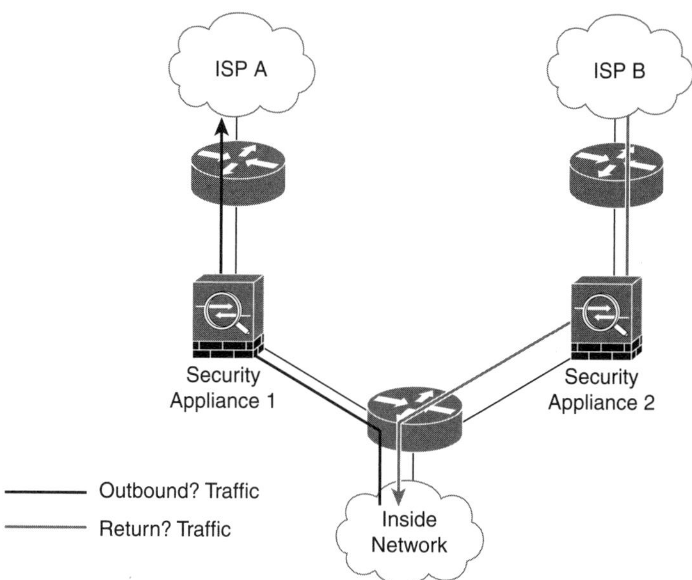

Figure 4-17 *ASA Asymmetric Flow*

By default, a stateful device drops this traffic by design, but you can disable this functionality on the ASA. In Example 4-23, TCP state checking is turned off for any traffic originating from the 10.1.1.0/27 network.

Example 4-23 *Disabling TCP State Checking on the ASA*

```
asa(config)# access-list tcp_bypass extended permit tcp 10.1.1.0 255.255.255.224 any
asa(config)# class-map tcp_bypass
asa(config-cmap)# description "TCP traffic that bypasses stateful firewall"
asa(config-cmap)# match access-list tcp_bypass

asa(config-cmap)# policy-map tcp_bypass_policy
asa(config-pmap)# class tcp_bypass
asa(config-pmap-c)# set connection advanced-options tcp-state-bypass

asa(config-pmap-c)# service-policy tcp_bypass_policy outside
```

Policy Based Routing (PBR)

PBR on the ASA is a new feature that was introduced in the 9.4 release. PBR has long been available in IOS and is another routing feature that was imported into the ASA code train. As in IOS, in the ASA PBR creates a policy in which packets are sent to a destination that is not in the routing table. Packets matching the PBR policy effectively override the global routing table. PBR is commonly used when multiple egress paths are present and there is a need to differentiate routing policy. It is also used on the ASA to assign QoS values for traffic classification.

In the example shown in Figure 4-18, an ASA is connected to two service providers, A and B. There is a requirement for Host A to only use Provider A and Host B to only go through Provider B. PBR on the ASA allows this to happen.

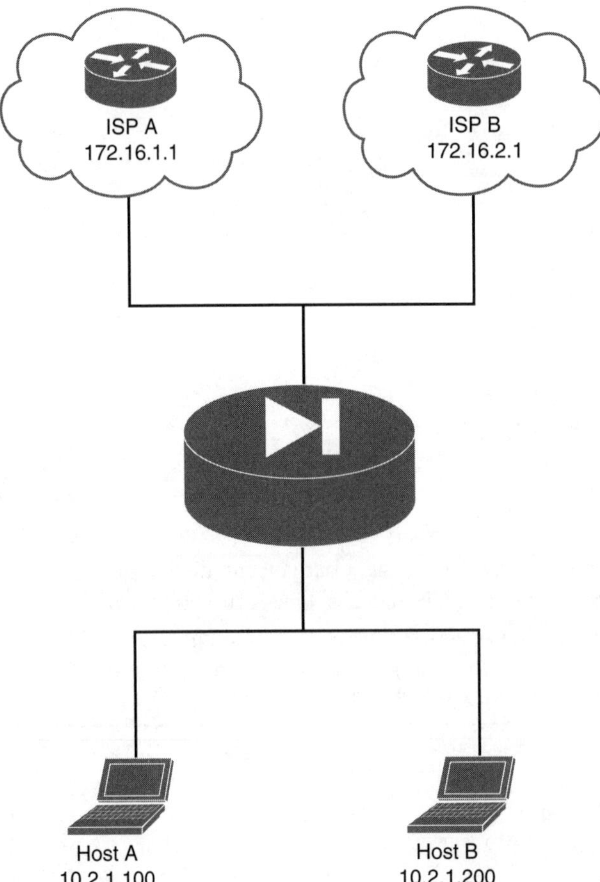

Figure 4-18 *PBR on the ASA*

Much as in IOS, with the ASA, **route-map** statements are used to define the match criteria and action to take. In this example, you set the next hop to the ISP gateway based on the host source address:

Step 1. Create an access list that defines the matching criteria. In this case you need an access list for each host:

```
asa(config)# access-list HOST_A extended permit ip host 10.2.1.100 any
asa(config)# access-list HOST_B extended permit ip host 10.2.1.200 any
```

Step 2. Create a route-map entry. Route-maps are processed in top-down order, using sequence numbers:

```
asa(config)# route-map PBR-MAP permit 10
asa(config-route-map)# match ip address HOST_A
```

Step 3. Create an action for matching traffic using the **set** keyword. In this example, you want Host A to use Provider A's gateway address, 172.16.1.1:

```
asa(config-route-map)# set ip next-hop 172.16.1.1
```

Step 4. Create a route-map entry for Host B and set the next-hop address to Provider B:

```
asa(config)# route-map PBR-MAP permit 20
asa(config-route-map)# match ip address HOST_B
asa(config-route-map)# set ip next-hop 172.16.2.1
```

Step 5. Apply the policy to at least one interface:

```
asa(config)# interface Gigabit0/1
asa(config-int)# policy-route route-map PBR-MAP
```

Unmatched traffic falls through the policy map and is routed according to the global routing table.

Threat Detection

Threat detection is an ASA Layer 3/Layer 4 feature that analyzes and baselines traffic patterns in ASA code 8.04 and later. This analysis is used to protect both the ASA and the network devices behind it. It is intended for environments that don't have dedicated deep-packet inspection (DPI) capabilities in place, such as an IDS or IPS.

Basic threat detection is enabled by default and tracks many different statistics, such as packet format, connection limits, incomplete sessions, and traffic dropped by an ACL, to name a few. Its performance impact is negligible, as it measures statistics for drop rates over a period of time. There are two configurable thresholds: the average rate and the burst rate. When a basic threat is detected, the ASA generates a syslog message as a result.

The **show threat-detection rate** command shows the average, current, trigger, and total events per category.

By using advanced threat detection, you can track traffic at the object level so the ASA has a concise picture for individual hosts, ports, and protocols. Only traffic that is going through the ASA is tracked; traffic destined for the ASA itself is not tracked, and only ACL statistics are enabled by default with advanced threat protection. Working with another ASA feature, TCP Intercept, advanced threat detection can track more detailed statistics on top servers to be considered under attack. Various rate limits can be fine-tuned to provide more useful information.

Advanced threat detection is optionally enabled via the **threat-detection statistics** command, as shown in Example 4-24.

Example 4-24 *ASA Threat Detection Configuration*

```
asa(config)# threat-detection statistics ?
configure mode commands/options:
 access-list     Keyword to specify access-list statistics
 host            Keyword to specify IP statistics
 port            Keyword to specify port statistics
 protocol        Keyword to specify protocol statistics
 tcp-intercept   Trace tcp intercept statistics
```

Care should be taken on what is measured via advanced threat detection as its usage can be resource-intensive. For a good view of how much memory is consumed by threat detection, use the **show memory app-cache threat-detection [detail]** command.

A third category of threat detection is designed to mitigate risks by malicious network scanning. It is enabled via the **threat-detection scanning-threat** command. Much as with basic threat detection, capture rates can be adjusted via **threat-detection rate.** Using the optional **shun** keyword with scanning threat detection allows the ASA to temporarily block traffic from the attacker. The ASA shunning feature allows for exceptions to the shunning action but should be used with care on a production network.

Troubleshooting the ASA

Troubleshooting the ASA is easier if you have an understanding of some of the built-in tools and **show** commands. In addition, having an understanding of the life of a packet through the ASA is helpful. Much as with other devices, for the ASA to forward traffic, it needs to be able to determine some basic networking information, such as egress interface and the routing next hop. This is obvious to any experienced network engineer. What may not be so obvious, however, is the order in which these checks are applied.

With few exceptions, the ASA checks these items in the following order:

1. Route lookup
2. Ingress access list lookup

3. NAT rules
4. Egress access list lookup
5. Redirection to an internal module (if present)
6. Egress interface

The following are some of the useful commands to help determine packet flow details at each stage:

```
show interface
show conn
show access-list
show xlate
show service-policy inspect
show run static
show run nat
show run global
show nat
show route
show arp
```

Note Using syslog is also a useful method for tracking connection state. For more information, see *Cisco ASA Series Syslog Messages* on cisco.com.

As mentioned earlier in this chapter, ASA Packet Tracer is an excellent built-in troubleshooting utility that can be accessed via the command line or via ASDM. It provides a detailed step-by-step walkthrough of a virtual packet in the ASA, from ingress to egress, and allows real-time debugging when source, destination, and port and protocol information are input.

Packet Tracer command line syntax is as follows:

```
packet-tracer input [src_int] protocol src_addr src_port dest_addr
dest_port [detailed] [xml]
```

Example 4-25 shows sample output from the Packet Tracer utility.

Example 4-25 *ASA Packet Tracer Output*

```
asa(config)# packet-tracer input inside tcp 10.2.1.10 53 8.8.8.8 53

Phase: 1
Type: ROUTE-LOOKUP
Subtype: Resolve Egress Interface
Result: ALLOW
Config:
```

```
Additional Information:
found next-hop 172.16.3.3 using egress ifc  outside

Phase: 2
Type: NAT
Subtype:
Result: ALLOW
Config:
object network Lab-Mgmt-Net
 nat (any,outside) dynamic interface
Additional Information:
Dynamic translate 10.2.1.10/53 to 172.16.1.100/53

Phase: 3
Type: NAT
Subtype: per-session
Result: ALLOW
Config:
Additional Information:

Phase: 4
Type: IP-OPTIONS
Subtype:
Result: ALLOW
Config:
Additional Information:

Phase: 5
Type: NAT
Subtype: per-session
Result: ALLOW
Config:
Additional Information:

Phase: 6
Type: IP-OPTIONS
Subtype:
Result: ALLOW
Config:
Additional Information:

Phase: 7
Type: FLOW-CREATION
```

```
Subtype:
Result: ALLOW
Config:
Additional Information:
New flow created with id 304980, packet dispatched to next module

Result:
input-interface: inside
input-status: up
input-line-status: up
output-interface: outside
output-status: up
output-line-status: up
Action: allow
```

The ASDM Packet Tracer under the Tools menu provides a visual tool for troubleshooting. Functionally, it works the same as the command-line version. The ASDM Packet Tracer is shown in Figure 4-19.

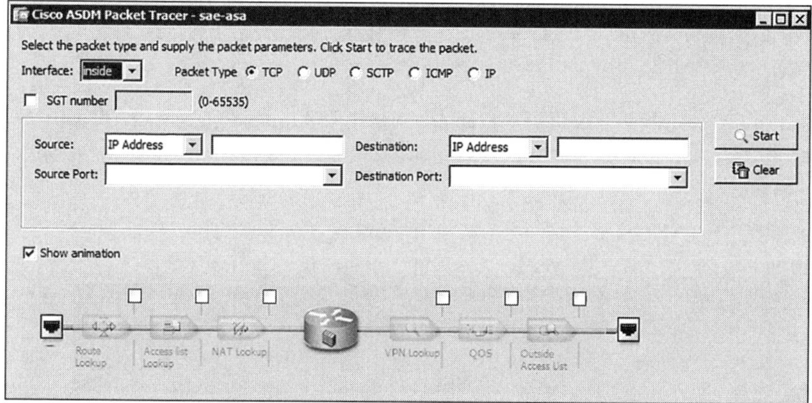

Figure 4-19 *ASDM Packet Tracer Utility*

Packet Capture

ASA Packet Capture is available at the command line or via a tool in ASDM. Only its command-line use is discussed here. As the name implies, Packet Capture is an ASA troubleshooting tool for capturing live packets as they transit the firewall. Unlike with a traditional SPAN port, ASA Packet Capture can record traffic on the ASA backplane as well as traffic that is dropped due to policy (**asp-drop**). Both of these are extremely useful when troubleshooting the ASA. An additional benefit is that you can export the Packet Capture file as a .pcap for detailed analysis via Wireshark by pointing any browser to https://*ASA_IP*/admin/capture/*capture_name*/pcap.

For more detailed troubleshooting, the Packet Capture utility offers different capture types. Some of the most useful ones are listed here:

- **asa_dataplane:** Useful for tracking packets between the ASA and a service module.
- **asp-drop:** The accelerated security path is useful for showing packets dropped by policy.
- **ethernet-type:** As implied, this is useful for troubleshooting EtherType issues.
- **real-time:** Use this with care on slow console connections to avoid overwhelming the serial buffer.
- **trace:** Similar to the Packet Tracer feature, this shows a step-by-step method for each packet.

Packet Capture Configuration

The configuration of Packet Capture consists of creating a capture file, binding it to an interface, and optionally providing matching criteria.

This is an example of a capture file named **capin** on the inside interface matching traffic between hosts 192.168.10.10 and 203.0.113.3:

```
asa# capture capin interface inside match ip 192.168.10.10 255.255.255.255
203.0.113.3 255.255.255.255
```

Optionally, another capture file could be created on the ASA outside interface. To view the capture, simply issue a **show capture** command that references the specified capture file (for example, capin).

To clear the buffer, use the **clear capture** ***capture_name*** command. This clears the contents but keeps the capture active. To stop the capture, use the **no** version of the command.

Summary

Since its release in 2005, the ASA firewall has continually added new features to expand its reach. It now has physical, virtual, and cloud-based versions that serve a wide range of customer deployment scenarios. This chapter highlights many of the core features of the ASA, including advanced tuning and configuration.

This chapter starts with the initial ASA configuration, highlighting the usage of security levels and zones and how a virtual lab ASA could be beneficial for CCIE study. Routing and transparent mode are covered, with common deployment scenarios and configuration provided for each. The benefits of multi-context mode and a treatment of the two high-availability options and ASA clustering are discussed. Wide routing protocol support is still a recent development on the ASA. Use cases and configuration examples are provided.

The importance of NAT cannot be understated in today's networks. The ASA offers a robust set of NAT configuration options, which give it maximum flexibility for advanced use cases. Best practices for troubleshooting NAT are shared in this chapter, as well as techniques to validate its operation.

Advanced ASA features such as policy maps and their usage are introduced in this chapter. The chapter also covers ways to manipulate traffic on the ASA, such as TCP state bypass and the built-in threat detection capabilities.

This chapter also covers general troubleshooting such as Packet Tracer and Packet Capture, and how they can be effective in debugging a broken firewall. The configuration examples in this chapter combined with hands-on practice will help a CCIE candidate maximize preparation for the lab exam.

References

"ASA Configuration Guides," https://www.cisco.com/c/en/us/support/security/asa-5500-series-next-generation-firewalls/products-installation-and-configuration-guides-list.html

"Release Notes for the ASA Series, 9.4(x)," https://www.cisco.com/c/en/us/td/docs/security/asa/asa94/release/notes/asarn94.html

"Cisco Firewalling Support Forums," https://supportforums.cisco.com/t5/firewalling/bd-p/5966-discussions-firewalling

"Configuring Network Address Translation," https://www.cisco.com/c/en/us/td/docs/security/security_management/cisco_security_manager/security_manager/4-1/user/guide/CSMUserGuide_wrapper/NATchap.pdf

"ASA 8.3 NAT Configuration" YouTube, https://www.youtube.com/watch?v=R6TMlH9U2pE

"Cisco Virtual Internet Routing Lab," https://learningnetworkstore.cisco.com/virtual-internet-routing-lab-virl/cisco-personal-edition-pe-20-nodes-virl-20

"ASA NAT Migration to Version 8.3," https://www.cisco.com/c/en/us/td/docs/security/asa/asa83/upgrading/migrating.html

"Cisco TrustSec Overview," http://www.cisco.com/c/en/us/solutions/enterprise-networks/trustsec/index.html.

Chapter 5

Next-Gen Firewalls

Firewalls have been around for decades and, by comparison, next-generation firewalls (NGFWs) are a more recent evolution of basic firewalls. Today it is generally accepted that a legacy firewall is a packet filter that provides access control based on ports and protocols. An NGFW, on the other hand, includes all the basic firewall functionality with an added benefit of application inspection and other advanced features. Gartner published a definition along these lines but added the additional capabilities of intrusion detection and intelligence from outside the firewall (for example, correlation and analytics capabilities). (See https://www.gartner.com/it-glossary/next-generation-firewalls-ngfws.)

Cisco's Adaptive Security Appliance (ASA) is considered a legacy firewall because it can filter based on ports and protocols. It has some application capability that has evolved over the years, but Cisco acquired Sourcefire in 2013 primarily to add NGFW and next-generation intrusion prevention system (NGIPS) offerings to its portfolio. Cisco now offers multiple options that blur the lines between firewall and NGFW functionality, based on differences in hardware platforms.

The Cisco Firepower system is a set of network security products that run as purpose-built appliances or as virtual machines. Providing a wide range of options, Firepower refers to features and products that include the ASA firewall and the Sourcefire security portfolio. For example, it is possible to deploy a native ASA firewall, an ASA firewall with Firepower next-generation security services, a Firepower NGIPS, or Firepower Threat Defense (FTD), which combines the ASA firewall and NGFW features. These devices are controlled by one of the following managers:

- Firepower Management Center (FMC)
- Cisco Security Manager (CSM)
- Firepower Device Manager
- Adaptive Security Device Manager (ASDM)

In addition, the Firepower 4100 and 9000 series chassis have a GUI-based Chassis Manager that is used for initial configuration of those platforms. This chapter focuses on the NGFW features that are part of FTD and managed by using the FMC.

Note Firepower Device Manager is not covered in this chapter as it is not included in the latest CCIE Security blueprint. For more information on using Firepower Device Manager, please see the online documentation at https://www.cisco.com/c/en/us/td/docs/security/firepower/610/fdm/fptd-fdm-config-guide-610.html.

Firepower Deployment Options

Firepower Services for ASA (FSA) adds the NGIPS features of network discovery and access control to the ASA. Firewall policy is built in the ASA, while NGIPS policy is built in the FSA system. Both the ASA and Firepower can inspect traffic, but the ASA must explicitly redirect traffic to the Firepower inspection engine using a service policy for this to occur. Functionally, FSA consists of two images residing on the local disk on a single appliance. Depending on the ASA platform, FSA may be run from an external module. The ASA configuration is managed using the CLI or ASDM, while FSA is configured in the FMC. The FMC does not have visibility into the ASA configuration, as they are separate systems running in the same appliance.

FTD is a merger between ASA and Firepower code. Unlike FSA, FTD is a single system image that is managed by using the FMC and has feature parity with the ASA and Firepower images separately. The major difference is that FTD images are not configured using the CLI. Instead, they are configured from the FMC. This is a big change for those who have a long history with Cisco security products.

Note For a complete listing of supported features, please refer to the latest *Firepower Management Center Configuration Guide* (https://www.cisco.com/c/en/us/td/docs/security/firepower/601/configuration/guide/fpmc-config-guide-v601.html).

FTD is supported on the following platforms:

- Firepower 9300 chassis
- Firepower 4100 chassis
- Firepower 2100 chassis
- ASA 5512-X through 5555-X
- ASA 5508-X and 5516-X
- ASA 5506-X series
- On an ISR module

- As a virtual machine in VMware vSphere
- As a virtual machine in KVM
- Virtually in Amazon Web Services (AWS)
- Virtually in Microsoft Azure

Note The terms *FTD* and *NGFW* are used interchangeably throughout this chapter, but it should be noted that FTD contains more than just NGFW functionality. Other chapters in this book cover the additional features.

What Is the Firepower Management Console?

As mentioned earlier in this chapter, the FMC is a fault-tolerant centralized console for managing multiple Cisco Firepower security devices. It provides a comprehensive portal for all security and network-related configuration. In addition to allowing for device management and configuration, the FMC aggregates and correlates network traffic events. It provides a single-pane view of network security posture, which helps in making rapid threat assessment decisions. You access the FMC by using a web browser, which means there is no need for a dedicated client installation. The FMC monitors the health of all managed devices and includes a licensing database for advanced security features.

The FMC runs on a dedicated physical appliance or virtually on VMware vSphere or KVM hypervisors. There is also an FMC version available for AWS. Larger deployments will prefer a dedicated appliance due to local processing of events and threat data. Virtual FMC platforms are best suited for small deployments, including CCIE study labs.

The FMC features depend on the license, the platform, and the user role. User access can be defined by domains, which allows multitenant deployment options. The FMC has advanced capabilities to provide a comprehensive network map. Hosts, operating systems, users, files, and geolocation data are captured in order to provide a granular security view of the network as a whole. These can be broken into different policy categories:

- Identity policies collect information on the network users and provide authentication services.
- Network discovery policies collect network, host, and application data.
- Access control policies enable advanced traffic inspection and logging capabilities.
- Intrusion policies inspect traffic for malicious behavior or signatures.
- SSL inspection policies provide options for handling encrypted traffic.
- Advanced Malware Protection (AMP) policies provide additional controls through network or agent-based tools.

The remainder of this chapter focuses on policy configuration and advanced features in the FMC. But first you need to get your FTD appliance bootstrapped and configured, as discussed in the following section.

Note For a comprehensive list of device support, management platforms, and software releases, see the *Cisco Firepower Compatibility Guide*, at https://www.cisco.com/c/en/us/td/docs/security/firepower/compatibility/firepower-compatibility.html#reference_A0CAB7C28A2B440F8F901D316D6684F4.

Configuring Firepower Threat Defense

FTD combines features and functionality from the Cisco ASA and the Sourcefire products into a single image. Configuration and troubleshooting can be confusing because of changes in the data plane to accommodate this new architecture. With the FMC being the main configuration component (remember that CLI configuration is no longer possible), it is necessary to cover some of the changes in the data plane in the FTD system.

FTD inherited two device modes and two interface modes from the ASA. These are commonly associated with the NGFW configuration process:

- Device modes:
  - Routed mode deployment
  - Transparent mode deployment
- Interface modes:
  - Routed mode interface configuration
  - BVI mode interface configuration (for transparent mode)

FTD also inherited interface modes from Firepower. These are commonly associated with the NGIPS configuration process:

- Passive mode
- Passive (ERSPAN) mode
- Inline pair
- Inline pair with tap

The FTD deployment mode and interface mode combination affects which engines will process traffic. For example, traffic cannot be dropped in every combination. Table 5-1 provides a summary of these options.

Table 5-1 *FTD Interface and Deployment Modes*

FTD Interface Mode	FTD Deployment Mode	Description	Can Traffic Be Dropped?
Routed	Routed	Full LINA engine and Snort engine checks	Yes
BVI	Transparent	Full LINA engine and Snort engine checks	Yes
Inline pair	Routed or transparent	Partial LINA engine and Snort engine checks	Yes
Inline pair with tap	Routed or transparent	Partial LINA engine and Snort engine checks	No
Passive	Routed or transparent	Partial LINA engine and Snort engine checks	No
Passive (ERSPAN)	Routed	Partial LINA engine and Snort engine checks	No

The information in this table is from "Configuring Firepower Threat Defense Interfaces in Routed Mode," https://www.cisco.com/c/en/us/support/docs/security/firepower-ngfw/200908-configuring-firepower-threat-defense-int.html.

FTD Initial Configuration

As mentioned previously, FTD runs on a wide variety of physical and virtual platforms. The exact steps to bootstrap a device and prepare it to be managed using the FMC vary by platform, but this section covers the common steps.

We recommend a console connection to the device during first boot in order to provide the initial configuration. Virtual devices require access to the virtual console. A second option is to use SSH and go to the default IP address 192.168.45.45. Once connected, upon first boot, FTD needs login credentials, and you can use the default username admin and the password Admin123. Upon successful login, a configuration wizard starts and prompts for the following information required by the system:

- Accept the EULA.
- Set a new admin password.
- Verify the DHCP settings.
- Set the management IP address (IPv4 and/or IPv6) and mask.
- Specify the system name.

- Specify the gateway.
- Verify the DNS settings.
- Verify the proxy settings.
- Specify the management mode (standalone or managed).
- Specify the firewall mode (routed or transparent).

Pay special attention to the last two prompts listed here as they are the most important and require advance planning. Because the CCIE lab includes the FMC, you should install only managed devices. In order to use the FMC for management, you must answer No to the prompt regarding local device management mode; otherwise, the device can only be managed using Firepower Device Manager.

Note Some devices, like the Firepower 4100 and 9300, require additional configuration with the Chassis Manager configuration.

Chapter 4, "Firewalling with the ASA," covers firewall modes on the ASA. Because FTD inherited ASA functionality, it also supports routed and transparent modes, which are equivalent to their operation on the ASA. Similarly, you may remember that changing the firewall mode after the initial setup erases the running configuration—so choose wisely.

Warning Changing the firewall mode after the initial configuration erases the running configuration.

The following sections look at some of the differences between the firewall modes to help you complete the initial configuration.

Routed Mode

In routed mode, FTD acts like a routed hop in the network path, with each interface in a different subnet, and is typically deployed at the network edge. A common example of this would be a NGFW deployed at the boundary of a trusted network and an untrusted network (such as the Internet). Routed mode also supports VPN termination and is the default mode for a new install. A routed mode NGFW has interfaces in different subnets and routes packets that pass access control policy through the device. In routed mode, a NGFW could act as a default gateway for hosts, provide DHCP services, and/or exchange routing protocols with another Layer 3 device. Figure 5-1 illustrates a common routed mode configuration where the NGFW is routing between the outside Internet network and the inside trusted network.

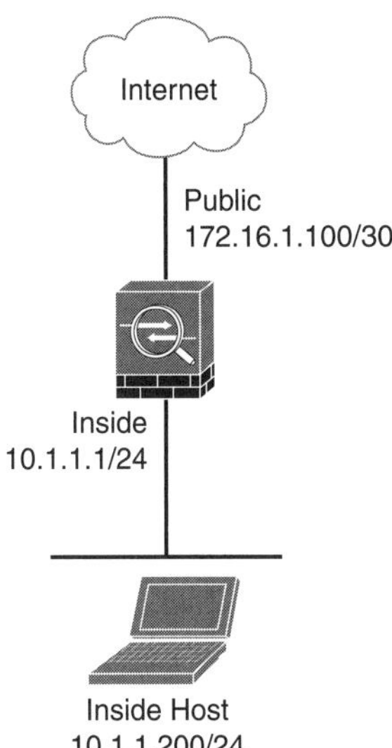

Figure 5-1 *NGFW in Routed Mode*

Transparent Mode

A NGFW in transparent mode is inserted at Layer 2, which allows it to function as a "bump in the wire," inspecting and bridging traffic between two or more VLANs. This mode (also known as Layer 2 mode) offers a unique insertion method but requires an understanding of the nuances of this mode of operation as it introduces the concept of bridge groups and the Bridge Virtual Interface (BVI).

A *bridge group* is a group of two or more interfaces where the NGFW bridges traffic. Traffic moving from one interface to another is controlled by using policy. Each bridge group has only one BVI, and it must be in the same subnet as the bridge group member interfaces. The BVI address is used for sourcing frames from the bridge group. Traffic in a bridge group is isolated from traffic in other bridge groups.

Note Because the BVI requires a valid address in the subnet, it is not possible to use /30 network masks.

An FTD NGFW in transparent mode actually bridges between two broadcast domains (VLANs). Unlike devices from other firewall vendors, where both interfaces reside in the same VLAN, an FTD device in transparent mode has interfaces in *different* VLANs. These interfaces, however, are mapped to each other as being part of the *same* bridge group. Due to the unique nature of transparent mode, a CCIE candidate must have an understanding of how Layer 2 protocols like ARP and BPDUs work.

Figure 5-2 shows a basic configuration of two bridge groups, 1 and 2. Note that the subnets are the same on either side of the NGFW.

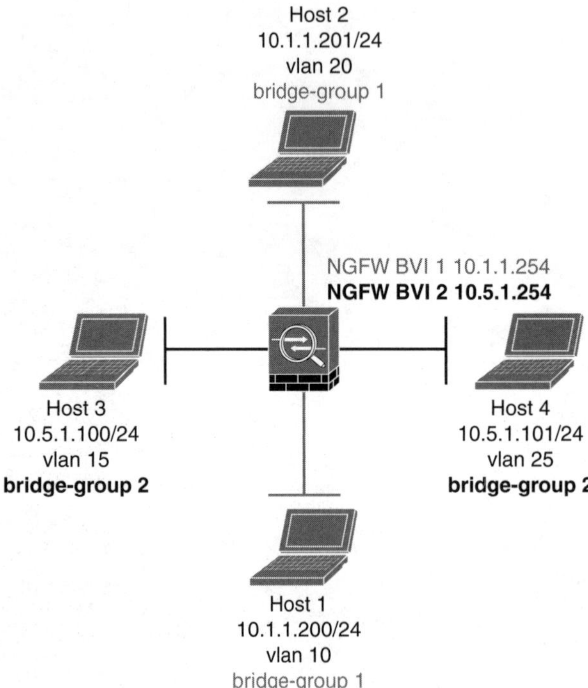

Figure 5-2 *NGFW in Transparent Mode*

The BVI interface allows flexibility for a NGFW in transparent mode. For example, it is possible for the NGFW to act as a DHCPv4 server and perform NAT in this mode of operation. Also consider the following:

- ARPs are allowed through the bridge group in both directions without an access rule. ARP traffic can be controlled by ARP inspection.
- Broadcast and multicast traffic can be passed using access rules.
- Using EtherType rules, AppleTalk, IPX, BPDUs, and MPLS can be allowed.
- Dynamic routing protocols and VPN traffic can be passed through the ASA in Layer 2 mode.
- Management interfaces cannot be members of a bridge group.

This last item is important to note as the NGFW is not actually participating in the VPN traffic or routing protocol when configured in transparent mode. Instead, it is allowing the traffic to pass between the two entities. It is a common data center deployment to place a transparent mode NGFW between two routers. The routers are peered to each other, but the NGFW provides stateful inspection and access control of traffic.

BPDUs are passed by default to prevent spanning-tree loops. However, when using failover, it may be beneficial to block BPDUs using an EtherType rule in order to minimize switch ports from going into a blocking state. More details on that can be found later in this chapter, in the section "High Availability."

Note Some features, such as DHCP relay and remote access VPN termination, are not supported in transparent mode.

Adding a Device to the FMC

After choosing a firewall mode, the system configuration is processed, and then you can add the device to the FMC. This requires registering the FTD device with the management center by using the following command:

```
configure manager add FMC hostname/address registration {key}
```

The *registration-key* must be the same in both the device and the FMC. After the process completes successfully, you are ready to log in to the FMC and add the FTD device to the FMC, using the appropriate key. Select the proper licensing to complete the registration process.

Figure 5-3 illustrates the relationship between the FMC and a managed device.

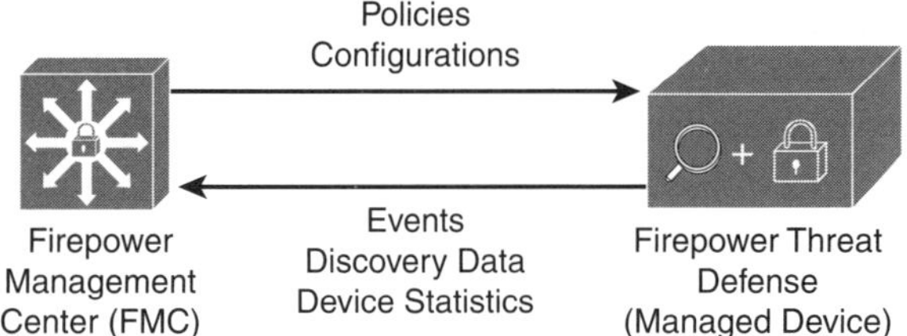

Figure 5-3 *FMC Communication with a Managed Device*

Once the managed FTD device is properly registered, you are ready to configure your NGFW by using the FMC.

Interface Configuration

A big change with FTD is that configuration is managed by using the FMC and not the CLI. With little exception, nearly all device configuration is managed by using the FMC. The advantage to this model is that the FMC manages the policy configurations for multiple devices while simultaneously collecting event data and statistics. Depending on the hardware platform, limited CLI functionality is available through the console, but configuration is controlled by the FMC.

Note Different platforms have different options when it comes to management interfaces. Some use shared physical interfaces. Please consult the *Cisco Configuration Guide* for more information at https://www.cisco.com/c/en/us/td/docs/security/firepower/601/configuration/guide/fpmc-config-guide-v601.html.

Before we get too deep into the NGFW discussion, you need to ensure that your management interfaces are properly configured. You have already set up the management interface as part of the initial first boot process, since it is required for FMC communication. This connectivity was confirmed during the FMC device registration process. If the FMC is not able to reach the device, go back to the console CLI and check the configuration. If needed, change the device management address in the CLI by using the **configure network** command.

The diagnostic interface is an optional secondary management interface that can be used for RADIUS and LDAP external authentication, SNMP, syslog, or inbound SSH. It consumes a physical port on the device (device-dependent) and is often used when security policy does not allow other data interfaces to receive inbound authentication requests, such as SSH.

Figure 5-4 shows the diagnostic interface on a lab FTD device under Devices > Device Management > Interfaces.

Device | Routing | Interfaces | Inline Sets | DHCP

Sta...	Interface	Logical Name	Type	Security
	Ethernet1/5		Physical	
	Ethernet1/6		Physical	
	Ethernet1/8	diagnostic	Physical	
	Ethernet1/2	inside	Physical	inside
	Ethernet1/1	outside	Physical	outside

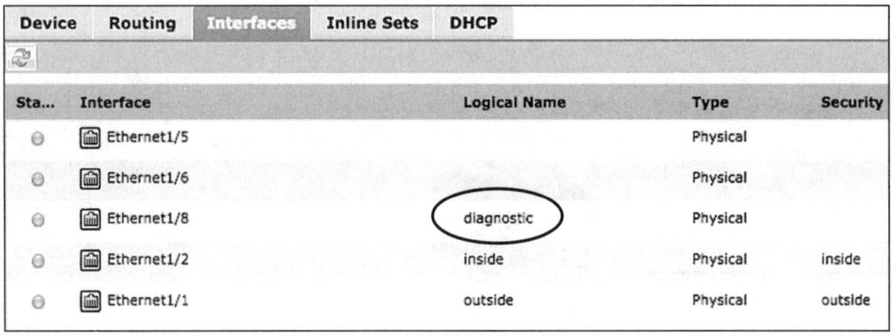

Figure 5-4 *FTD Diagnostic Interface*

Now you are ready to configure the NGFW data interfaces. As you saw earlier in this chapter, the firewall mode determines how the data interfaces function. There are two interface modes:

- Regular firewall mode
- IPS-only mode

Interface modes outline the capabilities of an interface. Firewall mode interfaces function like a traditional firewall by normalizing traffic, maintaining TCP state, and so on. IPS mode bypasses many of the firewall checks and allows the interface to support NGIPS security policies. IPS-only interfaces are deployed in two ways:

- Inline set with optional tap mode
- Passive or ERSPAN passive

An *inline set* is an interface pair that acts as a "bump in the wire." The interface pairs are transparent to adjacent network devices and retransmit traffic out of the inline set unless that traffic is dropped due to policy. The optional tap mode functions in a similar manner except that it receives a copy of the traffic. Inline sets actively process live traffic, while tap mode analyzes copied traffic but still processes it with inline rules.

Passive or ERSPAN passive is similar to tap mode except that it requires a switch SPAN or mirror port to function. Whereas inline sets with tap mode copy the traffic that is seen through the inline set, passive mode interfaces are dependent on the switch or mirror port to supply the traffic source. This allows FTD greater flexibility where security inspection is required but due to other reasons can't be deployed actively inline. ERSPAN is a method of routing SPAN traffic through the network with GRE encapsulation. ERSPAN interfaces are allowed only in NGFW routed mode.

The choice between inline set interfaces and passive interfaces is usually governed by the balance between security policy and network efficiency. For example, an inline set may add latency to network traffic, which may be undesirable in high-transaction, low-latency networks. Passive mode allows traffic from other parts of the network to be directed for security inspection.

Figure 5-5 shows the interface type configuration drop-down box. The option None implies a firewall mode interface. This is configured in the FMC under Devices > Device Management > Interfaces.

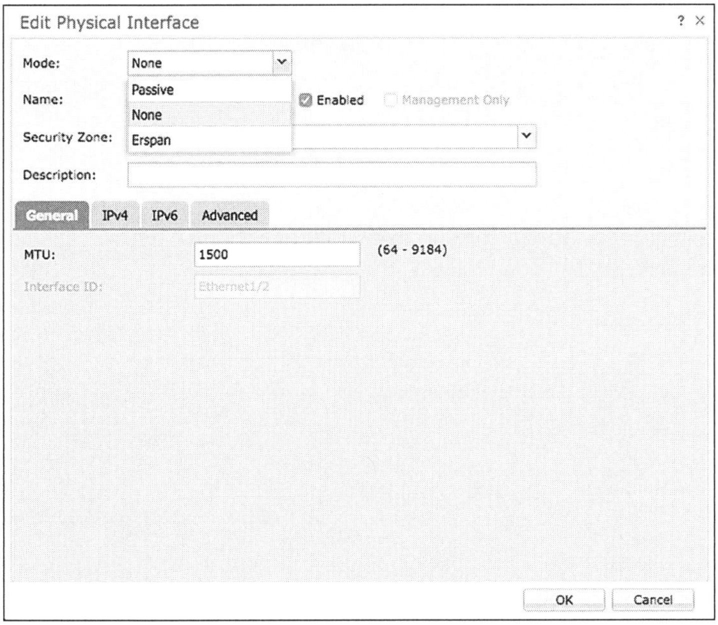

Figure 5-5 *FTD Interface Mode Selection*

Security Zones

The Firepower NGFW uses a zone-based security policy model in which each interface must be part of a security zone. Policy is applied to each zone in a single direction. Unlike with the ASA, there is no concept of security levels in Firepower because traffic is applied directionally to a security policy, and traffic is never permitted in any direction by default.

Zones are configured by using the Objects > Object Management page or during interface configuration.

Figure 5-6 shows the interface configuration under Objects > Object Management > Interface.

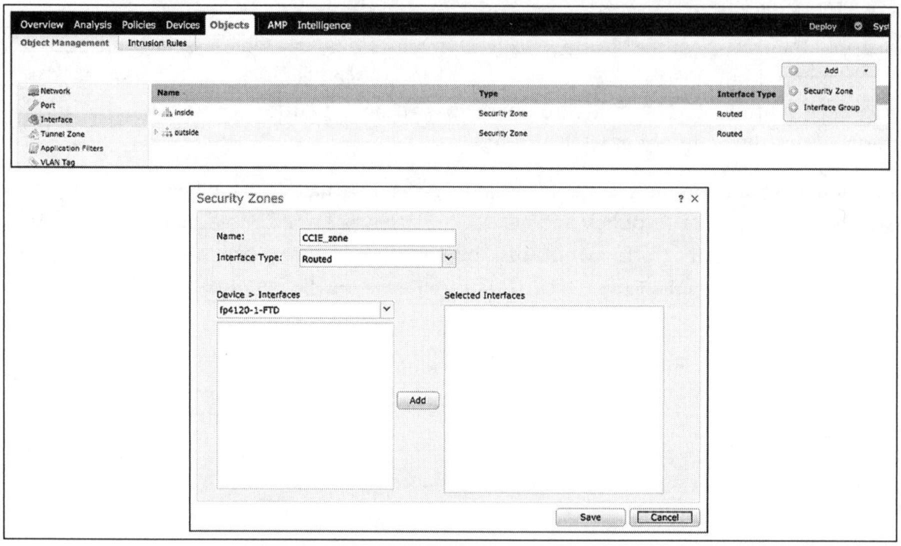

Figure 5-6 *FTD Security Zone Configuration*

Interface Addressing

Once the physical characteristics of an interface are set, you can configure address information and verify security zones. IPv4 and IPv6 addresses are configured by using the Edit Physical Interface page, as shown in Figure 5-7.

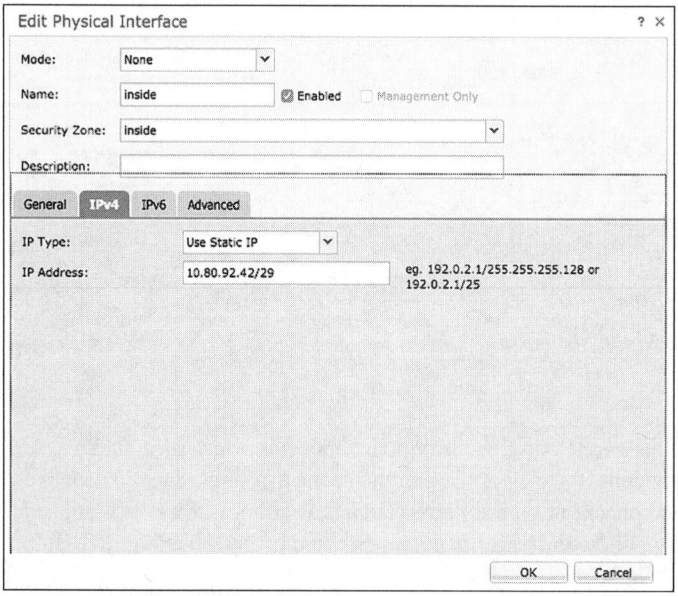

Figure 5-7 *FTD Zone and Address Configuration*

High Availability

In today's networks, there is little room for a single point of failure. Network redundancy and system high availability are required in order to meet requirements for application assurance. The Cisco NGFW offers a robust set of high-availability features to meet customer needs, as discussed in the following sections.

NGFW Interface High Availability

There are two options for high-availability interface configuration on a NGFW: EtherChannel and redundant interfaces.

EtherChannels are 802.3ad standard port channels where interfaces are bundled together in a channel group, creating a logical interface. The port channel provides link aggregation and interface redundancy. The traffic load is shared across the port channel based on a user-configurable algorithm. Link Aggregation Control Protocol (LACP) is a protocol that dynamically allows interfaces to join or leave a port channel. Without the benefit of LACP, interfaces are statically configured, which adds complexity and operational overhead when trying to modify a port channel as LACP does accommodate this automatically.

Note The chassis-based FTD devices configure EtherChannels by using the Chassis Manager.

Figure 5-8 shows a typical NGFW setup with two port channels (1 and 2) connected to separate switches.

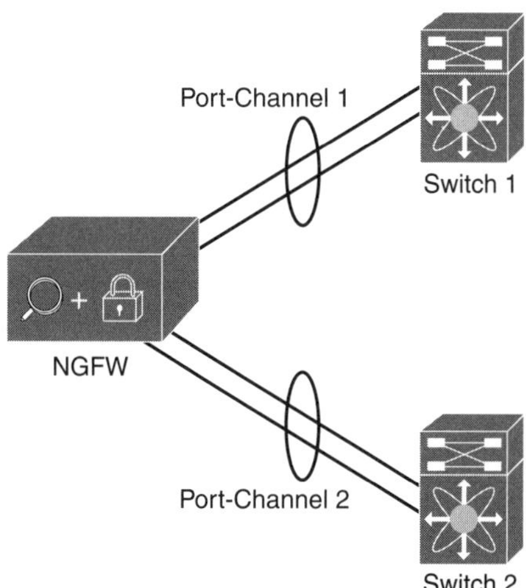

Figure 5-8 *NGFW Port Channels*

A redundant interface is a pair of interfaces that act as a single logical interface. One interface is active, and the other is standby. The standby becomes active only if the previously active interface fails. The downside to using redundant interfaces is that twice the number of physical interfaces are required because the standby interfaces can only be used to monitor the active interface. Therefore, using 802.3ad EtherChannel port channels with LACP is the recommended best practice.

Note The 4100 and 9300 chassis-based devices do not support redundant interfaces.

NGFW System High Availability

Much like the ASA, discussed in Chapter 4, FTD supports both Active/Standby failover on all platforms and clustering on the Firepower 4100 and 9300 platforms. FTD devices do not support Active/Active mode. The operation of Active/Standby on the NGFW is functionally equivalent to the same mode on the ASA. The active unit is actively processing traffic, while the standby unit is standing by in case the active unit fails. A failover condition occurs when the health of the active unit is degraded based on user-configurable options. To maintain continuity if a failover occurs, device configuration is continuously synchronized from the active unit to the standby.

To be configured in a failover pair, the NGFWs must meet some basic requirements. They must be the same model and have the same number and type of physical interfaces. They must run the same software version and be in the same firewall mode (routed or transparent), and they must both be managed devices in the FMC.

Both devices must be reachable to each other with a dedicated network interface. If both devices are in the same data center, it is best practice to connect them with an Ethernet cable. This link, called the *failover link*, is a control plane connection between the two units. The failover link is used for configuration sync, control messages, and other health data to ensure the reachability of the mate. It cannot be used for security inspection. It is possible to connect the two NGFW devices by using a single switch or multiple switches, but Cisco has very specific recommendations.

Failover is, by default, stateless, but stateful failover is an option. Similar to the failover link described earlier, the stateful failover link is a network connection between the two NGFW devices. It is recommended that, if enough physical interfaces exist, this should be a dedicated physical interface on each device in the pair to mitigate potential oversubscription issues between the failover pair. However, if needed, Cisco supports combining both failover and stateful links on the same physical interface. The NGFW supports Auto-MDI/MDIX, so either a straight-through or crossover cable may be used.

Note For a list of recommended options for connecting the failover and stateful failover links across the network, see https://www.cisco.com/c/en/us/td/docs/security/firepower/601/configuration/guide/fpmc-config-guide-v601/fpmc-config-guide-v601_chapter_01100110.html.

High-Availability Configuration

When the two NGFWs are cabled and properly registered to the FMC, you can start the high-availability configuration. Make sure the appropriate licenses are installed on the soon-to-be primary NGFW. The standby unit will receive copies of the licenses from the primary and release any licenses it's currently using back into the Smart Licensing pool. To start the high-availability process, go to Device > Device Management and choose Add High Availability. Next, specify the name of the high-availability pair, the device type, and the primary and secondary units, as shown in Figure 5-9.

Figure 5-9 *NGFW Adding High-Availability Pair*

When finished, click Continue to move to the next window, where you configure the high-availability and optional state interfaces. You need to specify the address and mask information for both peers and determine whether you want the peer communications to be encrypted using IPsec. There is an option to use the same physical interface pair for both the high-availability link and state. The state and failover link configurations are shown in Figure 5-10.

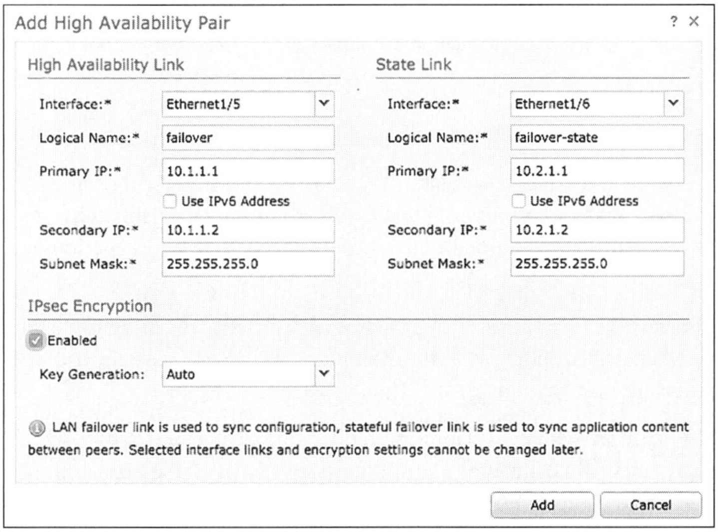

Figure 5-10 *NGFW High Availability Link Configuration*

As mentioned earlier in this chapter, FTD clustering is supported only on the Firepower 4100 and 9300 chassis. This feature is covered for the ASA in detail in Chapter 4. It should not surprise you that FTD clustering is functionally identical to ASA clustering since this feature was ported from ASA. Because this feature is covered in Chapter 4, we provide a summary of operations and highlight the differences in this section.

Tip The Firepower 4100 and 9300 interfaces are configured using the Chassis Manager, not using the FMC.

Clustering provides three advantages over Active/Standby failover:

- All units are actively forwarding traffic.
- Clustering is deployed between two or more units.
- Capacity can be expanded as needed.

Much like A/S, clustering syncs the configuration from the primary to the secondary unit(s). This allows the cluster to be managed as one logical entity, which simplifies operations. Just as with the ASA, the cluster has three different roles for operation: Director, Owner, and Forwarder. Asymmetric traffic flows are redirected back to the Owner unit through the cluster control plane link.

There are some differences between ASA clustering and FTD clustering. For example, FTD supports intra-chassis clustering (that is, between units in the same chassis) and inter-chassis clustering. The clustering configuration is deployed by using the Chassis Manager and then added to the FMC when the individual units are registered with the FMC.

Note See Chapter 4 for a more detailed discussion of the clustering feature.

Routing in FTD

Like any other network device, the Firepower NGFW supports both static and dynamic routing. Static routes are manually configured, and dynamic routes are exchanged by routing protocols. Transparent firewall mode does not route as the NGFW is functioning as a traditional bridge at Layer 2.

As is standard on security devices, FTD separates management interface routing from data interface routing. Management interfaces (for example, SSH) do not route traffic through the NGFW; they are merely for accessing the device.

Like the ASA, a NGFW supports equal-cost multipath (ECMP) routing. Traffic is load-balanced across up to three equal cost routes configured statically or learned dynamically. Unlike with some Cisco devices, ECMP is not supported across multiple interfaces on a NGFW.

Configuring static routing is straightforward in the FTD. Use the Devices > Device Management menu and click the Add Route button to open a configuration page, as shown in Figure 5-11.

> **Note** There are much more definitive guides on how these routing protocols work on Cisco's website. This section only briefly covers their use in terms of the configuration.

Figure 5-11 *NGFW Static Route Configuration*

Static routes are configured by interface. The destination networks are represented by objects in the GUI. The green plus sign allows you to configure new network objects without leaving the window. In Figure 5-11, the static route is pointing to the DMZ network through a gateway at 10.1.1.254. Route tracking could optionally be enabled. Unlike dynamically learned routes, static routes remain in the routing table unless the associated NGFW interface goes down. Route tracking is a feature whereby ICMP echo requests are sent to a monitoring address. Typically this is an address on the gateway or ISP. As long as ICMP echo replies are received, the route is installed; otherwise, the backup route is used.

FTD supports the most common routing protocols in use today: OSPFv2 and OSPFv3, RIPv1 and RIPv2, and BGP. All routing protocol support is configured by using Devices > Device Management on the Routing tab.

OSPF Non-Stop Forwarding (NSF) support allows the NGFW to support both IETF and Cisco NSF capabilities. The router can continue forwarding known routes if the NGFW experiences a failover scenario. NSF preserves uptime and reachability for network hosts. The NGFW also supports two OSPF processes running concurrently, which allows two separate OSPF databases to be learned. This is commonly found in scenarios where a router is required to play a different OSPF role in two different OSPF networks.

BGP is supported for both IPv4 and IPv6 networks. Compared to configuration on IOS devices, the BGP configuration on a NGFW is considerably easier—assuming that the user has a good working knowledge of BGP. Figure 5-12 shows a NGFW BGP configuration.

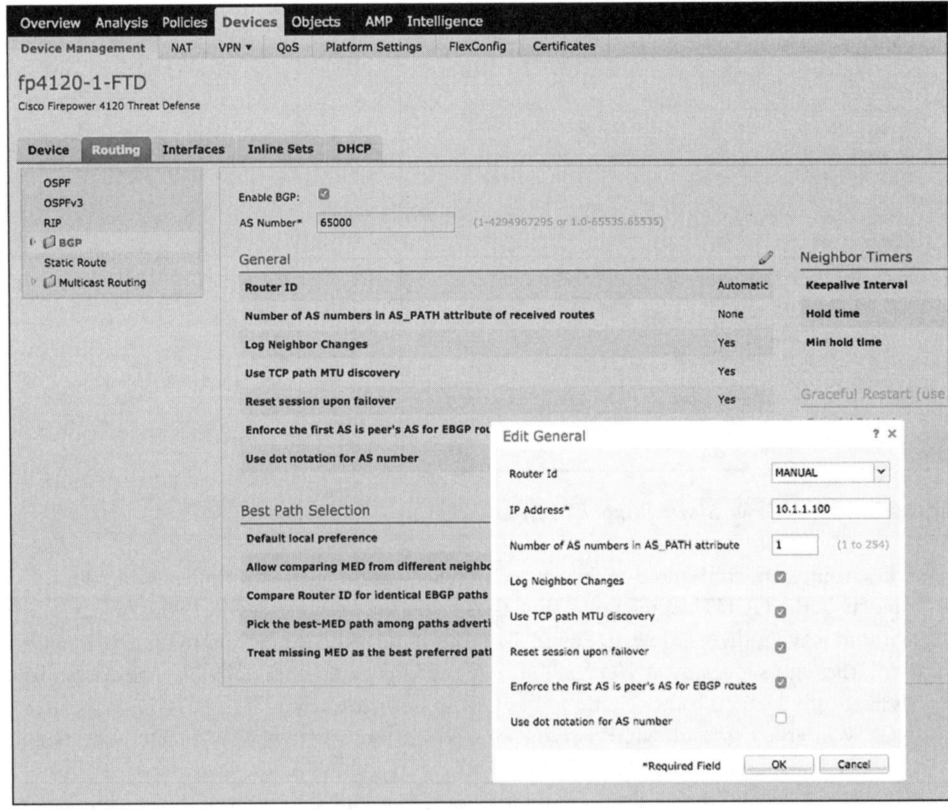

Figure 5-12 *NGFW BGP Configuration*

RIP is seen much less in production networks than are OSPF and BGP. This is mainly due to its perceived inability to scale for large networks. Unlike OSPF and BGP, RIP is very easy to configure and requires very little planning. FTD supports both RIPv1 and RIPv2, as shown in Figure 5-13. Notice how much less configuration is required for RIP than is needed for BGP and OSPF.

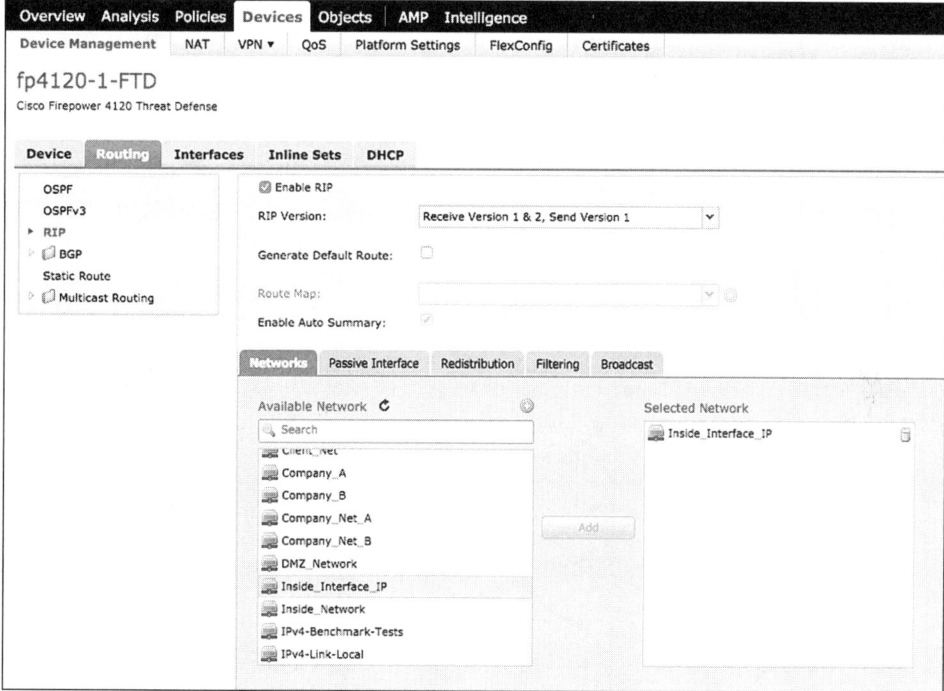

Figure 5-13 *NGFW RIP Configuration*

Note FTD supports EIGRP configuration by using the FMC FlexConfig option. FlexConfig isn't covered here because it is a newer feature not supported in the current lab blueprint.

Network Address Translation (NAT)

NAT is covered in both Chapter 4 (for the ASA) and Chapter 7, "IOS Firewall and Security Features." Both of those chapters go into detail, highlighting its usage and operation as well as different types of NAT (for example, static versus dynamic NAT, PAT, and so on). This section summarizes the NAT options for NGFW, assuming that you already have an understanding of the basic types of NAT and their differences.

The FMC supports two different types of NAT policies: Firepower NAT policy and Threat Defense NAT policy. FTD supports only the latter because the former is only compatible with the 7000 and 8000 series Firepower appliances. The NAT features in FTD were inherited from the ASA code, so the functionality is nearly identical. It may be helpful to refer to Chapter 4, which provides considerable detail on NAT rule order and functionality. This section summarizes the points for clarity.

The NGFW supports two types of NAT: auto NAT and manual NAT. Auto NAT is recommended for basic NAT functions since the NAT policy is applied to a network object. Each rule applies to either the source or destination of a packet but not both. Unlike the ASA CLI, the auto NAT rules are not visible when viewing the network object. You apply NAT to an interface or to a wildcard by using the keyword **any**. Proxy ARP is enabled by default but can be disabled if necessary. This function is discussed in detail in Chapter 4.

Manual NAT combines both source and destination addresses in a single rule, but the destination address is optional. This allows for more complex configuration as different translations can be manipulated based on source and destination address matches. Manual NAT also scales better than Auto NAT because its policies can be associated with network object groups. Auto NAT can only be associated with the individual objects.

NGFW NAT is applied on a top-down, first-match basis, so the order of the rules is important. There are three sections in the NAT rule table:

- **NAT Rules Before:** This is recommended for the most specific match.
- **Auto NAT Rules:** Static rules are matched first and then dynamic rules.
- **NAT Rules After:** This is recommended for the least specific match.

This order is shown in the NGFW NAT table in Figure 5-14 under Devices > NAT.

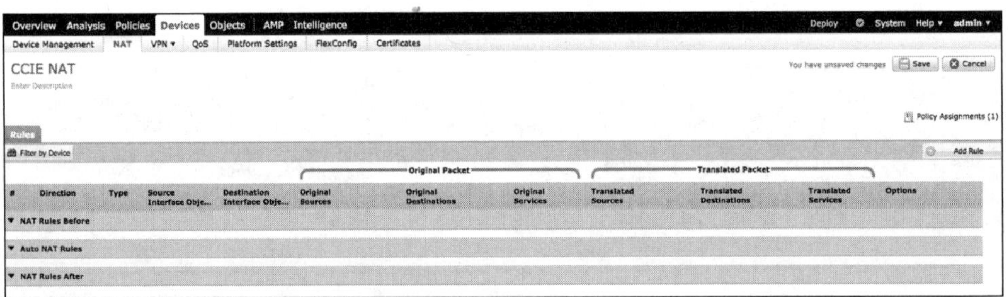

Figure 5-14 *NGFW Empty NAT Table*

The easiest and most common NAT configuration is dynamic PAT. PAT is the most address-conservative of the NAT options because it requires only a single global IP address. Port numbers are used to differentiate the return traffic and translate it back to the originating host. It is common to use the NGFW interface address for PAT and conserve another address from the global pool. Figure 5-15 shows a dynamic PAT configuration with a source of network object **Inside_Network**, using the interface IP address for translation when traffic is destined for anything on interface **outside**.

> **Note** This NAT configuration requires the use of interface names, which should not be confused with security zones that have the same names.

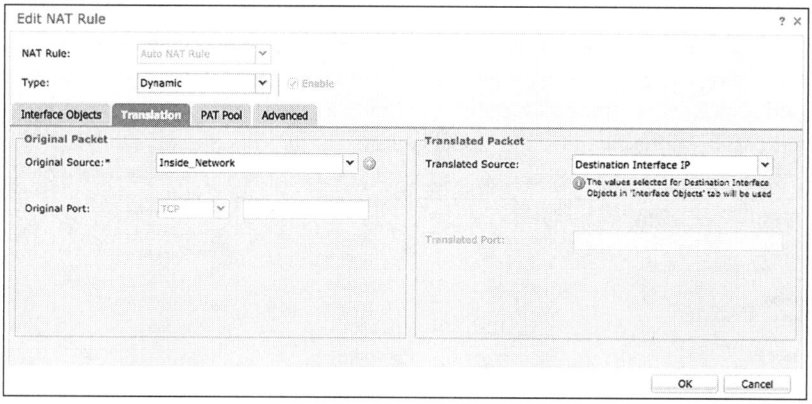

Figure 5-15 *NGFW Dynamic PAT Configuration*

Recall that dynamic NAT uses a pool of global addresses that are dynamically assigned to source addresses requiring translation. They are not statically defined because the NAT engine is pulling addresses from the global pool. This configuration is less common for Internet connectivity due to the shortage of globally routable IPv4 addresses but is a good option for connectivity when two companies have overlapping address space. Because most companies use RFC 1918 addresses for internal hosts, there is more chance of overlapping addresses. Dynamic NAT is also used because some applications do not work properly with PAT. Multimedia applications often open ephemeral ports after the initial handshake, and for that reason, dynamic or static NAT is required.

Figure 5-16 shows a dynamic NAT policy in a NGFW that translates from the Trusted_Hosts network to NAT_Pool-2.

Note The NGFW NAT configuration does not permit the translated source to be a subnet. It must be a network object with a range of addresses.

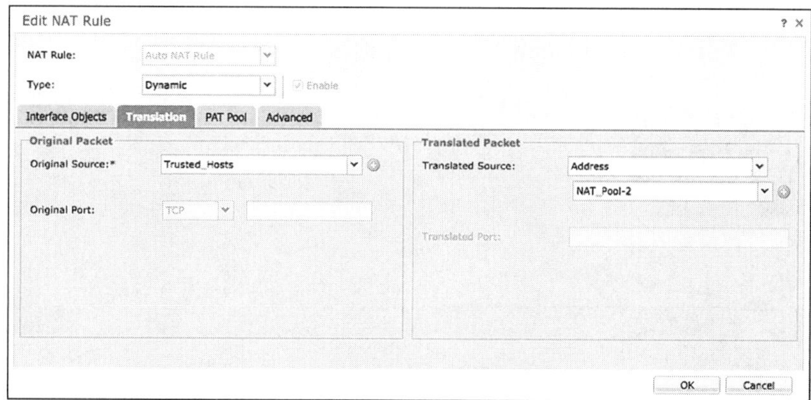

Figure 5-16 *NGFW Dynamic NAT Configuration*

Static NAT can be configured through auto NAT or manual NAT. In the static auto NAT example shown in Figure 5-17, you want host Server_A to be reachable using global address Server_A_WWW. This allows any host on the outside interface to access Server_A by the statically defined global address. Any outbound traffic sourced by Server_A will also be represented by the global address.

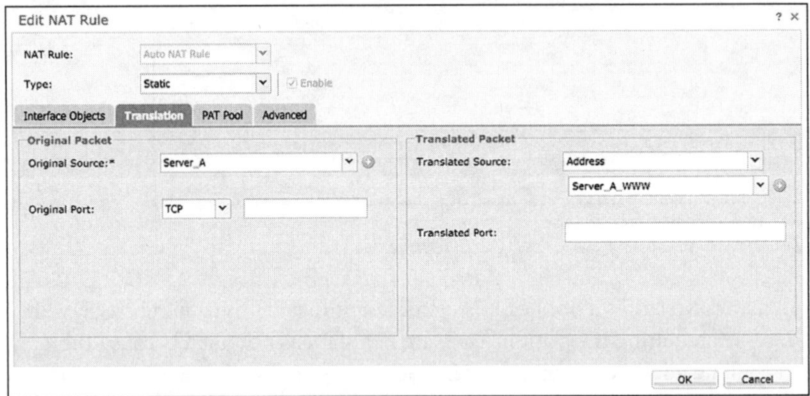

Figure 5-17 *NGFW Static Auto NAT Configuration*

Sometimes the translation rules get more complex. In the topology shown in Figure 5-18, the NGFW is connected to two different companies, A and B. Web Host requires a NAT policy that translates its address into an address based on the destination network. Manual NAT is capable of doing this.

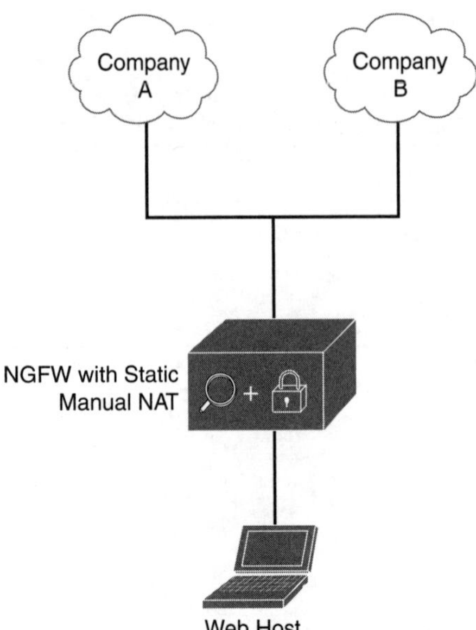

Figure 5-18 *Web Host Manual NAT Example*

When Web Host goes to Company_A, it gets translated into the Net_A address space, but if Web Host communicates to Company_B, it gets translated to the Net_B space. In both cases, the NAT policy is based on the destination address. For this to work properly, you need two manual NAT statements configured. Prior to the NAT configuration, network objects were created to represent the destination network (Companies A and B) and the translated addresses (Net_A and Net_B).

The first NAT statement is shown in Figure 5-19.

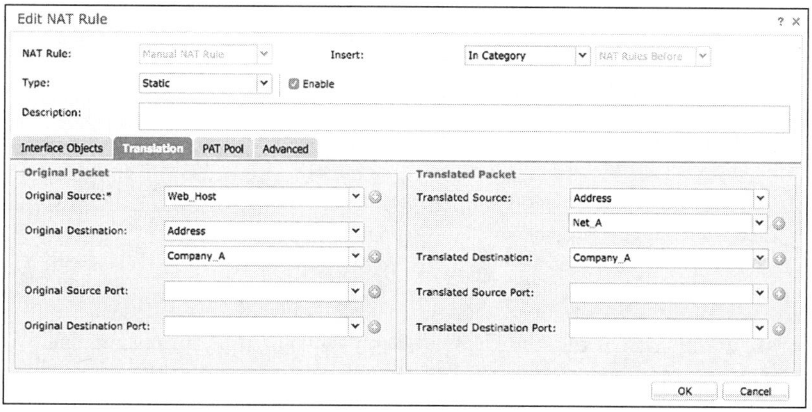

Figure 5-19 *NGFW Manual NAT Configuration, Part 1*

The second NAT statement is shown in Figure 5-20. Notice that you can disable manual NAT rules by deselecting the Enable check box. There is also an option to place the manual NAT above or below a rule in a different section, if necessary, as shown in Figure 5-20.

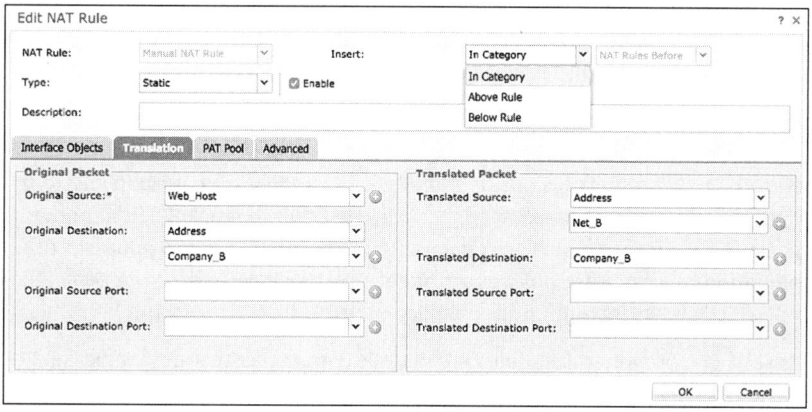

Figure 5-20 *NGFW Manual NAT Configuration, Part 2*

Figure 5-21 shows the complete NAT table. Note that the two manual NAT statements are at the top of the table, in the NAT Rules Before section. You could have placed them in the NAT Rules After section, but that would be less efficient. The auto NAT rules land in the Auto NAT Rules section. Pay attention to the directional arrows on the left-hand side that indicate the direction of the NAT translation.

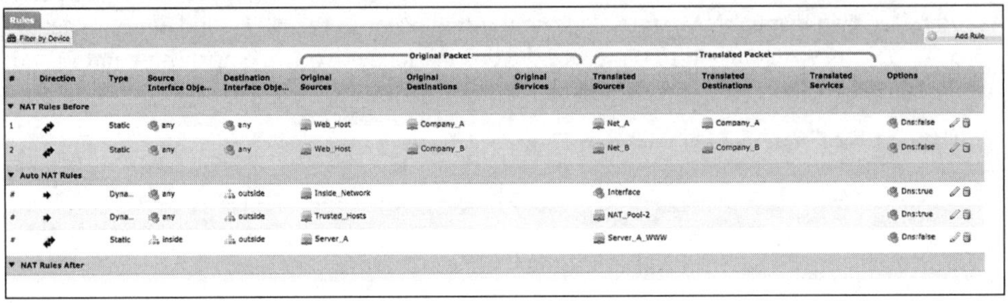

Figure 5-21 *NGFW NAT Table*

When you are satisfied that the NAT table looks accurate, click Save to allow the NAT policy to be used by managed devices.

Note Changes made in the FMC are pushed to the managed devices only after you have deployed the configuration by clicking the Deploy button. Clicking the Save button saves the configuration changes, but you need to click Deploy in order to put them into service.

Access Control Policies

Access policies are very important in the FTD architecture as they dictate the inspection actions for network traffic. There are different types of policies available in the FTD, but the most important type is access control policies. Other access policies supplement access control by enabling more inspection engines and providing additional configuration parameters for advanced traffic inspection. It's easiest to think of an access control policy as the master configuration that relies on subpolicies when advanced inspection methods are required.

A policy can optionally define a set of rules that are processed according to their numeric value, starting at number one. Only one policy can be deployed per managed device, and the FMC alerts you if a policy is out of date. Policies can be hierarchical in nature (if using domains) and may support top-down inheritance in order to streamline the policy creation process. Newly installed systems contain a base policy in order to jump-start the policy configuration process. Base policies are like templates because they can be copied and exported, which allows for a more scalable deployment.

Policies consist of one or more rules. Rules provide the *conditions* that determine the match criteria and *actions* that determine how to process the traffic. For traffic to match a given rule, all conditions must be met, so it is a recommended practice to put the most specific rules at the top of the policy (with the lowest numbers).

Rule type as part of policy is important as it determines the rule order processing. Security intelligence traffic filtering, SSL inspection, and user identification all occur before access control rules evaluate traffic. The reason for this is to make traffic inspection more efficient by evaluating traffic with policies that do not consume many resources. For example, a security intelligence policy applies a blacklist (known bad traffic) before other more computationally intensive policies. After all, why waste CPU on traffic that you already know is bad?

There are seven possible rule actions:

- **Allow:** Matching traffic is allowed but with more inspection.
- **Trust:** Matching traffic is allowed without further inspection.
- **Monitor:** Traffic is tracked and logged but is otherwise not affected, as it continues to be inspected.
- **Block:** Matching traffic is blocked without further inspection.
- **Block with Reset:** Intrusion policy that blocks traffic and sends a TCP reset.
- **Interactive Block:** Forces users to click through a block page in order to reach website.
- **Interactive Block with Reset:** Same as Interactive Block above but resets connection.

If traffic does not match a rule, the rule resorts to a preconfigured default action. There are three types of default system policy actions:

- **Access Control: Block All Traffic:** Blocks traffic with no further inspection.
- **Network Discovery Only:** Allows traffic and is used for discovery process.
- **Intrusion Prevention:** Blocking and allowing are determined by an intrusion policy.

Access control policies are configured under Policies > Access Control > Access Control. Figure 5-22 shows how to create a new access control policy.

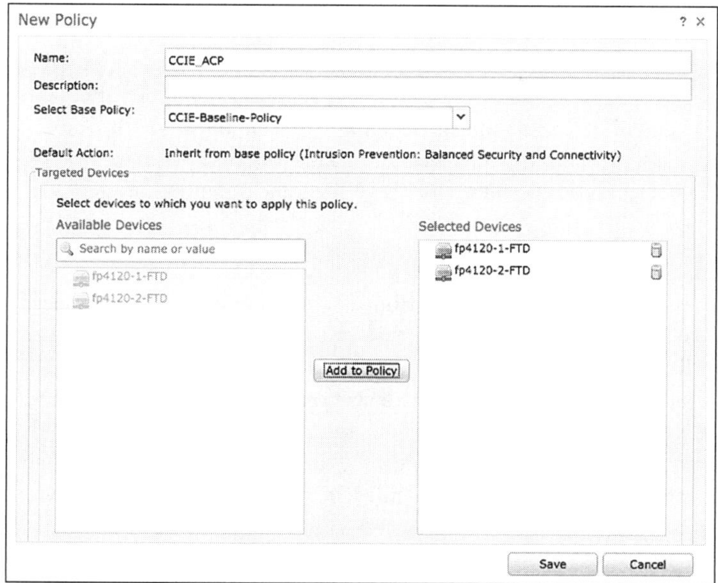

Figure 5-22 *New Access Control Policy Configuration*

Each policy must have a unique name and may optionally use a base policy. Figure 5-22 uses CCIE-Baseline-Policy as the base policy, as it has already been preconfigured with default rule settings. This is completely optional—but in the real world it saves a lot of effort tuning policies and rules.

Notice what happens when you deselect the base policy. As shown in Figure 5-23, you now have to choose a default action for the policy.

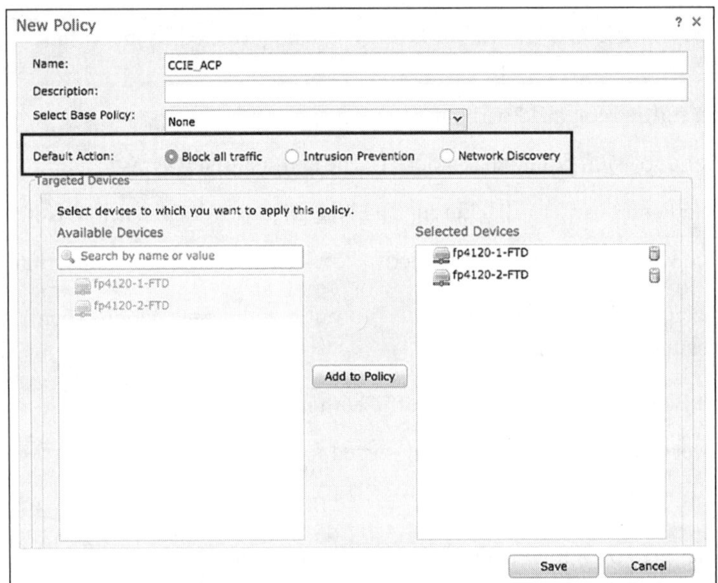

Figure 5-23 *Default Action Policy Configuration*

Remember that the default action applies to traffic that does not match a rule. The new policy in this example does not have rules configured yet, so this is an important choice. Network discovery, by default, attempts to map all applications on the network. Your next choice is to decide which devices receive the new policy. Because you use the FMC to manage all security devices, your devices could have the same policy or different versions of the same policy.

You can take a look at some rules in your baseline policy by choosing the edit icon (the pencil) in the Policies > Access Control > Access Control window. Figure 5-24 provides an overview of CCIE-Baseline-Policy. You can see two rules applied, numbered 1 and 2. Both rules are under the Mandatory section, and no rules are in the Default section. All access control rules must appear in one of these two sections. Mandatory rules must be processed first. Usually a mandatory rule is inherited from another policy configuration. If traffic does not match any of the mandatory rules, traffic is checked against the default rules, if present. These identifiers make it easy to prioritize rule order when policy configurations are nested, such as with a global policy and a local policy.

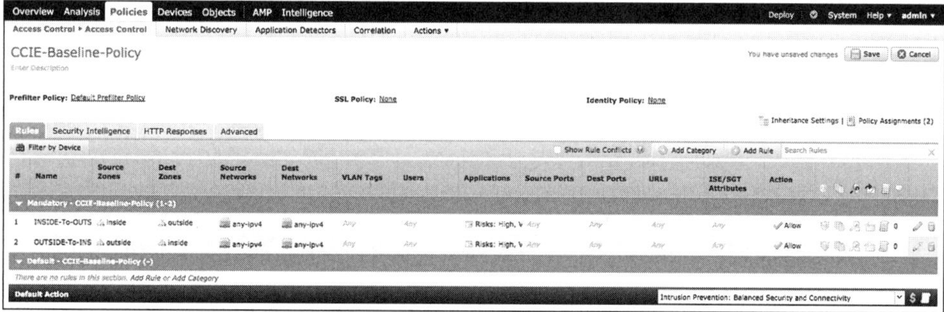

Figure 5-24 *Rules Configuration*

There is a lot of detailed information on this page, despite the fact that it has only two rules. You can see that traffic is processed in both directions, between zones inside and outside for any IPv4 traffic. The only additional condition check is for applications that are high risk or very high risk. You can drill down by clicking the pencil icon to open the Editing Rule window, shown in Figure 5-25.

> **Tip** In the Rules Editor you can move individual rules by clicking and dragging them to new locations. Right-clicking a rule allows you to cut, copy, or paste it. You can also individually enable or disable rules by using this method.

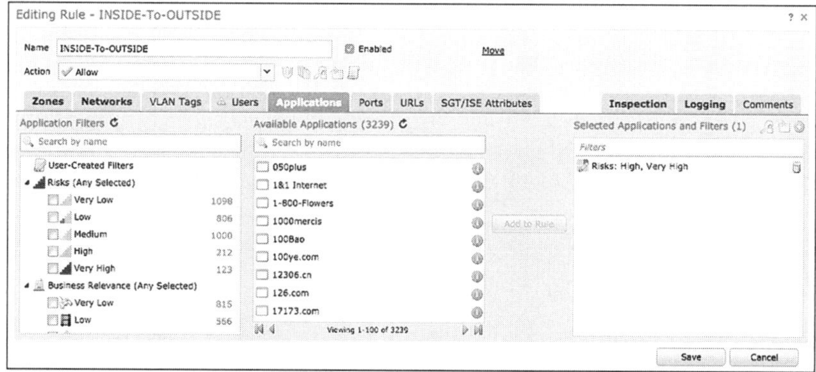

Figure 5-25 *Rule Conditions Configuration*

It may be difficult to see in Figure 5-25, but the name of any tab that has been changed from the default is in bold. This rule is matching on security zone, network address, and application. It also has an intrusion policy set (on the Inspection tab), and logging has been enabled. If all these conditions are met, the traffic action is **Allow**, which subjects the traffic to more inspection, as defined in the intrusion policy. As shown here, rule conditions can be very specific or very general. Now you're ready to dive into the different policy types and their configuration.

Prefilter Policy

The prefilter policy is an access control policy feature that is allowed a priority first pass at inspection. Technically, it's the first phase of the access control policy. It is only supported in FTD and is built on the premise that efficient traffic classification will improve the overall performance of the NGFW. It doesn't have all the advanced features of the standard access control policy, and for that reason, it can reach a verdict much more quickly. Prefiltering is focused on encapsulated (that is, tunneled) traffic. It examines the outer headers while letting more advanced inspection occur on the inner headers. It is configured under Policies > Access Control > Prefilter.

The system uses the default prefilter policy if no custom prefilter policy is configured. The default prefilter policy has a default action to analyze all tunnel traffic. Prefilter rules have three possible actions:

- **Analyze:** Passes traffic to standard access control policies for deeper inspection on inner header
- **Block:** Drops traffic
- **Fastpath:** Permits traffic, with no action taken

Figure 5-26 shows the configuration of a prefilter rule.

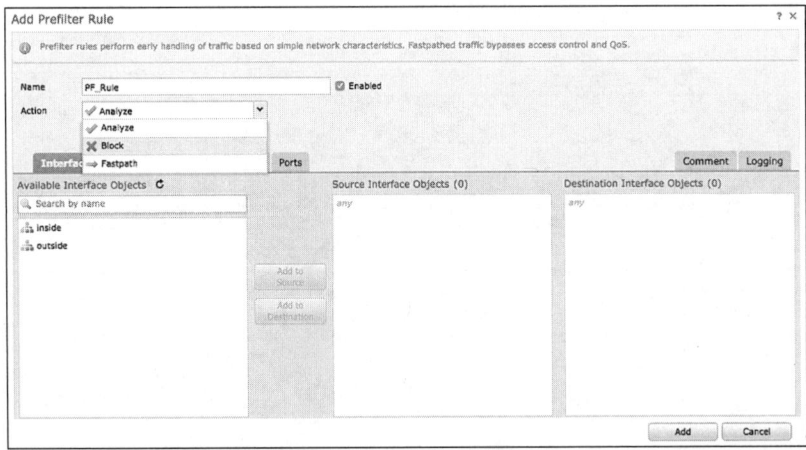

Figure 5-26 *NGFW Prefilter Policy Configuration*

Prefilter policies are unidirectional, and access control policies are bidirectional. Prefilter policies conserve resources that can be used for deeper inspection later in policy processing.

Objects

Similar to the ASA, FTD uses containers called *objects* to build policy. The section "Network Address Translation (NAT)," earlier in this chapter, introduces objects as they are a vital part of NAT policy. Objects in the general sense allow for human-readable descriptions to be placed on data to make it easier to use and understand. Nearly every part of the FMC GUI uses these objects as part of the configuration.

There are many types of objects used in FTD, and they are defined under Objects > Object Management. Many FTD configuration windows have a green plus sign, which allows you to define an object without leaving that configuration area. Figure 5-27 shows the Object Management page.

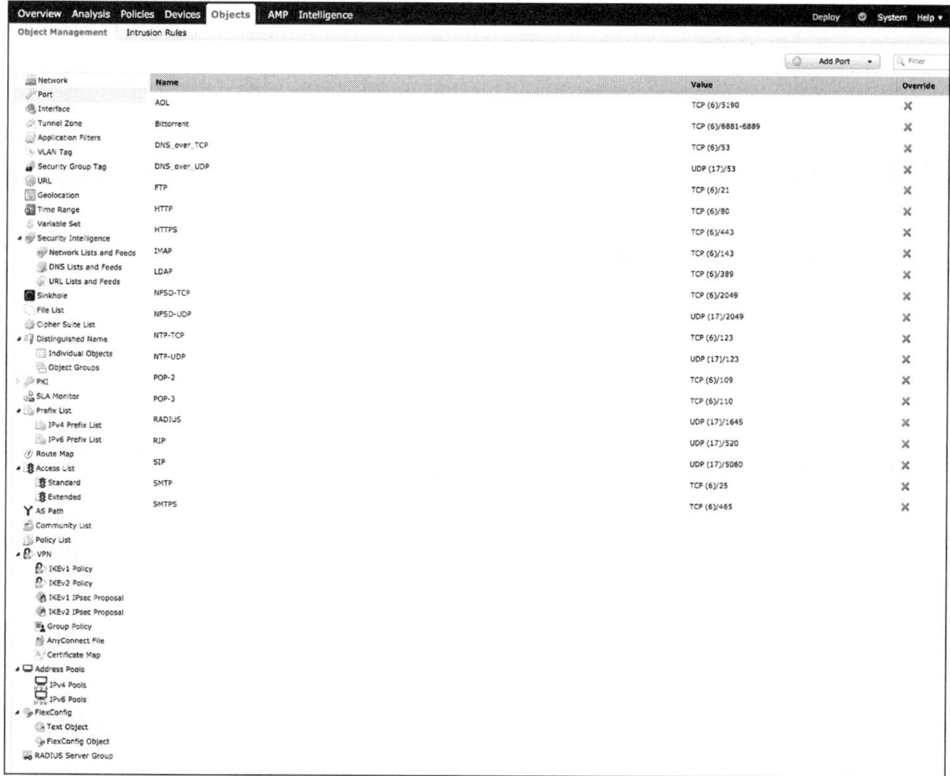

Figure 5-27 *NGFW Object Manager*

An object group is multiple objects within a single construct. Network object groups can be nested up to ten levels deep. Figure 5-28 shows the configuration of a new network group object called All_Company_Nets, which contains multiple network objects.

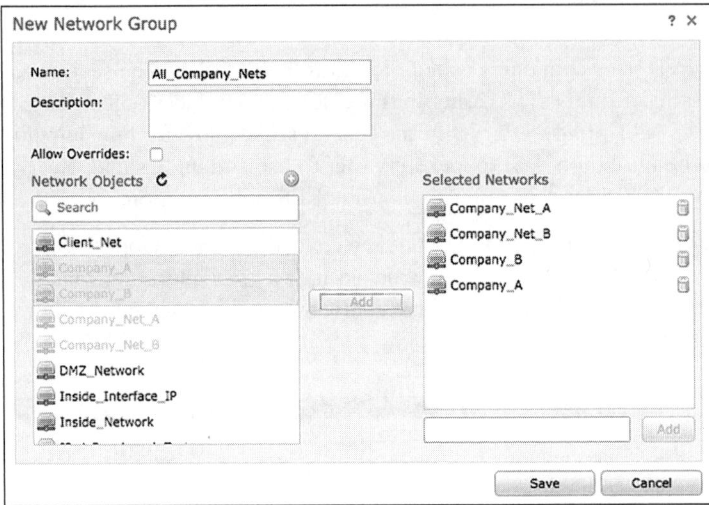

Figure 5-28 *NGFW Network Group Object Configuration*

Object overrides allow an alternate value to be defined for an object to extend its usage. In this manner, an object functions more like a container in that the value defined can pivot based on circumstance.

Note Objects are very powerful tools in FTD. For a much deeper look at how they work, see the latest *FMC Configuration Guide* at https://www.cisco.com/c/en/us/td/docs/security/firepower/601/configuration/guide/fpmc-config-guide-v601.html.

Network Discovery Policy

One of the benefits to FTD is that it can map a network based on the traffic it sees passing through its interfaces. How this process works and to what degree are controlled by the network discovery policy, found under Policies > Network Discovery > Networks. The network discovery policy contains a single rule that is set to discover all application traffic by default. This action is user-configurable and can be modified to discover network assets and users as well. Figure 5-29 shows the network discovery rule being updated to include hosts and user information for all networks.

Network discovery can include NetFlow exported data. The only requirement is that a NetFlow device be defined under Policies > Network Discovery > Advanced. This then adds an additional configuration tab under the Edit Rule option where the NetFlow device is defined. Figure 5-30 shows this configuration option.

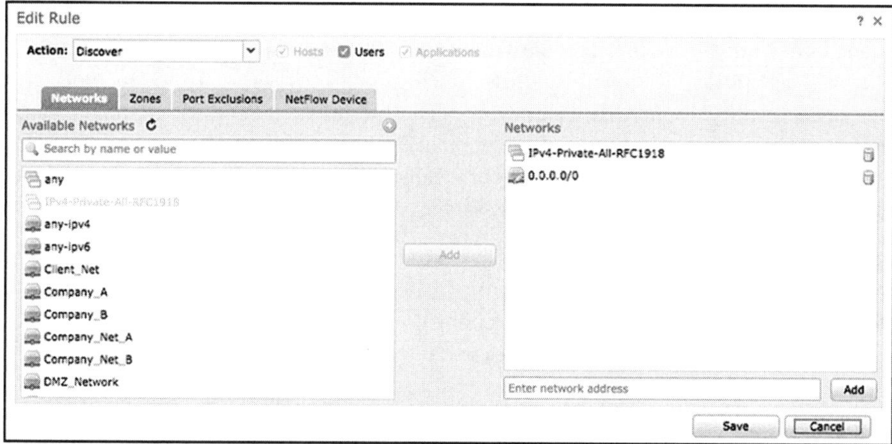

Figure 5-29 *Network Discovery Rule Modification*

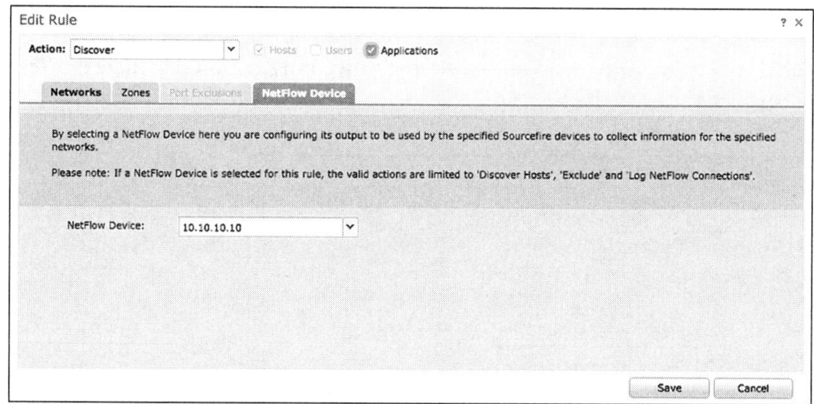

Figure 5-30 *Network Discovery Using NetFlow*

Note The rule enabling NetFlow collection does not support user data collection.

Be aware that the network discovery policy sees only what the access control policy allows it to see; traffic dropped by the access control policy is not processed by network discovery, so having them properly configured is vital for proper network discovery.

Identity Firewall

The previous section highlights the detection features of FTD and how they are configured. A NGFW can be configured to detect network users by analyzing data fields in applications for this information. These users can be mapped into policies and also tied to sources of traffic in order to provide a more comprehensive threat outlook. Security policy was historically based on IP address, which, as you know, is not a good method for determining identity. To increase its efficacy, FTD uses both active and passive methods to validate user identity. An identity policy determines which method is invoked and the order in which conditions are met. Before configuring any policy, make sure that time is synchronized between the FMC and any directory servers with which it will communicate.

The first step in configuring an identity policy is to ensure that at least one realm is configured. A *realm* is one or more Active Directory (AD) or LDAP servers that share the same credentials. At least one realm is required for any user and user group queries, user controls, or active authentication. Once the realm is configured, you can configure the identity policy.

> **Note** For the latest information on which versions of LDAP and AD are supported, consult the *FMC Configuration Guide* at https://www.cisco.com/c/en/us/td/docs/security/firepower/601/configuration/guide/fpmc-config-guide-v601.html.

Realms are configured in the FMC under System > Integration. Figure 5-31 shows a properly configured AD realm. Note that under the Directory configuration tab, there is a Test button you can click to verify the bindings.

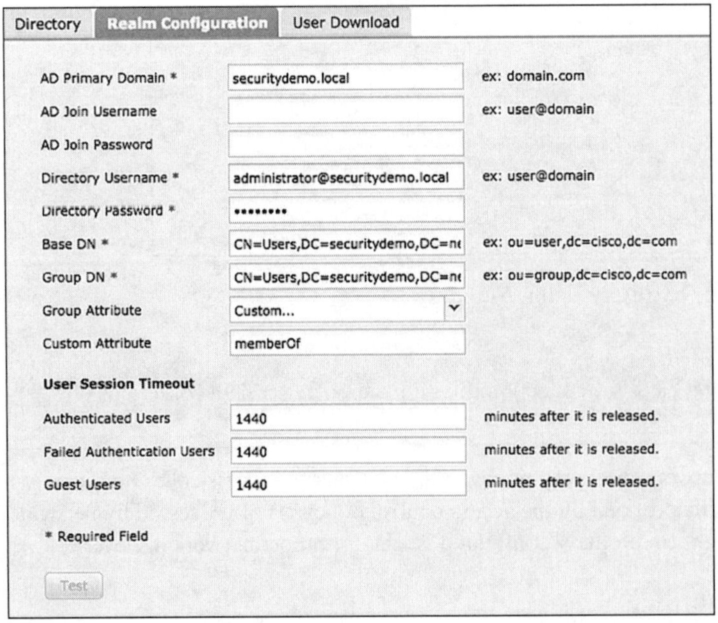

Directory | Realm Configuration | User Download

AD Primary Domain * securitydemo.local ex: domain.com
AD Join Username ex: user@domain
AD Join Password
Directory Username * administrator@securitydemo.local ex: user@domain
Directory Password * ••••••••
Base DN * CN=Users,DC=securitydemo,DC=n ex: ou=user,dc=cisco,dc=com
Group DN * CN=Users,DC=securitydemo,DC=n ex: ou=group,dc=cisco,dc=com
Group Attribute Custom...
Custom Attribute memberOf

User Session Timeout

Authenticated Users 1440 minutes after it is released.
Failed Authentication Users 1440 minutes after it is released.
Guest Users 1440 minutes after it is released.

* Required Field

Test

Figure 5-31 *Realm Configuration*

Once the realm is verified, it is possible to query the directory server and get a current list of users and groups. These users and groups are then used as condition elements in an access control policy rule. Figure 5-32 shows an example of a list retrieved from a lab server.

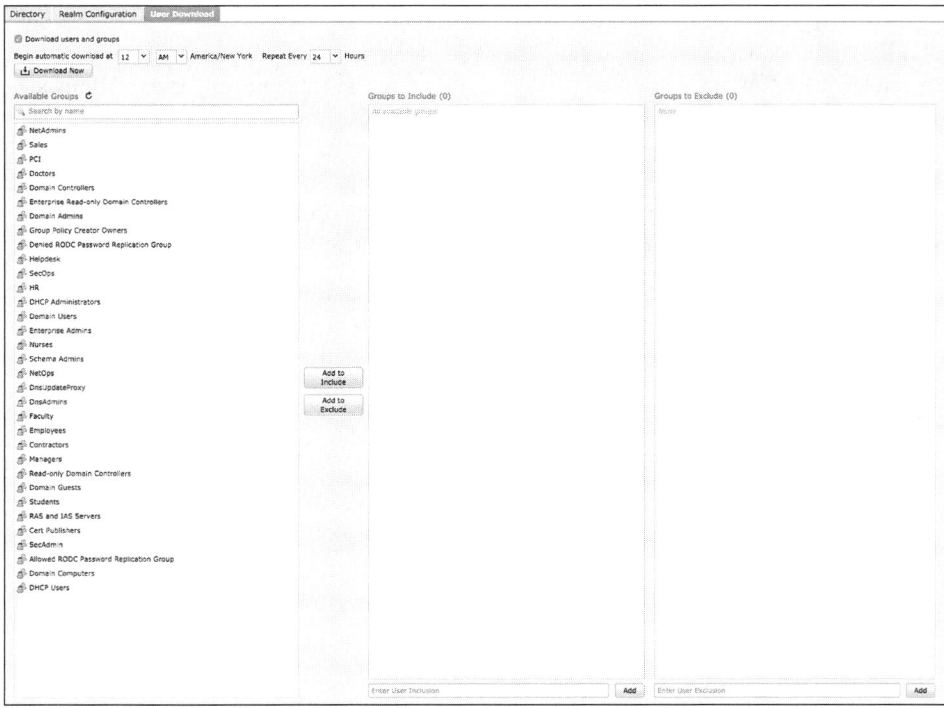

Figure 5-32 *User and Group Query*

Figure 5-33 shows a simple rule that permits any member of group Faculty access to a resource. This is an example of Identity Firewall because the access is granted based on the user and group information in AD and not on the IP address.

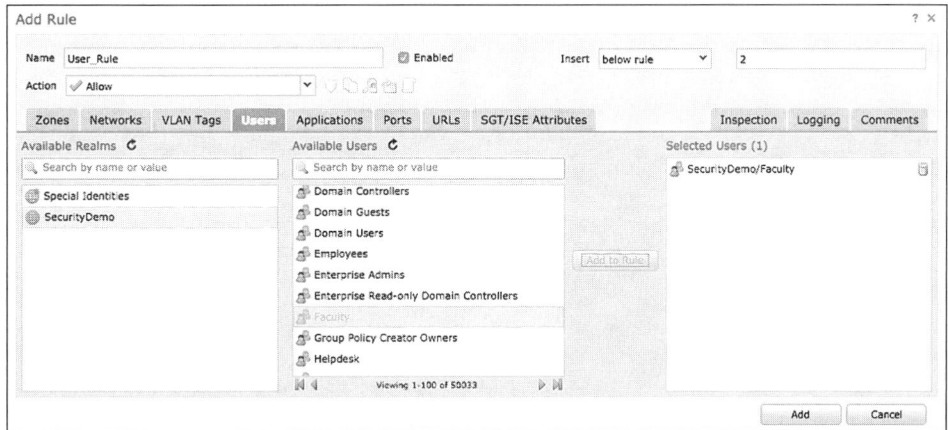

Figure 5-33 *Access Control Based on User Group*

Active Authentication

FTD supports only one method for active authentication: Captive Portal. This portal intercepts traffic and then prompts the user for an access credential in his or her browser. Most people experience this when they are in a public place and want to get Wi-Fi. The portal redirects the user's browser in order to determine the user's identity. FTD works in a similar manner. It requires routed mode interfaces, and the NGFW queries the user for credentials. Only HTTP and HTTPS traffic types are supported. HTTPS traffic requires an additional SSL policy to decrypt the traffic.

The first step in configuring active authentication in a NGFW is to verify the configuration on the Active Authentication tab at Policies > Access Control > Identity. Figure 5-34 shows basic information about web redirection configuration.

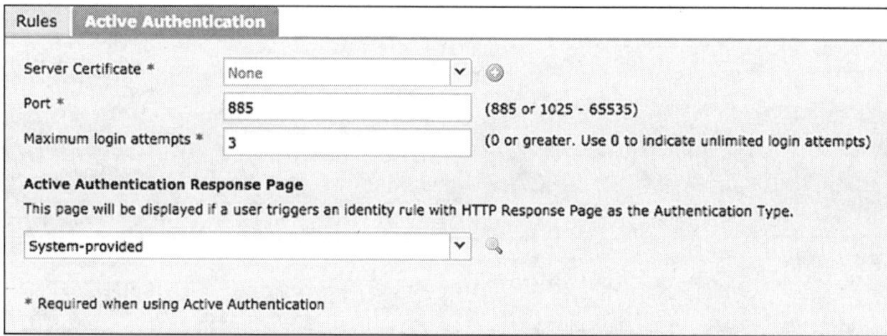

Figure 5-34 *Active Authentication Tab Configuration*

You are now ready to configure your first identity rule under Policies > Access Control > Identity. Figure 5-35 shows a rule named CaptivePortal_Rule that authenticates any traffic sourced from the inside zone against an Active Directory realm named Security Demo, using HTTP Basic.

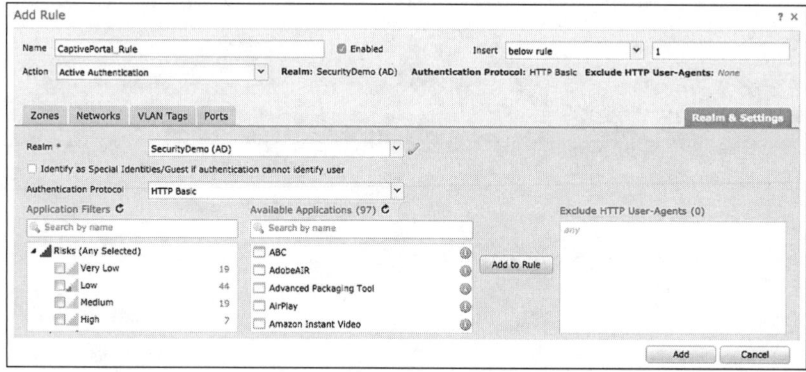

Figure 5-35 *Captive Portal Configuration*

Passive Authentication

Passive authentication relies on other data sources to make informed decisions about user identity, and FTD supports two methods: the user agent and ISE. The User Agent identity source requires a software agent running on a trusted host and some configuration on the Active Directory server. ISE is Cisco's Identity Services Engine, which allows rich metadata to be used as part of policy creation.

> **Tip** Ensure that time is synchronized between the FMC and the directory servers; otherwise, user control policies may not work.

The User Agent option relies on an agent running on a trusted host to gather user logon and logoff information from AD, using Windows Management Instrumentation (WMI). The host must have a configured user account that has privileges to use WMI. Next, the host is configured to point to up to five management consoles with which it will exchange user information. The FMC needs to be configured to point to the host with a hostname or an IP address. This can be found under System > Integration > Identity Sources > User Agent. Figure 5-36 shows this menu and configuration window.

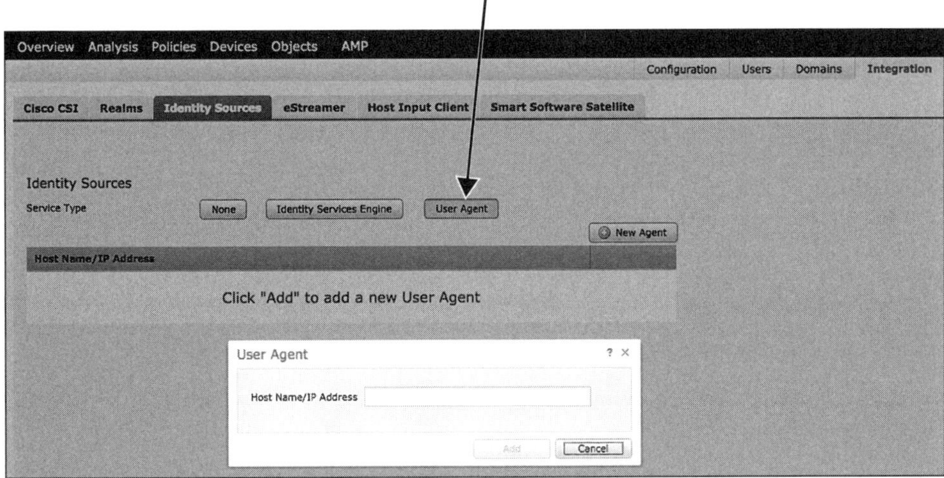

Figure 5-36 *User Agent Configuration*

The user agent monitors users as they log in to the network or authenticate against AD. This includes interactive logins, Remote Desktop logins, file share authentication, and computer accounts. Because this monitoring is happening in real time, it's considered authoritative; that is, new user-to-IP mappings will overwrite previous mappings. The FMC continually checks the user activity database for existing users. If a user is not found, the new user is added to the database. This keeps the identity rules in the access control policy up to date with the latest user information.

Note Please refer to the latest *User Agent Configuration Guide* (https://www.cisco.com/c/en/us/td/docs/security/firesight/user-agent/23/config-guide/Firepower-User-Agent-Configuration-Guide-v2-3.html) for supported host systems and other requirements.

ISE is also considered an authoritative source that uses passive authentication. FTD only supports user control for users authenticated with ISE to AD, despite ISE having the ability to authenticate using other methods. Using ISE as an identity source provides an additional benefit in that ISE attribute data can be used by the FMC. These attributes include security group tags (SGTs), endpoint location attributes (which indicate where the device is), and endpoint profiles (which indicate what the device is). ISE has a built-in API called pxGrid that allows trusted communication between ISE and other nodes.

Note For more information on pxGrid, search Cisco.com and see *Integrated Security Technologies and Solutions, Volume II.*

You can configure FMC-to-ISE communication by clicking the System > Integration > Identity Sources > Identity Services Engine. Figure 5-37 shows FMC-to-ISE configuration details.

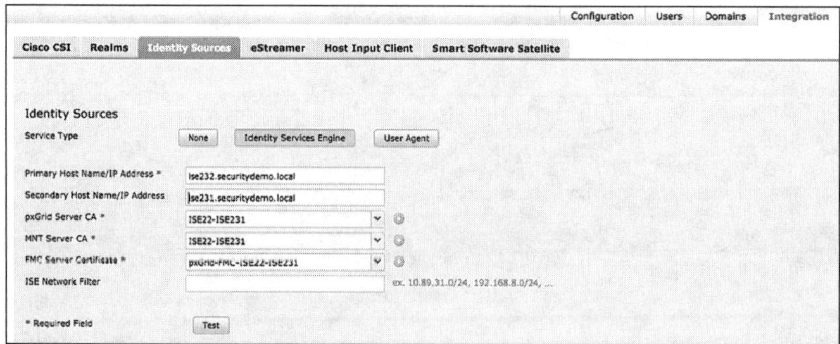

Figure 5-37 *FMC-to-ISE Configuration*

FMC-to-ISE communication is encrypted and therefore requires a trusted certificate authority (CA) to issues keys and signing requests. The CA could be the ISE server or an enterprise root CA such as Verisign. For more information on creating signing requests and installing certificates, see the latest *FMC Configuration Guide* at https://www.cisco.com/c/en/us/td/docs/security/firepower/601/configuration/guide/fpmc-config-guide-v601.html.

Application Visibility and Control (AVC)

One of the things that separates a firewall from a next-generation firewall is the latter's ability to detect and control application usage. Modern security devices are required to provide application inspection. A NGFW has a robust AVC capability as part of its access control policy. Configuring AVC is one of the rule conditions in access control.

One of the biggest differences with NGFW AVC is that detection is based on the application, regardless of the port number. This is performed through analysis of the application, even if it's communicating over nonstandard or ephemeral ports, without the need for custom signatures.

As with any NGFW traffic inspection rule, applications can be trusted, allowed, blocked, or monitored. Applications can be blocked in the singular or as part of an application category, which is a grouping of similar applications. In addition, AVC can use risk level and business relevance as rule conditions. For networks with custom-written applications, there is the capability to create custom application definitions, as discussed in the next section.

Let's look at a simple AVC policy that blocks the Telnet application for any traffic sourced from inside with a destination of outside. In order to accomplish this, you need to create a new rule or modify an existing one.

Tip Right-clicking a rule allows you to copy, cut, or paste it.

After right-clicking the rules table, you click Insert New Rule to open a new Add Rule window, as shown in Figure 5-38.

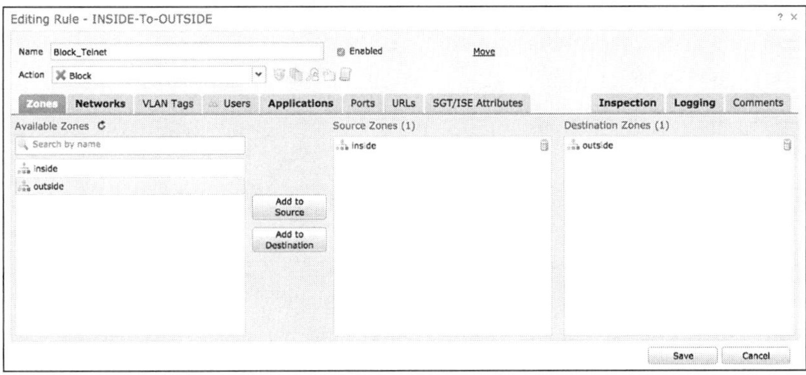

Figure 5-38 *AVC Rule Example*

Just as with any other access control rule, first you need to give it a unique name and choose an action. If you choose Block, the Intrusion Policy and File Policy options are automatically cleared because block actions do not subject the traffic to any more inspection after a match is made. This allows the NGFW to more efficiently inspect traffic by not subjecting dropped traffic to further inspection.

You now are ready to configure the source zone (Inside), the destination zone (Outside), and the source (any-ipv4) and destination addresses (any). When you're done with this, you can skip over to the Applications tab and search for the application Telnet, as shown in Figure 5-39.

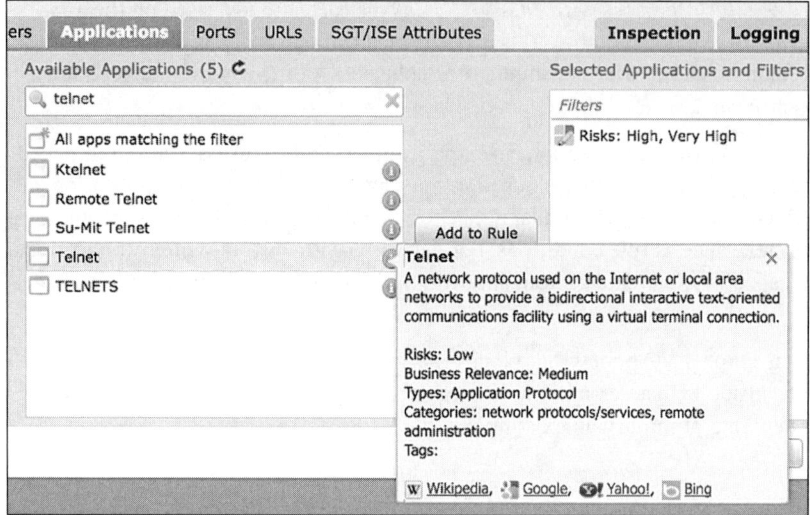

Figure 5-39 *Add Rule Dialog Applications Tab*

Because there are multiple matches on the search word "telnet," you can choose to get more information by clicking on the associated information button. A new window appears, providing a short description of the application, its risk rating, the application categories it appears in, and any custom tags that are configured. You can get more details in a new browser window by clicking one of the hyperlinks.

Tip Enable rule logging for tuning an access control policy. Rule logging is disabled by default. The recommended best practice is to enable logging for policy visibility and validation.

Custom Application Detectors

FTD has a library of more than 5,000 application detectors that can be used for classification of the most common applications. You may recall that, by default, FTD maps applications on the network. This data is used as part of a comprehensive threat profile. A NGFW can detect three types of applications:

- Application protocols used for communication, such as HTTP and SSH
- Client applications such as web browsers and email applications
- Web applications accessed using web browsers, such as YouTube and Facebook

These are considered system-provided detectors because they are maintained by Cisco and included in each FTD release. Sometimes, for a variety of reasons, detection cannot validate a certain type of application. These applications remain unclassified and can fall into one of three states:

- **Pending:** The FMC doesn't have enough data to make a match.
- **Unknown:** The FMC can't match the application.
- **Blank:** The FMC can't determine whether this is application traffic (for example, raw data).

Many networks rely on custom-built applications for specific purposes or business workflows and require them to be included in a security inspection policy. For these applications, FTD has user-configurable custom application detectors to classify custom application traffic, which can then be included in policy rules.

Tip There are two types of detectors: basic and advanced. Basic detectors are configured using the FMC web interface, and advanced detectors are created externally and uploaded as custom .lua files.

Custom applications are defined in Policies > Application Detectors. Applications can be added as part of a known application protocol or as part of a completely custom application. Figure 5-40 shows how you build a custom application detector called OldApp that uses Telnet for transport.

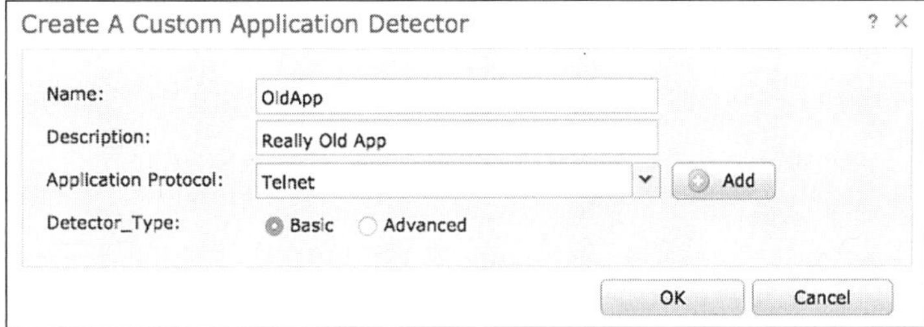

Figure 5-40 *Custom Application Detector*

After defining the new custom application, you can optionally specify in the FMC the detection pattern for the custom application. The recommended practice is to verify the string match with a packet capture, as shown in Figure 5-41.

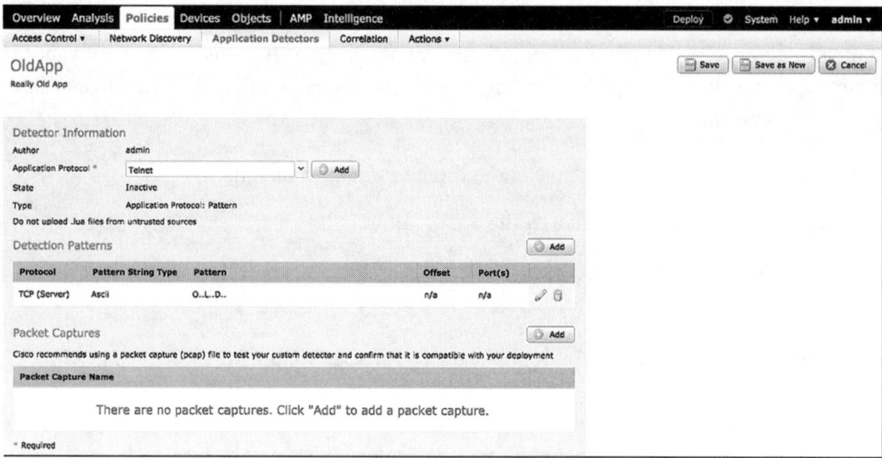

Figure 5-41 *Application Protocol Pattern Configuration*

It is also possible to define a new application in the custom Application Detector configuration window. Click the Add button next to Application Protocol (Figure 5-41) to open a new window. Figure 5-42 shows how you create NewApp-Protocol as a custom application protocol. Because it's a business-related protocol, you define the business relevance as high and the risk as very low. You can then define a new custom application, NewApp, that is built on this new protocol.

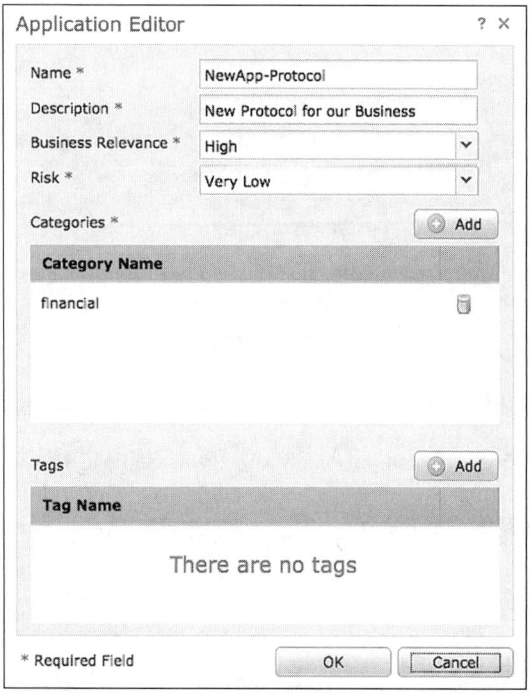

Application Editor

Name * NewApp-Protocol

Description * New Protocol for our Business

Business Relevance * High

Risk * Very Low

Categories * Add

Category Name

financial

Tags Add

Tag Name

There are no tags

* Required Field OK Cancel

Figure 5-42 *Custom Application Protocol Configuration*

Note Custom application protocol configuration requires a restart of the Snort process, which interrupts traffic inspection. Depending on policy configuration, traffic may get dropped as a result.

OpenAppID was announced by Cisco in 2014 as a way for Snort users to share application detectors in an open community. The security community benefits as a whole from this sharing of knowledge because Snort still has an incredibly large installation base. For more information about the OpenAppID project, see the Snort blog: http://blog.snort.org/search/label/openappid.

URL Filtering

URL filtering is a licensed feature that blocks inappropriate and malicious domains based on web reputation and a dynamic website database from Webroot BrightCloud. This database groups URLs into categories, which can then be applied to an access control policy. URL categories become another policy element in a rule and can be blocked or permitted. Custom URLs and URL lists may also be added as objects as part of a custom URL policy.

Figure 5-43 shows the URL Filtering configuration page at System > Integration > Cisco CSI.

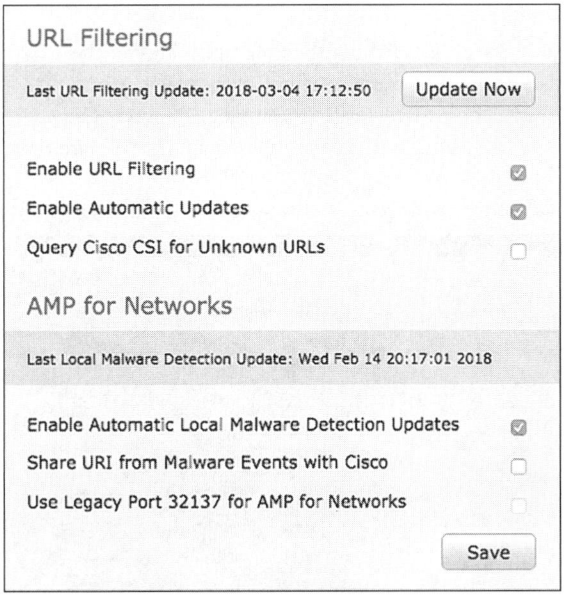

Figure 5-43 *NGFW URL Filtering*

Check the box to enable automatic updates to keep the URL database up to date. If you do, the database is checked every 30 minutes by default, or you can initiate a manual check by clicking the Update Now button. If a URL cannot be found in the local database, there is an option to classify the URL by querying the Cisco database on demand. This is enabled by using the Query Cisco CSI for Unknown URLs check box.

Figure 5-44 shows a new access control rule that blocks any website classified as Adult and Pornography.

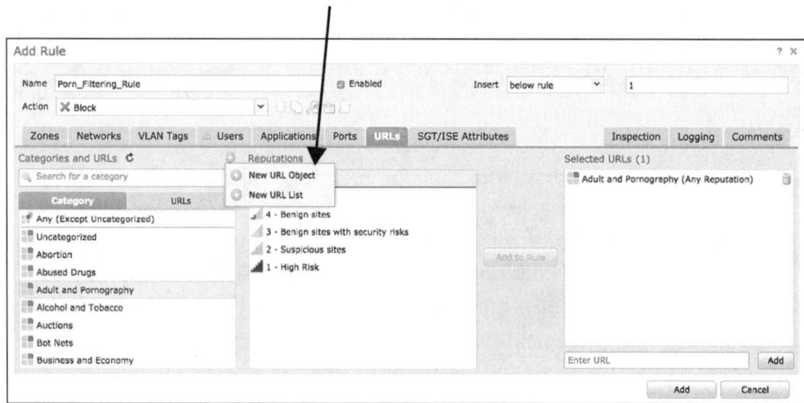

Figure 5-44 *NGFW Rule to Block Adult Websites*

You can configure custom URL objects by either clicking the green plus sign in the rule, as shown in Figure 5-44, or by using the Object Manager. Custom URL groups are made up of custom URL objects. These are also configured under Objects > Object Management > URL. Figure 5-45 shows a custom URL object named CCIE_Website that points to a specific URL.

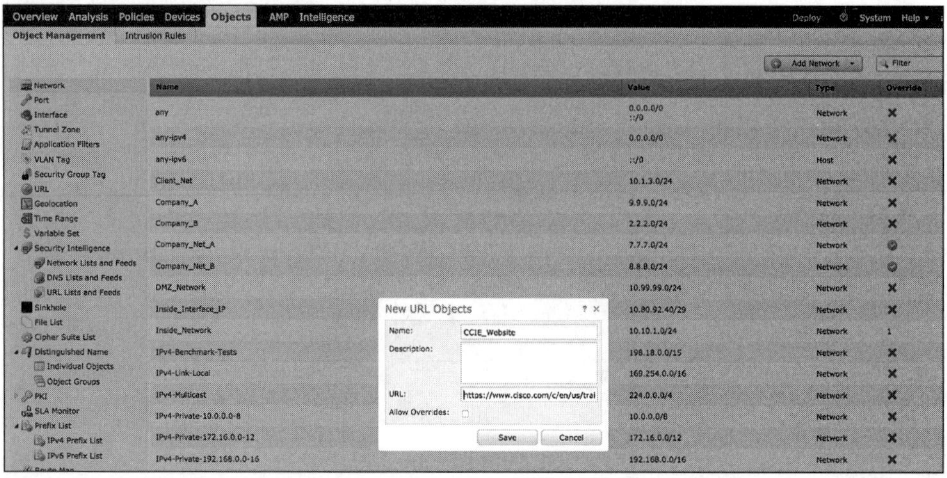

Figure 5-45 *NGFW Custom URL Object Configuration*

In Figure 5-46, a custom URL group called CCIE_URL_Group is created, and it contains multiple custom URL objects, including the CCIE_Website object. Additional custom objects can be added to the group over time.

Figure 5-46 *NGFW Custom URL Group*

Now you are ready to add the custom URL group CCIE_URL_Group to a new rule in your access control policy. In this example, you are whitelisting (that is, allowing) the URLs in the group, as shown in Figure 5-47.

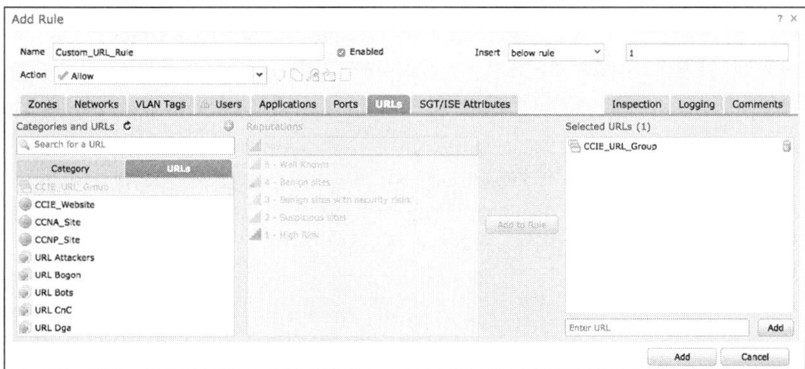

Figure 5-47 *NGFW Custom URL Rule Configuration*

Network Reputation

Reputation scoring is a first line of defense in protecting hosts and users from malicious content. Cisco offers security feeds where reputation data is updated in real time in order to protect against rapidly spreading threats. This feature is configured under Objects > Object Management > Security Intelligence. Security intelligence works by blocking traffic to IP addresses, URLs, or domain names that have known bad reputations. This traffic is dropped and not subject to any further inspection. Cisco Talos offers a constantly updated feed of reputation and threat data. The FMC can optionally point to a third-party feed as well. Figure 5-48 shows Cisco-Intelligence-Feed under Security Intelligence. Notice the timestamp; by default, it is updated every two hours with threat data.

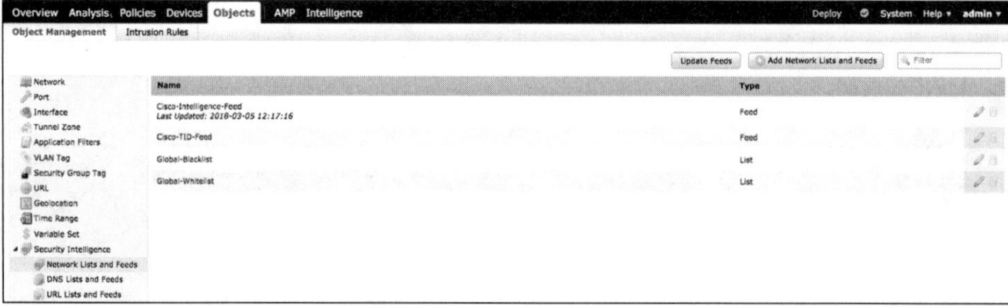

Figure 5-48 *NGFW Security Intelligence Feeds*

Security intelligence also includes an option to configure custom URL feeds and custom URL lists. Feeds are dynamically updated files, and a list is a file that is uploaded once. Feeds can be supplied by third parties or custom-built. Using URL lists is recommended when the number of custom URL objects grows to a large size. Both are text files limited to 500 MB in size. They are made up of IP addresses and blocks, domain names, and URLs.

Configuring a URL feed or a URL list is straightforward, under Objects > Object Management > Security Intelligence. Figure 5-49 shows configuration of a sample feed called CCIE_Feed.

Security Intelligence for Network List / Feed ? ×

Name: CCIE_Feed
Type: Feed
Feed URL: www.example.com/securityfeed/
MD5 URL: (optional)
Update Frequency: 30 minutes

Save Cancel

Figure 5-49 *Custom URL Feed Configuration*

SSL Inspection

Each day, more websites on the Internet move to SSL/TLS for greater security and privacy. Malicious traffic is often encrypted to hide its payload. FTD has features that inspect SSL traffic as part of access control. SSL policies determine how the system handles encrypted traffic and are configured as part of an access control policy. SSL rules are processed before any access control rules because most are expecting only unencrypted traffic.

Like any other policy in FTD, default actions determine how to handle traffic that does not match any rule. Once encrypted traffic is detected, the NGFW determines if it can decrypt it. If the system can decrypt the traffic, it either uses a known private key or re-signs the server certificate with a predefined certificate. Both options require use of a certificate authority that is trusted by both the NGFW and the servers.

The newly decrypted traffic is then processed for more inspection to see if the traffic matches any rule conditions, as per standard operation. If the NGFW determines that it cannot decrypt, it defaults to one of three actions:

- **Block:** Blocks the SSL session, with no further inspection
- **Block with Reset:** The same as above but adds a TCP reset
- **Do Not Decrypt:** Passes the traffic to access control for more inspection, including decryption, if possible

SSL inspection is supported only on interfaces that can modify the flow of traffic. These include interfaces deployed inline or routed on the NGFW. Passive and tap mode interfaces are not supported.

NGFW SSL policy is configured under Policies > Access Control > SSL. Figure 5-50 shows the default actions configured as part of a new SSL policy. Once the policy is created, you can add SSL rules.

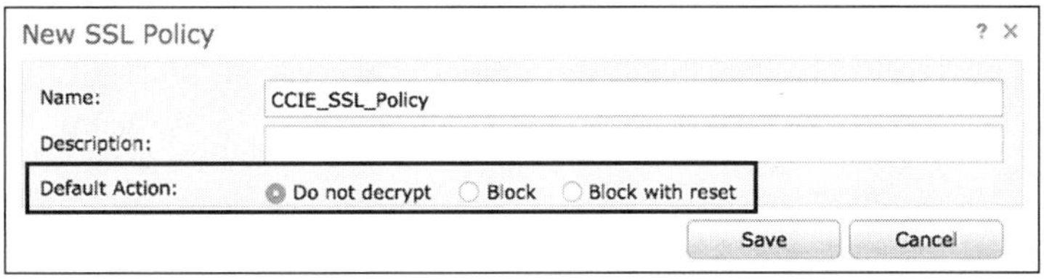

Figure 5-50 *SSL Policy Default Actions*

Figure 5-51 shows the SSL policy Add Rule window, which includes the configurable actions for this sample rule.

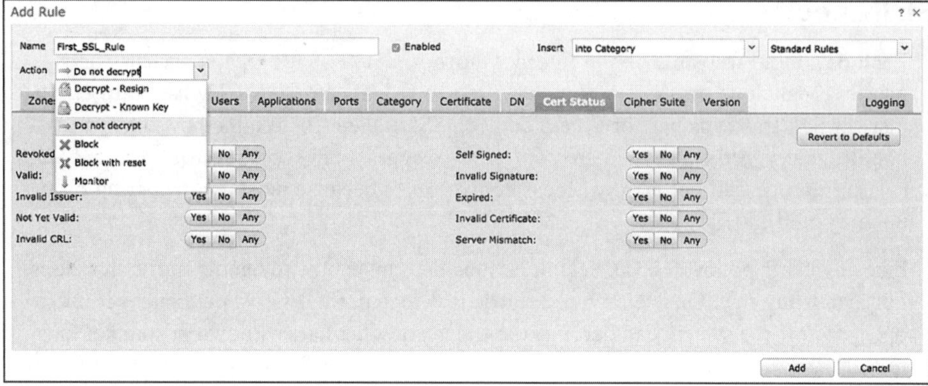

Figure 5-51 *SSL Policy Add Rule Actions*

Pay attention to the level of detail as part of the configurable conditions in an SSL rule. In Figure 5-51, for example, the Cert Status tab is visible, with a wide variety of certificate options to define the matching condition.

It is possible to deploy an SSL policy without any configured rules. This approach involves passing all traffic to the default action, at which point all inspection ceases. In certain cases, however, traffic is determined to be undecryptable. For such traffic, there are configurable response actions. Figure 5-52 shows that you can either have each line inherit the default action defined for the policy or choose an alternate action from the drop-down box.

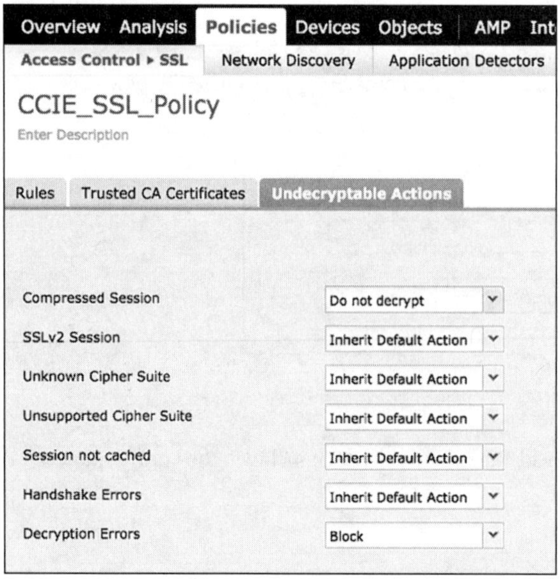

Figure 5-52 *Undecryptable Actions Configuration*

Analysis and Reporting

The FMC supports a wide variety of analysis and reporting capabilities. Understanding how they work is helpful for a CCIE candidate who is troubleshooting a deployment or configuration. The following sections cover dashboards, the Context Explorer, the Event Log (Connection Events), and the User Activity pages.

Dashboards

An FTD dashboard is a highly customizable monitoring tool that can provide a quick overview for a wide variety of system and network-related status. Dashboards provide a wealth of data collected from all managed devices. Dashboards are pages that consist of widgets displayed in a three-column layout. Widgets are independent, customizable graphical applications that display data. Like any other graphical window, they can be minimized or maximized or completely rearranged.

> **Note** Dashboards are visible only to users with appropriate role privileges. By default, this is limited to administrator, maintenance user, security analyst, and security analyst (read-only).

The system installs by default with predefined dashboards that are completely customizable. They are accessed at Overview > Dashboards. Admin users see the default Summary Dashboard page, as shown in Figure 5-53.

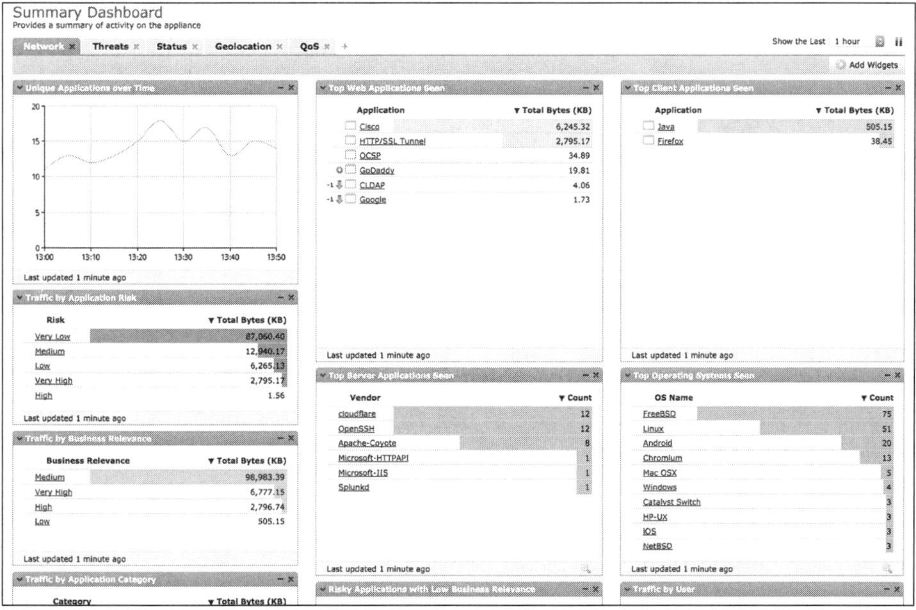

Figure 5-53 *Summary Dashboard View*

The Summary Dashboard page opens to the Network tab, by default, and includes widgets that provide a Top X overview of network events. The Threats tab (see Figure 5-54) is typically used by security operations for viewing IOCs that may require responses.

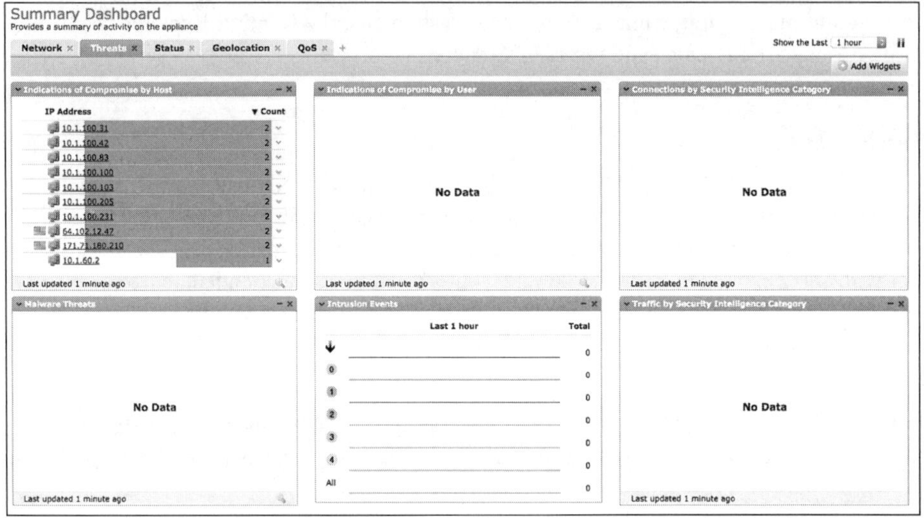

Figure 5-54 *Summary Dashboard Threats Tab*

The Status tab (see Figure 5-55) provides an overall system health summary. It shows software versions and a live feed from the Cisco Threat Research Blog.

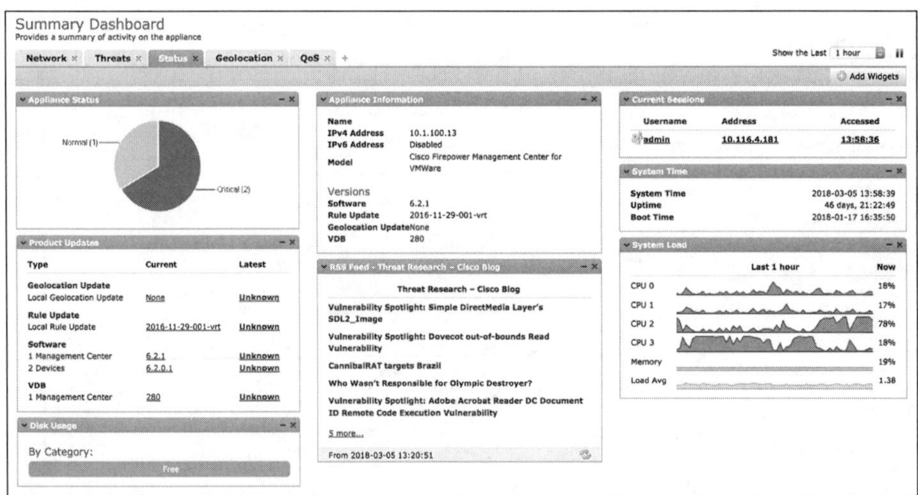

Figure 5-55 *Summary Dashboard Status Tab*

The Application Statistics dashboard under Overview > Dashboards is very helpful for a high-level view of discovered applications on the network (see Figure 5-56). It is no surprise that, just as in the real world, the most prevalent application in this lab network is HTTP.

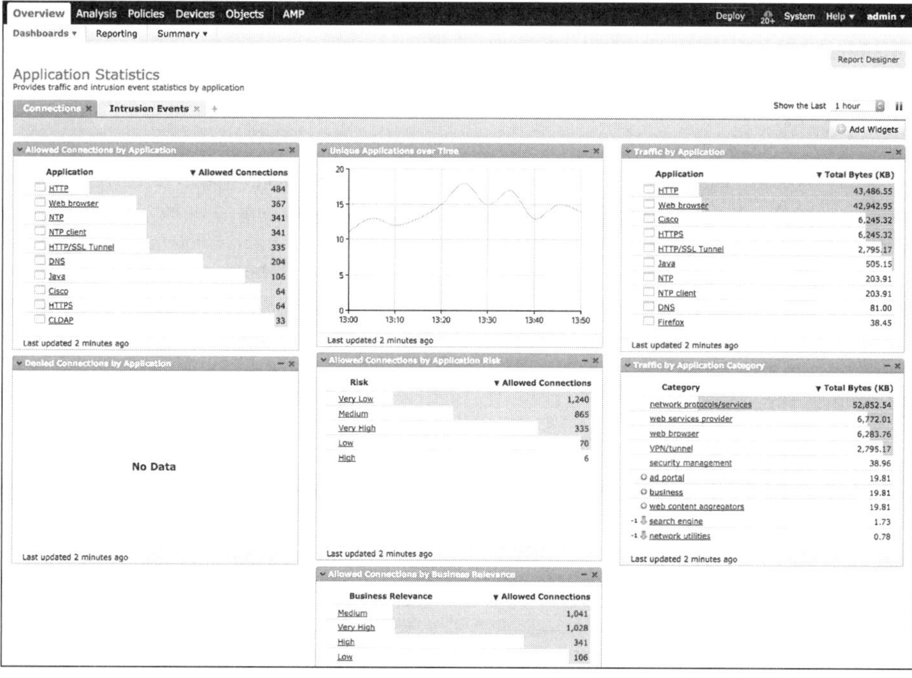

Figure 5-56 *Application Statistics Dashboard*

All dashboards are customizable. Clicking the Add Widgets button in the upper-right corner of a dashboard launches a utility for creating customized views (see Figure 5-57).

Add Widgets
Application Statistics - Connections

Categories
All Categories (16)
Analysis & Reporting (5)
Miscellaneous (1)
Operations (10)

Appliance Information
This widget displays local appliance information including software versions, Remote Management, and High Availability status.
Add

Appliance Status
This widget displays the current Health Monitoring appliance status.
Add

Correlation Events
This widget displays Correlation events
Add

Current Interface Status
This widget displays the current status of all local network interfaces.
Add

Current Sessions
This widget displays a list of the user sessions currently logged-in to this appliance.
Add

Custom Analysis
The Custom Analysis widget shows the top or bottom set of events (5, 10, 15, 20, or 25 events) from a user-selectable event table, search, and field.
Add
7 on Tab

Figure 5-57 *Add Widgets Page*

In summary, dashboards provide a quick look at various data points. You can use the predefined dashboards to build custom dashboards as necessary.

Context Explorer

Context Explorer is a graphical utility in the FMC that provides a wealth of data on the network, applications, connections, IOCs, users and URLs, and much more. It allows user-configurable filters, based on time range, to provide a summary view of data. Unlike dashboards, Context Explorer is a manual query into the FMC database in order to provide clarity for a specific aspect related to the system or network.

Context Explorer, found in the FMC under Analysis > Context Explorer, displays as a scrolling page of graphs and bar charts. It works by presenting a time-based general data set with options to filter on specific metadata for analysis. Each graphical element optionally links to a menu (accessed with a mouse click) that includes or excludes metadata from the query. With only a few clicks, an operator can drill many layers deep into the data.

Figure 5-58 shows the Context Explorer page from a lab network.

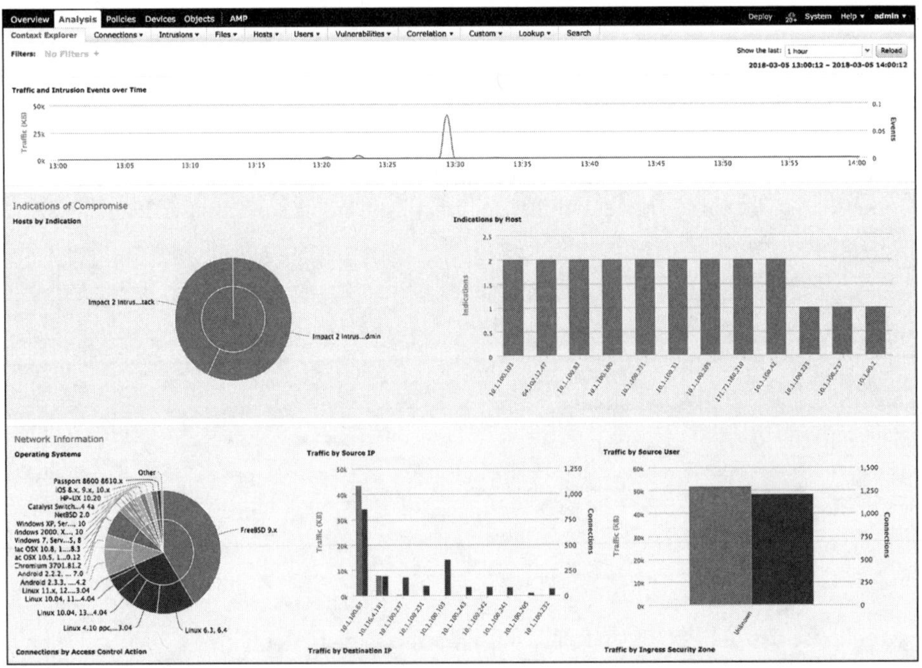

Figure 5-58 *Context Explorer Summary Page*

Figure 5-59 shows the Add Filter configuration page, which you access from the upper-left corner of the Context Explorer window. As you can see, there are several data types to choose from.

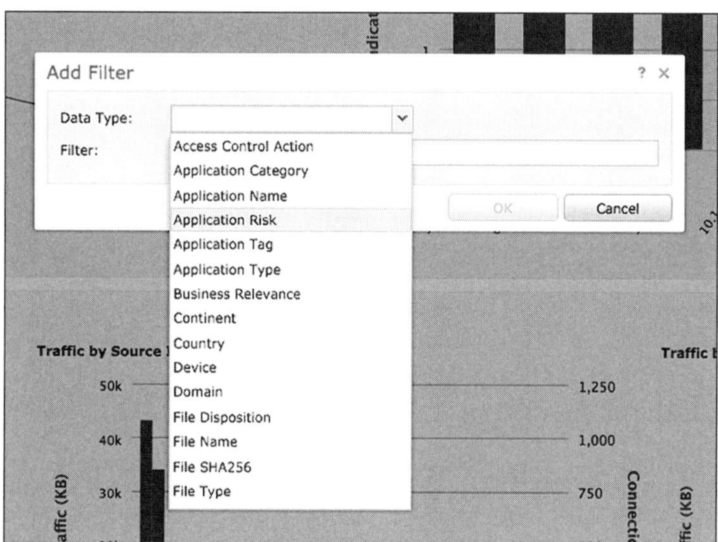

Figure 5-59 *Context Explorer Add Filter*

Context Explorer is an excellent tool for quickly digging through large amounts of data. Unlike dashboards, which update in real time, Context Explorer provides a snapshot based on a user-configurable time range.

Connection Events

The Connection Events page, found under Analysis > Connections > Events, provides a real-time event viewer that is valuable for testing rule configuration and general troubleshooting. This viewer displays a running log generated by managed devices for detected network connections. It provides a lot of detail in one place and can be very useful if you know where to look.

A special type of connection event, called a security intelligence event, is accessed on the Analysis > Connections > Security Intelligence Events page. You may recall from earlier in this chapter that security intelligence uses reputation-based blacklists to block malicious traffic. It occurs very early in the packet inspection process to prevent more advanced inspection engines from wasting resources on known bad traffic. These special events are security intelligence events, and they provide visibility into traffic dropped due to security intelligence rules.

Event logging is disabled by default in the base policy, so it must be explicitly enabled as part of the NGFW policy and rule configuration. Figure 5-60 shows the Logging tab of a typical access policy rule. The rule action is set to allow matching traffic with logging enabled.

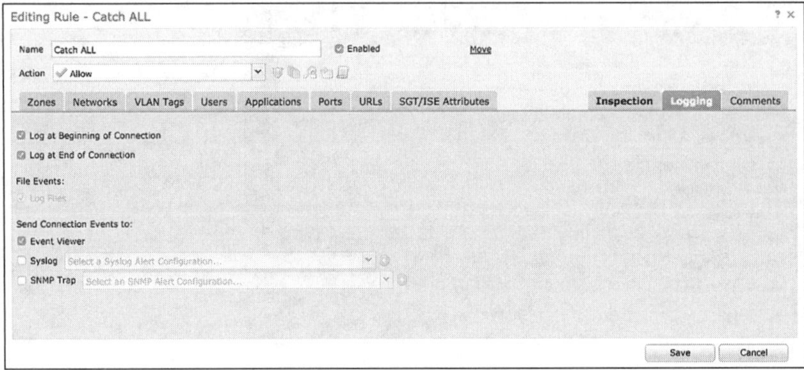

Figure 5-60 *Access Control Rule Logging Tab*

Let's look more closely at this page. The first two checked boxes enable logging for the beginning and end of every connection matched by this rule. This data populates the Connection Events page. Note that traffic blocked due to policy (including blacklists) is dropped immediately and does not generate an end-of-connection event. All other monitored traffic, however, generates end-of-connection events.

A little further down, the Event Viewer check box is selected. This setting allows events to be sent to the Connection Events page. Syslog and SNMP options are also available on this configuration page.

The Connection Events page from a live lab network is presented in Figure 5-61.

Figure 5-61 *Connection Events Page*

The Connection Events page shows tremendous detail for all connections, including geolocation data and known applications. This viewer includes many options for quickly drilling into the data fields. For example, right-clicking on either a source or destination IP address opens up a new context window with multiple options:

- Open in New Window
- Open up in Context Explorer
- Whois
- View Host Profile
- Blacklist IP Now
- Whitelist IP Now
- Exclude

You can also use the check boxes on the left side of the page to focus on a subset of events. In addition, a search function is useful when you are looking for very specific matches (for example, IP address, username).

The Connection Events page is a powerful tool that assists in troubleshooting and policy validation. Using it is the best way to get quick event-based feedback. The Connection Events page contains many more capabilities than are highlighted here. For a complete walkthrough of every feature and option, see the latest *FMC Configuration Guide* at https://www.cisco.com/c/en/us/td/docs/security/firepower/601/configuration/guide/fpmc-config-guide-v601.html.

User Activity

For security operations, it is necessary to associate a user with an event. Having a tool that can provide detailed information on users in an efficient manner speeds up troubleshooting and threat analysis. The FMC correlates user data passively as part of the network discovery process or actively from directory servers. There is tremendous operational value in linking users, hosts, and network events. The FMC offers this linkage in two ways: user awareness and user control. *User awareness* is the process of collecting users and the devices they are connecting to and from. This is the main focus of this section. *User control* is the ability to permit or deny access to resources based on user and group information, as discussed earlier in this chapter in the "Identity Firewall" section.

The FMC provides convenient event pages that focus on user activity and are found under Analysis > Users. There are four subpages available: Active Sessions, Users, User Activity, and Indications of Compromise.

The Analysis > Users > Users page lists the users discovered by the managed devices. In the lab shown in Figure 5-62, most of the users were discovered through FTP. Because

FTP is unencrypted traffic, the NGFW devices are able to detect the username in the FTP protocol initial exchange.

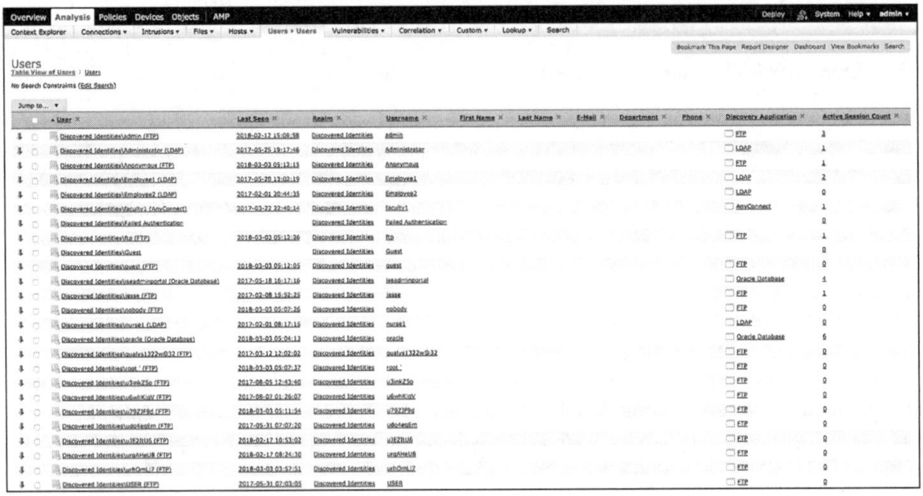

Figure 5-62 *Analyzing Users*

The Analysis > Users > Active Sessions page lists the current active user sessions, their current IP addresses, and the discovery device (see Figure 5-63). This is a very helpful utility for quickly narrowing a username and address.

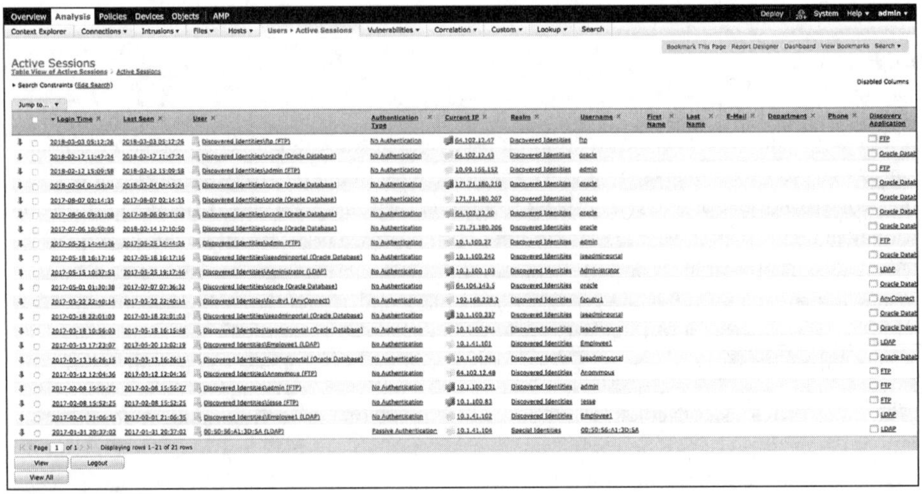

Figure 5-63 *Active Sessions*

The Analysis > Users > User Activity page provides a list of user login info, authentication type, and the realm users are associated with in the FMC (see Figure 5-64). It shows both passive and active authentication types.

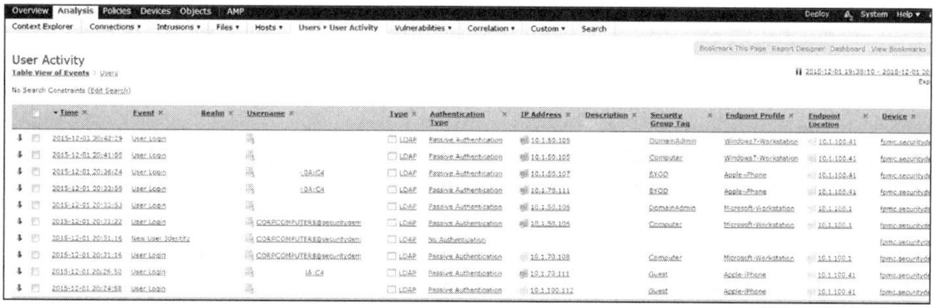

Figure 5-64 *Analyzing User Activity*

The FMC includes powerful reporting and dashboard utilities that can assist with policy validation and troubleshooting. This section highlights a few of the most popular options, but there are many more pages and tools that are not covered here. For a detailed overview of all the analysis event viewers in the FMC, see the latest *FMC Configuration Guide* at https://www.cisco.com/c/en/us/td/docs/security/firepower/601/configuration/guide/fpmc-config-guide-v601.html.

Summary

This chapter provides an overview of the functionality of the Firepower Management Console and the various configuration options of a NGFW. Since the release of Firepower Threat Defense, the vast majority of device configuration is performed using the FMC GUI. This chapter begins by providing an overview of NGFWs and how FTD fits into the Firepower portfolio. It also briefly covers the initial configuration and the important design choice of firewall mode. Routing and high-availability options as well as NAT configuration round out the information on NGFW configuration.

This chapter also looks at access control, policy creation, and rules. Network objects are introduced, along with their role in access control policy. Identity firewall features with AD and ISE are discussed, including how the NGFW detects user and application information by using network discovery. SSL decryption policy and URL filtering are covered as advanced inspection features.

Finally, this chapter highlights the analysis and reporting tools available in the FMC and how they can be used for policy validation and troubleshooting. This chapter discusses ways to get data out of the FMC, including user and address mapping. Knowing how to use these tools efficiently is valuable for both lab preparation and the real world.

References

"Firepower Management Console Configuration Guide, Version 6.0.1," https://www.cisco.com/c/en/us/td/docs/security/firepower/601/configuration/guide/fpmc-config-guide-v601.html

"Firepower Management Console Release Notes," https://www.cisco.com/c/en/us/support/security/defense-center/products-release-notes-list.html

"Firepower User Agent Configuration Guide, Version 2.3," https://www.cisco.com/c/en/us/td/docs/security/firesight/user-agent/23/config-guide/Firepower-User-Agent-Configuration-Guide-v2-3.html

"Gartner IT Glossary - Next-Gen Firewalls," https://www.gartner.com/it-glossary/next-generation-firewalls-ngfws

Chapter 6

Next-Gen Intrusion Detection and Prevention

This chapter provides details about Cisco's Firepower next-generation intrusion prevention system (NGIPS). An NGIPS can stop the exploits, vulnerabilities, and threats used by most attacks. This chapter explores the differences between legacy intrusion prevention systems (IPSs) and NGIPSs, placement of NGIPSs, the appliances that can be used, and the configuration and operations available. You will learn how to create signatures, policies, and rules, as well as how to tune those signatures for an organization, using dashboards, the Context Explorer, reporting, and rules.

NGIPS Overview

In 2013, Cisco acquired Sourcefire to expand its capabilities around continuous advanced threat protection. NGIPS allows an organization to see what is on the network in terms of threats, vulnerabilities, devices, operating systems, applications, users, and network behaviors. Once the system has the information, it can correlate the data contextually and make automatic decisions to protect the organization's environment. By deploying a NGIPS, an organization is able to identify, classify, and stop malicious traffic—including worms, spyware/adware, network viruses, and application abuse—before it affects business continuity.

Legacy IDSs/IPSs Versus NGIPSs

Intrusion detection systems (IDSs) were first developed starting in the 1980s to provide a list of rules to constantly scan network traffic against a list of known threats. Very quickly, this expanded into what is known today as intrusion prevention systems (IPSs) because once an organization was able to know a threat was on the network, it wanted to prevent it from being dangerous to the environment. As the security industry evolved to become better at detecting and preventing threats with IDSs/IPSs, attackers became better at evading IDSs/IPSs. Techniques such as encoding, fragmentation, encryption, and polymorphism added to the challenges faced by security teams.

As attacks evolved, the effectiveness of legacy IPSs decreased. Writing signatures to accommodate additional samples and evasive techniques created false positives, where legitimate network traffic would match threat signatures. At the same time, networks were becoming faster and had become mission-critical to the organization. The plethora of events created an overwhelming burden on security teams. NGIPSs were created to solve the number-one problem in the IPS space: finding the needle (in this case the real threat) in the haystack (a very large data set). It is not uncommon to see a legacy IPS with hundreds or thousands of events in a single second. Even with a large team of security operators, the events generated could not be reviewed or evaluated. A NGIPS allows an organization to correlate thousands of events with the target's context, including the host operating system, applications, and vulnerabilities, to prioritize the threats that matter most and associate users and devices with the intrusion events to speed investigations. Figure 6-1 illustrates the differences between a NGIPS and a legacy IPS.

Categories	Samples	NGIPS	Legacy IPS
Threats	Attacks, Anomalies	✔	✔
Users	AD, LDAP, POP3	✔	✗
Web Applications	Facebook, YouTube	✔	✗
Application Protocols	HTTP, SMTP, SSH	✔	✗
Client Applications	Firefox, IE, Chrome	✔	✗
Network Servers	Apache 2.3.1, IIS4	✔	✗
Operating Systems	Windows, Linux	✔	✗
Routers & Switches	Cisco, Nortel	✔	✗
Wireless Access Points	Linksys, Netgear	✔	✗
Mobile Devices	iPhone, Android	✔	✗
Printers	HP, Xerox, Canon	✔	✗
VoIP Phones	Cisco, Avaya	✔	✗
Virtual Machines	VMware, Xen	✔	✗

Figure 6-1 *NGIPS Versus Legacy IPS*

A NGIPS can use the additional information gleaned above and beyond what legacy IPSs can handle to increase operational efficiency and provide better threat defense.

Contextual Awareness

Context refers to the ability to understand and analyze important environmental factors. With the additional context data correlated with events, a NGIPS can provide better speed, accuracy, flexibility, and value to an organization. The following list describes the types of contextual awareness each host discovered by a NGIPS contains. The contextual information is contained in a host profile on the Firepower Management Center (FMC). A host profile provides a complete view of all the information the system has gathered about a single host and includes the following:

- **Host OS:** Windows 10, MAC OS X 10.9, Centos 6, and so on.
- **Users:** Learned from Active Directory, Identity Services Engine (ISE), or passive traffic (FTP, HTTP, MDNS, SIP, and so on). The FMC shows the last 24 hours of user activity on the host; for example, it might indicate that jamie@securitydemo.net was logged in from 8 a.m. to 4 p.m.
- **Clients and web applications:** Applications communicating from the host (for example, Dropbox, Firefox, Java).
- **Server applications:** Applications receiving traffic on the host (for example, IIS, Apache, OpenSSH).
- **Protocols:** Type of protocols being used (for example, TCP, UDP, ICMP, IGMP).
- **Vulnerabilities:** Based on the discovered OS and applications (for example, CVE 2009-1862).
- **Malware detected in a network transfer on the host:** Whitelist violations associated with a host, recent malware events for a host, and Nmap scan results for a host.

To access a host profile, navigate from any network map view or navigate from any event view that includes the IP addresses of hosts on monitored networks. Figure 6-2 shows an example of a host profile.

Notifications based on discovery of hosts allow administrators to spot rogue hosts, anomalies, policy violations, and more. Contextual awareness affords the possibility of changing the interpretation of security events and is the basis for other NGIPS features.

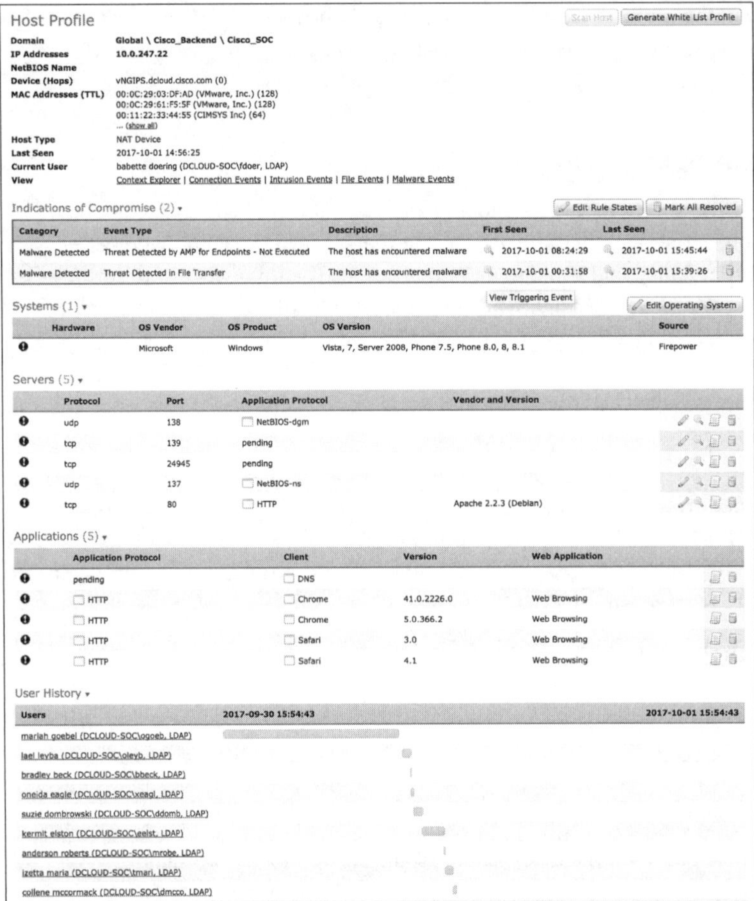

Figure 6-2 *FMC Host Profile*

Impact Assessment

An IPS may generate so much noise that a security operator may have a difficult time assessing the event. Even if an IPS sees a packet that matches a signature, it may not have sufficient context to make the correct assessment. Putting an event in the right context is critical to finding the types of events that require action. To help evaluate the impact an event has on the network, the FMC displays an impact level alongside each intrusion event. The impact level indicates the correlation between intrusion data, network discovery data, and vulnerability information.

Note The vulnerability database (VDB) is a database on the FMC of known vulnerabilities to which hosts may be susceptible, as well as fingerprints for operating systems, clients, and applications. Updates to this database happen frequently as new vulnerabilities are discovered all the time.

Figure 6-3 describes the impact levels and recommended responses to them.

Impact Level	Vulnerability	Admin Action	Color	Description
0	Unknown	Good to Know, Unknown Network	gray	Neither the source nor the destination host is on a network that is monitored by network discovery.
1	Vulnerable	Act Immediately, Vulnerable	red	Either: • the source or the destination host is in the network map, and a vulnerability is mapped to the host • the source or destination host is potentially compromised by a virus, trojan, or other piece of malicious software
2	Potentially Vulnerable	Investigate, Potentially Vulnerable	orange	Either the source or the destination host is in the network map and one of the following is true: • for port-oriented traffic, the port is running a server application protocol • for non-port-oriented traffic, the host uses the protocol
3	Currently Not Vulnerable	Good to Know, Currently Not Vulnerable	yellow	Either the source or the destination host is in the network map and one of the following is true: • for port-oriented traffic (for example, TCP or UDP), the port is not open • for non-port-oriented traffic (for example, ICMP), the host does not use the protocol
4	Unknown Target	Good to Know, Unknown Target	blue	Either the source or destination host is on a monitored network, but there is no entry for the host in the network map.

Figure 6-3 *Impact Levels*

Along with passive vulnerability mapping, the FMC can also integrate with third-party vulnerability assessment tools. This allows for privileged scan data to be used for higher-efficacy vulnerability data inside the FMC, thus creating even more valuable impact levels.

Operators and analysts dealing with event overload (that is, too many events to handle) can prioritize their efforts by focusing on impact level 1 and 2 events, as shown in Figure 6-4. By going to Analysis > Intrusions > Events and clicking Switch Workflow, the administrator can display intrusion events based on impact and priority, impact and source, and impact to destination.

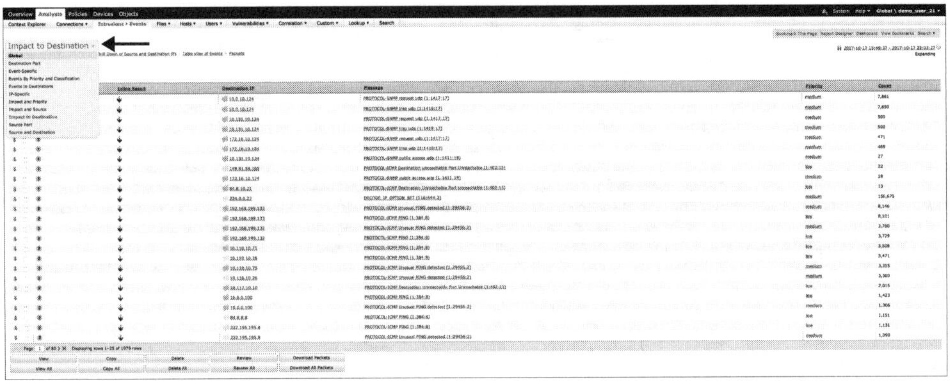

Figure 6-4 *Impact to Destination Intrusion Events Workflow*

Security Intelligence

The Internet is an ever-evolving landscape of good and bad hosts and devices. One major defense technique for networks is to filter traffic based on malicious observed behavior that has previously happened. Security intelligence works by blocking traffic to or from IP addresses, URLs, or domain names that have a known bad reputation. Sometimes referred to as *reputation filtering* or *blacklisting*, security intelligence in the context of NGIPSs is the ability to provide global intelligence to detect or prevent malicious connections. Talos is the global threat intelligence organization at Cisco that generates the security intelligence lists for known malicious IP addresses, DNS names, and URLs. These intelligence lists are updated very frequently and can change multiple times during a single day.

Sites representing security threats such as malware, spam, botnets, and phishing are added and removed faster than an administrator could research and manually update and deploy custom configurations.

The following are some of the different types of intelligence feeds and features that a NGIPS uses:

- **Cisco Talos–provided feeds:** Cisco provides access to regularly updated intelligence feeds—sites representing security threats such as malware, spam, botnets, and phishing.

- **Third-party threat intelligence feeds:** An organization may have third-party feeds or custom feeds that are generated by its security operations team. The FMC provides the ability to bring in third-party dynamic lists by downloading from a URL on a regular basis.
- **Global and custom blacklists:** Unlike a feed, a blacklist is a static list that an organization can use to block specific IP addresses, URLs, or domain names.
- **Whitelists to eliminate false positives:** When a security intelligence list preemptively blocks traffic that needs further analysis with the rest of access control, the blacklist can be overridden with a custom whitelist.
- **Monitoring instead of blacklisting:** Monitoring is especially useful in passive deployments and for testing feeds before enforcement. Monitoring options provides the ability to monitor and log the violating connections instead of blocking them.

More information on configuration and monitoring of security intelligence can be found later in this chapter.

Indications of Compromise (IOCs)

A NGIPS spotlights systems being compromised by using indications of compromise (IOC). IOCs allow for automated compromise analysis and prioritized response and remediation. A NGIPS uses IOC rules in the network discovery policy to identify a host as being likely to be compromised by malicious means. When a host meets the conditions specified in these system-provided rules, the system tags it with an IOC. Each IOC rule corresponds to one type of IOC tag. The IOC tag specifies the nature of the likely compromise. The FMC can tag the host involved by correlating information in intrusion, connection, security intelligence, and file or malware events. IOC rules can be viewed by going to Policies > Network Discovery > Advanced > Indications of Compromise Settings and clicking the edit icon. All rules and IOCs are enabled by default; Figure 6-5 shows some of the rules.

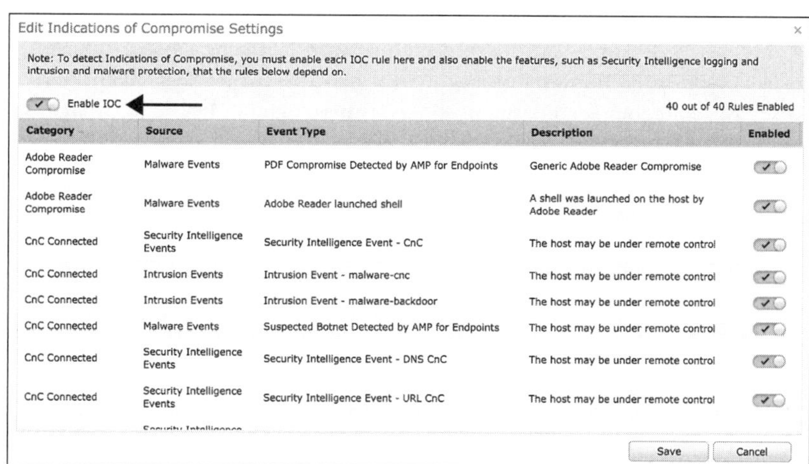

Figure 6-5 *Indications of Compromise Rules*

IOCs give an organization a new way to operationalize threats in the environment. Instead of simply reviewing a single event at a time, a security operator can prioritize IOCs based on hosts or users. For instance, if an impact level 1 IPS event occurs, it is interesting, but if that same host also reaches out to a malicious domain, noted by a security intelligence event, then FMC will mark two different IOCs for that host. In most cases those two separate events correlated in IOCs would be compelling evidence of a security incident. The same would be true if a single user were seen with a browser exploit and subsequently downloaded malware. As you can see, using IOCs is a powerful and effective way to manage risk and threats with a NGIPS.

User-based IOCs help organizations prioritize threats based on the risk of the user involved. If Lilianna from sales shows an IOC at the same time as the chief financial officer (CFO), for example, the security team can focus its efforts where the biggest risk exists.

Automated Tuning

One of the biggest challenges most organizations face in regard to IPS deployment and operations is correctly creating a customized rule set based on their unique operating environment. Administrators can use Firepower recommended rules to associate the operating systems, servers, and client application protocols detected on the organization's network with rules specifically written to protect those assets. The system makes an individual set of recommendations for each intrusion policy. It typically recommends rule state changes for standard text rules and shared object rules, but it can also recommend changes for preprocessor and decoder rules. By using recommended rules an organization can do the following:

- Reduce manual work in tuning the NGIPS
- Help prevent IPS evasions
- Maximize sensor resources

For example, if a NGIPS determines that a protected network segment is only running Windows systems supporting IIS web services and Exchange email services, Firepower recommended rules can recommend disabling any rules pertaining to UNIX hosts and services, such as Apache and SSHD. Auto-tuning is designed to maximize protection and sensor performance and significantly reduce, or virtually eliminate, the manual and ongoing effort required to tune the NGIPS. Rule recommendations can be implemented with or without human intervention. When generating rule state recommendations, the default settings can be used, or the advanced settings can be modified to suit the needs of the organization. Advanced settings allow administrators to do the following:

- Redefine which hosts on the network the system monitors for vulnerabilities
- Influence which rules the system recommends, based on rule overhead
- Specify whether to generate recommendations to disable rules

Figure 6-6 shows the recommended changes to the IPS policy and the advanced settings found under Policies > Intrusion > Firepower Recommendations.

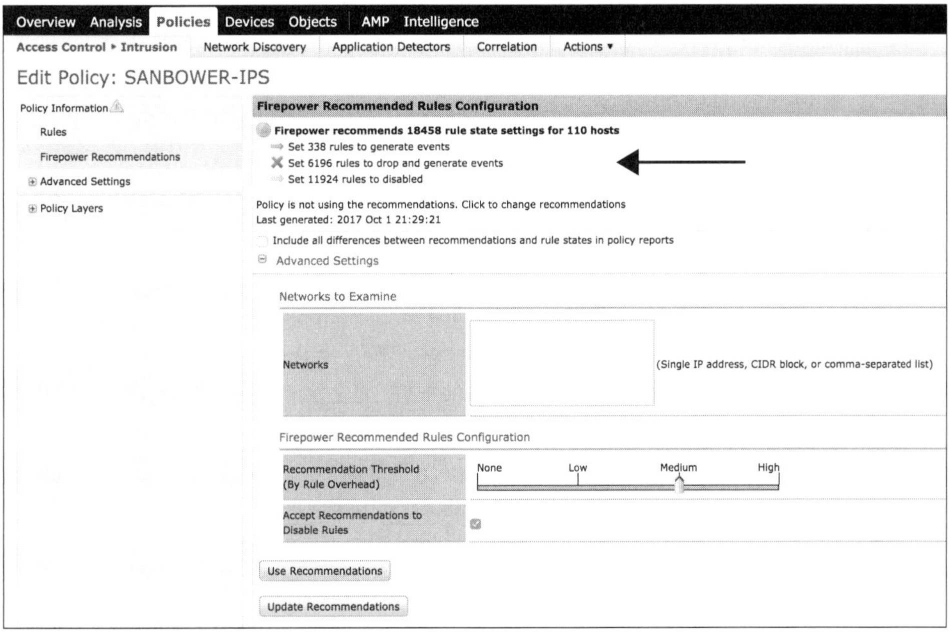

Figure 6-6 *Firepower Recommended Rules*

After generating the rules, an organization can choose to use the recommendations immediately or to review the recommendations (and affected rules) before accepting them. Figure 6-7 shows recommended changes to the IPS policy.

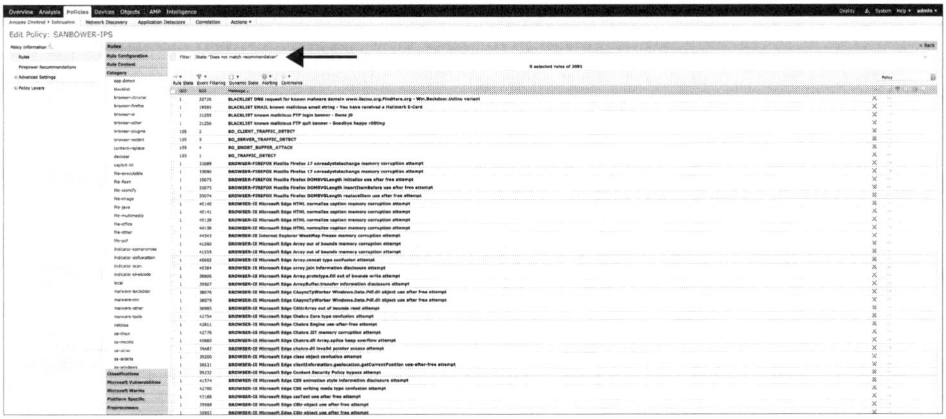

Figure 6-7 *Firepower Recommended Rule Changes*

Choosing to use the recommended rule states adds a read-only Firepower recommendations layer to the intrusion policy, and subsequently choosing not to use the recommended rule states removes the layer. Automatic recommendations can be scheduled as a task to generate automatically based on the most recently saved configuration settings in the intrusion policy.

Cisco NGIPS Appliances

Cisco NGIPSs run on the following appliances:

- **Cisco Firepower 7000 and 8000 series appliances:** 50 Mbps to 60 Gbps of IPS throughput, running standalone NGIPS software
- **Cisco NGIPS Virtual for VMware:** Virtual machine running standalone NGIPS software that allows for inspection of virtual traffic or private cloud environments
- **Cisco NGFWv for Public Cloud:** Firepower Threat Defense (FTD) running in Amazon Web Services (AWS) or Microsoft Azure, which allows for inspection of public cloud traffic
- **Cisco ASA5500-X with Firepower Services:** Industry-leading Cisco ASA with NGIPS running in software or hardware (5585X only)
- **Cisco Firepower 2100/4100/9300 Series:** 2 Gbps to 133 Gbps of IPS throughput, running FTD

Note Throughput information in this list is based on the published datasheet performance numbers at the time this book was published.

All Firepower 7000/8000 series appliances and Firepower 4100/9300 devices can contain configurable bypass interfaces, also known as fail-to-wire (FTW) interfaces. Configurable bypass inline sets allow an organization to select how traffic is handled if a hardware or software failure occurs. An interface pair configured for bypass allows all traffic to flow if the device fails. The traffic bypasses the device and any inspection or other processing by the device. Bypass allows un-inspected traffic across the network segment but ensures that the network connectivity is maintained. Bypass is configured when pairing interfaces into inline sets.

Firepower Clustering

Firepower clustering, which is applicable only for Firepower 7000 and 8000 series appliances, is a way of providing Active/Standby high availability for dedicated NGIPS devices. Clustering of devices provides redundancy of configuration and networking functionality between two devices or stacks. The FMC treats devices in a cluster as a single device and applies policies to a cluster rather than to each device individually. Clusters are stateful, and state sharing allows the clustered devices or clustered stacks to synchronize the states so that if one of the devices or stacks fails, the other peer can take over with no interruption of traffic flow. Failover in a cluster can happen manually or automatically. Manual failover happens when a clustered device or stack is put in maintenance mode. Clustering is not preemptive, which means if the active cluster member goes into maintenance mode and the active member fails over to the standby member, when the original active cluster member is restored to normal operation, it does not automatically reclaim the active role.

In order to use clustering, the high availability link interfaces on both devices must be enabled, and both devices must be the same hardware models, contain the same network modules in the same slots, and have the same licenses, software version, and VDB version. Figure 6-8 shows how the FMC sees clusters.

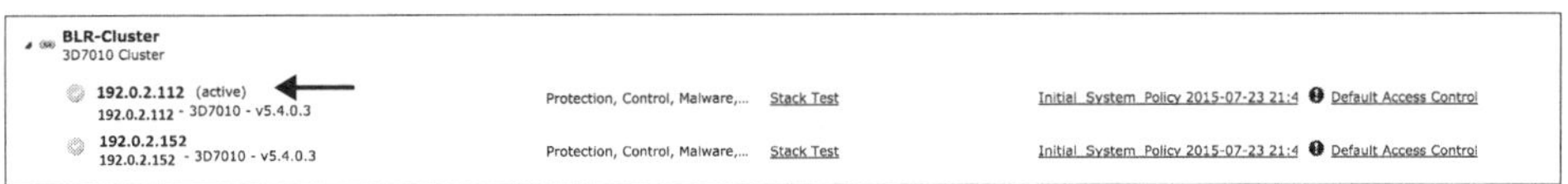

Figure 6-8 *Firepower Cluster*

Firepower Stacking

Stacking allows resources to be combined on multiple Firepower 8000 series appliances in a single shared configuration. Up to four physical devices can be stacked to allow for combined throughput. This allows an organization to increase the amount of traffic inspected on a network segment. In a stack deployment, one of the devices connected to the network segments is designated as the primary device, and all other devices are designated as secondary devices and are deployed to provide additional resources to the primary device. Only the primary device is connected to the network, and it is the only device used to pass traffic. The secondaries are used to provide the primary with CPU and memory resources only. If the primary fails, no traffic is passed to the secondary devices.

Stacking modules are used to connect the primary device to the stacking interfaces on the secondary devices using the stacking cables. Figure 6-9 highlights the stacking module.

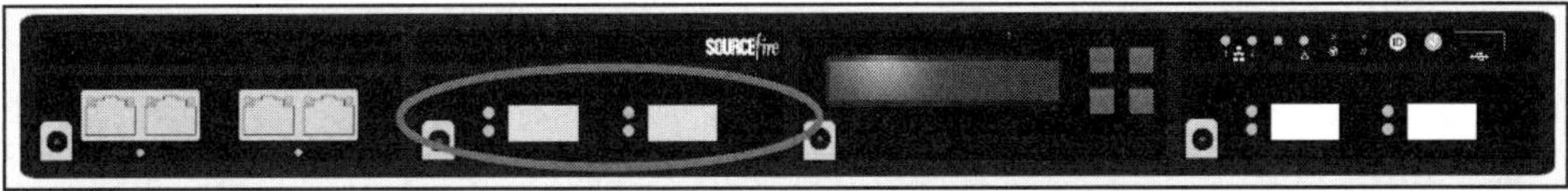

Figure 6-9 *Firepower Stacking Module*

Each secondary device is connected directly to the primary device using the stacking interfaces. Even though the primary holds all of the network data plane, each secondary must have management interfaces configured. All devices in the stack need to be the same hardware model, run the same software, and have the same licenses. Figure 6-10 shows how the stack appears in the FMC.

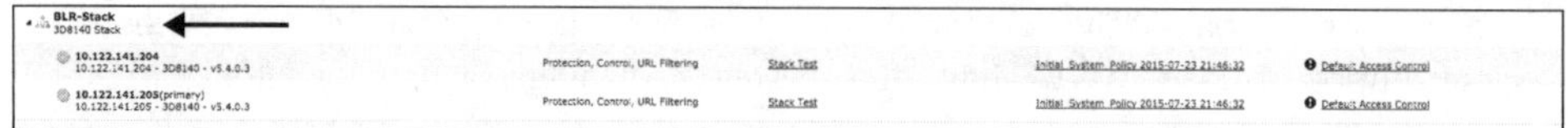

Figure 6-10 *Firepower Stack in the FMC*

Firepower Management Center (FMC)

The FMC is used to manage one or more NGIPS appliances. FMC is responsible for policy management and configuration, correlation of discovery events, event analysis, and monitoring of device statistics and health. The FMC in a NGIPS deployment should be sized for the appropriate number of IPS events; for example, FMC 4500 supports up to 300 million IPS events.

Figure 6-11 illustrates the bidirectional communication between a NGIPS device and the FMC.

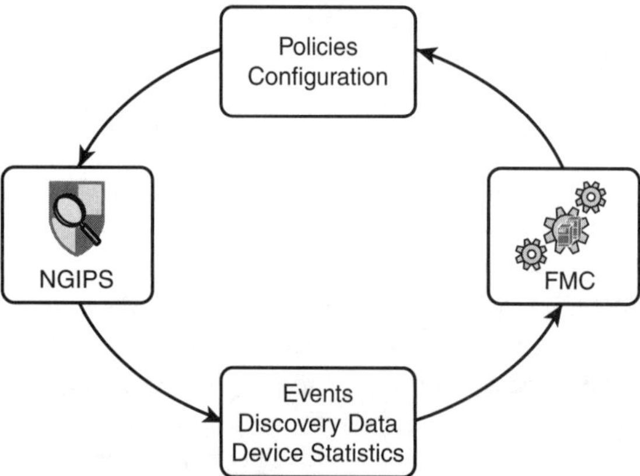

Figure 6-11 *FMC Communication*

NGIPS Deployment Options

In today's organizations, attacks come from everywhere. As networks evolve, many organizations struggle to have intrusion prevention or other security architecture evolve at the same pace. Visibility is everything: A NGIPS must be able to detect and respond to threats before they cause significant damage. Placement of NGIPS services is just as important as the rules and configuration that reside on the system. Where a NGIPS is placed is typically driven by compliance requirements (for example, PCI, HIPAA, NIST), risks, threats, and vulnerabilities specific to the organization. For example, a hospital might want to focus on protecting electronic health records (EHRs) and medical devices, which in turn would require NGIPSs in between all devices that store or process EHRs or medical devices. Some organizations might have connected devices that cannot be patched, such as an audiovisual system. NGIPS would be essential in reducing risk associated with any unpatched systems because those are the most susceptible to attacks and malware.

Industry best practices normally encourage organizations to at a minimum have NGIPSs for perimeter protection, demilitarized zones (DMZs), data centers, and critical network segments. Figure 6-12 illustrates some of the typical locations used for inline NGIPS deployments.

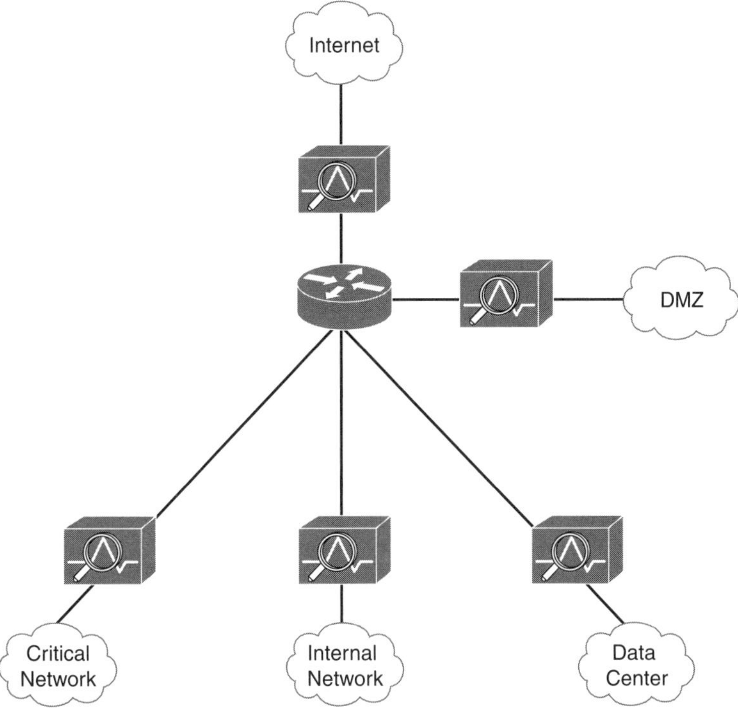

Figure 6-12 *Typical NGIPS Deployment Locations*

After determining where protection is required, the next step is to determine what type of NGIPS deployment is appropriate for the desired location. All deployment characteristics regarding networking are configured for the device in question under Devices > Device Management. The following types of deployments are supported:

- **Passive IPS deployments:** This type of deployment monitors traffic flowing across a network using a switched port analyzer (SPAN) or mirror port. This provides the system visibility within the network without being in the flow of network traffic. When configured in a passive deployment, a system cannot take certain actions, such as blocking. Passive interfaces receive all traffic unconditionally, and no traffic received on these interfaces is retransmitted.

- **Inline IPS deployments:** This type of deployment is transparently inserted on a network segment by binding two ports together. This allows the system to be installed in any network environment without the configuration of adjacent network devices. Inline interfaces receive all traffic unconditionally, but all traffic received on these interfaces is retransmitted out of an inline set unless explicitly dropped. An inline IPS deployment may be configured in one of several modes:
  - **Transparent inline mode:** This option allows the device to act as a "bump in the wire," and the device forwards all the network traffic it sees, regardless of the source and destination. In order to configure transparent inline mode, each interface must be set to use an inline set, as shown in Figure 6-13. Configuration of the inline set is the same as shown in Figure 6-14 except that the Failsafe check box is not selected.

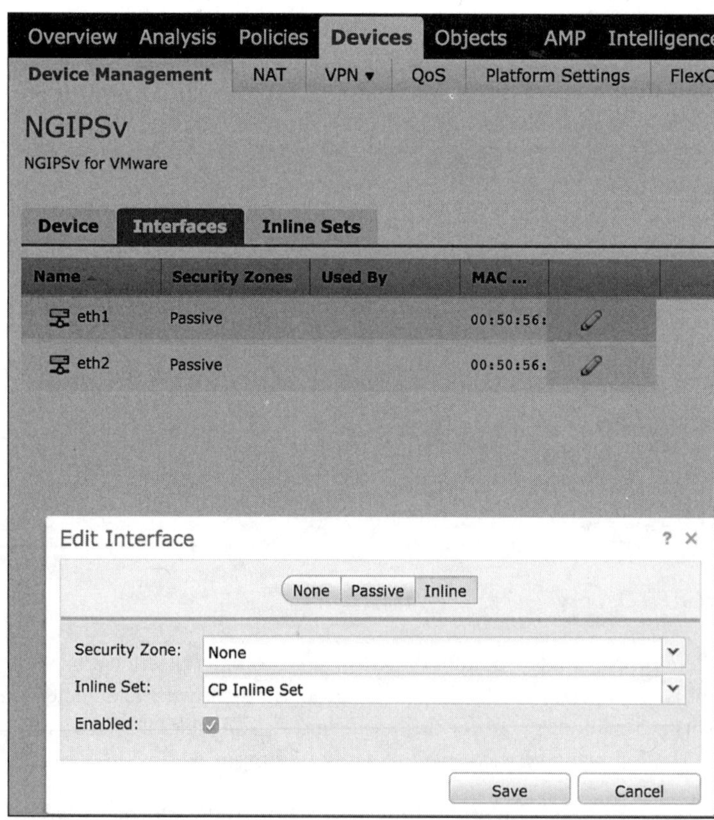

Figure 6-13 *Assigning Interfaces to an Inline Set*

  - **Bypass mode:** This setting determines how the relays in the inline interfaces respond when an interface fails. Bypass mode allows traffic to continue to pass through the interfaces. A non-bypass mode blocks traffic. Bypass mode is configured as FailSafe under the inline set configuration, as shown in Figure 6-14.

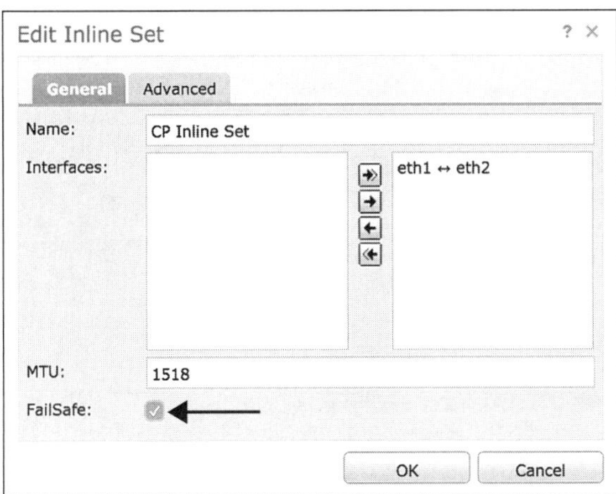

Figure 6-14 *Editing an Inline Set and Assigning Bypass Mode*

- **Tap mode:** When you create an inline interface set, the device is deployed inline, but instead of the packet flow passing through the device, a copy of each packet is sent to the device, and the network traffic flow is undisturbed. Rules that are set to drop and rules that use the replace keyword do not affect the packet stream because the device only has a copy of the packet and is not in the data plane. However, rules of these types do generate intrusion events when they are triggered. This mode is typically used in an initial deployment to minimize the risk of dropping traffic. Figure 6-15 shows how tap mode is configured under the advanced settings on the inline set configuration.

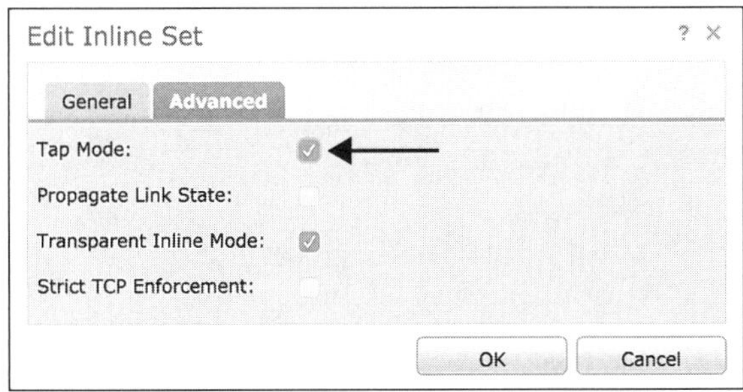

Figure 6-15 *Enabling Tap Mode*

- **Firepower Threat Defense(FTD) deployments:** When deploying a NGIPS using FTD software, the same modes of firewall deployments are available for use: transparent or routed. Also, IPS-only interface modes are available. This allows for FTD to be configured with inline pair, inline pair with tap, passive mode, or passive encapsulated remote switched port analyzer (ERSPAN). ERSPAN interfaces are allowed only when a device is in routed firewall mode. Figure 6-16 shows how an unused interface on a Firepower 2100 running FTD in routed mode can be used as a passive NGIPS interface. More detail on FTD firewall deployments, including interface configuration and routed/transparent setups, can be found in Chapter 5, "Next-Gen Firewalls."

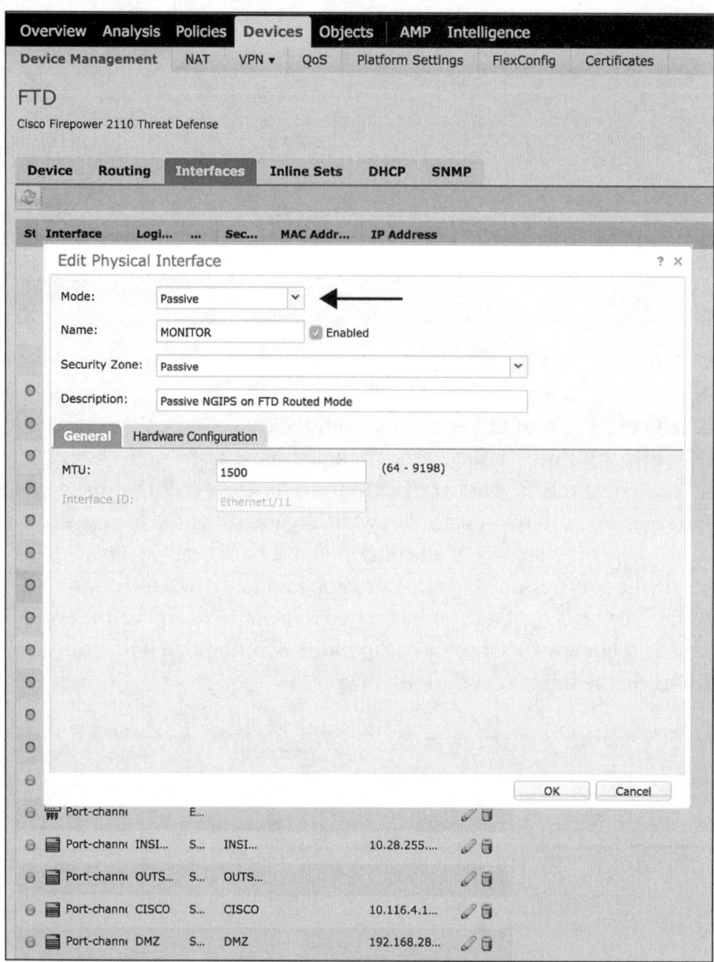

Figure 6-16 *Assigning an Interface to Passive Mode*

On Firepower 7000 and 8000 series appliances, sensing interfaces can be set to virtual switch, virtual router, or hybrid on the device. These options were originally designed for firewall deployments on 7000 and 8000 series devices. Today, the options are still available to support customers that previously deployed these appliances, but they are not recommended for greenfield deployments.

Switched interfaces can be configured on a Firepower appliance in a Layer 2 deployment to provide packet switching between two or more networks. Switched interfaces can have either a physical or logical interface configuration. The big difference is that a physical interface handles untagged VLAN traffic, and a logical interface associates an interface and a VLAN tag. After assigning the physical interface as switched, as shown in Figure 6-17, the virtual switch can be created and assigned, as shown in Figure 6-18. These interfaces will be associated with a virtual switch, which uses the media access control (MAC) address from a host to determine where to send packets.

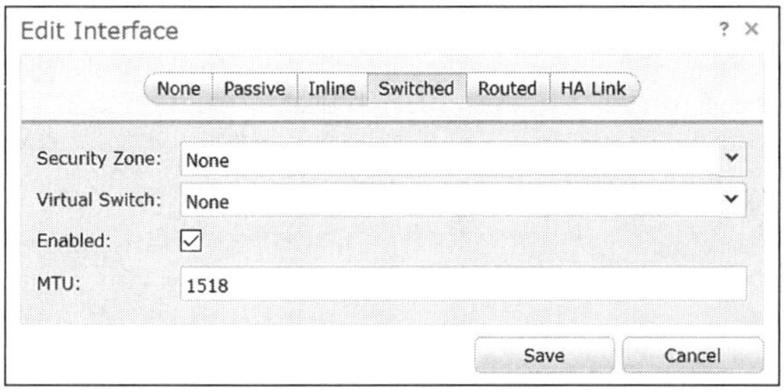

Figure 6-17 *Assigning Interface to Switched Mode*

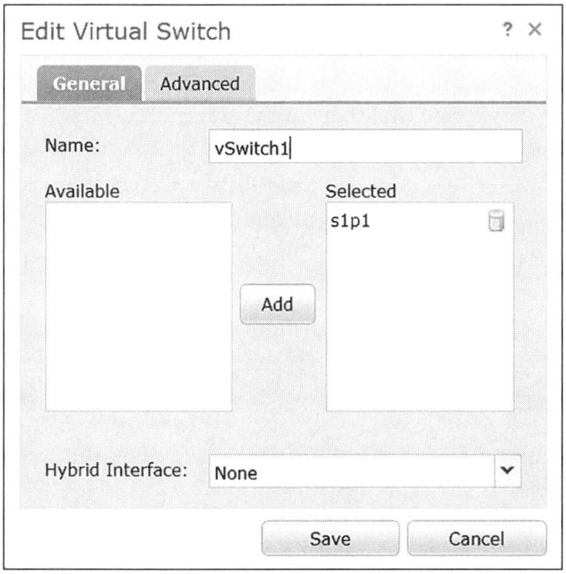

Figure 6-18 *Creating a Virtual Switch*

Routed interfaces can be used in a Layer 3 deployment so that the Firepower appliance routes traffic between two or more interfaces. Each interface must have an IP address assigned, and the interface must be assigned to a virtual router. The virtual router uses the destination IP address to route packets by making packet forwarding decisions. Figure 6-19 shows how dynamic routing can also be used with the virtual router option.

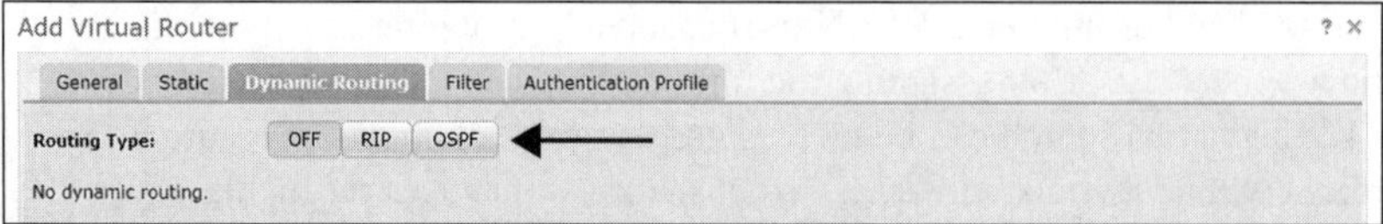

Figure 6-19 *Dynamic Routing on a Virtual Router*

Logical hybrid interfaces also can be configured on Firepower appliances to allow bridging of traffic between virtual routers and virtual switches. If IP traffic received on interfaces in a virtual switch is addressed to the MAC address of an associated hybrid logical interface, the system handles it as Layer 3 traffic and either routes or responds to the traffic, depending on the destination IP address. If the system receives any other traffic, it handles it as Layer 2 traffic and switches it appropriately.

Snort

Snort is an open source network intrusion detection and prevention system created by Martin Roesch in 1998. It is widely known for its ability to detect malicious traffic and its universal rule language. Many classes on intrusion detection and prevention use Snort to educate individuals on how to write intrusion rules, also known as signatures, to detect malicious content. This has created a following of Snort community members who also contribute the detection content they create to the rest of the community. More information on open source Snort, the community, and documentation is available at www.snort.org.

Snort is now developed by Cisco and, while it still remains a very popular open source platform, it is also the rules engine for Cisco's NGIPS. It is responsible for looking at traffic received by the NGIPS and evaluating that traffic against its compiled rules to determine whether the traffic is malicious.

Note Snort is modified, tuned, and enhanced to run in the commercially available NGIPS.

Snort Rules

A Snort rule, or intrusion rule, is a specific set of keywords and arguments used as matching criteria to identify security violations, known network attacks, and IPS evasion techniques. The system analyzes and compares network traffic against the conditions specified in each rule. If the data matches all the conditions specified in a rule, the rule triggers. The action field in the rule specifies what should be done next. For example, if the rule is an alert rule, it generates an intrusion event. If it is a pass rule, it ignores the traffic.

There are two types of intrusion rules: shared object rules, which are rules only Cisco Talos can create to detect attacks using methods that traditional standard text rules cannot detect, and standard text rules, which are rules that anyone can create. This section focuses on standard text rules.

A rule contains two logical sections: the rule header and rule body. The rule body consists of keywords and arguments to define the criteria on which to trigger an alert. Figure 6-20 illustrates the header and body of one of the rules in the Firepower system.

Rule Header

```
alert tcp $EXTERNAL_NET any -> $HOME_NET $HTTP_PORTS \
```

Rule Body

```
(msg:"SQL union select - possible sql injection attempt - GET parameter"; \
flow:to_server,established; content:"union"; fast_pattern:only; http_uri; \
content:"select"; nocase; http_uri; pcre:"/union\s+(all\s+)?select\s+/Ui"; \
metadata:policy max-detect-ips drop, policy security-ips drop, service http; \
reference:bugtraq,14876; reference:cve,2011-1667; \
reference:url,osvdb.org/show/osvdb/71463; \
classtype:misc-attack; sid:13990; rev:24; gid:1; )
```

Figure 6-20 *Intrusion Rule Anatomy*

The rule header is the portion of the rule that identifies how to match traffic based on the action, protocol, source IP, source port, operator, destination IP, and destination port. For every rule, these parameters and arguments make up the rule header. Restricting packet inspection to the packets originating from specific IP addresses, ports, directions, and protocols reduces the amount of packet inspection the system must perform. This also reduces false positives by making the rule more specific and removing the possibility of the rule triggering against packets whose matching criteria do not indicate malicious behavior. The following list describes each of the arguments that make up the rule's header:

- **Action:** This argument is the action the system takes when a packet triggers a rule. A rule with the action set to alert generates an intrusion event against the packet that triggered the rule and logs the details of that packet. A rule with the action set to pass does not generate an event against, or log the details of, the packet that triggered the rule.

- **Protocol:** This argument is the protocol of the traffic the rule inspects. Internet Control Message Protocol (ICMP), Internet Protocol (IP), Transmission Control Protocol (TCP), and User Datagram Protocol (UDP) are all network protocols that can be specified for analysis. If you use IP, all other protocols will be inspected.

- **Source and destination IP address:** This argument is a single IP address, **any**, IP address lists, CIDR notation, prefix lengths, a network variable, or a network object or network object group can be used in the source or destination IP address fields. In addition, a **!** tells the rule to exclude a specific IP address or set of IP addresses. When specifying IPv6 addresses, you can use any addressing convention defined in RFC 4291. Some examples of IP attributes in the header are **192.168.28.0/24**, **!192.168.28.1**, **$HOME_NET**.

- **Source and destination ports:** specifies the relevant source and destination ports for the rule. Ports can be listed by separating the ports with commas, by using a hyphen for a range, or by using ports defined by a port variable. Additionally, a ! tells the rule to exclude the ports defined; for example, **!21**, **80-81**, **$HTTP_PORTS**.

- **Direction:** This argument is the direction that the packet must travel for the rule to inspect it. Directional, denoted with **->**, looks for only traffic from the specified source IP address to the specified destination IP address. Bidirectional, denoted with **<->**, looks at all traffic traveling between the specified source and destination IP addresses.

The rule body, sometimes referred to as *rule options*, is where the real power of the intrusion rules language comes in. This is where the rule can very specifically drill into a packet and get to the content that actually signals malicious or suspicious activity. The rule keywords section contains event messages, patterns that a packet's payload must match to trigger the rule, and specifications of which parts of the packet the detection engine should inspect. A rule can contain multiple keyword or content references. Rules with multiple content options are treated as an AND operation for the rule to trigger, meaning both options must be matched for the rule to trigger. Some examples are **content:"union";**, **nocase;**, **content:"select";**, and **nocase;**.

The rule body is composed of the following:

- **Message:** The message is meaningful text that appears as a message when the rule triggers. The message gives immediate insight into the nature of the threat, vulnerability, or information that the rule detects.
- **Keywords and arguments:** Keywords and their associated values, called arguments, dictate how the system evaluates packets and packet-related values that the rules engine tests. The Firepower system currently supports keywords that allow you to perform inspection functions, such as content matching, protocol-specific pattern matching, and state-specific matching. You can define up to 100 arguments per keyword, and you can combine any number of compatible keywords to create highly specific rules. This helps decrease the chance of false positives and false negatives and focuses the intrusion information you receive.
- **Priority:** By default, the priority of a rule derives from the event classification for the rule. However, you can override the classification priority for a rule by adding the **priority** keyword to the rule and selecting a high, medium, or low priority. For example, to assign a high priority for a rule that detects web application attacks, add the **priority** keyword to the rule and select high as the priority.
- **Reference:** You can add references to external websites and additional information about the event. A reference provides analysts with an immediately available resource to help them identify why a packet triggered a rule or what vulnerabilities or threats a rule is finding. The following are some of the external systems that can provide data on known exploits and attacks: Bugtraq, the Common Vulnerabilities and Exposure page, McAfee, Microsoft Security Bulletin, Nessus, URLs, and secure URLs.
- **Classification:** For each rule, an attack classification can be specified that appears in the packet display of the event. There were 38 rule classifications at the time this book was published—everything from policy-violation and attempted-recon to malware-cnc and web-application-attack. For more customized content for the packet display description of the events generated by a custom rule, a custom classification can be defined.

Note It is recommended that you try to classify custom rules with a type that complements the built-in rules. This allows for easier operations in the future.

- **Snort ID (SID):** This indicates whether the rule is a local rule or a system rule. When a new rule is created, the system assigns the next available SID for a local rule. SID numbers for local rules start at 1000000, and the SID for each new local rule is incremented by 1.
- **Revision number (REV):** For a new rule, the revision number is 1. Each time a rule is modified, the revision number increments by 1.
- **Generator ID (GID):** For all standard text rules, this value is 1.

Understanding the format of the body is significant because the very specific syntax must be taken into account. Poorly formatted rules will not save or run. Rules can be defined in a single line or multiple lines, using a backslash (\) at the end of each line. Text rules are placed in a file and uploaded to the FMC. Rules can also be created or edited via the GUI on the FMC. Figure 6-21 shows an example of a rule on the FMC found under Objects > Intrusion Rules.

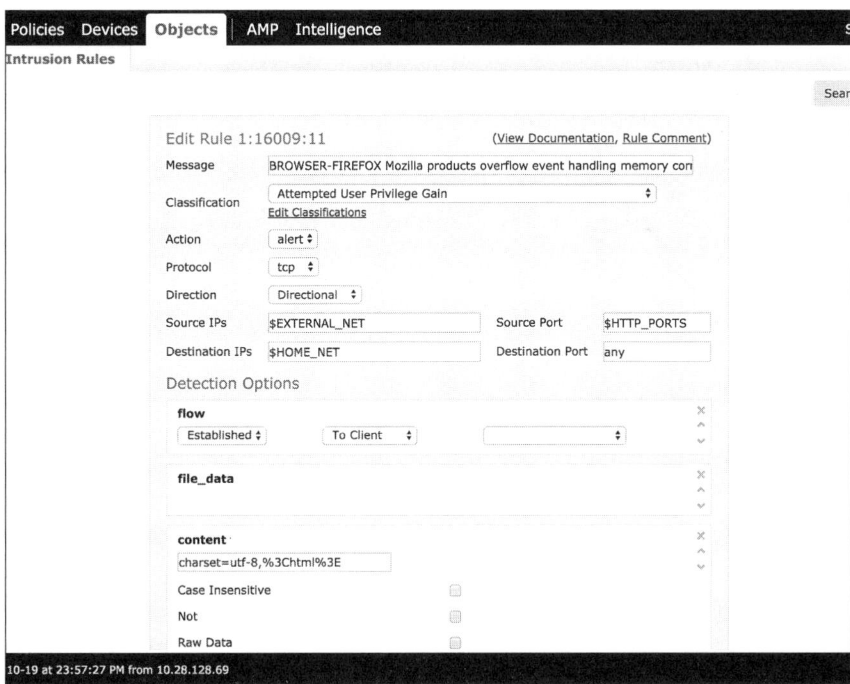

Figure 6-21 *Intrusion Rule Example in the FMC*

Options, Keywords, and Arguments in Rules

A rule's language allows matching of specific behavior in a rule by combining keywords. Keywords and their parameters dictate how the system evaluates packets and values against which the detection engine tests them. Snort supports keywords that allow performing inspection functions, such as content matching, protocol-specific pattern matching, and state-specific matching. The entire body is enclosed in parentheses. Each rule option ends in a semicolon, including the last option. If multiple arguments apply to a keyword, they are separated by commas. Options that act on content apply to the previous content string, as identified by the content keyword (for example, **content:"root";, nocase;**). Compatible keywords can be combined to create highly specific rules, which can help decrease the chance of false positives and false negatives and focus the alert feedback you receive.

In the following example, packets from the **$TELNET_SERVERS** variable with TCP port 23 going to any host in the variable **$EXTERNAL_NET** on any port will be checked to see if the string **"login: root"** occurs, regardless of case:

```
alert tcp $TELNET_SERVERS 23 -> $EXTERNAL_NET any \
(msg:"PROTOCOL-TELNET root login"; flow:to_client,established; \
content:"login|3A| root"; fast_pattern:only; metadata:ruleset community, service
telnet; \
classtype:suspicious-login; sid:719; rev:15; gid:1; )
```

The alert will include the message **"PROTOCOL-TELNET root login"**.

The **content** keyword can be used to specify content to detect in a packet. The detection engine searches the packet payload or TCP stream for that string. For example, if you enter **/etc/passwd** as the value for the **content** keyword, the detection engine searches the packet payload for that string. Figure 6-22 shows an event firing after a custom signature is added matching /etc/passwd on any port or protocol.

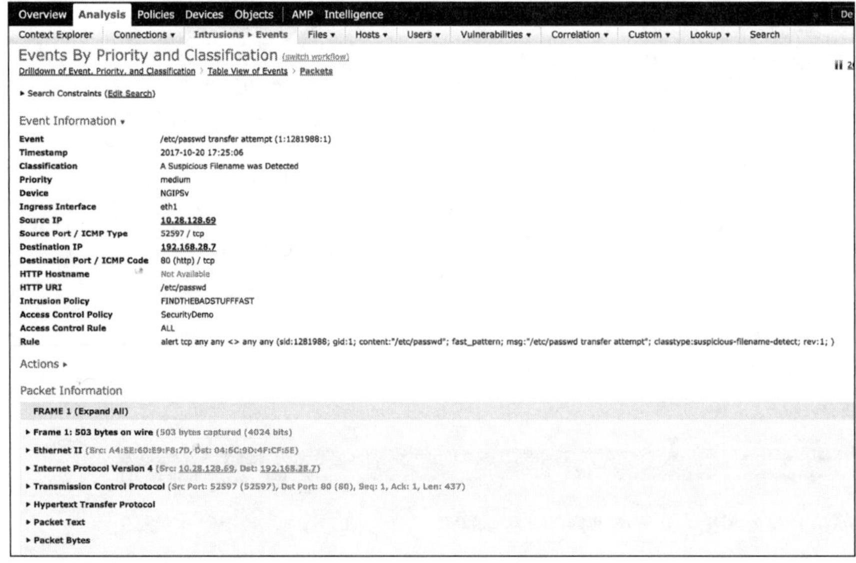

Figure 6-22 *Content Matching Custom Rule*

Content matches can use an ASCII string, hexadecimal content, or a combination of the two. Hexadecimal content is always surrounded by pipe characters (**|**). The following signature uses the content match of "**|28|C|29| Copyright 1985-**", which uses hexadecimal to denote the parentheses around the C:

```
alert tcp $HOME_NET !21:23 -> $EXTERNAL_NET any \
(msg:"INDICATOR-COMPROMISE Microsoft cmd.exe banner"; \
flow:established; content:"Microsoft Windows"; depth:18; \
content:"|28|C|29| Copyright 1985-"; distance:0; content:"Microsoft Corp.";
distance:0; \
metadata:policy max-detect-ips drop, ruleset community; reference:nessus,11633; \
classtype:successful-admin; sid:2123; rev:12; gid:1; )
```

Multiple content matches can be used in a single rule to indicate that content matches must be found in the packet payload or TCP stream for the rule to trigger. The **content** keyword is almost always followed by a modifier that indicates where the content should be searched for, whether the search is case sensitive, and other options. Matches can also be negated or can exclude content. In other words, you can specify that content *not* be present in the payload of the packets that are inspected. This is done by using the negation character (**!**).

You can constrain the location and case-sensitivity of content searches with options that modify the **content** keyword. The **nocase** argument instructs the detection engine to ignore case when searching for content matches in ASCII strings. The **offset** keyword specifies where the detection engine should start searching for content within a packet, measured in bytes. The byte count always starts at byte 0. For example, if you added a content match with an offset value of 5, the detection engine would start searching for the content at the fifth byte, counting from 0. Using the **offset** keyword promotes more efficient searches by constraining the portion of the packet payload that is searched; this is useful in instances where you know that the matching content will not appear in the first part of the packet. Conversely, you should be sure not to set the offset value too stringently because the detection engine will not inspect the bytes that appear before the specified offset value.

The **depth** keyword allows you to specify the maximum search depth, in bytes, from the beginning of the offset value, or, if no offset is configured, from the beginning of the payload. The **distance** keyword instructs the detection engine to identify subsequent content matches that occur a specified number of byes after the previous content match. For example, if you set a **distance** value of **4**, the detection engine starts searching for content matches 4 bytes after the previous content match. The **within** keyword indicates that, to trigger the rule, the next content match must occur within the specified number of bytes after **distance**. However, if no distance is defined, the value is from the end of the previous content match. For example, if you specify a **within** value of **8** and no **distance**, the next content match must occur within the next 8 bytes of the previous content match, or it does not meet the criteria that triggers the rule. In the following rule for UPnP service discovery, the rule uses a depth of 9 before it searches for the SSDP discovery message:

```
alert udp $EXTERNAL_NET any -> $HOME_NET 1900 \
(msg:"INDICATOR-SCAN UPnP service discover attempt"; flow:to_server; \
```

```
content:"M-SEARCH "; depth:9; content:"ssdp|3A|discover"; fast_pattern:only; \
metadata:policy max-detect-ips drop, ruleset community; classtype:network-scan; \
sid:1917; rev:15; gid:1; )
```

The **flow** keyword can be used to leverage the work performed by the stream reassembly preprocessor. Note that if you enabled stream processing of UDP or ICMP in the stream preprocessor, you can use this option for those protocols as well, even though they are not connection-oriented protocols. The **flow** keyword allows you to specify the direction of the traffic flow to which a rule applies, and you can apply rules to either the client flow or server flow.

Along with content matches, **pcre** (which refers to Perl Compatible Regular Expressions) may be used to write more variable content matches. **pcre** can be used to avoid writing multiple rules to match slight variations of the same content. Regular expressions are useful when searching for content that could be displayed in a variety of ways. The content may have different attributes that you want to account for in your attempt to locate it within a packet's payload. The following example uses **pcre** to match a Social Security number with dashes on any port or protocol:

```
alert tcp any any -> any any (sid:1281987; gid:1; pcre:"/[0-9]{3,3}\-[0-9]{2,2}\-
[0-9]{4,4}/"; \

msg:"SSN in Clear Text"; classtype:string-detect; rev:1; )
```

Custom Intrusion Rules

Many organizations have unique applications, threats, or vulnerabilities or simply want to get notifications when something occurs. Administrators can define custom rules that are specific to their system. Before starting writing rules, consider these practical tips:

- Review existing system rules to learn how Cisco Talos typically writes rules.
- Poorly written intrusion rules may seriously affect the performance of the system, so make sure to use a controlled network environment to test any custom intrusion rules before deploying the rules in a production environment.
- Using keyword modifiers in your rules will enhance overall performance by consuming less system resources.
- Instead of being written to detect specific exploits, the most successful rules target traffic that may attempt to exploit known vulnerabilities rather than specific known exploits.
- Some rule keywords and arguments require that traffic first be decoded or preprocessed in a certain way. If the preprocessor is a required preprocessor, the system automatically uses it with its current settings, although the preprocessor remains disabled in the network analysis policy web interface.

To add custom rules through the GUI, go to Objects > Intrusion Rules > Create Rule and fill out the form, which includes all header and body information (see Figure 6-23). Detection options allow for multiple content entries and all the previously discussed options.

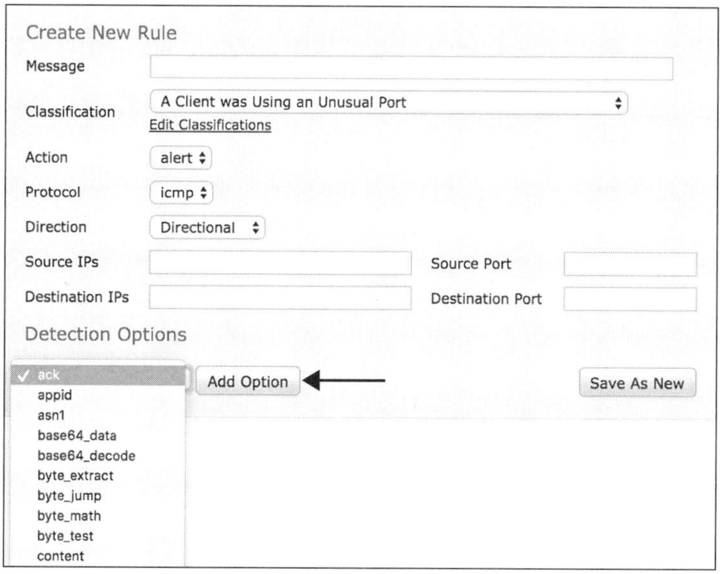

Figure 6-23 *Add a Custom Intrusion Rule Through the GUI*

Some organizations and advanced users want to create multiple rules at once. In order to do this, the rules must be written in text format and saved as a plaintext file with ASCII or UTF-8 encoding.

Let's look at an example of a scenario that might require a custom rule. Say that you have a web application that is used to allow external users to access an online portal (portal.securitydemo.net, 192.168.28.7) and malicious users are trying to access the administrative side of the application (/admin/portaladmin.jsp). The attackers' tools are using HTTP Post and have a unique user agent that always contains **"BB Wrecker"**. The developers of the web application will take months to fix the rights to the portal, so you want to write a rule to prevent external users from accessing it. The rule might look as follows:

```
alert tcp $EXTERNAL_NET any -> 192.168.28.7 $HTTP_PORTS (content:"POST";
http_method; \
content:"BB Wrecker"; http_header; nocase; uricontent:"/admin/portaladmin.jsp"; \
msg:"Security Demo Portal Admin Access Attempt"; classtype:attempted-admin;)
```

This custom intrusion rule allows the admin page to continue to function but stops the malicious attackers from accessing it with their tools. In Figure 6-24, the text file containing the custom rule is uploaded to the FMC at System > Updates > Rule Updates, and Figure 6-25 displays the update log, which shows that the rule was successfully installed.

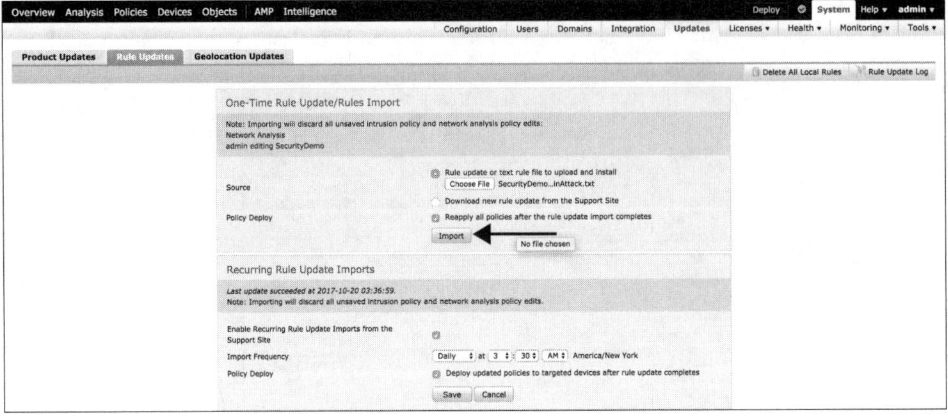

Figure 6-24 *Add a Custom Intrusion Rule Through Text File Upload*

Product Updates | Rule Updates | Geolocation Updates

Rule Update Log

Rule Update Import Log
Table View of Rule Update Import Log

▸ Search Constraints (Edit Search Save Search)

Disabled Columns

Time	Name	Type	Action	GID	SID	Rev	Policy	Details	Count
2017-10-20 21:49:06	Policy Reapply - access control policies	policy apply	apply				All	Policy Reapply transaction posted	1
2017-10-20 21:49:00	Security Demo Portal Admin Access Attempt	rule	new	1	1281989	1	All		1
2017-10-20 21:49:00	/var/sf/SRU/SecurityDemoAdminAttack.txt	Text Rule File Import	new					Installed successfully	1

Figure 6-25 *Rule Update Import Log*

After the import, the rule must be enabled in the intrusion policy to start enforcing, as discussed later in the chapter. Figure 6-26 illustrates the event that resulted from the custom rule.

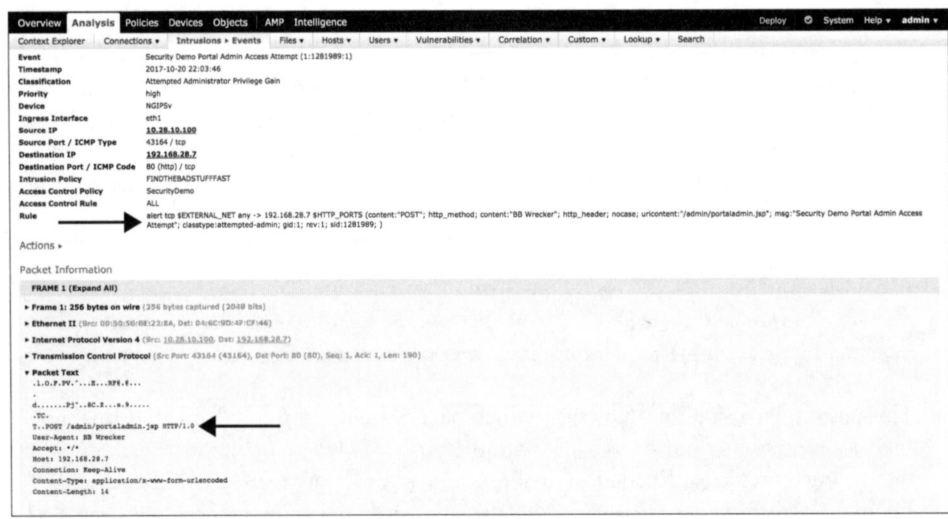

Figure 6-26 *Security Demo Custom Rule Event*

Preprocessors and Network Analysis

Preprocessors prepare traffic to be further inspected by normalizing traffic and identifying protocol anomalies. Preprocessors can generate preprocessor events when packets trigger preprocessor options that have been configured. The base policy for the network analysis policy determines which preprocessors are enabled by default and the default configuration for each.

Preprocessors do one or more of the following:

- Provide detection for attacks and activity that is not able to be done by standard Snort rules
- Provide normalization services to present data in a standardized format
- Provide reassembly services so that detection can be performed against a complete message

By default, the system uses the Balanced Security and Connectivity network analysis policy to preprocess all traffic handled by an access control policy. However, a different default network analysis policy can be chosen to perform this preprocessing. The system provides a choice of several nonmodifiable network analysis policies, which are tuned for a specific balance of security and connectivity by Cisco Talos. A custom network analysis policy with custom preprocessing settings can also be created and used.

> **Note** In most cases, configuring preprocessors requires specific expertise, and a preprocessor typically requires little or no modification. Tailoring preprocessing, especially using multiple custom network analysis policies, is an advanced task. Because preprocessing and intrusion inspection are so closely related, the network analysis and intrusion policies examining a single packet must complement each other.

To configure network analysis policies, go to Policies > Access Control and click Network Analysis Policy. You can then view your current custom network analysis policies or create a new policy, as shown in Figure 6-27.

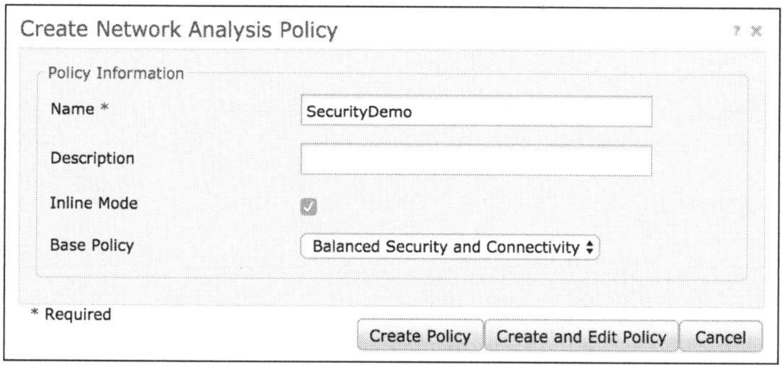

Figure 6-27 *Create a New Network Analysis Policy*

Network analysis policies have preprocessors for Back Orifice detection, checksum verification, DCE/RPC configuration, DNS configuration, FTP and Telnet configuration, GTP command channel configuration, HTTP configuration, IP defragmentation, packet decoding, SMTP configuration, SSH configuration, SSL configuration, Sun RPC configuration, TCP stream configuration, and UDP stream configuration. Normally, only a few of these settings are modified, and typically those changes are based on customizations per organization, such as specifying uncommon ports for inspection or IP addresses/CIDR blocks for targets of the preprocessor. Figure 6-28 illustrates changing the ports and targets for the FTP and Telnet preprocessor.

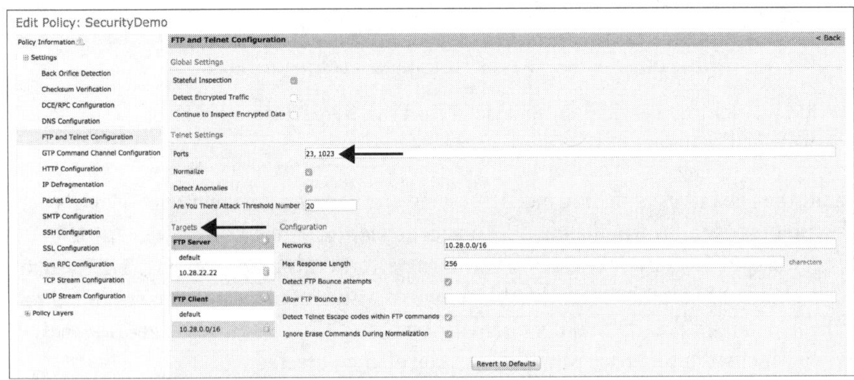

Figure 6-28 *FTP and Telnet Preprocessor Configuration*

For networks that contain asymmetric traffic and where the NGIPS sees only unidirectional traffic (or half of the traffic), you can use the TCP stream configuration to handle it by selecting Asynchronous Network (see Figure 6-29). When this option is enabled, the system does not reassemble TCP streams to increase performance. While in some environments there are no other alternatives, this setting does limit the ability of the NGIPS to detect certain threats and evasive techniques by not providing visibility into the full symmetric traffic.

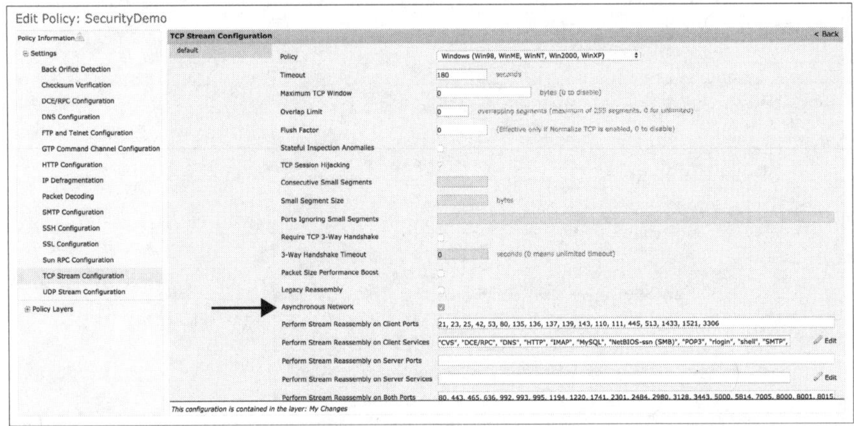

Figure 6-29 *Asynchronous Network Configuration in TCP Stream Preprocessor*

To assign the newly created network analysis policy, go to Policies > Access Control > Edit > Advanced > Network Analysis and Intrusion Policies. Along with the network analysis policy, you need to set the default intrusion policy to initially inspect traffic before the system can determine exactly how to inspect that traffic. This is needed because sometimes the system must process the first few packets in a connection and allow them to pass before it can decide which access control rule (if any) will handle the traffic. By default, the default intrusion policy uses the default variable set. A default intrusion policy is especially useful when performing application control and URL filtering because the system cannot identify applications or filter URLs before a connection is fully established between the client and the server. For example, if a packet matches all the other conditions in an access control rule with an application or URL condition, it and subsequent packets are allowed to pass until the connection is established and application or URL identification is complete, usually three to five packets. The system inspects these allowed packets with the default intrusion policy, which can generate events and, if placed inline, block malicious traffic. After the system identifies the access control rule or default action that should handle the connection, the remaining packets in the connection are handled and inspected accordingly. Figure 6-30 illustrates the default intrusion policy and network analysis policy configuration.

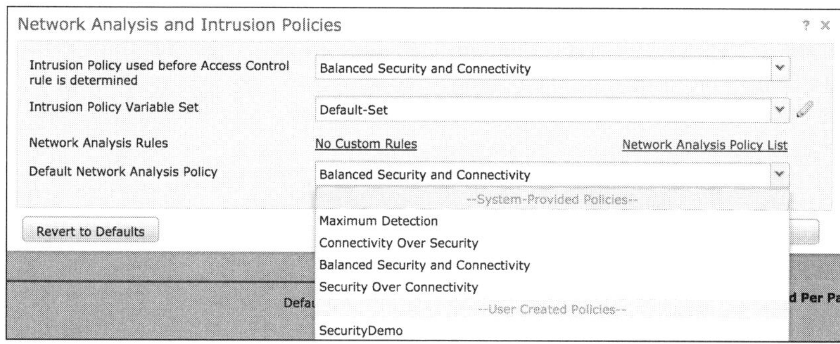

Figure 6-30 *Network Analysis and Intrusion Policies*

Configuring a NGIPS

When you understand the basics of a NGIPS and how the rules work, configuration is typically easily accomplished. The following basic steps are required to configure and enable the Firepower NGIPS:

Step 1. Add a custom intrusion policy or use a system default policy (for example, Balanced Security and Connectivity).

Step 2. Configure a variable set to be used with the intrusion policy.

Step 3. Create or modify an access control policy to reference the intrusion policy and variable set.

Step 4. Configure security intelligence on the access control policy in use.

Step 5. Deploy changes to sensors.

Intrusion Policies

Intrusion policies configure all rules, their associated states (generate events, drop and generate events, or disable), policy layers, and advanced settings.

System-Provided Intrusion Policies

The Firepower system provides several out-of-the-box intrusion policies provided by Cisco Talos. For these policies, Talos sets intrusion and preprocessor rule states and also provides the initial configurations for preprocessors and other advanced settings. The system-provided policies can be used as-is, or they can be used as a base for creating custom policies. When using a system-provided policy as the base, importing rule updates may modify settings in the base policy. However, the policy can be configured so that a base policy change does not automatically affect the custom policy. This allows administrators to update system-provided base policies manually, on a schedule independent of rule updates. In either case, changes that a rule update makes to the base policy do not change or override settings in My Changes or any other policy layer, meaning even if a signature is turned off with a rule update, you will still see that you changed the rule manually from Generate Events to Drop and Generate Events.

No system-provided policy covers all network environment, traffic mix, or defensive posture requirements. Each policy covers common cases and network setups that provide a starting point for a well-tuned defensive policy. Although you can use system-provided policies as-is, Cisco strongly recommends that you use them as the base for custom policies that are tuned to suit your organization's network.

Note Even if system-provided network analysis and intrusion policies are used, administrators should configure the system's intrusion variables to accurately reflect the network environment. At a minimum, modify key default variables in the default set, such as **HOME_NET**. Many rules in the system use **HOME_NET** and **EXTERNAL_NET** to represent outside connections traversing to the inside network. If variables are not defined, many key protections are not effective.

As new vulnerabilities become known, Talos releases intrusion rule updates. These rule updates can modify any system-provided intrusion policy and can provide new and updated intrusion rules and preprocessor rules, modified states for existing rules, and modified default policy settings. Rule updates may also delete rules from system-provided policies and provide new rule categories, and they may modify the default variable set. If a rule update will affect the deployment, the GUI marks the affected intrusion and network analysis policies, as well as their parent access control policies, as out of date. An updated policy must be redeployed for its changes to take effect. The rule updates can be configured to automatically redeploy affected intrusion policies, either alone or in combination with affected access control policies. Figure 6-31 shows the configuration required to accomplish redeploying policies under System > Updates >

Rules Updates. This allows the system to easily and automatically keep the deployment up-to-date to protect against recently discovered exploits and intrusions.

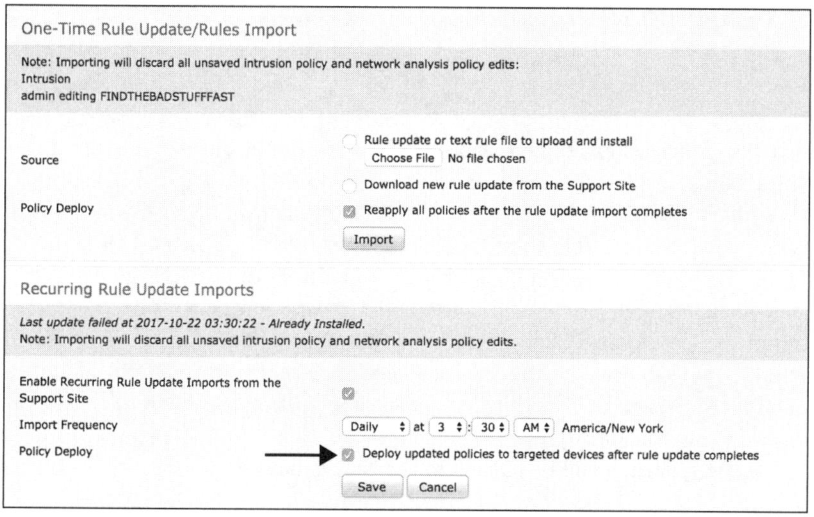

Figure 6-31 *Policy Deploy Settings After Rule Updates*

Cisco delivers the following network analysis and intrusion policies with the Firepower system:

- **Balanced Security and Connectivity:** This policy is built for both speed and detection. It serves as a good starting point for most organizations and deployment types. The system uses the Balanced Security and Connectivity policies and settings as defaults in most cases.

- **Connectivity Over Security:** This policy is built for organizations where connectivity (that is, being able to get to all resources) takes precedence over network infrastructure security. This intrusion policy enables far fewer rules than those enabled in the Security over Connectivity policy. Only the most critical rules that block traffic are enabled.

- **Security over Connectivity:** This policy is built for organizations where network infrastructure security takes precedence over user convenience. This intrusion policy enables numerous network anomaly intrusion rules that could alert on or drop legitimate traffic.

- **Maximum Detection:** This policy is built for organizations where network infrastructure security is given even more emphasis than is given by the Security over Connectivity policy, with the potential for even greater operational impact. For example, this intrusion policy enables rules in a large number of threat categories, including malware, exploit kits, old and common vulnerabilities, and known in-the-wild exploits.

- **No Rules Active:** In this intrusion policy, all intrusion rules and advanced settings are disabled. This policy provides a starting point for creating your own intrusion policy instead of basing it on the enabled rules in one of the other system-provided policies. Typically, this is performed only by advanced users.

Policy Layers

Layers in intrusion policies allow organizations to differentiate the changes made to a base policy. Administrators can create and edit intrusion policies without consciously using layers. While modifying policy configurations, the system automatically includes the changes in a single configurable layer that is initially named My Changes. Optionally, up to 200 layers can be added, and any combination of settings can be configured. User layers can be copied, merged, moved, and deleted, and, most importantly, shared with other policies of the same type. Figure 6-32 shows two built-in layers, one for the base policy, Security Over Connectivity, and one for Firepower Recommended Rules, along with a single user layer that represents all changes the administrator made to the base policy. At the top, the policy summary helps represent all the layers put together and what intrusion policy configuration will be pushed to the NGIPS device.

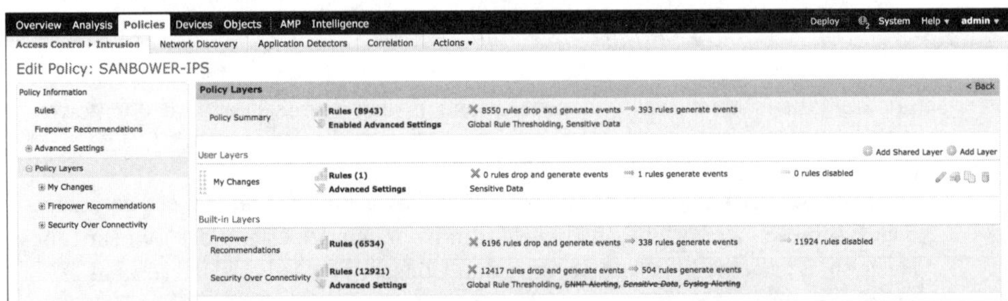

Figure 6-32 *Default Policy Layers with Firepower Recommended Rules Configured*

Each policy layer contains complete configurations of all intrusion rules and advanced settings in the intrusion policy. The lowest, base, policy layer includes all the settings from the base policy that was selected when the policy was created. A setting in a higher layer takes precedence over the same setting in a lower layer. Features not explicitly set in a layer inherit their settings from the next highest layer where they are explicitly set. The system flattens the layers—that is, it applies only the cumulative effect of all settings—when it handles network traffic.

A *sharable layer* is a layer that is created on one policy and is allowed to be shared with another. To create a sharable layer, simply click the edit icon on the layer in the policy and select Allow This Layer to be Used by Other Policies, as shown in Figure 6-33. The advanced settings can also be shared or inherited from the policy.

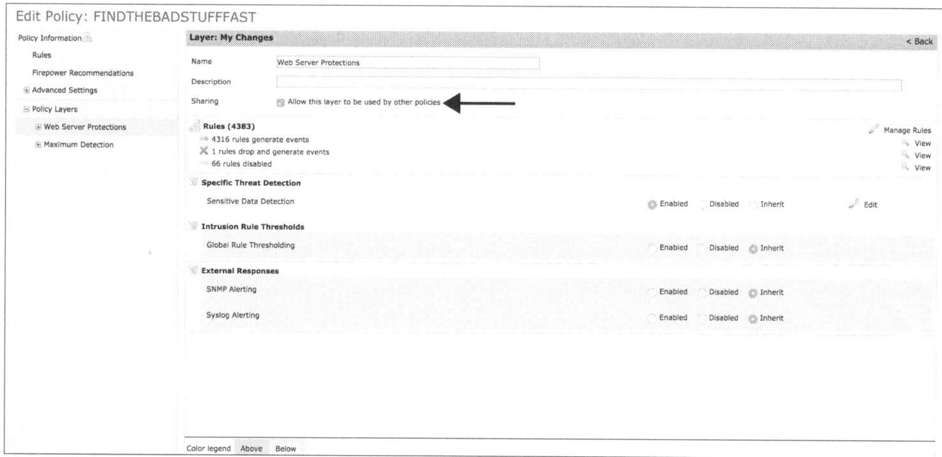

Figure 6-33 *Sharing an Intrusion Policy Layer*

After sharing the layer, you can add the new sharable layer by editing the target policy and clicking Add Shared Layer and selecting the shared layer. Figure 6-34 illustrates adding a sharable layer to a new policy.

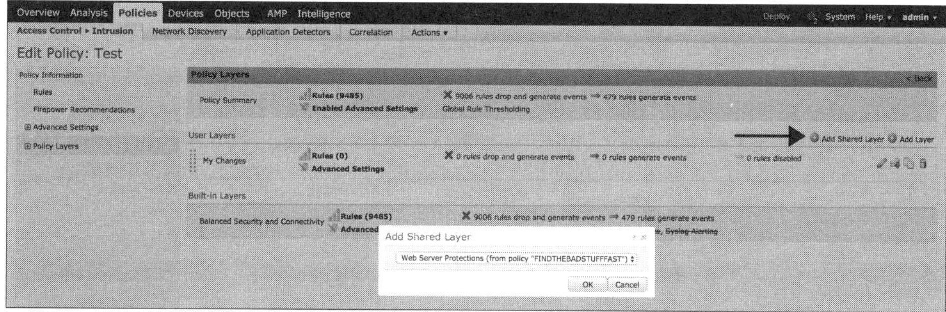

Figure 6-34 *Using a Sharable Layer in an Intrusion Policy*

Many organizations use a master policy where they create the companywide templated policies and allow them to be shared. Then the appropriate layers can be added as shared layers to the policies for all applicable intrusion policies. The companywide layer in the master policy includes settings applicable to all use cases. A use case layer, such as Web Server Protection Layer, includes settings specific to that use case. For example, in the case of a web server layer, this would be enabled for policies that are protecting web servers and would need to have rules specific to protecting those assets from web application attacks. Figure 6-35 shows how the master policy could have sharable layers that would be reused in an intrusion policy written for DMZ and data center use cases.

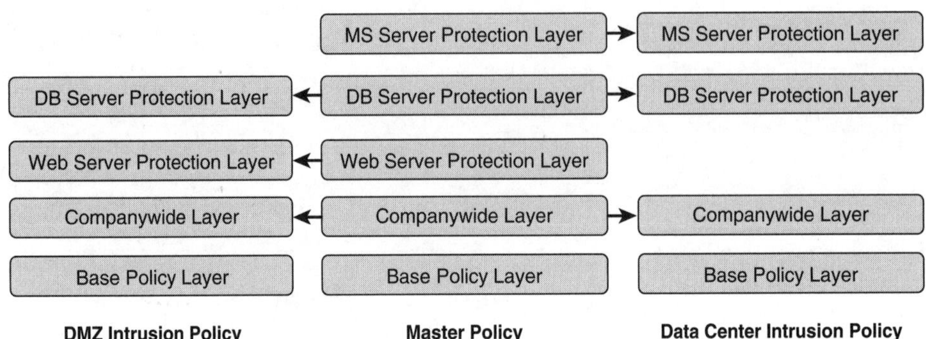

Figure 6-35 *Master Policy Sharing Layers with Use Case Policies*

Many other layer configurations are possible. For example, you could define policy layers by company, by department, by network, or even by location. In the case of an intrusion policy, you could also include advanced settings in one layer and rule settings in another.

Advanced Settings

The base policy for the intrusion policy determines which advanced settings are enabled by default and the default configuration for each. When Advanced Settings is chosen in the navigation panel of an intrusion policy, the policy lists its advanced settings by type. On the Advanced Settings page, you can enable or disable advanced settings in the intrusion policy, and you can also access advanced setting configuration pages. An advanced setting must be enabled in order to be configured. Figure 6-36 shows the Advanced Setting page on the FMC found under Policy > Intrusion > Edit Policy > Advanced Settings.

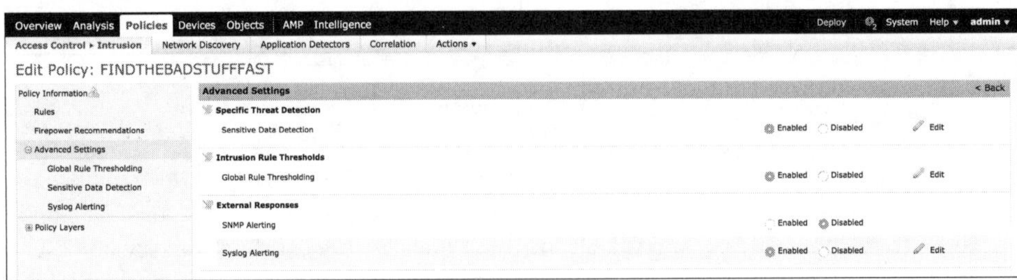

Figure 6-36 *Intrusion Policy Advanced Settings*

In the Specific Threat Detection section, you can see the sensitive data preprocessor, which detects sensitive data such as credit card numbers and Social Security numbers in ASCII text. The advanced options of this preprocessor are shown in Figure 6-37. The other preprocessors that detect specific threats (Back Orifice attacks, several port scan types, and rate-based attacks that attempt to overwhelm your network with excessive traffic) are configured in network analysis policies.

Sensitive Data Detection
< Back
Configure Rules for Sensitive Data Detection
Global Settings
Mask (Obscure all but the last four credit card or Social Security numbers.)
Networks
Global Threshold 25 (Total occurrences across all data types combined before generating a global threshold event.)
Targets
Data Types
Credit Card Numbers
Email Addresses
U.S. Phone Numbers
U.S. Social Security Numbers (w/out dashes)
U.S. Social Security Numbers (with dashes)
Configuration
Data Type Credit Card Numbers
Threshold 20 (Total occurrences of this data type before generating an event.)
Destination Ports 21,25,80,110,143
Application Protocols "FTP Data", "HTTP", "IMAP", "POP3", "SMTP" Edit
Revert to Defaults

Figure 6-37 *Sensitive Data Detection Configuration*

Another advanced and useful setting is global rule thresholding. It can prevent the system from being overwhelmed with a large number of events by allowing administrators to use thresholds to limit the number of times the system logs and displays intrusion events. The global rule threshold sets limits for event logging for an intrusion policy. Organizations can set a global rule threshold across all traffic to limit how often the policy logs events from a specific source or destination and displays those events per specified time period. When a global threshold is set, that threshold applies for each rule in the policy that does not have an overriding specific threshold.

Every intrusion policy contains a default global rule threshold that applies by default to all intrusion rules and preprocessor rules. This default threshold limits the number of events on traffic going to a destination to one event per 60 seconds. Figure 6-38 shows the default thresholds.

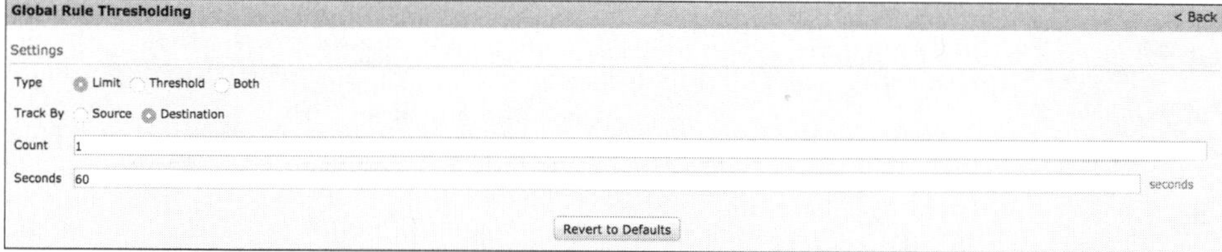

Figure 6-38 *Sensitive Data Detection Configuration*

> **Note** You can customize thresholds on a per-signature basis by selecting Event Filtering and Threshold while the rule in question is selected.

In addition to the various views of intrusion events within the GUI, external responses can also be configured in the advanced settings of the intrusion policy to enable logging to system log (syslog) facilities or sends event data to an SNMP trap server. Per policy, you can specify intrusion event notification limits, set up intrusion event notification to external logging facilities, and configure external responses to intrusion events.

Note While using syslog is pretty standard in most organizations, the recommended way of receiving intrusion alerts external to the FMC is to use the Event Streamer (eStreamer). The FMC eStreamer uses a message-oriented protocol to stream events and host profile information to client applications, such as security information and event management (SIEM) systems.

Committing Changes

After making changes to an intrusion policy, all changes must be either committed or discarded on the Policy Information page. In the FMC configuration, settings on this page control whether administrators are prompted (or required) to comment on the intrusion policy changes when they commit them and whether changes and comments are recorded in the audit log. Figure 6-39 illustrates the commit process. In order for all changes to take effect, a deployment to the corresponding devices must be performed.

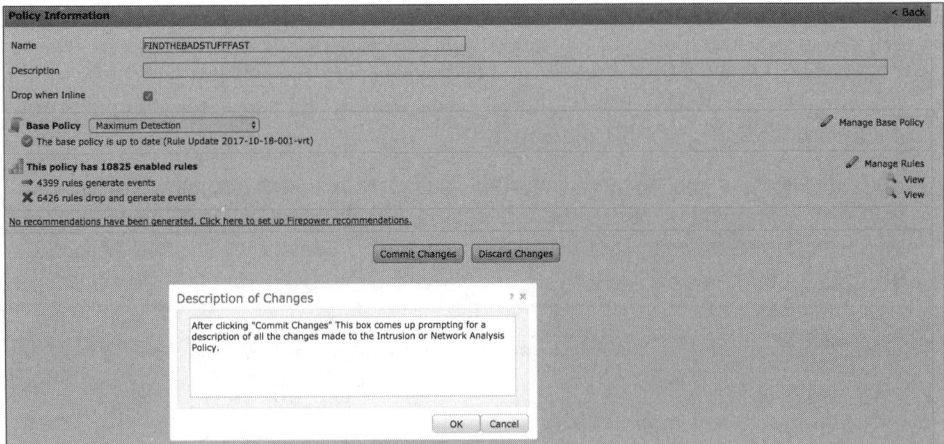

Figure 6-39 *Committing Changes to Intrusion Policy*

The system caches one intrusion policy per user. While editing an intrusion policy, if a user chooses any menu or other path to another page, the changes stay in the system cache even if the user leaves the page. While editing a network analysis or intrusion policy, if the user exits the policy editor without saving the changes, the system caches those changes. Those changes are cached even when the user logs out of the system or experiences a system crash. The policy must be committed or discarded before the user can edit another policy of the same type.

Variables

Variables are values commonly used in intrusion rules to identify source and destination IP addresses and ports. They allow objects to be reused without requiring IP addresses and ports to be typed out every time they are needed. Variables can also be used in intrusion policies to represent IP addresses in rule suppressions, adaptive profile updates, and dynamic rule states. Variable sets are used to manage, customize, and group the variables. The default variable set provided by the system can be used, or a custom set can be created. In any set, the predefined default variables can be modified, and user-defined variables can be added or modified.

Most of the shared object rules and standard text rules that the Firepower system provides use predefined default variables to define networks and port numbers. For example, the majority of the rules use the variable **$HOME_NET** to specify the protected network and the variable **$EXTERNAL_NET** to specify the unprotected (or outside) network. In addition, specialized rules often use other predefined variables. For example, rules that detect exploits against web servers use the **$HTTP_SERVERS** and **$HTTP_PORTS** variables.

Rules are most effective when variables accurately reflect the organization's network environment. At a minimum, the default variables in the default set should be modified to accurately reflect the target environment. By ensuring that a variable such as **$HOME_NET** correctly defines the network and **$HTTP_SERVERS** includes all web servers on the network, processing is optimized and all relevant systems are monitored for suspicious activity. Figure 6-40 shows how to create a new custom variable set by going to Objects > Object Management > Variable Set and clicking Add Variable Set. For this variable set, the **HOME_NET** variable has been changed to include the two internal networks, as shown in Figure 6-41.

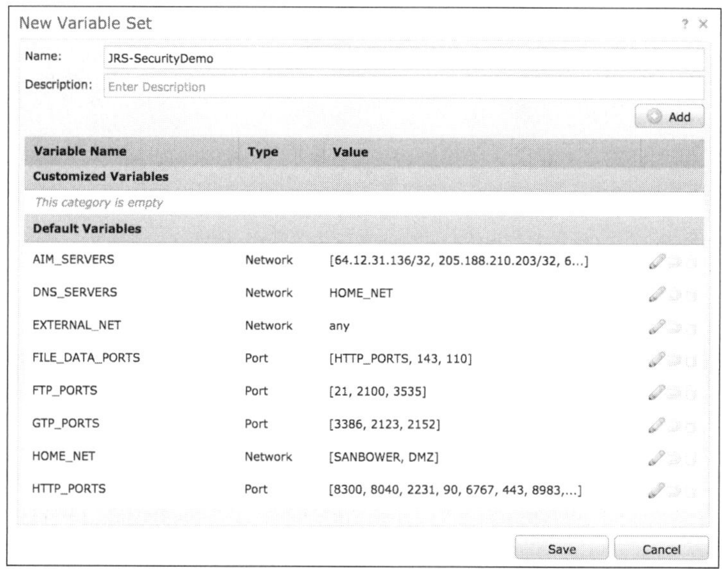

Figure 6-40 *Custom Variable Set*

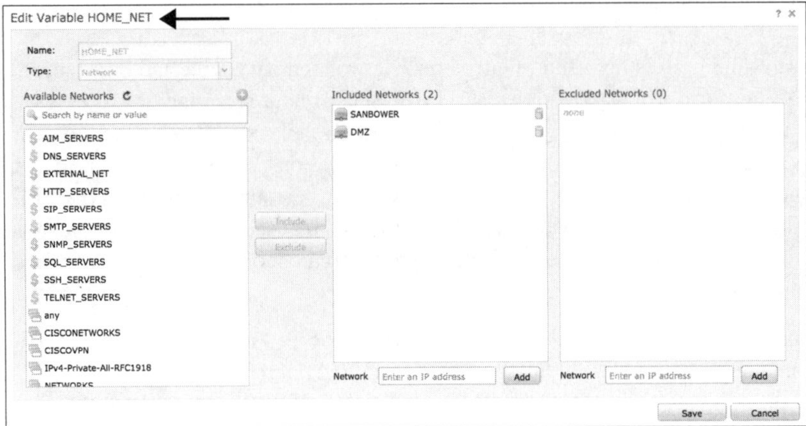

Figure 6-41 *Modifying* HOME_NET *Variable*

To use custom variables, the variable sets must be linked to intrusion policies associated with access control rules or with the default action of an access control policy. By default, the default variable set is linked to all intrusion policies used by access control policies. Figure 6-42 shows selecting the custom variable set created previously for the access control policy.

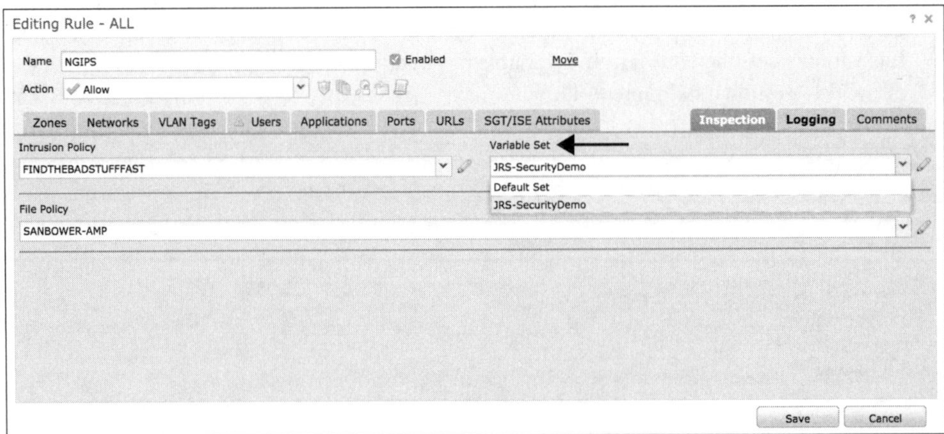

Figure 6-42 *Network Analysis and Intrusion Policies*

If you add a variable to any set adds, it is added to all sets; that is, each variable set is a collection of all variables.

Initially, the Firepower system provides a single default variable set composed of predefined default values. Each variable in the default set is initially set to its default value, which for a predefined variable is the value set by Cisco Talos and provided in rule updates.

You could work with variables only in the default set, but in many cases, you can benefit most by adding one or more custom sets, configuring different variable values in different sets, and perhaps even adding new variables. For example, you might have a variable set for a data center NGIPS and a different variable set for the Internet edge. When using multiple sets, it is important to remember that the current value of any variable in the default set determines the default value of the variable in all other sets. When you select Variable Sets on the Object Manager page, the object manager lists the default variable set and any custom sets you created. It is also recommended to create a new variable set rather than modify the default to make it clear that the variables have been changed.

Access Control Policies

Chapter 5 introduces access control policies (ACPs) in the context of firewalls, applications, and URL rules. This chapter explores ACPs for NGIPS rules. You use access control rules to tell the Firepower system to inspect traffic using intrusion policies. Rules within an ACP afford the opportunity to customize which intrusion policy is applied to certain traffic. For example, traffic for internal users connecting to the Internet does not necessarily need to be inspected for web server threats, but traffic to the DMZ does. By not using the same intrusion policy for all traffic, the system can be optimized to inspect traffic with only necessary rules, thus saving critical resources for other processing the appliance performs. As described in the "Preprocessors and Network Analysis" section, earlier in this chapter, the default intrusion policy also is used to initially inspect traffic before the system can determine exactly how to inspect that traffic.

If a NGIPS is also performing the task of a NGFW, then typically IPS policies are added to the rule associated with permitting traffic to certain services. Figure 6-43 shows an example of a rule created to allow external users to DMZ web servers but that also enables intrusion prevention for traffic matching the rule and using the assigned variable set. To add a new rule in the FMC, go to Policy > Access Control > Edit ACP > Add Rule. Intrusion policy is configured on the Inspection tab.

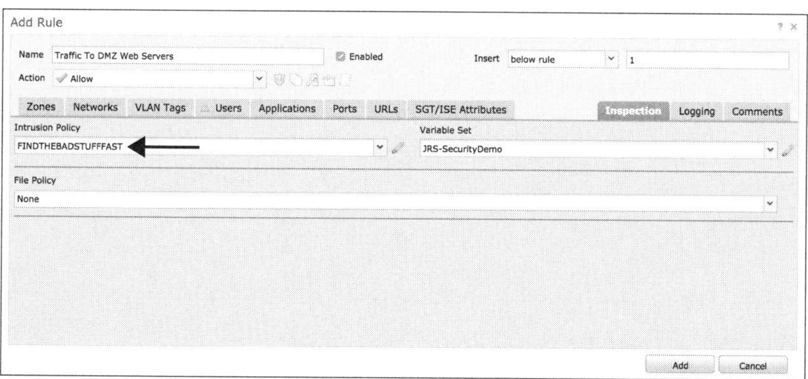

Figure 6-43 *New Access Control Rule Specifying an Intrusion Policy*

The same type of rule could be used in NGIPS-only deployments and typically would focus on what to inspect and what to allow and then inspect, as seen with firewall rules. Each access control rule can be used to match traffic based on zones, networks, geolocation, VLAN tags, users, applications, ports, URLs, and SGT/ISE attributes. This flexibility gives administrators the ability to match any of those characteristic and differentiate intrusion policy to match the use case the rule matches. The granularity is vast, and combinations of rules are endless. For example, a rule could be created to apply an intrusion policy customized for contractors on Android devices, coming from the Washington, DC, location, and connecting to social media applications hosted in all countries except the United States. Most organizations probably do not need to be this specific in their policies, but the fact that you can be is important to understand. Many organizations have regulatory and security compliance requirements that determine the level of inspection and rules associated with different use cases and flows. This documentation should be used to help configure intrusion policies.

As a NGIPS deployment best practice, it is typically recommended that you create a policy that justifies a separate intrusion policy. For example, most organizations apply different policies to different places in the network (for example, one policy for the Internet edge outbound and another for the Internet edge DMZ).

When it comes to logging, intrusion events are controlled by the intrusion policy, but if an organization wants to see connection events for allowed or blocked traffic, logging must be configured on the access control rule under the Logging tab.

Performance Settings

A NGIPS provides several features for improving the performance of the system as it analyzes traffic for attempted intrusions. In the advanced settings of the access control policy, a few of the sections are specific to intrusion performance settings. The section Performance Settings offers the following configurable options:

- **Pattern Matching Limits:** You can configure the maximum pattern states to analyze per packet (see Figure 6-44).

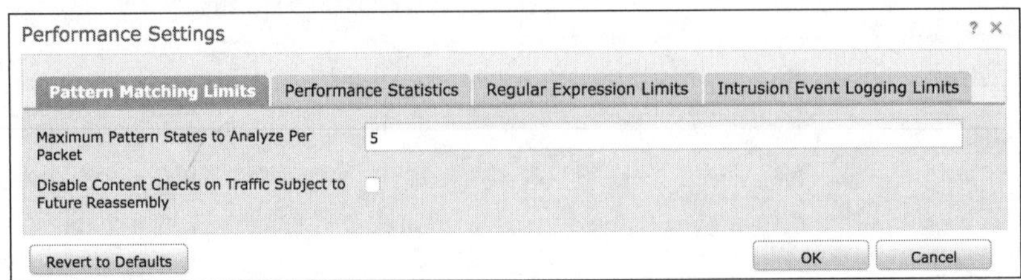

Figure 6-44 *Pattern Matching Limits*

- **Performance Statistics:** You can configure the basic parameters of how devices monitor and report their own performance. You can specify the intervals at which the system updates performance statistics on your devices.

Note It is recommended that you not enable the items under Troubleshooting Options in the Performance Statistics section without explicit instructions from Cisco TAC (see Figure 6-45).

Performance Settings
Pattern Matching Limits | Performance Statistics | Regular Expression Limits | Intrusion Event Logging Limits
Sample time (seconds) 300
Minimum number of packets 0
Troubleshooting Options
Log Session/Protocol Distribution
Summary
Revert to Defaults | OK | Cancel

Figure 6-45 *Performance Statistics*

- **Regular Expression Limits:** You can override default match and recursion limits on PCRE that are used in intrusion rules to examine packet payload content (see Figure 6-46).

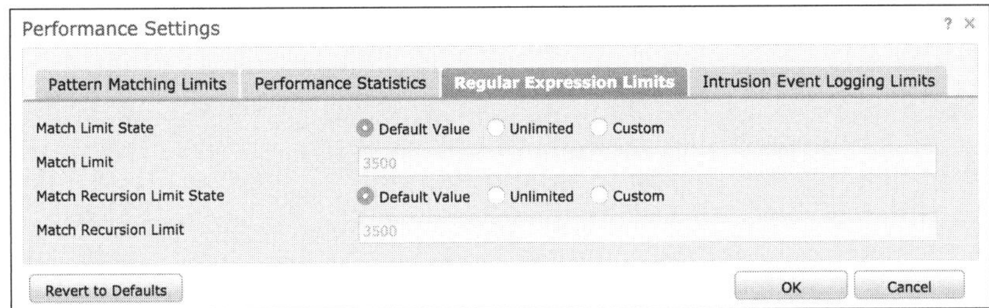

Figure 6-46 *Regular Expression Limits*

- **Intrusion Event Logging Limits:** You can specify the number of packets to allow in the event queue. You can also, before and after stream reassembly, enable or disable inspection of packets that will be rebuilt into larger streams (see Figure 6-47).

Performance Settings
Pattern Matching Limits | Performance Statistics | Regular Expression Limits | Intrusion Event Logging Limits
Maximum Events Stored Per Packet 8
Maximum Events Logged Per Packet 5
Prioritize Events Logging By Content Length
Revert to Defaults | OK | Cancel

Figure 6-47 *Intrusion Event Logging Limits*

A NGIPS also has latency-based performance settings that balance security with the need to maintain device latency at an acceptable level with packet and rule latency thresholding. Each access control policy has latency-based settings that use thresholding to manage packet and rule processing performance. Packet latency thresholding measures the total elapsed time taken to process a packet by applicable decoders, preprocessors, and rules, and it ceases inspection of a packet if the processing time exceeds a configurable threshold. Rule latency thresholding measures the elapsed time each rule takes to process an individual packet, suspends the violating rule along with a group of related rules for a specified time if the processing time exceeds the rule latency threshold a configurable consecutive number of times, and restores the rules when the suspension expires. By default, the system takes latency-based performance settings from the latest intrusion rule update deployed on a system. You configure latency-based performance settings in the advanced section of the access control policy, but you will rarely change them unless you're working with support.

Intelligent Application Bypass (IAB) identifies applications that are trusted to traverse the network without further inspection if performance and flow thresholds are exceeded. For example, if a nightly data transfer significantly impacts system performance, you can configure thresholds that, if exceeded, trust traffic generated by the high-throughput application. The system implements IAB on traffic allowed by access control rules or the access control policy's default action before the traffic is subject to deep inspection. A test mode allows administrators to determine whether thresholds are exceeded and, if so, to identify the application flows that would have been bypassed if you had actually enabled IAB. Figure 6-48 shows the IAB configuration parameters.

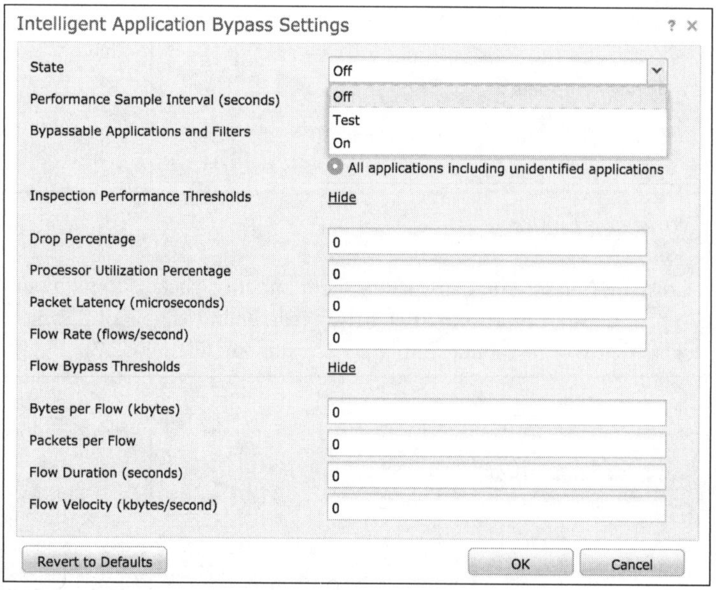

Figure 6-48 *Intelligent Application Bypass Configuration*

Security Intelligence

Security intelligence happens before resource-intensive deep packet inspection (DPI) is performed, which can improve performance because it is much easier to match connection information than it is to match an intrusion rule. By default, each ACP allows the global whitelist and denies the global blacklist for networks, URLs, and DNS security intelligence lists. All other lists are not configured by default. The following data is included in the various types of security intelligence lists:

- **Network lists/feeds:** An IP address or network (in CIDR format), such as 192.168.28.0/24
- **DNS lists/feeds:** A domain name, such as securitydemo.net
- **URL lists/feeds:** A specific URL, such as http://www.securitydemo.net/maliciouspage.htm

All three types of lists are important because they are used to selectively block a malicious threat at the correct level of detail. For example, you wouldn't want to blacklist an IP address if it were for a shared web server (where multiple websites share the same server IP address). DNS-based security intelligence could specify a single web server that is hosting malicious content. You also wouldn't want to block an entire DNS name if only a specific page hosted malicious content—hence the ability to use URL-based security intelligence lists or feeds. Generally, organizations should use the most specific list type based on the threat presented.

To configure network-based security intelligence, go to Policy > Access Control > Edit > Security Intelligence and select the Talos-provided feeds and Add to Blacklist. Figure 6-49 illustrates the policy with all categories added to the blacklist. To change a category from Block to Monitor-only, right-click the category after adding it to the blacklist. Figure 6-49 shows this happening for URL and Network Tor_exit_node. To add URL-based security intelligence monitoring, simply click the URLs tab next to Networks to select those lists and click Add to Blacklist.

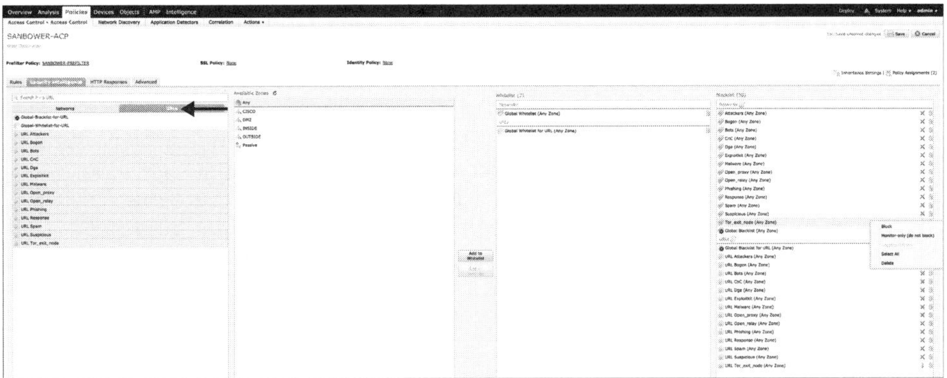

Figure 6-49 *Network and URL Security Intelligence*

Organizations can configure DNS-based security intelligence by using a DNS policy and associated DNS rules. To deploy the configuration of the DNS policy to NGIPS devices, the DNS policy must be associated with an access control policy and then deployed to managed devices. This is configured under Policy > Access Control > DNS > Edit DNS Policy or Add New. Click Add DNS Rule and define matching criteria, such as zones, networks, VLAN, or tags. Every DNS rule has one of the following actions that determines the handling and logging for matching traffic:

- **Whitelist:** This action allows matching traffic to pass DNS policy, but the traffic is also subject to further inspection either by a matching access control rule or the access control policy's default action.
- **Monitor:** Similarly to IP and URL configuration, the monitor action does not affect traffic flow, but it logs at the end of the connection.
- **Drop:** Similarly to IP and URL blacklists, this action drops the DNS request.
- **Domain Not Found:** This action returns a nonexistent Internet domain (NXDOMAIN) response to the DNS query, which prevents the host from resolving the DNS request and, as a result, does not transfer data.
- **Sinkhole:** This action returns a sinkhole IPv4 or IPv6 address in response to the DNS query. The sinkhole server can log or log and block. To use the sinkhole action, a sinkhole object also needs to be configured under Objects > Object Management > Sinkhole. Sinkholes provide administrators the ability to redirect malicious traffic to a host for which additional logging has been enabled, which can lead to a better understanding of the threat to the organization.

Figure 6-50 shows a DNS rule blocking all the Cisco-provided DNS-based security intelligence feeds.

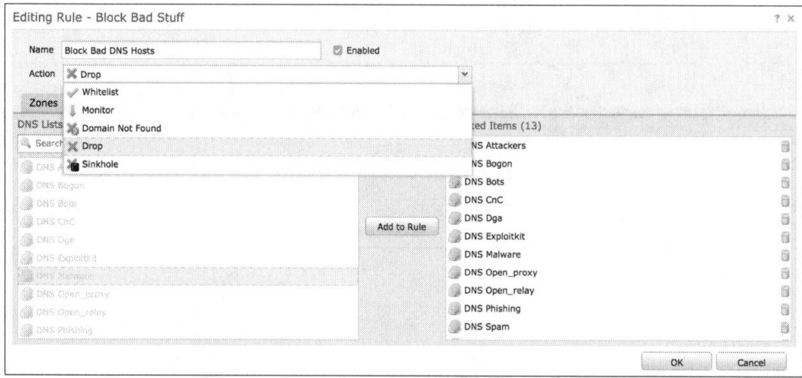

Figure 6-50 *DNS-Based Security Intelligence*

> **Note** Only devices deployed inline can blacklist traffic, and passive deployments should use the monitor-only option for security intelligence.

Monitoring Security Intelligence

Once security intelligence is configured, administrators can monitor the events generated. Figure 6-51 shows the Security Intelligence Statistics dashboard, found under Overview > Dashboards > Security Intelligence Statistics.

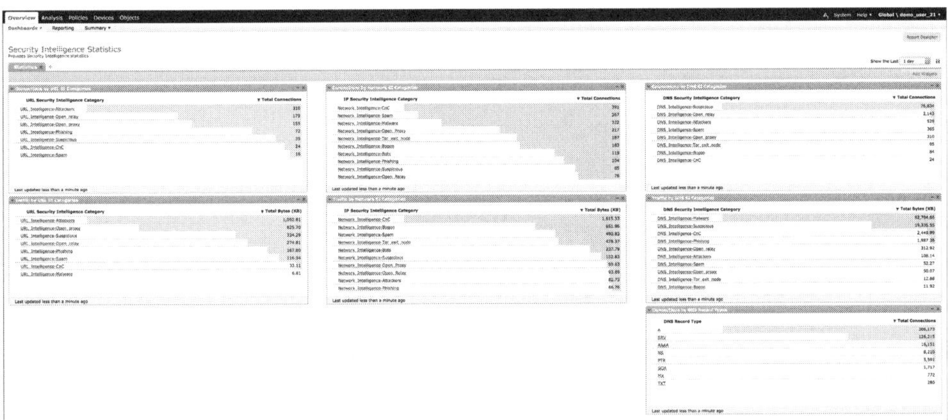

Figure 6-51 *Security Intelligence Statistics Dashboard*

You can click any of the entries on the dashboard to expand all the relative events associated with the row clicked. You can also see a detailed view of all events by going to Analysis > Connections > Security Intelligence Events.

Operationalizing a NGIPS

Once a NGIPS is configured, the important work begins. An IPS is normally not a set-it-and-forget-it tool. Dashboards, dynamic notifications and actions, tuning, and rules updates are all just as important as initial deployment and configuration. The FMC has a rich set of dashboards, the Context Explorer, incident framework, correlation engine, and reports to make operations of NGIPS easier for administrators and analysts.

Dashboards and Custom Dashboards

An FMC dashboard provides an overview of current system status, including data about the events collected and generated by the system. Keep in mind that the information a dashboard provides depends on the licensing, configuration, and deployment of the system. A dashboard is a useful, highly customizable monitoring feature that provides actionable data.

A dashboard uses tabs to display widgets: small, self-contained components that provide insight into different aspects of the system. For example, Figure 6-52 shows the Intrusion Events tab on the Detailed Dashboard, which is included in all FMC deployments and is found at Overview > Dashboards > Detailed Dashboard.

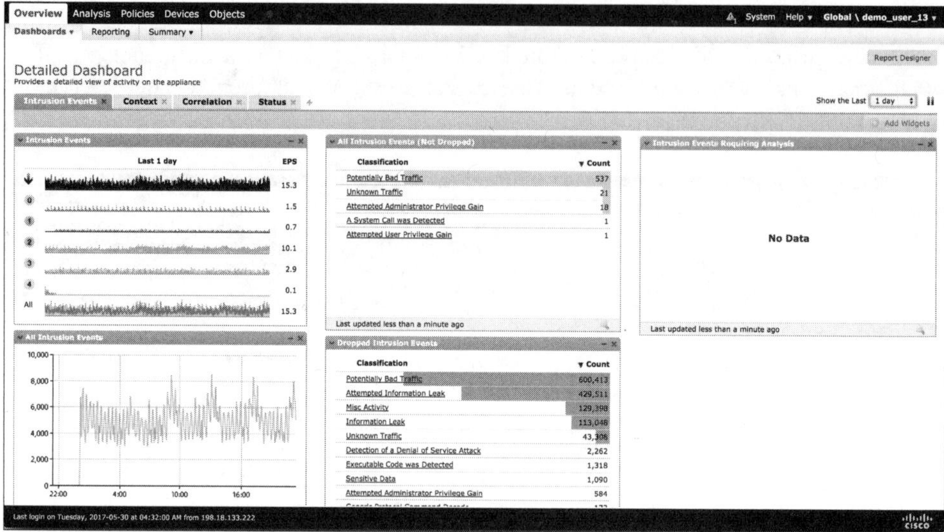

Figure 6-52 *Intrusion Event Tab on the Detailed Dashboard*

The widgets on the Intrusion Events tab show the different impact level events per second (EPS), the total number of events during the timeframe shown, all intrusion events dropped and not dropped, and any intrusion events that have been marked as requiring analysis. The FMC constrains widgets on the dashboard by time range, which can be changed to reflect a period as short as the last hour or as long as the last year.

The system is delivered with several predefined dashboards, which can be used and modified to meet the organization's needs. The predefined dashboards can be used as the base for custom dashboards, which can either be shared or restricted as private. A user who does not have administrator access cannot view or modify private dashboards created by other users.

The Intrusion Events widget shows the rate of intrusion events that occurred over the dashboard time range. This includes statistics on intrusion events with dropped packets and different impacts. Depending on the kind of data that a custom analysis widget is configured to display, you can invoke an event view (that is, a workflow) that provides detailed information about the events displayed in the widget.

When you invoke an event view from the dashboard, the events appear in the default workflow for that event type, constrained by the dashboard time range. This also changes the appropriate time window for the appliance, depending on how many time windows you have configured and depending on what type of event you are trying to view.

Context Explorer

The Firepower system Context Explorer displays detailed, interactive graphical information in context about the status of the monitored network, including data on applications, application statistics, connections, geolocation or country information, indications of compromise, intrusion events, hosts, servers, security intelligence, users, files (including malware files), and relevant URLs. Figure 6-53 shows Context Explorer, found at Analysis > Context Explorer. The top section in the Context Explorer is Traffic and Intrusions over Time, which shows a line chart of traffic and event counts over time and provides an at-a-glance picture of recent trends in the network's activity. The bottom section of the window, Indications of Compromise, provides a quick view of IOCs by indication and by host.

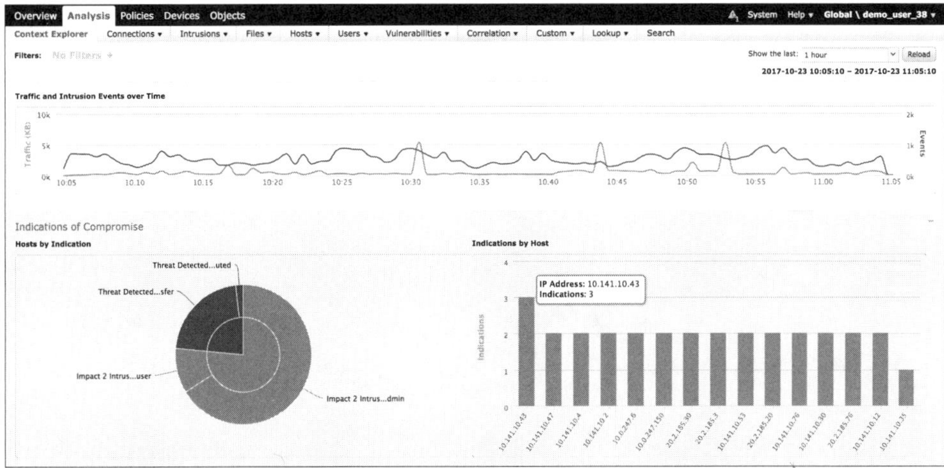

Figure 6-53 *Context Explorer Overview*

Context Explorer also includes additional information about the following:

- **Operating systems/device types:** You can see a breakdown of devices' passively learned operating systems, as shown in Figure 6-54.
- **Traffic:** As shown in Figure 6-54, you can look at traffic by IP address, user, zone and access control action.

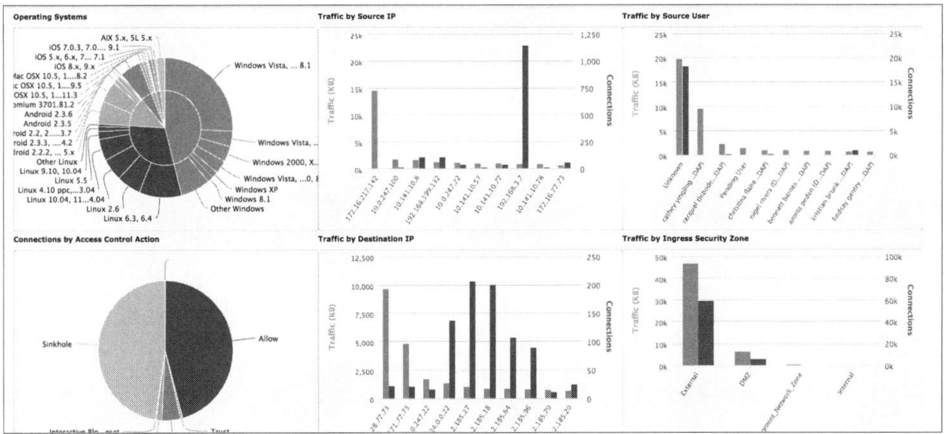

Figure 6-54 *Context Explorer: Operating Systems and Device Types*

- **Application protocol information:** As shown in Figure 6-55, you can see an application protocol, client application, and web application breakdown of traffic by risk/app, intrusion events by risk/app, and hosts by risk/app.

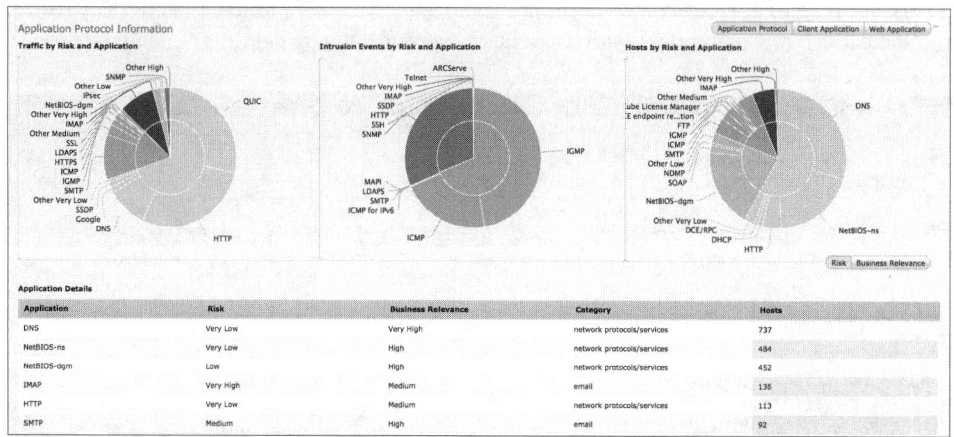

Application	Risk	Business Relevance	Category	Hosts
DNS	Very Low	Very High	network protocols/services	737
NetBIOS-ns	Very Low	High	network protocols/services	484
NetBIOS-dgm	Low	High	network protocols/services	452
IMAP	Very High	Medium	email	136
HTTP	Very Low	Medium	network protocols/services	113
SMTP	Medium	High	email	92

Figure 6-55 *Context Explorer: Application Protocol Information*

- **Security intelligence:** As shown in Figure 6-56, you can see security intelligence by category, source IP address, and destination IP address.

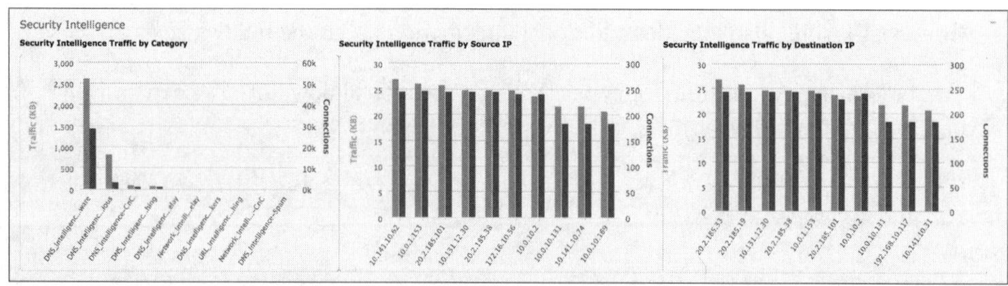

Figure 6-56 *Context Explorer: Security Intelligence*

- **Intrusion information:** As shown in Figure 6-57, you can see events by impact, events by priority, top attackers, top targets, top users, and top ingress security zones.

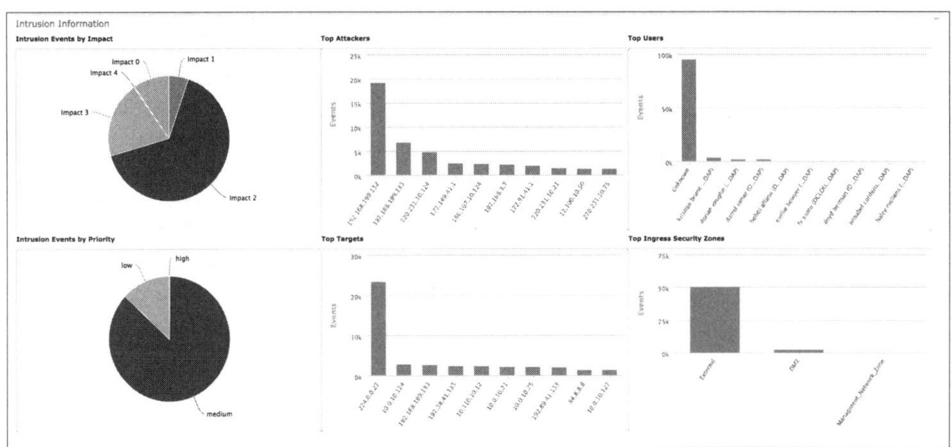

Figure 6-57 *Context Explorer: Intrusion Information*

- **Geolocation information:** As shown in Figure 6-58, you can see connections by initiator country, intrusion events by source country, and file events by sending country.

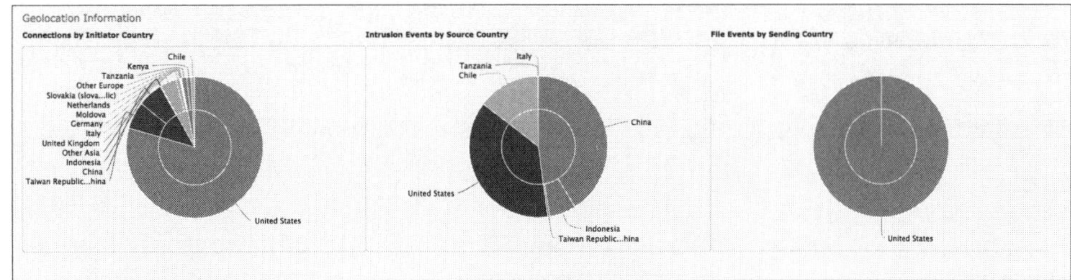

Figure 6-58 *Context Explorer: Geolocation Information*

- **URL information:** As shown in Figure 6-59, you can see traffic by URL, URL category, and URL reputation.

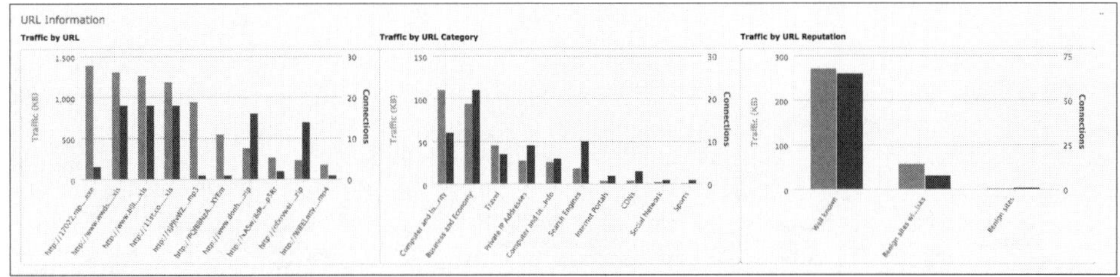

Figure 6-59 *Context Explorer: URL Information*

One way organizations have been able to leverage Context Explorer is by using custom filters to fine-tune their analysis. Any of the information shown above, including IP addresses, applications, users, and so on, can be used as a filter to show only information regarding the respective data. For example, you could see all Context Explorer information for Linux systems only or look at information regarding your data center resources only. The Context Explorer's time range can be configured to reflect a period as short as the last hour or as long as the last year.

Reporting

The FMC provides a flexible reporting engine that allows administrators to quickly and easily generate multiple-section reports with the event views or dashboards.

A report is a document in PDF, HTML, or CSV format with content chosen to represent information to different levels within the organization. A report template specifies the data searches and formats for the report and its sections. Figure 6-60 shows the default reports that are available in the FMC. To run a report, go to Overview > Reporting > Report Templates and click the Generate Report icon.

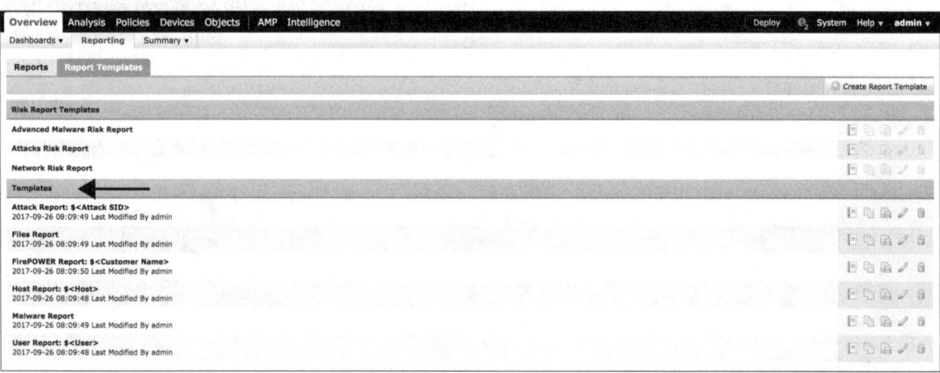

Figure 6-60 *Report Templates*

As an example, Figure 6-61 shows the Host report, which shows the intrusion events for a specific host, along with other relevant information on other pages of the report.

CISCO

Intrusion Events Destined to This Host

Time Window: *2017-10-16 16:42:17 - 2017-10-23 16:42:17*
Constraints: *Destination IP = 192.168.28.7*

This table lists intrusion events that this host has been the target of.

Impact	Classification	Message	Source IP	Destination Port / ICMP Code	Count
Impact 2	Misc Attack	SQL union select - possible sql injection attempt - GET parameter (1:13990:24)	10.28.128.10	80 (http) / tcp	4
Impact 2	Misc Attack	SQL union select - possible sql injection attempt - GET parameter (1:13990:24)	10.28.10.100	80 (http) / tcp	4
Impact 2	Access to a Potentially Vulnerable Web Application	Christi Rule (1:1281985:1)	10.28.10.100	80 (http) / tcp	3
Impact 2	Web Application Attack	SQL url ending in comment characters - possible sql injection attempt (1:19438:13)	10.28.128.10	80 (http) / tcp	3
Impact 2	Attempted Denial of Service	SERVER-WEBAPP Imatix Xitami web server head processing denial of service attempt (1:43238:2)		80 (http) / tcp	3
Impact 2	Access to a Potentially Vulnerable Web Application	SERVER-WEBAPP robots.txt access (1:1852:11)		80 (http) / tcp	2
Impact 2	Misc Attack	SQL union select - possible sql injection attempt - GET parameter (1:13990:24)	10.28.128.160	80 (http) / tcp	2
Impact 2	Attempted Administrator Privilege Gain	SERVER-APACHE Apache Struts remote code execution attempt (1:41818:2)		80 (http) / tcp	2
Impact 2	Attempted Administrator Privilege Gain	SERVER-APACHE Apache Struts remote code execution attempt (1:41818:2)		80 (http) / tcp	2
Impact 2	Access to a Potentially Vulnerable Web Application	SERVER-WEBAPP Setup.php access (1:2281:15)		80 (http) / tcp	1

Figure 6-61 *Host Report*

The Attack report provides information regarding top source and destination around a specific Snort ID. This is extremely useful in researching a specific threat to the organization.

One very powerful tool is the report designer, which automates the design of a report template. Any of the content on any event view table or dashboard graphic displayed in the web interface can be used as the base of the report template. Simply click the Report Designer button on the page that needs to be turned into a report and customize the format.

There is no hard limit on the number of report templates created. Each report template defines the individual sections in the report and specifies the database search that creates the report's content, as well as the presentation format (table, chart, detail view, and so on) and the timeframe.

To schedule a report to be run daily, weekly, and so on, go to System > Monitoring > Scheduling and click Add Task. Figure 6-62 shows a new task to run a weekly Firepower report, which includes information on risky applications, unauthorized anonymizers and proxies, low-business-relevance applications, malicious URLs, and intrusion impact alerts.

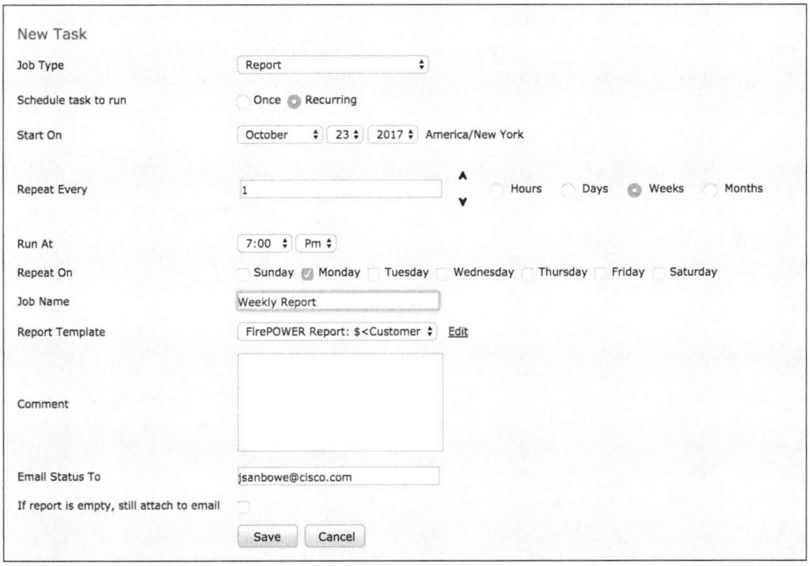

New Task
Job Type: Report
Schedule task to run: Once / Recurring
Start On: October 23 2017 America/New York
Repeat Every: 1 Hours Days Weeks Months
Run At: 7:00 Pm
Repeat On: Sunday Monday Tuesday Wednesday Thursday Friday Saturday
Job Name: Weekly Report
Report Template: FirePOWER Report: $<Customer Edit
Comment
Email Status To: jsanbowe@cisco.com
If report is empty, still attach to email
Save Cancel

Figure 6-62 *Scheduling a Task to Generate a Weekly Report*

Intrusion Event Workflows

When Firepower identifies a possible intrusion, it generates an intrusion event, which is a record of the date, time, and type of exploit, as well as contextual information about the source of the attack and its target. For packet-based events, a copy of the packet or packets that triggered the event is also recorded. Access an intrusion event workflow by going to Analysis > Intrusions > Events. The default workflow is Events by Priority and Classification, but other workflows can be selected (see Figure 6-63).

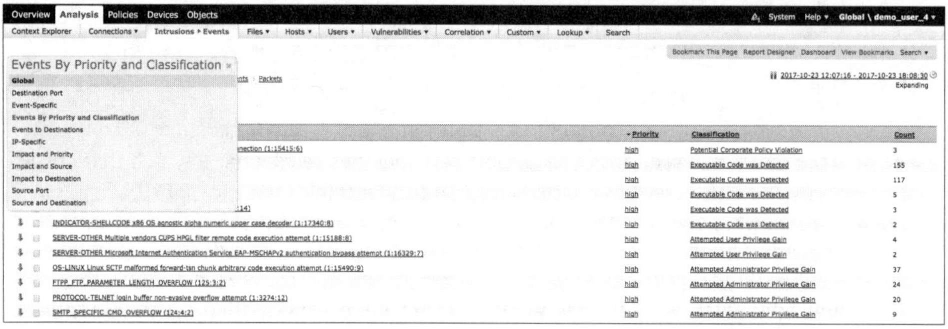

Figure 6-63 *Intrusion Events Workflows*

You can click on an event, a classification, or a count or select specific events and click View to open a table view of the events, as shown in Figure 6-64. The table view provides additional details above and beyond the workflow view, including impact, inline result, source and destination IP addresses, source and destination ports, source and destination countries, VLAN ID, SSL status, source user, application protocol, client, web application, IOCs, application risk, business relevancy, ingress and egress security zones, domain, device, ingress and egress interfaces, intrusion policy, access control policy and rule, and network analysis policy.

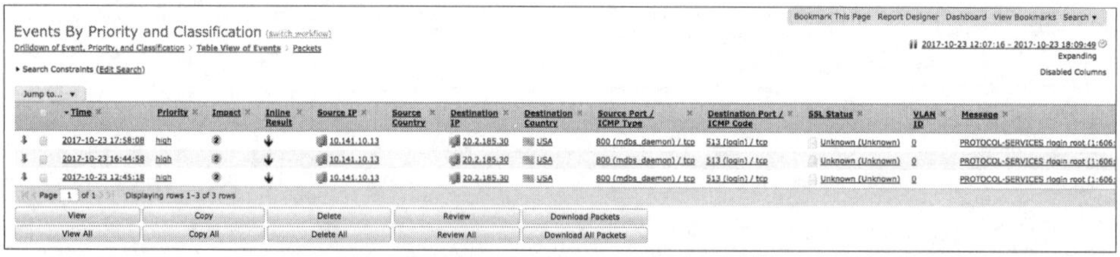

Figure 6-64 *Table View of Intrusion Events*

By using the table view, security analysts can better understand multiple events in great detail. If a single incident is selected, a packet view is shown, which gives similar information to the table, along with some actions (discussed in the "IPS Tuning" section, later in this chapter) and packet information, as shown in Figure 6-65.

Figure 6-65 *Packet View of Intrusion Events*

On all intrusion event views, if you want to go deeper, you can download a copy of a packet capture in PCAP format for a single event or multiple events by selecting multiple events in the table view. If you are confident that an intrusion event is not malicious, you can mark the event as reviewed. Normally you use a reviewed event only if you are confident that the event does not represent a threat to the network security (for example, because you know that none of the hosts on your network are vulnerable to the detected exploit). Reviewed events are stored in the event database and are included in the event summary statistics but no longer appear in the default intrusion event pages. The name of the user who marks the events as reviewed appears as the reviewer name.

Events can be deleted from multiple views, which permanently deletes them from the database. The system also allows you to add an event, or multiple events, to the clipboard so the event(s) can be transferred to an incident (that is, the response an organization takes when a threat or violation of policy happens) at a later time. The FMC includes features to support analysts as they collect and process information that is relevant to an investigation of an incident. The incident feature can be used to gather intrusion events, packet data, and notes about any activity that is taken regarding the incident (for example, mitigation or investigation activities). There is also a built-in incident life cycle management function that allows users of the FMC to change incident status throughout the response to an attack. Incidents are configured at Analysis > Intrusions > Incidents, as shown in Figure 6-66.

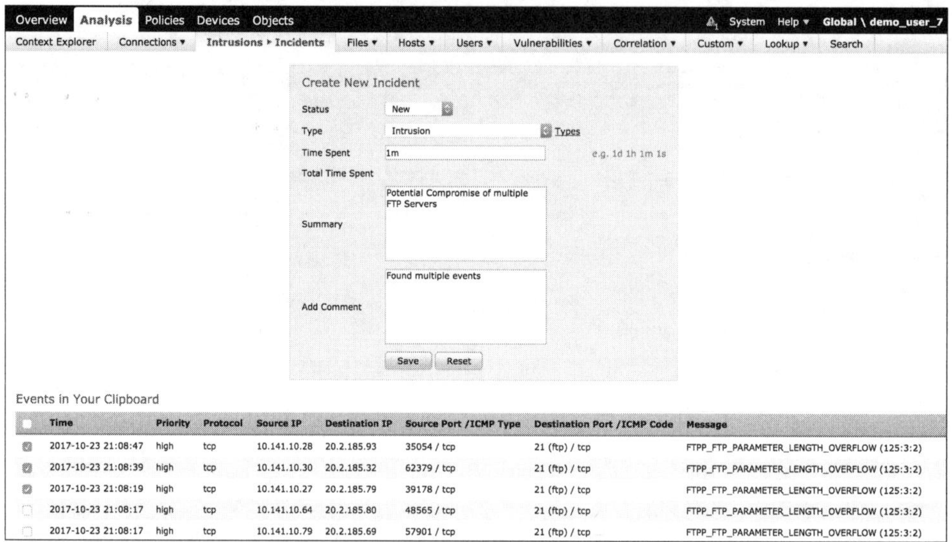

Figure 6-66 *Creating a New Incident*

Correlation Engine

The correlation engine in the FMC provides the ability to create dynamic real-time responses based on many event and data types. When a correlation rule in an active correlation policy triggers, the system generates a correlation event. Correlation rules can trigger when the system generates a specific type of event (connection, intrusion, malware, discovery, user activity, and so on) or when network traffic deviates from its normal profile.

Responses to correlation policy violations include simple alerts and various remediations (such as scanning a host). Each correlation rule can be associated with a single response or group of responses. A *remediation* is a program that the FMC launches in response to a correlation policy violation. When a remediation runs, the system generates a remediation status event. Remediation status events include details such as the remediation name, the correlation policy and rule that triggered it, and the exit status message. The FMC supports several remediation modules:

- **Cisco ISE pxGrid Mitigation:** Quarantines, unquarantines, or shuts down traffic sent to a host or network involved in a correlation policy violation
- **Cisco IOS Null Route:** Blocks traffic sent to a host or network involved in a correlation policy violation (requires Cisco IOS Version 12.0 or higher)
- **Nmap Scanning:** Scans hosts to determine running operating systems and servers
- **Set Attribute Value:** Sets a host attribute on a host involved in a correlation policy violation

The FMC also allows for custom remediation modules, so that anyone can write a module and use it as a response to an event. More information on the correlation engine and integration with ISE and other products can be found in *Integrated Security Technologies and Solutions, Volume II.*

To configure correlation, go to Policies > Correlation > Rule Management and add a new rule. Figure 6-67 illustrates a rule designed to match any impact level 1 intrusion events or to match when the host IOC tag is set.

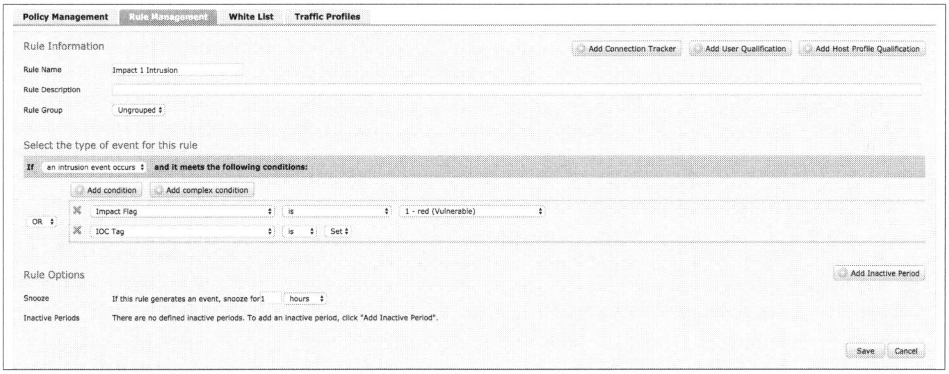

Figure 6-67 *Correlation Rule*

You can navigate to the Policy Management tab to add a new correlation policy, as shown in Figure 6-68. This policy tells the FMC to send an email any time the correlation rule is matched. The policy allows for multiple actions as a result of a correlation rule firing. Using correlation policies is also an easy way to configure dynamic notification (for example, if a NGIPS sees over 500 MB from inside to outside, send an email to the ticket system with the subject "Suspect Data Loss").

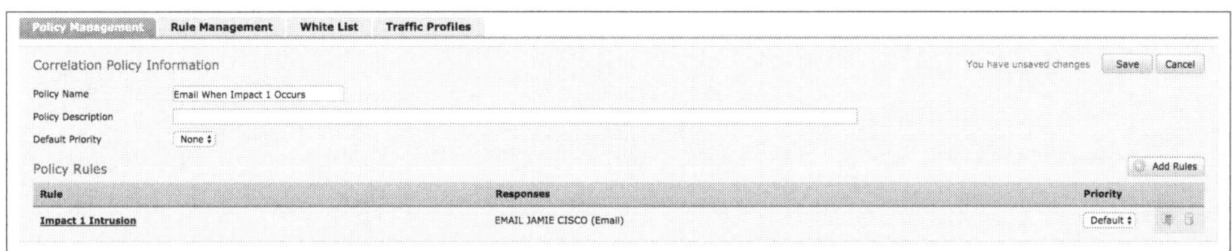

Figure 6-68 *Correlation Policy*

IPS Tuning

Cisco Talos does a great job tuning the default policies in a NGIPS to allow organizations to focus on investigating malicious activities rather than spending countless hours tuning their sensors. With that said, there may still be times when an organization needs to do some tuning. Intrusion detection and prevention devices can generate events that fall into these four categories:

- **True positive:** The system identifies traffic as an attack, and the traffic is actually an attack. This means the system is doing the right thing.
- **True negative:** The system identifies traffic as normal behavior, and the traffic is actually normal. Again, the system is doing its job.
- **False positive:** The system identifies traffic as an attack, but the activity is acceptable traffic. A false positive is a false alarm and is an inconvenience at best, but false positives can cause significant issues if not dealt with over time.
- **False negative:** The system identifies traffic as acceptable when the traffic is actually an attack. This event type is the most serious and dangerous because the security analyst has no idea that an attack took place.

False negatives normally come up in environments where a sensor is not seeing malicious traffic, so no event is registered. If a sensor is seeing the traffic, then the next logical step is to ensure proper configuration of rules, preprocessors, and policies. If all of the above proves correct and an organization is still experiencing a false negative, a support case should be created for Cisco to review packet captures and configurations. If the attack is unknown (known as a zero-day attack), signatures, IOCs, and security intelligence rules can be created to detect the malicious traffic.

For false positives, there are a few options available to tune policies, depending on the type of event:

- **Use global whitelisting:** If a false positive is created because an IP address, DNS name, or URL is marked as malicious and blocked, the item can be added to the global whitelist to allow traffic. Whitelisting can be configured by going to Objects > Object Management > Security Intelligence and editing the global whitelist or adding a custom whitelist. (*Caution:* Most data in security intelligence is there because it was discovered actively attacking other organizations, is hosting malicious content, or is associated with nefarious activities. It is recommended that you verify the reason the organization believes it is experiencing a false positive with security intelligence events.)
- **Monitor the SI category:** Some organizations are aggressive with their policies to start with and might have enabled blocking a category like Open_proxy that is actually required by the organization. If only a limited number of services are required, whitelisting might be a better option. To change a category from blocking to monitor-only, the policy is configured under the access control policy at Policies > Access Control > Edit > Security Intelligence.
- **Disable unnecessary rules:** Organizations can disable intrusion rules that target old and patched vulnerabilities. Doing so improves performance and reduces false

positives. Using Firepower recommendations can assist with this task as well. In addition, rules that frequently generate low-priority alerts or alerts that are not actionable may be good candidates for removal from an intrusion policy. Rules can be disabled by going to Policies > Intrusion > Edit, selecting the rule in question, and selecting Disable under Rule State.

- **Set a threshold:** A threshold can be used to reduce the number of intrusion events. This is a good option to configure when a rule is expected to regularly trigger a limited number of events on normal traffic but could be an indication of a problem if more than a certain number of packets match the rule. You can use this option to reduce the number of events triggered by noisy rules. Thresholds can be configured by going to Policies > Intrusion > Edit, selecting the rule in question, and selecting Threshold under Event Filtering (see Figure 6-69).

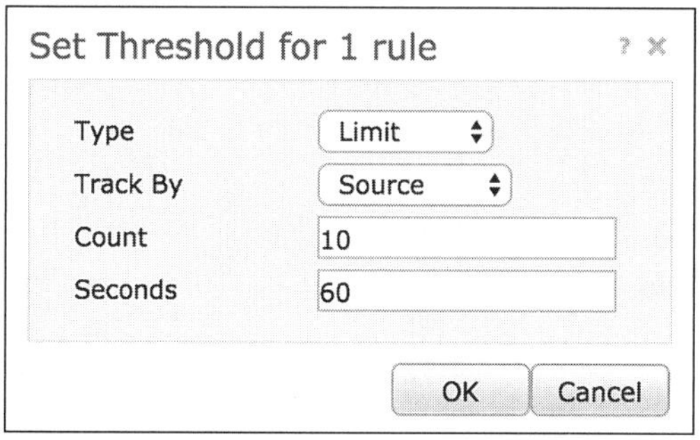

Figure 6-69 *Rule Threshold*

- **Configure suppression:** Suppression is used to completely eliminate the notification of events. It is configured similarly to the Threshold option.

> **Caution** Suppression can lead to performance issues because while no events are generated, Snort still has to process the traffic.

- **Use pass rules:** In order to prevent a specific rule from triggering on traffic from a certain host (while other traffic from that host needs to be inspected), you can use a *pass* type Snort rule. By default, pass rules override alert rules. You add pass rules the same way you add any other rules: Go to Objects > Intrusion Rules, click Add Rule, and select Pass for the action.
- **Use trusted flow:** The best option for permitting trusted traffic to pass through a NGIPS without inspection is to enable a trust or allow action without an associated intrusion policy. To configure a trust or allow rule, navigate to Policies > Access Control > Add Rule.

- **Report to Cisco TAC:** If you find a Snort rule that triggers alerts on benign traffic, report it to Cisco Technical Support. A customer support engineer will escalate the issue to Cisco Talos for review.

Updating Rules and the Vulnerability Database (VDB)

Rule updates play an important part in keeping intrusion rules up to date. Cisco Talos provides frequent updates to the rules to ensure that each organization has the latest and greatest threat prevention. To update rules, go to System > Updates > Rule Updates. You can manually update rules by downloading new rules automatically from Cisco or manually with a file. Also, you can schedule recurring rule update imports on the same page. The option Deploy Updated Policies to Targeted Devices After Rule Update Completes allows organizations to automatically apply the latest protections.

As new vulnerabilities become known, Cisco Talos releases VDB updates. To update the VDB, use the System > Updates > Product Updates page and either manually upload an update package or click Download Updates to download packages from Cisco.

Note The same method is used to perform FMC and Firepower software updates. To apply an update, click the apply icon on the right of the screen (see Figure 6-70).

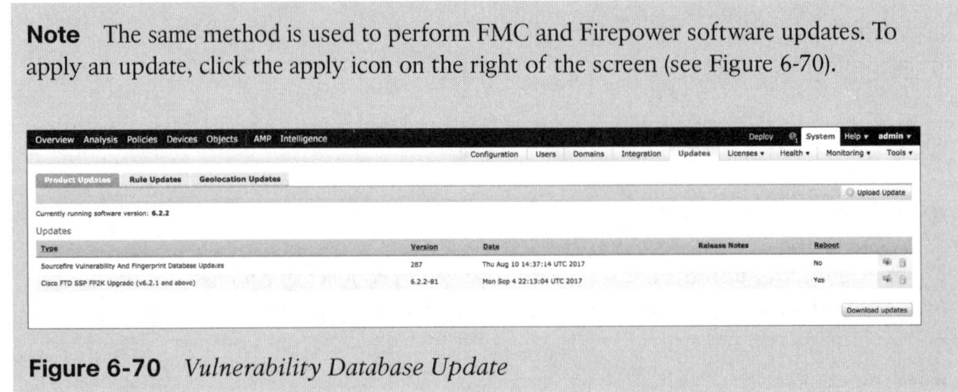

Figure 6-70 *Vulnerability Database Update*

To automatically download and/or install VDB updates, a task can be scheduled.

Summary

In this chapter, you have learned all about the Cisco NGIPS for performing threat prevention. You learned about deployment options and placement of the Firepower NGIPS. You examined the Snort rules language and learned the configuration steps required to enable NGIPS features on Firepower systems. Finally, you found out how to operationalize the data from the FMC.

References

"Firepower Management Center Configuration Guide, Version 6.2", https://www.cisco.com/c/en/us/td/docs/security/firepower/620/configuration/guide/fpmc-config-guide-v62.html

"Custom Local Snort Rules on a Cisco FireSIGHT System", https://www.cisco.com/c/en/us/support/docs/security/firesight-management-center/117924-technote-firesight-00.html

"Writing Snort Rules", http://snort.datanerds.net/writing_snort_rules.htm

Chapter 7

IOS Firewall and Security Features

Cisco's venerable IOS, which has been around since the 1980s, is used in the majority of Cisco networking devices today. Over the years, IOS has evolved to include forks and multiple versions, such as IOS XE and IOS XR. IOS can now be run in a virtualized environment, which makes it very useful for CCIE preparation. This environment, called the Virtual Internet Routing Lab (VIRL), is part of the 5.0 lab blueprint. VIRL runs on a hypervisor and supports the following Cisco virtual images:

- OSv and IOSvL2
- NX-OSv and NX-OS 9000v
- IOS XRv and IOS XRv 9000
- IOS XE (CSR1000v)
- ASAv

This chapter uses the Cloud Services Router (CSR) for all sample configurations.

Note For more information about setting up and running VIRL, visit http://virl.cisco.com.

Network Address Translation (NAT)

Chapter 5, "Next-Gen Firewalls," covers the configuration and troubleshooting of NAT on the ASA firewall. This section describes how to configure NAT in IOS XE and highlights differences between the two. While the concepts of NAT are the same on both, the commands for configuration and troubleshooting are the focus in this section.

IOS XE has some restrictions in terms of configuring NAT:

- NAT, Zone-Based Firewall, and WCCP cannot coexist on the same network.
- NAT Virtual Interfaces (NVIs) are not supported in the Cisco IOS XE software.
- For access lists used for NAT configuration, the **permit ip any any** command is not supported.

NAT Terminology

Cisco uses specific terminology to explain NAT. It is built on concepts of *inside* and *outside*, *local* and *global*:

- Inside local addresses are addresses prior to translation. They are often found on the inside, or private-side, network.
- Inside global addresses are addresses that an inside local address is translated into. They most commonly use global address space addresses that are routable on the Internet.
- An outside local address is the address of an outside host as it appears to the inside network. It is allocated from the address space that is routable on the inside.
- Outside global addresses are assigned to a host on the outside by the network owner and usually allocated from the global address space.

Even for CCIEs, these definitions are ambiguous at best. To keep it simple, remember that addresses are either *local* or *global* in nature, while NAT relies on the terms *inside* and *outside* for configuration.

A helpful command to help sort out these terms is **show ip nat translations**. Example 7-1 shows sample output from this command. It labels each address in the appropriate column to make it very easy to discern.

Example 7-1 show ip nat translations *Command*

```
csr(config)# do sh ip nat trans
Pro  Inside global         Inside local          Outside local         Outside global
---  172.16.1.20           10.1.1.1              ---                   ---
Total number of translations: 1
```

This command is a great help in a CCIE lab to ensure that your NAT translations are what you intended. (The next section examines in more detail the multiple ways that NAT is configured.)

NAT is configured either dynamically, statically, or both. Let's examine the differences:

- **Dynamic Port Address Translation (PAT):** With PAT, also called NAT Overload, real addresses are translated to a single mapped address (many to one). Often using the egress interface address, ports are used to differentiate between real hosts.

- **Dynamic NAT:** With dynamic NAT, real addresses are translated to mapped addresses (many to many). Dynamic NAT is commonly used for Internet access, as an example.
- **Static NAT:** Static NAT involves static mapping between a local address and a global address (one to one). These hosts will always translate bidirectionally. Static NAT is common for mail servers, web servers, and so on.

NAT Configuration

The first requirement in configuring NAT is to define the NAT criteria for operation:

- What are the NAT inside and outside interfaces?
- Which type of NAT is required: static or dynamic?
- What are the matching criteria for NAT operation (source, destination, and so on)?

After gathering this information, it is possible to begin the initial NAT configuration. Figure 7-1 shows the virtual CSR lab topology used for the NAT examples in this chapter.

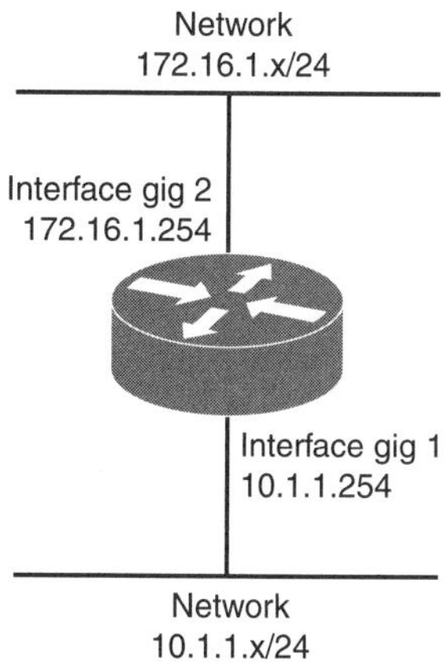

Figure 7-1 *Virtual Lab Topology*

NAT Overload

NAT Overload uses the outside interface address as the source address, which allows many-to-one translation from the inside network to the outside network. Ports are used to differentiate the return path traffic back to the originating host. An access list defines the source addresses defined for translation. Addresses are dynamically returned to the pool when connections are closed or time out. The vast majority of routers today use NAT Overload to connect hosts to the Internet because of its flexibility and ease of configuration.

Figure 7-2 illustrates NAT Overload.

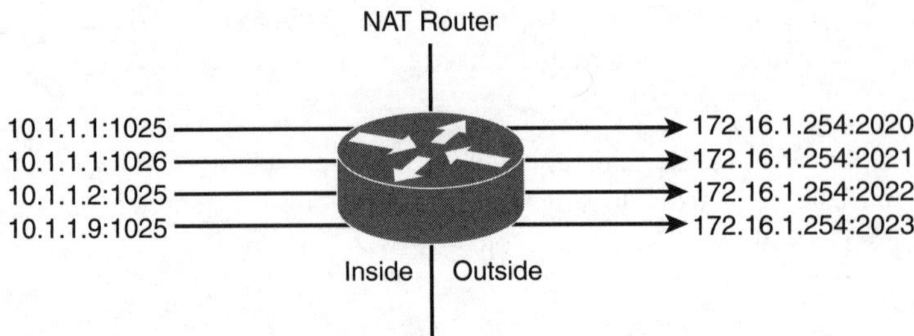

Figure 7-2 *NAT Overload*

Let's walk through the configuration of NAT Overload:

Step 1. Ensure that both interfaces are up and addressed properly:

```
csr# sh ip int brief
Interface              IP-Address      OK? Method Status       Protocol
GigabitEthernet1       10.1.1.254      YES NVRAM  up           up
GigabitEthernet2       172.16.1.254    YES NVRAM  up           up
```

Step 2. Define the inside and outside interfaces in the NAT configuration. In this case, interface Gig1 is the inside interface, and Gig2 is the outside interface. Optionally, you could define more inside interfaces, if necessary:

```
csr(config)# int g1
csr(config-if)# ip nat inside
csr(config-if)# int g2
csr(config-if)# ip nat outside
```

Step 3. Define an access list that specifies the inside source network so the NAT engine will know what traffic is to be translated or ignored. This access list can be named or numeric. Recommended best practice is to use named access lists where possible in order to minimize any confusion during the lab.

In this case, the inside network is 10.1.1.x/24, as defined by **access-list INSIDE-NET**:

```
csr(config)# ip access-list standard INSIDE-NET
csr(config-std-nacl)# permit 10.1.1.0 0.0.0.255
```

Step 4. Configure the interface overload statement and bind it to the **INSIDE-NET** source list.

```
csr(config)# ip nat inside source list INSIDE-NET interface
GigabitEthernet2 overload
```

Alternatively, you could use a static global address instead of the interface address. For example, if you wanted to map to the 172.16.1.199 address, you would have to define a NAT pool with a single IP address:

```
csr(config)# ip nat pool SINGLENAT 172.16.1.199 172.16.1.199 prefix 24
```

Note The **prefix** part of the command here ensures that the address range falls within the same subnet. For example, **prefix 32** is not allowed.

Step 5. Configure the NAT pool for overloading and bind it to the **INSIDE-NET** source list:

```
csr(config)# ip nat inside source list INSIDE-NET pool SINGLENAT overload
```

NAT Overload (dynamic PAT) has some minor drawbacks:

- Some multimedia applications and protocols do not work with PAT if their control plane is different from the data plane.
- Network traffic analytics with NAT Overload show a large amount of traffic from a single address. This might affect thresholds for network packet dispersion.

Dynamic NAT

Dynamic NAT is very similar to NAT Overload except that instead of using a single IP address for the global address (interface or otherwise), the NAT engine pulls addresses from a pool of global addresses. This is a common scenario when an ISP has provided a block of globally routable address space or when NAT Overload isn't a good fit. Figure 7-3 illustrates basic dynamic NAT, which you configure as follows:

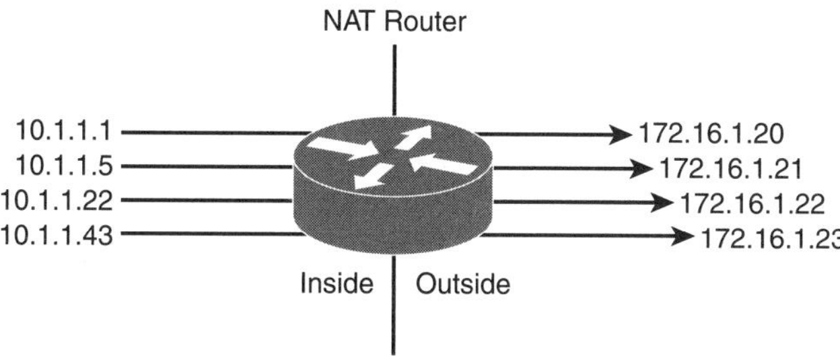

Figure 7-3 *Dynamic NAT*

Step 1. As in the steps in the section "NAT Overload," define the inside and outside interfaces and a source access list:

```
csr(config)# int g1
csr(config-if)# ip nat inside
csr(config-if)# int g2
csr(config-if)# ip nat outside
```

Tip For completeness, this configuration shows a numeric access list for a lab's inside network. Using it is functionally the same as using the named access list in the previous configuration example and defines the source addresses to be translated.

Step 2. Define the access list:

```
csr(config)# access-list 100 permit ip 10.1.1.0 0.0.0.255 any
```

Step 3. Define the outside global address pool, which NAT uses for the dynamic translations:

```
csr(config)# ip nat pool DYNPOOL 172.16.1.100 172.16.1.125 prefix 24
```

Step 4. Tell the NAT engine to use **DYNPOOL** and bind it to source access list 100:

```
csr(config)# ip nat inside source list 100 pool DYNPOOL
```

A shortcoming of dynamic NAT is that it is limited to the size of the NAT pool for outside translated addresses. In the example above, there are 26 addresses (172.16.1.100 to 172.16.1.125) available for translation. Once these addresses are in use, no other inside hosts will be able to access resources outside until an existing inside host times out or closes its connection.

One way to prevent this from happening is to configure both dynamic NAT and NAT Overload at the same time. NAT Overload fills any translation requests if the dynamic pool gets depleted.

Step 5. (Optional) If necessary, add **overload** to the configuration statement:

```
csr(config)# ip nat inside source list 100 pool DYNPOOL overload
```

Static NAT

Static NAT is used when a continuous bidirectional address mapping is required for a host. Unlike dynamic NAT, where mapped addresses are pooled, static NAT creates a one-to-one relationship to the host. It is therefore commonly used when hosts need to be reachable from outside the network.

Static NAT operation is outlined in Figure 7-4. Note the direction of the arrows.

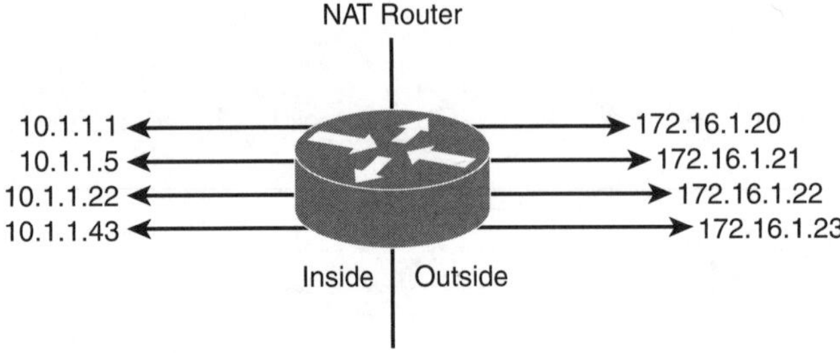

Figure 7-4 *Static NAT*

Static NAT can statically map ports as well as addresses. This provides more flexibility when a variety of network services are being offered, and it is a typical deployment when traffic is received on a well-known port and redirected to a different port number, as detailed in Figure 7-5.

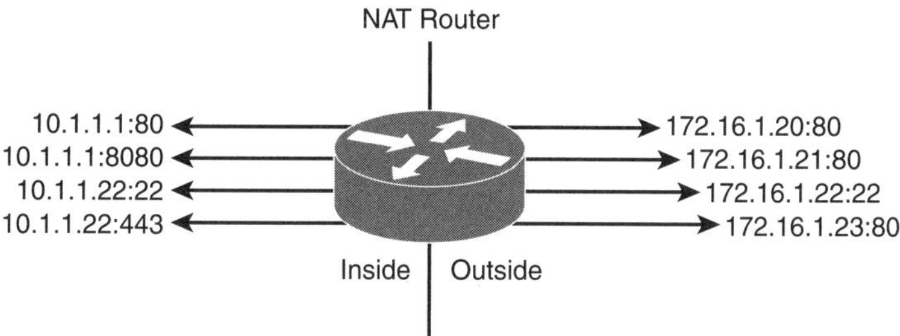

Figure 7-5 *Static NAT with Port Redirection*

The sample configurations continue with the NAT inside as Gig1 and the NAT outside as Gig2. Because you have already configured that previously, it is not shown again here. The biggest difference with an IOS-XE static NAT configuration is how the NAT statement is defined. For example, if you need to statically map 10.1.1.1 to 172.16.1.20, use this NAT statement:

```
csr(config)# ip nat outside source static 10.1.1.1 172.16.1.20
```

This tells the NAT engine to send any traffic (all ports and protocols) on the outside destined to 172.16.1.20 to the inside host 10.1.1.1. It creates a bidirectional binding between the inside local address and the outside global address. Confirm the mapping by using the **show ip nat translations** command:

```
csr(config)# do sh ip nat trans
Pro  Inside global         Inside local          Outside local         Outside global
---  172.16.1.20           10.1.1.1              ---                   ---
Total number of translations: 1
```

In many cases, you may want NAT only for specific services or you might even need to redirect services from one port to another. This allows more granular control where the NAT boundary is connected to untrusted networks such as the Internet. The security best practice is to allow only services advertised to the outside that are required. For example, instead of allowing all traffic to inside host 10.1.1.1, you can restrict it to just SSH because that is the only service allowed to access this host from the outside. That configuration is shown here:

```
csr(config)# ip nat inside source static tcp 10.1.1.1 22 172.16.1.20 22
```

You get confirmation of the configuration change. Note that the port numbers are visible now:

```
csr(config)# do sh ip nat trans
Pro  Inside global         Inside local          Outside local         Outside global
tcp  172.16.1.20:22         10.1.1.1:22           ---                   ---
Total number of translations: 1
```

It is also possible to redirect port numbers by using NAT. This is a common scenario with web servers that are accessed using proxies. The following example redirects **tcp 8080** to **tcp 80** on the outside and vice versa on the inside:

```
csr(config)# ip nat inside source static tcp 10.1.1.1 8080 172.16.1.20 80
```

Remember that static translations are mapped in both directions. Here's how you can verify the configuration:

```
csr# sh ip nat trans
Pro  Inside global         Inside local          Outside local         Outside global
tcp  172.16.1.20:80        10.1.1.1:8080         ---                   ---
Total number of translations: 1
```

Troubleshooting NAT

Most feel that the NAT configuration in IOS-XE is easier to follow than NAT configuration on the ASA. However, troubleshooting a complex NAT configuration on any device can be daunting. CCIE candidates need to know the order of operation and must have an understanding of the commands to use to quickly verify NAT operation. For more detailed troubleshooting, it may necessary to use NAT **debug** commands.

Note Like any other **debug** commands, use the NAT **debug** commands with care as the amount of output can be significant on a loaded device.

Table 7-1 illustrates the NAT order of operation discussed in this section.

Table 7-1 *NAT Order of Operation*

NAT: Inside to Outside	NAT: Outside to Inside
Apply Ingress ACL (If Present)	Apply Ingress ACL (If Present)
Routing Decision to Determine Egress Interface	NAT Operation Outside to Inside
NAT Operation Inside to Outside	Routing Decision to Determine Interface
Apply Egress ACL (If Present)	Apply Egress ACL (If Present)

Understanding the order of operation for NAT is critical for understanding where to look when troubleshooting. IOS-XE NAT is based on the concept of an inside and outside. Sometimes it is easy to determine which is which when configuring NAT for Internet connectivity. However, in the lab exam, it may not be easy to discern direction, which leads to some important points:

- Know the NAT boundaries for both inside and outside interfaces. Remember that there can be more than one of each but not both on the same interface.

- Traffic entering the inside NAT interface is always routed first, before any NAT takes place. This makes sense because the router has to forward the packet somewhere before NAT can be applied. For example, if the egress interface cannot be determined by the router (suggesting a routing issue), it is pointless to troubleshoot the NAT configuration until that is resolved.
- Traffic entering the outside NAT interface is always translated first, before routing takes place. This is less obvious but follows logically as the NAT configuration requires the router to route based on the properties of the translated address. At this point, you need to understand that enabling NAT does a few things in the background of the router that do not show up in the running configuration.
- NAT installs an IP alias and an ARP entry when the inside global address is matched to the local interface that is on the NAT outside. The router then uses proxy ARP for these addresses. To see this in your practice lab, configure NAT and then issue the **show ip alias** command. The output should show dynamic mappings that allow the router to respond to packets received in the outside global address space.
- Proxy ARP often leads to unintended behavior, as is the case here for a host on the outside network pinging to an address that is mapped to an inside local host. With proxy ARP, the router responds on behalf of the host without actually forwarding traffic and receiving a legitimate response. This can be very dangerous in both the real world and the CCIE lab if you do not understand what is taking place.

Cisco allows you to change this default behavior in the NAT configuration by using the **no-alias** keyword:

```
csr(config)# ip nat inside source static tcp 10.1.1.1 8080 172.16.1.20 80 no-alias
```

This disables the auto-generated ARP table entries.

What happens when a NAT router is configured for both inside and outside static translations? This creates an interesting scenario, where static routes are required for the return path traffic (NAT outside to inside, in order of operation: NAT first, then routing). Without these static routes, traffic does not flow properly with translation (with a major caveat, as discussed next).

NAT Virtual Interface (NVI)

NVI was introduced as a way to simplify the logic behind NAT operation based on the legacy inside and outside NAT configuration. It eliminates the concept of inside and outside (hereafter referred to as the *legacy method*) and instead defines an interface as NAT-enabled or not. This simplifies the NAT logic by providing a more consistent order of operation because translation rules occur after routing decisions and are not dependent on the traffic direction (inside or outside), as in the legacy method.

Configuring NVI is very similar to the legacy method. Because there is no concept of inside and outside, you simply must enable NAT on the interface as shown here (with any **inside** or **outside** statements removed):

```
csr(config)# int g1
csr(config-if)# ip nat enable
```

The NAT statement is exactly the same except for the lack of the **inside** or **outside** keyword.

```
csr(config)# ip nat source static tcp 10.1.1.1 22 172.16.1.20 22
```

NVI provides an additional benefit in that the static routes discussed in the previous section under the legacy method are no longer required. The recommended practice is to use NVI where allowed as it reduces complexity by not requiring you to define the NAT inside and outside interfaces.

ACLs and NAT

CCIE candidates should have a solid understanding of how NAT and ACLs behave when configured on the same interface. Access lists add complexity when troubleshooting NAT configurations. Once again, before any troubleshooting can begin, the direction of NAT processing must be determined. This is because access lists are affected by the order of operation of traffic in the router:

- Inbound ACLs are always processed *before* routing and NAT. This makes logical sense as the router does not forward any packets that are being dropped due to an ingress ACL in order to conserve resources.
- Outbound ACLs are processed *after* routing and NAT. This creates interesting scenarios when determining which network to include in the egress ACL. Depending on the source ACL, this will either be the outside local address or the outside global address.

Helpful Troubleshooting Commands

show ip nat translations is the starting point for verifying and troubleshooting any NAT configuration. It provides a concise summary of addresses being used by the NAT engine.

Many additional keywords can may be added to **show ip nat translations** in order to drill down into a specific area for troubleshooting. For example, the **verbose** keyword adds details that are helpful when diagnosing static and dynamic NAT timeouts.

Having a strong working knowledge of the other commands related to **show ip nat** is essential for rapid troubleshooting in the CCIE lab. Example 7-2 shows the options in a lab virtual router.

Example 7-2 show ip nat *Options*

```
csr# show ip nat ?
  bpa            Bulk Port Allocation information
  limits         Limit statistics
  pool           Pool and port statistics
  portblock      TCP/UDP port blocks allocated for NAT
  statistics     Translation statistics
  translations   Translation entries
```

clear ip nat translation * is useful when it is necessary to clear the NAT table. Remember that NAT translations stay active until the connection tears down and a timer expires. Changes to the NAT configuration may not be immediately apparent unless you clear the translation table first. The best practice is to create an alias so this command can be used without worrying about typos.

For a step-by-step visual of the NAT engine process, use **debug ip nat**. When used in conjunction with **debug ip packet**, this command provides a verbose walkthrough of the packet order of operation on the router.

Warning The use of any **debug** commands on a loaded router could lead to a tremendous volume of output that could adversely affect the console. Ensure that adequate bandwidth is available through your serial connection.

There are many nuances and dark corners that the CCIE lab exam could explore when it comes to NAT configuration. It tests a candidate's understanding of the NAT process at a deep level by layering in multiple services. Having a solid understanding of the NAT order of operation and the commands required to verify and troubleshoot the configuration quickly is mandatory for a strong CCIE candidate.

Zone-Based Firewall (ZBF)

The IOS firewall and related security functions are designed to give customers greater flexibility in how to deploy security services in their network. In some cases, there are advantages to deploying security features on network devices. Cisco obviously offers dedicated standalone security gear as well. CCIE candidates need to have an understanding of both and the configuration differences between the platforms.

ZBF was released to improve the legacy stateful firewall functions in the IOS routers. Prior to the release of ZBF, Cisco routers had a set of features known as Content-Based Access Control (CBAC). ZBF offers a more robust feature set and a less complex configuration than CBAC. As the name implies, ZBF allows groups of interfaces to be defined as a zone, and then policy is applied to the zone in a logical manner. This is an improvement over CBAC because there is no requirement to create policy based on unique interfaces. ZBF inherits a new configuration construct that is based on Class-Based

Policy Language (CPL), which is built on definitions of class maps and policy maps. An example of a typical ZBF is shown in Figure 7-6.

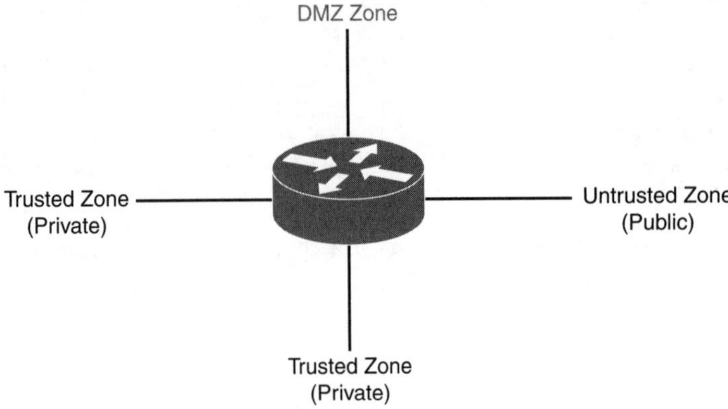

Figure 7-6 *A Typical ZBF*

As with any other Cisco feature, a CCIE candidate needs to have an understanding of the requirements for configuration of ZBF. Accordingly, ZBF has several rules that govern interface behavior, such as the traffic moving between zone member interfaces:

- A zone must be configured before interfaces can be assigned to the zone.
- An interface can be assigned to only one security zone.
- All traffic to and from a given interface is implicitly blocked when the interface is assigned to a zone, except traffic to and from other interfaces in the same zone and traffic to any interface on the router.
- Traffic is implicitly allowed to flow, by default, among interfaces that are members of the same zone.
- In order to permit traffic to and from a zone member interface, a policy allowing or inspecting traffic must be configured between that zone and any other zone.
- The self-zone is the only exception to the default deny all policy. All traffic to any router interface is allowed until traffic is explicitly denied.
- Traffic cannot flow between a zone member interface and any interface that is not a zone member. Pass, inspect, and drop actions can be applied only between two zones.
- Interfaces that have not been assigned to a zone function as classical router ports and might still use classical stateful inspection/CBAC configuration.
- If it is required that an interface on the box not be part of the zoning/firewall policy, it might still be necessary to put that interface in a zone and configure a pass-all policy (sort of a dummy policy) between that zone and any other zone to which traffic flow is desired.

- From the preceding, it follows that if traffic is to flow among all the interfaces in a router, all the interfaces must be part of the zoning model (that is, each interface must be a member of one zone or another).

ZBF Configuration Steps

Many of the concepts discussed in this section are covered in Chapter 4 as well, but for clarity they are discussed again here. Class maps and policy maps are the building blocks of CPL and ZBF configuration. Class maps define the traffic that is governed by ZBF policy, and policy maps describe the action taken on this traffic matched by policy. These commands are nested within the configuration.

Here is the recommended order for configuration:

1. Define zones.
2. Assign interfaces to zones.
3. Define zone pairs.
4. Define class maps.
5. Define policy maps.
6. Apply the policy maps to zone pairs.

The following sections examine these elements in detail, starting with defining zones.

Defining Zones

Zones are named constructs. They can contain useful names such as DMZ, WWW, or TrustedNet. They are then applied to interfaces as part of the zone configuration. An interface can be a member of only one zone.

Configuring Zone Pairs

Zone pairs are also named constructs. It is common to name them according to the zones that make up the pair (for example, TrustedNet-WWW). A zone pair defines the pairing of zones and a direction. Policy is then applied with the **policy-map** command.

Defining the Class Map(s)

Class maps are the workhorses of the ZBF configuration as they define the traffic to which policy is applied. Typically, an access list is defined that specifies the match criteria. The ACL can be standard, extended, or named. Class maps can also match on Layer 4 protocols (for example, TCP, UDP, and ICMP) and Layer 7 services (such as HTTP or SMTP). The **not** keyword negates matching for more advanced configuration. This is especially useful because class maps can include other embedded class maps as part of their configuration.

Class maps provide two options for defining the matching criteria: **match-any** and **match-all. match-any** is valid if any of the match criteria are met, and **match-all** requires that all elements be met in order for a match to be valid.

It is very important that multiple match criteria be configured from the most specific to the least specific. This is helpful for matching on protocols where secondary channels are used after a primary channel has been established.

To make configuration easier, there is a class called **class-default** that, as its name implies, is a default, catch-all class for traffic. It is applied as part of an inspect-type policy map, as discussed in the next section.

Defining the Policy Map(s)

Policy maps apply firewall actions to one or more class maps as traffic traverses from one zone to another. Three actions can be taken:

- **Drop traffic:** Dropping traffic is the default action for all traffic, as applied by the class default. Other class maps can be configured to drop traffic. There is an option to send dropped traffic notifications with syslog using the **log** keyword, but otherwise the drops are silent. This is analogous to an ACL deny action.
- **Pass traffic:** Passing traffic allows traffic to move from one zone to another in one direction only. It exempts traffic from inspection, but an additional corresponding policy must be created for bidirectional traffic. This option is useful for allowing encrypted protocols such as IPsec and SSH through the router. This is analogous to an ACL permit action.
- **Inspect traffic:** Inspecting traffic is the most commonly configured option and is where the actual state-based traffic control is applied. Application control applied with the **inspect** option is an additional option. Without using **inspect**, traffic would either pass or be dropped and would never be processed by stateful policy control.

Configuring ZBF

This section walks through a simple ZBF configuration of a router with three interfaces (see Figure 7-7).

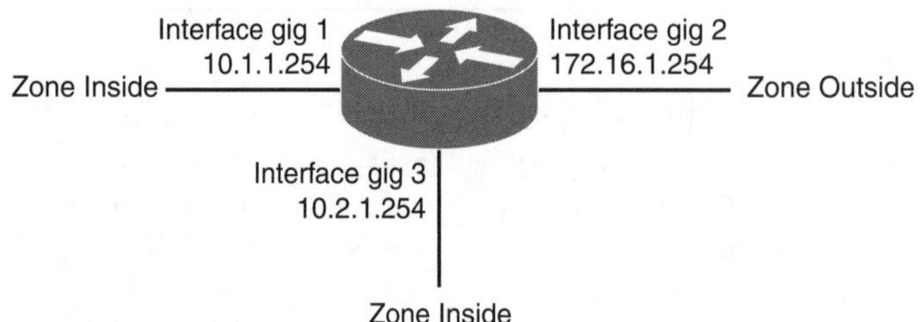

Figure 7-7 *ZBF Configuration with Three Interfaces*

Note Remember that *interzone* communication is denied by default in the absence of firewall policy and that *intrazone* traffic is permitted. For example, both interfaces defined as part of zone inside have no restrictions on traffic sourced and destined to zone inside.

Follow these steps to configure ZBF in the scenario shown in Figure 7-7:

Step 1. Define two zones, named **INSIDE** and **OUTSIDE**:

```
csr(config)# zone security INSIDE
csr(config)# zone security OUTSIDE
```

Note The zone names are not required to be all caps (for example, **INSIDE**), but making them all caps is suggested in order to make the configuration easier to read.

Step 2. Assign the router interfaces to the previously created zones:

```
csr(config)# int gig1
csr(config)# zone-member security INSIDE
csr(config)# int gig3
csr(config)# zone-member security INSIDE
csr(config)# int gig2
csr(config)# zone-member security OUTSIDE
```

Step 3. Configure the zone pairs, or traffic will never pass inside to outside or vice versa:

```
csr(config)# zone pair security ZP-IN-OUT source INSIDE destination
OUTSIDE
```

Some prefer to configure the zone pairs last, after the class maps and policy maps have been defined. It is a matter of preference which order is used. In this example we will come back to the zone pairs and apply the policy maps afterward.

Step 4. Configure the matching policy (class map) and the action policy (policy map). To keep things simple for this example, allow WWW, ICMP, and DNS traffic outbound for both inside interfaces:

```
csr(config)# ip access-list extended IN-OUT-ACL
csr(config-ext-nacl)# permit tcp 10.1.1.0 0.0.0.255 any eq www
csr(config-ext-nacl)# permit tcp 10.2.1.0 0.0.0.255 any eq www
csr(config-ext-nacl)# permit icmp 10.1.1.0 0.0.0.255 any
csr(config-ext-nacl)# permit icmp 10.2.1.0 0.0.0.255 any
csr(config-ext-nacl)# permit udp 10.1.1.0 0.0.0.255 any eq dns
csr(config-ext-nacl)# permit udp 10.2.1.0 0.0.0.255 any eq dns
```

Note You could easily use a numbered access list instead of a named access list for the same outcome. However, in the CCIE lab, it is a best practice to use named access lists if allowed in order to minimize confusion.

Step 5. Create the class map and determine the match criteria (**match-all** or **match-any**). It is helpful to add the element type (ACL, class, and so on) in the name to minimize confusion. As you have learned, the class map defines the match criteria. Because you have already created an ACL (**IN-OUT-ACL**), you now need to apply it in the class map:

```
csr(config)# class-map type inspect match-all IN-OUT-CMAP
csr(config-cmap)# match access-group name IN-OUT-ACL
```

This example uses **match-all** for strict processing of the ACL. But what if your ACL were growing large and unwieldy? You could change your class map to match on protocols instead, as in this configuration:

```
csr(config)# class-map type inspect match-any IN-OUT-CMAP
csr(config-cmap)# match protocol http
csr(config-cmap)# match protocol dns
csr(config-cmap)# match protocol icmp
```

Note the use of **match-any** to inspect any of the policies listed.

Step 6. Apply the class map to a policy map and define the action (in this case, inspecting traffic):

```
csr(config)# policy-map type inspect IN-OUT-PMAP
csr(config-pmap)# class type inspect IN-OUT-CMAP
csr(config-pmap-c)# inspect
```

Step 7. Don't forget to apply the zone pair to the policy map that you just created. This requires defining a new construct, the zone pair, and applying it to the policy map:

```
csr(config)# zone-pair security ZP-IN-OUT source INSIDE destination
OUTSIDE
csr(config-sec-zone-pair)# service-policy type inspect IN-OUT-PMAP
```

Let's pause here for a quick review. You have configured an ACL (**IN-OUT-ACL**) that is defining the match criteria for traffic to be inspected. It uses the ACL to determine the fine details (such as port and protocol) for a match. This is a valid ZBF configuration. The downside is that if there is a need to add more matching criteria (for example, subnet, port, protocol), this ACL will continue to grow. As you also know, the ordering of an ACL can be critical as it relates to policy. This adds a level of complexity that may not be warranted, and there might be an easier way. You could define a protocol as part of a class map, as discussed in more detail in the next section.

Nested Class Maps

For greater efficacy, multiple class maps can be created. They are processed like any access list, in top-down order. The following example builds on the earlier example where all hosts from the **INSIDE** zone are allowed HTTP, ICMP, and WWW access to the **OUTSIDE** zone. In this case you will modify the configuration to only allow WWW and DNS traffic from the proxy servers (.100 and .101, respectively):

Step 1. Create a new access list to specify the addresses of the proxy servers:

```
csr(config)# ip access-list extended PROXY-SRVS
csr(config-ext-nacl)# permit ip host 10.1.1.100 any
csr(config-ext-nacl)# permit ip host 10.1.1.101 any
```

Step 2. Redefine the top-level class map, keeping the match logic to **match-all**:

```
csr(config)# class-map type inspect match-all IN-OUT-CMAP
csr(config-cmap)# match access-group name PROXY-SRVS
```

Step 3. Define the child class map, which is inspecting DNS and HTTP traffic only:

```
csr(config)# class-map type inspect match-any DNS-WEB-CMAP
csr(config-cmap)# match protocol dns
csr(config-cmap)# match protocol http
```

Step 4. Create the policy map with the new class map included:

```
csr(config)# policy-map type inspect IN-OUT-PMAP
csr(config-pmap)# class type inspect DNS-WEB-CMAP
csr(config-pmap-c)# inspect
```

The policy map is now modified to allow ICMP outbound from any host captured by the **IN-OUT-ACL** and any TCP/80 or UDP/53 traffic from the two proxy servers defined in the **PROXY-SRVS** access list.

Example 7-3 shows the relevant configuration. Note the addition of the system-defined class named **class-default**, which is a catch-all for any traffic that does not match the class maps above it. **class-default** is always the last class in an inspect policy, and its default action is to drop. Alternatively, **class-default** could be configured to pass traffic much the way a **permit any** operates at the end of an access list.

Example 7-3 *Policy Map Sample Configuration*

```
class-map type inspect match-all IN-OUT-CMAP
  match access-group name PROXY-SRVS
class-map type inspect match-any DNS-WEB-CMAP
 match protocol dns
 match protocol http
!
policy-map type inspect IN-OUT-PMAP
 class type inspect IN-OUT-CMAP
  inspect
 class type inspect DNS-WEB-CMAP
  inspect
 class class-default
  drop
!
zone security INSIDE
zone security OUTSIDE
zone-pair security ZP-IN-OUT source INSIDE destination OUTSIDE
 service-policy type inspect IN-OUT-PMAP
!
interface GigabitEthernet1
 ip address 10.1.1.254 255.255.255.0
 zone-member security INSIDE
 negotiation auto
!
interface GigabitEthernet2
 ip address 172.16.1.254 255.255.255.0
 zone-member security OUTSIDE
 negotiation auto
!
interface GigabitEthernet3
 ip address 10.2.1.254 255.255.255.0
 zone-member security INSIDE
 negotiation auto
!
ip access-list extended PROXY-SRVS
 permit ip host 10.1.1.100 any
 permit ip host 10.1.1.101 any
```

The Self-Zone

As mentioned earlier in this chapter, there is another zone, the *self-zone*, created automatically during the ZBF configuration. This refers to the router itself and includes any management plane and control plane traffic where the router is the source or destination. ZBF policies define actions to take on transit traffic, or traffic that is passing *through* the router. The self-zone refers to traffic destined *to* the router (or *from* it). It's important to point out that in the absence of any self-zone policy, all traffic is permitted by default to and from the router. However, once a zone-pair mapping is applied to the self-zone, explicit configuration is required for traffic to reach the router control and management plane. This is typically configured with an **inspect** or **pass** statement in the ZBF policy.

> **Note** In this chapter, for ease of interpretation, we use all caps for the policy elements (for example, **INSIDE**). The system reserved name **self** must be all lowercase. Careful attention should be paid to ensure that any configuration for the self-zone uses this form.

Self-Zone Configuration

It's important to know what a policy is trying to achieve and the direction to which the policy is applied. This section shows a basic configuration that only allows SSH and ICMP traffic from the **INSIDE** zone to the self-zone and vice versa. Because the self-zone is already defined and assigned to interface(s), you can skip that step. Follow these steps:

Step 1. Define an access list of the permitted traffic types:

```
csr(config)# ip access-list extended MGMT-ACL
csr(config-ext-nacl)# permit tcp any any eq 22
csr(config-ext-nacl)# permit icmp any any
```

Because you don't specify where the traffic is sourced from, it will be allowed from any interface defined on zone **INSIDE**. Building the ACL in this manner allows you to easily add to it in the future, if necessary.

Step 2. Define the class map as per a standard ZBF configuration:

```
csr(config)# class-map type inspect match-any MGMT-CMAP
csr(config-cmap)# match access-group name MGMT-ACL
```

Step 3. Create a policy map in which you define an **inspect** statement:

```
csr(config)# policy-map type inspect MGMT-PMAP
csr(config-pmap)# class type inspect MGMT-CMAP
csr(config-pmap-c)# inspect
```

Step 4. Configure the zone pair to complete the configuration (remembering to leave **self** lowercase):.

```
csr(config)# zone-pair security ZP-IN-SELF source INSIDE destination self
csr(config-sec-zone-pair)# service-policy type inspect MGMT-POLICY
```

Proper Use of the Self-Zone

Common uses of the self-zone are to protect the control plane and management plane from unwanted traffic when it is necessary to have interface-specific policies. Unlike Control Plane Policing (CoPP), ZBF allows for granular policy control to an interface. A different policy could be defined in ZBF for each interface.

The self-zone becomes critically important when ZBF is combined with other services that terminate on the router. Some of these may include secure tunnels using IPsec or routing protocols such as BGP or OSPF. It is also important to consider traffic sourced from the router such as RADIUS, TACACS+, or SNMP.

Port-to-Application Mapping (PAM)

ZBF includes built-in application inspection and control for specific applications such as POP3, IMAP, SMTP/ESMTP, RPC, and P2P file-sharing applications. This enhances the capability of the router running ZBF as it can natively match an application's behavior for a more granular security policy. For example, security policy may restrict the use of file-sharing applications such as BitTorrent and Gnutella. The ZBF can be configured to block this type of traffic based on the applications in the PAM list. Refer to the Cisco Zone-Based Policy Firewall Design and Application Guide for specifics on this configuration (https://www.cisco.com/c/en/us/support/docs/security/ios-firewall/98628-zone-design-guide.html).

Verifying ZBF

To verify proper configuration, use the **show** commands, especially if multiple service policies exist:

show zone security <zone-name> shows interfaces bound to the specified zone.

show zone-pair security shows all the zone pairs and associated policy.

show policy-map type inspect without any modifiers shows all inspection policy maps.

show policy-map type inspect zone-pair <zone-pair-name> shows all inspection sessions created as part of the specified zone pair.

It is easy to confuse policy elements from one to the other, especially in the CCIE lab.

Troubleshooting ZBF

Troubleshooting ZBF always starts with understanding how the class maps and policy maps work. There are many nuances to ZBF that change over time. Make sure to know and comprehend the configuration guides and release notes for the code in the latest exam blueprint, which provide detailed descriptions of how features are intended to work as well as any new or deprecated features as of that specific release.

ZBF continues to evolve with each IOS release, adding features and complexity, especially when combined with other features, such as NAT and IPsec VPNs. The only way to truly understand how it works is to practice configurations in your study lab that layer in multiple services with ZBF and see how they interact.

Use care when mixing interface ACLs and ZBF. Access lists configured on interfaces that are mapped to zones are processed prior to any ZBF policy. Likewise, if the ZBF engine permits stateful return traffic but there is an interface ACL denying the traffic, the traffic is dropped.

Unsupported Features with ZBF

At the time of this writing, multicast and the legacy CBAC firewall features are not supported in conjunction with and are not compatible with the ZBF inspection engine. The list of supported features changes over time, which is why the release notes are helpful. They outline the new features and bug fixes in a specific release. They also contain other information that is critical for a CCIE candidate.

IOS Advanced Security Features

In addition to traditional security features like firewall and packet inspection, Cisco has expanded the capabilities of the router to protect its control plane from exploitation. These advanced features allow the router to both defend itself and the hosts behind it. Other features like policy-based-routing and WCCP give the router additional deployment flexibility. Let's examine some of the more common configurations.

TCP Intercept

The TCP Intercept feature is introduced in Chapter 4, "Firewalling with the ASA," for the ASA. In that chapter you learned how denial-of-service (DoS) exploits attempt to overwhelm a server by sending a flood of TCP SYN packets, knowing that the state of these packets is held in memory while the connection completes the three-way handshake. Memory, being a finite resource, fills up, and legitimate connections are denied access—hence the name denial of service.

TCP Intercept works by validating TCP connection requests on behalf of legitimate hosts, as defined by an extended access list. The feature establishes a connection with the client on behalf of the destination server, and, if successful, it establishes the connection with the server on behalf of the client and joins the two half-connections together transparently. Because SYN floods are generated from bogus client addresses, these connections will never complete, which protects the server from the malicious traffic. The combination of TCP Intercept and aggressive timers that rapidly age out the TCP half-open connections protects the servers from exploitation. To increase deployment flexibility, TCP Intercept also offers a passive option called watch mode that closes the TCP half-open connections after a preconfigured amount of time.

TCP Intercept Configuration

In order to operate, TCP Intercept requires a trigger access list. This ACL can specify the source, destination, or both source and destination traffic to be intercepted. Typically, the source is **any**, and the destination hosts or subnet is defined as the destination. In the following example, the server subnet is 10.2.1.x/24, and a single host is at 10.3.1.200/32. Follow these steps to configure TCP Intercept:

Step 1. Create the trigger access list:

```
csr(config)# access-list 101 permit tcp any 10.2.1.0 0.0.0.255
csr(config)# access-list 101 permit tcp any host 10.3.1.200
```

Step 2. Apply the access list to TCP Intercept:

```
csr(config)# ip tcp intercept list 101
```

Step 3. Define either intercept (active) or watch (passive) mode:

```
csr(config)# ip tcp intercept mode ?
  intercept  Intercept connections
  watch      Watch connections
```

TCP Intercept allows very granular tuning of the various timers associated with TCP three-way handshake. For example, watch mode by default waits 30 seconds for a connection to reach the established state before sending a reset to the server. You could reduce the timer to 20 seconds, as shown here:

```
csr(config)# ip tcp intercept watch-timeout 20
```

By default, TCP Intercept samples the connection rate every 60 seconds. Two rates are monitored: the total number of incoming connection requests and the number of incomplete (half-open) connections. Once a specified threshold is exceeded, TCP Intercept goes into aggressive mode, which leads to the following:

- Each new connection causes the oldest partial connection to be deleted. (You can change to a random drop mode.)
- The initial retransmission timeout is reduced by half, to 0.5 seconds, and so the total time trying to establish the connection is cut in half. (When not in aggressive mode, the code does exponential back-off on its retransmissions of SYN segments. The initial retransmission timeout is 1 second. The subsequent timeouts are 2 seconds, 4 seconds, 8 seconds, and 16 seconds. The code retransmits four times before giving up, so it gives up after 31 seconds of no acknowledgment.)
- If in watch mode, the watch timeout is reduced by half. (If the default is in place, the watch timeout becomes 15 seconds.)

These timers can be configured as shown in Example 7-4:

Example 7-4 *TCP Intercept Timers*

```
csr(config)# ip tcp intercept ?
  connection-timeout  Specify timeout for connection info
  drop-mode           Specify incomplete connection drop mode
  finrst-timeout      Specify timeout for FIN/RST
  list                Specify access-list to use
  max-incomplete      Specify maximum number of incomplete connections before
                      clamping
  mode                Specify intercepting mode
  one-minute          Specify one-minute-sample watermarks for clamping
  watch-timeout       Specify timeout for incomplete connections in watch mode
```

Using **show** commands is the best way to verify TCP intercept operation. **show tcp intercept connections** and **show tcp intercept statistics** are especially helpful.

Unicast Reverse Path Forwarding

A common technique used by DoS attacks is to spoof the source address in order to hide the identity of the attacker. The Unicast Reverse Path Forwarding (uRPF) feature was designed to mitigate these attacks by checking the Forwarding Information Base (FIB) in the CEF table to match the ingress interface on the router to the source address (that is, a "reverse" lookup). The default action was to drop packets received where the interface had no reverse route to the source address. Traffic that matched up was passed normally.

Over time this uRPF method became known as "strict" mode due to the strict nature in which it dropped non-conforming packets. However, it became apparent that this mode had weaknesses, especially where routers were multihomed and traffic flowed asymmetrically. Legitimate traffic was often dropped due to the inability of the router to match the interface with a corresponding FIB entry. Because of this, it became apparent that a less strict method was required. uRPF "loose" mode was created in response to this need. It removes the ingress interface match requirement but automatically drops and detects source traffic that doesn't exist in the FIB. This mode still provides effective defense against DoS attacks by dropping sourced traffic from which there is no matching entry.

uRPF Configuration

uRPF is very simple to configure on an interface, but it does require CEF to be enabled on the router in order to operate. Follow these steps to configure uRPF in loose mode:

Step 1. Enable CEF:

```
csr(config)# ip cef
```

Step 2. Apply the uRPF configuration to the interface:

```
csr(config)# int gig1
csr(config-if)# ip verify unicast source reachable-via any
```

Step 3. Optionally, if you require strict mode, modify the interface command as shown here:

```
csr(config-if)# ip verify unicast source reachable-via rx
```

Two helpful **show** commands enable you to verify uRPF operation, as shown in Examples 7-5 and 7-6.

Example 7-5 show cef interface *Output*

```
csr# sh cef inter g2
GigabitEthernet2 is up (if_number 8)
  Corresponding hwidb fast_if_number 8
  Corresponding hwidb firstsw->if_number 8
  Internet address is 172.16.1.254/24
  ICMP redirects are always sent
  IP unicast RPF check is enabled
  Input features: Virtual Fragment Reassembly, uRPF, NAT Outside
  Output features: Post-routing NAT Outside
  IP policy routing is disabled
```

Example 7-6 show ip traffic *Output*

```
csr# sh ip traffic
IP statistics:
  Rcvd:  16065 total, 6291 local destination
         0 format errors, 0 checksum errors, 0 bad hop count
         0 unknown protocol, 0 not a gateway
         0 security failures, 0 bad options, 0 with options
  Opts:  0 end, 0 nop, 0 basic security, 0 loose source route
         0 timestamp, 0 extended security, 0 record route
         0 stream ID, 0 strict source route, 0 alert, 0 cipso, 0 ump
         0 other, 0 ignored
  Frags: 0 reassembled, 0 timeouts, 0 couldn't reassemble
         0 fragmented, 0 fragments, 0 couldn't fragment
         0 invalid hole
  Bcast: 1377 received, 6 sent
  Mcast: 116 received, 0 sent
  Sent:  4260 generated, 0 forwarded
  Drop:  5 encapsulation failed, 0 unresolved, 0 no adjacency
         0 no route, 41 unicast RPF, 0 forced drop, 0 unsupported-addr
         0 options denied, 0 source IP address zero
```

Policy-Based Routing (PBR)

PBR is a Cisco router feature that allows the default behavior of next-hop routing to be overridden when a specified condition or conditions are met. For example, consider a multihomed router that is connected to two networks: one that is the primary connection using the company MPLS network and another that is a backup broadband Internet connection. Say that the company prefers to send guest network traffic over the broadband Internet connection, leaving the company MPLS uplink uncluttered. PBR could send the guest traffic over the backup link, saving valuable bandwidth on the corporate MPLS network. PBR also can mark quality of service (QoS) on traffic, which could then be prioritized at other points in the network. In short, PBR offers incredible flexibility.

PBR Operation

PBR is enabled by using a route map defined on an interface. The route maps are configured globally and are made up of **match** and **set** statements specifying the match criteria and corresponding action. The route maps are processed in top-down order, based on sequence number. The following occurs for a permit statement:

- If the decision reached is **permit**, the PBR logic executes the action specified by the **set** command on the packet.
- If the decision reached is **deny**, the PBR action is *not* applied. Instead, the processing logic moves forward to look at the next route-map statement in the sequence. If no next statement exists, PBR processing terminates, and the packet is routed using the default IP routing table.

The following occurs for a deny statement:

- If the criteria decision is **permit**, the PBR processing terminates, and the packet is routed using the default IP routing table.
- If the criteria decision is **deny**, the PBR processing logic moves forward to look at the next route-map statement in the sequence (the statement with the next higher sequence number). If no next statement exists, PBR processing exits, and the packet is routed normally, using the default IP routing table.

When using any combination of these commands in a policy, the commands are evaluated in the following order:

```
set ip next-hop
set interface
set ip default next-hop
set default interface
```

PBR Configuration

The following PBR configuration is based on the example with a multihomed router, as shown in Figure 7-8:

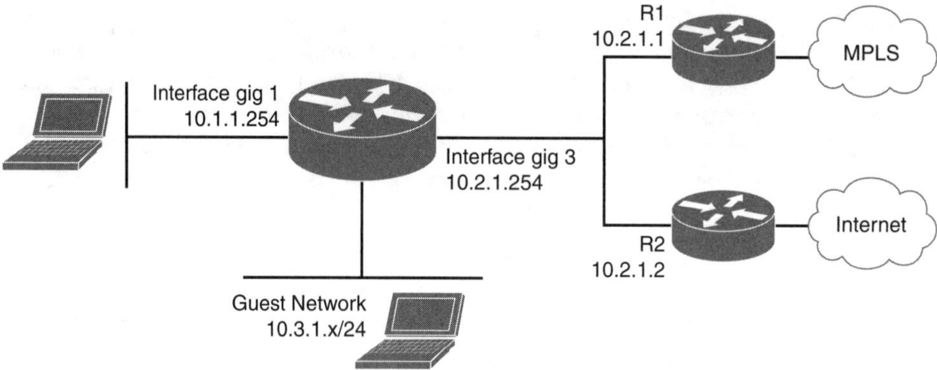

Figure 7-8 *Multihomed Router*

Step 1. Create the access list that will define the PBR action:

```
csr(config)# access-list 101 permit 10.3.1.0 0.0.0.255 any
```

Here your objective is to use PBR to send the guest network traffic to R2, which is acting as a broadband Internet backup link. Your access list uses the guest network as the source address matching criteria.

Step 2. Create the route-map:

```
csr(config)# route-map GUEST-PBR permit 10
```

Step 3. Apply the match condition for PBR:

```
csr(config-route-map)# match ip address 101
```

Step 4. Define the action for the guest network:

```
csr(config-route-map)# set ip next-hop 10.2.1.2
```

Step 5. Apply the route-map to interface Gig2:

```
csr(config-if)# ip policy route-map GUEST-PBR
```

By modifying the sequence numbers in the route-map statement, you could easily prepend or append more route-map clauses to **GUEST-PBR**.

PBR Troubleshooting

Remember that a normal routing table is used for all packets that do *not* match a route-map statement. Therefore, in order to troubleshoot PBR efficiently, it is critical to understand what routes are in the routing table.

show ip route <network> shows detailed information about a route, and **debug ip policy** shows which packets are policy-routed:

```
IP: s=10.3.1.4 (GigabitEthernet3), d=172.16.1.199, len 100, policy match
IP: route map GUEST-PBR, item 10, permit
IP: s=200.200.200.4 (GigabitEthernet3), d=172.16.1.199 (GigabitEthernet2),
    len 100, policy routed
```

Web Cache Communication Protocol (WCCP)

WCCP is a client/server protocol that allows a router to intercept IPv4 traffic that meets certain conditions. This traffic is then redirected to a destination other than the one specified in the IP packet. Certain configurations allow for load balancing and fault tolerance. The most common use of WCCP involves redirecting traffic destined for a web server to a web cache or proxy where the content is cached or a security policy is applied. Figure 7-9 shows a typical WCCP network topology.

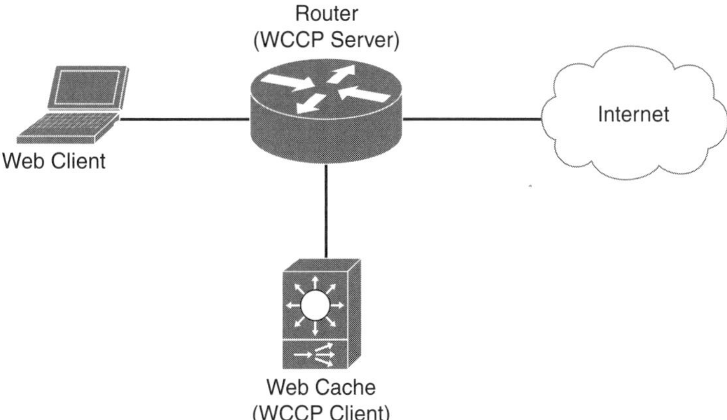

Figure 7-9 *WCCP*

The WCCP client is the cache or proxy that is receiving the redirected traffic, and the WCCP server is the redirecting router. WCCP communication is always initiated by the client to the server. The server (router) listens for WCCP client announcements.

WCCP Protocol Capabilities

WCCP provides the capability to load balance among clients. This is very common in large networks where multiple egress points exist. Two assignment methods exist for load balancing: hash and mask.

The hash method involves creating a value from one of the following fields in the traffic that is to be redirected: source port, destination port, source IP address, or destination IP address. A byte-wise XOR yields an 8-bit index into the hash table, which determines if the packet should be redirected, not redirected, or rehashed.

The mask assignment method involves using all the same fields as the hash method (source port, destination port, source IP address, or destination IP address) in an AND operation to create a 96-bit value. This value is compared to a list associated with the mask to determine whether to forward to the web proxy. If there is no match, the traffic is not forwarded.

Forwarding Method

The forwarding method determines how traffic is redirected from the WCCP router to the web proxy. This is either through GRE or Layer 2 and is negotiated as part of WCCP capabilities exchange. WCCP has the ability to ensure that redirected traffic leaves and returns using the same egress WCCP router, even if multiple WCCP routers exist.

GRE redirection involves using a GRE header and a redirect header that contains the service ID and hash bucket matched. GRE forwarding allows the router and Web Security Appliance (WSA) to be separated by multiple Layer 3 hops.

Layer 2 uses the original IP packet with a rewritten MAC address of the WCCP client. This is generally desirable over using GRE due to hardware switching at line rates for performance. However, not all Cisco WCCPD-capable devices support Layer 2 forwarding.

Using Layer 2 as a forwarding method allows direct forwarding to the web proxy without further lookup. Layer 2 redirection requires that the router and caches be directly connected—that is, on the same IP subnet.

Return Method

Also referred to as bypass traffic, the return method determines how traffic is forwarded from the web proxy to the router. In Cisco WSA terms, this is traffic that falls under "proxy bypass." For technical reasons, the WSA "returns" traffic back to the WCCP router in the same method that it was received, regardless of what was negotiated in the capabilities exchange. WSA configuration is covered in more detail in Chapter 8, "Content Security and Advanced Threat Protection."

Some devices are able to forward using Layer 2 but only return using GRE. The WCCP redirection method does not have to match the return method.

WCCP uses either GRE or Layer 2 to redirect or return IP traffic. GRE uses an additional header to encapsulate the traffic, which increases computational overhead. Layer 2 redirection involves using the MAC address of the WCCP client (typically the router) by overwriting the original MAC address of the web client. Layer 2 can use hardware acceleration and is preferred for performance reasons when the router is connected to a switch.

WCCP Version 1 only allows for redirection of TPC port 80, while WCCP Version 2 can redirect any TCP and UDP traffic. Version 2 is more scalable, supporting up to 32 routers and 32 caches, with an added benefit of MD5 hashing to protect the WCCP client/server relationship.

WCCP Configuration

A simple WCCP configuration requires only a few commands, but before any traffic redirection can occur, the WCCP client/server relationship must be established. First, you specify the WCCP version (preferably Version 2):

```
csr(config)# ip wccp version 2
```

Then you enable the service on a router interface:

```
csr(config)# int gig1
csr(config-if)# ip wccp web-cache redirect in
```

At this point WCCP is configured, but you haven't provided any parameters. The **web-cache** keyword by default redirects TCP 80 traffic only. To redirect other ports/protocols, you need to create a service ID. In the following example, service ID 90 is defined. The **in** keyword implies that traffic is redirected on ingress to the interface.

It is a best practice to limit the match criteria for redirection by using an access list; otherwise, the router will redirect all traffic. An extended access list serves the purposes of this example, where you define the hosts/subnets to be redirected and use **deny** statements to exempt protocols and addresses from redirection. For this lab, the web clients are on subnet 10.1.1.x/24, and you only redirect TCP 80 and 443. Note the structure of the source and destination of the access list. Here are the steps to build a typical WCCCP configuration:

Step 1. Create the access list for traffic that requires redirection:

```
csr(config)# access-list extended WEB-CLIENTS
csr(config-ext-nacl)# deny ip any 10.1.1.0 0.0.0.255
csr(config-ext-nacl)# ! deny traffic destined for the subnet from
redirection
csr(config-ext-nacl)# permit tcp 10.1.1.0 0.0.0.255 any eq www
csr(config-ext-nacl)# permit tcp 10.1.1.0 0.0.0.255 any eq 443
```

Tip It is also a best practice to deny the web proxy source addresses to avoid a redirect loop.

Step 2. Now enable the web service with service ID 90 and have it use the access list **WEB-CLIENTS** to determine matching hosts and protocols:

```
csr(config)# ip wccp 90 redirect-list WEB-CLIENTS
```

Step 3. Apply the web service to your interface:

```
csr(config-if)# ip wccp 90 redirect in
```

Step 4. Validate the configuration as shown in Example 7-7.

Example 7-7 *Verifying WCCP Operation*

```
csr# sh ip wccp 90
Global WCCP information:
    Router information:
        Router Identifier:                      10.1.1.254

    Service Identifier: 90
        Protocol Version:                       2.00 (minimum)
        Number of Service Group Clients:        1
        Number of Service Group Routers:        1
        Total Packets Redirected:               44376
          Process:                              0
          CEF:                                  44376
          Platform:                             0
        Service mode:                           Open
        Service Access-list:                    -none-
        Total Packets Dropped Closed:           0
        Redirect access-list:                   WEB-CLIENTS
        Total Packets Denied Redirect:          0
        Total Packets Unassigned:               0
        Group access-list:                      -none-
        Total Messages Denied to Group:         0
        Total Authentication failures:          0
        Total GRE Bypassed Packets Received:    0
          Process:                              0
          CEF:                                  0
          Platform:                             0
```

WCCP Troubleshooting

Troubleshooting WCCP on Cisco devices requires the use of both **show** and **debug** commands. WCCP is based on a simple protocol message exchange that is easy to follow by using **debug** commands. As usual, use **debug** commands with caution on loaded devices.

> **Note** Due to differences in Cisco device WCCP capabilities, the output in this section may not exactly match your lab setup.

The following are useful **show** commands:

```
show ip wccp
show ip wccp interface detail
show ip wccp <service> detail
show ip wccp <service> view
show ip wccp <service> service
```

The following are useful **debug** commands:

```
debug ip wccp events
debug ip wccp packets
```

The **debug** commands in Example 7-8 show the state change between the web cache and a switch. This example shows the WCCP handshake and then a change in the assignment method. The important part of the exchange is the usable WCCP client messages indicating that the WCCP handshake has properly completed.

Example 7-8 *WCCP Debug Output*

```
6w5d: %WCCP-5-SERVICEFOUND: Service web-cache acquired on WCCP Client 192.168.254.2
6w5d: WCCP-PKT:S00: Received valid Here_I_Am packet from 192.168.254.2 w/rcv_id
  00000006
6w5d: WCCP-EVNT:wccp_change_router_view: S00
6w5d: WCCP-EVNT:wccp_change_router_view: deallocate rtr_view (24 bytes)
6w5d: WCCP-EVNT:wccp_change_router_view: allocate hash rtr_view (1564 bytes)
6w5d: WCCP-EVNT:wccp_change_router_view: rtr_view_size set to 72 bytes
6w5d: WCCP-EVNT:S00: Built new router view: 1 routers, 1 usable WCCP clients,
  change # 00000002
6w5d: WCCP-PKT:S00: Sending I_See_You packet to 192.168.254.2 w/ rcv_id 00000007
6w5d: WCCP-EVNT:wccp_update_assignment_status: enter
6w5d: WCCP-EVNT:wccp_update_assignment_status: exit
6w5d: WCCP-EVNT:wccp_validate_wc_assignments: enter
6w5d: WCCP-EVNT:wccp_validate_wc_assignments: not mask assignment, exit.
6w5d: WCCP-PKT:S00: Sending I_See_You packet to 192.168.254.2 w/ rcv_id 00000008
6w5d: WCCP-EVNT:wccp_clear_hash_info: enter
6w5d: WCCP-EVNT:wccp_clear_hash_info: enter
6w5d: WCCP-EVNT:wccp_clear_hash_info: exit
6w5d: WCCP-EVNT:wccp_change_router_view: S00
6w5d: WCCP-EVNT:wccp_change_router_view: deallocate rtr_view (72 bytes)
6w5d: WCCP-EVNT:wccp_change_router_view: allocate hash rtr_view (1564 bytes)
6w5d: WCCP-EVNT:wccp_change_router_view: rtr_view_size set to 72 bytes
6w5d: WCCP-EVNT:S00: Built new router view: 1 routers, 1 usable WCCP clients,
  change # 00000002
```

If the assignment method is changed, the WCCP process tears down and attempts to reestablish, using the new parameters, as shown in Example 7-9.

Example 7-9 *WCCP Debug Output After Changing Proxy Mask Assignment*

```
6w5d: WCCP-EVNT:S00: Here_I_Am packet from 192.168.254.2 w/bad assign method
  00000002, was offered 00000001
6w5d: WCCP-EVNT:wccp_free_wc_assignment_memory: enter
6w5d: WCCP-EVNT:wccp_free_wc_assignment_memory: deallocate orig info (40 bytes)
6w5d: WCCP-EVNT:wccp_free_wc_assignment_memory: deallocate current info (40 bytes)
6w5d: WCCP-EVNT:wccp_free_wc_assignment_memory: exit
6w5d: WCCP-EVNT:wccp_free_mask_assignment_memory: enter
6w5d: WCCP-EVNT:wccp_free_mask_assignment_memory: exit
6w5d: %WCCP-1-SERVICELOST: Service web-cache lost on WCCP Client 192.168.25
6w5d: WCCP-EVNT:wccp_change_router_view: S00
6w5d: WCCP-EVNT:wccp_change_router_view: deallocate rtr_view (72 bytes)
6w5d: WCCP-EVNT:wccp_change_router_view: allocate hash rtr_view (1564 bytes)
6w5d: WCCP-EVNT:wccp_change_router_view: rtr_view_size set to 28 bytes
6w5d: WCCP-EVNT:S00: Built new router view: 1 routers, 0 usable WCCP clients,
  change # 00000003
6w5d: WCCP-EVNT:S00: Here_I_Am packet from 192.168.254.2 with incompatible
  capabilities
6w5d: WCCP-EVNT:wccp_copy_wc_assignment_data: enter
6w5d: WCCP-EVNT:wccp_copy_wc_assignment_data: allocate orig mask info (28 bytes)
6w5d: WCCP-EVNT:wccp_copy_wc_assignment_data: exit
6w5d: WCCP-EVNT:wccp_change_router_view: S00
6w5d: WCCP-EVNT:wccp_change_router_view: deallocate rtr_view (28 bytes)
6w5d: WCCP-EVNT:wccp_change_router_view: allocate mask rtr_view (60 bytes)
6w5d: WCCP-EVNT:wccp_change_router_view: copy orig info (28 bytes)
6w5d: WCCP-EVNT:S00: Built new router view: 1 routers, 1 usable WCCP clients,
  change # 00000004
```

You can validate that the web cache is usable, as shown in Example 7-10.

Example 7-10 *Web Cache Validation*

```
show ip wccp web-cache detail
WCCP Client information:
      WCCP Client ID: 192.168.254.2
      Protocol Version: 2.0
      State:           Usable
      Redirection:        L2
      Packet Return:     L2
      Packets Redirected:    0
      Connect Time:        00:00:21
      Assignment:         MASK
```

This section provides an introduction to basic WCCP configuration in IOS. There are many nuances and features in WCCP that are code-and platform-dependent. There is a wealth of information online about these features and requirements to provide much more detail than is allowed here. WCCP, like any other service, is bound to an order of operation. It is recommended that CCIE candidates need to have a strong working knowledge of this order and the options available for WCCP configuration. Before taking the exam, a CCIE candidate should use a virtual Web Security Appliance (WSAv) in order to practice WCCP configuration with a virtual CSR.

Summary

The security features in IOS and IOS XE products continue to evolve to meet the growing needs of customer deployment. Because they are offered in both physical and virtual options, they are versatile for today's networks. All the configuration examples in this chapter were built using a virtual Cloud Services Router, which is our recommendation for CCIE lab study.

This chapter begins with a discussion on NAT, including where it is used and recommended methods for troubleshooting. This chapter also discusses the benefits of ZBF configuration, with special attention to the self-zone. This chapter introduces the class map and policy map constructs, which are required for the ZBF features.

This chapter covers some advanced security features and their usage. Understanding the methods for protecting the router control plane is vital for both lab study and the real world. TCP Intercept and uRPF are features that can be deployed on a router in order to achieve this. PBR is an option when special circumstances require steering traffic outside the global routing table. WCCP is the protocol standard for redirecting traffic to a web proxy. It offers very granular configuration options, depending on the level of scale required. Having experience with these options and knowing how to quickly validate their proper configuration is required for a CCIE candidate. Understanding their compatibility and configuration methodology will pay dividends during the lab exam.

References

"Cisco CSR 1000v Cloud Services Router Software Configuration Guide," https://www.cisco.com/c/en/us/td/docs/routers/csr1000/software/configuration/b_CSR1000v_Configuration_Guide.html

"IP Addressing: NAT Configuration Guide, Cisco IOS XE Release 3S," https://www.cisco.com/c/en/us/td/docs/ios-xml/ios/ipaddr_nat/configuration/xe-3s/nat-xe-3s-book/iadnat-addr-consv.html

"Cisco Virtual Internet Routing Lab Personal Edition (VIRL PE) 20 Nodes," https://learningnetworkstore.cisco.com/virtual-internet-routing-lab-virl/cisco-personal-edition-pe-20-nodes-virl-20

"Cisco Zone-Based Policy Firewall Design and Application Guide," https://www.cisco.com/c/en/us/support/docs/security/ios-firewall/98628-zone-design-guide.html

Part III

<HTML> EHLO. You have threat in content </HTML>

Chapter 8

Content Security and Advanced Threat Protection

This chapter provides details about content security, as it relates to content filtering, inspection, and advanced threat protection. This chapter explores the Web Security Appliance (WSA), Email Security Appliance (ESA), and Content Security Management Appliance (SMA). You will learn how to proxy traffic with the WSA, using transparent and explicit forwarding modes, along with how to forward traffic to and from the ESA. This chapter reviews basic configuration along with policy configuration.

Content Security Overview

It is well known that email and the web are two of the top threat vectors in security. The main reason is that email and web protocols are the most popular protocols used by individuals in business and personal computing. If an email comes in, looking like it is from a loved one and has a file attached, most individuals click on that email. They are also likely to click links friends have posted on social media, which can lead to their computers becoming infected. While security awareness training helps a little, the most effective way to minimize the risk of web and email threats is to configure content filtering and security.

Chapter 5, "Next-Gen Firewalls," explores the Cisco next-generation firewall's (NGFW's) URL filtering and Application Visibility and Control (AVC) features. While some organizations decide that using a NGFW for content filtering and security is adequate and meets their needs, others opt for a dedicated solution or an additional layer of security, with a dedicated secure web gateway, sometimes referred to as a *proxy server*.

Cisco's WSA and ESA are purpose-built content security devices designed to provide strong protection, complete control, and operational visibility into threats to an organization. The WSA and ESA receive threat intelligence from Cisco Talos, Cisco's industry-leading threat intelligence team that protects organizations from active adversaries. The Talos team collects more than 16 billion web requests and 300 billion email messages per day. This data is used to create the comprehensive protection and detection content for content security appliances.

Cisco Async Operating System (AsyncOS)

AsyncOS is the underlying OS platform powering the WSA, ESA, and SMA. Crafted using a FreeBSD-based kernel, AsyncOS was modified to address some of the limitations of traditional Linux and UNIX operating systems. One focus was overcoming the limit of 100 simultaneous connections by creating a stackless threading model that allows the OS to support more than 10,000 simultaneous connections. AsyncOS has a high-performance file system and an I/O-driven scheduler optimized for the asynchronous nature of messaging and communication—hence the name AsyncOS. It also has no user-accessible UNIX shell, which makes the system secure and much simpler to administer. Users interact with a web-based GUI or fully scriptable command-line interface (CLI).

Web Security Appliance

The WSA is an integrated solution that includes web proxy, antimalware, threat analytics, policy management, and reporting in a single appliance. Enterprises use the WSA to protect their employees/users from accessing and being infected by malicious web traffic, websites, and viruses or malware. The WSA provides deep visibility into evolving application and micro-application content, along with granular control over those applications and usage behavior.

Administrators can give employees access to the sites they need to do their jobs while denying risky activities such as games and file transfers. Organizations can control their environments with actionable reporting that simplifies analysis, speeds troubleshooting, and identifies potential security policy refinements. Identifying potential web security issues becomes easy thanks to performance and bandwidth anomaly reporting.

Figure 8-1 illustrates the scanning and filtering that take place on the WSA. Now let's look at what each of those functions does:

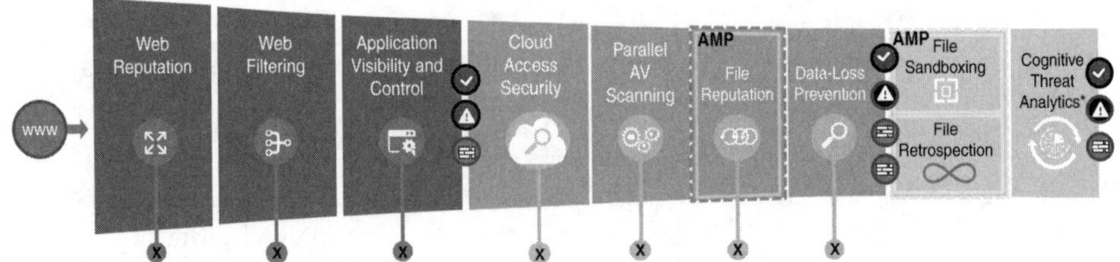

Figure 8-1 *WSA Scanning Engines*

- **Web Reputation:** The Cisco WSA analyzes and categorizes unknown URLs and blocks those that fall below a defined security threshold. The instant a web request is made, Web Reputation filters analyze more than 200 different parameters related to web traffic and the network to determine the level of risk associated with a site. Web Reputation tracking differs from a traditional URL blacklist or whitelist. It analyzes a broad set of data and produces a highly granular score of –10 to +10. This granular score offers administrators increased flexibility by helping them obtain more detail than the binary "good" or "bad" categorizations and allows them to implement different security policies based on different Web Reputation score ranges.

- **Web filtering:** WSA combines traditional URL filtering with real-time dynamic content analysis and allows for granular policy (AUP, warning, quota, bandwidth) and security scanning engine selection.
- **AVC:** AVC allows the WSA to inspect and even block applications that are not allowed by the corporate security polity. For example, an administrator can allow users to use social media sites like Facebook but block micro-applications such as Facebook games.
- **Cloud access security:** The WSA can find and stop hidden threats lurking in cloud apps by leveraging built-in AVC along with partnerships with cloud access security brokers (CASBs).
- **Antivirus scanning:** Webroot, McAfee, and Sophos are all options when configuring WSA antivirus scanning.
- **File reputation:** File reputation threat intelligence is updated every three to five minutes, using threat information from Cisco Talos.
- **Data-loss prevention (DLP):** Third-party DLP integration redirects all outbound traffic to a third-party DLP appliance, allowing deep content inspection for regulatory compliance and data exfiltration protection. It enables an administrator to inspect web content by title, metadata, and size and even to prevent users from storing files to cloud services, such as Dropbox and Google Drive.
- **File sandboxing:** If an unknown file is detected, the Cisco AMP capabilities can put the file in a sandbox to inspect its behavior. This inspection can be combined with machine-learning analysis to determine the threat level. More information about file reputation and file sandboxing can be found in Chapter 10, "Protecting Against Advanced Malware."
- **File retrospection:** After an unknown file has been downloaded, the WSA continues to cross-examine files over an extended period of time. If a file goes from Unknown to Malware status, the WSA notifies the administrator.
- **Cognitive threat analytics:** The WSA allows for anomaly detection of HTTP and HTTPS traffic. The results adjust based on new information, allowing the WSA to discover 100% confirmed threats in an environment even when HTTPS traffic inspection has been disabled.

Proxy Basics

The WSA is typically placed either on the inside of the corporate firewall or in a demilitarized zone (DMZ). This allows for centralized proxying and minimum appliances. The WSA can be deployed as a physical appliance, as an S-Series appliance, or as a virtual machine running on VMware's ESX, KVM, or Microsoft's Hyper-V. The goal of a proxy is to be the proxy between HTTP clients and HTTP servers. This specifically means that the WSA as a web proxy has two sets of TCP sockets per client request: one connection from the client to the WSA and another connection from the WSA to the web server.

Each WSA appliance and virtual appliance contains one or more of the following interface types:

- **M1:** Used for management, the M1 interface can be used for data traffic if the organization does not use a separate management network. This is also referred to as a *one-armed installation*.
- **P1/P2:** These are the data interfaces, which are used for web proxy traffic. When both P1 and P2 are enabled, they must be connected to different subnets. A combination of M1 and P1 could be used, where M1 receives proxy requests and P1 is used to send traffic to the Internet. When multiple interfaces are used for proxying, static routes must be used to direct the traffic to the correct interface.
- **T1/T2:** These ports are used for Layer 4 traffic monitoring to listen to all TCP ports. T1/T2 ports do not have an IP configuration. They are promiscuous monitoring ports only. T1 can be configured alone for duplex communication, or T1 and T2 can be configured together in simplex mode. For example, T1 can connect to the network to receive all outgoing traffic (from clients to the Internet), and the T2 interface can receive all incoming traffic (from the Internet to clients).

Regardless of the form factor or placement of the appliance, to get clients' traffic to the WSA, organizations can deploy one or both proxy modes on the WSA:

- **Explicit forward mode:** The client is configured to explicitly use the proxy and sends all web traffic to the proxy.
- **Transparent mode:** The clients do not know there is a proxy that they must work through. The infrastructure is configured to forward traffic to the proxy.

Explicit Forward Mode

In explicit forward mode, the client intentionally connects to a proxy. The proxy resolves the server name in the URL and communicates with the remote web server on behalf of the client. Because the client knows what is going on, issues such as authentication failures are relatively easy to troubleshoot.

It is important to note that because the client knows there is a proxy and sends all traffic to the proxy, the client does *not* perform a DNS lookup of the domain before requesting the URL. The WSA is responsible for resolving and requesting the page on behalf of the client.

Explicit mode requires no network infrastructure to redirect client requests, but each client configuration must change. An example of the setup for explicit proxy on Apple OS X is shown in Figure 8-2.

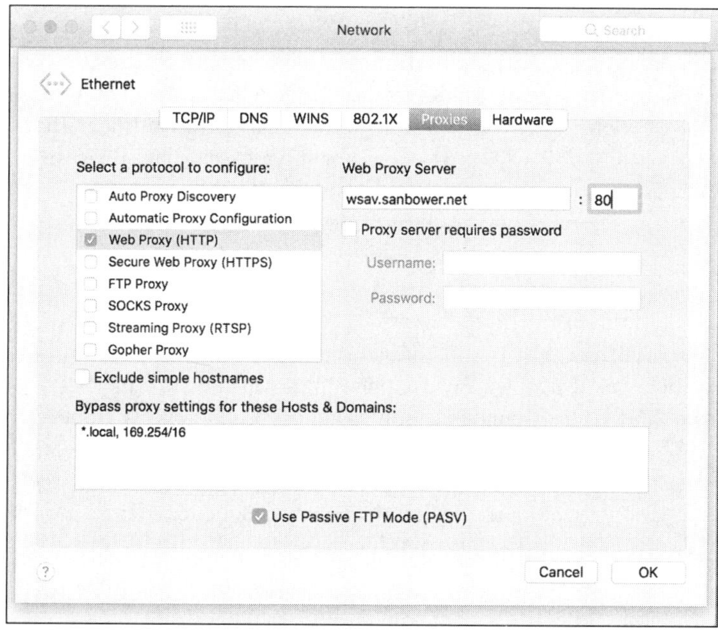

Figure 8-2 *Apple OS X Proxy Settings*

One misconception when it comes to deploying a proxy in explicit mode is that the only way to deploy a proxy in explicit mode is to manually define the settings within each client's browser. It is possible to configure proxy settings on the bowser using DHCP or DNS, with the help of proxy auto-configuration (PAC) files, or with Microsoft Group Policy Objects (GPOs).

Browser proxy settings can be locked down—for example, by using Microsoft GPOs. Furthermore, if the enterprise firewall is configured correctly, web traffic that is not coming from the proxies should be blocked. Therefore, even if the user manages to change the proxy settings, he or she will not be able to surf the web.

A simple way to advertise and configure web browsers with PAC settings is by using Web Proxy Auto-Discovery (WPAD) protocol. WPAD uses the auto-detect proxy settings found in every modern web browser. Proxy server location(s) can be provided to clients through DHCP option 252 with the URL as a string in the option (for example, http://domain.com/wpad.dat) or with DNS by creating an A host record for wpad.domain.com.

Another misconception is that deploying an explicit forward proxy does not provide failover or load balancing. Again, the solution lies in the use of PAC files. In fact, PAC files can offload the load balancing and failover processing to each client.

The WSA also includes a SOCKS proxy to process SOCKS traffic. The client contacts the SOCKS proxy server and, by exchanging messages defined by the SOCKS protocol, negotiates a proxy connection. When a connection is established, the client communicates with the SOCKS server by using the SOCKS protocol. The external server communicates with the SOCKS server as if it were the actual client.

In order to use SOCKS proxy, a SOCKS policy must be created. SOCKS policies are the equivalent of access policies that control SOCKS traffic. The SOCKS protocol only supports direct forward connections. The SOCKS proxy does not support (that is, does not forward to) upstream proxies. The SOCKS proxy does not support scanning services, which are used by AVC, DLP, and malware detection. Also, the SOCKS proxy does not decrypt SSL traffic; it tunnels traffic from the client to the server.

Transparent Mode

In transparent mode deployments, the network infrastructure redirects web traffic to the proxy. This can be done using policy-based routing (PBR), which is available on many routers, or Cisco's Web Cache Communication Protocol (WCCP) on Cisco routers, switches, or the ASA firewall. The client is unaware its traffic is being proxied and, as a result, the client uses DNS to resolve the domain name in the URL and send the web request destined for the web server (not the proxy). Transparent mode requires a network choke point with a redirection device to redirect traffic to proxy.

With transparent mode, administrators are able to force all traffic to the proxy if desired, without end-user interaction, and load balancing is inherent without use of hardware load balancers or PAC files. It is also easier to deploy in phases by using access control lists (ACLs) with PBR or WCCP. This also makes it easier to back out during deployment, by simply removing the redirection configuration.

Transparent Proxy Traffic Redirection with WCCP

WCCP is a Cisco-developed content-routing protocol that provides a mechanism to redirect traffic flows in real time. It has built-in load balancing, scaling, fault tolerance, and service-assurance (failsafe) mechanisms. WCCP typically puts only about 2% additional CPU load onto the redirection device.

Enabling WCCP can sometimes be cumbersome, and it requires review of routing/switching/firewall release notes and caveats. For example, Cisco ASA firewalls require that the WSA and clients be within the same security zone. Switches might have a number of caveats based on hardware and supervisory cards (for example, "sdm prefer routing"). The point is that you should always review caveats listed in software advisory or release notes before deploying WCCP.

Example 8-1 shows configuration of WCCP on a switch, and this configuration should work on most routers as well.

Example 8-1 *Configuring WCCP on a Switch*

```
! Match HTTP Traffic
ip access-list extended HTTP-TRAFFIC
permit tcp 10.28.28.0 0.0.0.255 any eq www
permit tcp 10.28.128.0 0.0.0.255 any eq www
deny ip 10.28.28.0 0.0.0.255 any
deny ip 10.28.128.0 0.0.0.255 any

! Match HTTPS Traffic
ip access-list extended HTTPS-TRAFFIC
permit tcp 10.28.28.0 0.0.0.255 any eq 443
permit tcp 10.28.128.0 0.0.0.255 any eq 443
deny ip 10.28.28.0 0.0.0.255 any
deny ip 10.28.128.0 0.0.0.255 any

! Match FTP Traffic
ip access-list extended FTP-TRAFFIC
permit tcp 10.28.28.0 0.0.0.255 any eq ftp
permit tcp 10.28.28.0 0.0.0.255 any range 11000 11006
permit tcp 10.28.128.0 0.0.0.255 any eq ftp
permit tcp 10.28.128.0 0.0.0.255 any range 11000 11006
deny ip 10.28.28.0 0.0.0.255 any
deny ip 10.28.128.0 0.0.0.255 any

! Where do you want to send the Traffic - WSA IP
ip access-list standard WSA
permit 10.28.20.130

! Create WCCP Lists
ip wccp web-cache redirect-list HTTP-TRAFFIC group-list WSA
ip wccp 60 redirect-list FTP-TRAFFIC group-list WSA
ip wccp 70 redirect-list HTTPS-TRAFFIC group-list WSA

! Configure Redirection of Traffic on Source Interface
interface Vlan28
ip wccp web-cache redirect in
ip wccp 60 redirect in
ip wccp 70 redirect in
interface Vlan128
ip wccp web-cache redirect in
ip wccp 60 redirect in
ip wccp 70 redirect in
```

Example 8-2 shows configuration of WCCP on an ASA firewall. This configuration could also be applied through FlexConfig on the Firepower Management Center (FMC) to provide WCCP on Firepower Threat Defense (FTD) systems.

Example 8-2 *Configuring WCCP on an ASA Firewall*

```
! Define HTTP Traffic
access-list HTTP-TRAFFIC extended permit tcp 10.28.28.0 255.255.255.0 any eq www
access-list HTTP-TRAFFIC extended permit tcp 10.28.128.0 255.255.255.0 any eq www
access-list HTTP-TRAFFIC extended deny ip 10.28.28.0 255.255.255.0 any
access-list HTTP-TRAFFIC extended deny ip 10.28.128.0 255.255.255.0 any

! Define HTTPS Traffic
access-list HTTPS-TRAFFIC extended permit tcp 10.28.28.0 255.255.255.0 any eq https
access-list HTTPS-TRAFFIC extended permit tcp 10.28.128.0 255.255.255.0 any eq https
access-list HTTPS-TRAFFIC extended deny ip 10.28.28.0 255.255.255.0 any
access-list HTTPS-TRAFFIC extended deny ip 10.28.128.0 255.255.255.0 any

! Define FTP Traffic
access-list FTP-TRAFFIC extended permit tcp 10.28.28.0 255.255.255.0 any eq ftp
access-list FTP-TRAFFIC extended permit tcp 10.28.28.0 255.255.255.0 any range 11000
  11006
access-list FTP-TRAFFIC extended permit tcp 10.28.128.0 255.255.255.0 any eq ftp
access-list FTP-TRAFFIC extended permit tcp 10.28.128.0 255.255.255.0 any range
  11000 11006
access-list FTP-TRAFFIC extended deny ip 10.28.28.0 255.255.255.0 any
access-list FTP-TRAFFIC extended deny ip 10.28.128.0 255.255.255.0 any

! Where do you want to send the Traffic - WSA IP
access-list WSA extended permit ip host 10.28.20.130 any

! Create WCCP Lists
wccp web-cache redirect-list HTTP-TRAFFIC group-list WSA
wccp 60 redirect-list FTP-TRAFFIC group-list WSA
wccp 70 redirect-list HTTPS-TRAFFIC group-list WSA

! Configure Redirection of Traffic on Source Interface
wccp interface inside web-cache redirect in
wccp interface inside 60 redirect in
wccp interface inside 70 redirect in
```

Logically, traffic goes through the following steps when using the ASA for redirection (see Figure 8-3):

Step 1. A user initiates a web request.

Step 2. The ASA firewall redirects the request to the WSA.

Step 3. The WSA checks the request and replies directly to the client if the request violates policy or the security engine flags it.

Step 4. The WSA initiates a new connection to the web server.

Step 5. The web server replies with content that is sent to the WSA.

Step 6. The WSA checks for malicious or inappropriate content and blocks it, if needed.

Step 7. If the content is acceptable, the WSA forwards the content to the client. (Note that the content doesn't actually go back to or through the ASA.)

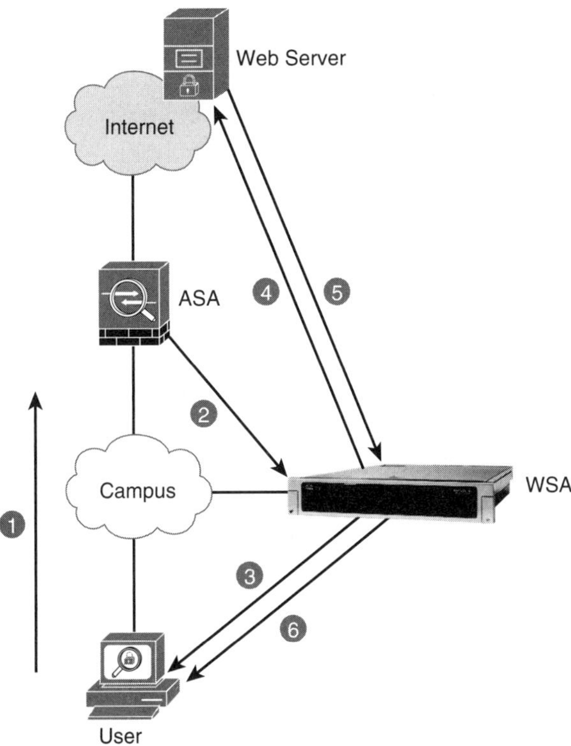

Figure 8-3 *Logical Traffic Flow Using WCCP*

> **Note** If there is HTTP, HTTPS, or FTP traffic destined for internal networks, it is still redirected. To exclude redirection or bypass the proxy for internal traffic, an administrator can add **deny ip** statements for internal subnets to the beginning of the HTTP, HTTPS, and FTP redirect ACLs.

On the WSA, WCCP must be configured to accept redirection. To configure WCCP on the WSA, navigate to Network > Transparent Redirection and click Edit Device. Choose WCCP v2 Router from the drop-down and click Submit. Then click Add Service to add a new WCCP redirection service, as shown in Figure 8-4. WCCP can be customized to use different service IDs for different traffic. Each service ID needs a separate entry on the WSA.

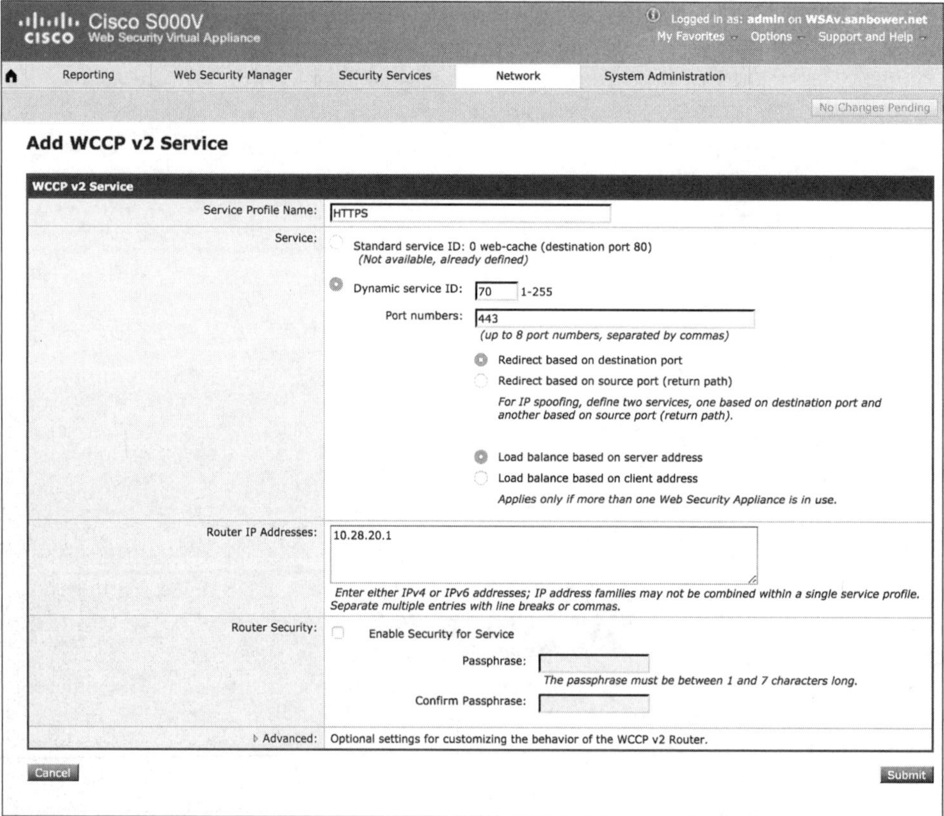

Figure 8-4 *Adding WCCP Service*

Transparent Proxy Traffic Redirection with PBR

It is possible to use PBR to redirect web traffic to the WSA. This is achieved by matching the correct traffic (based on TCP ports) and instructing the router or switch to redirect this traffic to the WSA. PBR can be resource-intensive for a switch or router if performed in software, so be sure to review the appropriate documentation to determine any impact.

When the WSA is configured in transparent mode using a Layer 4 switch (configured under Network > Transparent Redirection), no additional configuration is needed on the WSA. The redirection is controlled by the Layer 4 switch (or router).

Example 8-3 shows a PBR policy that matches traffic from two source subnets (10.28.28.0/24 and 10.28.128.0/24) with traffic being received on one interface (VLAN 28) and sends the traffic to the WSA (10.28.20.130).

Example 8-3 *PBR Policy*

```
! Match HTTP traffic
 access-list 100 permit tcp 10.28.28.0 0.0.0.255 any eq 80
 access-list 100 permit tcp 10.28.128.0 0.0.0.255 any eq 80
 ! Match HTTPS traffic
 access-list 100 permit tcp 10.28.28.0 0.0.0.255 any eq 443
access-list 100 permit tcp 10.28.128.0 0.0.0.255 any eq 443
!
route-map ForwardWeb permit 10
  match ip address 100
  set ip next-hop 10.28.20.130
!
Interface Vlan28
  ip policy route-map ForwardWeb
```

Note If the WSA loses connectivity, the switch or router still forwards traffic to the WSA, based on the PBR statement. Other features, such as IP service-level agreements, could be used to check reachability of the WSA and stop forwarding traffic if the WSA stopped responding to requests.

Web Proxy IP Spoofing

When a web proxy forwards a request, it changes the request source IP address to match its own address by default. This increases security, but administrators can change this behavior by implementing IP spoofing so that requests retain their source address and appear to originate from the source client rather than from the WSA.

IP spoofing works for transparent and explicitly forwarded traffic. When the web proxy is deployed in transparent mode, you have the choice of enabling IP spoofing for transparently redirected connections only or for all connections (transparently redirected and explicitly forwarded). If explicitly forwarded connections use IP spoofing, you should ensure that you have appropriate network devices to route return packets back to the web security appliance.

When IP spoofing is enabled and the appliance is connected to a WCCP router, you must configure two WCCP services: one based on source ports and one based on destination ports.

WSA System Setup

After the system has booted, from the console, the first task typically needed is to assign a static IP address to the management interface to allow for web-based management. The default username on the WSA is **admin**, and the default password is **ironport**. After login, you can use the **interfaceconfig** CLI command to set an IP address, as shown in Figure 8-5.

```
WSAv.sanbower.net> interfaceconfig


Currently configured interfaces:
1. Management (10.28.20.130/24 on Management: WSAv.sanbower.net)

Choose the operation you want to perform:
- NEW - Create a new interface.
- EDIT - Modify an interface.
- DELETE - Remove an interface.
- DETAILS - Show details of an interface.
[]> EDIT

Enter the number of the interface you wish to edit.
[]> 1

Would you like to configure an IPv4 address for this interface (y/n)? [Y]> Y

IPv4 Address (Ex: 192.168.1.2 ):
[10.28.20.130]>

Netmask (Ex: "24", "255.255.255.0" or "0xffffff00"):
[24]>

Would you like to configure an IPv6 address for this interface (y/n)? [N]>

Hostname:
[WSAv.sanbower.net]>

Do you want to enable FTP on this interface? [N]> Y

Which port do you want to use for FTP?
[21]>

Do you want to enable SSH on this interface? [Y]>

Which port do you want to use for SSH?
[22]>

Do you want to enable HTTP on this interface? [Y]>

Which port do you want to use for HTTP?
[8080]>

Do you want to enable HTTPS on this interface? [Y]>

Which port do you want to use for HTTPS?
[8443]>

You have not entered an HTTPS certificate.  To assure privacy, run "certconfig" first.  You may use the demo, but this will not be secure.
Do you really wish to use a demo certificate? [Y]>
```

Figure 8-5 *WSA CLI Interface Configuration*

Once an IP address has been set, you can use **setgateway** to assign an IPv4 and/or IPv6 default gateway or router. With all the content security appliances, **commit** should be used to save the changes made.

After getting IP connectivity established, the fastest and recommended way to create a base configuration for the WSA is to browse to the web management interface at https://<wsaip or hostname>:8443/ and run the System Setup Wizard found under System Administration > System Setup Wizard.

Note After you configure settings in the wizard, you can later change them by going to individual components' configuration pages in the web GUI.

The wizard allows you to select the mode for WSA operation, as illustrated in Figure 8-6. Standard mode uses onsite web proxy services and Layer 4 traffic monitoring. In Cloud Web Security connector mode, the appliance connects to and routes traffic to a Cisco Cloud Web Security proxy, where web security policies are enforced. Finally, hybrid mode is a combination of standard and Cloud Web Security connector modes.

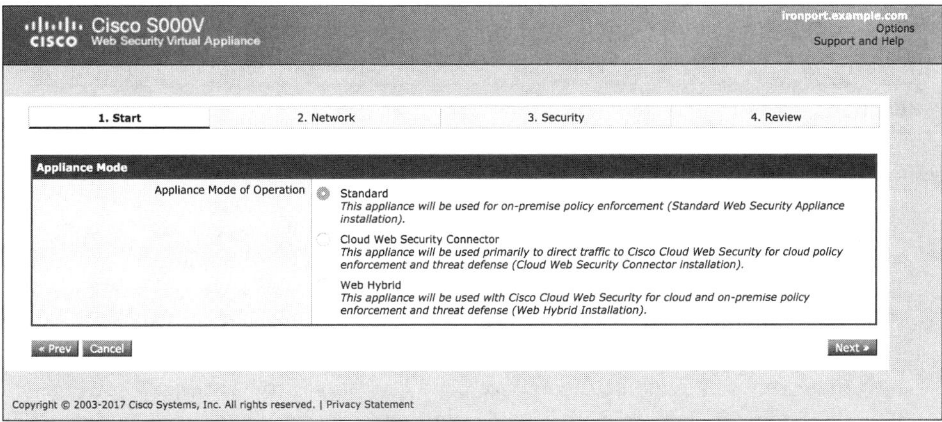

Figure 8-6 *WSA Appliance Mode of Operation*

Note Cisco Cloud Web Security subscriptions were announced to be end-of-sale in early 2018. For this reason, Cloud Web Security options are not reviewed in detail and should be used only for legacy deployments.

Figure 8-7 shows configuration of system settings, including the hostname, DNS servers, NTP, and time zone settings. Because the proxy is used to connect directly to Internet services through DNS hostnames, DNS is critical in establishing a working configuration. If internal HTTP, HTTPS, and other protocol requests go through the proxy, it is important to point to an internal DNS server that can resolve internal names (for example, intranet.securitydemo.local). If an organization prefers to use Internet DNS servers or Internet root DNS servers for Internet resolution, alternate DNS overrides can be configured for local domains under Network > DNS.

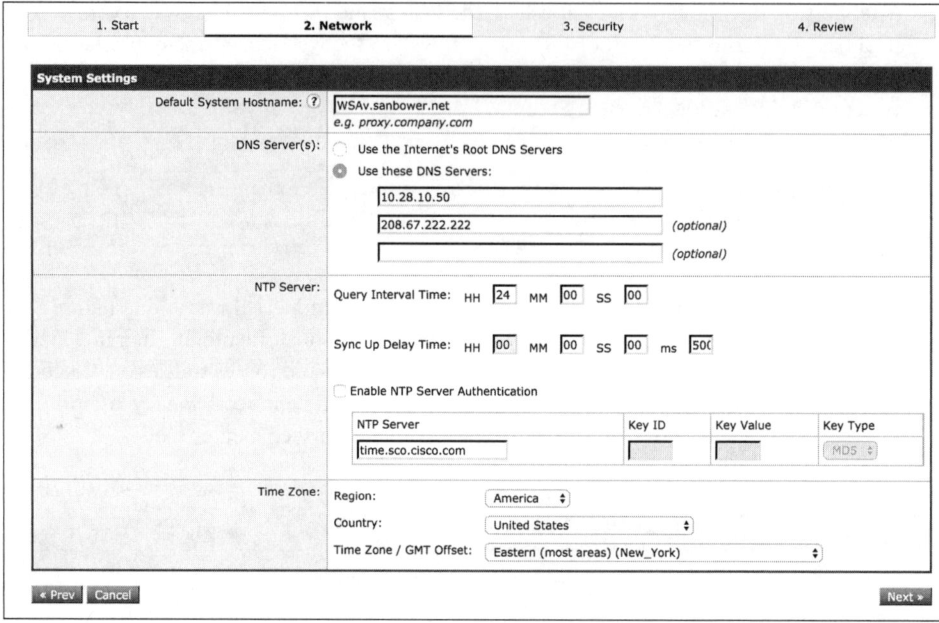

Figure 8-7 *WSA System Settings*

Some organizations have multiple proxy servers and would like to use them for both web content filtering and security. For such cases, the WSA has the ability to forward all Internet requests to another proxy. If deploying with multiple proxies, it is recommended that the WSA be deployed closest to client machines for logging and reporting purposes. Figure 8-8 illustrates the configuration options allowed for upstream proxies. Additional upstream proxy configuration can be accomplished by going to Network > Upstream Proxy. After proxy groups are configured, routing policies must be used to configure which traffic will be sent to the upstream proxy and which traffic can go directly.

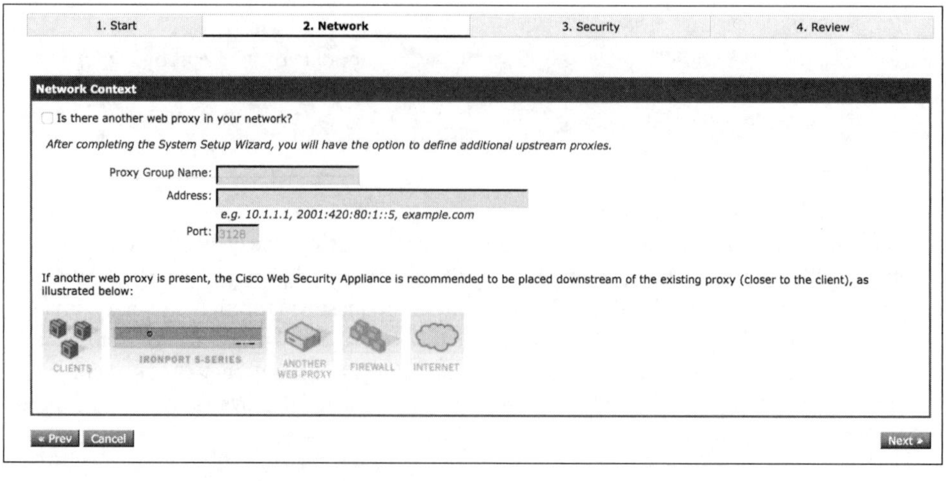

Figure 8-8 *WSA Network Context*

Next, interface configuration is required. While many organizations opt for a one-armed deployment using the M1 interface, some need to separate management and proxy traffic on different interfaces. A combination of M1/P1/P2 can be used to accomplish the requirements of the target network environment. Figure 8-9 shows basic configuration of the interfaces. If M1 is going to be used for management, only the check box can be selected to enable this option. IPv4 as well as IPv6 can be used on the WSA. Also, note that separate hostnames can be used for each interface, which allows administrators to help redirect users of the proxy to the appropriate interface.

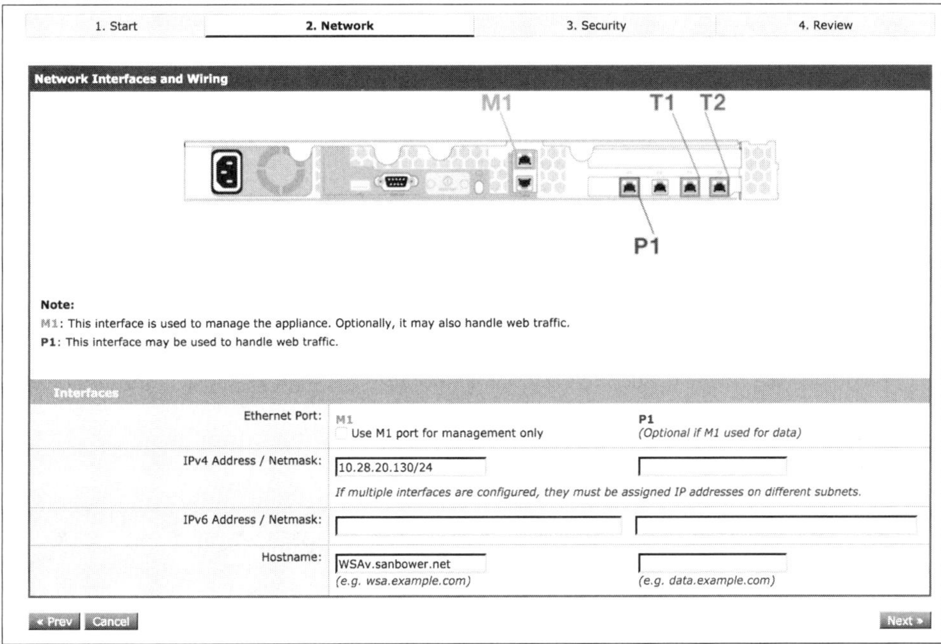

Figure 8-9 *WSA Network Interfaces and Wiring*

The WSA has integrated Layer 4 Traffic Monitor (L4TM) service that detects rogue traffic across all network ports and stops malware attempts to bypass port 80. When internal clients are infected with malware and attempt to phone home across nonstandard ports and protocols, L4TM prevents phone-home activity from going outside the corporate network. By default, L4TM is enabled and set to monitor traffic on all ports, including DNS and other services. L4TM uses and maintains its own internal database. To monitor Layer 4 traffic, connect the appliance to a test access port (TAP), switch, or hub after the proxy ports and before any device that performs Network Address Translation (NAT) on client IP addresses.

Even though traffic is only mirrored (copied) from the original sessions to the appliance, the WSA can still block suspicious traffic by either resetting a TCP session or sending ICMP "host unreachable" messages for UDP sessions.

WSA allows for the T1 port to be used for duplex (in/out) or for a combination of T1/T2 to be used for simplex (in on T1, out on T2), as shown in Figure 8-10.

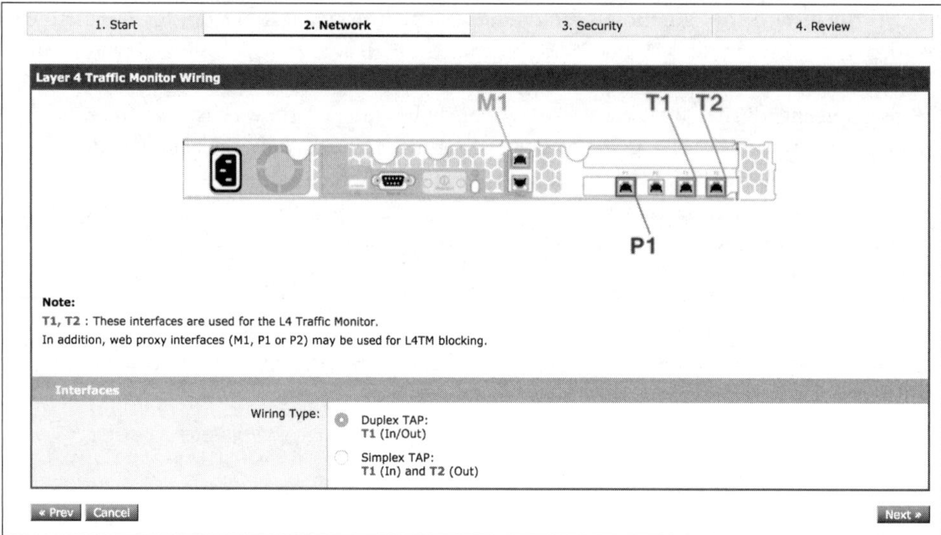

Figure 8-10 *WSA L4TM Wiring*

When using multiple interfaces on the WSA, the WSA uses static routes to determine which interface traffic should be routed in and out of. Figure 8-11 shows configuration of additional routes on the M1 interface, if required.

1. Start | 2. Network | 3. Security | 4. Review

IPv4 Routes for Management and Data Traffic (Interface M1: 10.28.20.130)

Default Gateway: 10.28.20.1

This will be the default route for external traffic as well as internal traffic with no static route below.

Static Routes Table

Optionally, add static routes for Management access to the Cisco Web Security Appliance as well as Data traffic. Depending on the appliance functions you enable, these routes will be used for monitoring by the Secure Web Proxy and optional blocking by the L4 Traffic Monitor.

Name	Internal Network	Internal Gateway
Identifying name for route	IPv4 Address (such as 10.1.1.10) or CIDR (such as 10.1.1.0/24)	IPv4 Address

Add Route

« Prev Cancel Next »

Figure 8-11 *WSA IPv4 Routes*

When deploying using transparent mode, the WSA requires an administrator to choose a redirection method, as shown in Figure 8-12. Two options are provided: Layer 4 Switch or No Device and WCCP v2 Router. You can still use WSA as an explicit proxy when using WCCP. If using WCCP, select WCCP v2 Router and enable the standard service, entering a password if needed. You need to configure your WCCP device with these same settings, as described earlier in this chapter. If you will be forwarding additional ports or doing SSL decryption with WCCP, you need to configure advanced options for WCCP after the setup wizard under Network > Transparent Redirection.

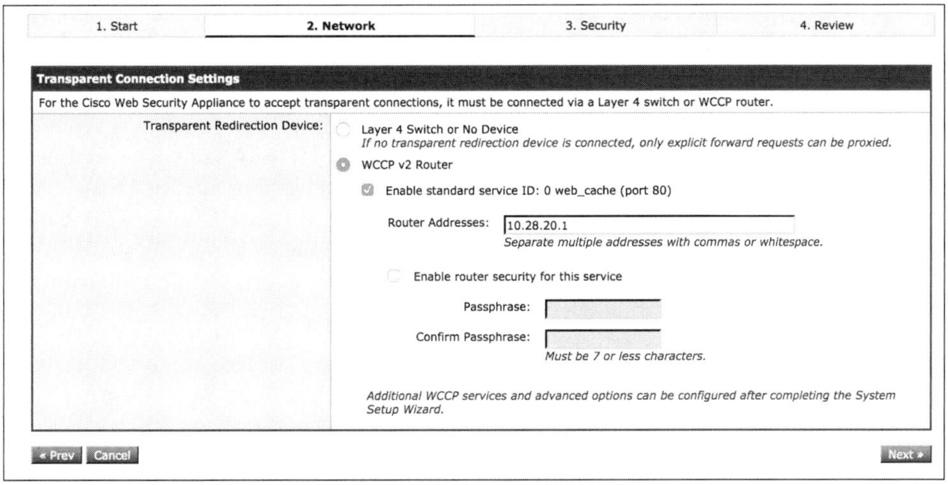

1. Start | 2. Network | 3. Security | 4. Review

Transparent Connection Settings

For the Cisco Web Security Appliance to accept transparent connections, it must be connected via a Layer 4 switch or WCCP router.

Transparent Redirection Device:

Layer 4 Switch or No Device
If no transparent redirection device is connected, only explicit forward requests can be proxied.

WCCP v2 Router

Enable standard service ID: 0 web_cache (port 80)

Router Addresses: 10.28.20.1
Separate multiple addresses with commas or whitespace.

Enable router security for this service

Passphrase:

Confirm Passphrase:
Must be 7 or less characters.

Additional WCCP services and advanced options can be configured after completing the System Setup Wizard.

« Prev | Cancel | Next »

Figure 8-12 *WSA Transparent Connection Settings*

The WSA requires the administrator to change the default password of the admin account. Administrative settings (see Figure 8-13) also give the option to set up a Simple Mail Transfer Protocol (SMTP) server and email address for notifications. The SensorBase Network Participation section allows you to share summary or full URL information with Cisco for threat intelligence use. The information organizations share helps Cisco Talos stay ahead of new threats that might appear on the Internet and create updated detection and classification content for all organizations running Cisco security products.

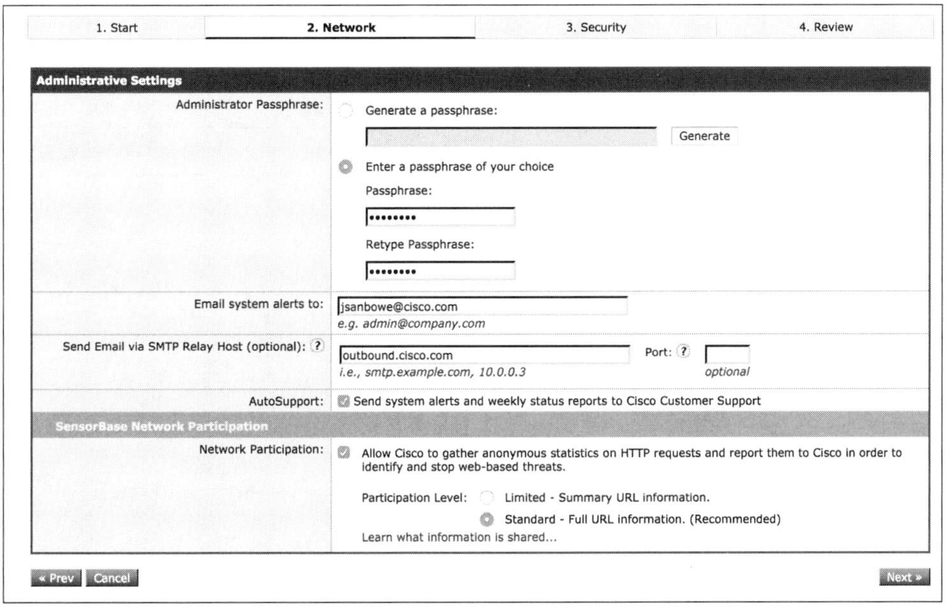

1. Start | 2. Network | 3. Security | 4. Review

Administrative Settings

Administrator Passphrase:

Generate a passphrase:

Generate

Enter a passphrase of your choice

Passphrase: ••••••••

Retype Passphrase: ••••••••

Email system alerts to: jsanbowe@cisco.com
e.g. admin@company.com

Send Email via SMTP Relay Host (optional): ? outbound.cisco.com
i.e., smtp.example.com, 10.0.0.3
Port: ? *optional*

AutoSupport: Send system alerts and weekly status reports to Cisco Customer Support

SensorBase Network Participation

Network Participation: Allow Cisco to gather anonymous statistics on HTTP requests and report them to Cisco in order to identify and stop web-based threats.

Participation Level: Limited - Summary URL information.
Standard - Full URL information. (Recommended)

Learn what information is shared...

« Prev | Cancel | Next »

Figure 8-13 *WSA Administrative Settings*

The WSA uses a global access policy that acts as a catch-all for connections that do not match other access policies. Administrators can configure the global access policy to either monitor or block all traffic. Typically, it is recommended that you monitor until an organization has deemed that all permitted traffic is matching other access policies first.

Figure 8-14 shows the security settings that determine which features the organization would like to enable globally and whether a feature should block or monitor by default. By default, Acceptable Use Controls, Reputation Filtering, Advanced Malware Protection, Malware and Spyware Scanning with Webroot and Sophos, and Cisco Data Security Filtering are all enabled. The Wizard allows you to selectively turn off any scanning not required by your organization.

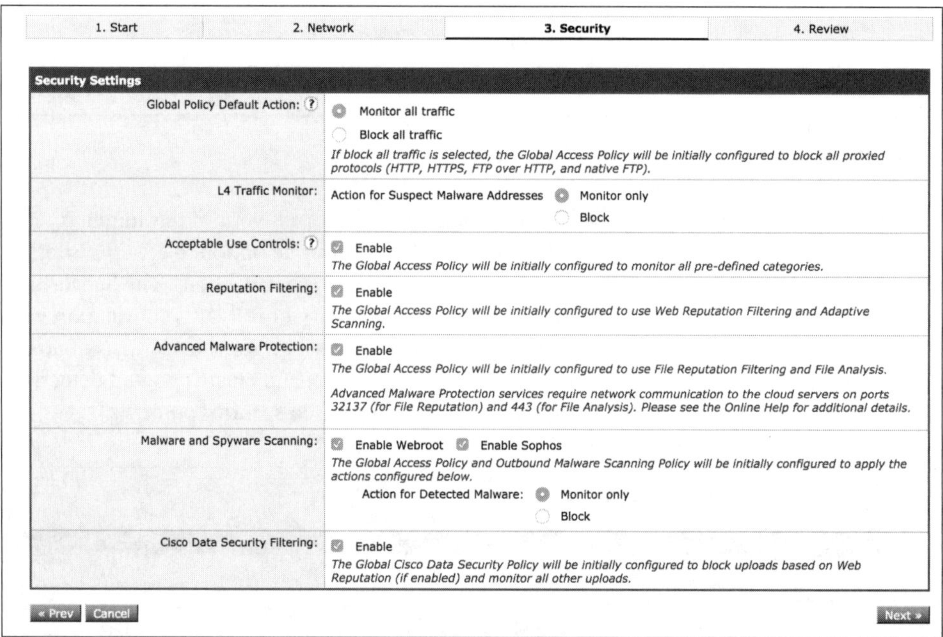

Figure 8-14 *WSA Security Settings*

After the wizard has prompted for all required configuration, it presents a review of the configuration selections made and allows an administrator to either install the configuration, go back and make changes, or cancel completely (see Figure 8-15).

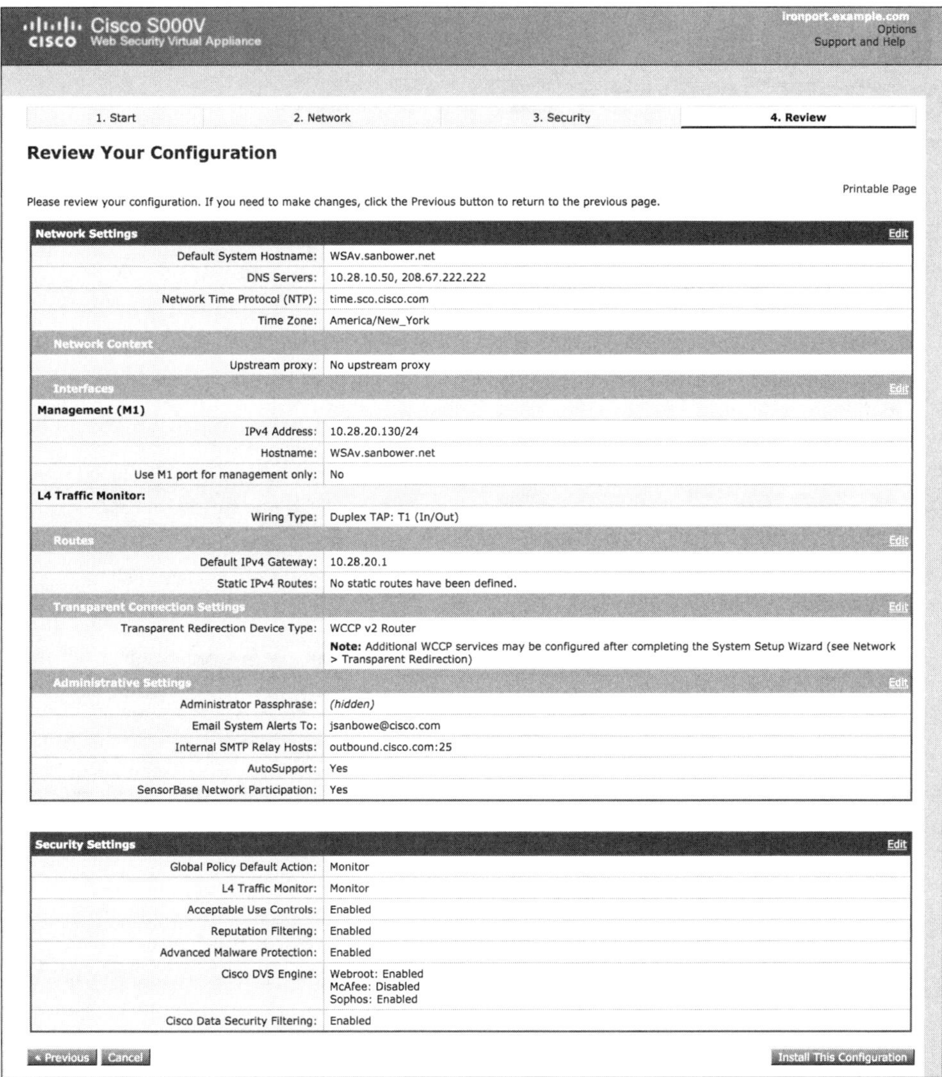

Figure 8-15 *WSA System Configuration Changes Review*

Committing changes after configuration is a required step for all of the configuration to take effect and ensure that the configuration is retained after reboots. The Commit Changes button at the top right is highlighted yellow (see Figure 8-16) when uncommitted changes are in memory. It is very important to remember to commit your changes.

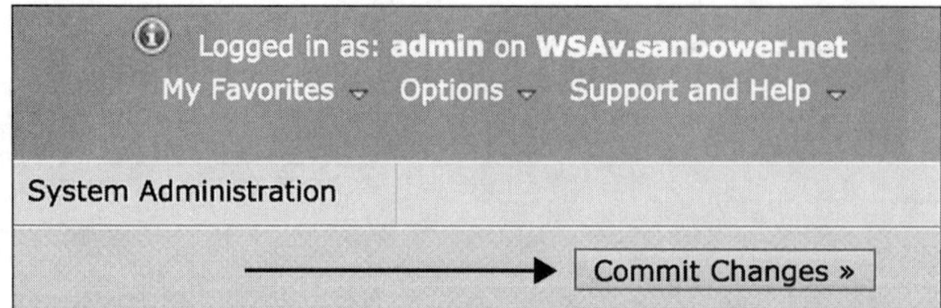

Figure 8-16 *WSA Commit Changes Notification*

For all configuration changes, an administrator must confirm the changes by using the Commit Changes button shown in Figure 8-17. Any changes may be reviewed and/or abandoned as well.

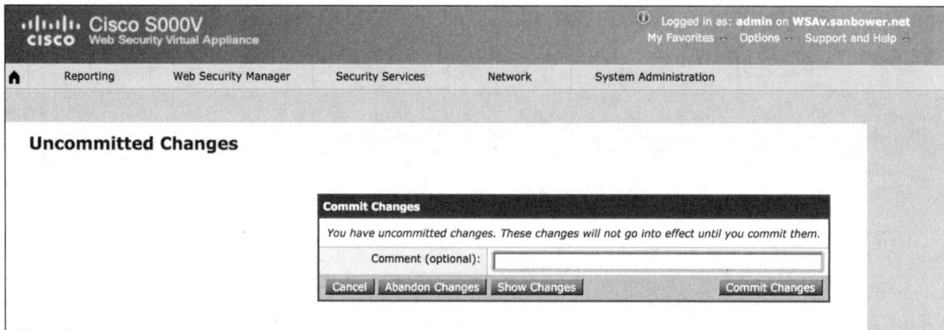

Figure 8-17 *WSA Uncommitted Changes*

WSA Policy Configuration

Policies are the means by which the WSA identifies and controls web requests. When a client sends a web request to a server, the web proxy receives the request, evaluates it, and determines to which policy it belongs. Actions defined in the policy are then applied to the request. The WSA policies are evaluated from the top down, like a firewall ACL. It is recommended that you attempt to place the most accessed or used policies at the top to exit the policy layer more quickly. This increases performance and puts less stress on the appliances.

When a user creates a web request, the configured WSA intercepts the request and manages the process by which the request travels to get to its final outcome—be that accessing a particular website, accessing an email, or even accessing an online application. In configuring the WSA, policies are created to define the criteria and actions of requests made by users.

Identification Policies

Identification policies are about trying to authenticate devices if an organization would like to identify the users behind web proxy requests. This allows for policy and reporting of users and groups rather than just based on the IP address of the machine or device. The WSA integrates directly with Lightweight Directory Access Protocol (LDAP) or Active Directory (AD). LDAP supports only basic authentication, while AD supports NTLM, Kerberos, and basic authentication.

Traditionally, users are identified by entering a username and passphrase. These credentials are validated against an authentication server, and then the web proxy applies the appropriate policies to the transaction, based on the authenticated username. However, the WSA can be configured to authenticate users transparently—that is, without prompting the end user for credentials. Transparent identification involves authenticating the user by means of credentials obtained from another trusted source, with the assumption that the user has already been authenticated by that trusted source, and then applies the appropriate policies.

Transparent authentication creates a single sign-on environment so users are not aware of the presence of a proxy on the network. It also allows administrators to apply authentication-based policies to transactions coming from client applications or devices that are incapable of displaying an authentication prompt to the device (for example, an IP phone). If transparent authentication fails, you can configure how to handle the transaction: You can grant the user guest access, or you can force an authentication prompt to appear to the user.

To configure authentication, browse to Network > Authentication and click Add Realm (see Figure 8-18) to create a new authentication realm. Then choose LDAP or AD.

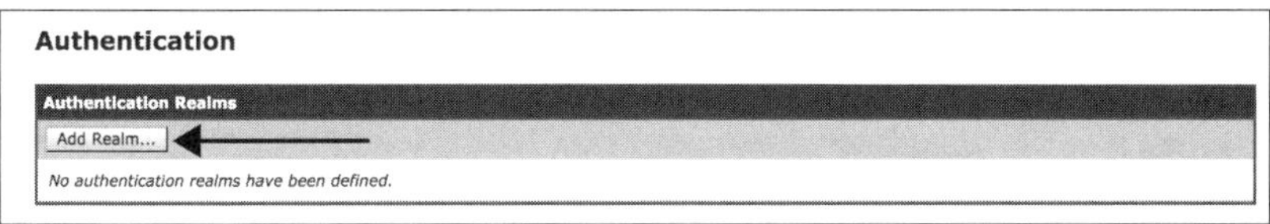

Figure 8-18 *WSA Add Realm*

If you choose Active Directory, the WSA allows administrators to input up to three AD servers and requires the domain name. Finally, click Join Domain, and the WSA asks for AD credentials. These credentials only need to be able to add computer objects to the domain. If successful, the WSA provides the message “Success — Computer Account <WSAHOSTNAME>$ successfully created.”

> **Note** DNS resolution of the domain, AD servers, and WSA hostname must be working for authentication to work correctly and for the WSA to join AD.

Once the computer object has been created, you can scroll down and click Start Test (see Figure 8-19) to test the communication with the AD server, compare time services, test communication with the authentication service, and test DNS records. If any items fail, you should repair and retest.

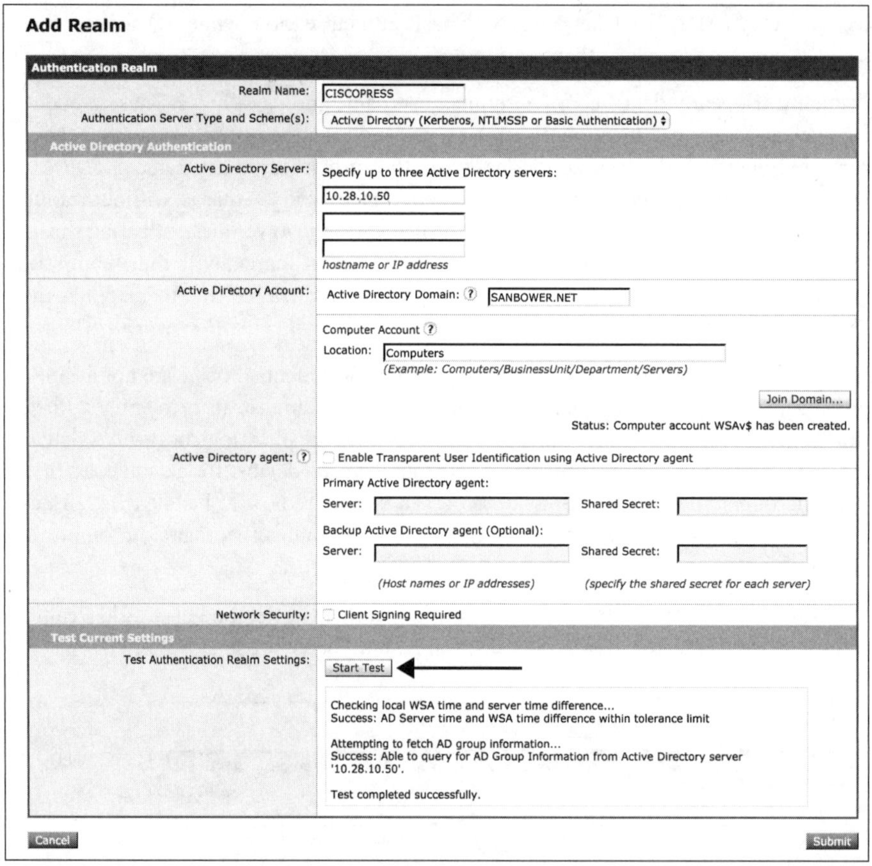

Figure 8-19 *WSA Add Realm*

To add transparent authentication, select the check box Enable Transparent User Identification Using Active Directory Agent, along with the server and shared secret for the Active Directory agents, such as Cisco's Context Directory Agent (CDA). CDA is necessary to query the Active Directory security event logs for information about authenticated users. The WSA communicates with the Active Directory agent to maintain a local copy of the IP address-to-username mappings. When the WSA needs to associate an IP address with a username, it first checks its local copy of the mappings. If no match is found, it queries an Active Directory agent to find a match.

The global authentication settings apply to all authentication realms, independent of their authentication protocols. The web proxy deployment mode affects which global authentication settings you can configure. More settings are available when the WSA is deployed in transparent mode than in explicit forward mode.

To configure global authentication settings, browse to Network > Authentication and click Edit Global Authentication Settings. You can then address key configuration items, such as the action that occurs if an authentication service is unavailable. Administrators can either permit traffic to proceed without authentication or block all traffic if user authentication fails. Figure 8-20 shows all the available global settings when the WSA is configured in transparent mode.

Edit Global Authentication Settings

Global Authentication Settings	
Action if Authentication Service Unavailable:	Permit traffic to proceed without authentication Block all traffic if authentication fails
Failed Authentication Handling:	Log Guest User by: IP Address User Name as Entered by End-User *User name as entered is available for NTLMSSP and Basic schemes. For Kerberos, IP address will always be logged for guest users, regardless of this setting.*
Re-authentication:	Enable Re-Authentication Prompt If End User Blocked by URL Category or User Session Restriction *If using Kerberos, to ensure that re-authentication can be performed, select an authentication surrogate for explicit forward requests in the applicable Identity policies*
Basic Authentication Token TTL:	3600 seconds
Authentication Settings	
Credential Encryption:	Use encrypted HTTPS connection for authentication
HTTPS Redirect Port:	443
Redirect Hostname:	*To achieve true single sign-on for Internet Explorer, use the short hostname or NetBIOS name instead of the fully qualified domain name.* WSAv.sanbower.net
Credential Cache Options:	Surrogate Timeout: 3600 seconds Client IP Idle Timeout: 3600 seconds *If this value is greater than the Surrogate Timeout value, this setting has no effect.* Cache Size: 8192 number of entries
User Session Restrictions:	Prohibit an authenticated user from accessing the Internet from a different IP address Restriction Timeout: 300 seconds *This value must be greater than the Credential Cache Surrogate Timeout.*
Advanced	*Upload SSL certificate for Credential Encryption*

Cancel Submit

Figure 8-20 *WSA Global Authentication Settings*

Re-authentication, configured under global authentication settings, allows for a user to authenticate again after being blocked from a website due to a restrictive URL filtering policy or due to being restricted from logging in to another IP address. If it is enabled, the end user sees a block page that includes a link that allows for entering new authentication credentials. If the user enters credentials that allow greater access, the requested page appears in the browser.

The Basic Authentication Token TTL setting controls the length of time that user credentials are stored in the cache before being revalidated with the authentication server. This includes the username, the passphrase, and the directory groups associated with the user.

After authentication and settings are configured, you can select which users will be forced to authenticate. This is handled by creating identities. To create an identity, select Web Security Manager > Identification Profiles, add a new identification policy, and give it a name. Under Identification and Authentication, select Authenticate Users. You can also select No Authentication if you specifically want to exempt users from authentication.

Finally, select the authentication realm that you already created and then select the scheme that you will use to authenticate, as shown in Figure 8-21.

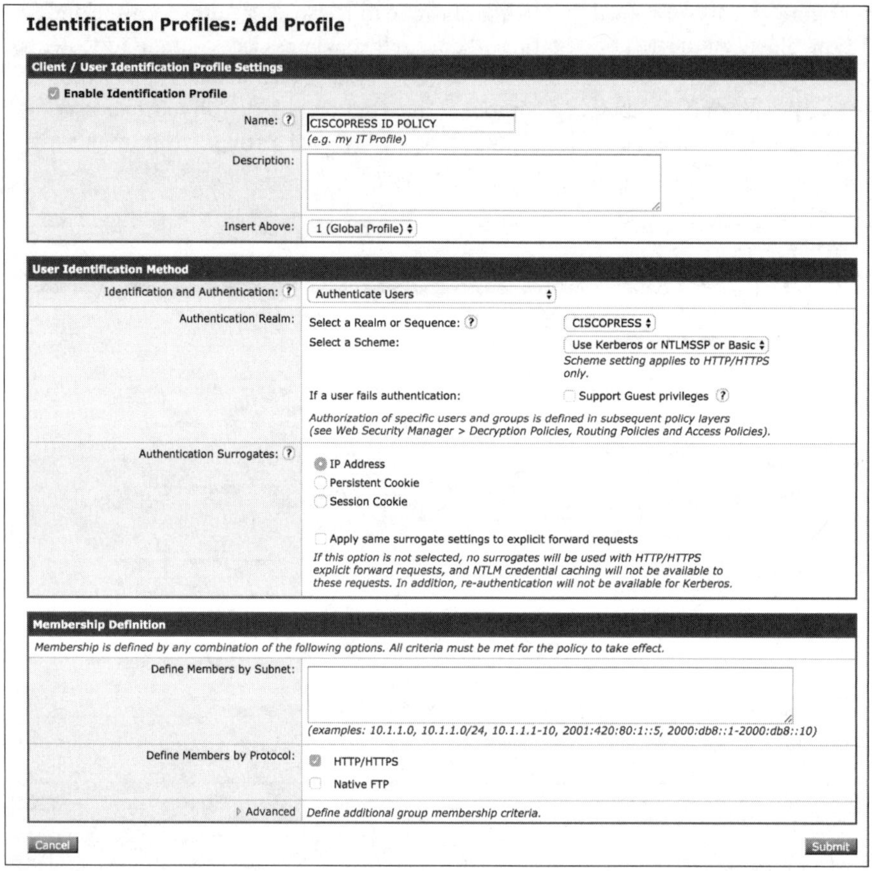

Figure 8-21 *WSA Identification Profile*

The WSA gives different options for schemes based on whether an AD or LDAP realm is chosen. For AD, the following are the available schemes:

- **Basic authentication:** This option is most compatible with all clients and devices. A browser window pops up, asking for credentials. Basic authentication is not transparent. Typically, basic authentication is in the clear; however, the WSA can encrypt credentials if necessary.
- **NTLMSSP:** This scheme is transparent authentication to the end user. NTLMSSP needs to be supported by the browser. It uses domain credentials for login and is typically used in Windows AD environments but will also work with MAC, with additional configuration on the client side.
- **Kerberos:** Primarily used with Windows clients, Kerberos is considered a more secure option.

As shown in Figure 8-21, the WSA allows for a combination of the different schemes for a wide range of client support.

The Authentication Surrogates options allow you to specify the way transactions will be associated with a user after the user has authenticated successfully. The WSA provides the following options:

- **IP Address:** The privileged user identity is used until the surrogate times out.
- **Persistent Cookie:** The privileged user identity is used until the surrogate times out.
- **Session Cookie:** The privileged user identity is used until the browser is closed or the session times out.

Identification policies also have a Define Members by Subnet option that you can use to ensure that the authentication policy is only applied to networks required to authenticate.

Advanced options allow matching of user agents for bypassing of authentication based on application (such as Windows Update).

The ID Policy Granularity option allows you to assign different policies to devices based on the matching criteria discussed earlier. For example, if all of your organization's guest devices are on a certain subnet, you could create an identity by subnet and apply URL filtering security and content control for all the guests.

Figure 8-22 illustrates multiple identification profiles and options.

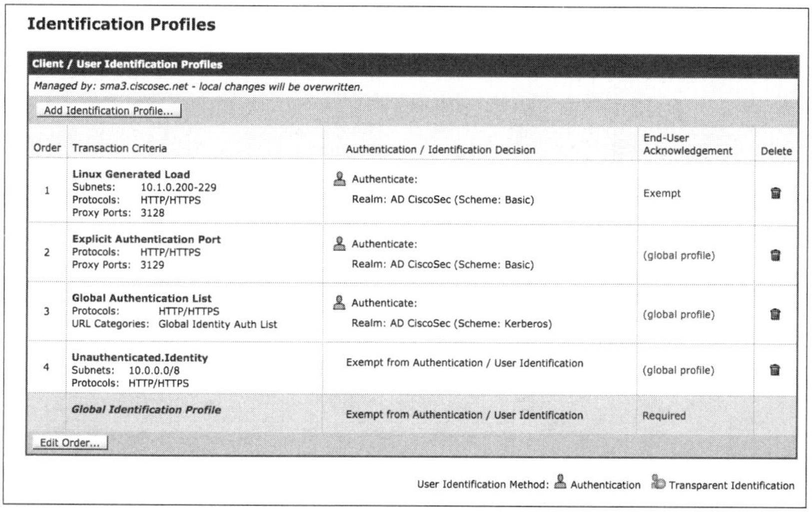

Identification Profiles

Client / User Identification Profiles

Managed by: sma3.ciscosec.net - local changes will be overwritten.

Add Identification Profile...

Order	Transaction Criteria	Authentication / Identification Decision	End-User Acknowledgement	Delete
1	**Linux Generated Load** Subnets: 10.1.0.200-229 Protocols: HTTP/HTTPS Proxy Ports: 3128	Authenticate: Realm: AD CiscoSec (Scheme: Basic)	Exempt	
2	**Explicit Authentication Port** Protocols: HTTP/HTTPS Proxy Ports: 3129	Authenticate: Realm: AD CiscoSec (Scheme: Basic)	(global profile)	
3	**Global Authentication List** Protocols: HTTP/HTTPS URL Categories: Global Identity Auth List	Authenticate: Realm: AD CiscoSec (Scheme: Kerberos)	(global profile)	
4	**Unauthenticated.Identity** Subnets: 10.0.0.0/8 Protocols: HTTP/HTTPS	Exempt from Authentication / User Identification	(global profile)	
	Global Identification Profile	Exempt from Authentication / User Identification	Required	

Edit Order...

User Identification Method: Authentication Transparent Identification

Figure 8-22 *WSA Multiple Identification Profiles*

Note Additional detailed information regarding configuration of the integration of the WSA with Cisco Identities Services Engine using pxGrid for transparent authentication can be found in *Integrated Security Technologies and Solutions, Volume II.*

Access Policies

Access policies map the identification profiles and users along with other characteristics, such as time-based restrictions, to ensure that the appropriate controls meet an organization's policies.

To add a new policy, go to Web Security Manager > Access Policies > Add Policy. The policy requires a unique name and mapping to identification profile settings and possibly advanced settings. Figure 8-23 shows the creation of a new policy.

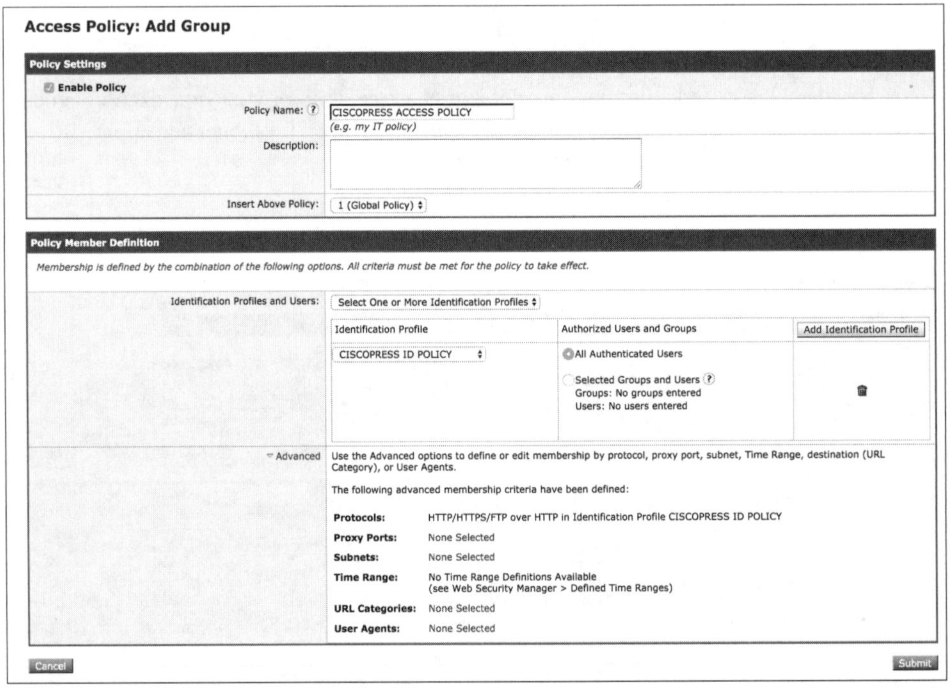

Access Policy: Add Group
Policy Settings
Enable Policy
Policy Name: CISCOPRESS ACCESS POLICY (e.g. my IT policy)
Description:
Insert Above Policy: 1 (Global Policy)
Policy Member Definition
Membership is defined by the combination of the following options. All criteria must be met for the policy to take effect.
Identification Profiles and Users: Select One or More Identification Profiles
Identification Profile | Authorized Users and Groups | Add Identification Profile
CISCOPRESS ID POLICY | All Authenticated Users
Selected Groups and Users
Groups: No groups entered
Users: No users entered
Advanced: Use the Advanced options to define or edit membership by protocol, proxy port, subnet, Time Range, destination (URL Category), or User Agents.
The following advanced membership criteria have been defined:
Protocols: HTTP/HTTPS/FTP over HTTP in Identification Profile CISCOPRESS ID POLICY
Proxy Ports: None Selected
Subnets: None Selected
Time Range: No Time Range Definitions Available (see Web Security Manager > Defined Time Ranges)
URL Categories: None Selected
User Agents: None Selected
Cancel
Submit

Figure 8-23 *WSA Access Policy*

After submitting the new policy, additional customization can be done to adjust how the access policy behaves compared to the global policy settings.

Protocols and user agents can be used to control policy access to protocols and configure blocking for particular client applications, such as instant messaging clients or web browsers. The WSA can also be configured to tunnel HTTP **CONNECT** requests on specific ports.

Each policy allows for customized URL filtering, which tells the WSA how to handle a transaction based on the URL category of a particular HTTP or HTTPS request. Using a predefined category list, organizations can choose to block, monitor, warn, or set quota-based or time-based filters. To configure URL filtering (see Figure 8-24), click the URL Filtering cell in the access policies table. You can then selectively block or allow URL categories based on policy.

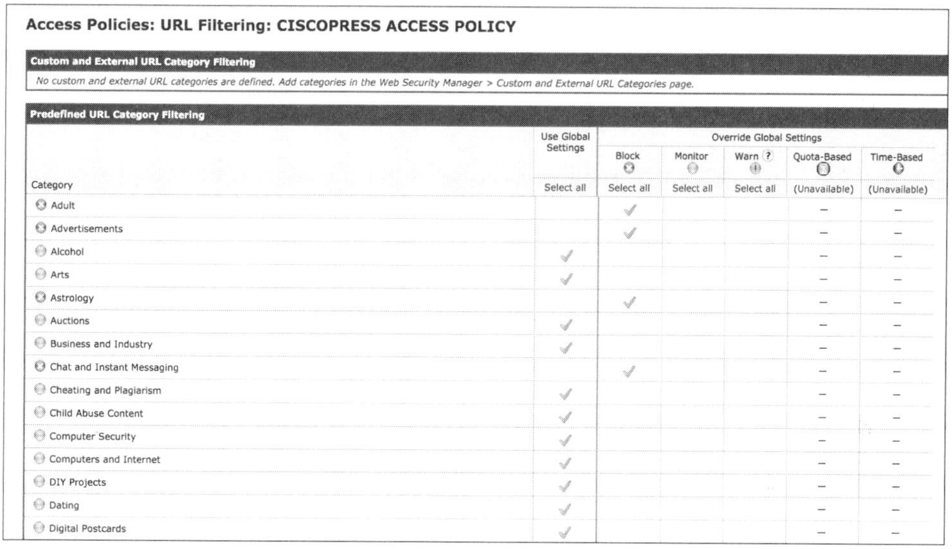

Access Policies: URL Filtering: CISCOPRESS ACCESS POLICY

Custom and External URL Category Filtering

No custom and external URL categories are defined. Add categories in the Web Security Manager > Custom and External URL Categories page.

Predefined URL Category Filtering

	Use Global Settings	Override Global Settings				
		Block	Monitor	Warn ?	Quota-Based	Time-Based
Category	Select all	Select all	Select all	Select all	(Unavailable)	(Unavailable)
Adult		✓			–	–
Advertisements		✓			–	–
Alcohol	✓				–	–
Arts	✓				–	–
Astrology		✓			–	–
Auctions	✓				–	–
Business and Industry	✓				–	–
Chat and Instant Messaging		✓			–	–
Cheating and Plagiarism	✓				–	–
Child Abuse Content	✓				–	–
Computer Security	✓				–	–
Computers and Internet	✓				–	–
DIY Projects	✓				–	–
Dating	✓				–	–
Digital Postcards	✓				–	–

Figure 8-24 *WSA URL Filtering*

While configuring URL filtering, you can also create custom URL categories and then choose to block, redirect, allow, monitor, warn, or apply quota-based or time-based filters for websites in the custom categories.

The AVC engine is an acceptable-use policy component that inspects web traffic to gain deeper understanding and control of web traffic used for applications. The WSA allows the web proxy to be configured to block or allow applications by application type and by individual applications. You can also apply controls to particular application behaviors, such as file transfers, within a particular application. To configure AVC for a policy, click the Applications cell in the access policies table, as shown in Figure 8-25. Make sure to select Define Applications Custom Settings from the drop-down at the top of the screen in order to customize the settings for the access policy in question. In this example, Blogger is allowed, but posting to Blogger is blocked.

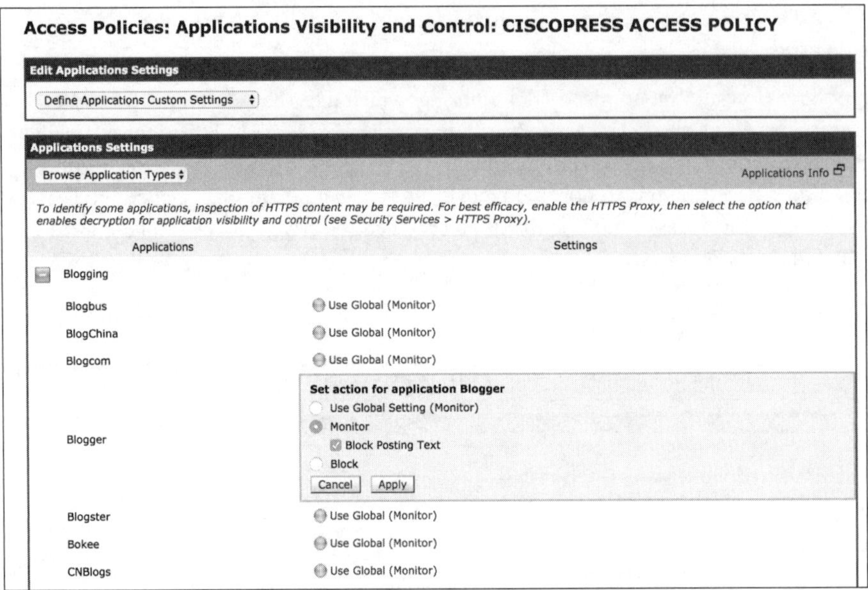

Figure 8-25 *WSA Application Visibility and Control Policy*

By configuring objects in access policies, administrators can configure the web proxy to block file downloads based on file characteristics, such as file size, file type, and MIME type. An object is generally any item that can be individually selected, uploaded, downloaded, or manipulated.

Access policies also allow for configuration of antimalware and reputation. Web Reputation filters allow for a web-based reputation score to be assigned to a URL to determine the probability that it contains URL-based malware. Antimalware scanning identifies and stops web-based malware threats. Advanced Malware Protection identifies malware in downloaded files. To modify the antimalware and reputation globally or for an individual policy, click the cell in the policies table in question and modify it as shown in Figure 8-26.

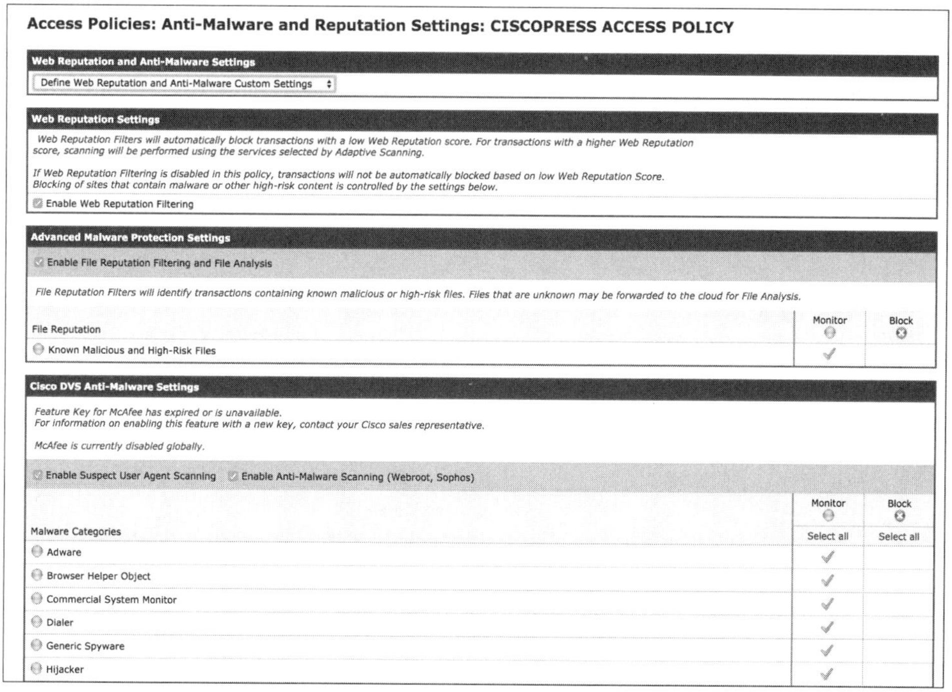

Access Policies: Anti-Malware and Reputation Settings: CISCOPRESS ACCESS POLICY

Web Reputation and Anti-Malware Settings

Define Web Reputation and Anti-Malware Custom Settings

Web Reputation Settings

Web Reputation Filters will automatically block transactions with a low Web Reputation score. For transactions with a higher Web Reputation score, scanning will be performed using the services selected by Adaptive Scanning.

If Web Reputation Filtering is disabled in this policy, transactions will not be automatically blocked based on low Web Reputation Score. Blocking of sites that contain malware or other high-risk content is controlled by the settings below.

Enable Web Reputation Filtering

Advanced Malware Protection Settings

Enable File Reputation Filtering and File Analysis

File Reputation Filters will identify transactions containing known malicious or high-risk files. Files that are unknown may be forwarded to the cloud for File Analysis.

File Reputation	Monitor	Block
Known Malicious and High-Risk Files	✓	

Cisco DVS Anti-Malware Settings

Feature Key for McAfee has expired or is unavailable.
For information on enabling this feature with a new key, contact your Cisco sales representative.

McAfee is currently disabled globally.

Enable Suspect User Agent Scanning   Enable Anti-Malware Scanning (Webroot, Sophos)

Malware Categories	Monitor Select all	Block Select all
Adware	✓	
Browser Helper Object	✓	
Commercial System Monitor	✓	
Dialer	✓	
Generic Spyware	✓	
Hijacker	✓	

Figure 8-26 *WSA Antimalware and Reputation Policy*

As more access policies are added, an organization can see URL, AVC, and antimalware policies on a single policy page, as illustrated in Figure 8-27, to prove compliance or represent an organization's web content filtering and security policies.

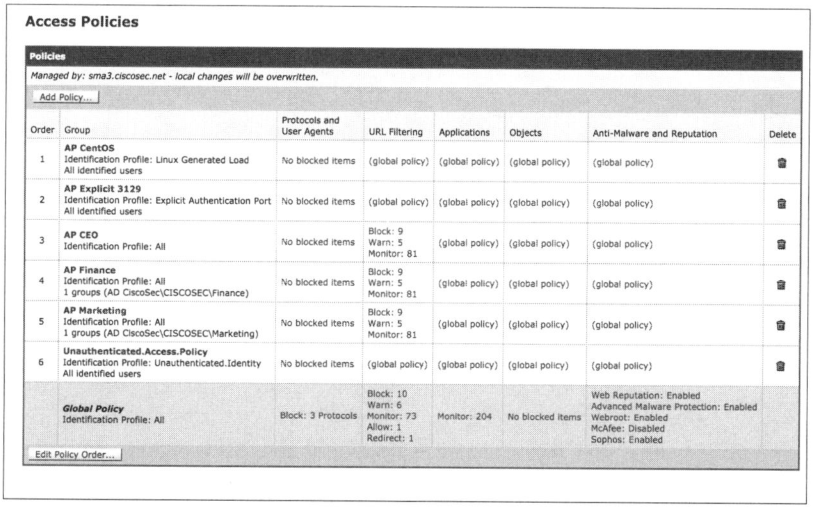

Access Policies

Policies

Managed by: sma3.ciscosec.net - local changes will be overwritten.

Add Policy...

Order	Group	Protocols and User Agents	URL Filtering	Applications	Objects	Anti-Malware and Reputation	Delete
1	**AP CentOS** Identification Profile: Linux Generated Load All identified users	No blocked items	(global policy)	(global policy)	(global policy)	(global policy)	🗑
2	**AP Explicit 3129** Identification Profile: Explicit Authentication Port All identified users	No blocked items	(global policy)	(global policy)	(global policy)	(global policy)	🗑
3	**AP CEO** Identification Profile: All	No blocked items	Block: 9 Warn: 5 Monitor: 81	(global policy)	(global policy)	(global policy)	🗑
4	**AP Finance** Identification Profile: All 1 groups (AD CiscoSec\CISCOSEC\Finance)	No blocked items	Block: 9 Warn: 5 Monitor: 81	(global policy)	(global policy)	(global policy)	🗑
5	**AP Marketing** Identification Profile: All 1 groups (AD CiscoSec\CISCOSEC\Marketing)	No blocked items	Block: 9 Warn: 5 Monitor: 81	(global policy)	(global policy)	(global policy)	🗑
6	**Unauthenticated.Access.Policy** Identification Profile: Unauthenticated.Identity All identified users	No blocked items	(global policy)	(global policy)	(global policy)	(global policy)	🗑
	Global Policy Identification Profile: All	Block: 3 Protocols	Block: 10 Warn: 6 Monitor: 73 Allow: 1 Redirect: 1	Monitor: 204	No blocked items	Web Reputation: Enabled Advanced Malware Protection: Enabled Webroot: Enabled McAfee: Disabled Sophos: Enabled	

Edit Policy Order...

Figure 8-27 *WSA Access Policies Example*

Decryption Policies

Many web services leverage SSL/TLS encryption. Many organizations find that more than half of their web traffic is encrypted. By default, the WSA only redirects and decodes port 80 HTTP traffic. The WSA must be configured to decrypt and evaluate SSL traffic if an organization expects to inspect it.

The WSA must have the HTTPS proxy enabled. To accomplish or verify this, go to Security Services > HTTPS Proxy and ensure that the proxy is enabled (see Figure 8-28).

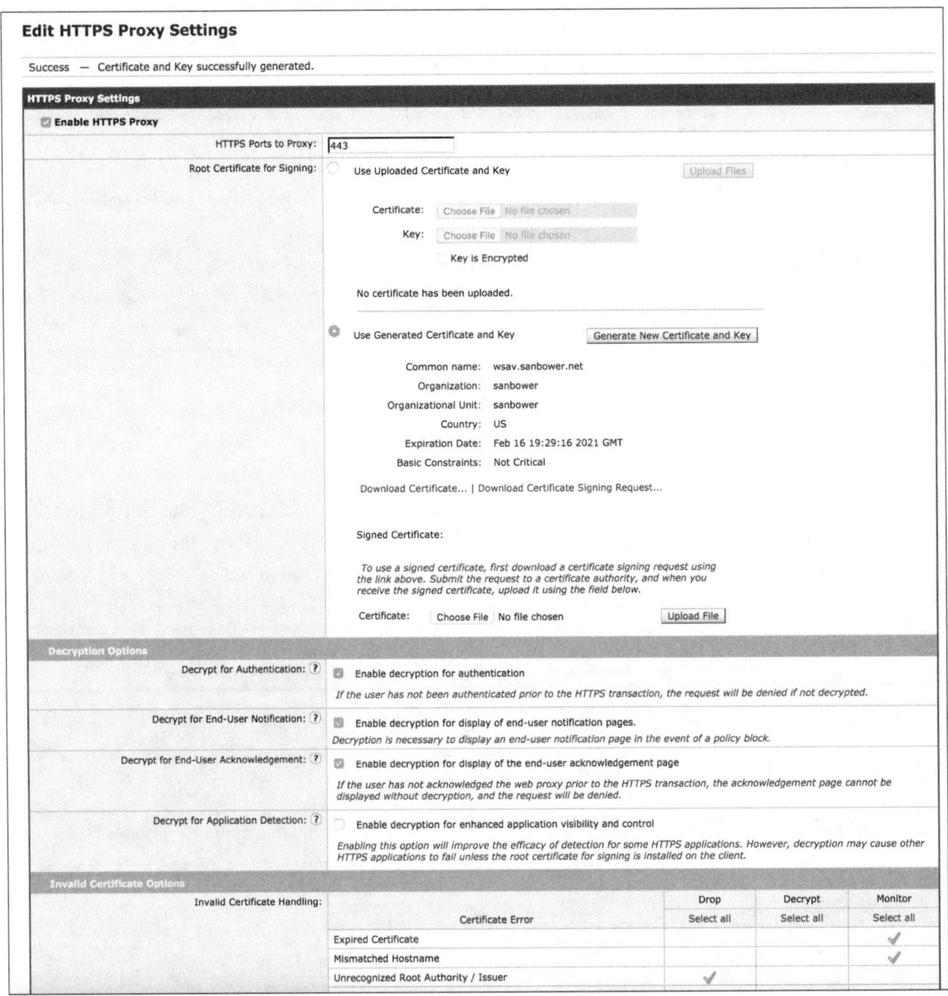

Figure 8-28 *WSA HTTPS Proxy*

A root certificate used to sign web traffic must be created or uploaded to the WSA. To upload a custom certificate, create an SSL private key and certificate signing request offline and submit it to the organization's PKI team for a subordinate CA certificate. Once approved, that certificate and private key can be uploaded to the WSA through use of the Use Uploaded Certificate and Key option. The certificate needs to be from a trusted root certificate authority in the organization because the client needs to trust the certificate in order to not receive a warning. (This will not be a public CA, as public CAs do not issue sub-CA certs.)

You can create a certificate on the WSA and then download the certificate and deploy the certificate to all clients in the organization.

HTTPS proxy also allows changing of the decryption options, invalid certificate handling, and OCSP options in the configuration. Once the HTTPS proxy is configured, a decryption policy needs to be added, or the global policy should be reviewed/edited. Figure 8-29 shows a new decryption policy being added to the WSA.

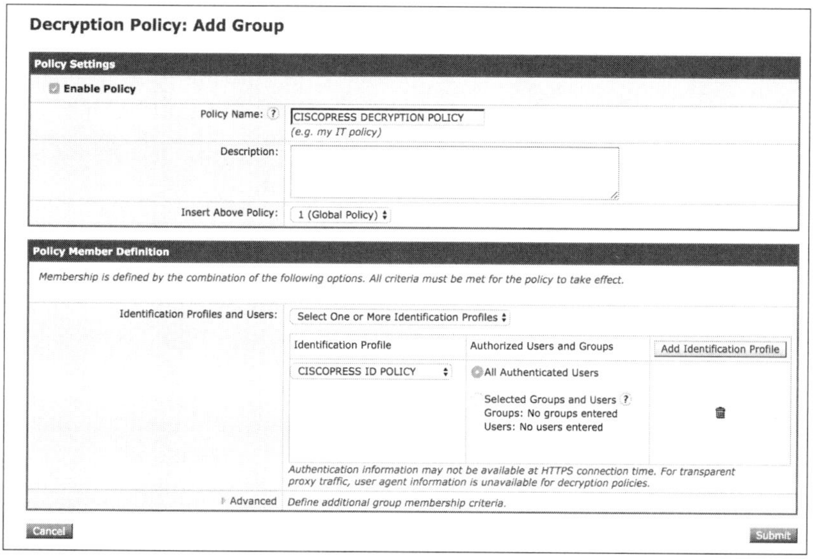

Figure 8-29 *WSA Decryption Policy*

After you add a policy, the variables regarding URL filtering, Web Reputation, and the default action become configurable in the decryption policies table. To edit a policy, click on the corresponding cell.

Unlike access policies, decryption policies provide additional actions, such as Decrypt, which allows the connection but causes the traffic content to be inspected. The appliance decrypts the traffic and applies access policies to the decrypted traffic as if it were a plaintext HTTP connection. By decrypting the connection and applying access policies, you can scan the traffic for malware.

It is recommended that you decrypt only categories that would need further fine-grained control, access policy processing, referrer exemption, or antivirus/antimalware scanning. It is important to pass through traffic that might be confidential, such as traffic at financial or banking sites.

Also, it is a good idea to drop the traffic that would have the block action applied by the corresponding access policy. If illegal, forbidden, and business-inappropriate content is blocked in an access policy, it should be dropped in the decryption policy. Otherwise, the WSA will spend cycles decrypting only for the access policy to drop that traffic anyway. Figure 8-30 illustrates a multiple-line decryption policy with customization of global policies.

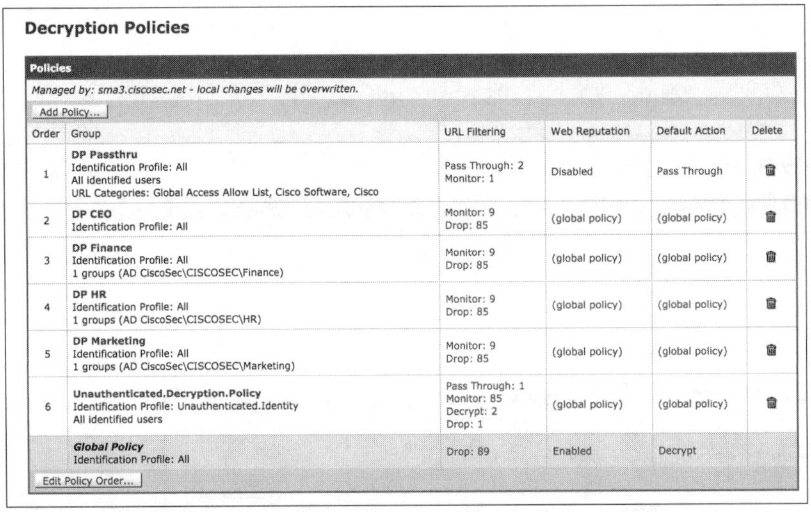

Decryption Policies

Policies

Managed by: sma3.ciscosec.net - local changes will be overwritten.

Add Policy...

Order	Group	URL Filtering	Web Reputation	Default Action	Delete
1	**DP Passthru** Identification Profile: All All identified users URL Categories: Global Access Allow List, Cisco Software, Cisco	Pass Through: 2 Monitor: 1	Disabled	Pass Through	
2	**DP CEO** Identification Profile: All	Monitor: 9 Drop: 85	(global policy)	(global policy)	
3	**DP Finance** Identification Profile: All 1 groups (AD CiscoSec\CISCOSEC\Finance)	Monitor: 9 Drop: 85	(global policy)	(global policy)	
4	**DP HR** Identification Profile: All 1 groups (AD CiscoSec\CISCOSEC\HR)	Monitor: 9 Drop: 85	(global policy)	(global policy)	
5	**DP Marketing** Identification Profile: All 1 groups (AD CiscoSec\CISCOSEC\Marketing)	Monitor: 9 Drop: 85	(global policy)	(global policy)	
6	**Unauthenticated.Decryption.Policy** Identification Profile: Unauthenticated.Identity All identified users	Pass Through: 1 Monitor: 85 Decrypt: 2 Drop: 1	(global policy)	(global policy)	
	Global Policy Identification Profile: All	Drop: 89	Enabled	Decrypt	

Edit Policy Order...

Figure 8-30 *WSA Decryption Policy*

Outbound Malware Policies

An outbound malware policy tells the WSA whether to scan uploads for malware. Figure 8-31 shows the options available for customization, including Do Not Scan Any Uploads, Scan All Uploads, and Scan Uploads to Specified Custom and External URL Categories.

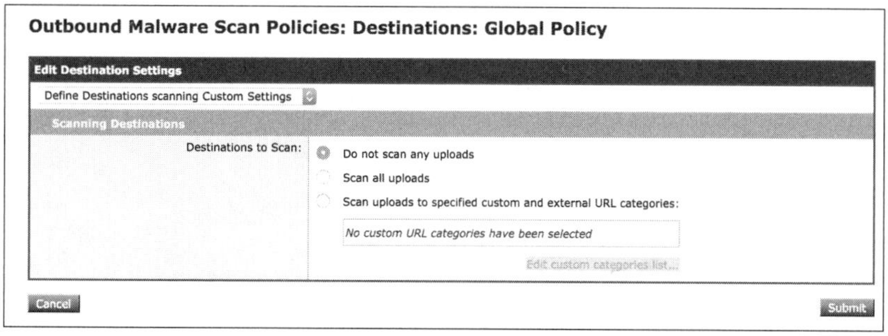

Outbound Malware Scan Policies: Destinations: Global Policy

Edit Destination Settings
Define Destinations scanning Custom Settings
Scanning Destinations
Destinations to Scan: Do not scan any uploads
Scan all uploads
Scan uploads to specified custom and external URL categories:
No custom URL categories have been selected
Edit custom categories list...
Cancel
Submit

Figure 8-31 *WSA Outbound Malware Policy*

The WSA allows for administrators to also choose which scanning engines are used to scan the uploads. Webroot, McAfee, and Sophos can be used to monitor or block files based on the malware categories configured in the policy.

Data Security Policies and DLP Policies

A data security policy manages data uploads to the web. Data security policies scan outbound traffic to ensure that it complies with company rules for data uploads, based on its destination and content. Data security policies use the WSA to scan and evaluate traffic and allow you to restrict the maximum file size for HTTP/HTTPS and FTP, which can help prevent data exfiltration of private data. It also allows for blocking of specific files or file types, as shown in Figure 8-32, where Windows executables are blocked.

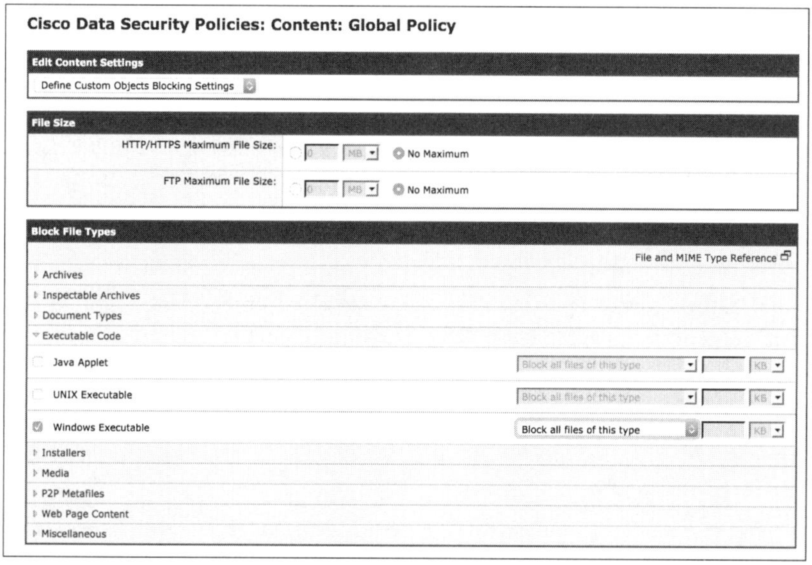

Cisco Data Security Policies: Content: Global Policy

Edit Content Settings
Define Custom Objects Blocking Settings
File Size
HTTP/HTTPS Maximum File Size: 0 MB No Maximum
FTP Maximum File Size: 0 MB No Maximum
Block File Types
File and MIME Type Reference
Archives
Inspectable Archives
Document Types
Executable Code
Java Applet — Block all files of this type — KB
UNIX Executable — Block all files of this type — KB
Windows Executable — Block all files of this type — KB
Installers
Media
P2P Metafiles
Web Page Content
Miscellaneous

Figure 8-32 *WSA Data Security Policy*

External DLP policies redirect outbound traffic to external servers for scanning. First an external DLP server must be defined by browsing to Network > External DLP Servers and configuring the server by selecting the communication protocol (ICAP or Secure ICAP) and setting the service address, service URL, and load balancing method, as shown in Figure 8-33.

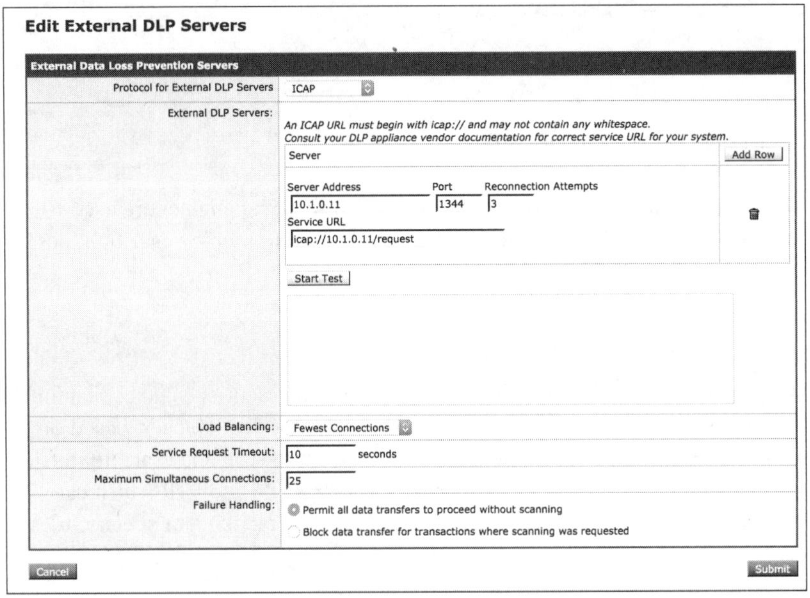

Figure 8-33 *WSA External DLP Server*

Note Internet Content Adaptation Protocol (ICAP) is a lightweight HTTP-like protocol used to forward HTTP requests to external content filters or scanners.

WSA Reporting

The WSA offers native on-box reporting with web usage and user reporting. Figure 8-34 shows the menu of reporting pages on the WSA on the Reporting tab.

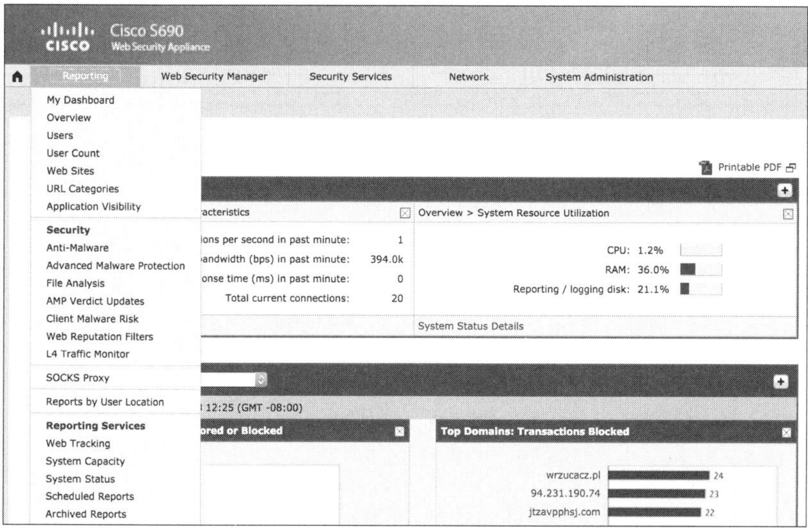

Figure 8-34 *WSA Reports*

While many of the reports and dashboards give quick indications of statistics, such as top malware or domains blocked, the WSA also gives administrators the ability to query specific requests. This can be crucial in troubleshooting allowed or blocked content. This is found by going to Reporting > Web Tracking. Figure 8-35 shows an example of a query searching for a specific user accessing a specific site. The access was blocked because of the reputation score of –7.4.

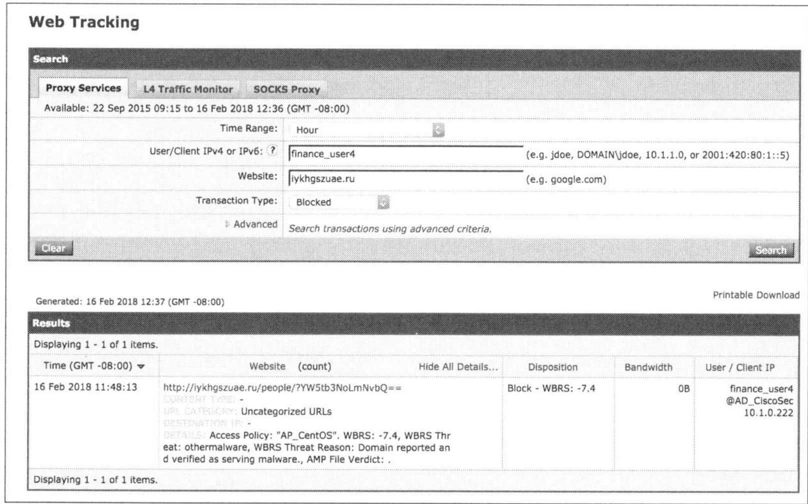

Figure 8-35 *WSA Web Tracking*

Note Logs can also be sent to third-party reporting, such as SIEM, for more granular reporting. The WSA uses the W3C log format.

Email Security Appliance

Today, businesses consider email one of their most important systems. People are more apt to send email than they are to make a phone call or send a text. Spam and malware are not going away any time soon, which means it is more important than ever before to use email security to protect an organization's sensitive data and meet industry compliance regulations.

The Cisco ESA acts as the email gateway to an organization, handling the transfer of all email connections, accepting messages, and relaying messages to the appropriate email servers. Email connections on the Internet use SMTP. The ESA services all SMTP connections for an organization and, by default, acts as the SMTP gateway.

Email Basics

Email leverages many protocols and components to operate effectively. The following are some of the most important ones:

- **Mail transfer agent (MTA):** Also known as a mail server, the MTA is the component responsible for moving email from the sending mail server to the recipient mail server.
- **Mail delivery agent (MDA):** The MDA is the component of an MTA that is responsible for the final delivery of a message to a local mailbox on disk.
- **Mail submission agent (MSA):** This is the component of an MTA that accepts new mail messages from an MUA, using SMTP.
- **Mail user agent (MUA):** An MUA is an email client or email reader used to access and manage a user's email.
- **Internet Message Access Protocol (IMAP):** IMAP is an email client communication protocol that allows users to keep messages on the server. An MUA using IMAP displays messages directly from the server, although a download option for archiving purposes is usually also available.
- **Post Office Protocol (POP):** POP is an application-layer protocol used by an MUA to retrieve email from a remote server.

A mail server is also known as an MTA, a mail transport agent, a mail router, or a mail exchanger (MX). When redirecting email from one server to another, DNS MX records are used to route the mail traffic on the Internet. An MX record is a type of verified resource record in the Domain Name System that specifies a mail server responsible for accepting email messages on behalf of a recipient's domain, and a preference value is used to prioritize mail delivery if multiple mail servers are available. The set of MX records of a domain name specifies how email should be routed with SMTP.

The following are the steps taken for inbound mail flow, as shown in Figure 8-36:

Step 1. The sender sends an email to jamie@securitydemo.net.

Step 2. The sending mail server looks up the securitydemo.net MX record and receives the hostname of the ESA (mail.securitydemo.net).

Step 3. The sending mail server resolves the ESA hostname (mail.securitydemo.net) to an IP address.

Step 4. The sending mail server opens an SMTP connection with the ESA.

Step 5. After inspection, the ESA sends the mail to the internal mail server.

Step 6. An employee retrieves the cleaned emails from the internal mail server by using IMAP or POP protocols.

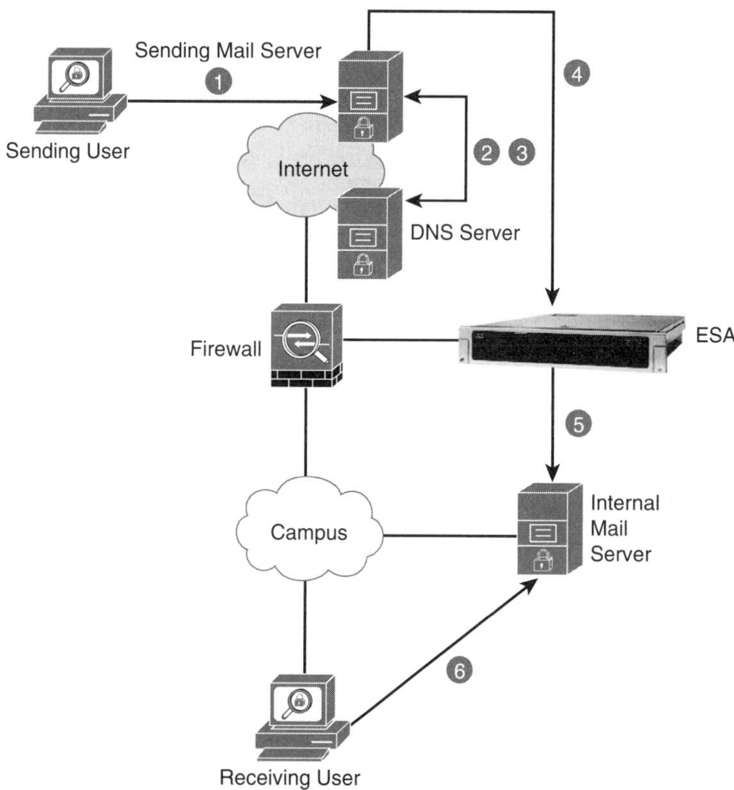

Figure 8-36 *ESA Mail Flow*

The Cisco ESA uses listeners to handle incoming SMTP connection requests. A listener defines an email processing service that is configured on an interface in the Cisco ESA. Listeners apply to email entering the appliance from either the Internet or internal systems.

The following listeners can be configured:

- Public listeners for email coming in from the Internet
- Private listeners for email coming from hosts in the corporate (inside) network

Cisco ESA listeners are often referred to as *SMTP daemons* running on a specific Cisco ESA interface. When a listener is configured, the hosts that are allowed to connect to the listener using a combination of access control rules must be configured. Also, the local domains for which public listeners accept messages need to be specified.

ESA System Setup

Like the WSA, the ESA can be used with a single physical interface to filter email to and from the organization's mail servers. The ESA could also be configured to use a two-interface configuration—one interface for email transfers to and from the Internet and the other for email transfers to and from the internal servers.

The Cisco ESA deployment is designed to be as easy as possible. The ESA is deployed into your existing mail delivery chain as a mail transfer agent. The ESA is the destination of the agency's email; as such, the public MX records (the DNS records that define where to send mail) must eventually point to the ESA's public IP address.

It is important that the ESA be accessible through the public Internet and that the ESA be the first hop in your email infrastructure. The sender's IP address is used by several of the ESA's processes and is one of the primary identifiers that SenderBase uses to determine the sender's reputation. If another device receives mail before forwarding it to the ESA, the ESA is not able to determine the sender's IP address, and filtering cannot be applied properly.

To create an initial configuration, browse to System Administration > System Setup on the ESA web GUI. Figure 8-37 shows the initial system configuration of the ESA's hostname, email alerts configuration, time zone, NTP, and administrator password.

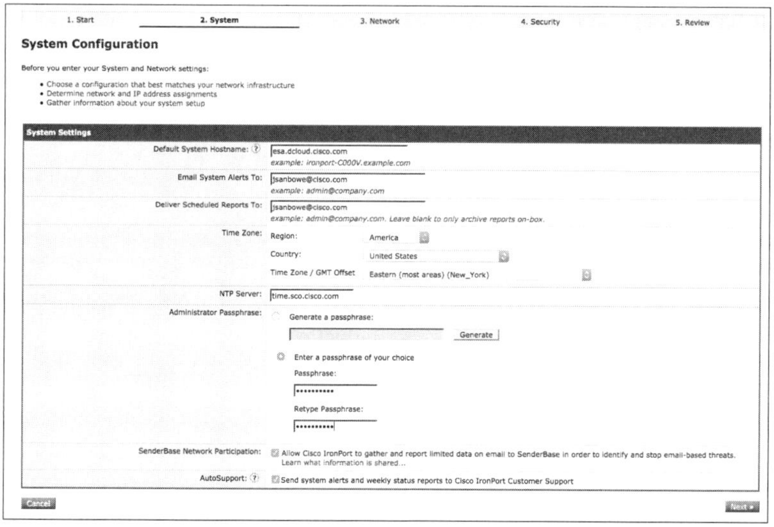

Figure 8-37 *ESA System Setup: System Configuration*

Next, the ESA requires configuration of IPv4 and IPv6 addresses, gateways, and DNS information. The incoming mail domain and destination and the outgoing mail relay are also configured on the Network Integration page, as shown in Figure 8-38.

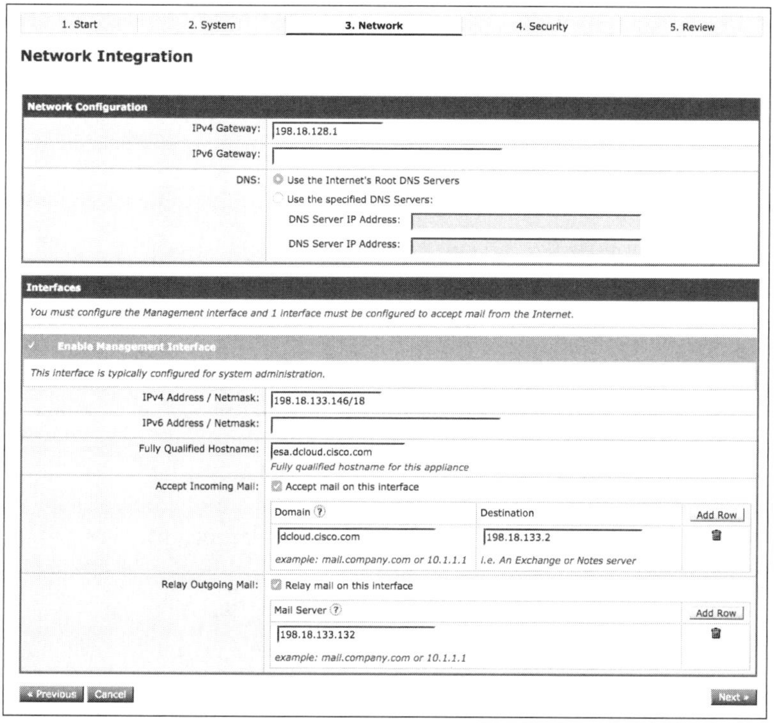

Figure 8-38 *ESA System Setup: Network Integration*

The Message Security page (see Figure 8-39) shows the order in which the security solutions are applied and allows administrators to enable, change, or disable the default security settings.

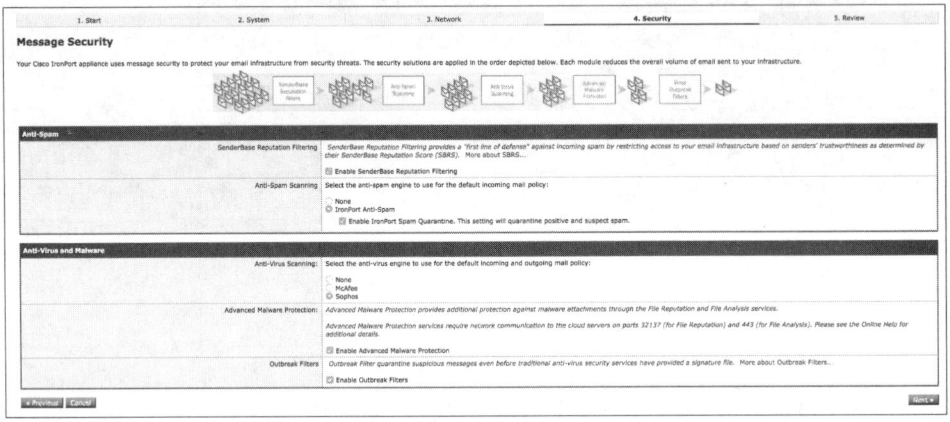

Figure 8-39 *ESA System Setup: Message Security*

SenderBase reputation filtering is the first layer of spam protection, allowing organizations to control the messages that come through the email gateway based on senders' trustworthiness, as determined by the Cisco SenderBase reputation service. The ESA can accept messages from known or highly reputable senders and deliver them directly to the end user without any content scanning. Messages from unknown or less reputable senders can be subjected to content scanning, such as antispam and antivirus scanning. Email senders with the worst reputation can have their connections rejected or their messages bounced, based on your preferences. Reputation on the ESA uses a –10 to +10 reputation score for email senders.

IronPort antispam uses conventional techniques and innovative context-sensitive detection technology to eliminate a diverse range of known and emerging email threats.

Cisco partnered with Sophos and McAfee to support their antivirus scanning engines for network antivirus capabilities on the ESA.

Outbreak filters, which are enabled by default, provide a dynamic quarantine, also called a DELAY quarantine, and can continue to hold or release back though antivirus and AMP for additional scans. Outbreak filters provide a significant catch rate for outbreaks over traditional scanning engines as they provide the "human" element after signature, heuristics, and hash-based scanning. On average, outbreak filters provide more than nine hours of lead time over antivirus engines for zero-day outbreaks.

After setting up the basic configuration, review the configuration, illustrated in Figure 8-40, to ensure that all settings meet the organization's requirements, and click Install This Configuration.

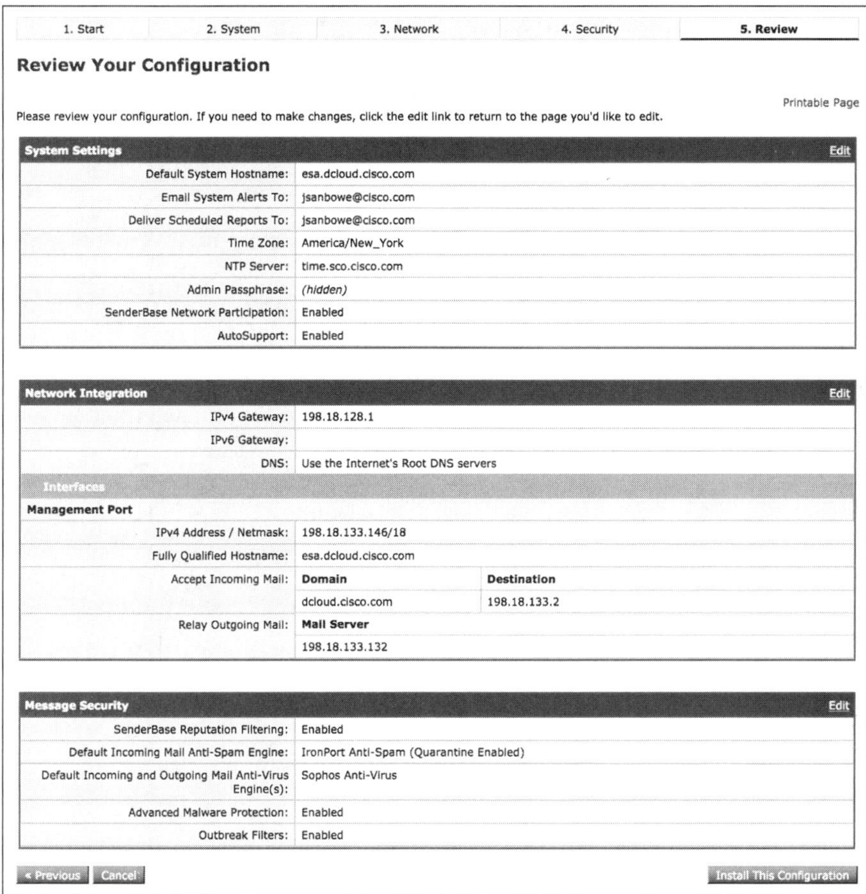

Figure 8-40 *ESA System Setup: Review and Install Configuration*

After installing the configuration, the ESA runs the Active Directory Wizard to connect the ESA to AD for verification of internal users. For example, when mail is destined for chad@securitydemo.net, the ESA will verify that the account exists in AD or LDAP. If the account doesn't exist, the mail will be dropped. The Active Directory Wizard requires the hostname or IP address of the AD server and credentials the ESA can use to connect. Figure 8-41 illustrates the required input to connect to AD.

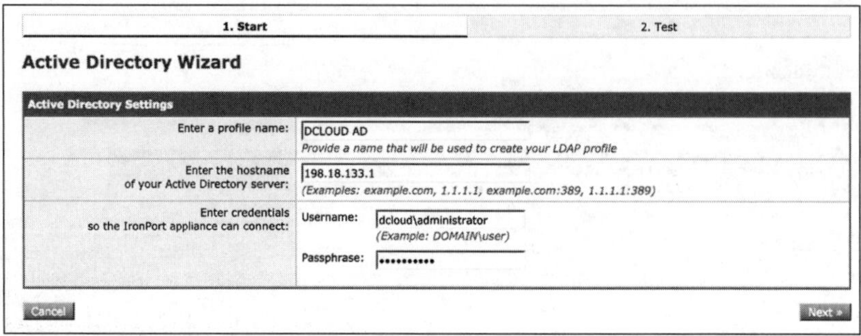

Figure 8-41 *ESA Active Directory Wizard*

In order to verify that the configuration is correct, the ESA allows the administrator to test the connection to AD, as shown in Figure 8-42.

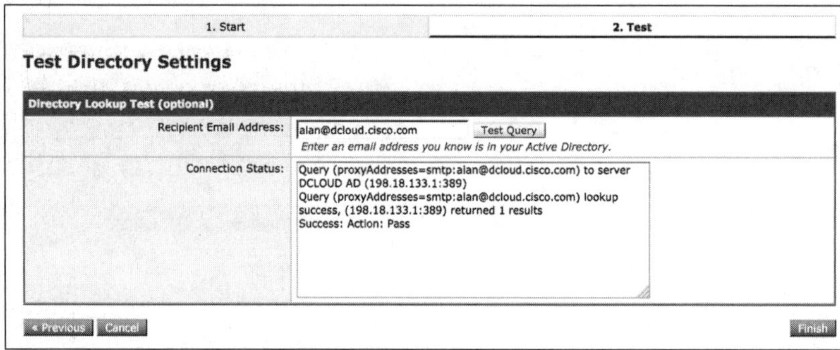

Figure 8-42 *ESA Active Directory Test*

To verify the configuration, the **mailconfig** CLI command can be used to send a test email containing the system configuration data that was entered in the System Setup Wizard.

ESA Policy Configuration

ESA has many different policies and settings that affect the mail flow for an organization. Figure 8-43 illustrates the email flow inside the ESA and the order in which policies are applied.

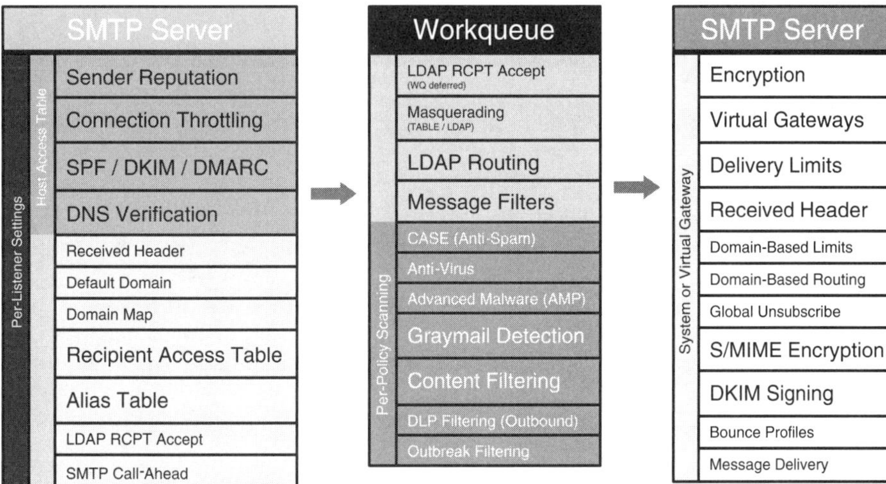

Figure 8-43 *ESA Mail Flow*

Incoming and Outgoing Mail Policies

The ESA enforces an organization's policies for messages sent to and from users through the use of mail policies. A mail policy is a set of rules that specify the types of suspect, sensitive, or malicious content that an organization may not want entering or leaving the network. This content may include the following:

- Spam
- Legitimate marketing messages
- Graymail
- Viruses
- Phishing and other targeted mail attacks
- Confidential corporate data
- Personally identifiable information (PII)

It is possible to create multiple mail policies that satisfy the disparate security needs of the different user groups in an organization. Figure 8-44 shows an example of an incoming mail policy that differentiates executives and IT security staff. Incoming mail policies are configured under Mail Policies > Incoming Mail Policies.

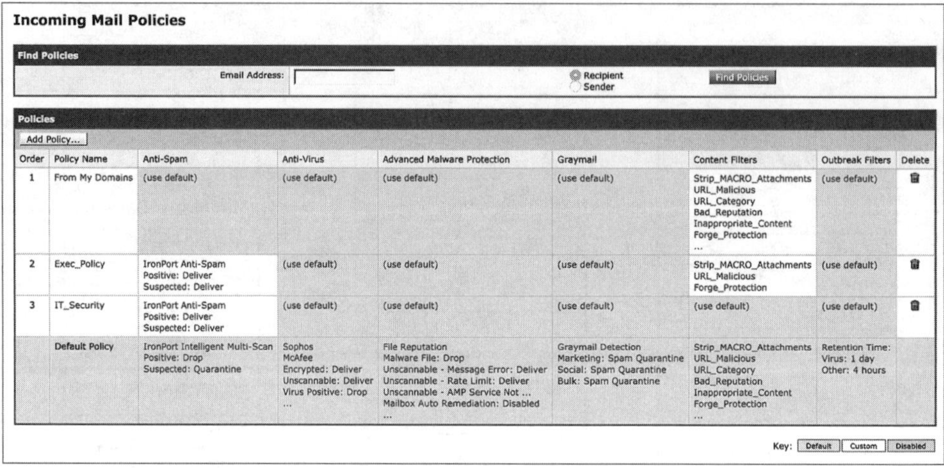

Figure 8-44 *ESA Incoming Mail Policies*

The ESA uses the rules defined in these policies to scan each message and, if necessary, perform an action to protect the user. For example, policies can prevent the delivery of suspected spam messages to everyone in the organization while allowing their delivery to IT security staff but with a modified subject to warn them of the content.

To add a new incoming mail policy, click Add on the Incoming Mail Policies page. Figure 8-45 shows the configuration of the new policy, which includes selecting a specific AD or LDAP group and naming the policy.

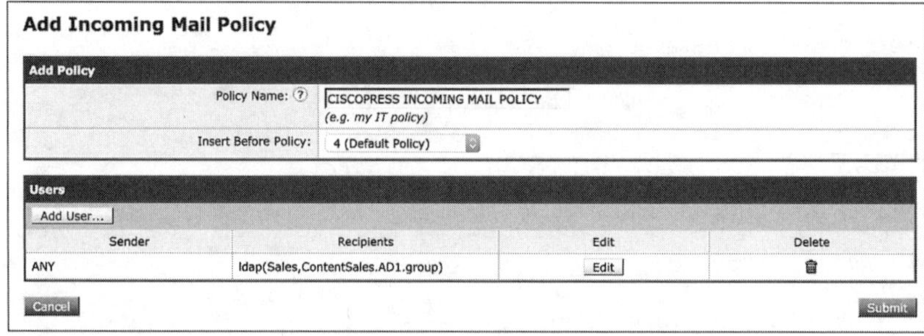

Figure 8-45 *ESA Add Incoming Mail Policy*

The process for adding an outbound mail policy is identical, except it is configured under Mail Policies > Outgoing Mail Policies. Figure 8-46 shows the configuration of a sample outgoing mail policy.

Outgoing Mail Policies

Find Policies

Email Address: Recipient Sender Find Policies

Policies

Add Policy...

Order	Policy Name	Anti-Spam	Anti-Virus	Advanced Malware Protection	Graymail	Content Filters	Outbreak Filters	DLP	Delete
	Default Policy	Disabled	Sophos McAfee Encrypted: Deliver Unscannable: Deliver Virus Positive: Drop ...	File Reputation Malware File: Drop Pending Analysis: Quarantine Unscannable - Message Error: Deliver Unscannable - Rate Limit: Deliver Unscannable - AMP Service Not	Disabled	Encrypt_Subject CorpControlledAttachments zixvpm_encryption zixport_encryption zixpxe_encrytion ...	Disabled	HIPAA and HITECH Confidential Documents CorpControlled PCI-DSS (Payment Card Industry... US GLBA (Gramm Leach Bliley Act)	

Key: Default Custom Disabled

Figure 8-46 *ESA Outgoing Mail Policy*

The most important part of the configuration of incoming and outgoing mail policies is the setting of security inspection applied to the mail. You can enable, modify, or disable each policy's security services by clicking in the cell of the associated policy or the default policy.

Antispam settings allow you to customize the action to a message, such as drop or deliver with the subject prepended with [SPAM]. Figure 8-47 illustrates the configuration of antispam settings.

Mail Policies: Anti-Spam

Anti-Spam Settings

Policy:	From My Domains
Enable Anti-Spam Scanning for This Policy:	Use Settings from Default Policy (IronPort Intelligent Multi-Scan) Use IronPort Anti-Spam service Use IronPort Intelligent Multi-Scan *Spam scanning built on IronPort Anti-Spam.* Disabled
Positively-Identified Spam Settings	
Apply This Action to Message:	Deliver Send to Alternate Host (optional):
Add Text to Subject:	Prepend [SPAM]
Advanced	Optional settings for custom header and message delivery.
Suspected Spam Settings	
Enable Suspected Spam Scanning:	No Yes
Apply This Action to Message:	Deliver Send to Alternate Host (optional):
Add Text to Subject:	Prepend [SUSPECTED SPAM]
Advanced	Optional settings for custom header and message delivery.
Spam Thresholds	
Spam is scored on a 1-100 scale. The higher the score, the more likely a message is a spam.	
IronPort Anti-Spam:	Use the Default Thresholds Use Custom Settings: Positively Identified Spam: *Score >* 90 *(50 - 100)* Suspected Spam: *Score >* 50 *(minimum 25, cannot exceed positive spam score)*

Figure 8-47 *ESA Mail Policies: Antispam*

Antivirus, while configured similarly to antispam, also requires setting which antivirus software to use—either McAfee or Sophos. The McAfee and Sophos engines contain the programming logic necessary to scan files at particular points, process and pattern-match virus definitions with data they find in files, decrypt and run virus code in an emulated environment, apply heuristic techniques to recognize new viruses, and remove infectious code from legitimate files. You can configure the appliance to scan messages for viruses, based on the matching incoming or outgoing mail policy, and, if a virus is found, to perform different actions on the message, including "repairing" the message of viruses, modifying the subject header, adding an additional X-header, sending the message to an alternate address or mailhost, archiving the message, or deleting the message.

Use *content filters* to customize handling of messages beyond the standard routine handling by the other content security features such as antivirus scanning or DLP. For example, you can use a content filter if the content warrants quarantining for later examination or if corporate policy requires certain messages to be encrypted before delivery. A content filter scans either incoming or outgoing messages. A filter cannot be defined that scans both types of messages. To add a new content filter, go to Mail Policies > Incoming Content Filters or Mail Policies > Outgoing Content Filters and click Add. Figure 8-48 shows an example of a content filter that checks for URLs that have a reputation between –10 and –6 and quarantines these message.

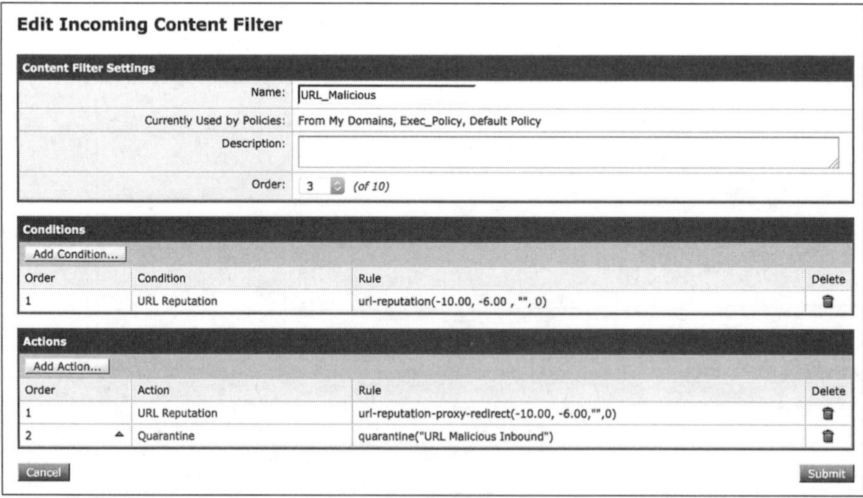

Figure 8-48 *ESA New Incoming Content Filter*

The variable conditions that ESA provides give content filters their ability to detect the correct message. Figure 8-49 shows all the conditions that can be matched in a content filter.

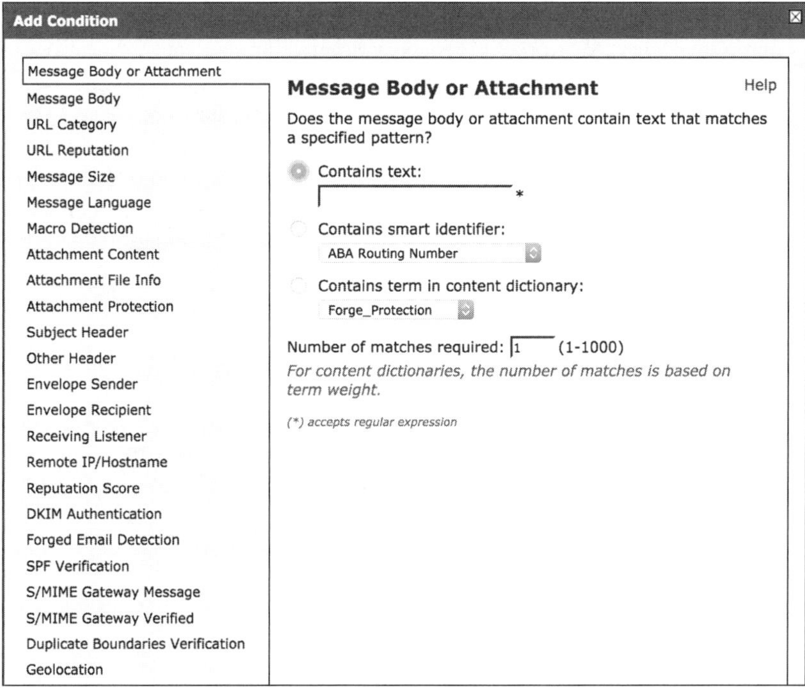

Figure 8-49 *ESA Content Filter Conditions*

When content filters are defined, you can enable them on an outgoing or incoming mail policy by going to the respective page, clicking the Content Filters cell, and selecting which content filters to enable, as shown in Figure 8-50.

Mail Policies: Content Filters

Content Filtering for Policy: From My Domains

Enable Content Filters (Customize settings)

Content Filters

Order	Filter Name	Description	Enable
1	Strip_MACRO_Attachments		☑
2	X-AMP-MALICIOUS		☐
3	URL_Malicious		☑
4	URL_Category		☑
5	Bad_Reputation		☑
6	Inappropriate_Content		☑
7	Forge_Protection		☑
8	McAfee_Caught		☑
9	Sophos_Caught		☑
10	SPF_Failure_My_Domain		☑

Cancel　　Submit

Figure 8-50 *ESA Enabling Content Filters in Policies*

Host Access Table

For every configured listener (Network > Listeners), you must define a set of rules that control incoming connections from remote hosts. The ESA allows you to configure which hosts are allowed to connect to the listener by using the host access table (HAT). The HAT maintains a set of rules that control incoming connections from remote hosts for a listener. Every configured listener has its own HAT. HATs are configured for both public and private listeners. Once a listener is defined, it cannot be changed. IP addresses and hosts are evaluated in the HAT top down, first match. Figure 8-51 shows the HAT Overview page for the 10.1.0.18 listener.

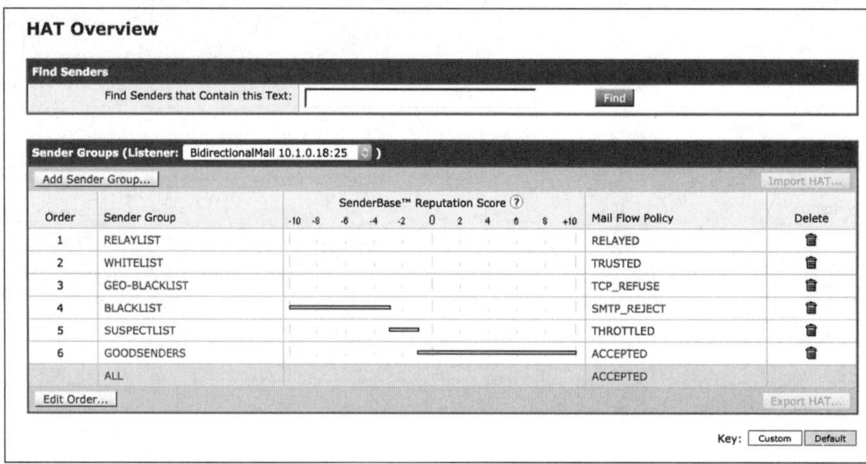

Figure 8-51 *ESA Host Access Table*

Each sender group can be modified or edited to match the appropriate criteria, based on requirements. Figure 8-52 illustrates the sender group BLACKLIST, which is matched based on an SBRS of –10 to –3.

Sender Group: BLACKLIST - BidirectionalMail 10.1.0.18:25

Sender Group Settings	
Name:	BLACKLIST
Order:	4
Comment:	Spammers are rejected
Policy:	SMTP_REJECT
SBRS (Optional):	-10.0 to -3.0
DNS Lists (Optional):	None
Connecting Host DNS Verification:	None Included

<< Back to HAT Overview Edit Settings...

Find Senders

Find Senders that Contain this Text: Find

Sender List: Display All Items in List

Add Sender...

There are no senders.

Figure 8-52 *ESA HAT Sender Group*

Mail Flow Policies

A mail flow policy allows you to control or limit the flow of email messages from a sender to a listener during an SMTP conversation. SMTP conversations are controlled by defining connection parameters, rate-limiting parameters, SMTP codes and responses, encryption, or authentication. Mail Flow policies are configured under Mail Policies > Mail Flow Policies, as illustrated in Figure 8-53.

Mail Flow Policies

Policies (Listener: BidirectionalMail 10.1.0.18:25)

Add Policy...

Policy Name	Behavior	Delete
ACCEPTED	Accept	?
RELAYED	Relay	
SMTP_REJECT	Reject	
TCP_REFUSE	TCP Refuse	
THROTTLED	Accept	
TRUSTED	Accept	
Default Policy Parameters		

Figure 8-53 *ESA Mail Flow Policies*

Figure 8-54 illustrates some of the parameters that can be configured in a mail flow policy.

Mail Flow Policy: THROTTLED - BidirectionalMail 10.1.0.18:25

Edit Policy Settings

Name:	THROTTLED	
Connection Behavior:	Accept	
Connections:	Max. Messages Per Connection:	Use Default (10) / 1
	Max. Recipients Per Message:	Use Default (50) / 25
	Max. Message Size:	Use Default (20M) / 10485760 (add a trailing K for kilobytes; M for megabytes)
	Max. Concurrent Connections From a Single IP:	Use Default (10) / 1
SMTP:	Custom SMTP Banner Code:	Use Default (220) / 220
	Custom SMTP Banner Text:	Use Default ()
	Override SMTP Banner Hostname:	Use Default (Use Hostname from Interface) / Use Hostname from Interface
Mail Flow Limits		
Rate Limit for Hosts:	Max. Recipients Per Hour:	Use Default (Unlimited) / Unlimited / 20
	Max. Recipients Per Hour Code:	Use Default (452)
	Max. Recipients Per Hour Text:	Use Default (Too many recipients received this hour)
Rate Limit for Envelope Senders:	Settings to define maximum recipients for envelope sender, per time interval.	

Figure 8-54 *ESA Edit Mail Flow Policy*

Recipient Access Table

The recipient access table (RAT) defines which recipients are accepted by a public listener. At a minimum, the table specifies the address and whether to accept or reject it. For example, some ESAs might accept mail from both securitydemo.com and securitydemo.net.

To configure the RAT, browse to Mail Policies > Recipient Access Table (RAT). Figure 8-55 shows the RAT page, which lists the entries in the RAT, including the order and default actions.

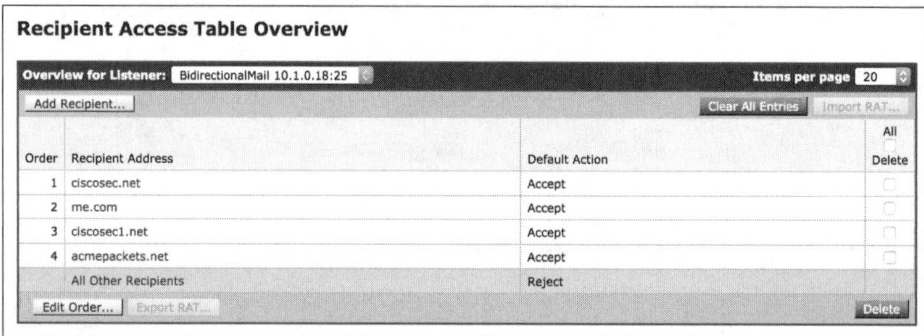

Figure 8-55 *ESA Recipient Access Table*

Data Loss Prevention

The DLP feature on the ESA focuses on securing the organization's proprietary information and intellectual property and enforces compliance with government regulations by preventing users from maliciously or unintentionally emailing sensitive data from the network. Administrators can define the types of data that employees are not allowed to email by creating DLP policies that are used to scan outgoing messages for any data that may violate laws or corporate policies.

To configure DLP, go to Security Services > Data Loss Prevention and enable the service, as shown in Figure 8-56. It is also recommended that you enable automatic updates.

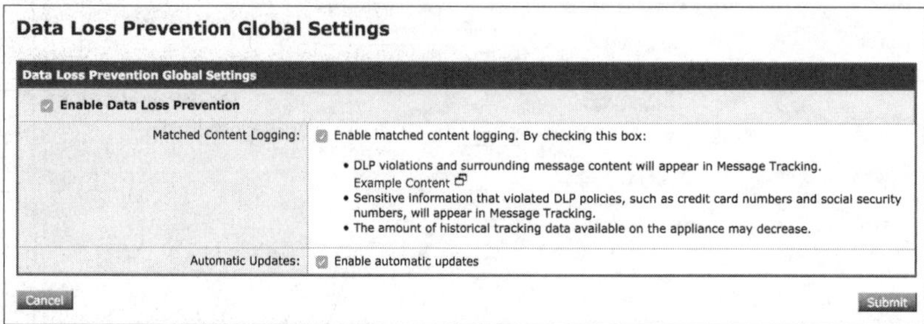

Figure 8-56 *ESA Data Loss Prevention Global Settings*

Next, go to Mail Policies > DLP Policy Manager (see Figure 8-57) and add DLP policies required to meet the organization's policy. Figure 8-58 illustrates adding a DLP policy for Payment Card Industry Data Security Standard (PCI-DSS). This policy identifies information protected by PCI regulatory compliance.

DLP Policy Manager

Active DLP Policies for Outgoing Mail

Add DLP Policy...

Order	DLP Policy	Duplicate	Delete
1	HIPAA and HITECH		
2	Confidential Documents CorpControlled		
3	PCI-DSS (Payment Card Industry Data Security Standard)		
4	US GLBA (Gramm Leach Billey Act)		

Edit Policy Order...

Advanced Settings

Custom DLP Dictionaries: (for use in Custom Policies only)	None Available

Figure 8-57 *ESA DLP Policy Manager*

Mail Policies: DLP: Policy: PCI-DSS (Payment Card Industry Data Security Standard)

Policy: PCI-DSS (Payment Card Industry Data Security Standard)

DLP Policy Name:	PCI-DSS (Payment Card Industry Data Security Standard)
Description:	Identifies information protected by the Payment Card Industry Data Security Standard (PCI-DSS).
Policy Matching Details:	*This policy identifies cardholder data, including but not limited to Primary Account Number (PAN), expiration dates, and magnetic stripe data.*
▷ Filter Senders and Recipients:	*Restrict this DLP policy by specific recipients and senders.*
▷ Filter Attachments:	*Restrict this DLP policy to detect specific attachment types.*
▷ Filter Message Tags:	*Restrict this DLP policy to detect message tags.*

Severity Settings

Critical Severity Incident:	PCI Quarantine
High Severity Incident:	Inherit Action from Critical Severity Incident
Medium Severity Incident:	Inherit Action from High Severity Incident
Low Severity Incident:	Inherit Action from Medium Severity Incident
Severity Scale:	

IGNORE	LOW	MEDIUM	HIGH	CRITICAL
0 - 14	15 - 52	53 - 72	73 - 87	88 - 100

Edit Scale...

Cancel Submit

Figure 8-58 *ESA PCI-DSS DLP Policy*

Finally, when the policy components are in place, DLP can be applied on the outgoing mail policies. Go to Mail Policies > Outgoing Mail Policies and click on the DLP cell for the policy that you want to modify. Figure 8-59 shows enabling DLP policies for outgoing mail.

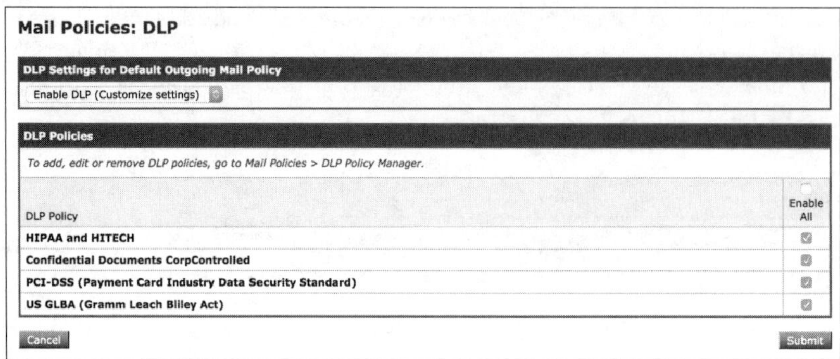

Figure 8-59 *ESA Enabling DLP Policies on Outgoing Mail*

> **Note** All policies inherit their settings from the default policy by default, so if the desire is to apply settings to all policies, modify the default.

SMTP Authentication and Encryption

Sender Policy Framework (SPF), specified in RFC 4408, allows recipients to verify sender IP addresses by looking up DNS records that list authorized mail gateways for a particular domain. SPF uses DNS TXT resource records. The ESA allows administrators to verify HELO/EHLO and MAIL FROM identity (FQDN) by using SPF.

When SPF is enabled, the ESA stamps headers in the message and allows organizations to gain additional intelligence on the sender. Effectiveness of SPF is based on participation. Organizations need to invest time to ensure that SPF records are up to date.

Many organizations are starting to implement SPF because some of the big email carriers claim they do not accept mail without SPF records. At the same time, if an organization starts dropping mail without an SPF record, it sees less spam, but some legitimate mail might be dropped if the sending organization hasn't configured SPF correctly.

Domain Keys Identified Mail (DKIM), specified in RFC 5585, has methods for gateway-based cryptographic signing of outgoing messages, makes it possible to embed verification data in an email header, and has ways for recipients to verify integrity of the messages. In addition, RFC 6376 on DKIM signatures, RFC 5863 on DKIM development, deployment, and operation, and RFC 5617 on Author Domain Signing Practices (ADSP) all provide additional details about DKIM operation. DKIM uses DNS TXT records to publish public keys.

SPF and DKIM verification is configured in mail flow policies. Under Mail Policies > Mail Flow Policy, click Default Policy Parameters. In the default policy parameters, view the Security Features section, shown in Figure 8-60.

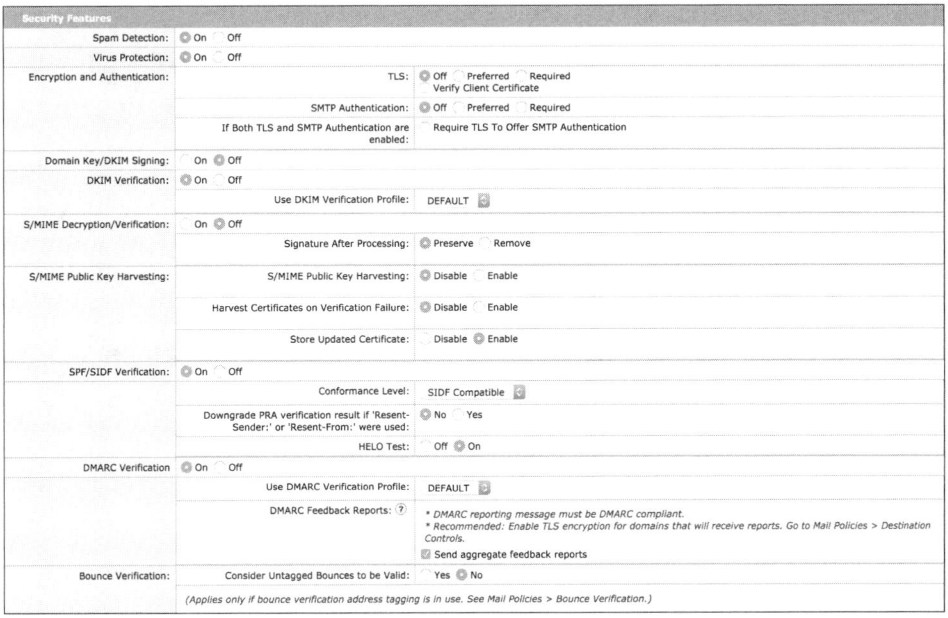

Figure 8-60 *ESA SPF and DKIM Authentication Settings*

Note To take action on SPF verification results, add a content filter.

The default action of DKIM is monitor. To customize the policy, go to Mail Policies > Verification Profiles and modify the default or add a new policy.

According to RFC 3207, "TLS is an extension to the SMTP service that allows an SMTP server and client to use transport-layer security to provide private, authenticated communication over the Internet. TLS is a popular mechanism for enhancing TCP communications with privacy and authentication." The STARTTLS implementation on the ESA provides privacy through encryption. It allows you to import an X.509 certificate and private key from a certificate authority service or use a self-signed certificate.

After uploading a certificate, in order to enable TLS encryption for receiving mail, the mail flow policies (refer to Figure 8-60) must have TLS set to Preferred or Required.

To enable TLS for delivery to hosts in remote domains, go to Mail Policies > Destination Controls. Add a new destination for the domain to which you will be using TLS and apply a TLS setting for the domain (that is, No, Preferred, or Required). Figure 8-61 shows the destination controls with TLS preferred for all domains except hotmail.com.

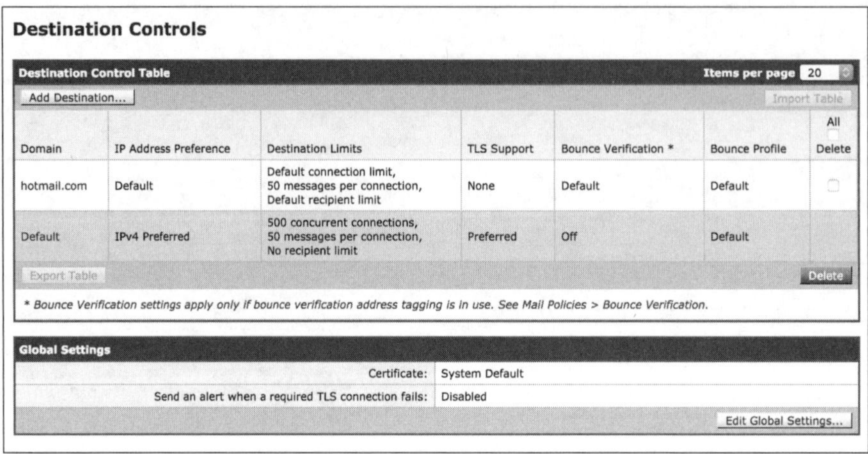

Figure 8-61 *ESA Destination Controls*

ESA Reporting

The ESA offers comprehensive dashboards and reports in the Monitor section of the GUI. You can find details related to incoming, outgoing, security scanning, and outbreaks in the reports available within the ESA. Figure 8-62 shows part of the Overview page, found under Monitor > Overview.

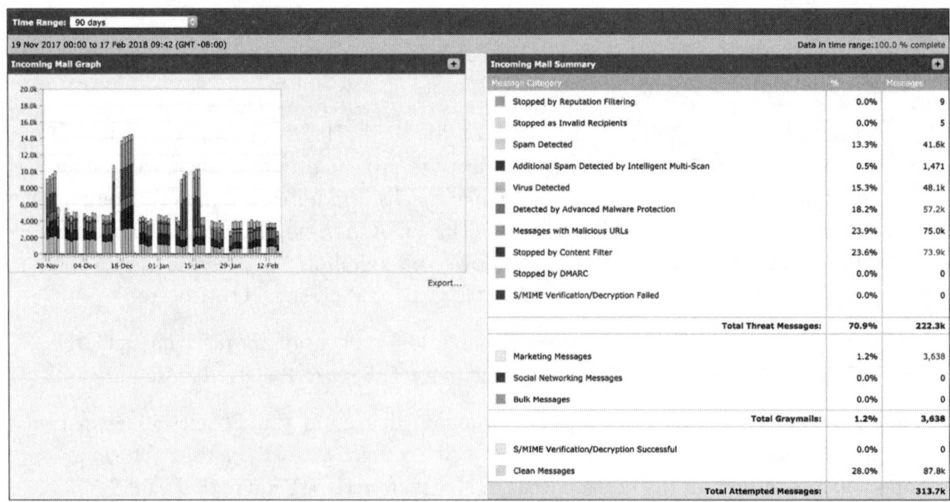

Figure 8-62 *ESA Monitor Overview*

Message tracking is one of the most useful tools in the Monitor section. It helps resolve help desk calls by giving a detailed view of message flow. For example, if a message was not delivered as expected, administrators can determine if it was found to contain a virus or placed in a spam quarantine or if it is located somewhere else in the mail stream.

A particular email message or a group of messages can be searched for the match criteria that are specified. Figure 8-63 shows an example of a search for DLP messages.

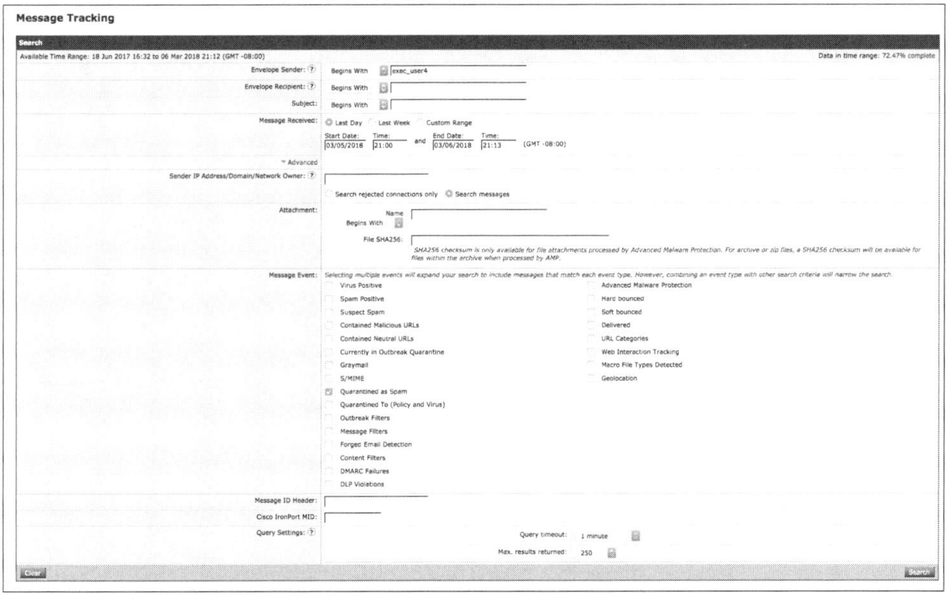

Figure 8-63 *ESA Message Tracking*

After reviewing the results, an administrator can click on any message to see additional details about the mail flow, as shown in Figure 8-64.

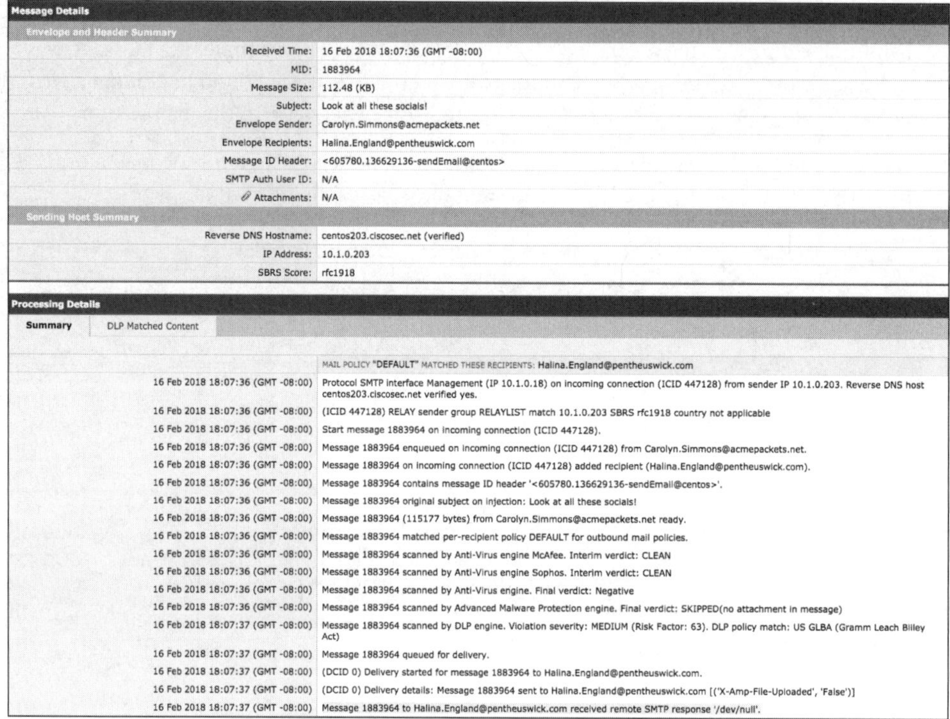

Figure 8-64 *ESA Message Tracking: Message Details*

Security Management Appliance

The Cisco Content SMA provides centralized management and reporting functions across multiple WSAs and ESAs. The integration of Cisco SMA with Cisco ESAs and WSAs simplifies the planning and administration of email and web security, improves compliance monitoring, makes possible a consistent enforcement of acceptable-use policies, and enhances threat protection.

SMA simplifies administration and planning by publishing policy settings and configuration changes from a single console to multiple appliances. Cisco SMA reports the number of transactions per second and the system's latency, response time, and proxy buffer memory.

Centralized reporting and tracking helps determine which users are in violation of acceptable use policies, identify policy infractions across any department or site, and monitor the use of Web 2.0 applications such as Facebook and YouTube as well as visits to URLs in specific categories such as "gambling" or "sports."

By centralizing the management of multiple appliances, administrators can enforce consistent acceptable use policies across the organization. The Cisco SMA delivers a comprehensive view of an organization's security operations, providing better threat intelligence, defense, and remediation. Important features include the centralized management of email spam quarantine, comprehensive threat monitoring across multiple web security gateways, Web Reputation scoring, and botnet detection.

Data is aggregated from multiple Cisco ESAs, including data categorized by sender, recipient, message subject, and other parameters. Scanning results, such as spam and virus verdicts, are also displayed, as are policy violations.

Summary

In this chapter, you have learned about deploying the Cisco WSA and ESA. You have seen how to initially deploy the WSA and ESA, how to redirect traffic, and how to use setup wizards. You have also learned how to manipulate policy to selectively filter and control content across web and email traffic.

References

"ESA FAQ: What Is a Listener?" https://www.cisco.com/c/en/us/support/docs/security/email-security-appliance/118236-configure-esa-00.html

"MX Record," https://en.wikipedia.org/wiki/MX_record

"20 Most Recent Virus Outbreaks from Email," https://www.talosintelligence.com/reputation_center/malware_rep#mal-outbreaks

Chapter 9

Umbrella and the Secure Internet Gateway

This chapter explores the fundamentals of Umbrella and the configuration of identities, policies, and reporting. You will learn how to forward DNS traffic to Umbrella and how to deploy the virtual appliance for local network and Active Directory integration. You will also learn about the policy components that can be applied to different identities.

Umbrella Fundamentals

Cisco Umbrella is a solution, delivered from the cloud, that blocks malicious destinations using Domain Name System (DNS). Resolving DNS is fundamental in connecting computers, services, or any other resource to the Internet, as all applications, ports, and protocols rely on DNS. Umbrella can be used on any device, including IoT devices, on any network, at any time. Implementation is very straightforward and can be accomplished by forwarding DNS queries to Umbrella on existing DNS servers, running the Umbrella virtual appliances, and using the Microsoft Windows or Mac OS X roaming client or the Cisco Security Connector for iOS.

Figure 9-1 illustrates a DNS request and Umbrella responding with a block page, essentially blocking all communication to a malicious or prohibited domain prior to any TCP or UDP data connection.

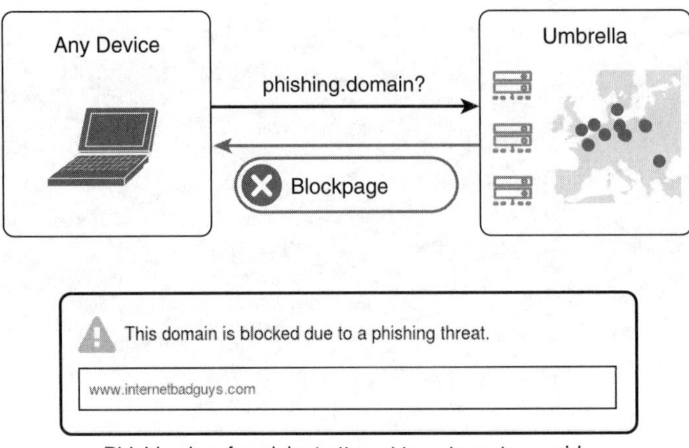

Figure 9-1 *Malicious Request to Umbrella*

Because most hosts use DNS to resolve the name-to-IP address mapping of hosts, Umbrella has the intelligence to see attacks before the application connection occurs. In most cases, this means limiting the load on a firewall or an IPS and reducing alerts, thus improving security operations and response. For this reason, Umbrella is often considered a first line of defense in an organization's security architecture.

Umbrella looks at the patterns of DNS requests from devices and uses them to detect the following:

- Compromised systems
- Command-and-control callbacks
- Malware and phishing attempts
- Algorithm-generated domains
- Domain co-occurrences
- Newly registered domains
- Malicious traffic and payloads that never reach the target

In real time, all Internet activity across an organization is logged, categorized by threat and content, and blocked when necessary. Umbrella can stop threats before a malware file is downloaded or before an IP connection over any port or any protocol is even established.

nslookup dnsbasics.securitydemo.net

As defined in RFCs 1034 and 1035, DNS is a foundational component of how the Internet works and is used by every device in a network to determine translations between domain names or hostnames and IPv4/IPv6 addresses. The DNS client/server architecture is based on query and response messages. Most queries of external name servers are DNS lookup Type A, which typically maps a domain's hostname to an IPv4 address. Figure 9-2 shows a packet capture of a DNS request and response. Most DNS queries consist of a single UDP request packet from the client, using destination port 53, followed by a single UDP reply packet from the server. When the response data size exceeds 512 bytes or for tasks such as zone transfers, TCP port 53 is typically used.

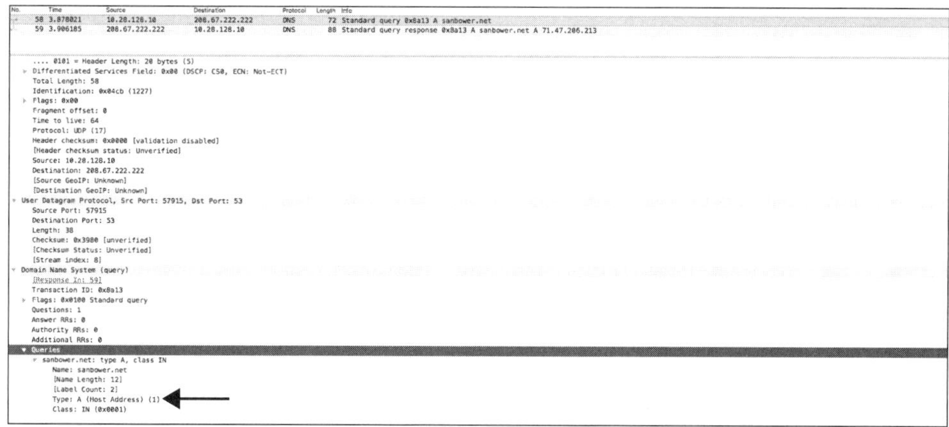

Figure 9-2 *Type A DNS Request*

Along with Type A, Table 9-1 describes some of the other DNS lookup types available and more commonly used on the Internet and internal networks for an organization.

Table 9-1 *DNS Lookup Types*

DNS Lookup Type	Description	Function
A	IPv4 address record	Returns a 32-bit IP address, which typically maps a domain's hostname to an IP address
AAAA	IPv6 address record	Returns a 128-bit IP address that maps a domain's hostname to an IP address
ANY	All cached records	Returns all records of all types known to the name server
CNAME	Canonical name record	Provides an alias of one name to another; the DNS lookup will continue retrying the lookup with the new name

DNS Lookup Type	Description	Function
MX	Mail exchange record	Stores information about where mail for the domain should be delivered
NS	Name server record	Delegates a DNS zone to use the specified authoritative name servers
PTR	Pointer record	Provides a pointer to a canonical name that returns the name only and is used for implementing reverse DNS lookups
SOA	Start of authority record	Specifies authoritative information about a DNS zone, including the primary name server, the email address of the domain administrator, the domain serial number, and several timers related to refreshing the zone
SRV	Service locator	Generalized service location record, used for newer protocols instead of creating protocol-specific records such as MX

On the Internet, recursive DNS nameservers are responsible for providing the proper IP address of the intended domain name to the requesting host. For example, when making a request to a website from your browser, the host or computer makes a request to a recursive DNS server to find the IP address associated with the website. This assumes that the operating system and web browser do not already have a response cached. From there, the recursive server checks to see if it has a cached DNS record from the authoritative nameserver and still has a valid time to live (TTL). If the recursive server does not have the DNS record cached, it begins the recursive process of going through the authoritative DNS hierarchy.

Authoritative DNS nameservers are responsible for providing answers to recursive DNS nameservers with the IP "mapping" of the intended website. The authoritative nameservers' responses to the recursive nameservers contain important information for each domain, such as corresponding IP addresses and other necessary DNS records. An authoritative nameserver is defined after registering a new domain with a domain registrar. Each domain name registrar allows organizations to set a primary name server and at least one secondary name server.

To better illustrate how the nameservers interact with each other, imagine that you are at your computer, and you want to search for a CCIE study guide, so you type www.google.com into your web browser to go to Google. However, your computer doesn't know where the server for www.google.com is located, so it sends a query to a recursive DNS nameserver (Umbrella) to locate the IP address of the website for you. The recursive DNS nameserver is now assigned the task of finding the IP address of the website you are searching for. If the recursive DNS nameserver does not already have the DNS record cached in its system, it queries the authoritative DNS hierarchy to get the answer.

Each part of a domain, like www.google.com, has a specific DNS nameserver (or group of redundant nameservers) that is authoritative. At the top of the tree are the root domain nameservers. Every domain has an implied/hidden . at the end that designates the DNS root nameservers at the top of the hierarchy. Root domain nameservers know the IP addresses of the authoritative nameservers that handle DNS queries for the top-level domains (TLDs), including .com, .edu, and .gov. The recursive DNS server first asks the root domain nameservers for the IP address of the TLD server—in this case .com (for google.com). Then it asks the authoritative server for .com, where it can find the google.com domain's authoritative server. Then google.com is asked where to find www.google.com. When the IP address is known for the website, the recursive DNS server responds to your computer with the appropriate IP address. The end result is that you are now happy because you can search for CCIE study guides all day long.

Umbrella Architecture

The Umbrella global infrastructure includes 25 data centers around the world that resolve more than 100 billion DNS requests from more than 85 million users across more than 160 countries every day. Umbrella data centers are peered with more than 500 of the top ISPs and content delivery networks to exchange BGP routes and ensure that requests are routed efficiently, without adding any latency over regional DNS providers. Anycast IP routing is used for reliability of the recursive DNS service Umbrella offers. All data centers announce the same IP address, and all requests are transparently sent to the fastest and lowest-latency data center available. Mostly due to anycast routing, Umbrella has had 100% uptime since its inception in 2006.

Its scale and speed give Umbrella a massive amount of data and, perhaps more importantly, a very diverse data set that is not just from one geography or one protocol. This diversity enables Umbrella to offer unprecedented insight into staged and launched attacks. The data and threat analytics engines learn where threats are coming from, who is launching them, where they are going, and the width of the net of the attack—even before the first victim is hit. Umbrella uses authoritative DNS logs to find the following:

- Newly staged infrastructures
- Malicious domains, IP addresses, and ASNs
- DNS hijacking
- Fast flux domains
- Related domains

Note Fast flux is a DNS technique used by botnets to hide phishing and malware delivery sites behind an ever-changing network of compromised hosts acting as proxies.

Umbrella is able to find these types of threats by using modeling inside the data analytics. Machine learning and advanced algorithms are used heavily to find and automatically block malicious domains. Here are a few examples of the dozens of available models:

- **Co-occurrence model:** This model identifies domains queried right before or after a given domain. This model helps uncover domains linked to the same attack, even if they're hosted on separate networks.
- **Traffic spike model:** This model recognizes when spikes in traffic to a domain match patterns seen with other attacks. For example, if the traffic for one domain matches the request patterns seen with exploit kits, you might want to block the domain before the full attack launches.
- **Predictive IP space monitoring model:** This model starts with domains identified by the spike rank model and scores the steps attackers take to set up infrastructure (for example, hosting provider, name server, IP address) to predict whether the domain is malicious. This identifies other destinations that can be proactively blocked before an attack launches.

Secure Internet Gateway

When Umbrella receives a DNS request, it first identifies which customer the request came from and which policy to apply. Next, Umbrella determines whether the request is safe or whitelisted, malicious or blacklisted, or "risky." Safe requests are allowed to be routed as usual, and malicious requests are routed to a block page. Risky requests can be routed to the cloud-based proxy for deeper inspection.

The cloud-based proxy is the basis for the secure Internet gateway (SIG). Before looking at the functionality of the proxy, it is helpful to understand what traffic is typically sent to the proxy. Most phishing, malware, ransomware, and other threats are hosted at domains that are classified as malicious. Yet some domains host both malicious and safe content; these are the domains that are classified as risky. These sites (such as reddit.com) often allow users to upload and share content, making them difficult to police.

Traditional web proxies or gateways examine all Internet requests, which adds latency and complexity. The Umbrella SIG proxy intercepts and inspects *only* requests for risky domains.

When SIG identifies a risky domain and begins to proxy that traffic, it uses the URL inspection engine to first classify the URL. SIG uses Cisco Talos threat intelligence, the Cisco web reputation system, and third-party feeds to determine if a URL is malicious. This means http://secdemo.net/url1.html can be clean, while http://secdemo.net/url2.html is malicious. An organization can create a list of custom URLs to be blocked based on the organization's intelligence and policies.

If the disposition of a web resource is still unknown after the URL inspection, if a file is present, SIG can also look at the file's reputation. The file is inspected by both antivirus (AV) engines and Cisco Advanced Malware Protection (AMP) to block malicious files based on known signatures before they are downloaded. Examples of file types include approximately 200 known file extensions, such as .PDF and .JPG. Finally, through AMP, if a file is later identified as malicious, customers can view retrospective details in a report to identify what systems might be infected.

Figure 9-3 summarizes the inspection capabilities of the intelligent proxy.

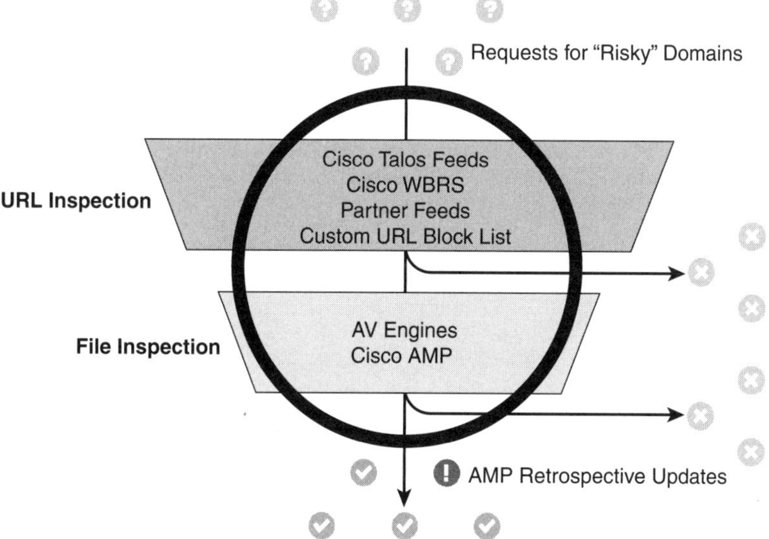

Figure 9-3 *Umbrella URL and File Inspection*

> **Note** More information about Cisco Advanced Malware Protection can be found in Chapter 10, "Protecting Against Advanced Malware."

SSL decryption is another important part of the Umbrella intelligent proxy. It allows the intelligent proxy to go beyond simply inspecting normal URLs and actually proxy and inspect traffic that is sent over HTTPS. The SSL decryption feature does require that the root certificate be installed on clients/computers that are using SSL decryption in their policies.

Umbrella Overview Dashboard

The Umbrella Overview dashboard gives an organization a quick view into what has happened during a defined time period. The time period for the dashboard defaults to the last 24 hours but can be set to show yesterday, the last 7 days, or the last 30 days.

Immediately upon browsing to the dashboard, you can see the number of malware and command-and-control requests that have been blocked for the time period set. As shown in Figure 9-4, general statistics on the numbers of active networks, roaming clients, and virtual appliances are also reported.

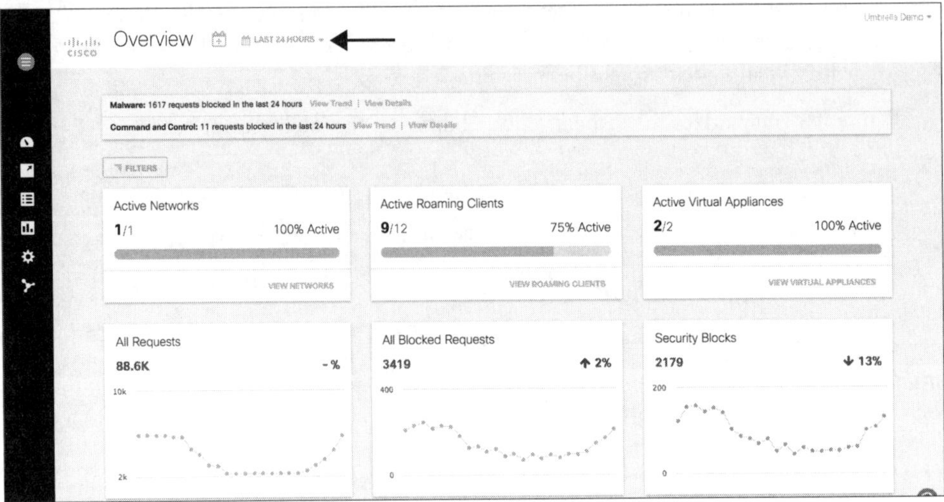

Figure 9-4 *Overview Dashboard*

You will also find that data summarizing all requests, all blocked requests, and security blocks is graphed to help illustrate any abnormal spikes or behavior for an organization.

In addition, the dashboard can show the top 10 security blocks by destination, identity, or type (see Figure 9-5).

Most Security Blocks

BY DESTINATION | BY IDENTITY | BY TYPE

Destination	Blocked Requests
binarycousins.com	334
mail.wavela.bid	242
iuqerfsodp9ifjaposdfjhgosurijfaewrwergwea.com	149
chart.apis.google.com.ref.ualibrary.org	144
goofooasdfasdfeeeee.com	105

Destination	Blocked Requests
zimagdcmasn.net	104
laryngectomy.cultivateward.eu	96
xing521.cn	86
bingbangboom.com	82
madingtoftling.com	81

VIEW BLOCKED REQUESTS 1 of 10

Figure 9-5 *Most Security Blocks by Destination*

Using the Overview dashboard is a great way to display high-level statistics about an organization's Umbrella deployment as well as give a pivot point to more detailed reports and information.

Deploying Umbrella

Umbrella is one of the simplest security solutions to deploy and manage. Because Umbrella is delivered from the cloud, there is no hardware to install or software to manually update, and the browser-based interface provides quick setup and ongoing management. Many organizations deploy enterprisewide in less than 30 minutes. Umbrella can be deployed for devices connected to the enterprise network/on-premises or devices outside the enterprise network/off-premises.

Identities

Umbrella identities are used to identify a device or network to an organization in the cloud. For example, a network is an identity in Umbrella and is defined by the public IP space of the network itself. All traffic originating from that IP space is identified as coming from that network in Umbrella. Thus, to add a network to Umbrella, you add the public IP address, or IP address range, to define the scope of the identity. This links the requests seen by that public IP address to the organization that has defined it in its Umbrella configuration.

To add a new network to Umbrella, go to Identities > Networks and click the **+** (see Figure 9-6). An organization should add to Umbrella each IP address or subnet that it uses. If the organization has the desire to apply different policies to different external IP addresses, then multiple networks should be created independently.

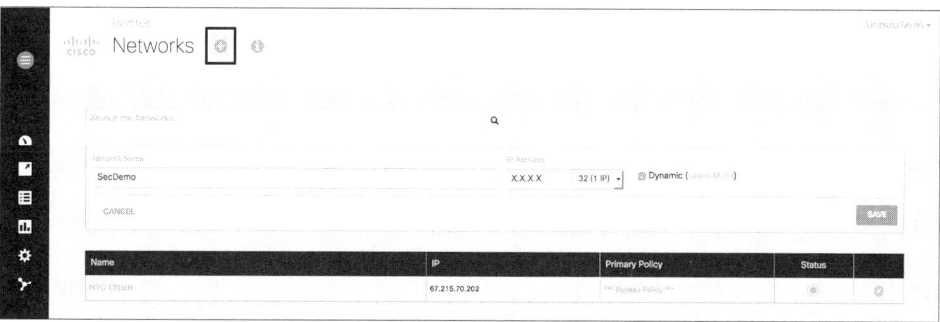

Figure 9-6 *New Network Identity*

Each network can have one IP address, as shown in Figure 9-6, or multiple IP addresses, where the number of IP addresses is changed when adding the network.

If your organization has dynamic IP addresses for Internet connectivity, you should select the Dynamic check box. This allows the organization's IP address to be updated automatically by the Umbrella Dynamic IP Updater. Without the IP updater, the Umbrella security settings no longer apply when an IP address change occurs because the IP address no longer matches the organization's account information. To avoid having to manually update IP address information, the Umbrella Dynamic IP Updater can be used on at least one computer in the network. The computer should remain powered on at all times and can be a Windows, Mac, or Linux system. The Umbrella Dynamic IP Updater automates the discovery and registration of a network's IP address to the organization's Umbrella account whenever the dynamic IP address changes.

Note If the Dynamic IP Updater is not used, the IP address must be updated manually each time it changes.

Forwarding DNS Traffic to Umbrella

When a network is configured, DNS traffic must be directed to Umbrella. The Umbrella IP addresses (IPv4) 208.67.222.222 and 208.67.220.220 are where DNS traffic should be directed. Forwarding DNS from an organization can be accomplished for on-network/on-premises devices in many ways. The most common method used in enterprise deployments is DNS forwarding on existing DNS servers. Both Windows (see Figure 9-7) and BIND DNS servers support forwarding requests to Umbrella and typically require only minimal configuration changes. Be sure to configure all internal DNS servers to forward requests. Also, by leveraging existing servers, no client configuration changes are typically required, and all internal DNS domains still operate as they did before the changes.

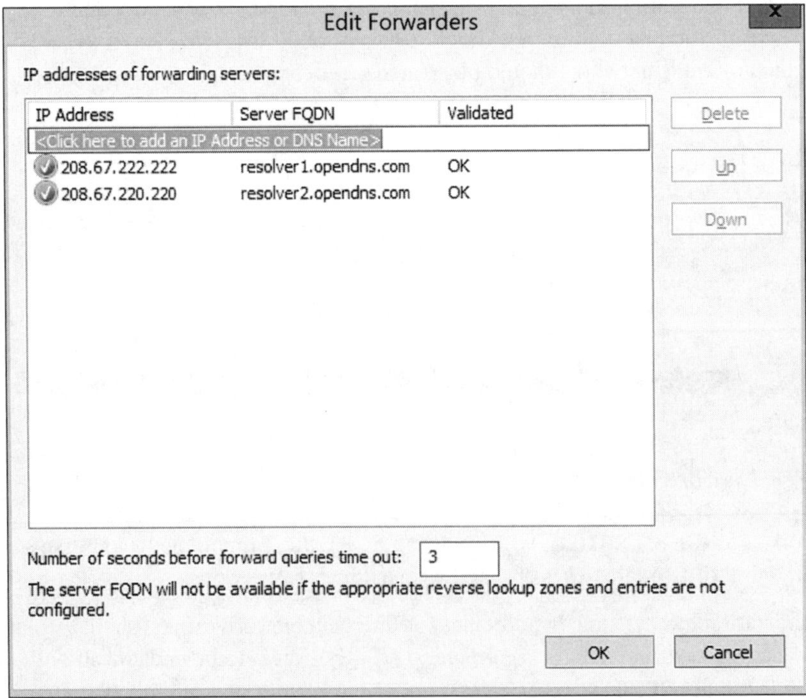

Figure 9-7 *Windows DNS Forwarders Configuration*

For smaller offices or offices without a local DNS server, the DHCP server, located on a dedicated DHCP server or network device, can be configured to assign Umbrella servers to clients. If static IP assignment is used at the location, the Umbrella servers can be manually configured on workstations and devices using DNS.

Another option for forwarding DNS is to perform network device integration. A network device is a physical piece of hardware that forwards DNS requests from client computers to Umbrella. Some of the major appliance types that support this type of integration are the Cisco Integrated Services Router (ISR), Meraki switches and access points, and Cisco wireless LAN controllers (WLCs). After registering a device with Umbrella, the device becomes an identity that can be managed and have policies set for it, with no need for any client device configuration at all. You accomplish this by providing authentication (either by entering the Cisco Umbrella username and password directly on the device or entering an API token obtained) and having a serial number added automatically or manually. To add a new network device, go to Identities > Network Devices and copy the API token. The token then can be used on the ISR or WLC, which will register to the appropriate Umbrella account, as shown in Figure 9-8.

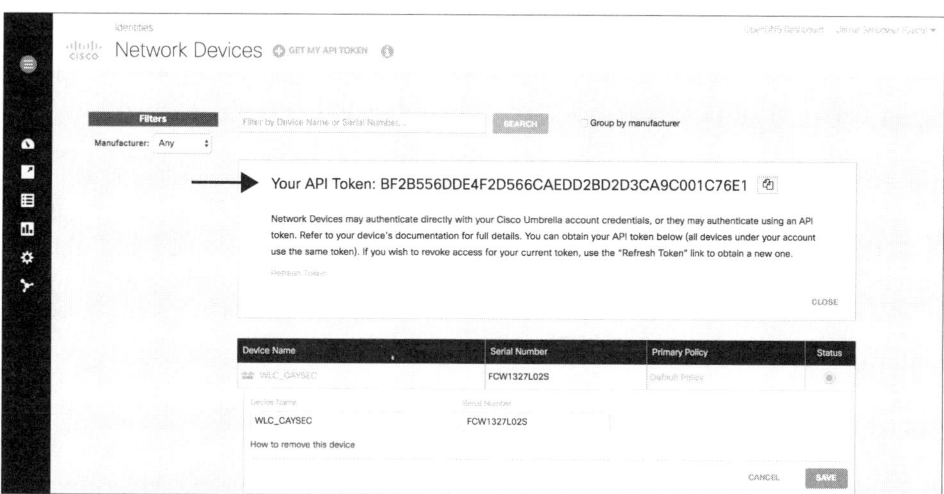

Figure 9-8 *Network Devices*

Umbrella uses an RFC-compliant mechanism for DNS, which allows the network device to securely embed VLAN identities within an RFC-compliant extension mechanism for DNS (EDNS) query that automatically is forwarded to Umbrella. For example, an administrator could define different policies for servers than for workstations in VLANs or for employees than for guests on wireless LANs. The administrator can do this even when it's the same network public IP or network device originating the query. With such configuration, reports provide more granularity by VLAN or WLAN.

Once forwarding of DNS is configured, browse to http://welcome.umbrella.com on any device in the network. If the DNS forwarding has been successfully pointed to the Cisco Umbrella servers, the green success page in Figure 9-9 appears.

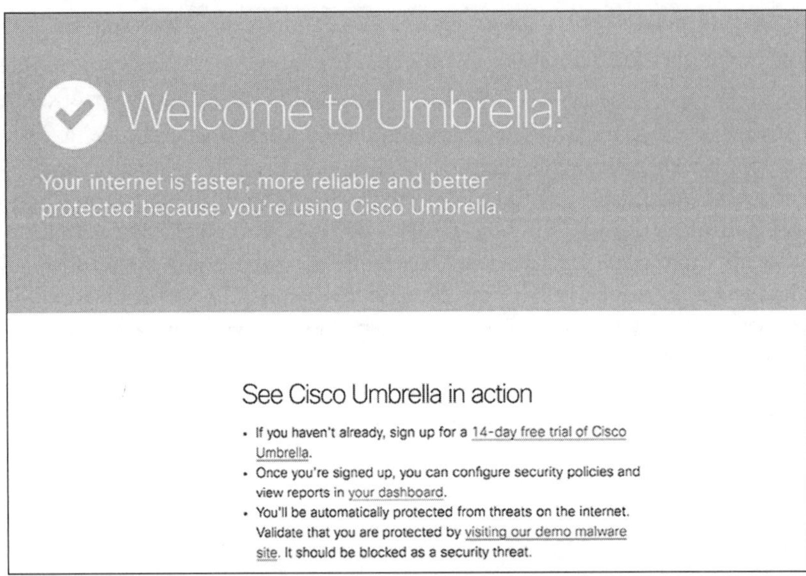

Figure 9-9 *Umbrella Configuration Success Page*

Umbrella Virtual Appliances

Umbrella Virtual Appliances (VAs) enable organizations to pinpoint devices within the network that are infected or being targeted by attacks. VAs are very lightweight virtual machines that are compatible with VMware ESX/ESXi and Windows Hyper-V hypervisors. When used as conditional DNS forwarders on an organization's network, VAs record the internal IP address information of DNS requests for use in reports, security enforcement, and content filtering policies in the Umbrella dashboard. In addition, VAs encrypt and authenticate DNS data for enhanced security.

A VA requires, at a minimum, 1 virtual CPU, 512 MB of RAM, and 7 GB of disk space. Each VA, when configured with the minimum specifications, is able to process millions of DNS requests per day, which equates to the ability to serve about 100,000 endpoints on average. VAs must be deployed in pairs for automatic updates to occur without downtime and to ensure redundancy at the DNS level.

A VA uses DNSCrypt between itself and the Umbrella resolvers. This means any information contained in the EDNS packets forwarded from the VA is encrypted by DNSCrypt and cannot be intercepted. This feature is enabled by default for the best protection.

Figure 9-10 illustrates a typical setup including an Umbrella VA, an internal DNS server, Umbrella public resolvers, an Internet gateway, and a laptop. In the example, the laptop would be configured to use the VA to resolve DNS. Any requests for the internal domain, securitydemo.net, would be forwarded by the VA to the internal DNS server. For all public domain requests from the laptop, the VA would insert the laptop's IP address (10.1.1.3), GUID, and organizational ID in an EDNS request and then encrypt and forward the request to the Umbrella cloud.

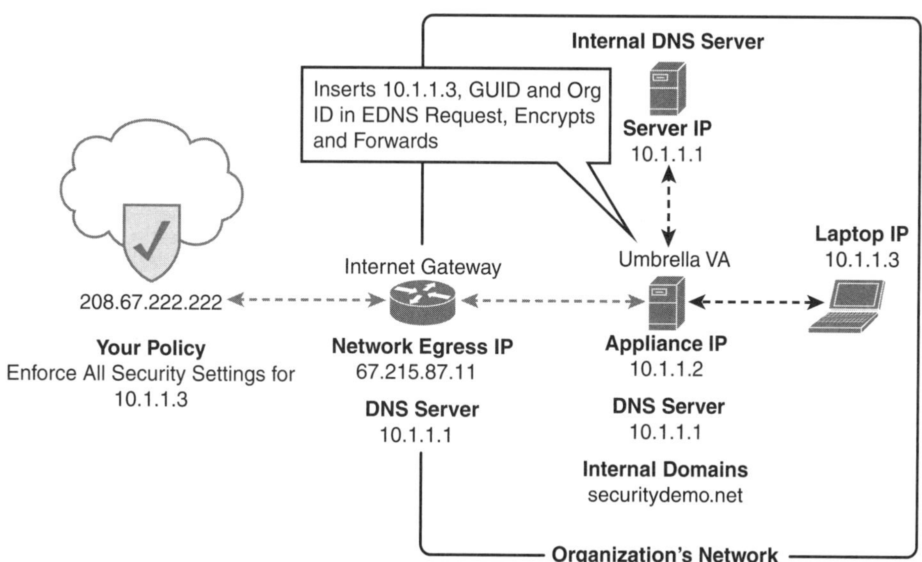

Figure 9-10 *Umbrella VA Example Topology*

To deploy a VA, go to Settings > Virtual Appliance > Sites and Active Directory and click Download Components (see Figure 9-11). You can open the Getting Started guide, next to the download, for step-by-step instructions for the preferred platform.

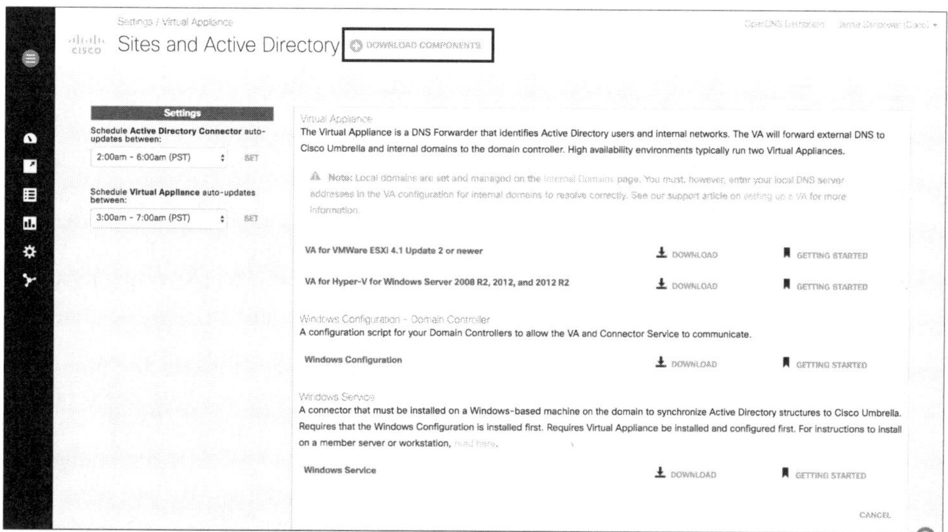

Figure 9-11 *Umbrella Virtual Appliance Download*

After installing a VA on ESX or Hyper-V, console into the VA through the hypervisor and configure the name, IP address, netmask, and gateway. If the organization has local DNS, then the local DNS servers should be configured to allow forwarding of local domain queries from the VA to the local DNS server. Make sure to save after making configuration changes. Figure 9-12 shows the console configuration of the VA.

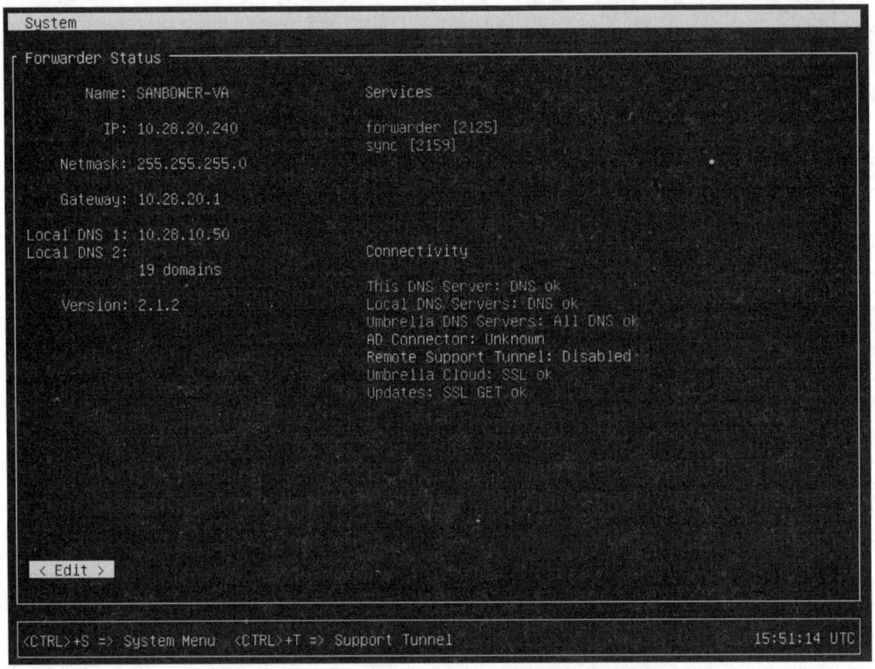

```
System
Forwarder Status

      Name: SANBOWER-VA              Services

        IP: 10.28.20.240             forwarder [2125]
                                     sync [2159]
   Netmask: 255.255.255.0

   Gateway: 10.28.20.1

Local DNS 1: 10.28.10.50
Local DNS 2:                         Connectivity
            19 domains
                                     This DNS Server: DNS ok
   Version: 2.1.2                    Local DNS Servers: DNS ok
                                     Umbrella DNS Servers: All DNS ok
                                     AD Connector: Unknown
                                     Remote Support Tunnel: Disabled
                                     Umbrella Cloud: SSL ok
                                     Updates: SSL GET ok

< Edit >

<CTRL>+S => System Menu  <CTRL>+T => Support Tunnel          15:51:14 UTC
```

Figure 9-12 *Umbrella Virtual Appliance Console Configuration*

After console configuration, it's normal for tests to fail for the first 60 seconds, but after that, the console should output sync messages indicating that the VA and the Umbrella service are communicating. Assuming that the sync completes without errors, the VA appears at Settings > Virtual Appliance > Sites and Active Directory with the name configured in the VA console configuration and a green/healthy status icon. Until a second VA is deployed, it is common to see the error message "This VA is not redundant within its site (2+ VA required per site)."

When the VAs receive queries that match domains or subdomains of a local DNS zone, the VA forwards those queries to the local DNS server for resolution instead of to Umbrella's public DNS resolvers. This is accomplished by defining local domain names in the Umbrella dashboard. To configure an internal domain, navigate to Settings > Internal Domains and click the + to add a new internal domain, as shown in Figure 9-13. Any DNS queries received by the VAs that match a domain on the internal domains list, or any subdomain thereof, will be forwarded to the local DNS server.

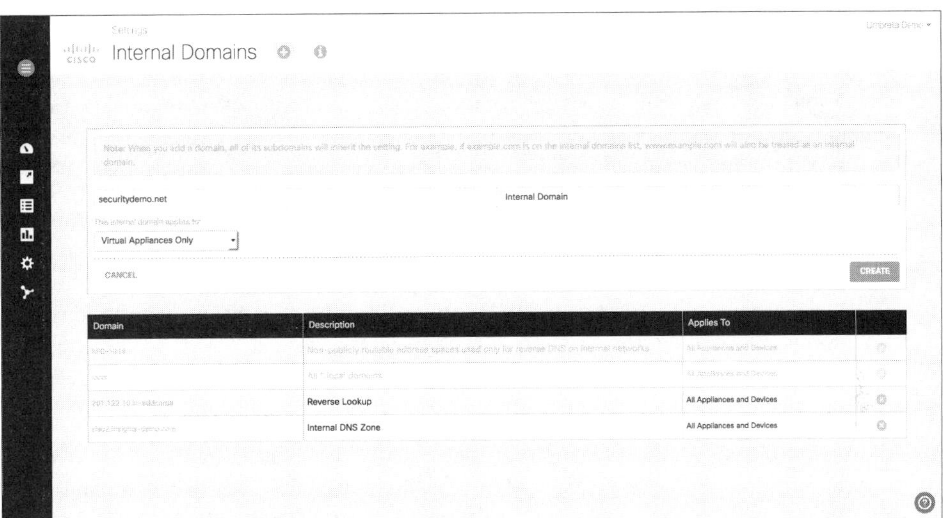

Figure 9-13 *Internal Domain Configuration*

To leverage the internal IP addresses the VA sends to Umbrella for customization of policies, an internal network needs to be configured to map single or multiple IP addresses assigned to endpoints. This configuration allows organizations to use a source IP address mapped to a policy (for example, 192.168.28.0/24 contains IoT devices and needs to have a very stringent security and content filtering policy applied). To add a new internal network, go to Identities > Internal Networks (see Figure 9-14).

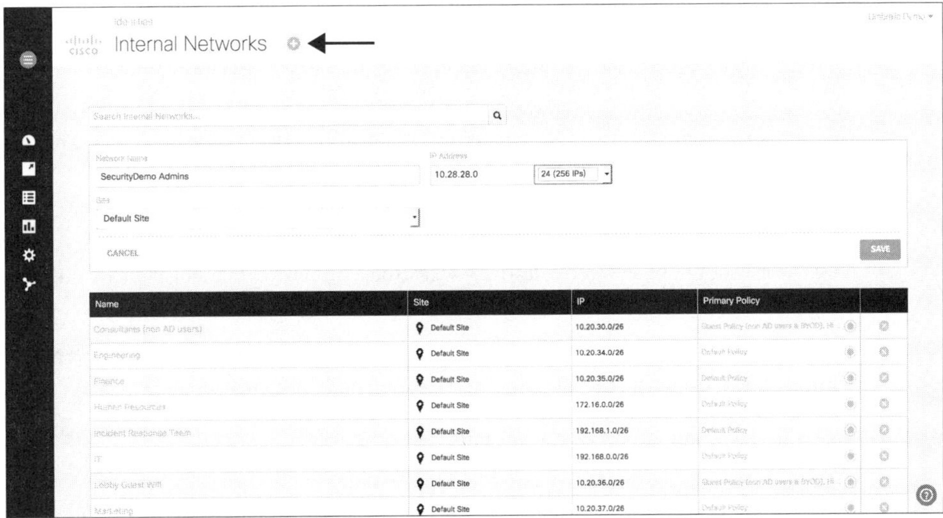

Figure 9-14 *Internal Network Configuration*

Active Directory

For even more granularity, Umbrella can be integrated with Active Directory (AD). AD integration provides organizations the ability to control and gain visibility per AD user, computer, or group. Extended control is provided through the ability to use AD information instead of internal subnets and IP addresses in Umbrella policy configuration. VAs are required for Active Directory integration, which expands on the functionality of the VAs.

AD Connector is deployed on an AD domain controller or a separate Windows server domain member. AD Connector is read-only software and syncs only the user and computer group memberships to the Umbrella cloud service. When a user authenticates, the connector also informs the VA about the AD user, AD computer, and internal IP address of the device from which the user authenticated. When devices make DNS requests, the VA, which can see its internal IP address, can now insert the AD user and computer name to the requests.

AD Connector requires Windows Server 2008 or 2008 R2, 2012 or 2012 R2, or 2016 with the latest service packs and 100 MB of free hard disk drive space. It also requires .NET Framework 3.5, 4.0, or 4.5. If a local antivirus application is running, the processes OpenDNSAuditClient.exe and OpenDNSAuditService.exe should be whitelisted.

Note Read Only Domain Controllers (RODCs) should not have the script run on them or have AD Connector installed. RODCs can be present in a domain and report as identities, but they should not be used for Active Directory integration and are not supported.

Only a single domain environment is supported. Child domains or trusts are currently not supported. Multidomain environments require a multi-dashboard experience, and support should be engaged in order for this to be configured.

For AD Connector to work properly, a new service user should be added to Active Directory with the following settings:

- The logon name (also known as the sAMAccountName) should be set to OpenDNS_Connector.
- The Password Never Expires box should be checked.
- A password should be entered without backslashes, quotation marks (single or double), greater-than or less-than "chevron" bracket characters (<, >), or colon characters.
- Make sure the OpenDNS_Connector user is a member of the following groups and, if not, add the missing ones:
  - Event Log Readers
  - Distributed COM Users
  - Enterprise Read-Only Domain Controllers

Each Active Directory domain controller needs to perform a one-time registration with the Cisco Umbrella API. To get started, run the Windows Configuration script on all of the domain controllers (DCs) at each site on the domain (excluding RODCs and DCs on other domains), which prepares them to communicate with AD Connector. Go to Settings > Virtual Appliance > Sites and Active Directory, select Download Components, and download the Windows configuration script to all AD controllers. Figure 9-15 shows the download page for the configuration script and the connector.

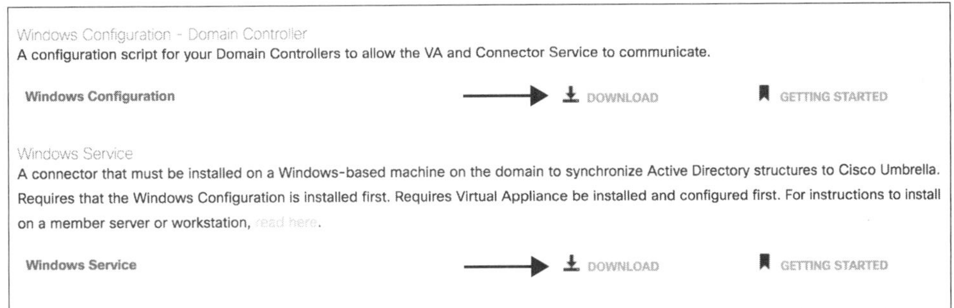

Figure 9-15 *AD Connector and Configuration Script*

As an administrator, run an elevated command prompt and enter **cscript** ***filename***, where ***filename*** is the name of the configuration script you downloaded. The script displays your current configuration and offers to auto-configure the domain controller for operation. If the auto-configure steps are successful, the script registers the domain controller with the Umbrella dashboard. Figure 9-16 illustrates the script being run on a domain controller and the resulting output.

```
Administrator: Command Prompt

c:\>cscript OpenDNS-WindowsConfigurationScript-20161118.wsf
Microsoft (R) Windows Script Host Version 5.8
Copyright (C) Microsoft Corporation. All rights reserved.

This is a Windows Server 2012 forest.
Testing configuration...

***********************************************
Local Platform Configuration

Local OS: Windows Server 2012
Functional Level: Server 2012 Forest
Local IP: 10.28.10.50
Domain:    SANBOWER.NET (SANBOWER)
Label:     AD
Firewall Enabled: False

Remote Admin Enabled: False
AD User Exists: True
WMI Permissions Set: False
RDC Permissions Set: False

Audit Policy Set: True
Manage Event Log Policy Set: False

Event Log Readers MemberOf: True
Distributed COM MemberOf: True
***********************************************

Your platform is supported for auto-configure.
Do you want us to auto configure this Domain Controller (y or n)? y

Configuring system...
Setting Remote Admin permissions on firewall...
Setting WMI permissions...
Setting RDC permissions...
Auto Config complete in full!
Registering Domain Controller in cloud...
Register Success!
Updating DC status in cloud...
Update success!

c:\>_
```

Figure 9-16 *Umbrella AD Configuration Script*

When you return to the dashboard, you see the hostname of the AD server you just ran the script on in the run state on the Active Directory Configuration page. When you click on the server, you get the message "This Domain Controller has never connected to a Connector." Repeat the preceding steps to prepare additional domain controllers in your single-domain environment to successfully communicate with AD Connector.

AD Connector can be installed on a domain controller or member server. As an administrator, extract the contents of the .zip file downloaded from the Umbrella cloud to a folder. Navigate to the extracted folder and run setup.msi. Enter the password configured for the OpenDNS_Connector user that was previously created. Follow the setup wizard prompts. When finished, click Close.

When you return to the dashboard, the hostname of the domain controller or other Windows machine that AD Connector was installed on is displayed on the Settings > Sites and Active Directory configuration page.

The Umbrella security cloud automatically configures and connects the VAs to the domain controllers via the connectors for each configured site, and the status of all of the organizations' VAs, AD servers, and connectors should change from Inactive to Active. Figure 9-17 shows the updated Sites and Active Directory page with AD Connector and servers.

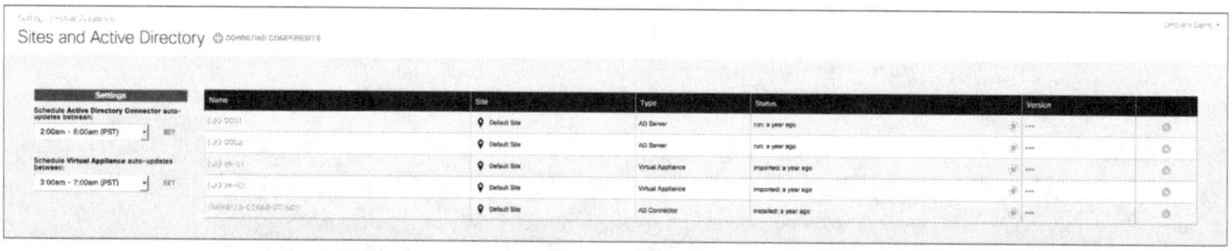

Figure 9-17 *AD Connector and Servers*

The domain controllers or other Windows machines should automatically synchronize user and computer group memberships, and any subsequent changes, with Umbrella via AD Connector. Organizations can verify that this has occurred successfully by clicking **+** to add a new policy and confirming that the groups are present.

To use the AD information about users, groups, or computers in policies, navigate to Configuration > Policies and click **+** to add a new policy. Under the selection of identities, AD groups, AD users, and AD computers should be listed along with the number of obtained objects from AD Connector. If AD Groups is selected, all the AD groups in the domain, including those nested within other groups, are shown in the identity picker of the policy wizard. Figure 9-18 shows the list of AD groups taken from AD Connector and includes selections for computers, users, and a group. Typically, policies are based on groups only for simplicity reasons and to reduce the number of policies, but both computers and users are useful for creating exception or override policies.

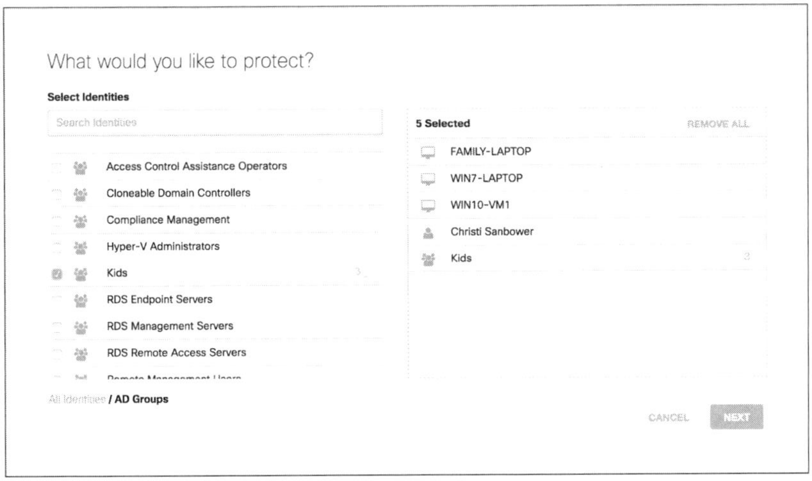

What would you like to protect?

Select Identities

Search Identities	5 Selected
Access Control Assistance Operators	FAMILY-LAPTOP
Cloneable Domain Controllers	WIN7-LAPTOP
Compliance Management	WIN10-VM1
Hyper-V Administrators	Christi Sanbower
Kids	Kids
RDS Endpoint Servers	
RDS Management Servers	
RDS Remote Access Servers	

All Identities / AD Groups

CANCEL NEXT

Figure 9-18 *Policy Using AD Computers, Users, and Group*

More information on policy configuration can be found in the "Policies" section, later in this chapter.

Roaming Devices

Umbrella Roaming extends DNS security and policy protection to employees and devices when they are disconnected from the corporate network or VPN. If an organization already uses Cisco AnyConnect for VPN connectivity, it can use a built-in integration to enable roaming security. Otherwise, it can use a lightweight, standalone client. With Umbrella Roaming, organizations gain always-on security without the hassle of an always-on VPN.

The Roaming client or AnyConnect Umbrella Roaming Security module provides per-computer granularity for both reporting and policy enforcement, extending protection to computers both on and off network. It is common to deploy the Roaming client on both laptops and desktops. The lightweight client sends DNS requests with embedded identity information directly to Cisco Umbrella on any network and gracefully handles local DNS requests. The DNS queries sent through the Roaming client are encrypted, authenticated, and subjected to security and content filtering, as dictated by the configured policy.

The Umbrella Roaming client binds to 127.0.0.1:53 (localhost) and sets itself as the exclusive DNS server on every network connection on a computer, ensuring that all DNS requests are directed to the closest Umbrella data center.

The following are the supported operating systems for Roaming clients:

- Umbrella Roaming client:
  - Windows 10 with .NET 4.5
  - Windows 8 (and 8.1) (64-bit) with .NET 4.5
  - Windows 7 (64-bit/32-bit) with .NET 3.5
  - Mac OS X 10.9 or newer
- AnyConnect Umbrella Roaming Security module:
  - Windows 7 (or later) x86 (32-bit) and x64 (64-bit) operating system
  - Mac OS X 10.9 (or later) operating system

To install the Roaming client or AnyConnect Umbrella Roaming Security module, go to Identities > Roaming Computers and click the **+** icon. You can now choose downloads and see step-by-step installation instructions (see Figure 9-19).

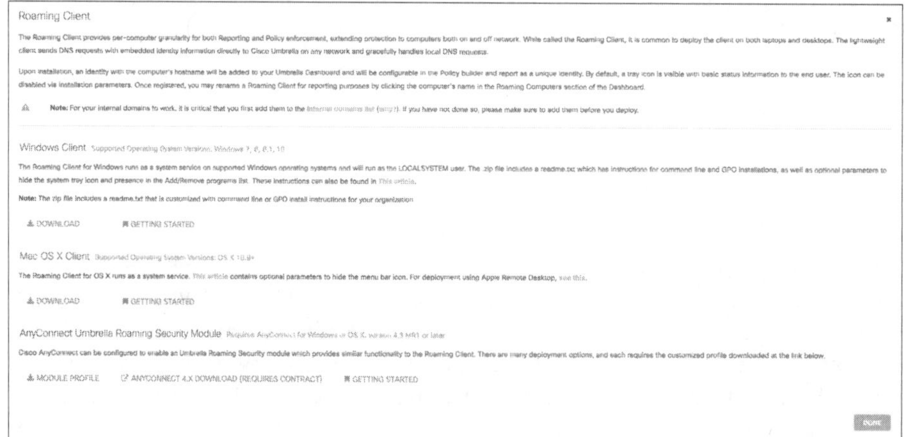

Figure 9-19 *Roaming Client Download and Installation*

The AnyConnect module profile, OrgInfo.json, is also available on the page shown in Figure 9-19. It associates each deployment with the corresponding service, and the corresponding protection features are enabled automatically.

After installation, an identity with the computer's hostname is added to the Umbrella cloud and configurable in the policy builder and report as a unique identity. To see a list of roaming computers, navigate to Identities > Roaming Computers (see Figure 9-20).

Figure 9-20 *Roaming Computers*

When using the Umbrella Roaming client, all DNS lookups are sent directly from the computer to Umbrella global network resolvers. However, in order to ensure that the Umbrella Roaming client directs internal DNS requests to an internal DNS server for resolution, local domain names must be added to the Internal Domains section, as discussed earlier in this chapter.

The Umbrella Roaming client syncs with the API every 10 minutes to check for new internal domains. This is a critical part of the setup process, and the list should be populated before an organization deploys the Umbrella Roaming client or the AnyConnect module.

Another benefit of using the Roaming client is IP-layer enforcement. At times malware authors use an IP address instead of a fully qualified domain name to host their malware; in such cases, IP-layer enforcement can protect users. IP-layer enforcement applies only to roaming computers with the Umbrella Roaming client installed on Windows or Mac and the Umbrella Roaming Security module for AnyConnect on Windows only. However, the IP-layer enforcement feature continues to be active and take effect when the Umbrella Roaming client is behind a VA on the corporate network.

The Roaming client retrieves a list of suspicious IP addresses from the Umbrella cloud and automatically checks the Umbrella API again for any new IP addresses every five minutes. Updates in the back end are provided every 45 minutes at a minimum, but the Umbrella Roaming client checks every 5 minutes to stay as up-to-date as possible and in case there are updates in the interim.

The information is downloaded to the local client and loaded into memory when the Umbrella Roaming client is running. The information about which IP addresses are being routed is not kept on disk but only in memory.

You configure IP-layer enforcement under Advanced Settings when creating or modifying a policy (see Figure 9-21).

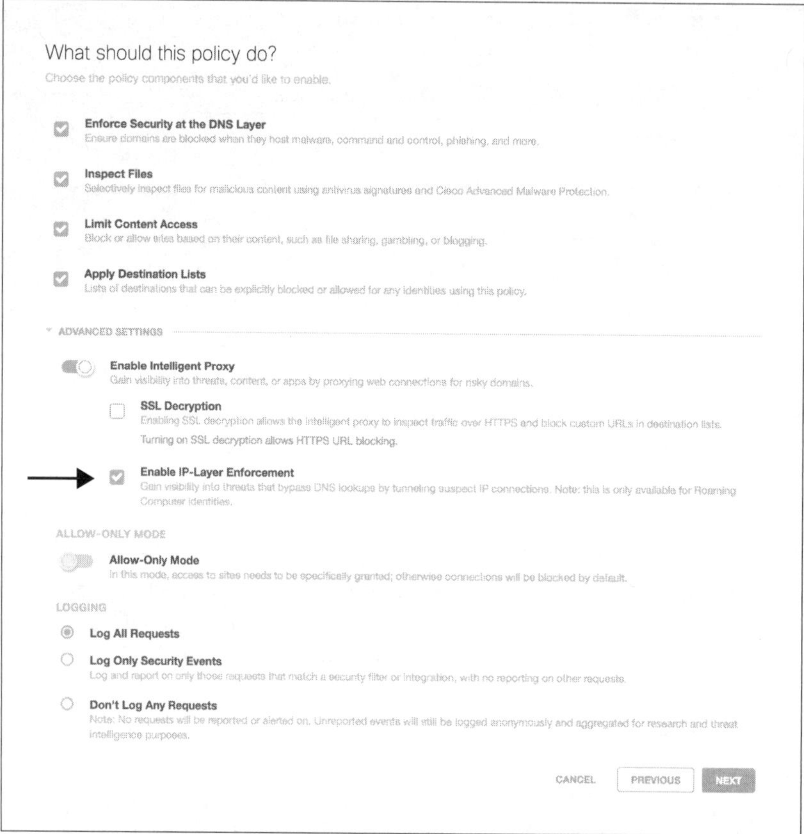

Figure 9-21 *IP-Layer Enforcement*

Note The Umbrella Roaming Security module and the Umbrella Roaming client are incompatible and should not be used/installed on the same machine.

Cisco Security Connector

Cisco Security Connector (CSC) is a solution that was developed in conjunction with Apple and provides protection to users on enterprise-owned Apple iOS devices in supervised mode. The Umbrella connector provides DNS-layer enforcement with customizable URL blocking through the intelligent proxy. This allows iOS to seamlessly integrate with Umbrella on or off the network. The CSC also provides Clarity, an AMP for Endpoints integration that provides metadata about all URLs and IP addresses connected to by all apps on supervised iOS endpoints.

The first release of CSC works seamlessly with the Meraki Systems Manager MDM, and installation/configuration is done primarily through Meraki. After installation, the CSC can show the status of the Umbrella integration (see Figure 9-22).

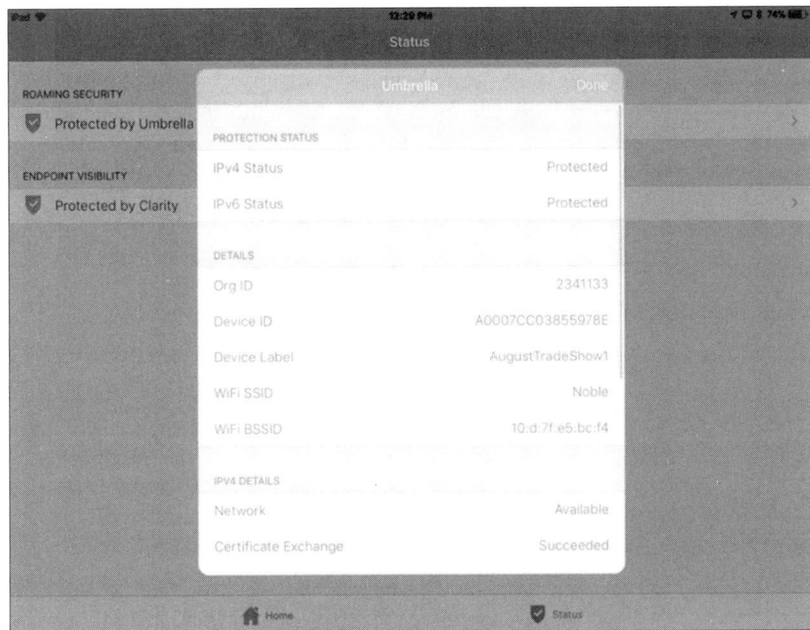

Figure 9-22 *Cisco Security Connector Umbrella Status*

In the Umbrella dashboard, admins can run reports and apply policies based on mobile device identities. All iOS devices connected to Umbrella can be viewed by navigating to Identities > Mobile Devices (see Figure 9-23).

Figure 9-23 *Mobile Devices*

Policies

Policies control the level of protection and logging, including which types of sites should be blocked and which additional levels of security, such as the Umbrella intelligent proxy, are enabled. The policy editor is designed to provide a step-by-step process to help answer the question "What do you want this policy to do?"

An organization's requirements and objectives for a deployment typically determine how simple or advanced the policy must be. Some organizations are able to simply utilize the default policy, which applies to all identities when no other policy above it covers an identity. In other words, the Umbrella default policy is a catch-all to ensure that all identities in an organization receive a baseline level of protection. The default policy can be modified to ensure that the appropriate settings around security, content filtering, block lists, file inspection, and block page are configured. Figure 9-24 shows the configuration of a default policy on the Policies > Policy List page.

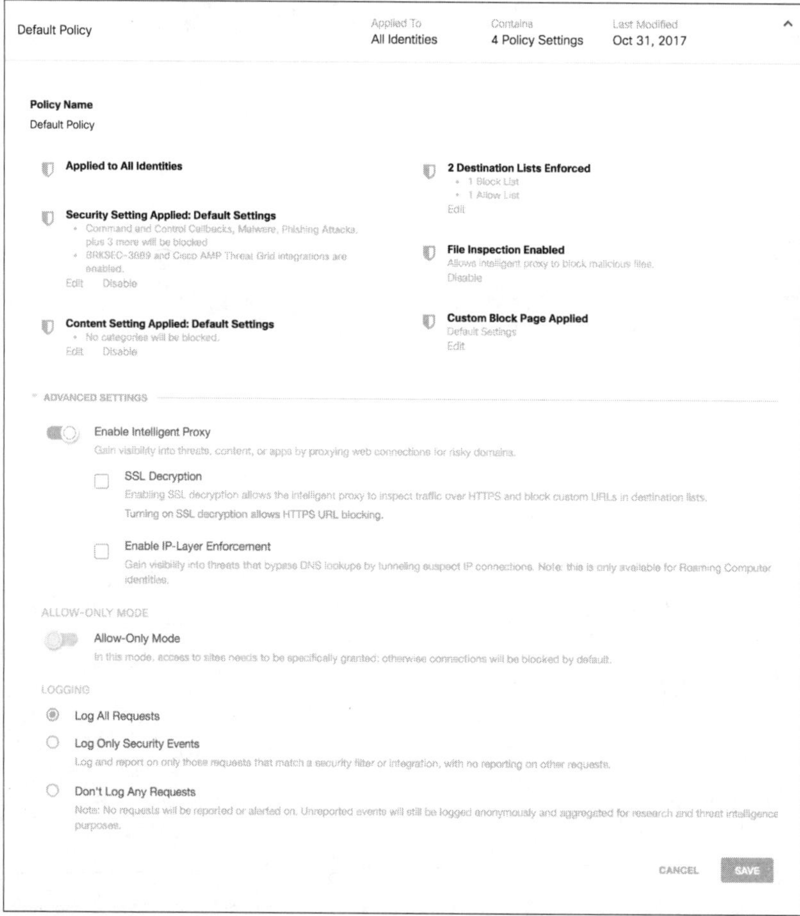

Figure 9-24 *Modifying the Default Umbrella Policy*

Policies are evaluated from the top to the bottom of the list. This means any specific rules should be placed at the top of the list to ensure that the appropriate policy is applied. For example, Figure 9-25 shows a list of nine policies. If a user is a part of marketing and an executive, the Marketing Policy applies to all traffic because it is the third rule evaluated and is applied prior to the Executive Policy.

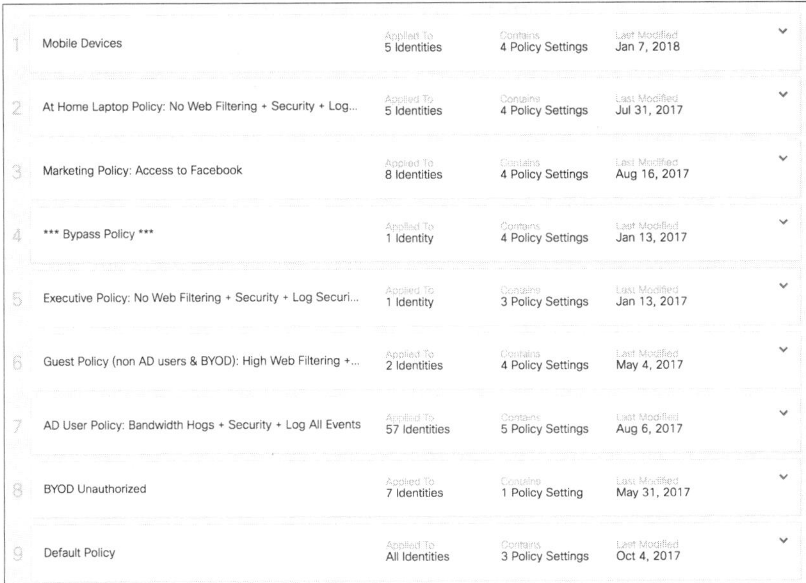

Figure 9-25 *Multiple Policies*

To add a new policy, click the **+** on the Policies > Policy List page. The Policy Wizard then walks you through the configuration steps required to create a new policy:

Step 1. On the What Would You Like to Protect? page, select the identities that should be protected with the policy. Identities, as discussed earlier in this chapter, include everything from networks to AD users and groups. Figure 9-26 shows a single user selected for protection.

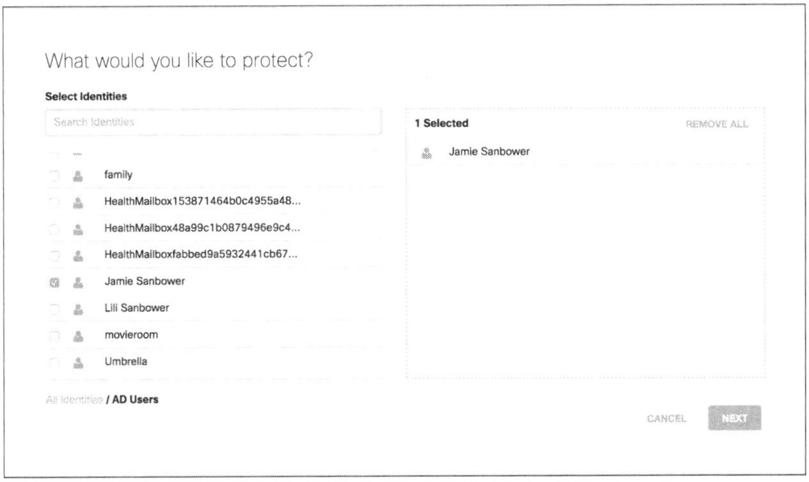

Figure 9-26 *Policy Wizard What Would You Like to Protect? Page*

> **Note** Top-level groups like All Networks and All Roaming Computers are special because they dynamically inherit new identities. This means that if you create a policy All Roaming Computers and then later provision a number of new mobile devices, they automatically have that policy applied without your having to do anything.

Step 2. On the What Should This Policy Do? page, select the types of inspections that should be applied, along with any advanced settings related to enabling the intelligent proxy and IP-layer enforcement (see Figure 9-27). Also configure logging to either log all events, log only security events, or log no events.

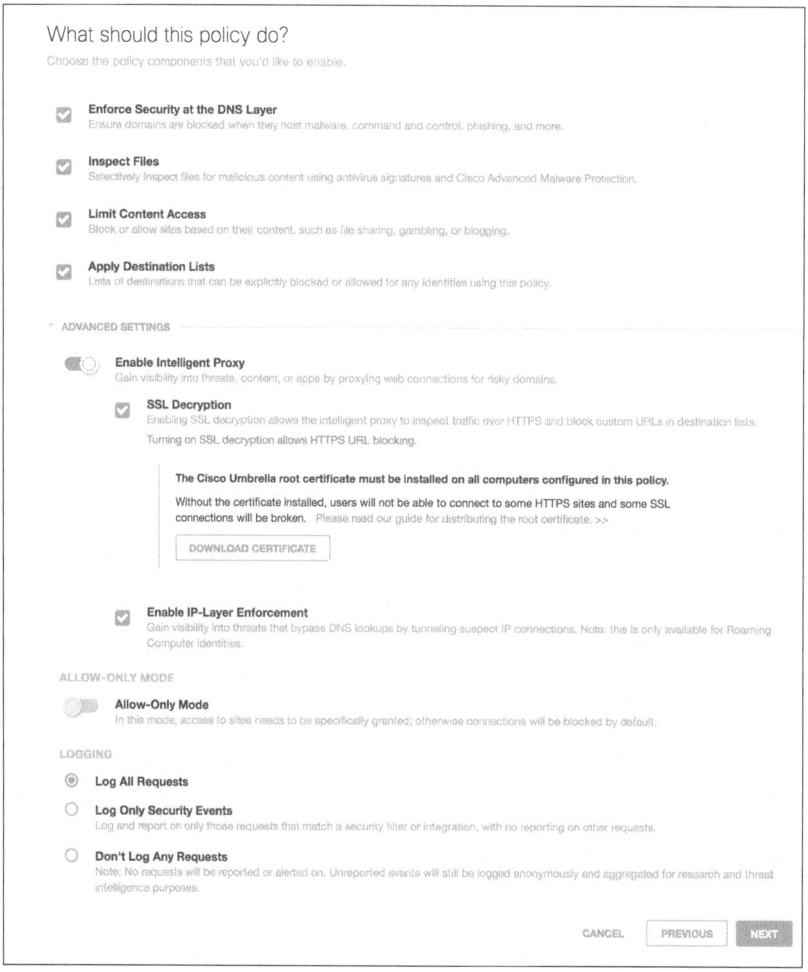

Figure 9-27 *Policy Wizard What Should This Policy Do? Page*

Step 3. The Security Settings page allows you to select a security settings policy component, which can be edited inline. This page includes the categories to block and integration that should be used (see Figure 9-28).

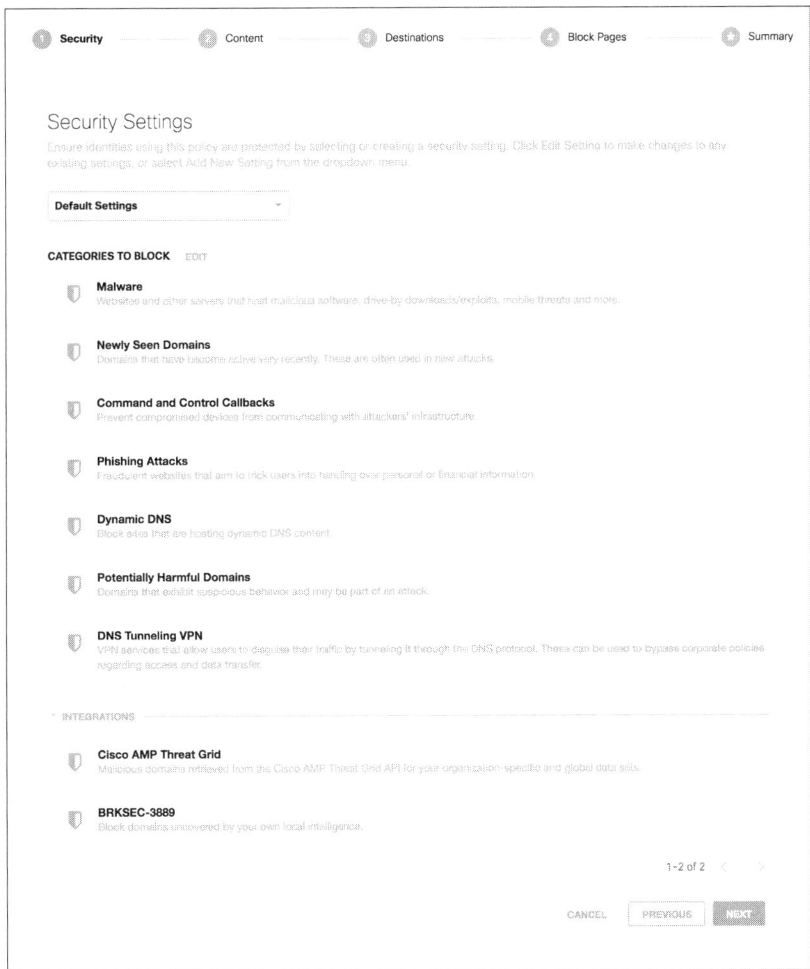

Figure 9-28 *Policy Wizard Security Settings page*

Step 4. On the Limit Content Access page, Umbrella provides three default content access settings—High, Moderate, and Low—that can be selected, or a custom grouping of categories can be used. Figure 9-29 illustrates the categories that are blocked when High is selected.

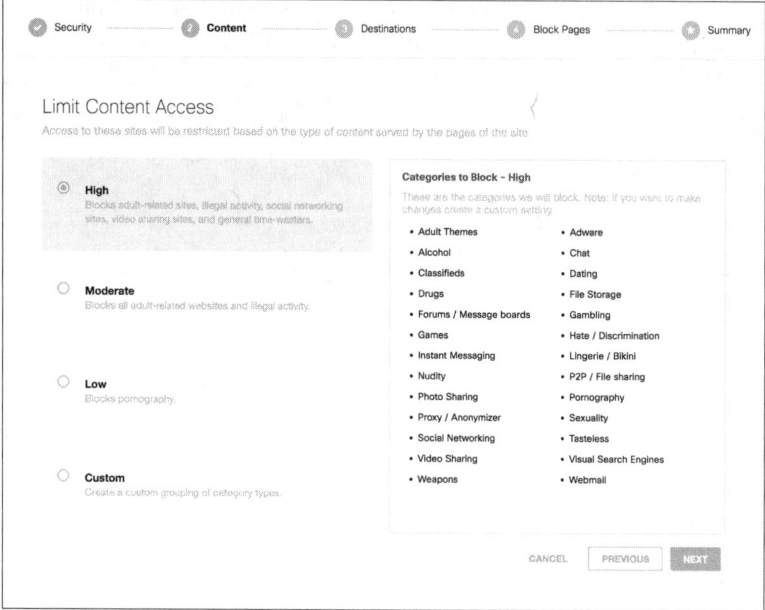

Figure 9-29 *Policy Wizard Limit Content Access Page*

Step 5. Specify the appropriate settings on the Apply Destination Lists page. In order to ensure that organizations have the ability to override content and security filtering, Umbrella provides destination lists, which can be configured to contain domains that should be blocked or allowed. By default, there is a global allow and block list, but custom lists can be added. Figure 9-30 shows how the policy wizard automatically allows the global allow list and blocks the global block list.

Figure 9-30 *Policy Wizard Apply Destination Lists Page*

Step 6. On the Set Block Page Settings page, customize the block page appearance and set bypass options. Bypass options allows granting of special permission to circumvent filtering settings. You can assign individual users, such as your IT managers, the ability to access specific filtering categories, such as social networking, or individual domains that are normally blocked on the network. Bypass privileges can be granted persistently on a per-user basis or through use of a bypass code, which grants access for timeframes ranging from 1 hour to 10 years. Figure 9-31 shows the Set Block Page Settings page.

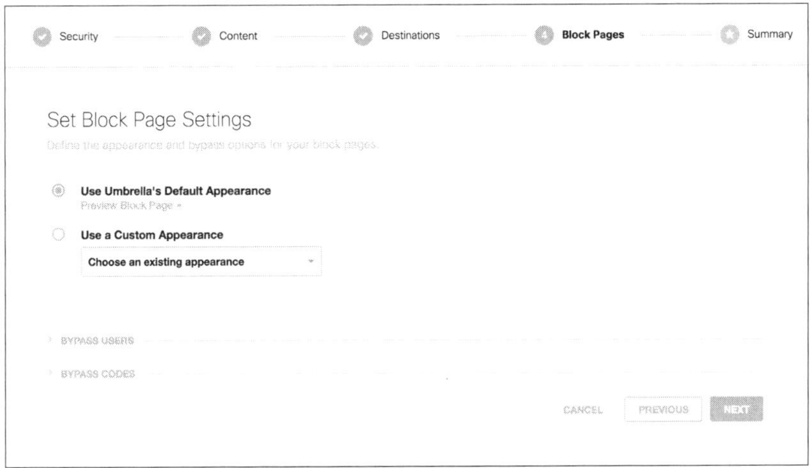

Figure 9-31 *Policy Wizard Set Block Page Settings Page*

Step 7. Give the new policy a name and click Save.

Umbrella allows administrators to add many different policies, depending on use cases and requirements. However, more policies leads to more difficult troubleshooting and more difficulty determining which policy was applied. The Policy Tester page, located at the Policies > Policy List page, enables you to determine whether a particular identity is blocked or allowed to go to a particular domain (see Figure 9-32). The policy tester can test the end state across all the policies the organization has configured to ensure that policies are working as desired.

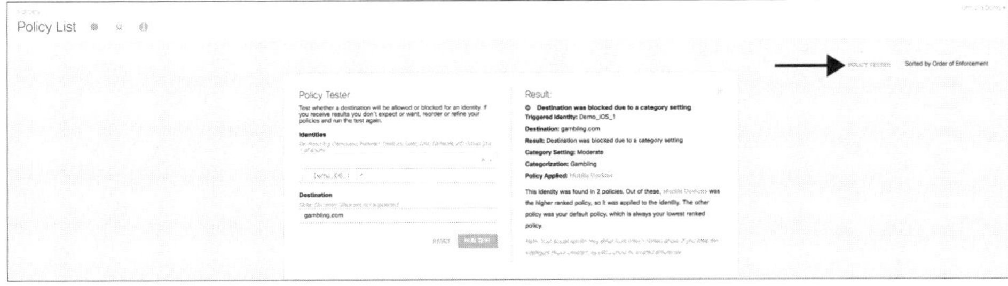

Figure 9-32 *Policy Tester*

Reporting

Umbrella's reports allow for better insights into request activity and blocked activity, as well as determining which identities are generating requests that are being blocked. Reports help build actionable intelligence in addressing security threats, including changes in trends over time.

One of the most popular reports is the activity search report, found under Reporting > Core Reports > Activity Search. This report shows all activity from the identities in the environment over a selected time period. Figure 9-33 shows how the report can be filtered by identity name, destination, source IP, response, content category, and security category.

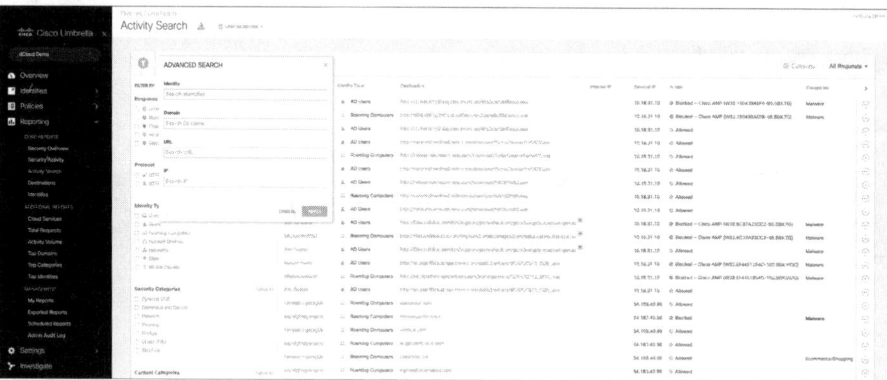

Figure 9-33 *Activity Search*

You can export any report to CSV format by selecting the download link on the page (highlighted in Figure 9-33).

Reports can also be scheduled. Go to Reporting > Scheduled Reports and click the **+** icon. The Scheduled Reports page opens, listing the reports that can be scheduled, as shown in Figure 9-34.

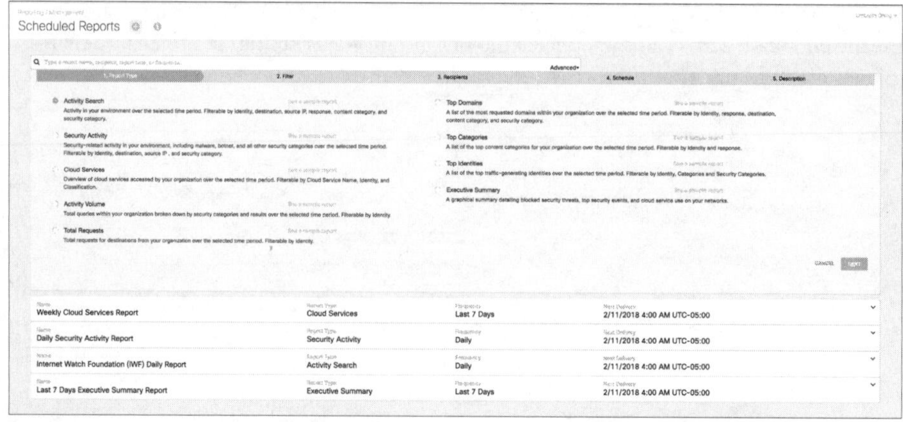

Figure 9-34 *Scheduled Reports*

Cisco Investigate

Many security products provide visibility into what's happening on an enterprise network. Cisco Investigate provides organizations access to global intelligence that can be used to enrich security data and events or help with incident response. Investigate provides the most complete view of an attacker's infrastructure and enables security teams to discover malicious domains, IP addresses, and file hashes and even predict emergent threats. Investigate provides access to this intelligence via a web console or an application programming interface (API). With the integration of Cisco's AMP Threat Grid data in Investigate, intelligence about an attacker's infrastructure can be complimented by AMP Threat Grid's intelligence about malware files, providing a complete view of the infrastructure used in an attack. Figure 9-35 illustrates a query of ciscopress.com using Investigate. You can use Investigate, if your Umbrella license allows, by going to https://investigate.umbrella.com.

Figure 9-35 *Umbrella Investigate*

Investigate provides a single, correlated source of intelligence and adds the security context needed to help organizations uncover and predict attacks. Investigate provides the following features:

- **Passive DNS Database:** This feature provides historical DNS data.
- **WHOIS Record Data:** This feature allows you to see domain ownership and uncover malicious domains registered with the same contact information.
- **Malware File Analysis:** This feature provides behavioral indicators and network connections of malware samples with data from Cisco AMP Threat Grid.
- **Autonomous System Number (ASN) Attribution:** This feature provides IP-to-ASN mappings.
- **IP Geolocation:** This feature allows you to see in which country an IP address is located.

- **Domain and IP Reputation Scores:** This feature allows you to leverage Investigate's risk scoring across a number of domain attributes to assess suspicious domains.
- **Domain Co-Occurrences:** This feature returns a list of domain names that were looked up around the same time as the domain being checked. The score next to the domain name in a co-occurrence is a measurement of requests from client IPs for these related domains. The co-occurrences are for the previous seven days and are shown whether the co-occurrence is suspicious or not.
- **Anomaly Detection:** This feature allows you to detect fast flux domains and domains created by domain generation algorithms. This score is generated based on the likeliness of the domain name being generated by an algorithm rather than a human. This score ranges from –100 (suspicious) to 0 (benign).
- **DNS Request Patterns and Geo Distribution of Those Requests:** This feature allows you to see suspicious spikes in global DNS requests to a specific domain.

Investigate helps an administrator really start to understand the threat associated with a malicious domain. For example, if internetbadguys.com is queried (see Figure 9-36), Investigate immediately shows that the domain is on the block list and that the domain has very low TTLs. Integration with AMP Threat Grid (see Figure 9-37) also provides administrators information that helps them determine which malware file samples have been seen on the domain in question. This information could then be used to quickly start an incident process and search for potential indicators based on the files that could have been downloaded.

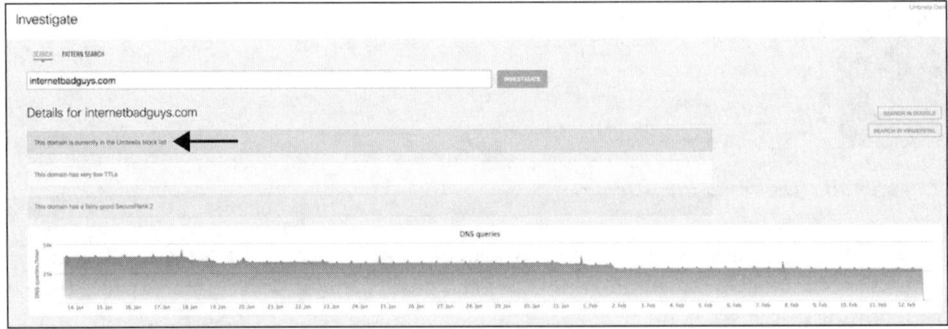

Figure 9-36 *Umbrella Investigate*

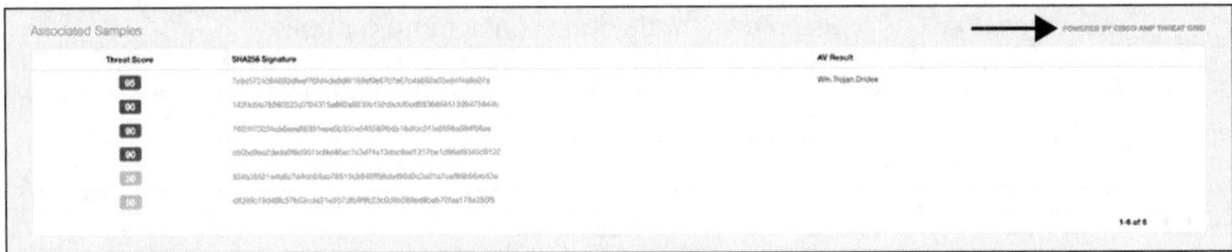

Figure 9-37 *Investigate/AMP Threat Grid Integration*

Summary

In this chapter, you have learned about Cisco Umbrella and how it can be the first line of defense in a security architecture. You examined how Umbrella uses identities to map IP addresses, users, computers, and groups to both policy and reporting. You found out all the ways to use customized policies for content filtering and security services. You also looked at how to turn policies into actionable intelligence with reporting and dashboards. Finally, you learned that Cisco Investigate can provide insights into attribution and statistics of IP addresses, domain names, and ASNs.

References

"Common DNS Request Types," https://support.umbrella.com/hc/en-us/articles/232252848-Common-DNS-Request-Types

"What Is the Difference Between Authoritative and Recursive DNS Nameservers?" https://umbrella.cisco.com/blog/2014/07/16/difference-authoritative-recursive-dns-nameservers/

"Fast Flux," https://en.wikipedia.org/wiki/Fast_flux

"Welcome to Cisco Umbrella," https://docs.umbrella.com/product/umbrella/

Chapter 10

Protecting Against Advanced Malware

This chapter provides details about the Cisco Advanced Malware Protection (AMP) solution, the AMP architecture, cloud types, and AMP connectors. This chapter dives into both public and private cloud architectures, comparing and contrasting their designs. You will learn how the different AMP connectors fit into a security architecture and how the connectors are designed to work, and you will also learn about the capabilities of each connector.

This chapter also focuses on configuration of AMP policies for the different connector types, as there are distinct differences in the connectors, based on the operating system or platform a connector is being used on.

Malware is a computer program or application designed to perform nefarious activities. There is no system in the world that is truly impervious to malware because it is custom-built software designed to operate on the target system. If someone has enough permissions to install the malicious software on a system, and that software is permitted to execute, then the system is not impervious.

Surely there are variations in the levels of risk associated with a system's susceptibility to malware, and there are varying degrees of "bad." Which is worse: software designed to send your list of contacts out to a server on the Internet or software designed to encrypt all the contents on a computer's hard drive and not decrypt it without a ransom payment for those decryption keys? Both are examples of real malware.

Introduction to Advanced Malware Protection (AMP)

Throughout this book, you have learned about the different Cisco next-generation security products and technologies. Your network's security technologies and processes should not only focus on detection but also should provide the ability to mitigate the impact after a successful attack. An organization must maintain visibility and control across the extended network during the full attack continuum: before the attack takes place, during an active attack, and after an attacker starts to damage systems or steal information.

AMP can enable malware detection, blocking, continuous analysis, and retrospective alerting with the following features:

- **File reputation:** AMP analyzes files inline and blocks or applies policies.
- **File sandboxing:** AMP analyzes unknown files to understand true file behavior.
- **File retrospection:** AMP continues to analyze files for changing threat levels.

There are major architectural benefits to using an AMP solution that leverages a cloud infrastructure for the heavy lifting.

The architecture of AMP can be broken down into three main components: the AMP cloud, AMP client connectors, and intelligence sources. AMP client connectors include AMP for Networks, AMP for Endpoints, AMP for content security appliances, and AMP for Meraki.

Figure 10-1 illustrates the cloud architecture, which receives intelligence from many sources, and a variety of client connectors.

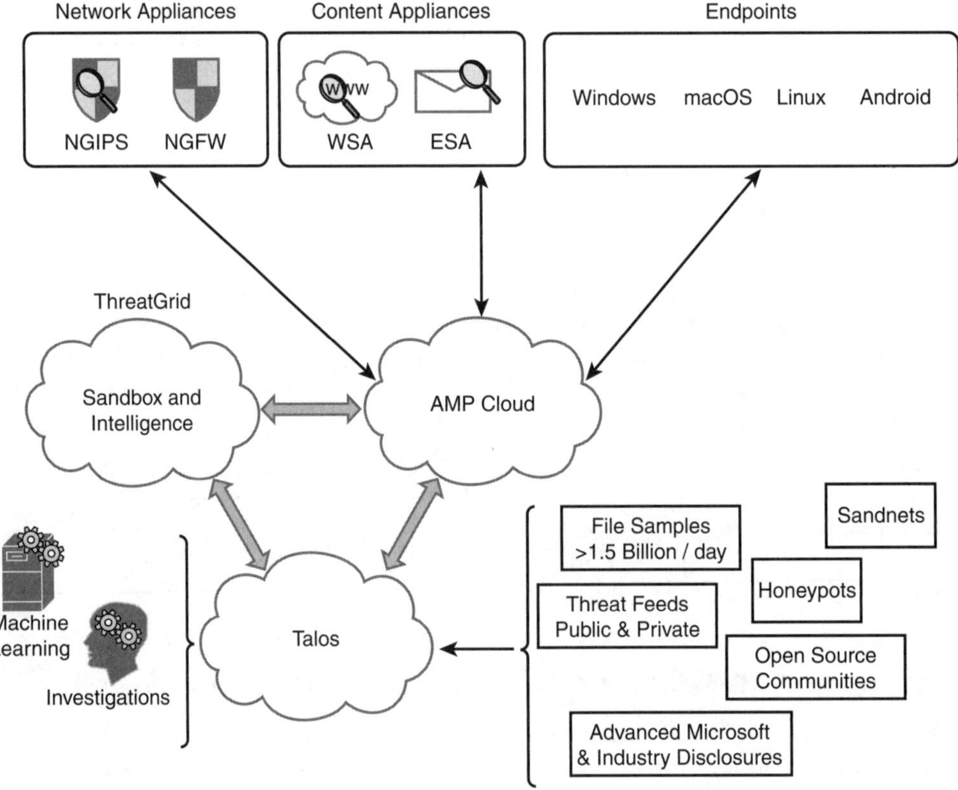

Figure 10-1 *AMP Architecture*

The AMP cloud contains many different analysis tools and technologies to detect malware in files, on the endpoint, and in transit, including the Threat Grid analysis solution. Cisco's research teams, including the famous Talos Security Intelligence and Research Group, feed information about malware into the AMP cloud. Threat intelligence from Cisco products, services, and third-party relationships is also sent to the AMP cloud. Consider the following examples:

- **Snort, ClamAV, and Immunet AV open source communities:** Users of these open source projects contribute threat information daily.
- **Talos:** The Cisco Talos Security Intelligence and Research Group is a team of leading threat researchers who contribute to the threat information ecosystem of Cisco security products. They get threat information from a variety of sources and their own internal research efforts. Talos maintains the official rule sets of Snort.org, ClamAV, SenderBase.org, and SpamCop. Talos is also the primary team that contributes to the Cisco Collective Security Intelligence (CSI) ecosystem. You can follow Talos on twitter @talos and subscribe to the official Talos blog at http://blogs.cisco.com/author/talos.
- **Threat Grid:** This deep threat analysis solution leverages many identification techniques, including sandboxing. Threat Grid is used to perform deep analyses of file samples that are submitted via AMP, through APIs, or manually uploaded through the web portal. The analysis results are fed into the AMP cloud and can be used in updating file disposition.
- **Over 100 TB of daily threat intelligence data:** A variety of sources contribute to the vast amount of data provided to Cisco through submitted malware samples, data from web and email traffic monitored by Cisco products, and other third-party sources.
- **1.6 million global sensors:** Cisco has programs designed to foster cooperation and information sharing of threat intelligence data. As such, Cisco has access to data from more than 1.6 million sensors worldwide.
- **Advanced Microsoft and industry disclosures:** Cisco has cooperative relationships with many industry-leading vendors of software products that yield advanced information about vulnerabilities and threats. AMP customers benefit from access to the vast amount of information gathered by Cisco through quick release of signature updates and threat protection.

Role of the AMP Cloud

The most foundational component of the AMP architecture is the AMP cloud itself. The word *cloud* tends to have people think of public infrastructure, but it doesn't have to be so. The AMP cloud has two deployment methods—public and private—and it plays the same role regardless of the deployment method.

The AMP cloud contains the database of files and their reputations, which are also known as *file dispositions*. A major benefit of storing and processing the files in the cloud is the major reduction in processing requirements on the endpoint and the much smaller footprint, since the bulk of the work is handled in the cloud.

An interesting and fairly unique feature of AMP is that administrators can create custom signatures in the cloud, and then those custom signatures are pushed out to the widely distributed connectors. In addition, the cross-referencing of files and signatures is done in the AMP cloud, so the cloud can be self-updating without having to transmit all the updates to the connectors every time. Contrast this with a traditional antivirus product, where the software on the endpoint has its own signature database and must be constantly updated and maintained.

The AMP cloud is also responsible for large-scale data processing—that is, big data. The data comes to the AMP cloud from multiple sources, including honeypots, threat feeds, open source communities, and antivirus solutions such as Immunet AV, ClamAV, and more. File samples are provided to the AMP cloud where they are processed. If the disposition (the result) of a sample file is deemed to be malicious, it is stored in the cloud and reported to the client connectors that see the same file. If the file is truly unknown, it can be sent to Threat Grid, where it's detonated in a secure environment and the behavior is analyzed.

Note It is important to note that customer data is never shared with any other entity.

Advanced analytics engines, including Threat Grid, are part of the AMP cloud and are constantly correlating the incoming data. The analytical results are used to update the AMP signatures. In addition to the advanced analytics, machine-learning engines further refine signatures and reevaluate detections that have already been performed. The cloud is not just a repository of signatures; rather, the decision making in the cloud is performed in real time, evolving constantly based on the data that is received and therefore capable of identifying malware that was previously thought to be clean.

Doing Security Differently

There is a brilliant engineer from Cisco Sourcefire named Eric Howard. Eric is one of the world's foremost experts in AMP, and he presents security—and the AMP solution—in a unique way that brings tremendous clarity. This section of the book is designed to mirror his presentation style.

Eric talks about the need to "do security differently." Companies need two security plans: Security Plan A, which is prevention, and Security Plan B, which is retrospection.

The Prevention Framework

Prevention is focused on keeping malware at bay, and the speed of prevention is critical. Prevention requires real-time, dynamic decisions to be made from real-world data. It must have high accuracy, with low false positives and false negatives. Prevention could also be viewed as the "security control mode."

As illustrated in Figure 10-2, the AMP cloud's prevention framework is made up of seven core components: one-to-one signatures, Ethos, Spero, indicators of compromise, device flow correlation, advanced analytics (including Cognitive Threat Analytics [CTA]), and dynamic analysis (Threat Grid).

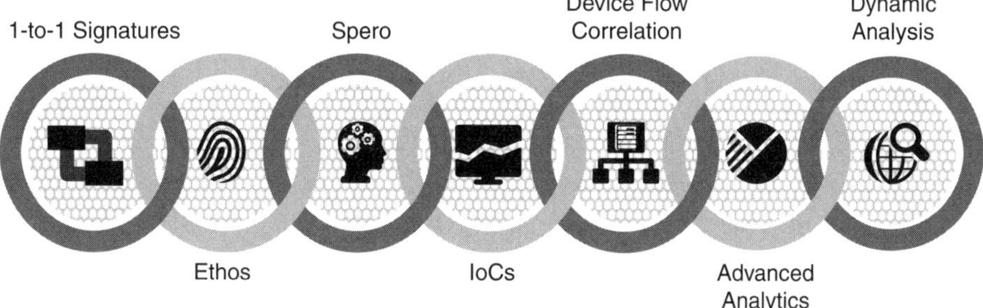

Figure 10-2 *The Protection Framework*

It is important for a security professional to understand that AMP is not a single technology and doesn't rely on any one single component to detect or prevent malware. Instead, AMP leverages the full framework of components, tools, and technologies illustrated in Figure 10-2, allowing any individual component or any combination of components to be the hero.

One-to-One Signatures

One-to-one signatures are a traditional technology that is used all over the security industry in one form or another. With these signatures, a hash is created of a file, and that hash is compared to a database that has the known files marked as malware. The benefit of this method is the speed at which malicious files can be identified and blocked. The downside is that a simple change to a file also changes the hash, thereby evading the signature.

AMP differentiates itself from other one-to-one signature solutions by storing the signature database in the cloud instead of in the client. The database is quite large; many other solutions cut corners by including only a subset of the signatures in the full database. Because the AMP database is stored in the cloud, the entire database can be leveraged. Comparing the files to the database can be quite resource-intensive. AMP does the comparison in the cloud, freeing those resources from the client connector. AMP is also able to collect, process, and detect in near real time.

Ethos Engine

The next phase of the protection framework is the Ethos engine. Ethos is a "fuzzy fingerprinting" engine that uses static or passive heuristics. The engine creates generic file signatures that can match polymorphic variants of a threat; this is necessary because when a threat morphs or a file is changed, the structural properties of that file are often the same, even though the content has changed.

Unlike most signature tools, Ethos has distributed data mining to identify suitable files. It uses in-field data for sources, which provides a highly relevant collection from which to generate the signatures. Ethos is completely automated and provides rapid generation of the generic signatures that are based on in-field data instead of relying on individual "rockstar" engineers to generate a limited number of generic signatures.

Note At the time this book was published, Ethos only applied to AMP for Endpoints.

Spero Engine

Spero is a machine learning–based technology that proactively identifies threats that were previously unknown. It uses active heuristics to gather execution attributes, and because the underlying algorithms come up with generic models, they can identify malicious software based on its general appearance rather than on specific patterns or signatures.

Indicators of Compromise

An indicator of compromise is something observed on a network or in an operating system that indicates a computer intrusion. There may be artifacts left on a system after an intrusion or a breach; they are known as indicators of compromise. Information in indicators of compromise describes how and where to detect the signs of an intrusion or a breach. Indicators of compromise can be host-based and/or network-based artifacts, but the scan actions are carried out on the host only.

Indicators of compromise are very high-confidence indicators, and they may describe numerous specific items, including FileItem, RegistryItem, EventLogItem, ProcessItem, and ServiceItem.

You could think of indicators of compromise as very advanced signatures that examine behaviors, and they have become some of the best and most reliable tools in the advanced threat security toolbox. Take the WannaCry ransomware worm for example. When that malware first landed, Talos immediately began analyzing it and identifying the Snort signatures they previously wrote that would protect customers. Talos accumulated all the file hashes of known files and wrote indicators of compromise to detect WannaCry based on the malware behavior. (For more on the WannaCry malware, check out the Talos blog for it: http://blog.talosintelligence.com/2017/05/wannacry.html.)

A company named Mandiant created an open framework for sharing threat intelligence indicators, known as Open Indicators of Compromise (OpenIOC). OpenIOC has become the industry standard for expressing threat intelligence in a behavioral signature model, and it is this standard that AMP uses.

Figure 10-3 shows an example of an indicator of compromise.

Downloads — -bash — 128×49

```
<?xml version="1.0" encoding="us-ascii"?>
<ioc xmlns:xsi="http://www.w3.org/2001/XMLSchema-instance" xmlns:xsd="http://www.w3.org/2001/XMLSchema" id="af2e8c80-13db-4a57-9
9ac-460ccd192333" last-modified="2012-06-04T21:33:52" xmlns="http://schemas.mandiant.com/2010/ioc">
  <short_description>Flamer,Skywiper</short_description>
  <description>IOCs to detect the presence of the Flamer framework</description>
  <authored_by>Jaime Blasco, Alienvault</authored_by>
  <authored_date>2012-06-04T15:15:17</authored_date>
  <links />
  <definition>
    <Indicator operator="OR" id="9aa42d5a-3bc6-446e-b19c-1b2a4b909b5a">
      <Indicator operator="AND" id="2e1b945c-2587-412c-9b9d-51a28d23f652">
        <IndicatorItem id="8be295c7-879c-4499-b1ee-ca03873decf8" condition="contains">
          <Context document="RegistryItem" search="RegistryItem/Path" type="mir" />
          <Content type="string">HKEY_LOCAL_MACHINE\SOFTWARE\Microsoft\Windows NT\CurrentVersion\Drivers32</Content>
        </IndicatorItem>
        <IndicatorItem id="4becb7bf-5f45-4c9b-8c7b-130a7e8cbe26" condition="contains">
          <Context document="RegistryItem" search="RegistryItem/Text" type="mir" />
          <Content type="string">wavesup3.drv</Content>
        </IndicatorItem>
        <Indicator operator="OR" id="1f4f8b85-b307-487a-897c-197492cb51f4">
          <IndicatorItem id="3d9496b4-10fa-4b65-b72b-8f289c914c91" condition="is">
            <Context document="RegistryItem" search="RegistryItem/ValueName" type="mir" />
            <Content type="string">wave9</Content>
          </IndicatorItem>
          <IndicatorItem id="c729ed47-513d-436d-b164-919ff4cd2d3d" condition="is">
            <Context document="RegistryItem" search="RegistryItem/ValueName" type="mir" />
            <Content type="string">wave8</Content>
          </IndicatorItem>
        </Indicator>
      </Indicator>
      <Indicator operator="AND" id="14868529-c95f-4576-af9c-23f9d2923107">
        <IndicatorItem id="5225f2f2-8293-42c5-92a7-fbb5afb1cda8" condition="contains">
          <Context document="RegistryItem" search="RegistryItem/Path" type="mir" />
          <Content type="string">\Control\Lsa\Authentication Packages</Content>
        </IndicatorItem>
        <IndicatorItem id="48c2cd98-5324-4780-a06c-0e6b7ecd780b" condition="contains">
          <Context document="RegistryItem" search="RegistryItem/Text" type="mir" />
          <Content type="string">mssecmgr.ocx</Content>
        </IndicatorItem>
      </Indicator>
      <Indicator operator="OR" id="c702bea5-317a-4232-855a-090cd61c8e5e">
        <IndicatorItem id="209070e1-50d7-489d-af11-e0f2b3df23d5" condition="contains">
          <Context document="ProcessItem" search="ProcessItem/HandleList/Handle/Name" type="mir" />
          <Content type="string">TH_POOL_SHD_PQOISNG</Content>
        </IndicatorItem>
        <IndicatorItem id="f64f68ac-5d94-49e2-b59d-d614db8dc122" condition="contains">
          <Context document="ProcessItem" search="ProcessItem/HandleList/Handle/Name" type="mir" />
          <Content type="string">microsoft shared_msaudio_wpgfilter.dat</Content>
        </IndicatorItem>
```

Figure 10-3 *Indicator of Compromise Example*

Device Flow Correlation

Device flow correlation provides a kernel-level view into network I/O. It allows for the blacklisting and whitelisting of communication with IPv4 networks as well as alerting on network activity. One of the most useful features of device flow correlation is that it can trace the network traffic back to the initiating process itself. Device flow correlation provides internal and external networks to be monitored, leverages IP reputation data, and does URL/domain logging; anyone performing threat hunting or incident response activities will be delighted to find that the flow points are included in the telemetry data.

Cisco provides intelligence on many malicious destinations, including generic command and control (CnC, also called C2) servers, phishing hosts, zero-access C2 servers, and more.

Advanced Analytics

A set of multifaceted engines provide big data context beyond a single host and beyond a single file. There are many facets to the advanced analytics category of the AMP framework. One of those facets is *prevalence*, which is the frequency at which a file has been executed within the organization. Prevalence can aid in surfacing previously undetected threats that may have only been seen by a small number of users, and AMP may even be configured to automatically send any files with low prevalence to Threat Grid for dynamic analysis.

However, an incredibly useful engine that cannot be overlooked and should not be minimized is Cisco's Cognitive Threat Analytics (CTA) platform. CTA leverages advanced machine learning capabilities to identify C2 communication from telemetry data such as NetFlow, encrypted traffic analytics (ETA), and incredibly valuable data coming from web traffic logs. The most common telemetry sources for CTA are the logs from web proxies such as the Cisco Web Security Appliance (WSA) or Blue Coat ProxySG, as well as web traffic and NetFlow telemetry from Cisco Stealthwatch.

Other engines can also factor into the advanced analytics component of the AMP protection framework, such as analyzing the age of a file in the entire install base, using algorithms that examine the relationship between dropped files, and leveraging the verdict from the VirusTotal service, which analyzes files against a multitude of antivirus products.

Dynamic Analysis with Threat Grid

Cisco's Threat Grid is not a single tool. It is a full solution for dynamic malware analysis and threat intelligence. It performs high-speed, automated analysis with adjustable run times while not exposing any tags or other indicators that malware could use to detect that it is being observed.

Threat Grid provides video playbacks, the Glovebox for malware interaction and operational troubleshooting, a process graph for visual representation of process lineage, and a threat score with behavior indicators. It searches and correlates all data elements of a single sample against billions of sample artifacts collected and analyzed over years, leveraging global and historic context. Threat Grid enables an analyst to better understand the relevancy of a questionable sample as it pertains to the analyst's own environment.

Threat Grid was architected from the ground up as a cloud solution with an API designed to integrate with existing IT security solutions and to create custom threat intelligence feeds. It can automatically receive submissions from other solutions and pull the results into your environment; it is also available in an appliance form factor.

Many think that Threat Grid is a sandboxing solution, but it is much more than that. However, sandboxing is a piece of the solution, and its sandbox functions are performed in a way that evades detection by malware. It uses an outside-in approach, with no presence in the virtual machine. The sandboxing's dynamic analysis includes an external kernel monitor, dynamic disk analysis that illuminates any modifications to the physical disk (such as the MBR), monitoring user interaction, video capture and playback, process information, artifacts, and network traffic.

Threat Grid supports the following list of samples and object types:

- **.bat:** Batch files. (*Note:* The file *must* have the .bat extension.)
- **.bz2:** bzip2 files; see .zip.
- **.chm:** Compiled HTML help or Microsoft compiled HTML help.
- **.dll:** See .pe32 and .pe32+.
- **.doc, .docx:** Microsoft Word files; see Office documents.
- **.exe:** See .pe32.
- **.gz:** gzip files; see .zip.
- **.hta:** HTML applications (*Note:* The file *must* have the .hta extension)
- **.hwp, .hwt, .hwpx:** Available on the win7-x64-kr VM *only* (specific to Hancom Office). (*Note:* Not available on Threat Grid appliances.)
- **.jar:** Java archives.
- **.js:** JavaScript files. (*Note:* The file *must* have the .js extension.)
- **.jse:** Encoded JavaScript files. (*Note:* The file *must* have the .jse extension.)
- **.jtd, .jtt, .jtdc, .jttc: Compressed document files.**
- **.lnk:** Windows shortcut files.
- **.msi:** Microsoft Installer files.
- **.mhtml:** MIME HTML files.
- Office documents (.doc, .docx, .rtf, .xls, .xlsx, .ppt, .pptx).
- **.pdf:** Portable Document Format files (detailed static forensics, including JavaScript resources).
- **.pe32:**
  - Executables (.exe).
  - Libraries (.dll).
- **.pe32+:** Available on the win7-x64 VM only.
  - Executables (.exe).
  - Libraries (.dll).

- **.ps1:** PowerShell. (*Note:* The file *must* have the .ps1 extension.)
- **.sep:** Tagged image file format; see .zip.
- **.swf:** Flash files.
- **.tar:** tar files; see .zip.
- **URLs:** As Internet Shortcut file or submit the URL directly. Detailed static forensics or JavaScript resources.
- **.vbe:** Encoded Visual Basic files. (*Note:* The file *must* have the .vbe extension.)
- **.vbn:** Virus bin files; see .zip.
- **.vbs:** VBScript files. (*Note:* The file *must* have the .vbs extension.)
- **.wsf:** Windows Script files. (*Note:* The file *must* have the .wsf extension.)
- **.xml:**
  - XML-based Office document types (.docx, .xlsx, .pptx).
  - **XML:** Extensible Markup Language (.xml).
  - XML that is from Office will be opened in the corresponding program (Office 2003).
  - All other XML will be opened in Internet Explorer.
- **.zip:** Archive and quarantine formats:
  - .zip archives may contain a maximum of 100 files. Archives with more than 100 files return no analysis and display an error stating that too many files were found. The maximum file size for each file within the .zip archive is 25 MB.
  - Quarantine (.sep, .vbn).
  - xz (.xz), gzip (.gz), bzip2 (.bz2), tar (.tar).

The Threat Grid user interface provides even more details. If you have questions, or for additional information on what is and what isn't supported, please see the online help.

As mentioned earlier in this section, the Threat Grid solution is designed to not allow malware to detect that it is being detonated in a sandbox solution. Again consider the WannaCry ransomware worm as an example. It has a built-in kill switch to shut down if it detects that it is in a sandbox. Many other sandboxing solutions triggered that kill switch, but Threat Grid did not. Threat Grid was able to analyze WannaCry completely.

The Retrospective Framework

Retrospection is the process of examining what has already transpired and tracking system behavior regardless of the file's disposition in an attempt to uncover malicious activity. It could also be viewed as the "incident response mode." The AMP cloud provides retrospection through its continuous analysis of files and ability to reactively act on a file that was assigned a clean disposition once but was later found to have a bad disposition.

The retrospective framework is designed to show the trajectory of the malicious file, with a goal of 30 days of telemetry data, as illustrated in Figure 10-4.

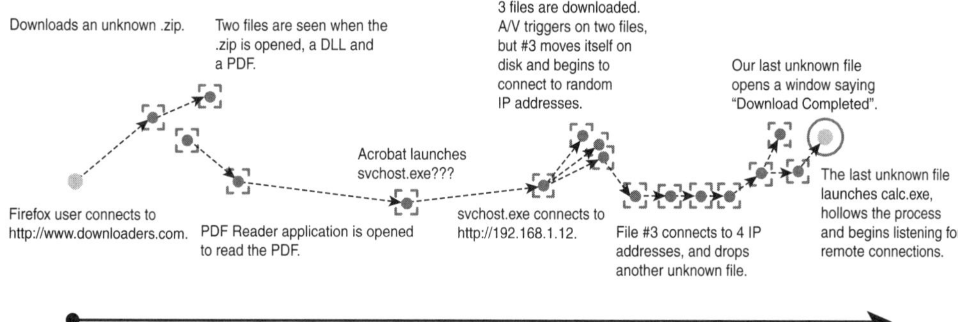

Figure 10-4 *Retrospection Trajectory*

The Cloud

As you will see throughout this chapter, the AMP cloud is the centralized brain for all file dispositions, and it is the centralized location for all management and reporting related to endpoint connectors. Figure 10-5 shows an example of the AMP cloud dashboard in use. The dashboard shows indicators of compromise and allows you to drill into them.

Endpoints can be provisioned from the AMP console, agents downloaded, endpoint policies configured, reports run, and more.

The cloud is where the main AMP intelligence exists. As far as the AMP cloud is concerned, there really is no difference between the connectors. AMP for Endpoints doesn't appear any different from AMP for Networks. Or, as Millard Arnold, one of the original founding engineers from Immunet, likes to say, "A connector is a connector is a connector."

The AMP cloud is available as a public cloud offering as well as a private cloud offering for installations where connectivity to the public cloud is not permitted.

Private Cloud

The AMP cloud is available in a private version that allows administrators to run their own cloud with many of the features from the public cloud—but not all of them. With the private cloud option, you may choose to host all components within your own data center.

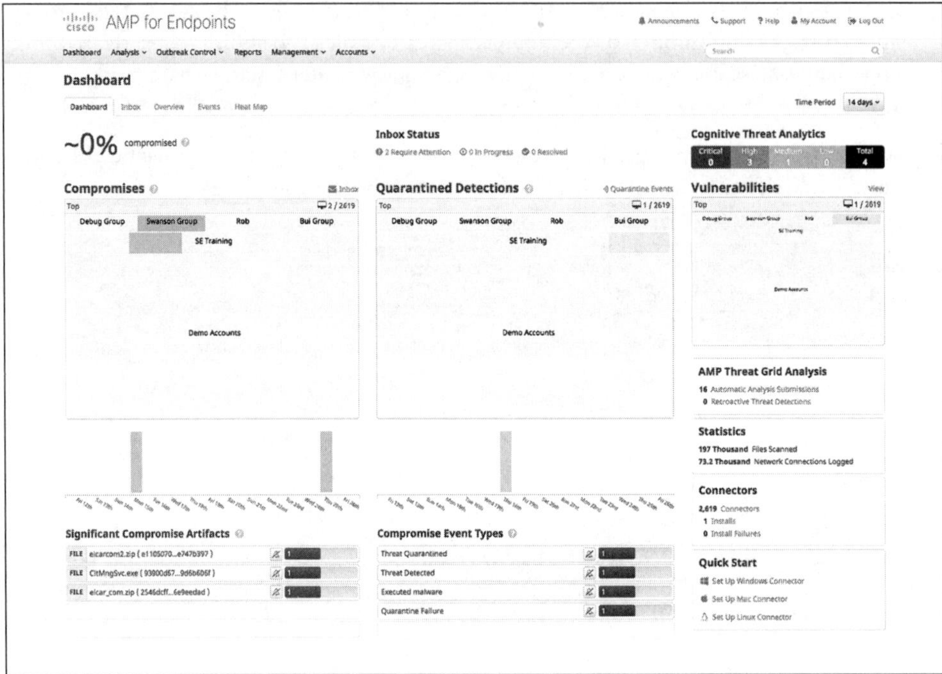

Figure 10-5 *The AMP Cloud Dashboard*

Organizations that reside outside the United States and have very strict controls on where data may reside often choose the option to host the AMP cloud in their own data center. In addition, organizations such as government agencies have their own requirements for data storage being on-premises.

It's important to note that as new features are developed for AMP, they are added to the public cloud first. The private cloud receives the relevant features but always lags behind the public cloud when it comes to feature velocity and feature adoption.

At the time this book was published, there were whispered rumors of a physical appliance, but the private cloud product itself was shipped only as a virtual machine that runs in a customer's own VMware environment, and that private cloud may be operated in one of two ways: cloud proxy mode or air gap mode.

Cloud Proxy Mode

Cloud proxy mode operates the private cloud within the confines of your own data center or other cloud infrastructure. The AMP connectors can be configured to leverage the private cloud, instead of one of Cisco's public clouds, for file disposition lookups. Even though the connectors leverage the locally installed private cloud, the private cloud maintains a connection to the public cloud for certain communications:

- **File disposition checks:** File disposition is still determined by the public cloud. The file hashes are passed on to the public cloud over an SSL session using TCP port 443 or TCP port 32137. The public cloud is known as the *upstream server*, and the FQDN that you connect to is cloud-pc.amp.sourcefire.com.
- **Product updates:** The AMP private cloud can be configured for automatic or manual updates, leveraging a Yum repository named packages.amp.sourcefire.com, which uses an SSL session over TCP port 443.
- **Support:** Cisco TAC is able to remotely access the device for diagnostic purposes and customer assistance. The remote access uses SSH and TCP port 443.

Figure 10-6 illustrates the cloud proxy mode.

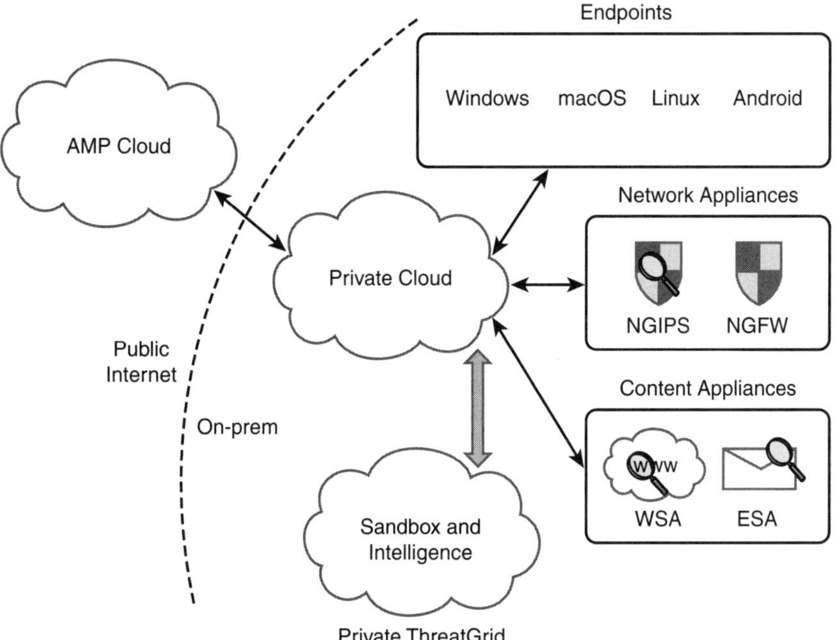

Figure 10-6 *Private Cloud Proxy Mode*

There are numerous architectural benefits to the proxy mode private cloud architecture, especially when you consider that the large database of file hashes and their dispositions is maintained in Cisco's public cloud, and therefore the data will always be as up-to-date as possible, the installation will continue to benefit immediately from all the other AMP customers and Talos research, and it keeps the data storage requirements of the private cloud VM to a minimum.

Cloud proxy mode is always the preferred and recommended mode for the private cloud where it is possible. However, in certain instances and environments, connection to the public Internet is simply prohibited or not feasible. For those instances and environments, there is air gap mode.

Air Gap Mode

In air gap installation mode, the private cloud instance is completely isolated and has no external access to the public cloud. Updates must be completed manually; remote support is very challenging. Yet this mode provides the highest levels of confidentiality.

The AMP administrator needs to have a separate Linux server to run a tool called amp-sync, which is a script that downloads a copy of the database with the file hashes and dispositions, known as the "protect database" (protect DB), from the public AMP cloud. The amp-sync utility saves the downloaded data into an .iso-formatted file to be imported into the air-gapped private cloud.

Figure 10-7 illustrates air gap mode, and Figure 10-8 illustrates the amp-sync utility.

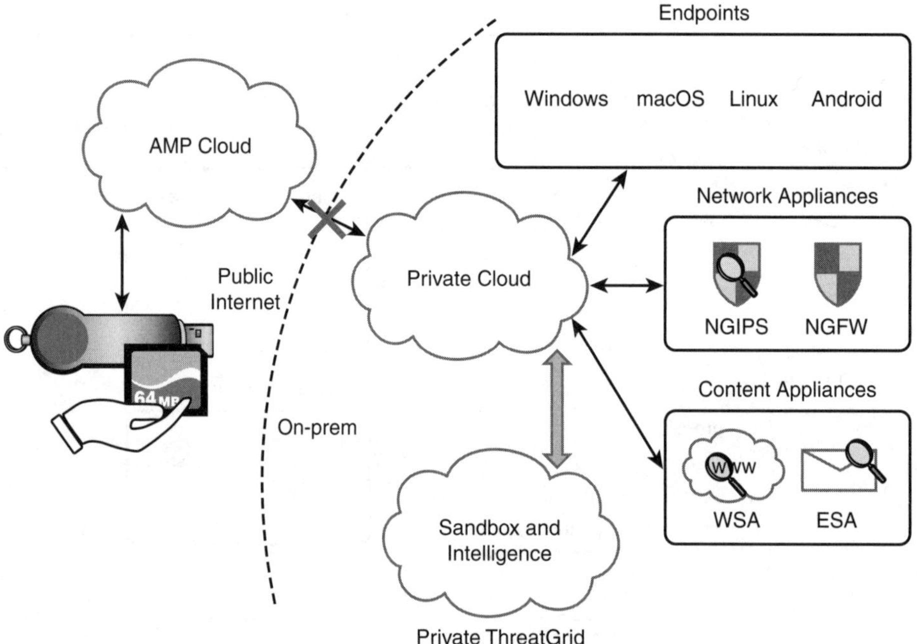

Figure 10-7 *Private Cloud Air Gap Mode*

As you can see in Figures 10-7 and 10-8, the process involved with air gap mode can be a little tedious, as well as time-consuming. When you first install an air gap mode private cloud, the database is completely empty. Depending on your geography, it could take a day or two to download the entire protect database and then another day to import the resulting .iso.

Table 10-1 lists the system requirements for proxy mode and air gap mode private clouds, as well as the amp-sync system.

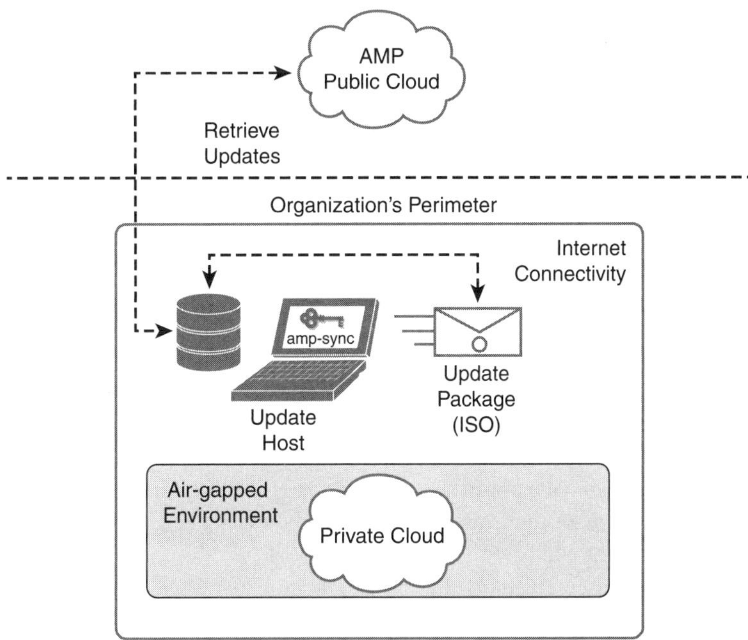

Figure 10-8 *amp-sync Utility*

Table 10-1 *System Requirements for Private Clouds and amp-sync*

	Proxy Mode	Air Gap Mode	amp-sync Host
OS	N/A (Appliance)	N/A (Appliance)	Dedicated host with CentOS 6.6 or Ubuntu
VMware	vSphere 5.x or higher	vSphere 5.x or higher	N/A
# CPUs	8 CPUs	8 CPUs	N/A
RAM	32 GB RAM	32 GB RAM	N/A
Free disk space	238 GB free SSD space	1 TB free SSD space	500 GB of disk space
RAID type	RAID 10 (striped mirror) with 4 drives	RAID 10 (striped mirror) with 4 drives	N/A
Read IOPS	Reads: 100,000 4K IOPS	Reads: 100,000 4K IOPS	N/A
Write IOPS	Writes: 90,000 4K IOPS	Writes: 90,000 4K IOPS	N/A
Software Packages	N/A	N/A	EPEL, curl, genisoimage, and xmlstarlet

> **Note** At the time this book was published, there were rumors that a physical appliance would be coming out and that the physical appliance would be preloaded with the protect DB, thereby speeding and easing the installation and eliminating the tedious initial download and import of the protect DB.

Threat Grid

The AMP cloud is not the only cloud in the solution or architecture. Threat Grid is an integral part of the AMP architecture, as it is the dynamic analysis and threat intelligence solution used to identify the behavior of a file when it executes or detonates on a system. Threat Grid runs the suspected malware in an isolated cleanroom virtual environment. It tracks everything that occurs in the cleanroom—every file that is created, every computer setting that is changed, every website it tries to communicate with. Threat Grid correlates the artifacts of the sample malware against billions of artifacts that have been collected and analyzed; it compares the malware artifacts to known malicious behaviors, including nearly 1,000 behavioral indicators.

Figure 10-9 shows the Threat Grid dashboard.

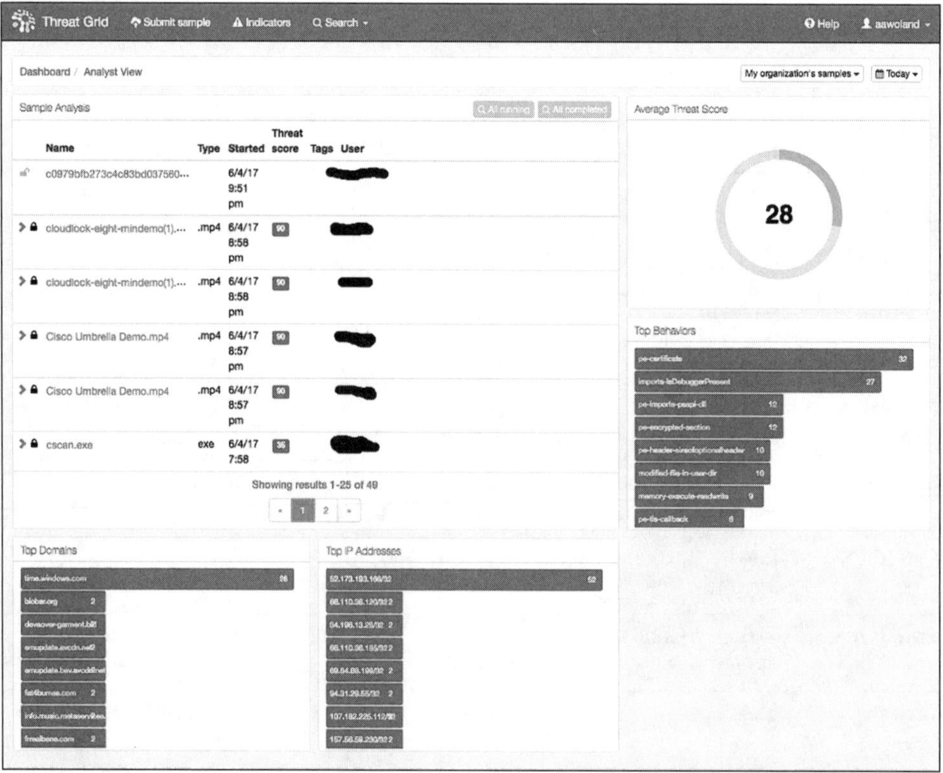

Figure 10-9 *The Threat Grid Dashboard*

One of the most fun features of Threat Grid is the way it records the activity in the virtual machine and provides video playback of the activities. There is also a feature called Glovebox, which allows the administrator to interact with the malware sample in real time—as if remotely controlling a virtual machine's console. (The name Glovebox refers to the sealed container that allows manipulation of objects using gloves while preventing atmospheric exposure, not the storage compartment of an automobile.)

After the sample has been run, Threat Grid outputs a threat score as well as a list of the behavioral indicators that were exhibited, allowing the analyst to see if the malware is behaving in a malicious, suspicious, or benign way.

Figure 10-10 shows an example of a report for an analyzed sample, and Figure 10-11 shows the video playback for that sample.

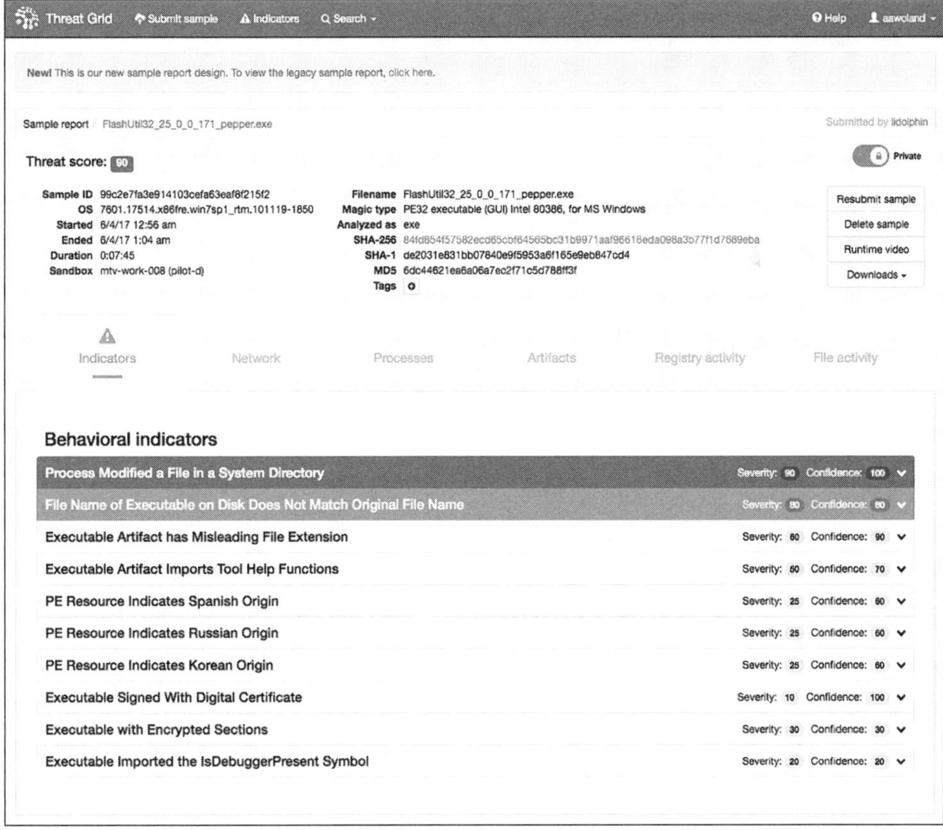

Figure 10-10 *Threat Grid Sample Report*

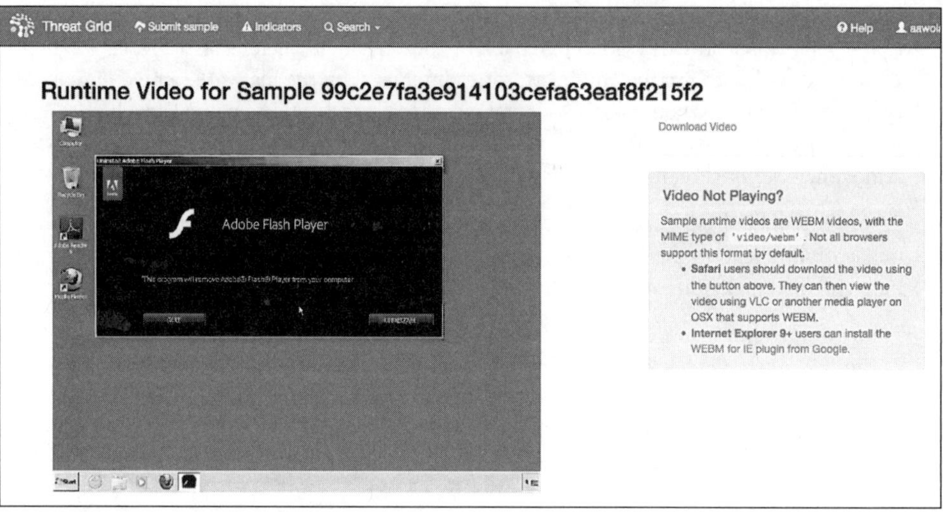

Figure 10-11 *Threat Grid Run-Time Video*

It is important to note that Threat Grid does not assign the disposition to files; AMP does. Threat Grid can be and is one of the sources of data that AMP leverages to determine the disposition.

The video playback, behavioral indicators, and report are not the only output from Threat Grid. As with any other good threat intelligence solution, robust feeds are required. Threat Grid provides feeds through detailed APIs, allowing for custom and batch feeds to be ingested by other security solutions. There are various data formats available, such as .json, .stix, .csv, and Snort.

There is even more information available. When interacting with a sample report, you can drill into Registry changes or additions, attempted network connections, and even a full list of processes that were running and what subprocesses were spawned as well as what files or Registry changes were made by those child processes. You can view the process data in a table format or in an interactive graphical process tree, as shown in Figure 10-12.

As you saw in Figures 10-1, 10-6, and 10-7, Threat Grid is offered in both public cloud as well as an on-premises offering for customers who are worried about sending files to the cloud or concerned about the bandwidth used to upload those files. Unlike the AMP private cloud, the on-premises Threat Grid offering comes in an appliance form factor only.

Threat Grid Cloud

When using the Threat Grid cloud, all samples are submitted and tagged as either private or public. All private data is isolated and is restricted to the submitting organization only. Public data benefits all Threat Grid and AMP customers, allowing them to pivot on the artifacts; however, all public data remains anonymous (that is, does not identify which organization submitted a sample).

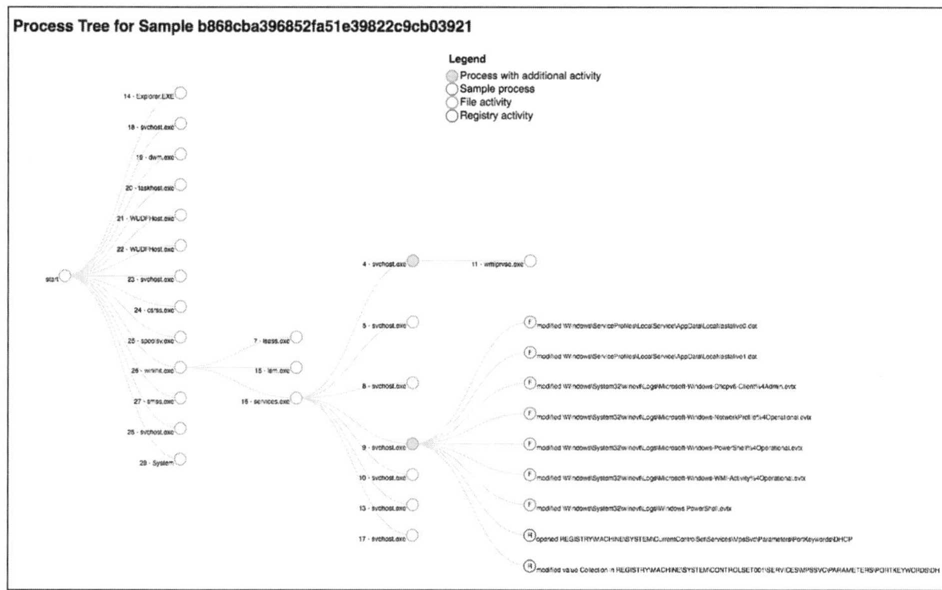

Figure 10-12 *Threat Grid Interactive Process Tree*

Private submissions may be converted to public. However, there is no way to change a publicly submitted sample to private. Customer submissions are limited to a specified number of samples per day. Many of the Cisco products that have AMP connectors are entitled to some number of Threat Grid submissions, and customers may purchase additional sample packs.

Threat Grid Appliance

When using a local appliance, all file samples and artifacts that are sent to Threat Grid are kept locally on-premises. No data at all is sent to the cloud. All pivoting on samples and artifacts is based on local data only.

There are two available appliances with differing capabilities in terms of the number of samples that can be analyzed per day:

- **TG 5004:** 1500 samples per day
- **TG 5504:** 5000 samples per day

The AMP cloud is not the only part of the solution where communication ports and protocols are important. If you're using an on-premises Threat Grid appliance, you need additional communication paths.

The appliance has three interfaces: clean, administrative, and dirty. These interfaces have different purposes and different connectivity requirements, as described in the following sections.

The Clean Interface

The clean interface is used for connectivity to the web-based user interface and to provide access to the API for file submissions. All the submitting devices must have access to this interface and its IP address. Ensure that TCP port 443, TCP port 8443, and TCP port 9443 are open from the internal network to the clean interface. The clean interface also needs to be able to reach rash.threatgrid.com on TCP port 19143.

The Administrative Interface

The administrative interface is used for setup and configuration of the appliance. All updates, backups, restores, and logging go through this interface. Ensure that both TCP port 443 and TCP port 8443 are open from the internal network.

Note The administrative interface uses Gigabit Ethernet small form-factor pluggable (SFP) transceiver modules, so if you want to use 1000BASET, you need to order a GLC-T module.

The Dirty Interface

The dirty interface's name perfectly fits the purpose of this interface. The dirty interface provides Internet connectivity for the virtual machines. It should be connected to a separate Internet connection, such as a DSL connection or a truly isolated DMZ. Remember that Threat Grid detonates live malware in the virtual machines, and that malware often needs to connect to the Internet to prove the malicious behavior.

The best option is to block TCP port 25 (SMTP) for all outbound traffic to prevent the malware from sending spam but otherwise to allow unrestricted access from the dirty interface to the outside world. It is impossible for Cisco to know exactly which protocols, ports, and destinations the malware needs to reach in order to successfully launch. Some organizations are prohibited from ever using a **permit ip any any** type of firewall rule due to regulatory compliance. That is another reason to use a separate Internet connection. However, if your organization is truly prohibited from using a wide-open rule for outbound traffic, you must ensure that TCP port 22 (SSH) and Threat Grid support ports TCP port 19791 and 20433 are allowed.

Comparing Public and Private Deployments

As you have read in this chapter, AMP and Threat Grid can both be deployed in the cloud or on-premises, and there can be a mixture, in which either AMP or Threat Grid is private or publicly deployed. Your deployment choices will have an impact on integrations with the connectors. Table 10-2 shows the four deployment variations and which ones work with the main AMP connectors.

Table 10-2 *Deployment Options*

	Deployment Options			
	Fully Public	**AMP Public Threat Grid Private**	**AMP Private Threat Grid Public**	**Fully Private**
Cisco ESA	Yes	Yes	No	Yes
Cisco WSA	Yes	Yes	No	Yes
Firepower	Yes	Yes	No	Yes
AMP for Endpoints	Yes	No	No	Yes

AMP for Networks

The network is a strategic place to gain visibility across an organization and to uncover and discover threats. It provides unprecedented visibility to activity at a macro-analytical level. However, to remediate malware, you need to be on the host. The importance of strategically locating sensors in the network and on the host is why AMP connectors exist in multiple form factors (AMP for Networks, AMP for Endpoints, AMP for content security appliances, and AMP for Meraki). Cisco likes to call the overall architecture *AMP Everywhere*.

What Is That Manager Called?

While AMP connectors are installed differently and act in different places in networks, they all speak to the AMP cloud. However, because the AMP connectors exist as part of different security products already, there can also be differing management platforms. AMP for Networks leverages a management platform that has unfortunately gone by a few different names since Cisco's acquisition of Sourcefire.

Thanks to Cisco's acquisition and branding strategy, you may see the management center referred to as Sourcefire Defense Center (SFDC), Cisco FireSIGHT Management Center (FMC), or even Cisco Firepower Management Center (FMC). At the time this book was published, the latest and hopefully final name for the management system was Cisco Firepower Management Center (FMC).

Form Factors for AMP for Networks

Cisco AMP for Networks is the AMP service that runs on an appliance and examines traffic flowing through the network. It can be installed as a service on a Firepower IPS, a Cisco ASA with Firepower services, or the Firepower Threat Defense (FTD) next-generation firewall (NGFW).

What AMP for Networks Does

AMP for Networks and all the AMP connectors are designed to find malicious files and provide retrospective analysis, illustrate trajectory, and point out how far malicious files may have spread.

The AMP for Networks connector examines, records, and tracks files, and it queries the cloud with the recorded information. It creates an SHA-256 hash of the file and compares it to the local file cache. If the hash is not in the local cache, the AMP for Networks connector queries the FMC. The FMC has its own cache of all the hashes that it has seen before, and if it hasn't previously seen this hash, the FMC queries the cloud. When a file is not in the FMC's local cache, that file can be analyzed locally on the network connector, and it doesn't have to be sent to the cloud for all analysis.

Figure 10-13 illustrates the many AMP for Networks connectors and sending the file hash to the FMC, which in turn sends it to the cloud if the hash is new. The connectors could be running as a service on a next-generation IPS (NG-IPS), an ASA with Firepower services, or even the newer NGFW known as Firepower Threat Defense (FTD).

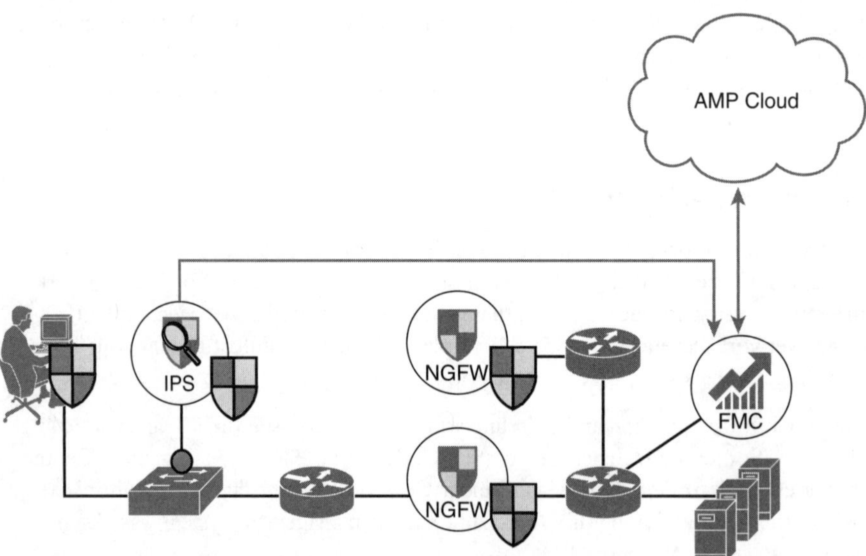

Figure 10-13 *AMP Connectors Talking to the FMC and the Cloud*

It's very important to note that only the SHA-256 hash is sent unless you configure the policy to send files for further analysis within Threat Grid.

AMP can also provide retrospective analysis. The AMP for Networks appliance keeps data about what occurred in the past. When the disposition of a file is changed, AMP provides a historical analysis of what happened, tracing an incident or infection. When AMP for Networks is combined with AMP for Endpoints, retrospection can reach out to that host and remediate the bad file, even though it was permitted in the past.

This capability of retrospection aids when a file is considered normal but is later reconsidered to be malicious.

AMP for Networks does not only deal with malicious files but also allows an organization to implement file control—whether malware is present or not.

In order for the AMP policies to be used, you must have one or more Firepower devices with an active malware license. Figure 10-14 shows an example of the license screen located at System > Licenses. Notice that there are two devices listed in this example—an ASA5515-X with Firepower services and a virtual Firepower NGIPS (NGIPSv)—both of which have malware licenses.

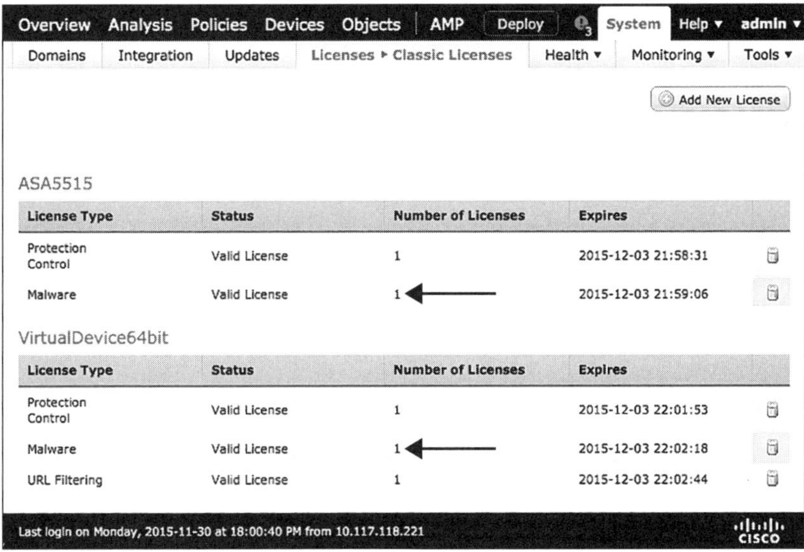

Figure 10-14 *Malware Licenses*

Where Are the AMP Policies?

The FMC user interface has a top-level menu item named AMP, as shown in Figure 10-15. However, that section of the UI is for configuring which AMP and Threat Grid cloud to connect to, not for configuring AMP policies.

The FMC is organized logically, and policies appear under the Policies top-level menu. However, if you take a look in the Policies menu, you won't see the AMP policies called by that same name. You must navigate to Policies > Access Control > Malware & File (see Figure 10-16).

You can create a new File Policy by clicking New File Policy in the upper-right corner and providing a name in the New File Policy dialog box (see Figure 10-17). Remember to add a detailed description that will help you understand the purpose of the policy. Click Save to create the policy and move into the configuration itself.

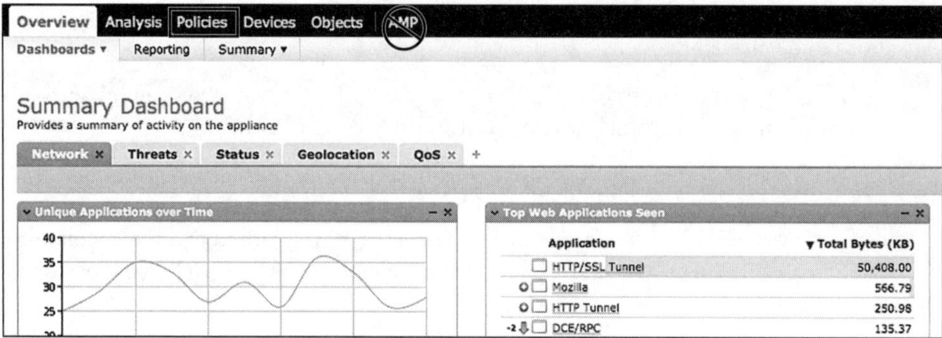

Figure 10-15 *Firepower Management Center User Interface*

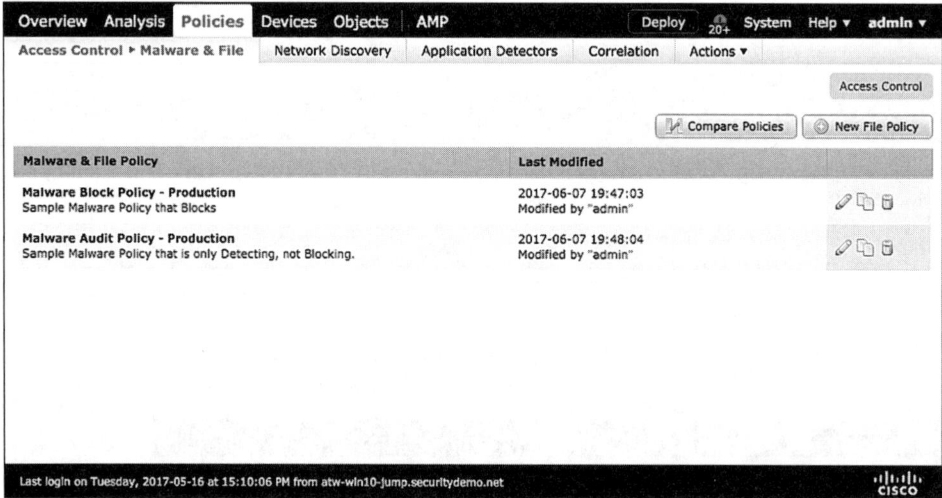

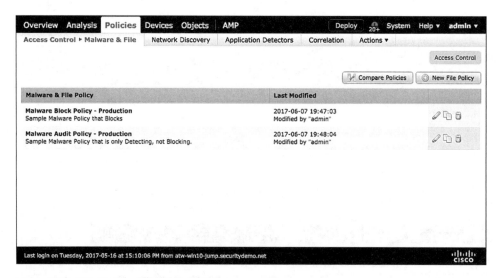

Figure 10-16 *Malware & File Policies*

Figure 10-17 *New File Policy Dialog*

You now have a brand-new file policy with no rules, as shown in Figure 10-18. To create your first rule in the new policy, click the Add Rule button.

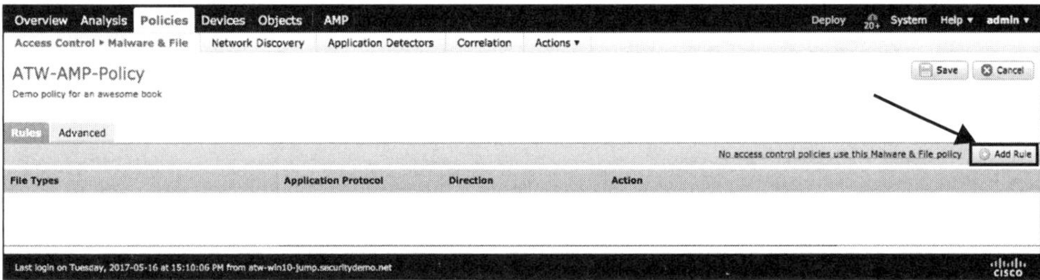

Figure 10-18 *A New File Policy Without Rules*

The Add Rule window appears (see Figure 10-19).

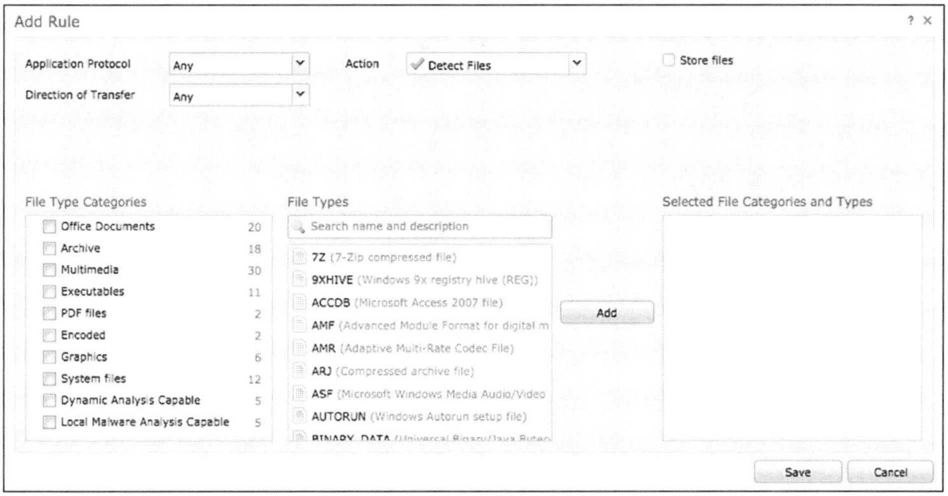

Figure 10-19 *Add Rule Window*

When creating a file rule, you first select the application protocol to inspect for files, and the more specific your rule, the better the performance will be. As shown in Figure 10-20, the choices are Any, HTTP, SMTP, IMAP, POP3, FTP, and NetBIOS-ssn (SMB).

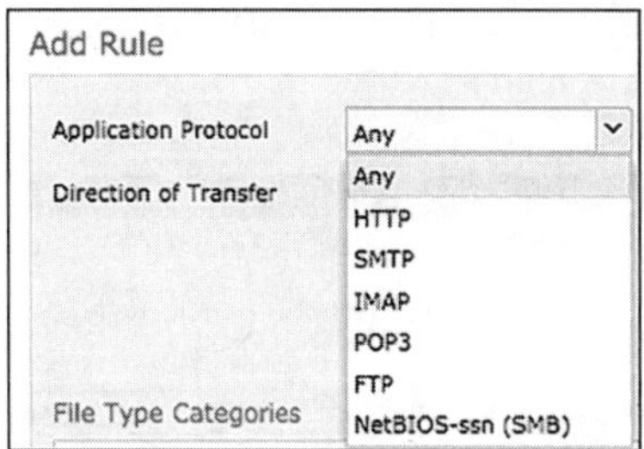

Figure 10-20 *Application Protocols*

You must also specify the direction of the file transfer through the network appliance. The choices are Any, Upload, and Download, as shown in Figure 10-21.

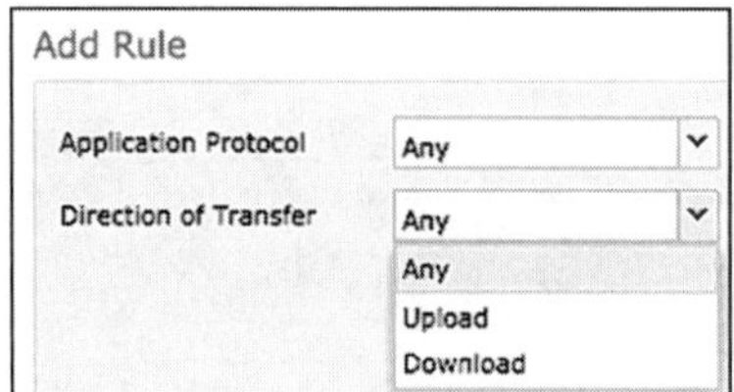

Figure 10-21 *Direction of Transfer*

The action determines what to do with files. The actions are Detect Files, Block Files, Malware Cloud Lookup, and Block Malware, as shown in Figure 10-22.

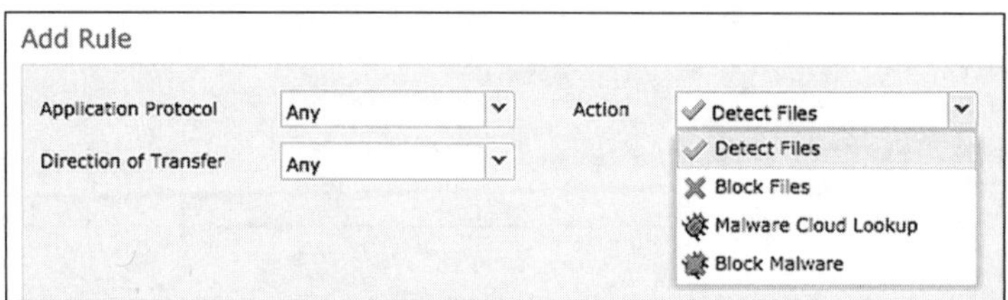

Figure 10-22 *File Rule Actions*

File Rules

The first traditional file rule action is Detect Files. With this action, upon detecting the files, AMP logs the detection of the specific files but does not interfere with the files' traversal through the network. Think of it as a "monitor mode," or audit-style rule. You can store the files that meet the rule for further evaluation.

The next traditional file rule action is Block Files, which resets the file transfer connection. Just like the Detect Files action, this blocking action has an option to store the files.

Malware Cloud Lookup is the first of the AMP rule actions, and it requires a valid malware license. This rule action is like a monitor mode or an audit rule for AMP, where the AMP connector obtains and logs the disposition of the file but does not stop the transmission of the files. As with the other rules, you have the ability to store the triggering files, only this time the options are to store file types: Malware, Unknown, Clean, and/or Custom.

Block Malware is an AMP rule action that, naturally, requires a valid malware license. This rule action works the same way as Malware Cloud Lookup, only it adds an option to reset the connection by sending a TCP reset.

With both malware lookup options, you have four choices:

- **Spero Analysis for EXEs:** Spero analysis is machine learning that leverages heuristics to determine zero-day malware.
- **Dynamic Analysis:** This sends the files to be analyzed by Threat Grid.
- **Capacity Handling:** When using dynamic analysis, and the cloud is not reachable, the files can be stored locally.
- **Local Malware Analysis:** With this option, AMP examines the file using a locally installed antivirus software; at the time this book was published, the antivirus software in use was ClamAV (an open source antivirus owned by Cisco Sourcefire).

File Disposition Types

As mentioned earlier in the chapter, there are four file disposition options: malware, clean, unknown, and custom. You may see a file being assigned any one of these file dispositions. The types are described as follows:

- **Malware:** Indicates that the AMP cloud categorized the file as malware and local malware analysis identified malware during the file scan using the local antivirus. Another possibility for this file disposition is that the file's threat score exceeded the malware threshold defined in the file policy.
- **Clean:** Indicates that the AMP cloud categorized the file as clean. It is also possible to manually add a file to the clean list, which also shows as the clean file disposition.
- **Unknown:** Indicates that the system queried the AMP cloud, but the AMP cloud has not categorized the file.
- **Custom:** Indicates that a user added the file to the custom detection list, possibly for DLP purposes or a static location of the file instead of a dynamic one.
- **Unavailable:** Indicates that the AMP for Networks system could not query the AMP cloud.

What Files to Match

The file rule must understand what file types to examine. To make it easier, the system organizes file types into categories. You can use the categories to help locate certain file types more easily. When you have the file types you want in the middle column (aptly named File Types), click the Add button to select them for matching in the rule.

You do not have to add the individual file types but can add an entire category. Simply select the category on the left and then click All Types in Selected Categories in the middle and click Add. The overall chosen categories and file types are maintained in the right column. Click Save to save the final file rule.

Figure 10-23 shows the file rule with file types and categories mixed together in the right-hand column.

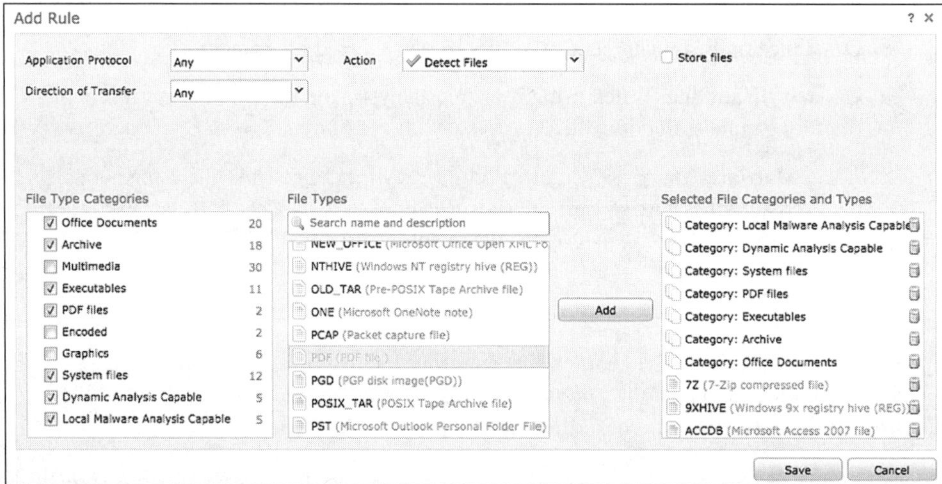

Figure 10-23 *The File Types to Match*

It's important to understand that AMP looks at the header information within the file to determine what the file type is. AMP does not look at the file extension. For example, if someone were to rename a file from atw.scr to atw.exe, that file would still be recognized as a .scr file, not as a .exe file.

What About Those "Zippy" Files?

.zip and other archive files contain other files within them. The contents of an archive file are examined, and the disposition of the archive file itself is assigned based on the files inside it.

If any of the files are determined to be malware, the archive file is assigned the malware disposition. If any of the files are unknown, the archive file is marked as unknown.

All the files within an archive must be found as clean in order for the overall archive to be assigned the clean disposition.

Advanced

A file policy is made up of one or more file rules. In addition, an Advanced tab allows you to set some global settings for all the file rules within a file policy. The advanced options are broken into two different sections:

- General section:
  - **First Time File Analysis:** If this option is disabled, all files detected for the first time are marked as unknown. With this option enabled, the files are analyzed based on the options selected in the file rule.
  - **Enable Custom Detection List:** If this option is enabled and a file is on the custom detection list, it is blocked.
  - **Enable Clean List:** If this option is enabled and a file is on the clean list, it is always allowed.
  - **Mark Files as Malware Based on Dynamic Analysis Threat Score:** From this drop-down list you select a threshold score. Files are considered malware when their score is equal to or worse than the threshold value.
- Advanced File Inspection section:
  - **Inspect Archives:** With this option disabled, AMP bypasses inspecting files of the archive file type, even when they are selected in the file rule.
  - **Block Encrypted Archives:** Because you will not be able to decrypt archives and examine the files within an archive, you can simply choose this option to treat all encrypted archives as possibly malicious and therefore block them.
  - **Block Uninspectable Archives:** Selecting this option allows you to block archive files with contents that the system is unable to inspect for reasons other than encryption, such as file corruption or an archive within an archive exceeding the specified maximum archive depth.
  - **Max Archive Depth:** This option allows you to specify how many levels of archive stacking you wish the system to decompress and examine. Think of it as a Russian stacking doll, where files can be in a .zip that is within a tar.gz file, which is in a .7zip compressed archive.

Figure 10-24 shows the advanced settings for file policies.

At the time this book was published, there was an upcoming capability to allow network connectors to be registered to the same cloud console as AMP for Endpoints. This was not meant to diminish the use of the FMC; rather, the cloud console was set to become the ultimate source for centralized control.

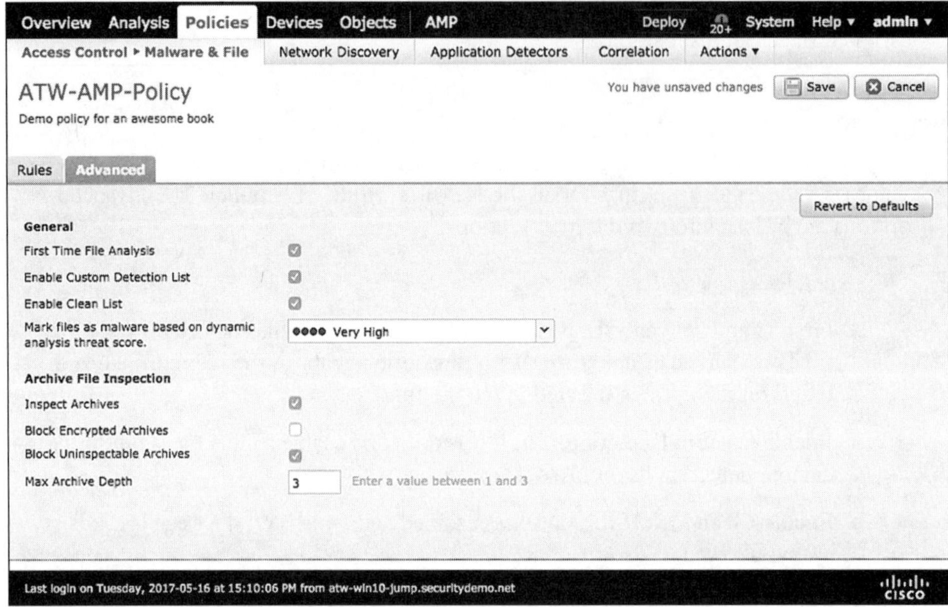

Figure 10-24 *File Policy Advanced Settings*

The ability for the network connector to be registered to the same organization as the endpoint connectors permits a centralized whitelist and simple custom detections. Eventually, those network connectors may even show up in the truly great incident response and investigative tools, such as file and device trajectory.

Figure 10-25 illustrates the shared centralized lists.

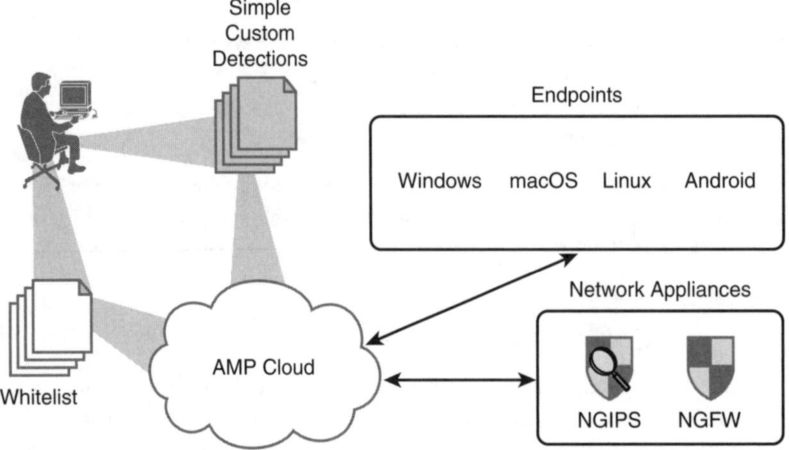

Figure 10-25 *Shared Whitelists and Simple Custom Detections*

AMP for Endpoints

Throughout this book, you have learned that security technologies and processes should not only focus on detection but also should provide the ability to mitigate the impact after a successful attack. An organization must maintain visibility and control across the extended network during the full attack continuum: before the attack takes place, during an active attack, and after an attacker starts to damage systems or steal information.

In this chapter, you have learned all about the components that make up the AMP architecture and the AMP cloud. You have learned how the AMP solution enables malware detection, blocking, continuous analysis, and retrospective views and actions with the following features:

- **File reputation:** AMP analyzes files inline and blocks or applies policies.
- **File sandboxing:** AMP analyzes unknown files to understand true file behavior.
- **File retrospection:** AMP continues to analyze files for changing threat levels.

Remember that the architecture of AMP can be broken down into three main components: the AMP cloud, AMP client connectors, and intelligence sources. This section focuses on the AMP for Endpoints client connector.

Figure 10-26 illustrates the cloud architecture, which receives intelligence from many sources, and a variety of client connectors.

AMP for Endpoints provides more than just endpoint-level visibility into files; it also provides cloud-based detection of malware, in which the cloud constantly updates itself. This enables very rapid detection of known malware because the cloud resources, rather than endpoint resources, are used.

This architecture has a number of benefits. With the majority of the processing being performed in the cloud, the endpoint software remains very lightweight. The cloud is able to provide a historical view of malware activity, which the AMP cloud segments into two activity types:

- **File trajectory:** What endpoints have seen the files
- **Device trajectory:** Actions that the files performed on a given endpoint

With the data storage and processing in the cloud, the solution is able to provide powerful and detailed reporting, as well as very robust management. The AMP for Endpoints agent is also able to take action. For example, it can prevent applications from running, it can quarantine executables and other files, and it can even block malicious network connections based on custom IP blacklists or intelligent dynamic lists of malicious IP addresses.

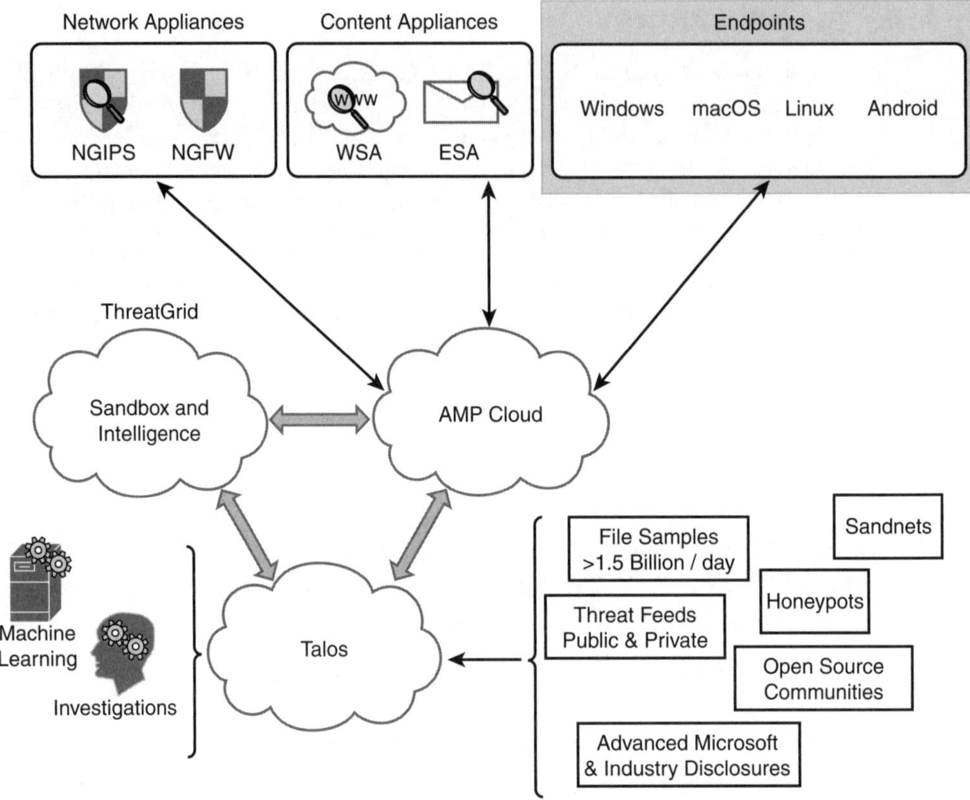

Figure 10-26 *AMP Cloud Architecture*

What Is AMP for Endpoints?

AMP for Endpoints is the connector that resides on (you guessed it) endpoints—Windows, Mac, Linux, and Android endpoints, to be precise. Unlike traditional endpoint protection software that uses a local database of signatures to match a known bad piece of software or a bad file, AMP for Endpoints remains lightweight, sending a hash to the cloud and allowing the cloud to make the intelligent decisions and return a verdict of clean, malicious, or unknown.

Figure 10-27 illustrates the AMP for Endpoints architecture.

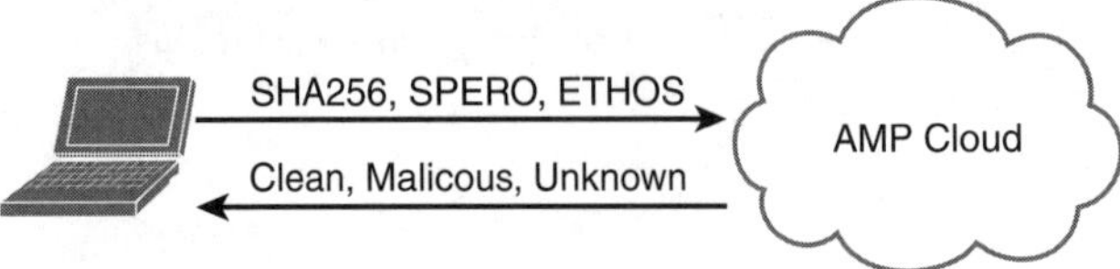

Figure 10-27 *AMP for Endpoints Architecture*

AMP for Endpoints is not completely reliant on the cloud. You can leverage an optional locally installed engine, called TETRA, that provides classic antivirus and scanning capabilities. At the time this book was published, AMP for Endpoints had just been approved to meet Payment Card Industry Data Security Standard (PCI DSS) and Health Insurance Portability and Accountability Act (HIPAA) compliance requirements.

Connections to the AMP Cloud

AMP for Endpoints connectors must be able to reach the AMP cloud to perform hash lookups, procure policy and configuration, obtain signature updates for the TETRA engine, and even update the agent software itself. Communicating to the cloud means the agents may have to be able to go through firewalls and proxy servers to reach the Internet.

If traversing a firewall and/or web proxy to reach the Internet, the connectors require connectivity to numerous servers on the Internet. There are three different public AMP clouds: one for the United States and North America, another for the European Union, and a third for Asia Pacific, Japan, and greater China.

U.S. and North American Cloud

Any firewalls or web proxy solutions must allow connectivity from the AMP connector to the following servers over HTTPS (TCP 443):

- **Event server:** intake.amp.cisco.com
- **Management server:** mgmt.amp.cisco.com
- **Policy server:** policy.amp.cisco.com
- **Error reporting:** crash.immunet.com
- **Endpoint indicator of compromise downloads:** ioc.amp.cisco.com
- **Advanced custom signatures:** custom-signatures.amp.cisco.com
- **Connector upgrades:** upgrades.amp.cisco.com
- **Remote file fetch:** console.amp.cisco.com

To allow the connector to communicate with Cisco cloud servers for file and network disposition lookups, the firewall must allow the clients to connect to the following server over TCP 443:

- **Cloud host:** cloud-ec.amp.cisco.com

With the AMP for Endpoints Windows connectors version 5.0 and higher, there are new servers servers, and those new servers are also using TCP 443:

- **Cloud host:** cloud-ec-asn.amp.cisco.com
- **Enrollment server:** cloud-ec-est.amp.cisco.com

If you have TETRA enabled on any of your AMP for Endpoints connectors, you must allow access to the following server over TCP 80 for signature updates:

- **Update server:** update.amp.cisco.com

European Union Cloud

For organizations leveraging the cloud in the European Union, any firewalls or web proxy solutions must allow connectivity from the AMP connector to the following servers over HTTPS (TCP 443):

- **Event server:** intake.eu.amp.cisco.com
- **Management server:** mgmt.eu.amp.cisco.com
- **Policy server:** policy.eu.amp.cisco.com
- **Error reporting:** crash.eu.amp.sourcefire.com
- **Endpoint indicator of compromise downloads:** ioc.eu.amp.cisco.com
- **Advanced custom signatures:** custom-signatures.eu.amp.cisco.com
- **Connector upgrades:** upgrades.amp.cisco.com
- **Remote file fetch:** console.eu.amp.cisco.com

To allow the connector to communicate with Cisco cloud servers for file and network disposition lookups, the firewall must allow the clients to connect to the following server over TCP 443 (the default) or TCP 32137:

- **Cloud host:** cloud-ec.eu.amp.cisco.com

With AMP for Endpoints Windows connectors version 5.0 and higher, there are different servers; however, those new servers are still using TCP 443:

- **Cloud host:** cloud-ec-asn.eu.amp.cisco.com
- **Enrollment server:** cloud-ec-est.eu.amp.cisco.com

If you have TETRA enabled on any of your AMP for Endpoints connectors, you must allow access to the following server over TCP 80 for signature updates:

- **Update server:** update.amp.cisco.com

Asia Pacific, Japan, and Greater China Cloud

For organizations leveraging the cloud in Asia Pacific, Japan, and greater China (APJC), any firewalls or web proxy solutions must allow connectivity from the AMP connector to the following servers over HTTPS (TCP 443):

- **Event server:** intake.apjc.amp.cisco.com
- **Management server:** mgmt.apjc.amp.cisco.com
- **Policy server:** policy.apjc.amp.cisco.com
- **Error reporting:** crash.apjc.amp.sourcefire.com
- **Endpoint indicator of compromise downloads:** ioc.apjc.amp.cisco.com
- **Advanced custom signatures:** custom-signatures.apjc.amp.cisco.com
- **Connector upgrades:** upgrades.amp.cisco.com
- **Remote file fetch:** console.apjc.amp.cisco.com

To allow the connector to communicate with Cisco cloud servers for file and network disposition lookups, the firewall must allow the clients to connect to the following server over TCP 443 (the default) or TCP 32137:

- **Cloud host:** cloud-ec.apjc.amp.cisco.com

With AMP for Endpoints Windows connectors version 5.0 and higher, there are different servers; however, those new servers are still using TCP 443:

- **Cloud host:** cloud-ec-asn.apjc.amp.cisco.com
- **Enrollment server:** cloud-ec-est.apjc.amp.cisco.com

If you have TETRA enabled on any of your AMP for Endpoints connectors, you must allow access to the following server over TCP 80 for signature updates:

- **Update server:** update.amp.cisco.com

Outbreak Control

With a solution as powerful and extensive as AMP for Endpoints, it is very difficult to determine the best place to start in describing how to configure and use the system. However, it makes logical sense to begin with outbreak control because the objects you create for outbreak control are key aspects of endpoint policies.

Outbreak control provides lists that allow you to customize AMP for Endpoints to your organization's needs. The main lists can be seen from the AMP cloud console by clicking the outbreak control menu, which opens a deep blue menu illustrating the different outbreak control options: Custom Detections, Application Control, Network, and Endpoint IOC (see Figure 10-28).

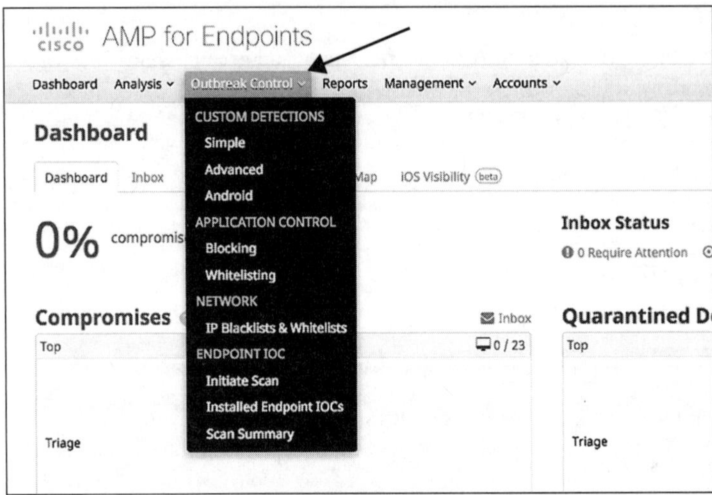

Figure 10-28 *Outbreak Control Menu*

Custom Detections

You can think of custom detections as a blacklist. You use them to identify files that you want to detect and quarantine. When a custom detection is defined, not only do endpoints quarantine matching files when they see them, but any AMP for Endpoints agents that have seen the file before the custom detection was created can also quarantine the file through *retrospection*, also known as *cloud recall*.

Simple custom detection allows you to add file signatures for files, while advanced custom detection is more like traditional antivirus signatures.

Simple Custom Detections

Creating a simple custom detection is similar to adding new entries to a blacklist. You define one or more files that you are trying to quarantine by building a list of SHA-256 hashes. If you already have the SHA-256 hash of the file, you can paste that hash directly into the UI, or you can upload files directly and allow the cloud to create the SHA-256 hash for you.

To create a simple custom detection, navigate to Outbreak Control > Custom Detections > Simple, and the list of all existing simple custom detections is displayed. To add a new one, you must type it in the Name box and click Save (see Figure 10-29), and it is added to the list below, as shown in Figure 10-30, and automatically edited—with the contents displayed on the right-hand side.

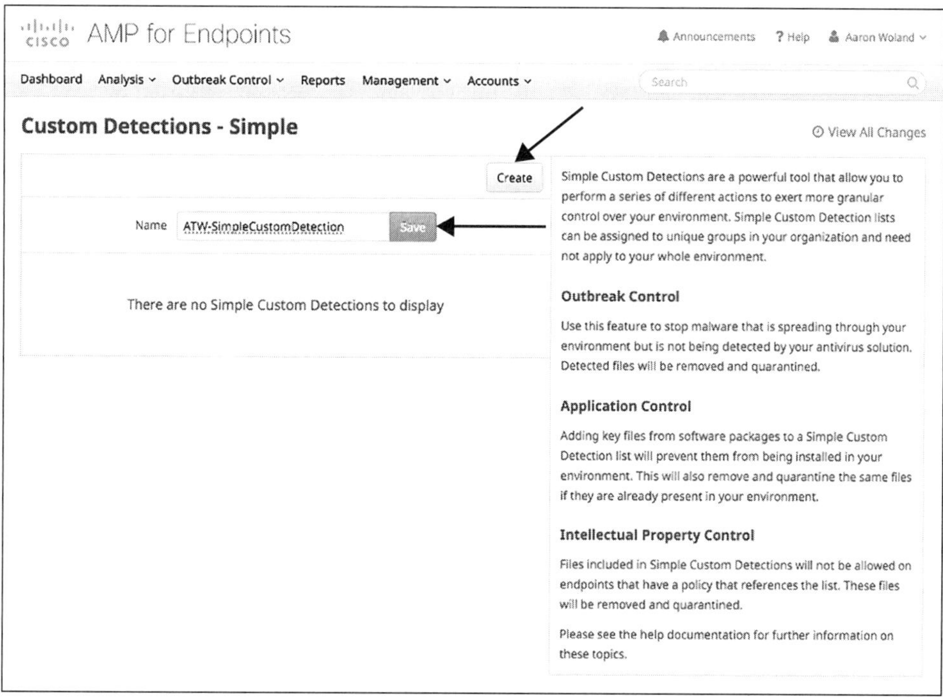

Figure 10-29 *Creating a Simple Custom Detection*

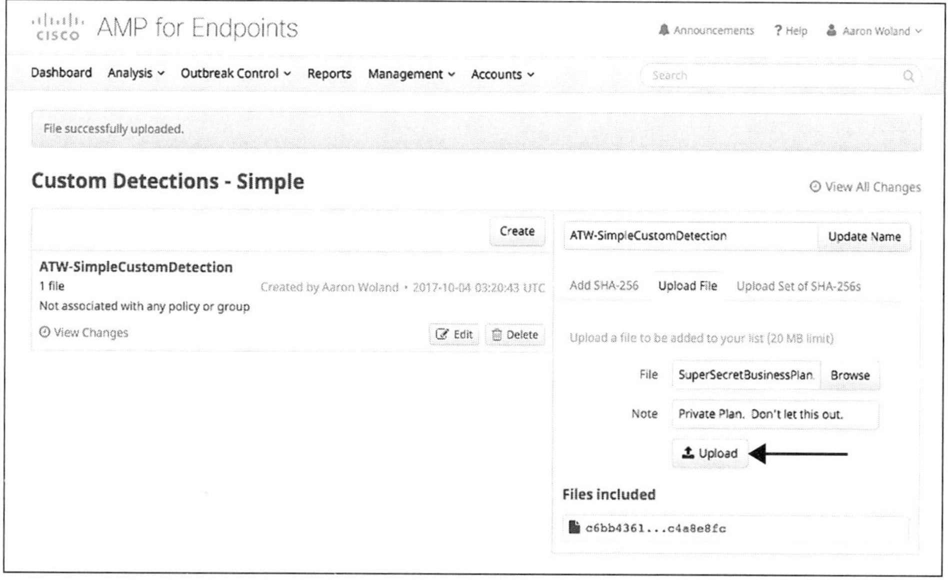

Figure 10-30 *Detection Added and Contents on the Right Side*

If you have the SHA-256 hash of a file already, simply paste it in, add a note, and click Save. Otherwise, you can upload a file, add a note, and click Upload (refer to Figure 10-30). When the file is uploaded, the hash is created and shown on the bottom-right side. You must click Save, or the hash will not be stored as part of your simple custom detection.

Advanced Custom Detections

Simple custom detections involve just looking for the SHA-256 hash of a file. Advanced custom detections offer many more signature types to the detection, based on ClamAV signatures, including the following:

- File body–based signatures
- MD5 signatures
- MD5 PE section–based signatures
- An extended signature format (wildcards, regular expressions, and offsets)
- Logical signatures
- Icon signatures

To create an advanced custom detection, navigate to Outbreak Control > Custom Detections > Advanced, and the list of all existing advanced custom detections is displayed, as shown in Figure 10-31.

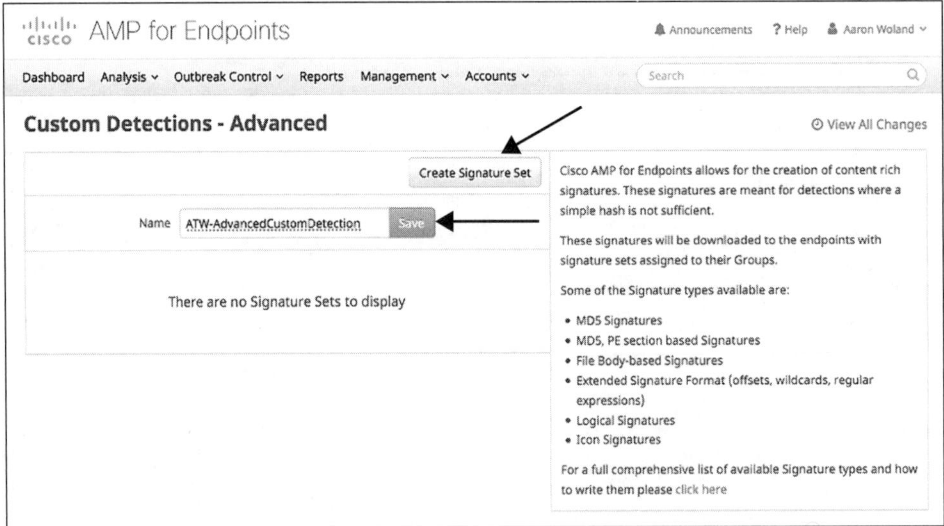

Figure 10-31 *Custom Detections—Advanced*

To add a new custom detection, you must type it in the Name box and click Save (refer to Figure 10-31), and it is added to the list below, as shown in Figure 10-32. Then click Edit to display the contents of the new advanced detection object on the right side.

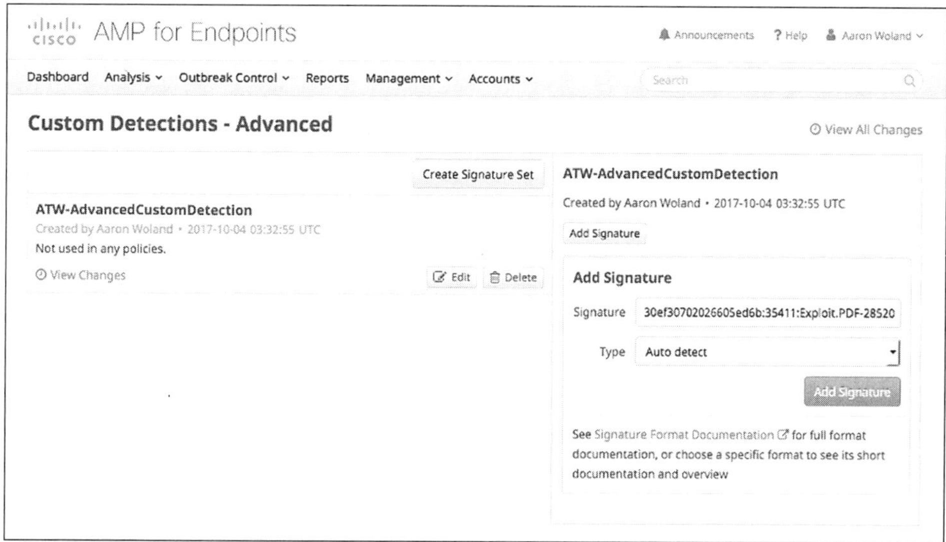

Figure 10-32 *Adding an Advanced Custom Detection*

As shown in Figure 10-33, the ClamAV signature types can be auto-detected or manually selected from the drop-down list.

ATW-AdvancedCustomDetection
Created by Aaron Woland • 2017-10-04 03:32:55 UTC
Add Signature | Build Database From Signature Set
Add Signature
Signature
Type Auto detect
Auto detect
cdb 3.6 Signatures based on container metadata
db3.3.3 Basic signature format
hdb3.1 MD5
hsbSHA1/SHA256
idb3.4 Icon signatures for PE files
ldb3.3.5 Logical signatures
mdb3.2 MD5, PE section based
msbSHA1/SHA256 PE section based
ndb3.3.4 Extended signature format
See Signatu
documenta
documenta
hdb: Exploit.

Figure 10-33 *ClamAV Signature Types*

Figure 10-34 shows what AMP for Endpoints looks like after the ClamAV signature string 5d47b318b55c130ef30702026605ed6b:35411:Exploit.PDF-28520 is pasted in, Auto Detect is selected as the type, and the Create button is clicked. You can see there that the UI has converted it correctly into hdb:Exploit.PDF-28520.UNOFFICIAL.

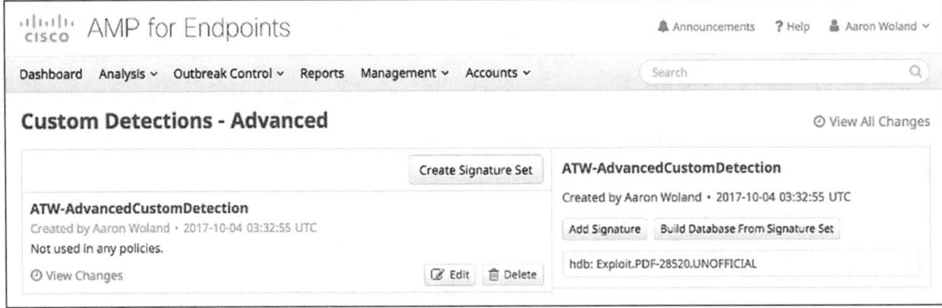

Figure 10-34 *Adding a Signature*

Next, click the Build Database from Signature Set button, and a success message is displayed, indicating the successful creation of the advanced custom detection signature set, as shown in Figure 10-35.

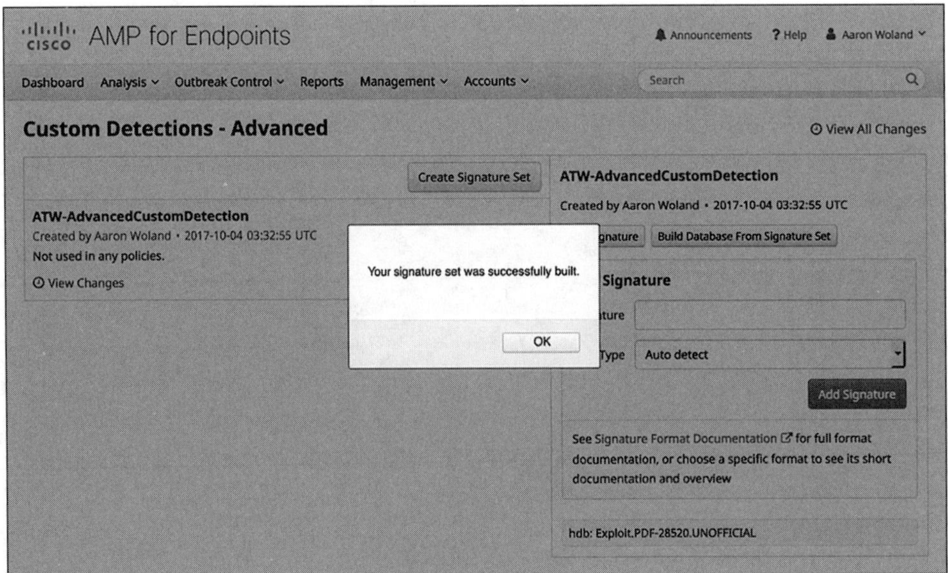

Figure 10-35 *Successfully Built Advanced Detection*

A View Changes link is visible with every custom detection, both simple and advanced. The AMP cloud maintains an audit log for each of the detection lists, and you can view it by clicking View Changes. Figure 10-36 shows an example of the audit log.

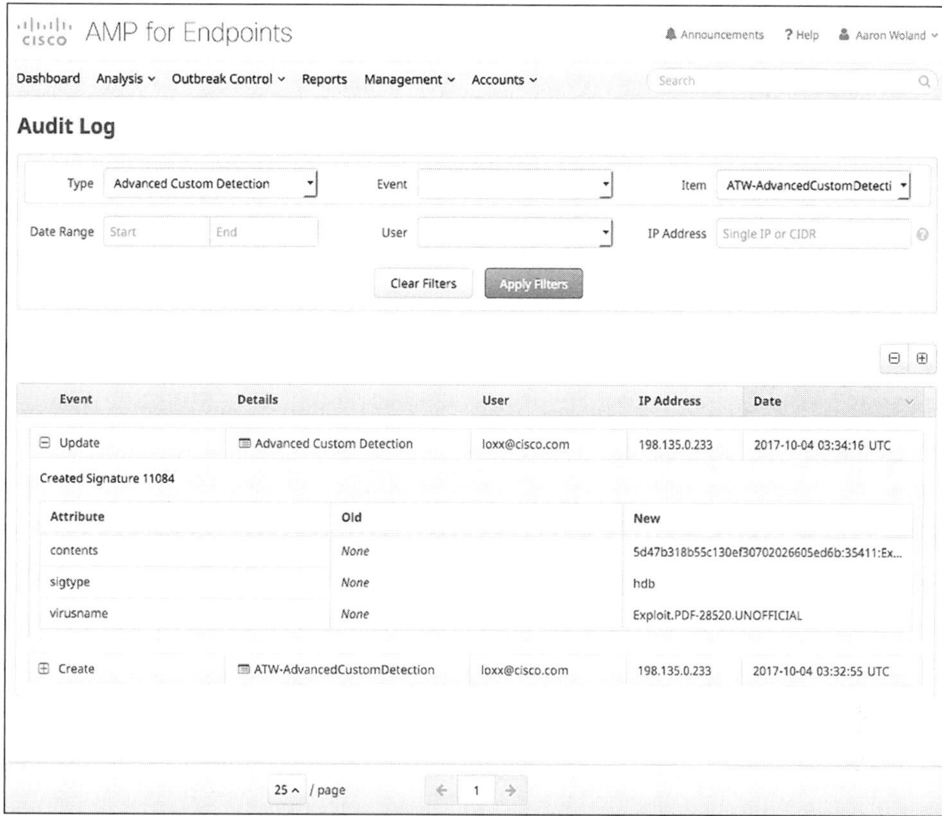

Figure 10-36 *Audit Log for an Advanced Custom Detection*

Android Custom Detections

Android detections are defined separately from the ones used by Windows or Mac. The detections look for specific applications, and you build a custom detection by either uploading the app's .apk file or selecting it from the AMP console's list of inventory.

You can choose to use these custom detections for two main functions: outbreak control and application control.

When using an Android custom detection for outbreak control, you are using the detections to stop malware that is spreading through mobile devices in your organization. When a malicious app is detected, the user of the device is notified and prompted to uninstall it.

You don't have to use these detections just for malware; you can also use them to stop applications that you don't want installed on devices in your organization. This is what the AMP console refers to as *application control*. Simply add to an Android custom detection list apps that you don't want installed, and AMP will notify the user of the unwanted application and prompt the user to uninstall it, just as if it were a malicious app.

To create an Android custom detection, navigate to Outbreak Control > Custom Detections > Android, and the list of all existing Android custom detections, if any exist, appears. Click Create to add a new one and provide it a name, as shown in Figure 10-37. Then click Save.

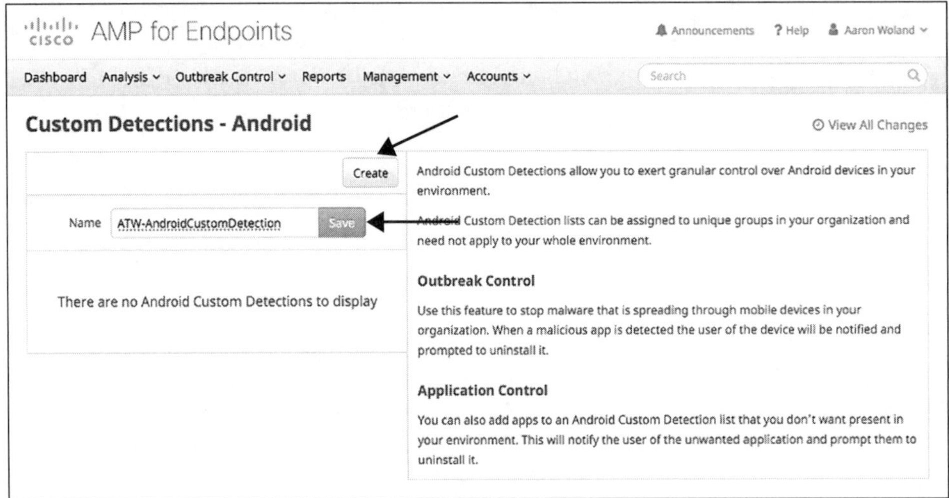

Figure 10-37 *Custom Detections—Android*

After the new Android detection is created, you can click Edit to add the Android apps you wish to detect as either malware or unwanted, as shown in Figure 10-38.

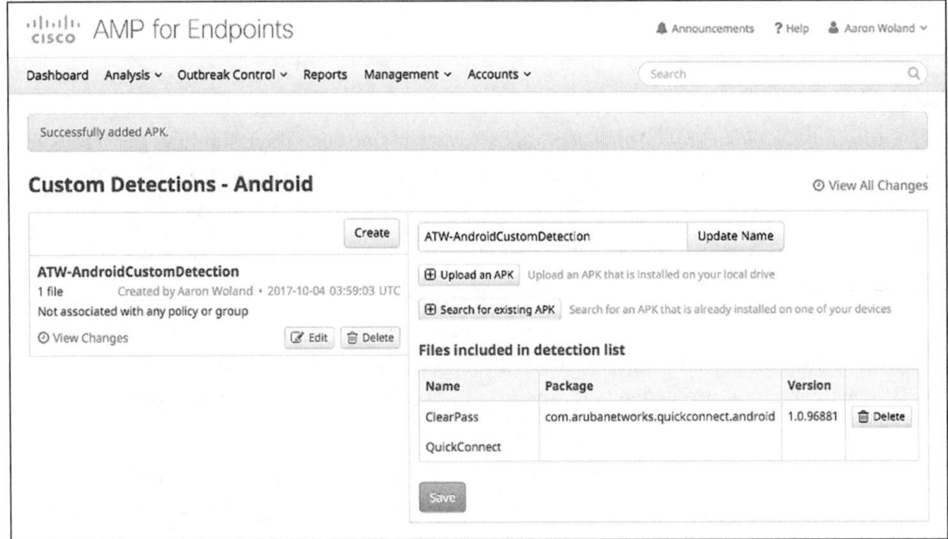

Figure 10-38 *Custom Detections—Android APK Uploaded*

Network IP Blacklists and Whitelists

Outbreak control IP lists are used in conjunction with device flow correlation (DFC) detections. DFC allows you to flag or even block suspicious network activity. You can use policies to specify AMP for Endpoints behavior when a suspicious connection is detected, and you can also specify whether the connector should use addresses in the Cisco intelligence feed, the custom IP lists you create yourself, or a combination of both.

You use an IP whitelist to define IPv4 addresses that should not be blocked or flagged by DFC. AMP bypasses or ignores the intelligence feeds as they relate to the IPv4 addresses in the whitelist.

You use an IP blacklist to create DFC detections. Traffic that matches entries in the blacklist is flagged or blocked as the DFC rule dictates.

To create an IP blacklist or whitelist, navigate to Outbreak Control > Network > IP Blacklists & Whitelists, as shown in Figure 10-39.

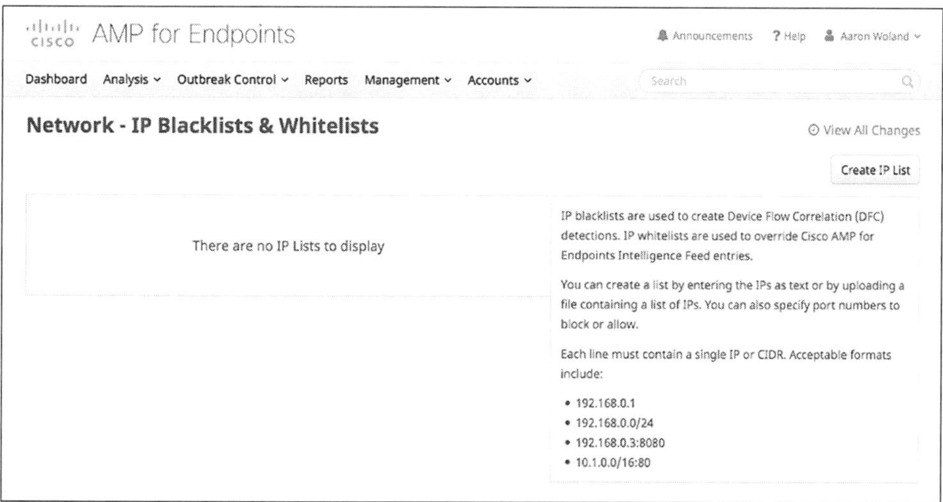

Figure 10-39 *Network—IP Blacklists & Whitelists*

Here you click Create IP List to start a new IP list, and you see the New IP List configuration screen, where you can create an IP list either by typing a name for the list, designating whether it should be a whitelist or blacklist, and entering the IPv4 addresses in classless inter-domain routing (CIDR) notation, or by uploading a file containing a list of IPs. You can also specify port numbers to block or allow. If you type the addresses, each line must contain a single IP or CIDR. Acceptable formats include:

- **10.1.100.0/24:** A standard network range designated by network/mask-length CIDR notation
- **192.168.26.26:** A single IPv4 address
- **10.1.250.254:443:** A single IPv4 address with a port specified (UDP and TCP)

- **10.250.1.1/16:8443:** A CIDR-notated network range with a port specified (UDP and TCP)

Figure 10-40 shows the New IP List screen with a mixture of entries entered as text. Once the list is created, you can edit it only by downloading the resulting file and uploading it back to the AMP console.

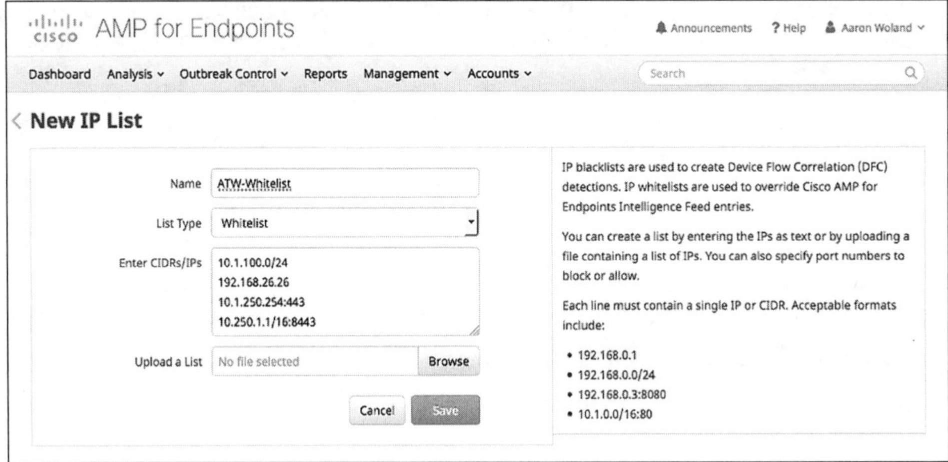

Figure 10-40 *New IP List*

You can click Create IP List to create the text file in the cloud console, and your new IP list will be shown on the screen. If you click Edit, you can change the name of the IP list only. In order to truly update the contents of the list, you must click Download, delete the list, and then create a new list with the same name and upload the modified file. IP lists can contain up to 100,000 lines or may be a maximum of 2 MB in size.

As with the custom detections, the AMP console maintains an audit trail for IP lists that you can view by clicking View Changes.

Application Control

Much like files, applications can be detected, blocked, and whitelisted. With application control, AMP is not looking for the name of the application but the SHA-256 hash, just as it is with other files.

To create a new application control list for blocking an application, navigate to Outbreak Control > Application Control > Blocking. The Sourcefire AMP team certainly understands the concept of consistency in GUIs: This GUI works just like so many other areas of the interface. If any existing blocking lists exist, they are displayed here. As you would expect, to create a new list, click Create (see Figure 10-41). You must name the list and click Save before you can add any applications to the blocking list.

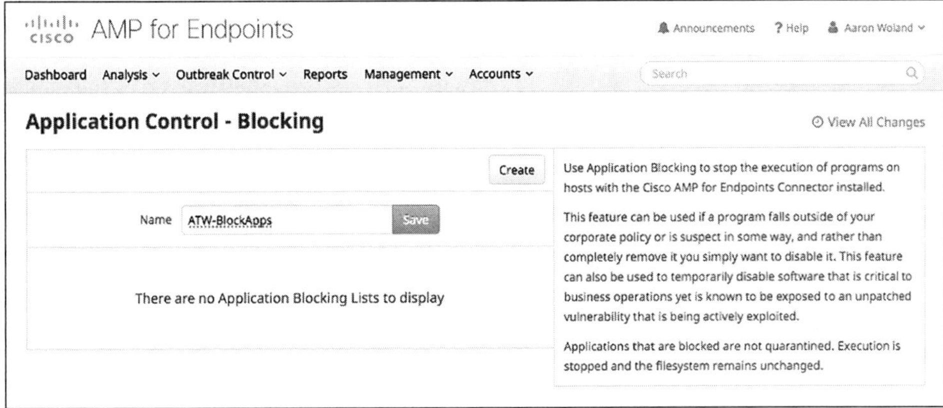

Figure 10-41 *Outbreak Control > Application Control > Blocking*

Once the list has been created and saved, click Edit to add any applications. If you already have the SHA-256 hash, add it. Otherwise, you can upload one application at a time and have the AMP cloud console calculate the hash for you, as long as the file is not larger than the 20 MB limit. You can also upload an existing list. Figure 10-42 shows a blocking list with an existing application hash shown at the bottom of the right-hand side, while another file is being uploaded for hash calculation.

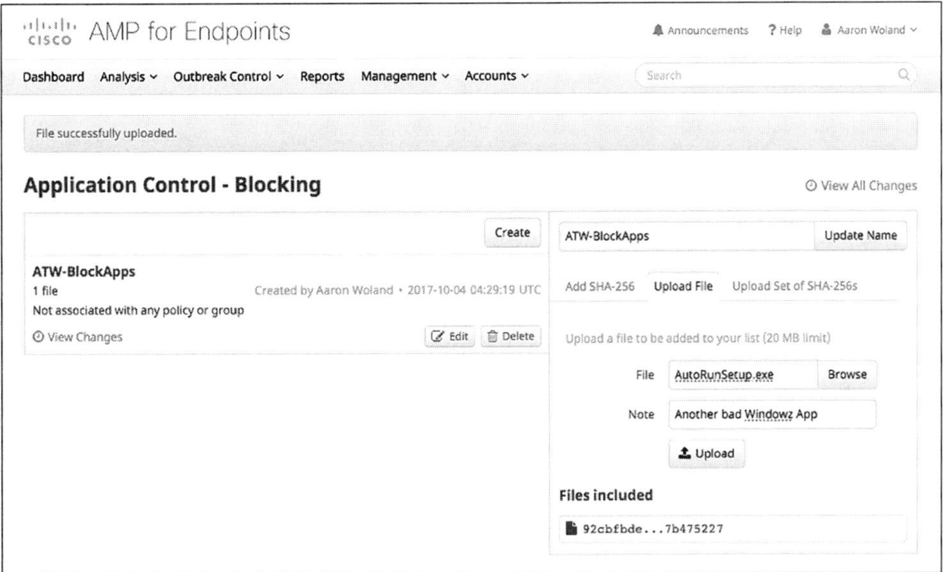

Figure 10-42 *Adding Application Hashes to the Blocking List*

Application whitelists work the same way. Navigate to Outbreak Control > Application Control > Whitelisting, and you see a list of any existing whitelists. Click Create to add a new one, provide it a name, and click Save.

Once the list has been created and saved, click Edit to add any applications. If you already have the SHA-256 hash, add it. Otherwise, you can upload one application at a time and have the AMP cloud console calculate the hash for you, as long as the file is not larger than the 20 MB limit. You can also upload an existing list. Figure 10-43 shows a whitelisting list that contains an existing application (SafeGuardPDFViewer.exe).

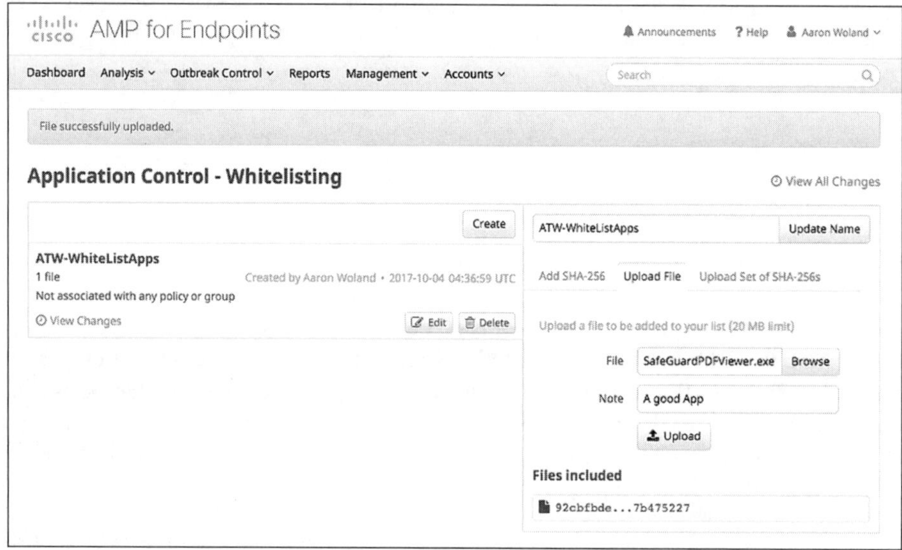

Figure 10-43 *Adding Application Hashes to the Whitelisting List*

Don't forget to click Save after adding the hash to the list.

Exclusions

There is one more object you should try creating before you build your policies: an exclusions list. An exclusions list is a set of directories, file extensions, or even threat names that you do not want the AMP agent to scan or convict as malware.

Exclusions can be used to resolve conflicts with other security products or mitigate performance issues by excluding directories that contain large files that are written to frequently, such as databases. If you are running an antivirus product on computers with the AMP for Endpoints connector, you will want to exclude the location where that product is installed. Microsoft Exchange is another application where you must exclude the directories where the exchange database and logs are stored.

It's important to remember that any files stored in a location that has been added to an exclusions list will not be subjected to application blocking, simple custom detections, or advanced custom detections.

The following are the available exclusion types:

- **Threat:** Exclude specific detections by threat name

- **Extension:** Exclude files with a specific extension
- **Wildcard:** Exclude files or paths using wildcards for filenames, extensions, or paths
- **Path:** Exclude files at a given path

For Windows, path exclusions may use constant special ID lists (CSIDL), which are Microsoft names for common file paths. For more on CSIDL, see https://msdn.microsoft.com/en-us/library/windows/desktop/bb762494%28v=vs.85%29.aspx.

To create a new exclusion set, navigate to Management > Exclusions. Here you see a list of any existing exclusions and can create new ones. Click Create Exclusion Set, provide a name for the set, and click Save. The contents of the exclusion set are automatically listed on the right-hand side.

As shown in Figure 10-44, new exclusion sets are created with some default exclusions. Many of these exclusions are specific to the default installation paths of antivirus products and designed to cover a large variety of installations. Figure 10-44 shows an example of a Windows exclusion set, and you can also see in this figure that there are default exclusion sets for Windows, Windows domain controllers, Windows servers, Mac, and Linux.

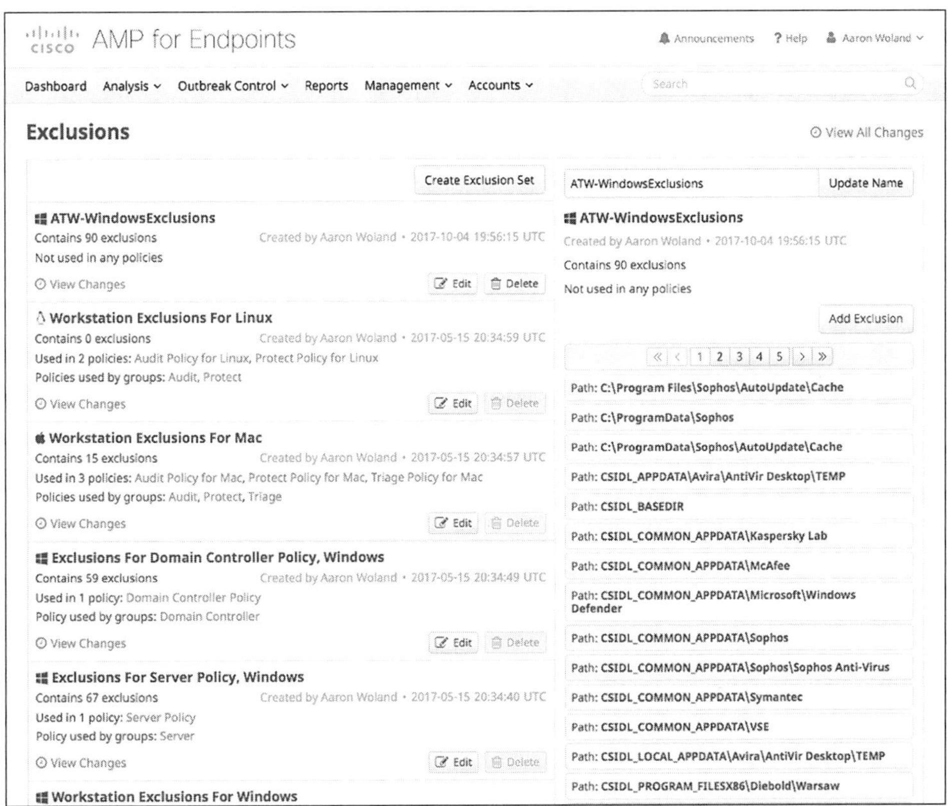

Figure 10-44 *Windows Exclusion Set*

The Many Faces of AMP for Endpoints

AMP for Endpoints is available for multiple platforms: Windows, Android, Mac, and Linux. You can see the available connectors from the cloud console by navigating to Management > Download Connector. Here you see the types of endpoints, as shown in Figure 10-45.

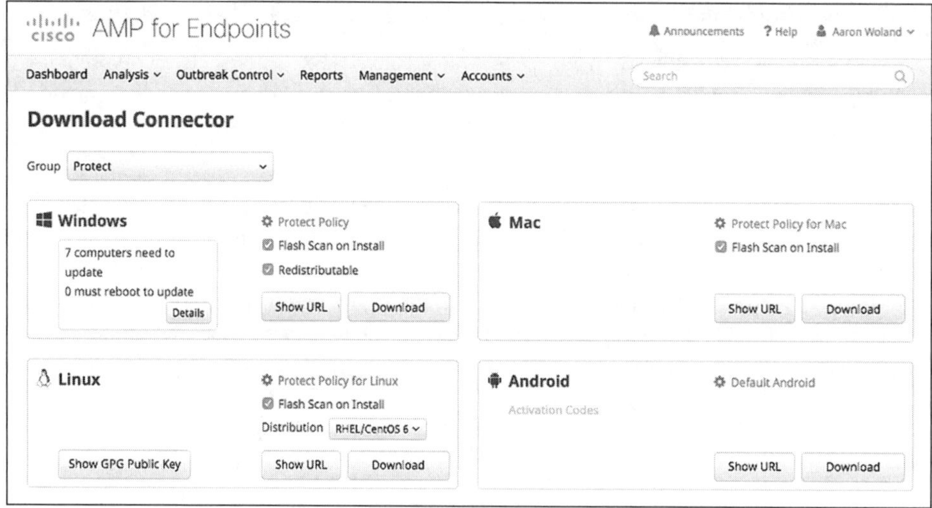

Figure 10-45 *AMP Connector Types*

The following sections go through the options for each of the operating systems shown in Figure 10-45, one-by-one.

> **Note** iOS is a very special type of connector, and is not downloaded or configured in the same way as the others.

AMP for Windows

The AMP for Endpoints connector on Windows monitors files as they are copied, moved, or executed, in addition to monitoring IP connections (TCP and UDP). AMP for Endpoints also performs scan operations to determine the parent, file, or IP disposition by first looking in the local cache and then querying the upstream cloud if the disposition is not in the cache or if the time to live (TTL) has expired.

If the file or parent disposition comes back as malicious, then it is checked against "guard rails" before being quarantined. The guard rails are a list of files defined by the AMP developers that should never be quarantined in order to ensure that AMP does not accidently quarantine files whose quarantine can render the system unusable.

Windows Policies

The Windows connector is certainly the connector with the most policy options. From the AMP cloud console, navigate to Management > Policies > Windows. In this screen, you can see existing AMP policies for Windows and also create new ones, as illustrated in Figure 10-46.

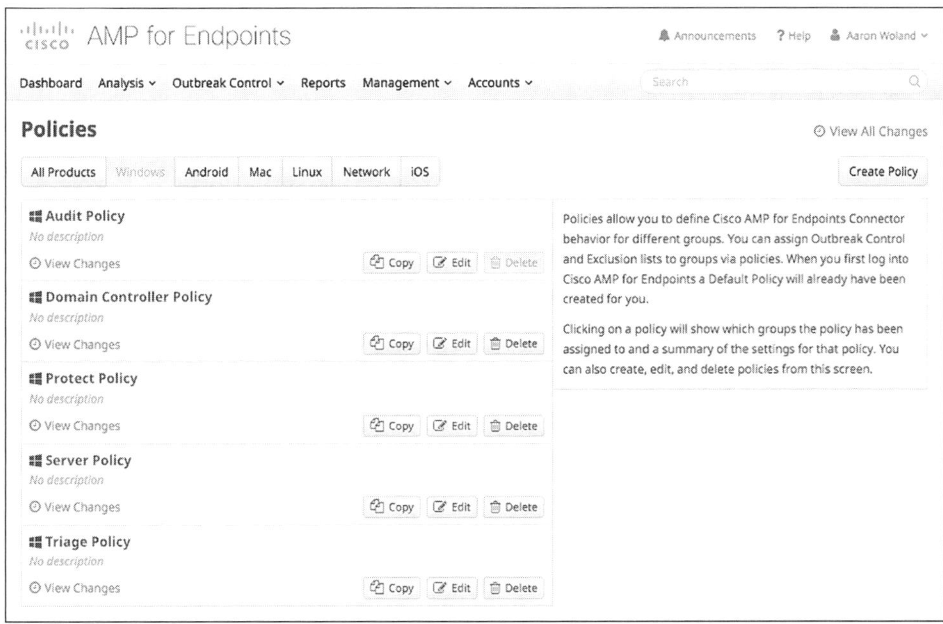

Figure 10-46 *Windows Policies*

In order to examine all the options available to a Windows AMP policy, this section works through the creation of a brand-new policy. To set Windows policies, click Create Policy, select Windows from the drop-down in the Create Policy dialog, and click Create Policy (see Figure 10-47).

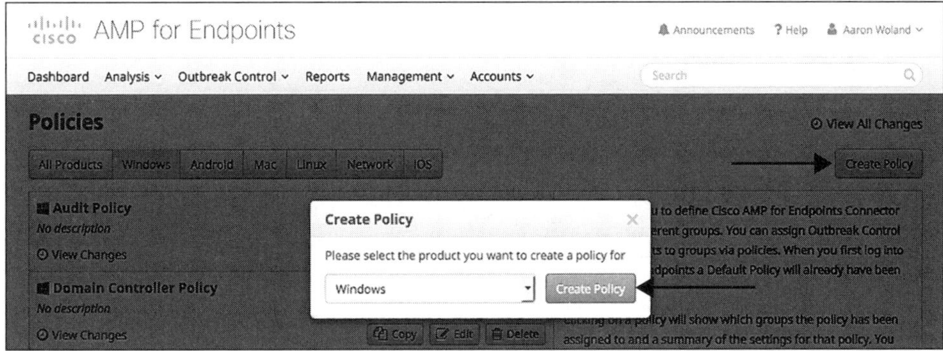

Figure 10-47 *Selecting the Connector OS*

You are now presented with the New Policy window, where a policy is broken into numerous sections, and the user interface is organized in an orderly manner. The main body of the policy contains many of the detections and controls created previously in this chapter, and there are separate tabs below for more specific options.

Start by naming the new policy and providing a description. Then select the custom detections, application control lists, whitelists, and exclusions you created earlier in this chapter, as shown in Figure 10-48. When they are all selected, click Create Policy to save the policy.

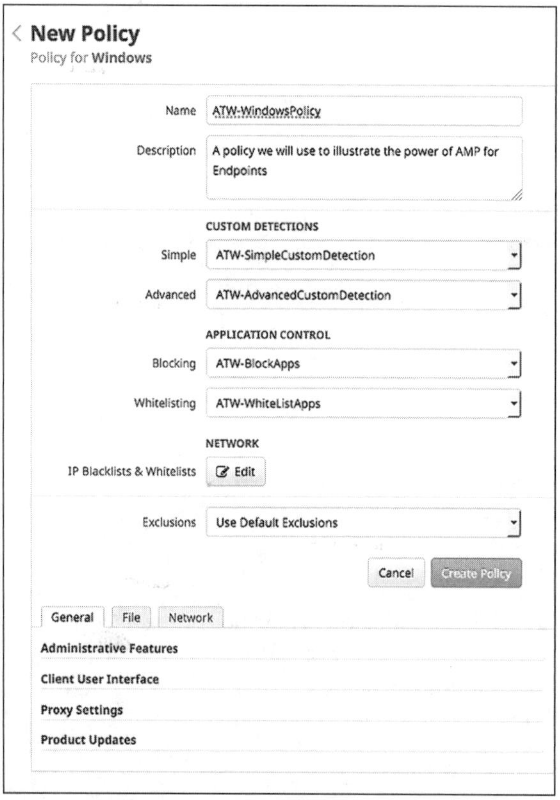

Figure 10-48 *Creating a Windows Policy*

Click Edit for the newly created Windows policy and scroll to the bottom of the screen. This is where a lot of the AMP agent configuration and customization takes place. There are three main types of AMP connector configurations: general, file, and network.

The General Tab

The General tab of a Windows policy has the basic settings for the AMP for Endpoints connector, such as proxy settings and update schedules. There are four component areas within the general settings tab: Administrative Features, Client User Interface, Proxy Settings, and Product Updates. These areas are explained in the next sections. One very nice UI feature here is that a blue informational icon shows whenever a default setting is changed, as shown in Figure 10-49.

Figure 10-49 *Windows Policy General Tab*

Administrative Features

As you can see in Figure 10-49, there are nine configurable settings in the administrative features section of the General tab:

- **Send User Name in Events:** This setting relates to the name of the user who launched the process. This is very useful for tracking down who was on a system that may be seeing malware.
- **Send Filename and Path Info:** This setting enables you to have the AMP agent send the filename and path information to the AMP cloud so that it is visible in the Events tab's device trajectory and file trajectory settings. Unchecking this setting stops this information from being sent.
- **Heartbeat Interval:** This setting allows you to configure how often the AMP agent should call home to the AMP cloud. During that call home connection, the agent checks whether there are any policy updates, any software updates to download or scans to perform, or any files to restore via the cloud recall or by the administrator.
- **Connector Log Level and Tray Log Level:** These settings allow you to change the default log level to debug when directed by Cisco TAC.

- **Connector Protection:** This setting allows you to require a password for stopping the AMP service or uninstalling the AMP agent.
- **Connector Protection Password:** This setting allows you to fill in the password for the connection protection, as the name implies.
- **Automated Crash Dump Uploads:** When this setting is enabled, the connector will automatically send crash dumps to Cisco for analysis in the event that the connector crashes.
- **Command Line Capture:** Selecting this setting allows the connector to capture command-line arguments (including usernames, filenames, passwords, and so on) used during file execution and send the information to AMP for Endpoints. This information becomes visible in device trajectory for administrators as long as they have two-step verification enabled.

> **Note** If Command Line Capture is enabled and Connector Log Level is set to Debug, you can use Command Line Logging to log captured command-line arguments to the local connector log file on the endpoint.

Client User Interface

This section allows you to configure what the end user sees on the Windows system. Many organizations prefer to show the agent icon in the system tray so that it is obvious that the agent is running, but they often choose to hide all notifications so that the users are not bothered by the connector. There are seven options in this section, as shown in Figure 10-50.

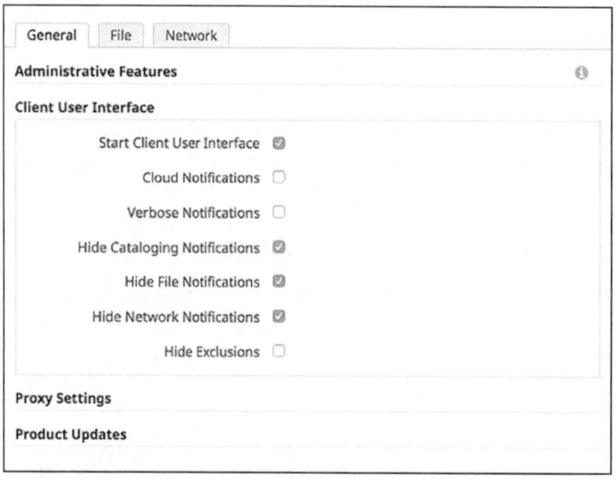

Figure 10-50 *Client User Interface*

- **Start Client User Interface:** This setting allows you to hide the user interface or show it. The agent is running either way, but this setting offers you the option of keeping it out of the system tray. If you change this option, the new setting takes effect at the next agent restart.
- **Cloud Notifications:** This setting allows you to enable those fun balloon pop-ups from the agent icon in the Windows system tray. If this setting is selected, a pop-up appears when the agent is successfully connected to the cloud, and it displays the number of users and detections registered to the cloud.
- **Verbose Notifications:** When this setting is enabled, the end user will be completely harassed by a series of text boxes that pop up from the Windows system tray icon, telling the user about nearly every file that traverses the AMP connector. *Leave this unselected* unless you are in the process of active troubleshooting or want to punish your end users.
- **Hide Cataloging Notifications:** This setting relates to endpoint indicator of compromise scans and hides the user notification about cataloging.
- **Hide File Notifications:** This setting allows you to hide malicious file notifications from being displayed when a file is convicted or quarantined by the AMP agent.
- **Hide Network Notifications:** Selecting this option means that messages are not displayed when a malicious network connection is detected or blocked by AMP.
- **Hide Exclusions:** Selecting this option means that the list of exclusions is not displayed to the end user through the user interface.

It is highly recommended that you keep any interactivity with the end user to an absolute minimum. End users can get frustrated and annoyed when burdened by notifications they don't understand or care to understand.

Proxy Settings

In today's world of mobile workstations, configuring a hard-coded proxy server may not always be the way to go for a best-practices configuration. However, with the wonderful cloud-based technologies available, such as Cisco's Cloud Web Security solution (blatant plug), you may wish to configure the AMP agent to always use that cloud proxy solution. Proxy servers and some of the complications that come along with them are covered in more detail later in this chapter, but in the meantime, let's take a look at the proxy settings section of the General tab, which is displayed in Figure 10-51.

By populating the section of this page, you can configure a hard-coded proxy server for the agents that receive this policy. As you can see in the figure, basic and NTLM authentications are both supported, as are straight HTTP and SOCKS proxies. If you use NTLM, be sure to use the DOMAIN\USER notation for the account.

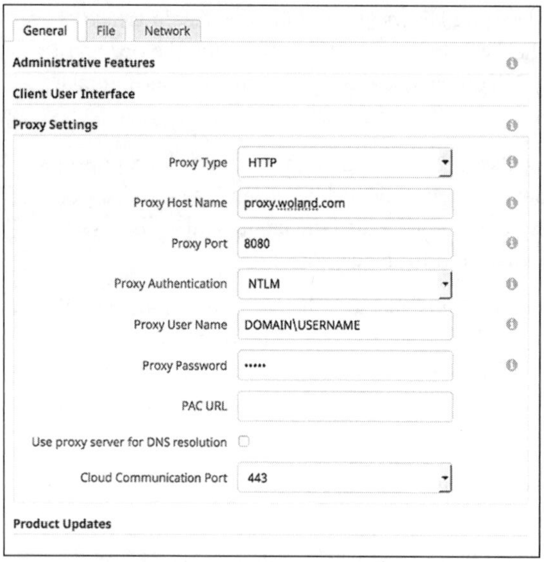

General | File | Network

Administrative Features

Client User Interface

Proxy Settings

Proxy Type: HTTP

Proxy Host Name: proxy.woland.com

Proxy Port: 8080

Proxy Authentication: NTLM

Proxy User Name: DOMAIN\USERNAME

Proxy Password: •••••

PAC URL

Use proxy server for DNS resolution

Cloud Communication Port: 443

Product Updates

Figure 10-51 *Proxy Settings*

Product Updates

The policy that is applied to the AMP connector tells it whether and when to update to a newer version. You select the version from the drop-down and choose a time window for the updates to occur. When selecting the update time window, the cloud server uses an algorithm to find the best interval for updating all the connectors within that designated time range. Figure 10-52 shows the product updates settings.

General | File | Network

Administrative Features

Client User Interface

Proxy Settings

Product Updates

Product Version: 5.1.13.10483

No computers require updates

Update Server: upgrades.amp.cisco.com

Start Update Window: 2017-10-06 12:37 UTC

End Update Window: 2017-10-08 00:00 UTC

Update Interval: 30 minutes

Block Update if Reboot Required

Reboot: Force reboot after...

Reboot Delay: 30 minutes

Figure 10-52 *Product Updates*

A reboot is required for the running AMP agent to reflect the upgrade. As shown in Figure 10-52, settings are available to not reboot the system, to ask the user if it's okay to proceed with a reboot, or to simply reboot the system.

The File Tab

You use the File tab to configure the settings and behavior of file scanning within the AMP for Endpoints agent. You can set which engines to use, a schedule for scans, and cache settings. There are six component areas of the File tab: Modes, Cache Settings, Ethos, Engines, Cloud Policy, and Scheduled Scans.

Figure 10-53 shows the File tab with the Modes component area expanded.

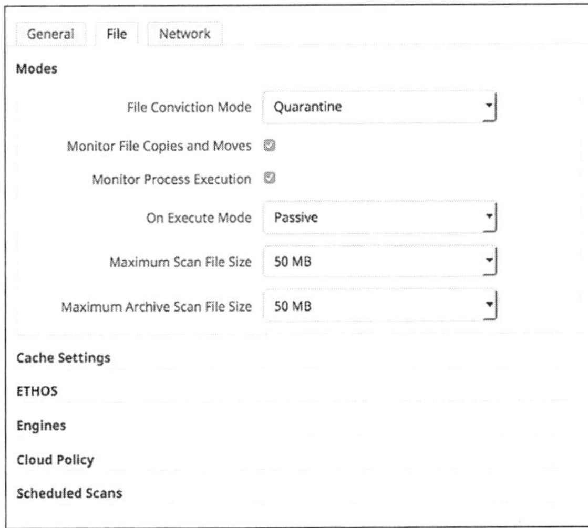

Figure 10-53 *File Tab, Modes Configuration*

Modes

The Modes section determines how the AMP connector should behave during file moves or copies as well as how it should behave when a file is executed. It includes the following settings:

- **File Conviction Mode:** You can choose either Audit or Quarantine. In other words, is this a monitor-only deployment, or should the AMP agent take action against the convicted file?
- **Monitor File Copies and Moves:** You can set this to be either on or off to indicate whether AMP should care about files when they are moved or copied within or off the system.
- **Monitor Process Execution:** You can set this to be either on or off to indicate whether AMP should take interest in executable files when they are run.

- **On Execute Mode:** You can set this to either Passive or Active to indicate whether the file lookup should happen before the executable is allowed to run or whether it should occur in parallel. When the endpoint has another antivirus product installed, it is best to leave this set to Passive to avoid performance issues.
- **Maximum Scan File Size:** Any file larger than this setting will not be scanned by AMP. 50 MB is the default size—and also the largest size available.
- **Maximum Archive Scan File Size:** Any archive file (.zip, .tar, and so on) larger than this setting will not be scanned by AMP. The default size is 50 MB, and the maximum archive size is 100 MB.

Cache Settings

As you know, the AMP connector focuses on the disposition that the AMP cloud assigns to the SHA-256 hash of a file. The hash and the disposition are stored in a local cache for better performance and reducing redundant lookups of the same hash value. The settings in the Cache Settings section of the File tab determine how long the hashes should remain in the cache. As Figure 10-54 shows, there are four different cache settings, all of which are configured with the number of seconds before checking those file hashes again:

Figure 10-54 *File Tab, Cache Settings*

- **Malicious Cache TTL:** How long to hold on to the disposition of a file hash when it has been deemed malicious. The default is one hour.
- **Clean Cache TTL:** How long to hold on to the information when a file has been assigned a clean disposition. The default is seven days.
- **Unknown Cache TTL:** How long to store the dispositions of files that receive an unknown disposition. The default is one hour.
- **Application Blocking TTL:** How long an Outbreak Control > Application Control > Blocking list is cached. The default is one hour.

Ethos

Ethos is a "fuzzy fingerprinting" engine that uses static or passive heuristics. Think of it as Cisco's file-grouping engine. It groups families of files together, and when variants of a malware are detected, it marks the Ethos hash as malicious, and entire families of malware are instantly detected.

Ethos can be a bit resource-intensive, and therefore it is enabled only for file move and copy by default, as shown in Figure 10-55. When scanning on copy or move, AMP allows the copy or move action to finish and then queues another thread to calculate the Ethos for a file. That same passive performance luxury is not available for On Execute or On Scan actions.

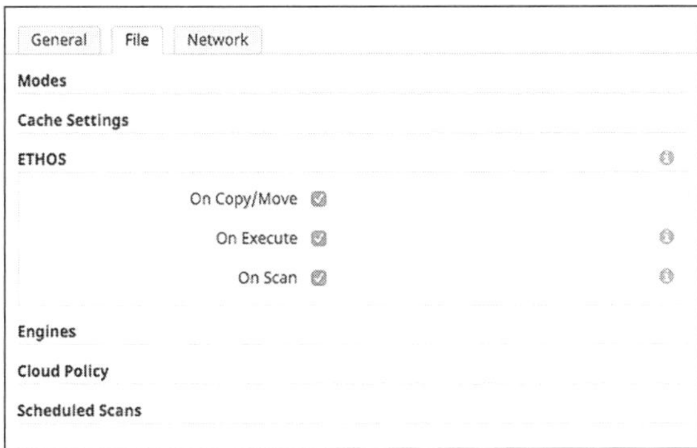

Figure 10-55 *File Tab, Ethos Settings*

Engines

As shown in Figure 10-56, the Engines section is used to configure the use of one or all of the three engines:

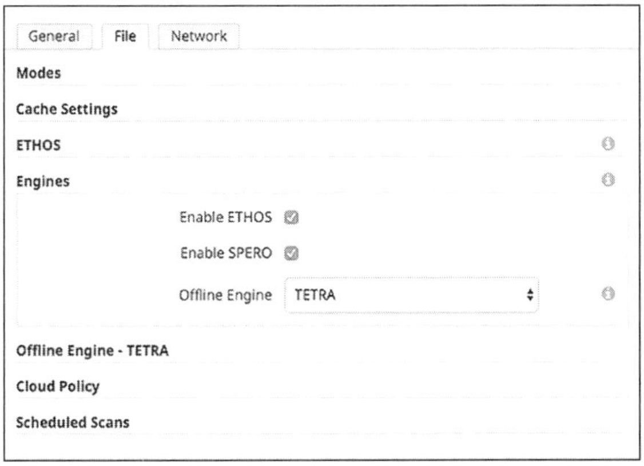

Figure 10-56 *File Tab, Engines Settings*

- **Ethos:** As mentioned in the preceding section, Ethos is a "fuzzy fingerprinting" engine that uses static or passive heuristics. Disabling Ethos in this section hides the Ethos menu from the File tab altogether.
- **Spero:** Spero is a machine learning–based technology that proactively identifies threats that were previously unknown. It uses active heuristics to gather execution attributes, and because the underlying algorithms come up with generic models, they can identify malicious software based on its general appearance rather than on specific patterns or signatures.
- **Offline Engine (TETRA):** You can set this option to be disabled or TETRA, which is a full client-side antivirus solution. Do not enable the use of TETRA if there is an existing antivirus product in place. The default AMP setting is to leave TETRA disabled, as TETRA changes the nature of the AMP connector from being a very lightweight agent to being a "thicker" software client that consumes more disk space for signature storage and more bandwidth for signature updates. When you enable TETRA, another configuration subsection is displayed, where you can choose what file-scanning options to enable, as shown in Figure 10-57.

As AMP moves from being an endpoint detection and response (EDR) tool to being a full-blown next-generation endpoint security product, TETRA has played a bigger and more important role. While it has always been a full endpoint antivirus product, it has been enhanced over time to include some more of the "table stakes" features of a desktop antivirus product:

- **Incremental updates:** It used to be that a TETRA update involved downloading the entire signature database from the cloud with each update. Incremental updates are now possible, so that the large antivirus signature database is downloaded only one time, and then only changes/additions are added to the signature database periodically.
- **Custom AMP update server:** Because AMP is a very cloud-centric endpoint security product, it naturally follows that the TETRA updates would come from that cloud. This means that every endpoint in your organization would be downloading exactly the same signature updates directly from the cloud, which is great for mobile devices but not so good when the majority of those devices are located on the same network.

Figure 10-57 shows the following TETRA settings:

- **Scan Archives:** You can specify whether the connector will open compressed files to scan the contents of the archive. The default limit is to not open archive files larger than 50 MB.
- **Scan Packed Files:** Files can be packed to decrease their size but also in an attempt to obfuscate the file type (such as hiding an executable). This setting indicates whether TETRA will unpack files and scan the contents.

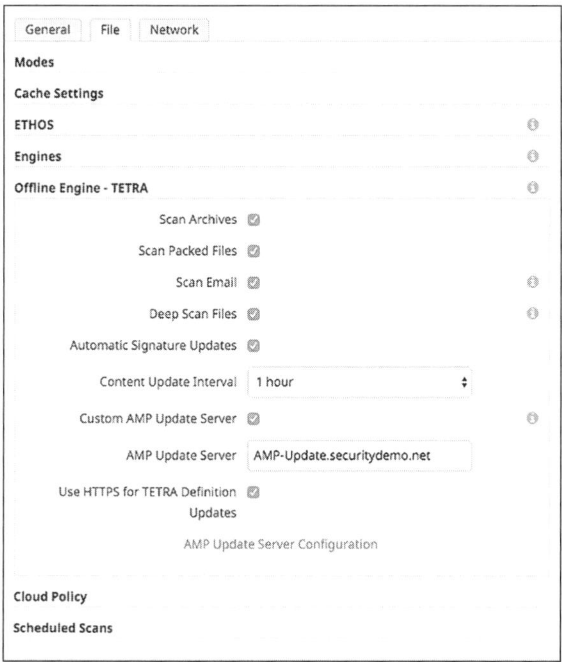

Figure 10-57 *File Tab, TETRA Settings (Optional)*

- **Scan Email:** This setting dictates whether the connector will scan the contents of supported client email stores. Supported email formats are Thunderbird 3.0.4, Outlook 2007, Outlook 2010, Windows Mail on x86, and Outlook Express.
- **Deep Scan Files:** This setting allows you to enable the scanning of product install and compiled HTML files (help files), also known as CHM files.
- **Automatic Signature Updates:** Without this setting selected, TETRA will not get incremental updates to the antivirus definitions.
- **Content Update Interval:** You can set how often TETRA should check for new signatures.
- **Customer AMP Update Server:** You can set the connector to get the TETRA updates from an on-premises AMP update server instead of the AMP public cloud.
- **AMP Update Server:** You can set the FQDN of the on-premises update server.
- **Use HTTPS for TETRA Definition Updates:** You can specify HTTPS instead of HTTP.
- **AMP Update Server Configuration:** This is a link to the AMP Update Server page, discussed next.

AMP Update Server Configuration

The AMP update server is an application for Windows Server 2012 64-bit and CentOS Linux release 6.9 x86_64 that is designed to reduce the high volume of network traffic consumed by TETRA while receiving definition updates from the AMP cloud.

Figure 10-58 shows the AMP Update Server page. Notice that it enables you to download the server for Windows and Linux and provides a button to download a configuration. The configuration tells the update server which organization or business the server belongs to, as well as the selected update interval that you chose before downloading the file.

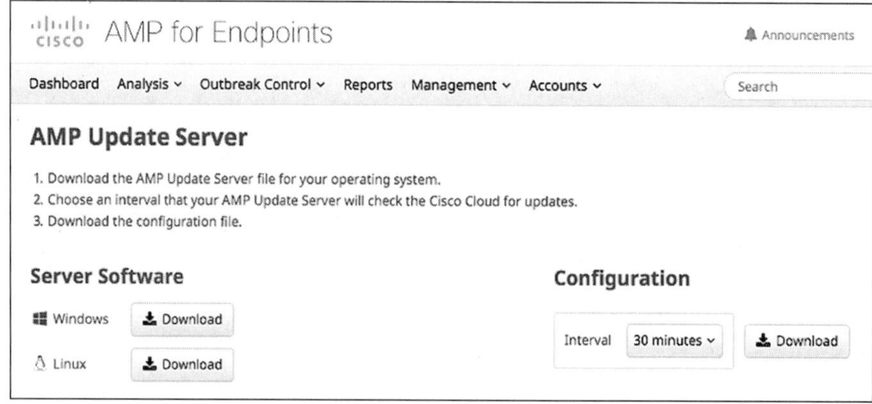

Figure 10-58 *AMP Update Server*

There are two modes of operation for the AMP update server:

- **Self-hosting:** In this mode, the AMP update server periodically downloads TETRA definitions and microdefinitions from the AMP servers to a user-specified location and hosts them using the built-in HTTP server.
- **Fetch only:** In this mode, the AMP update server is used only to fetch TETRA definition updates to a customer-specified location. The customer is responsible for setting up an HTTP server such as Apache, Nginx, or IIS to serve the downloaded content.

Figure 10-59 illustrates the AMP update server distributing updates to endpoints both on- and off-premises.

It is possible and expected that you may have more than one AMP update server to provide updates to a large enterprise. How do you determine which endpoints are assigned to the different servers? You assign endpoints to an update server by specifying the update server FQDN right in the Windows policy. To share the load of the endpoints across different update servers, simply assign those endpoints to groups and apply different policies to each group.

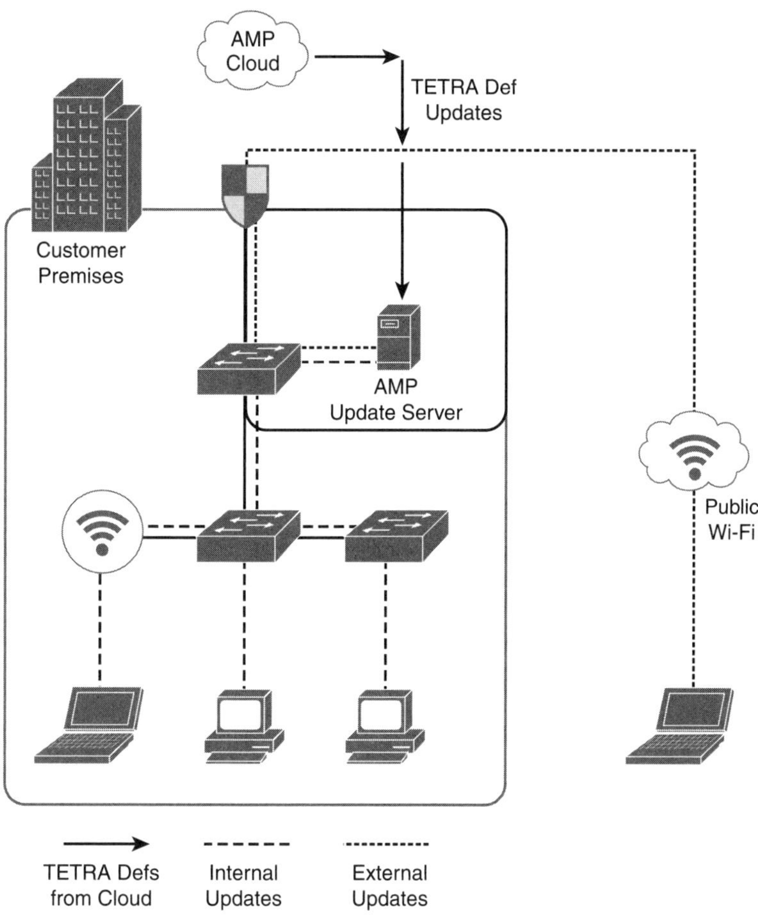

Figure 10-59 *AMP Update Server Distributing Updates*

> **Note** At the time this book was published, TETRA was the only supported update with the AMP update server, but there were plans to expand that functionality.

Cloud Policy

The Cloud Policy settings refer to the Ethos and Spero engines. Because both Ethos and Spero are classified as generic engines, you have the ability to tune how prone to false positives an Ethos or Spero hash is. The Cloud Policy page provides up to three configurable thresholds (see Figure 10-60):

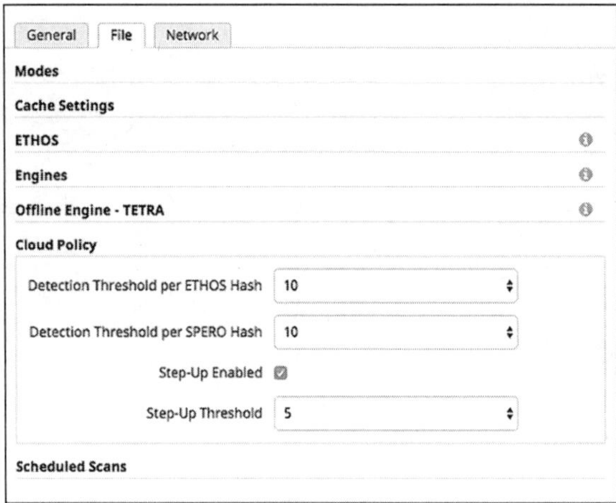

Figure 10-60 *File Tab, Cloud Policy Settings*

- **Detection Threshold per Ethos Hash:** When this option is set, a single Ethos hash can convict a single SHA of unknown disposition a maximum number of times. The default is 10, meaning that Ethos will not convict any SHA-256 seen 10 times in 24 hours by the entire community. If you encounter a situation where the detection threshold has been reached but feel that the detection is not a false positive and want to keep convicting the particular SHA, you should add it to a Custom Detections > Simple or Custom Detections > Advanced list.
- **Detection Threshold per Spero Hash:** This exactly the same as the Detection Threshold per Ethos Hash except that it refers to Spero.
- **Step-Up Enabled:** You can turn on additional Spero groupings if you are considered "massively infected." These Spero groupings, or trees, are more prone to false positives, but they do a better job of detecting malware. The definition of "massively infected" is based on the Step-Up Threshold setting.
- **Step-Up Threshold:** This setting determines whether a connector is "massively infected." The default is 5, meaning that if 5 SHA one-to-one detections are found in 30 seconds, you are considered "massively infected," and additional Spero trees will be enabled for the next 30 seconds.

Scheduled Scans

Scheduled scans are typically deemed unnecessary with AMP for Endpoints because files are scanned as they are moved, copied, or executed. In order to keep the processing low and the performance higher, no scans are scheduled by default. This does not, however, preclude you from turning that nerd-knob and configuring some scheduled scans per policy, as shown in Figure 10-61.

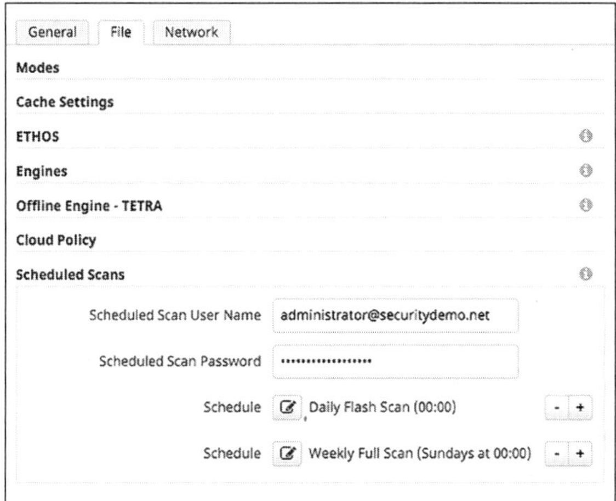

Figure 10-61 *File Tab, Scheduled Scans Settings*

Multiple scans can be configured to occur daily, weekly, and/or monthly. Each scan can be a flash, full, or custom scan, and scans can be configured to occur at specific times. Flash scans examine the processes running in memory, along with the files and Registry settings associated with those running processes. A full scan examines the processes running in memory, their associated Registry settings, and all the files on the entire disk. A custom scan is configured to look at files in a specific path.

The Network Tab

The Network tab is used to configure device flow correlation (DFC), and, in fact, DFC is the only configuration section in the Network tab. As described in the section "Network IP Blacklists and Whitelists," earlier in this chapter, DFC allows you to flag or even block suspicious network activity.

As shown in Figure 10-62, you can enable or disable DFC from the Network tab. In addition, you can specify whether the detection action should be Audit or Blocking—in other words, whether this policy should dictate a monitor-only mode or actually take action on the file. If you select Blocking mode, you can choose to terminate and quarantine the malicious file. Finally, you can set the DFC data source to be Cisco, Custom, or both.

General
File
Network
Device Flow Correlation (DFC)
Enable Device Flow Correlation
Detection Action
Blocking
Terminate and Quarantine
Blacklist Data Source
Custom and Cisco

Figure 10-62 *Network Tab*

AMP for macOS

The AMP for Endpoints connector on macOS monitors files as they are copied, moved, or executed, in addition to monitoring IP connections (TCP and UDP). AMP for Endpoints also performs scan operations to determine the parent, file, or IP disposition by first looking in the local cache and then querying the upstream cloud if the disposition is not in the cache or if the time to live (TTL) has expired.

Mac Policies

There are many policy options for Macs. From the AMP cloud console, navigate to Management > Policies > Mac. From this screen, you can see existing AMP policies for Mac as well as create new ones, as shown in Figure 10-63. To set Mac policies, click Create Policy, select Mac from the drop-down in the Create Policy dialog, and click Create Policy.

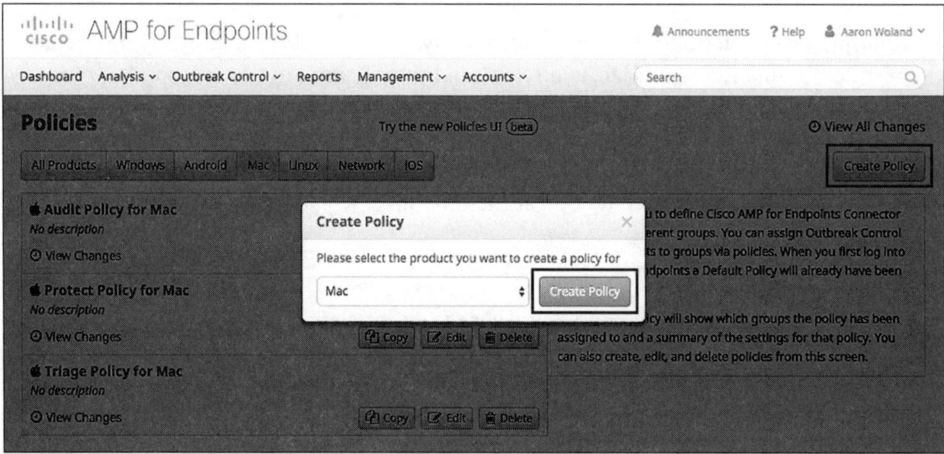

Figure 10-63 *Creating a Mac Policy*

In the New Policy window (see Figure 10-64), provide a name and select the custom detections, app blocking, whitelists, and exclusions you created earlier in this chapter. When they are all selected, click Create Policy to save the policy.

As you can see in Figure 10-64, the top section allows for the global whitelists and blacklists to be selected, and the macOS specific settings are at the bottom. Just as with the Windows policy, the AMP connector configurations are divided into three main areas: General, File, and Network.

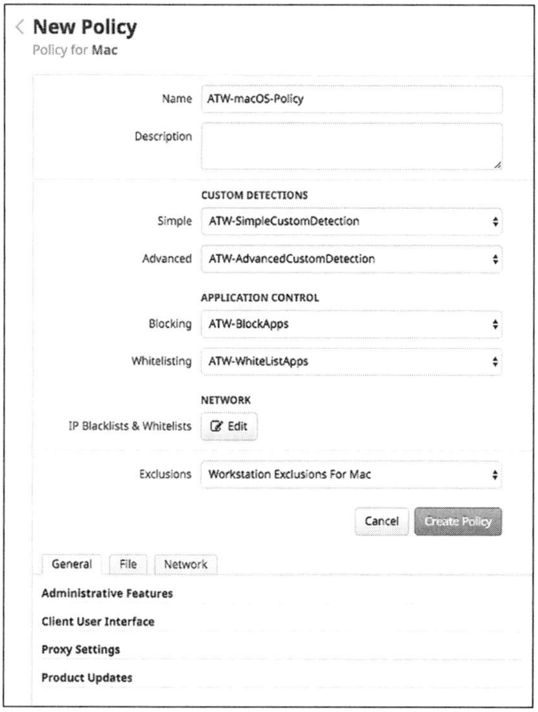

Figure 10-64 *Creating a New Mac Policy*

The General Tab

The General tab for a Mac policy contains the basic settings for the AMP for Endpoints connector, such as proxy settings and update schedules. As shown in Figure 10-65, there are four component areas in the General settings tab: Administrative Features, Client User Interface, Proxy Settings, and Product Updates. These areas are explained in the following sections.

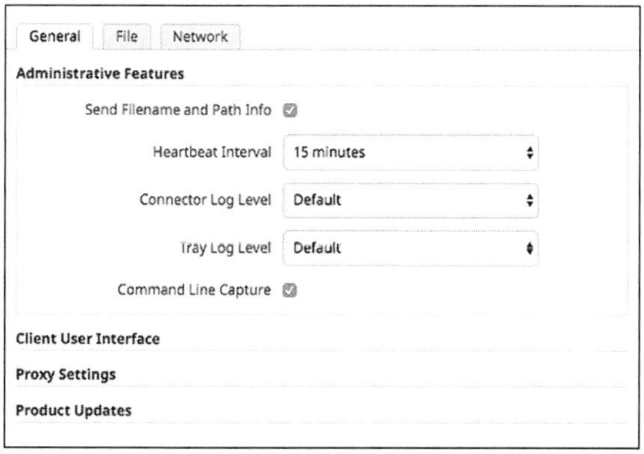

Figure 10-65 *Mac Policy General Tab, Administrative Features*

Administrative Features

As you can see in Figure 10-65, there are five configurable settings in the Administrative Features section of the General tab. (You can see that it has fewer settings than AMP for Windows. There is no option to send the username, there are no connector protection options, and there is no option to automate the sending of crash dumps, which are Windows-specific options.) There are five options for Mac:

- **Send Filename and Path Info:** Selecting this setting enables the AMP agent to send the filename and the file path information to the AMP cloud so that they are visible in the Events tab's device trajectory and file trajectory. Unchecking this setting stops this information from being sent.
- **Heartbeat Interval:** You can configure how often the AMP agent should call home to the AMP cloud. During that call home connection, the agent checks whether there are any policy updates, any updates or scans to perform, or any files to restore via the cloud recall or by the administrator.
- **Connector Log Level and Tray Log Level:** These settings allow you to change the default log level to debug when directed by Cisco TAC.
- **Command Line Capture:** Selecting this setting allows the connector to capture command-line arguments (including usernames, filenames, passwords, and so on) used during file execution and send the information to AMP for Endpoints. This information will be displayed in device trajectory for administrators as long as they have two-step verification enabled.

Client User Interface

This section allows you to configure what the end user is going to see on the Mac system. Many organizations prefer to show the agent icon in the menu bar so that it is obvious that the agent is running, but they often choose to hide all notifications so that users are not bothered by the agent. There are five options in this section, as shown in Figure 10-66:

Figure 10-66 *Client User Interface*

- **Start Client User Interface:** This setting allows you to hide the user interface or show it. The agent is running either way, but this setting offers you the option of keeping it out of the system tray. If you change this option, the new setting takes effect at the next agent restart.
- **Cloud Notifications:** This setting allows you to enable those fun balloon pop-ups from the agent icon in the Notification Center. A pop-out appears when the agent is successfully connected to the cloud, and it displays the number of users and detections registered to the cloud. Your end users will normally not thank you for these messages that don't make any sense to them.
- **Hide File Notifications:** This setting allows you to hide malicious file notifications from being displayed when a file is convicted or quarantined by the AMP agent.
- **Hide Network Notifications:** Selecting this option means that messages are not displayed when a malicious network connection is detected or blocked by AMP.
- **Hide Exclusions:** Selecting this option means that the list of exclusions is not displayed to the end user through the user interface.

It is highly recommended that you keep any interactivity with the end user to an absolute minimum. End users can get frustrated and annoyed when burdened by notifications they don't understand or care to understand.

Proxy Settings

This section is exactly the same as for the Windows connector. To do our part to save the planet and use less paper, please see the "Proxy Settings" section under "AMP for Windows," earlier in this chapter.

Product Updates

This section is exactly the same as for the Windows connector. To do our part to save the planet and use less paper, please see the "Product Updates" section under "AMP for Windows," earlier in this chapter.

The File Tab

You use the File tab to configure the settings and behavior of file scanning within the AMP for Endpoints agent. You can set which engines to use, a schedule for scans, and cache settings. There are five component areas of the file tab: Modes, Cache Settings, Engines, Offline Engine - ClamAV, and Scheduled Scans.

Modes

This section is exactly the same as for the Windows connector. To do our part to save the planet and use less paper, please see the "Modes" section under "AMP for Windows," earlier in this chapter.

Cache Settings

This section is exactly the same as for the Windows connector. To do our part to save the planet and use less paper, please see the "Cache Settings" section under "AMP for Windows," earlier in this chapter.

Engines

There are only two options in the Engines section: ClamAV or Disabled. ClamAV is the default, and disabling this setting hides the Offline Engine - ClamAV portion of the File tab.

Offline Engine - ClamAV

This section is available only when ClamAV has been selected for Offline Engine in the Engines portion of the File tab.

Whereas the Windows connector uses TETRA for offline scanning, the Mac connector uses ClamAV, which is an open source full antivirus product that is owned by Cisco Sourcefire and designed for UNIX-based systems like macOS and Linux. Just like TETRA, ClamAV is signature-based and requires more disk space and processor power.

As shown in Figure 10-67, the only configurable option for ClamAV is Content Update Interval. By default, AMP checks for new or updated antivirus signatures to be downloaded every 24 hours. Just as on Windows, compatibility with other antivirus software solutions can be an issue, so never enable the Offline Engine setting if another antivirus product is installed on the computer.

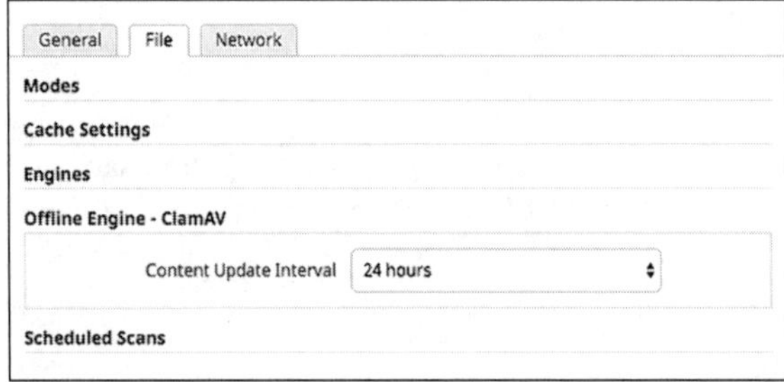

Figure 10-67 *Offline Engine - ClamAV*

Scheduled Scans

This section is exactly the same as for the Windows connector. To do our part to save the planet and use less paper, please see the "Scheduled Scans" section under "AMP for Windows," earlier in this chapter.

The Network Tab

Just as with the AMP for Windows connector, for Mac the Network tab is used to configure device flow correlation (DFC), and, in fact, DFC is the only configuration section in the Network tab. As described in the section "Network IP Blacklists and Whitelists," earlier in this chapter, DFC allows you to flag or even block suspicious network activity.

As you see in Figure 10-68, the options are even fewer for Mac than for Windows. DFC may be enabled or disabled, and the action may be configured to Audit or Block. Finally, you can set the DFC data source to be Cisco, Custom, or both.

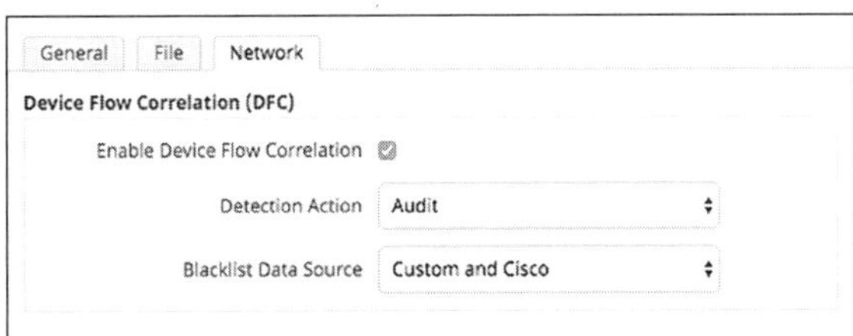

Figure 10-68 *Network Tab*

AMP for Linux

AMP for Linux is rather interesting. First of all, there are more flavors of Linux than one can count, and Cisco certainly cannot be expected to support and test every last one. At the time this book was published, only the 64-bit versions of CentOS and RedHat Linux variants were supported.

Note AMP for Linux may not install properly on custom kernels.

Linux Policies

Just as for Windows and Mac, there are many policy options for Linux. From the AMP cloud console, navigate to Management > Policies > Linux. On this screen, you can see existing AMP policies for Linux and also create new ones.

To set Linux policies, click Create Policy, select Linux from the drop-down in the Create Policy dialog, and click Create Policy.

In the New Policy window (see Figure 10-69), provide a name and select the custom detections, app blocking, whitelists, and exclusions you created earlier in this chapter. When they are all selected, click Create Policy to save the policy.

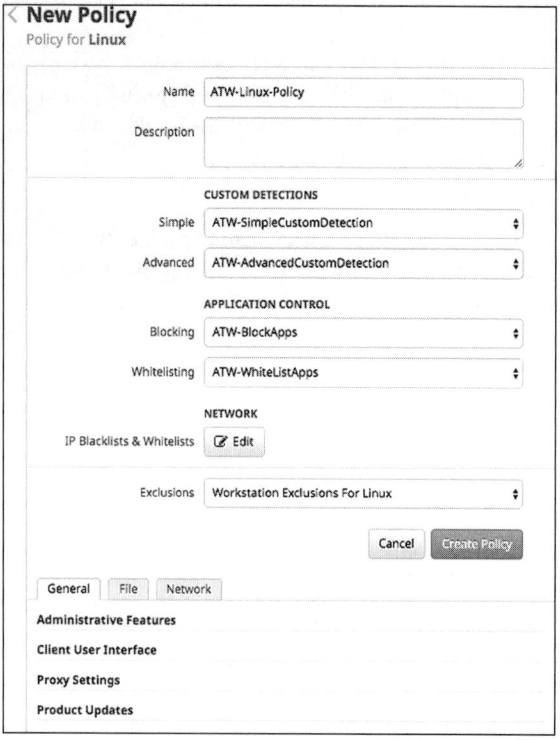

Figure 10-69 *Creating a New Linux Policy*

The General Tab

Just as with Windows and Mac, the General tab of a Linux policy contains the basic settings for the AMP for Endpoints connector, such as proxy settings and update schedules. (You have to hand it to the AMP team for being consistent!)

There are only four component areas in the General tab: Administrative Features, Client User Interface, Proxy Settings, and Product Updates. Only the items that are different from the Mac policy are discussed here. Please see the section "The General Tab" under "AMP for Windows" or "AMP for macOS," earlier in this chapter, for the other configuration option explanations.

Administrative Features

The only difference in configuration of administrative features for Linux as compared to Mac is the lack of a system tray log with which to set the level.

Client User Interface

The Client User Interface section provides three options: Hide File Notifications, Hide Network Notifications, and Hide Exclusions. As always, silence seems to be golden for the AMP connector, and hiding notifications may be wise for your environment.

The File Tab

The File tab for Linux is exactly the same as it is for the Mac connector. ClamAV is the antivirus product for Linux that is built in to the AMP connector, and it may be enabled and configured for periodic updates, just like the Mac connector.

The Network Tab

Just as for the Mac and Windows connectors, the Network tab for Linux is used to enable or disable DFC. However, Linux does not have a blocking mode for DFC; it is only capable of doing audits.

AMP for Android

The AMP for Android connector requires Android 2.1 or higher running on ARM and Intel Atom processors with 4 MB of free space on the device.

Unlike for Windows and Mac, there are simply not many policy options for Android. AMP for Android is not looking at files and hashes; instead, it is focused on the SHA-1 hash of Android applications (APKs) and maintaining an inventory of the APKs seen on the Android devices.

From the AMP cloud console, navigate to Management > Policies > Android. On this screen, you can see existing AMP policies for Android and also create new ones.

To set Android policies, click Create Policy, select Android from the drop-down in the Create Policy dialog, and click Create Policy.

In the New Policy window (see Figure 10-70), provide a name and select the custom detections you created earlier in this chapter. There is only one section with one option to configure at the bottom of the policy: Heartbeat Interval.

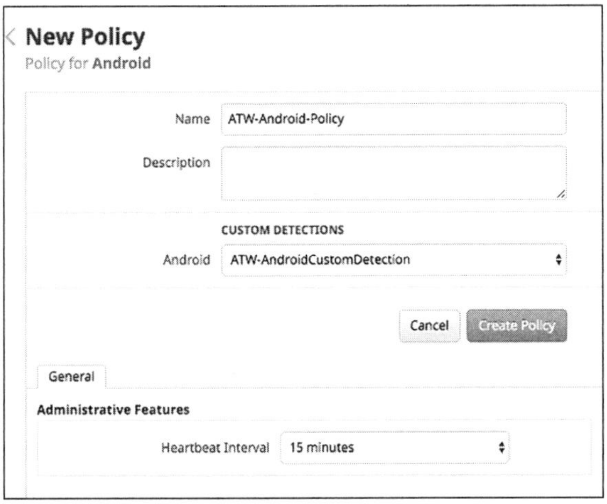

Figure 10-70 *Creating a New Android Policy*

Installing AMP for Endpoints

You have created policies for the different endpoints. The next step is to assign those policies to groups so you can begin to deploy the AMP connectors to the many endpoints in your organization.

Groups, Groups, and More Groups

Before moving into installing AMP for Endpoints onto your hosts, we should really discuss an important organizational component: groups. The AMP administrative console uses groups to organize and manage computers according to their function, location, or other criteria that you determine. Policies get assigned to groups and can inherit from parent groups for more granular control. For example, a group may be created per department or per line of business. However, there could be additional controls required based on the country of origin that the computer normally resides in.

Navigate to Management > Groups, and you see a list of all top-level groups within your organization. There are a number of default groups that AMP has prebuilt for new organizations, as you can see in Figure 10-71.

You can create, edit, or delete the groups from this screen. If a group has child groups within it, it is listed as pointed out in Figure 10-71.

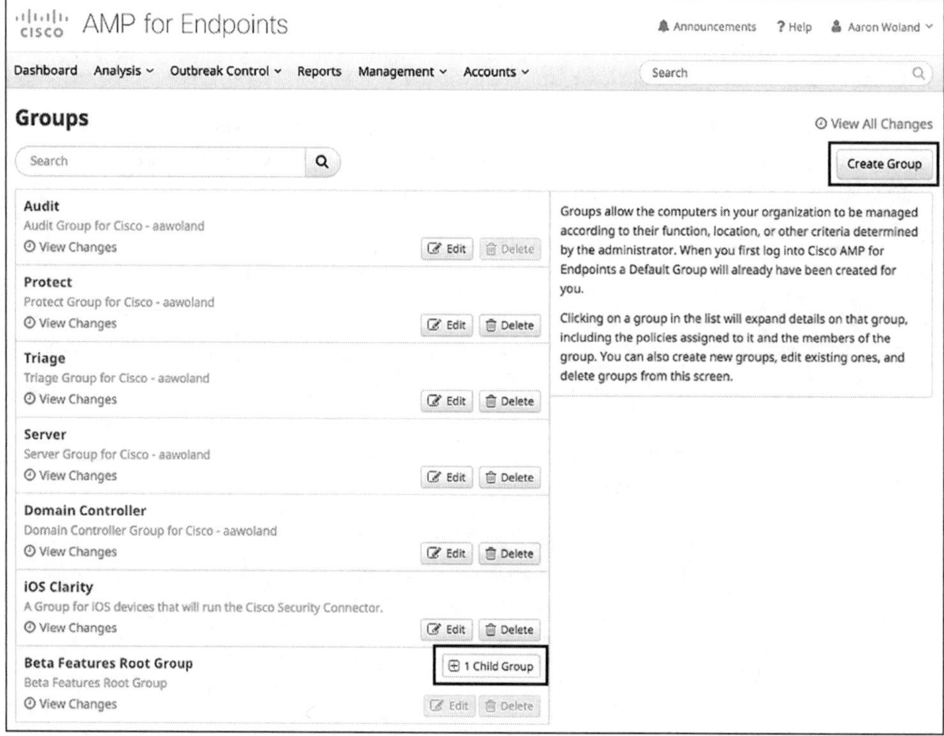

Figure 10-71 *Top-Level Groups*

To create a new group, click Create Group. When you create a new group, you provide a group name, description, and parent group (if any) and you can assign existing known computers to it, as shown in the upper right of Figure 10-72. At the bottom of the screen, you can make this new group a parent by assigning other existing groups to it as children.

In addition, you can see in Figure 10-72 that you can assign existing policies to the group. Here is where you should select the policies we have created in this chapter.

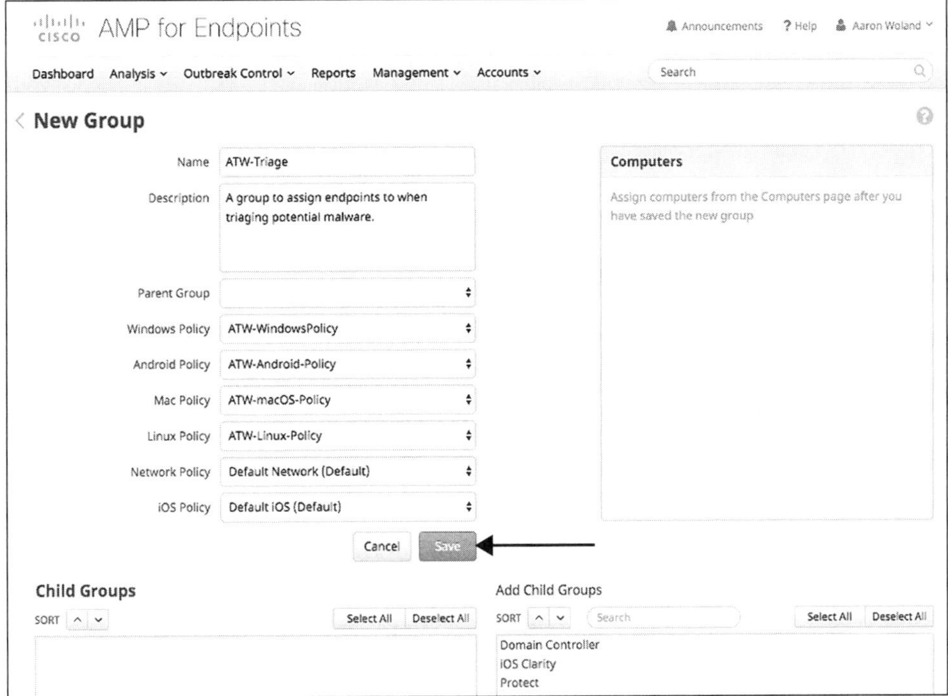

Figure 10-72 *Creating a New Group*

Click Save in order to save the new group.

The Download Connector Screen

Earlier in the chapter we took a look at the Download Connector screen located at Management > Download Connector. In this screen you can download installation packages for each type of AMP for Endpoints connector, or you can copy the URL from where those connectors may be downloaded, as shown in Figure 10-73. Before downloading a connector, select the appropriate group so that correct policies will be assigned and the installed computers will appear in the correct group.

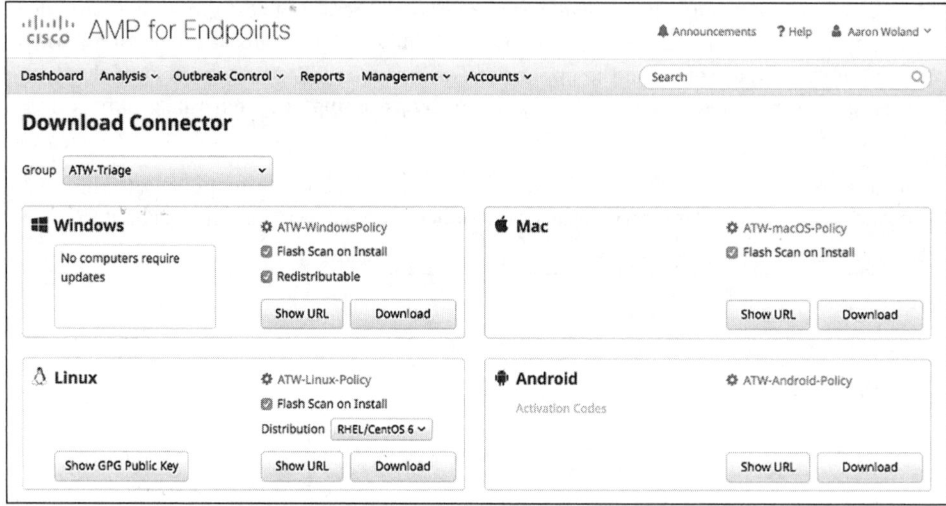

Figure 10-73 *Download Connector*

The installer may be placed on a network share, distributed via management software, or distributed via Cisco's AnyConnect Secure Mobility Client. The download URL can be emailed to users to allow them to download and install it themselves, which can be convenient for remote users.

Distributing via Cisco AnyConnect

At the time this book was published, the AMP connector was not part of Cisco's AnyConnect Secure Mobility Client, but an "AMP Enabler" add-on to AnyConnect could be used to aid in the distribution of the AMP connector to clients who use AnyConnect for remote access VPNs, secure network access, posture assessments with Cisco's Identity Services Engine, and more. Figure 10-74 shows the AnyConnect Secure Mobility Client with the AMP Enabler tile.

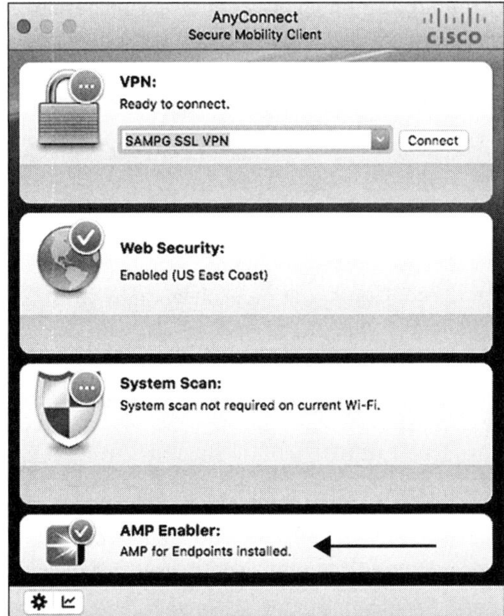

Figure 10-74 *AnyConnect Security Mobility Client*

Installing AMP for Windows

In the Download Connector screen (refer to Figure 10-73), Windows is the first operating system. As you can see in Figure 10-75, there are a few options to select when choosing to download the AMP installer for Windows.

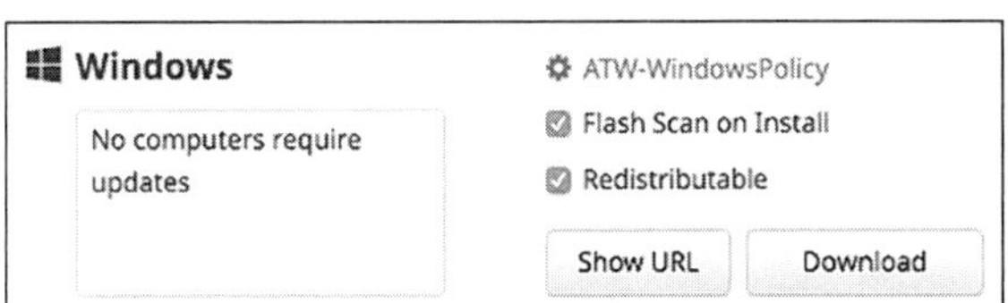

Figure 10-75 *Downloading AMP for Windows*

There is an option to have the connector perform a flash scan during the install process. The flash scan checks processes currently running in memory and should be performed on each install.

The second check box is an option to enable a redistributable. This option is enabled by default, and when you click Download with Redistributable disabled, you download a very small (around 500 KB) bootstrapper file to install the AMP connector. This type of installer is also referred to as a *stub installer*.

The stub installer determines whether the computer is running a 32- or 64-bit operating system and connects to the cloud to download and install the appropriate version of the AMP connector. The connector will be configured with your policies based on the group assignment.

If you select the Redistributable option and then click Download, you download a much larger executable (around 30 MB) that contains the full installation, both 32- and 64-bit versions.

The installer file can be placed on a network share or pushed to all the computers in a group by using a tool like Microsoft System Center Configuration Manager (SSCM) or Active Directory Group Policies in order to install the AMP connector on multiple computers. The bootstrapper and redistributable installer also both contain a policy.xml file, which contains your assigned policies, and those policy.xml files are used as the configuration files for the install.

Figure 10-76 shows the UI displaying the URL to send to the end users. Figure 10-77 shows an end user connecting to the installer stub through the download URL entered into a browser. The stub installer is downloaded as shown in Figure 10-77, and when it is executed, it will continue with installation and download the full agent with the policies, as is shown in Figure 10-78.

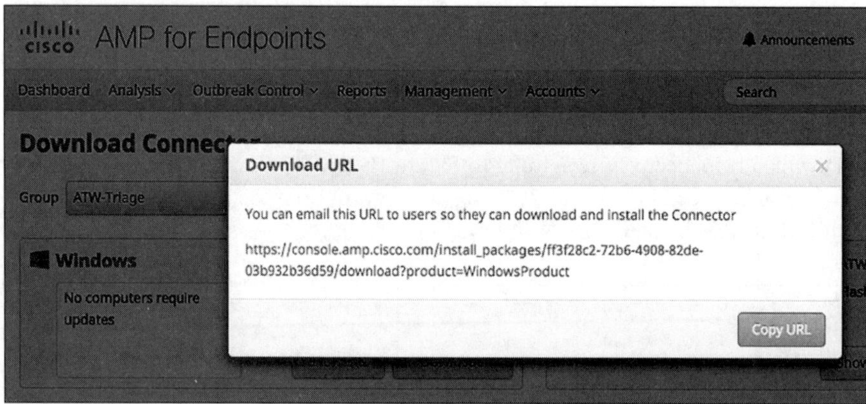

Figure 10-76 *The URL for End Users*

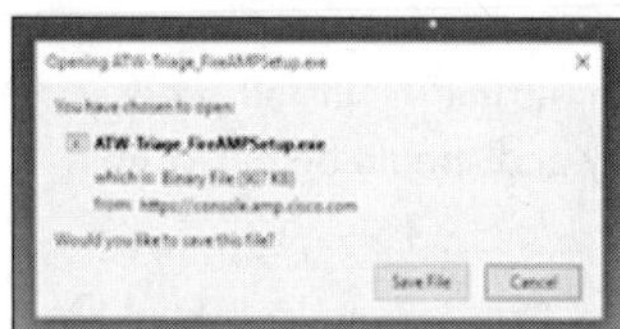

Figure 10-77 *Downloading the Stub Installer*

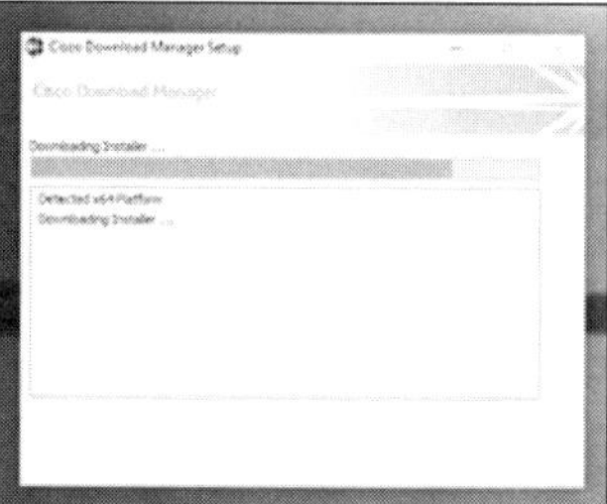

Figure 10-78 *Installing the Agent on Windows*

When the agent is installed on a Windows endpoint, and the user interface is configured to be visible, the AMP icon is in the system tray, and clicking on that system tray icon brings up the summary window, shown in Figure 10-79. As you can see in Figure 10-79, the summary window includes the current status of the connection to the AMP cloud, the last date the system was scanned, and the assigned policy.

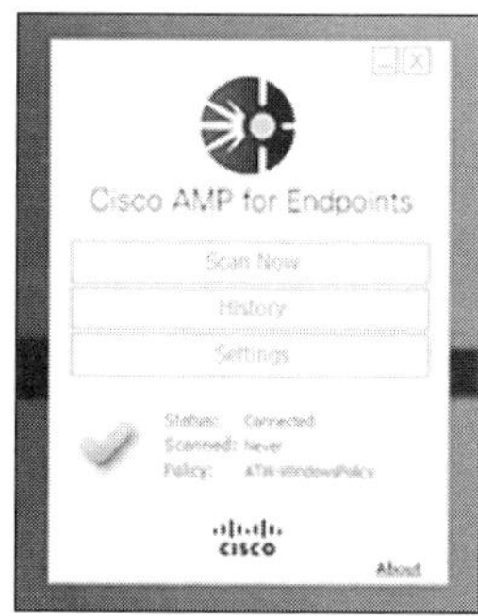

Figure 10-79 *Summary Window*

Installing AMP for Mac

The process of installing AMP for Mac is very similar to the process of installing AMP for Windows. First, you select the group, but instead of downloading a Windows executable file, you download a .pkg file to install the AMP connector. Or you can copy the URL, just as with Windows. Figure 10-80 shows the downloading of the .pkg file.

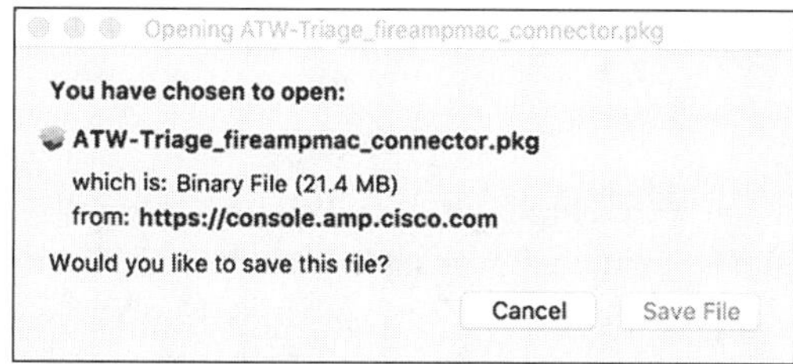

Figure 10-80 *Downloading the Mac .pkg File*

The .pkg file is only about 20 MB in size, as there is no "redistributable" equivalent. Once an end user has the .pkg file and runs it, he or she is walked through the installation step-by-step, as illustrated in Figure 10-81.

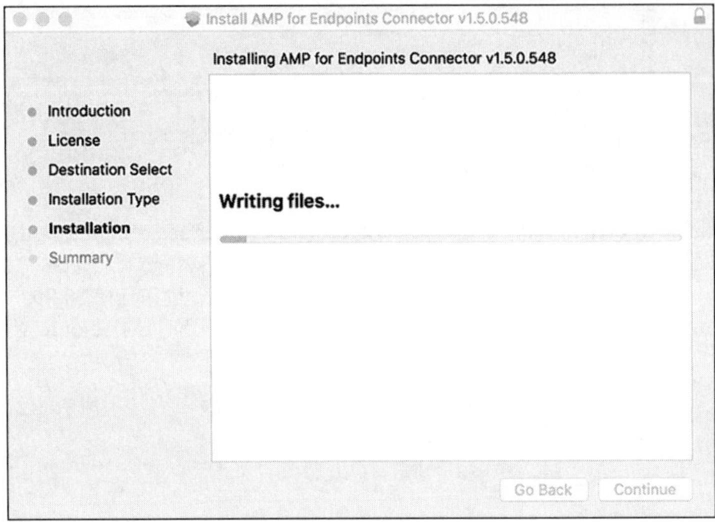

Figure 10-81 *Mac Installation GUI*

Once AMP is installed, if the user interface is configured to be visible, there will be an AMP icon in the menu bar. By clicking the menu bar icon, you can trigger an on-demand scan, sync the policy to the cloud, or get into the settings, as shown in Figure 10-82.

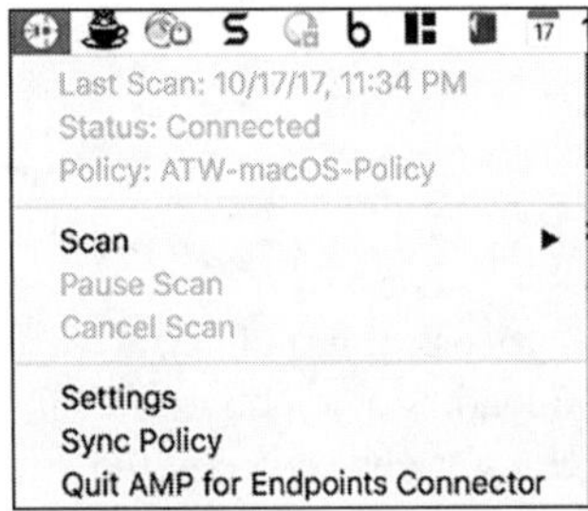

Figure 10-82 *Menu Bar Icon and Menu*

Installing AMP for Linux

Downloading the Linux connector provides you with an .rpm (that is, a Red Hat Package Manager, or an RPM Package Manager) file to be installed. The installer is about 16 MB and also contains the policy.xml file that is used as a configuration file to your settings. There is also a link to download the GPG keys, which are required for connector updates via the central policy. Figure 10-83 shows the screen where the GPG can be copied or downloaded.

Figure 10-83 *GPG Public Key*

You can install the .rpm file by using **rpm** or the **yum** toolset. To install by using **rpm**, use the **rpm -i** command and option. For **yum**, use **sudo yum localinstall** [*install-file*] **-y**. Figure 10-84 shows an example of using the **rpm** command.

```
root@atw-tme-CentOS-1:~/...    ~/Downloads (zsh)
[root@atw-tme-CentOS-1 AMP]# ls
ATW_Group_fireamplinux_connector.rpm  cisco.gpg
[root@atw-tme-CentOS-1 AMP]# rpm -i ./ATW_Group_fireamplinux_connector.rpm
warning: ./ATW_Group_fireamplinux_connector.rpm: Header V4 RSA/SHA1 Signature, k
ey ID f2fd178f: NOKEY
Installing to install prefix /opt
Verifying archive integrity... 100%   All good.
Uncompressing ampconnector installer  100%
[logger] Set minimum reported log level to error
[logger] Shutdown file logger for module:ampsupport
Shutting down system logger: [  OK  ]
Starting system logger: [  OK  ]
cisco-amp start/running, process 29158
[root@atw-tme-CentOS-1 AMP]# 
```

Figure 10-84 *Installing the Connector by Using* ***rpm***

If you plan on pushing connector updates via policy, you need to import the GPG key into your RPM database. Here's how you do this:

Step 1. Verify the GPG key by clicking the GPG Public Key link on the Download Connector page, which will display the GPG key as shown in Figure 10-83. Compare the key from that link to the one at /opt/cisco/amp/etc/rpm-gpg/RPM-GPG-KEY-cisco-amp.

Step 2. Run the following command from a terminal to import the key:

```
[sudo] rpm --import /opt/cisco/amp/etc/rpm-gpg/RPM-GPG-KEY-cisco-amp
```

Step 3. Verify that the key was installed by running the following command from a terminal:

```
rpm -q gpg-pubkey --qf '%{name}-%{version}-%{release} --> %{summary}\n'
```

Step 4. Look for a GPG key from Sourcefire in the output.

The Linux connector has a CLI, as shown in Figure 10-85.

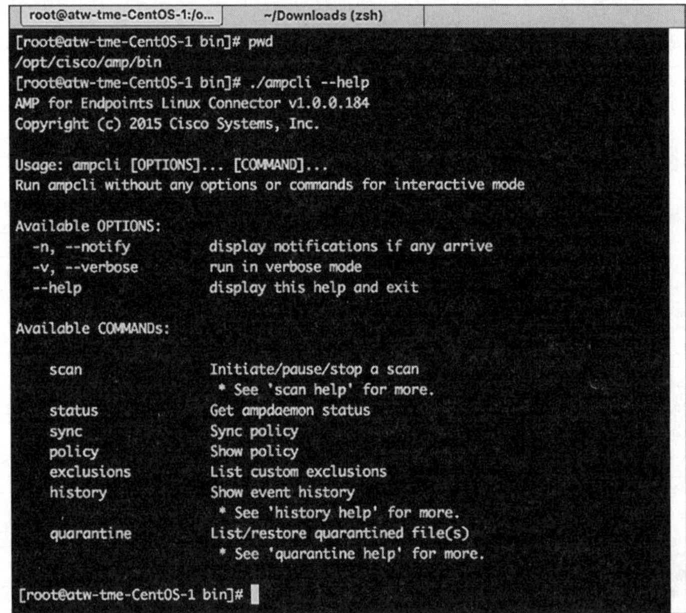

Figure 10-85 *Linux AMP CLI*

Installing AMP for Android

AMP for Android comes in the form of an app. You can send a link to the app to a user, sending the app directly, or even have the user download the app from the Google Play Store.

Android Activation Codes

Before you can successfully install the app on an Android endpoint, an activation code is required. These codes are generated in the console GUI and by default do not have expiration dates.

On the Download Connector screen, click Activation Codes in the Android box, as indicated in Figure 10-86.

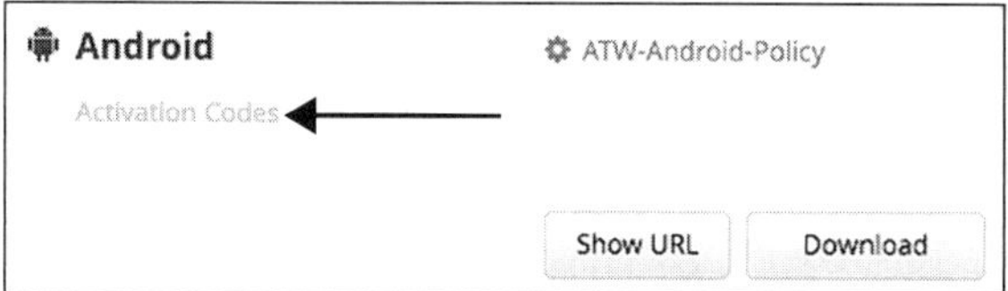

Figure 10-86 *Download Connector Screen: Android*

On the Android Activation Codes screen, click Create near the top of the screen (#1 in Figure 10-87) to generate a new code. The right-hand side of the screen is now populated with a small form for you to fill out, including the new code value. The Activation Limit setting is how many connectors may be activated using this license code. You can choose an expiration date for the use of the code to prevent any new activations with the code from this date forward. Setting an expiration date does not disable the connectors that were previously activated using that code.

Finally, select the group that will use the activation code. Keep in mind that only a single activation code can be applied to a group at a time, so you should make sure you have assigned a high enough activation limit for the number of devices in the group you are applying the code to. Don't worry, though. You can always return to the screen and edit the code to extend the activation limit. You can also delete the old code for a group and create a new code for that group. Again, deleting a code does not deactivate the connectors that were previously activated; it simply prevents any new users from activating their app with that code.

Click Create near the bottom of the screen (#2 in Figure 10-87) to create the new activation code. Be sure to make note of that code for use in the next steps.

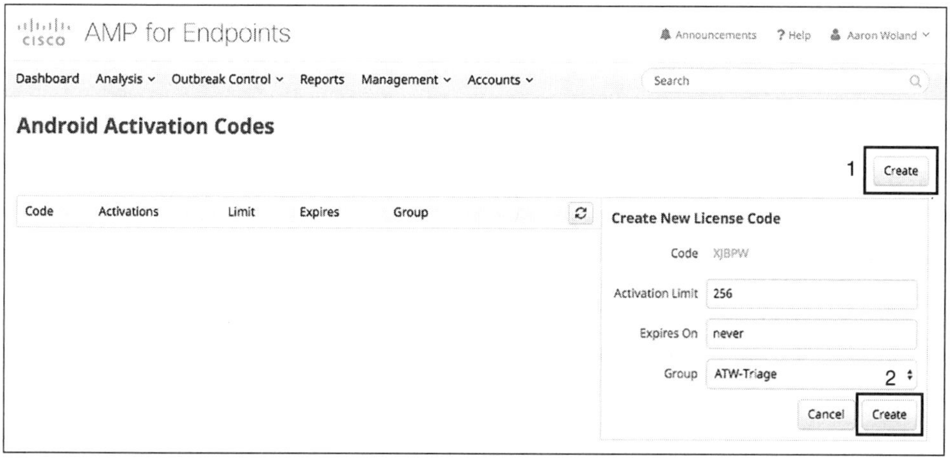

Figure 10-87 *Generating the AMP Connector Code*

Deploying the AMP for Android Connector

As mentioned earlier in this chapter, AMP for Android comes in the form of an app. Users can obtain the app by using a link you send to them, using the app you send to them directly, or downloading the app from the Google Play Store. Using The Play Store is often considered the easiest method since the Google Play Store is trusted by all Android devices by default and doesn't require changing security settings on the device to allow apps to be installed from other sources.

Figure 10-88 shows the app in the Play Store. Click Install to download and install the app.

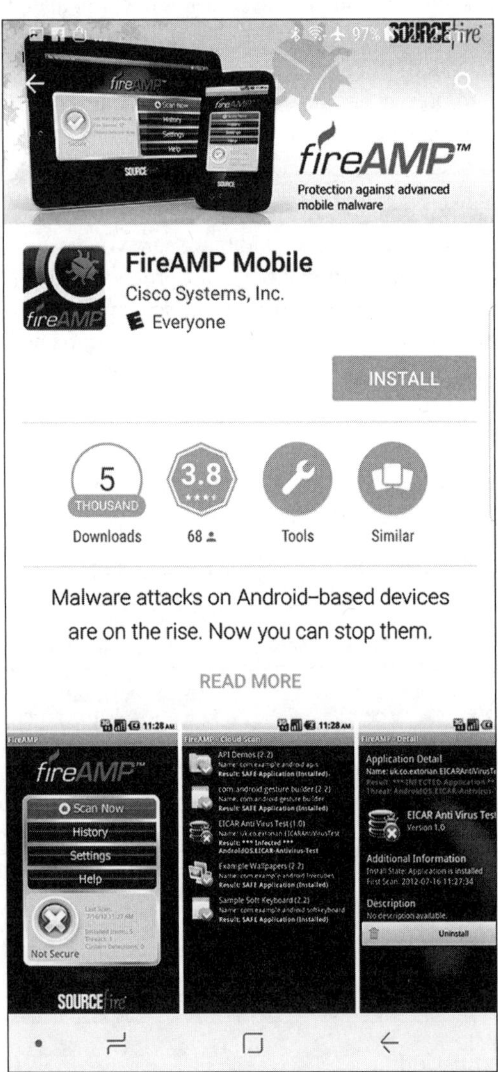

Figure 10-88 *Downloading the AMP Connector App*

When the installation is complete, open the app. You are prompted to accept the license agreement, as shown in Figure 10-89.

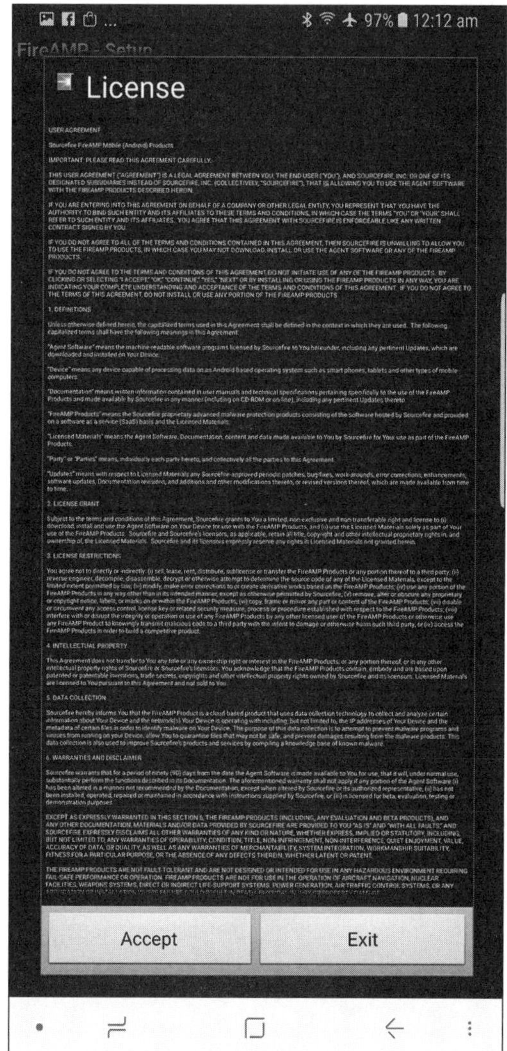

Figure 10-89 *License Agreement*

Next, you are asked to enter the activation code and provide an identifying name for the Android device, as shown in Figure 10-90.

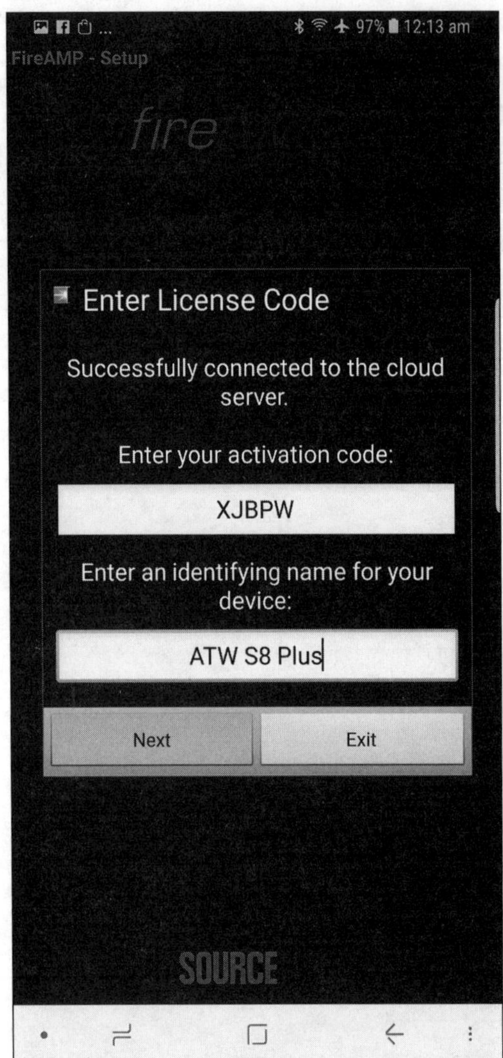

Figure 10-90 *Entering the License Code and Device Name*

If the code is active and valid, you see a success message and then the main AMP app window, as shown in Figure 10-91.

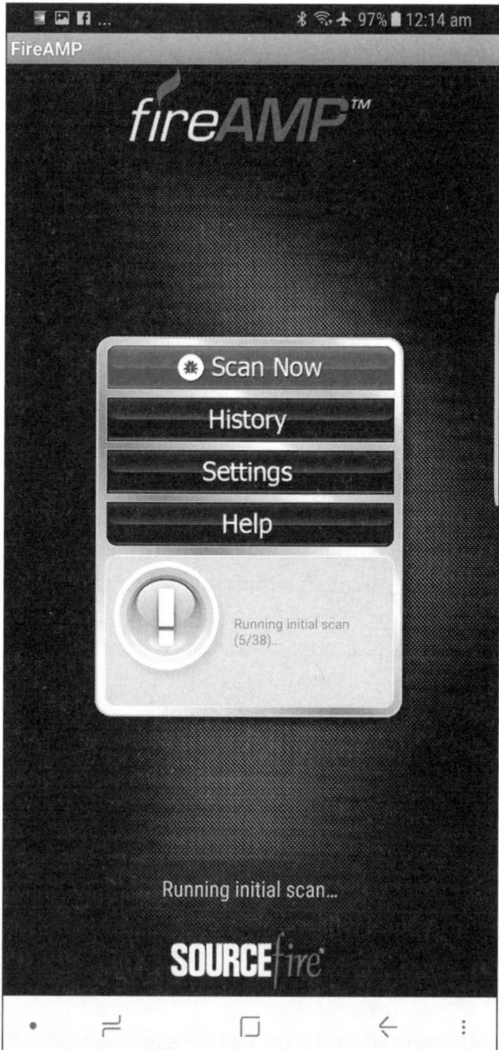

Figure 10-91 *The AMP Main App Window*

Proxy Complications

AMP for Endpoints needs to reach the AMP cloud through an Internet connection. That connection may need to traverse a proxy server—and sometimes complications arise.

Proxy Server Autodetection

AMP for Endpoints is able to use multiple mechanisms to support anonymous proxy servers. A specific proxy server or path to a proxy auto-config (.pac) file can be defined in policies, or the connector can discover the endpoint proxy settings from the Windows Registry.

The FireAMP connector can be set to discover endpoint proxy settings automatically. Once the connector detects proxy setting information, it attempts to connect to the FireAMP Management Server to confirm that the proxy server settings are correct. The connector at first uses the proxy settings specified in the policy. If the connector is unable to establish a connection to the FireAMP Management Server, it attempts to retrieve proxy settings from the Windows Registry on the endpoint. The connector attempts to retrieve the settings only from systemwide settings and not per-user settings.

If the connector is unable to retrieve proxy settings from the Windows Registry, it attempts to locate the .pac file. This can be specified in policy settings or determined using the Web Proxy Auto-Discovery protocol (WPAD). If the .pac file's location is specified in policy, it has to begin with HTTP or HTTPS. Note that the .pac files supported are only ECMAScript-based and must have a .pac file extension. If a .pac file is hosted on a web server, the proper MIME type, application/x-javascript-config, must be specified. Because all connector communications are already encrypted, HTTPS proxy is not supported. For Version 3.0.6 of the connector, a SOCKS proxy setting cannot be specified using a .pac file.

The connector attempts to rediscover proxy settings after a certain number of cloud lookups fail to ensure that when laptops are outside the enterprise network, the connector is able to connect when network proxy settings are changed.

Incompatible Proxy Security Configurations

Certain proxy/web security configurations are incompatible with AMP:

- **Websense NTLM credential caching:** The currently supported workaround for AMP is either to disable NTLM credential caching in Websense or allow the AMP connector to bypass proxy authentication exception.
- **HTTPS content inspection:** This also breaks the AMP endpoint agent's communication with the cloud, due to certificate pinning and strong authentication. The currently supported workaround is either to disable HTTPS content inspection or set up exclusions for the AMP connector.
- **Kerberos/GSSAPI authentication:** The AMP connector does not work with Kerberos and GSSAPI authentication methods. The currently supported workaround is to use either basic or NTLM authentication or to set up an authentication exception.

AMP for Content Security

Cisco's AMP architecture uses connectors that examine files on the endpoint or in transit to and from the network. Content security appliances play a key role in the perimeter security of a network, examining key traffic flows that represent common attack vectors, and they are therefore another perfect location for detecting and blocking malware.

Figure 10-92 illustrates a network with the many different AMP connectors on endpoints, next-generation IPSs, AMP appliances, Email Security Appliance (ESA) devices, and Web Security Appliance (WSA) devices.

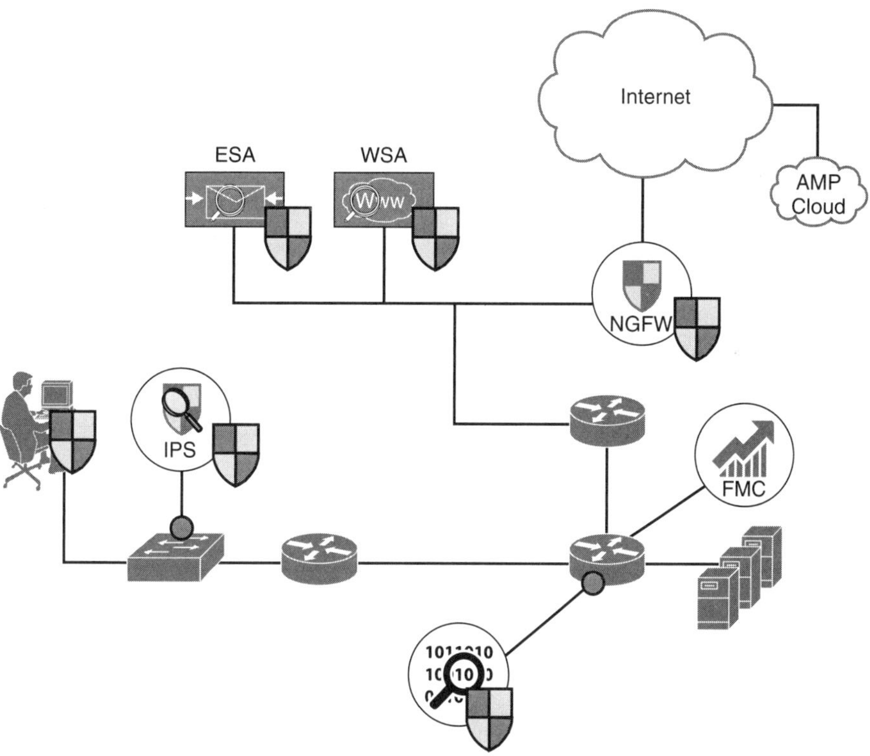

Figure 10-92 *Illustrated Network with Multiple AMP Connectors*

Content Security Connectors

AMP connectors are implemented in different ways. The AMP for Networks connectors that you learned about earlier in this chapter are managed by the FMC and configured through file policies.

Content security appliances rely heavily on a concept called *reputation scoring*—of websites, email senders, and now files. Therefore, it shouldn't come as a surprise that the AMP capabilities on content security appliances are referred to as *file reputation filtering* and *file analysis*.

The file evaluation used by content security AMP is illustrated in Figure 10-93. If the Web-Based Reputation Score (WBRS) is configured to scan, the appliance simultaneously scans the file for malware and sends an SHA-256 of the file to the AMP cloud. In addition, if it is a Microsoft .exe file, you also send along a Spero fingerprint of the PE header. If the file's reputation and scan results are both determined to be clean, the file gets released and delivered to the end user.

If the file is deemed to be malicious either through file reputation or based on the local scan result, the configured action is taken. If the file reputation is unknown, and it matches the criteria for file upload, the appliance uploads it to Threat Grid in the cloud.

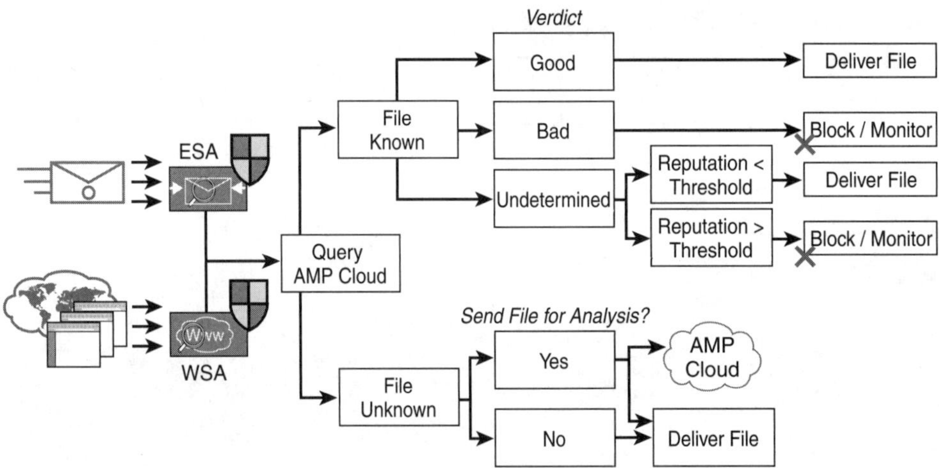

Figure 10-93 *Content AMP Flows*

Configuring AMP for Content Security Appliances

Before you can configure AMP for content security appliances, you must first have the correct licensing (known as "feature keys") on your appliances. The feature keys enable the service on the appliance and allow you to configure the settings for the AMP services.

Configuring the Web Security Appliance (WSA) Devices

There are two features in WSA that correspond to AMP: File Reputation and File Analysis. Figure 10-94 shows the feature keys for a WSA device and points out the File Reputation and File Analysis feature keys.

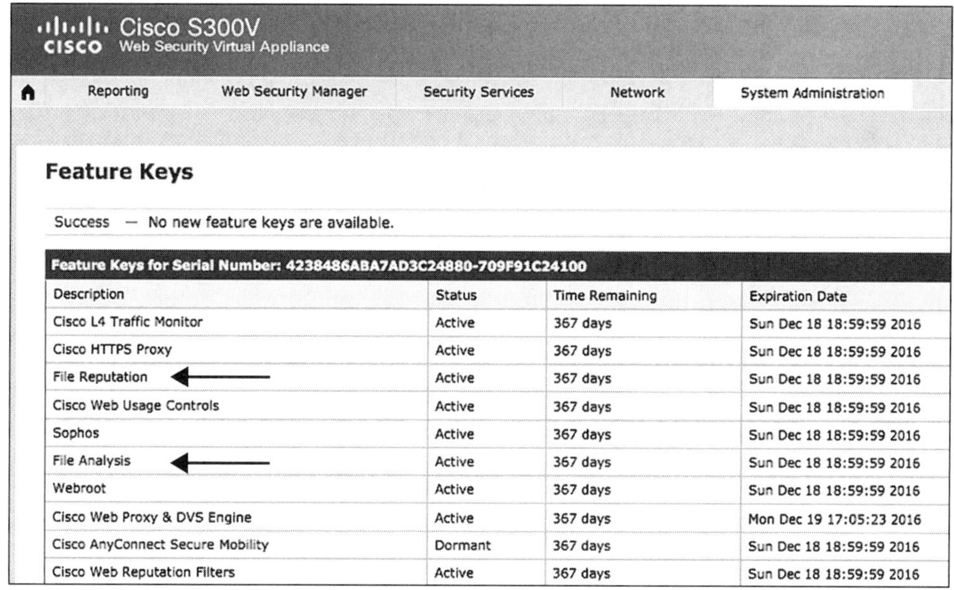

Figure 10-94 *AMP Feature Keys*

The WSA device must have access to reach the AMP cloud. Remember that the nomenclature used by each Cisco product may vary. The product documentation for WSA refers to the AMP cloud as "File Reputation and Analysis Services," but it's really still the AMP cloud. You configure the AMP cloud settings under Security Services > Anti-Malware and Reputation, as shown in Figure 10-95.

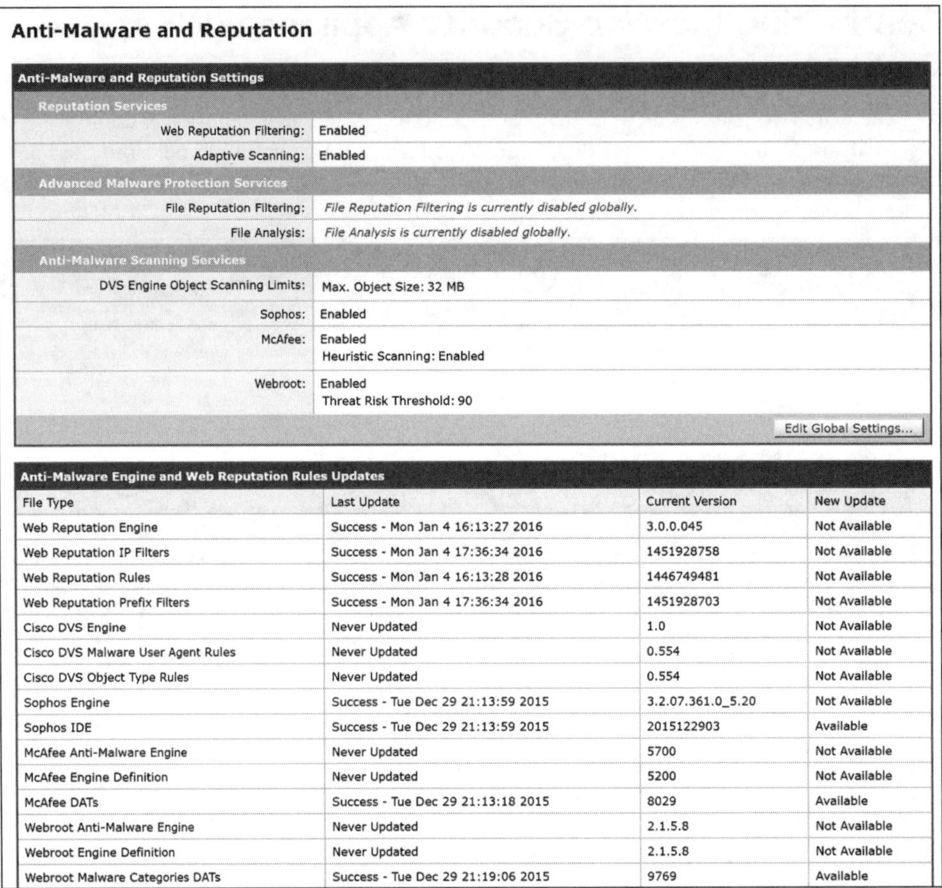

File Type	Last Update	Current Version	New Update
Web Reputation Engine	Success - Mon Jan 4 16:13:27 2016	3.0.0.045	Not Available
Web Reputation IP Filters	Success - Mon Jan 4 17:36:34 2016	1451928758	Not Available
Web Reputation Rules	Success - Mon Jan 4 16:13:28 2016	1446749481	Not Available
Web Reputation Prefix Filters	Success - Mon Jan 4 17:36:34 2016	1451928703	Not Available
Cisco DVS Engine	Never Updated	1.0	Not Available
Cisco DVS Malware User Agent Rules	Never Updated	0.554	Not Available
Cisco DVS Object Type Rules	Never Updated	0.554	Not Available
Sophos Engine	Success - Tue Dec 29 21:13:59 2015	3.2.07.361.0_5.20	Not Available
Sophos IDE	Success - Tue Dec 29 21:13:59 2015	2015122903	Available
McAfee Anti-Malware Engine	Never Updated	5700	Not Available
McAfee Engine Definition	Never Updated	5200	Not Available
McAfee DATs	Success - Tue Dec 29 21:13:18 2015	8029	Available
Webroot Anti-Malware Engine	Never Updated	2.1.5.8	Not Available
Webroot Engine Definition	Never Updated	2.1.5.8	Not Available
Webroot Malware Categories DATs	Success - Tue Dec 29 21:19:06 2015	9769	Available

Figure 10-95 *Anti-Malware and Reputation Screen*

To configure the AMP services, click Edit Global Settings. Figure 10-96 shows the resulting Anti-Malware and Reputation Settings screen. To enable AMP, simply select the check box next to Enable File Reputation Filtering.

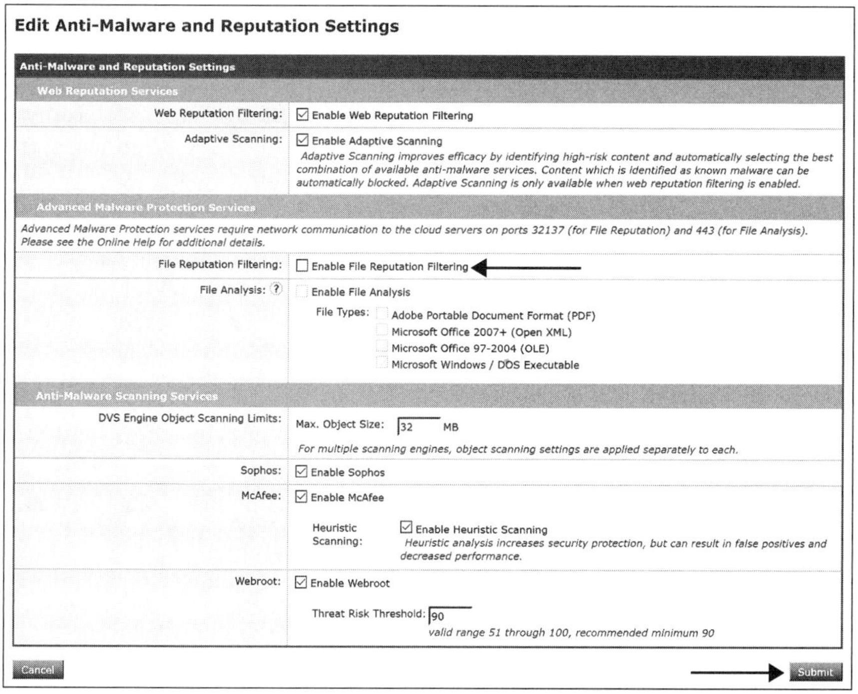

Edit Anti-Malware and Reputation Settings

Anti-Malware and Reputation Settings

Web Reputation Services

Web Reputation Filtering: ☑ Enable Web Reputation Filtering

Adaptive Scanning: ☑ Enable Adaptive Scanning
Adaptive Scanning improves efficacy by identifying high-risk content and automatically selecting the best combination of available anti-malware services. Content which is identified as known malware can be automatically blocked. Adaptive Scanning is only available when web reputation filtering is enabled.

Advanced Malware Protection Services

Advanced Malware Protection services require network communication to the cloud servers on ports 32137 (for File Reputation) and 443 (for File Analysis). Please see the Online Help for additional details.

File Reputation Filtering: ☐ Enable File Reputation Filtering

File Analysis: ☐ Enable File Analysis
File Types: ☐ Adobe Portable Document Format (PDF)
☐ Microsoft Office 2007+ (Open XML)
☐ Microsoft Office 97-2004 (OLE)
☐ Microsoft Windows / DOS Executable

Anti-Malware Scanning Services

DVS Engine Object Scanning Limits: Max. Object Size: 32 MB
For multiple scanning engines, object scanning settings are applied separately to each.

Sophos: ☑ Enable Sophos

McAfee: ☑ Enable McAfee
Heuristic Scanning: ☑ Enable Heuristic Scanning
Heuristic analysis increases security protection, but can result in false positives and decreased performance.

Webroot: ☑ Enable Webroot
Threat Risk Threshold: 90
valid range 51 through 100, recommended minimum 90

Cancel Submit

Figure 10-96 *Anti-Malware and Reputation Settings Screen*

You are redirected to the license agreement page, shown in Figure 10-97, where you must click Accept.

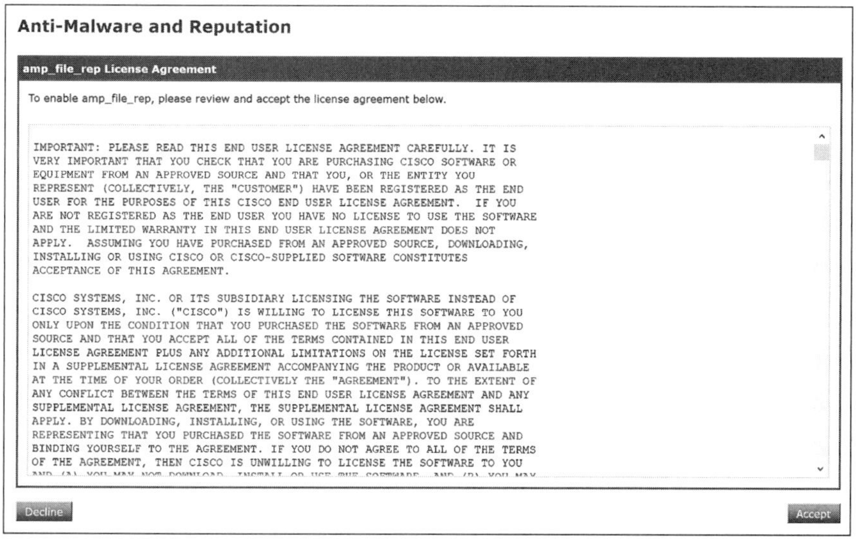

Anti-Malware and Reputation

amp_file_rep License Agreement

To enable amp_file_rep, please review and accept the license agreement below.

IMPORTANT: PLEASE READ THIS END USER LICENSE AGREEMENT CAREFULLY. IT IS VERY IMPORTANT THAT YOU CHECK THAT YOU ARE PURCHASING CISCO SOFTWARE OR EQUIPMENT FROM AN APPROVED SOURCE AND THAT YOU, OR THE ENTITY YOU REPRESENT (COLLECTIVELY, THE "CUSTOMER") HAVE BEEN REGISTERED AS THE END USER FOR THE PURPOSES OF THIS CISCO END USER LICENSE AGREEMENT. IF YOU ARE NOT REGISTERED AS THE END USER YOU HAVE NO LICENSE TO USE THE SOFTWARE AND THE LIMITED WARRANTY IN THIS END USER LICENSE AGREEMENT DOES NOT APPLY. ASSUMING YOU HAVE PURCHASED FROM AN APPROVED SOURCE, DOWNLOADING, INSTALLING OR USING CISCO OR CISCO-SUPPLIED SOFTWARE CONSTITUTES ACCEPTANCE OF THIS AGREEMENT.

CISCO SYSTEMS, INC. OR ITS SUBSIDIARY LICENSING THE SOFTWARE INSTEAD OF CISCO SYSTEMS, INC. ("CISCO") IS WILLING TO LICENSE THIS SOFTWARE TO YOU ONLY UPON THE CONDITION THAT YOU PURCHASED THE SOFTWARE FROM AN APPROVED SOURCE AND THAT YOU ACCEPT ALL OF THE TERMS CONTAINED IN THIS END USER LICENSE AGREEMENT PLUS ANY ADDITIONAL LIMITATIONS ON THE LICENSE SET FORTH IN A SUPPLEMENTAL LICENSE AGREEMENT ACCOMPANYING THE PRODUCT OR AVAILABLE AT THE TIME OF YOUR ORDER (COLLECTIVELY THE "AGREEMENT"). TO THE EXTENT OF ANY CONFLICT BETWEEN THE TERMS OF THIS END USER LICENSE AGREEMENT AND ANY SUPPLEMENTAL LICENSE AGREEMENT, THE SUPPLEMENTAL LICENSE AGREEMENT SHALL APPLY. BY DOWNLOADING, INSTALLING, OR USING THE SOFTWARE, YOU ARE REPRESENTING THAT YOU PURCHASED THE SOFTWARE FROM AN APPROVED SOURCE AND BINDING YOURSELF TO THE AGREEMENT. IF YOU DO NOT AGREE TO ALL OF THE TERMS OF THE AGREEMENT, THEN CISCO IS UNWILLING TO LICENSE THE SOFTWARE TO YOU

Decline Accept

Figure 10-97 *License Agreement Screen*

After you accept the license agreement for file reputation, the GUI redirects you to the main Anti-Malware and Reputation screen. You need to click Edit Global Settings again to go back and select the Enable File Analysis check box. When you enable the file analysis service, the GUI asks you to accept the license for that service, and after you click Accept, you are redirected to the main Anti-Malware and Reputation screen again.

You must click Edit Global Settings one more time if you want to change the file types that will be analyzed. There is also a small area for more advanced configuration, such as changing the cloud server to use for file reputation and which cloud (public or private) to send the file to for analysis. The reputation threshold is also configured here, and it defaults to using whatever threshold is being conveyed by the cloud. Normally you would leave these settings at their defaults.

Figure 10-98 shows the final file reputation and file analysis settings for WSA.

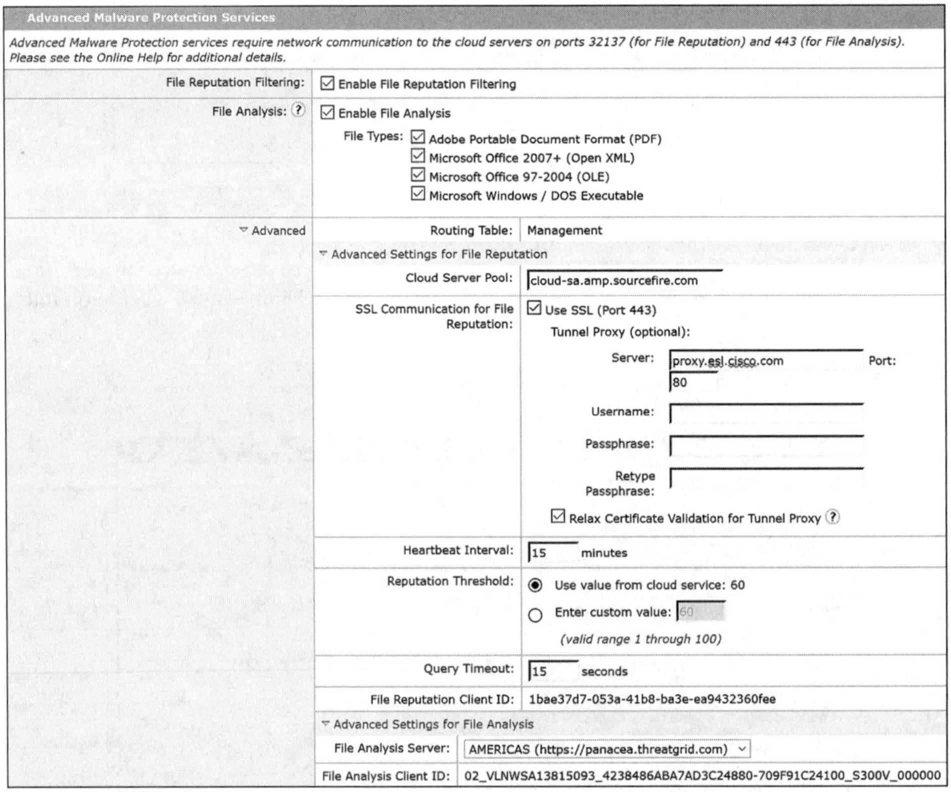

Figure 10-98 *Final AMP Settings*

Configuring the Email Security Appliance (ESA) Devices

Just like WSA, ESA has two feature keys: File Reputation and File Analysis. Figure 10-99 shows the feature keys for a Cisco ESA and points out the File Reputation and File Analysis feature keys, as well as the menu item for configuring AMP.

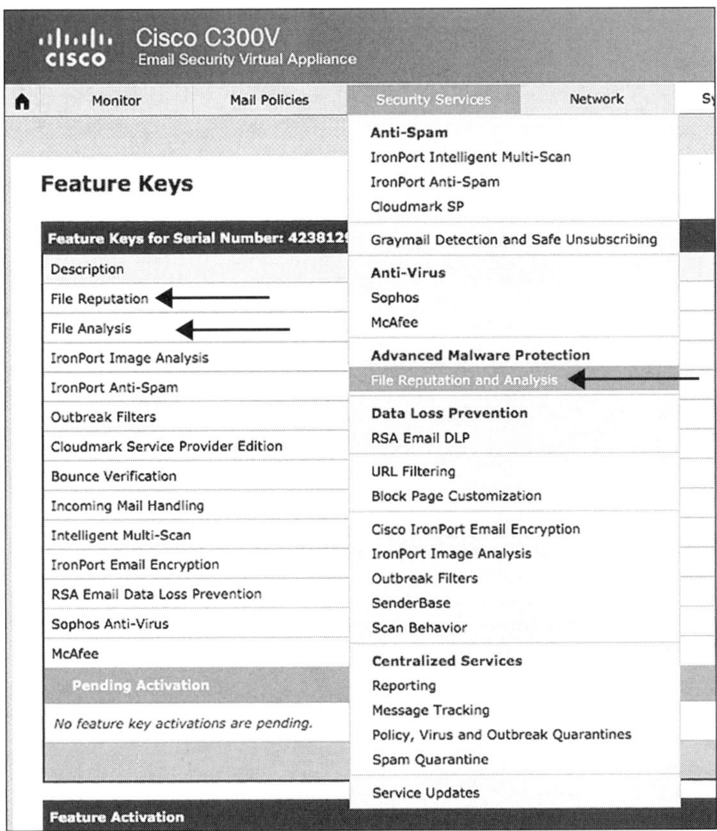

Figure 10-99 *ESA Feature Keys and Menu*

An ESA device must have the ability to reach the AMP cloud. Just like WSA, ESA refers to the AMP cloud as "File Reputation and Analysis Services." As you saw in Figure 10-99, you configure the AMP cloud settings under Security Services > File Reputation and Analysis. Initially, the service is disabled, as shown in Figure 10-100.

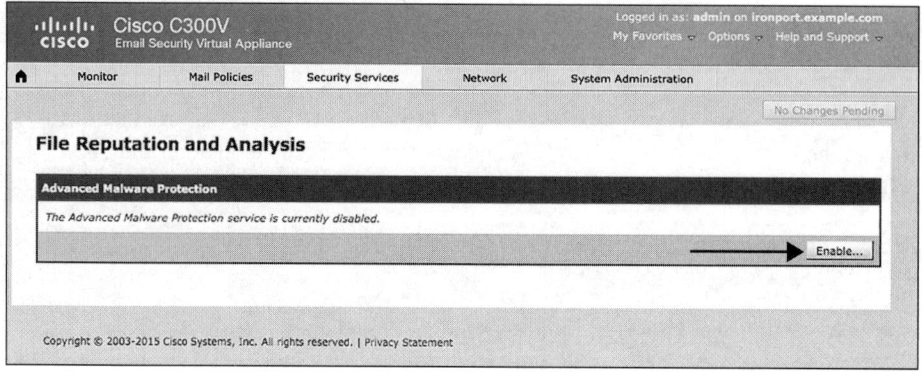

Figure 10-100 *Security Services > File Reputation and Analysis*

Configuring File Reputation and Analysis requires clicking the Enable button shown in Figure 10-100. You are then prompted to accept the license agreement, as shown in Figure 10-101.

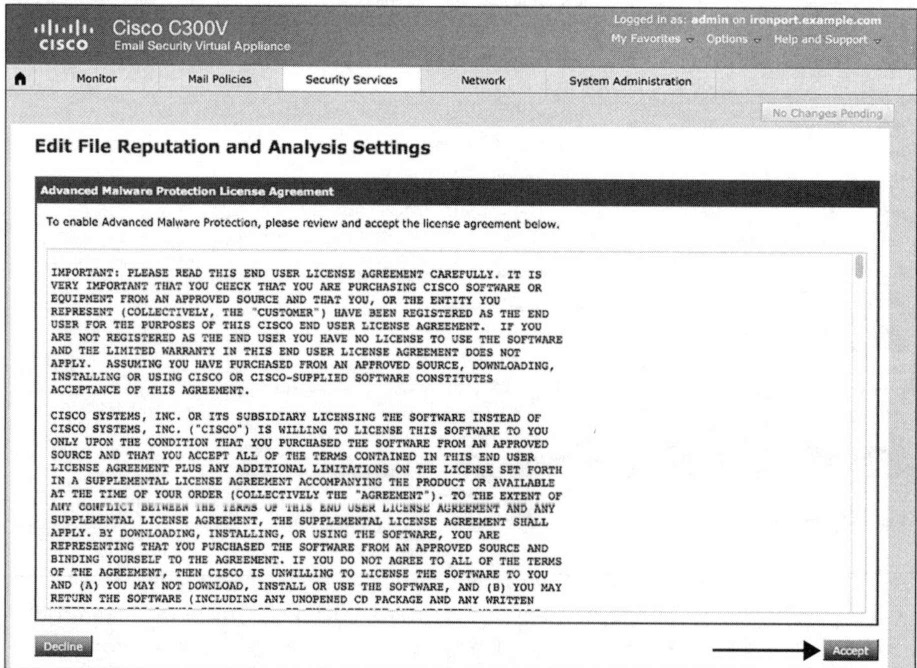

Figure 10-101 *Accepting the License Agreement*

After you accept the license agreement, the AMP service is enabled for both File Reputation and File Analysis, as shown in Figure 10-102.

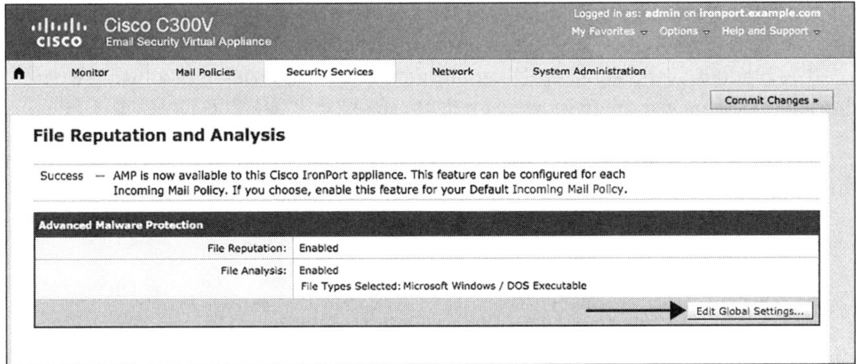

Figure 10-102 *AMP Services Enabled*

To configure the enabled services, click Edit Global Settings, and all the settings for AMP are displayed, as shown in Figure 10-103.

Cisco C300V
Email Security Virtual Appliance
Logged in as: admin on ironport.example.com
My Favorites Options Help and Support
Monitor | Mail Policies | Security Services | Network | System Administration
Commit Changes »

Edit File Reputation and Analysis Settings

Advanced Malware Protection

Advanced Malware Protection services require network communication to the cloud servers on ports 32137 or 443 (for File Reputation) and 443 (for File Analysis). Please see the Online Help for additional details.

File Reputation Filtering: Enable File Reputation
File Analysis: Enable File Analysis
File Types: Microsoft Windows / DOS Executable
Advanced Settings for File Reputation
Cloud Domain: a.immunet.com
Cloud Server Pool: cloud-sa.amp.sourcefire.com
SSL Communication for File Reputation: Use SSL (Port 443)
Tunnel Proxy (Optional):
Server: Port:
Username:
Password:
Retype Password:
Relax Certificate Validation for Tunnel Proxy
Heartbeat Interval: 15 minutes
Reputation Threshold: Use Value from Cloud Service (60)
Enter Custom Value: 60
(Valid range 1 through 100)
Query Timeout: 15 seconds
Processing Timeout: 120 seconds
File Reputation Client ID: e74c763f-540e-41ec-92f1-28bc2889d6e8
Advanced Settings for File Analysis
File Analysis Server URL: AMERICAS (https://panacea.threatgrid.com)
File Analysis Client ID: 01_4238129EC2F54929EF54-453C40E7AE02_C300V_00000000000000000000
Cancel
Submit

Figure 10-103 *AMP Settings*

There is also a small area for more advanced configuration, such as changing the cloud server to use for file reputation and which cloud (public or private) to send the file to for analysis. The reputation threshold is also configured here, and it defaults to using whatever threshold is being conveyed by the cloud. Normally you would leave these settings at their defaults.

As with all other configuration changes with content security appliances, you must click Commit Changes before the configuration take effect.

AMP Reports

A number of reports help you keep an eye on AMP-related activity. Figure 10-104 shows an example of an AMP report from ESA. Summaries are in the charts at the top, and the files identified as threats are listed at the bottom.

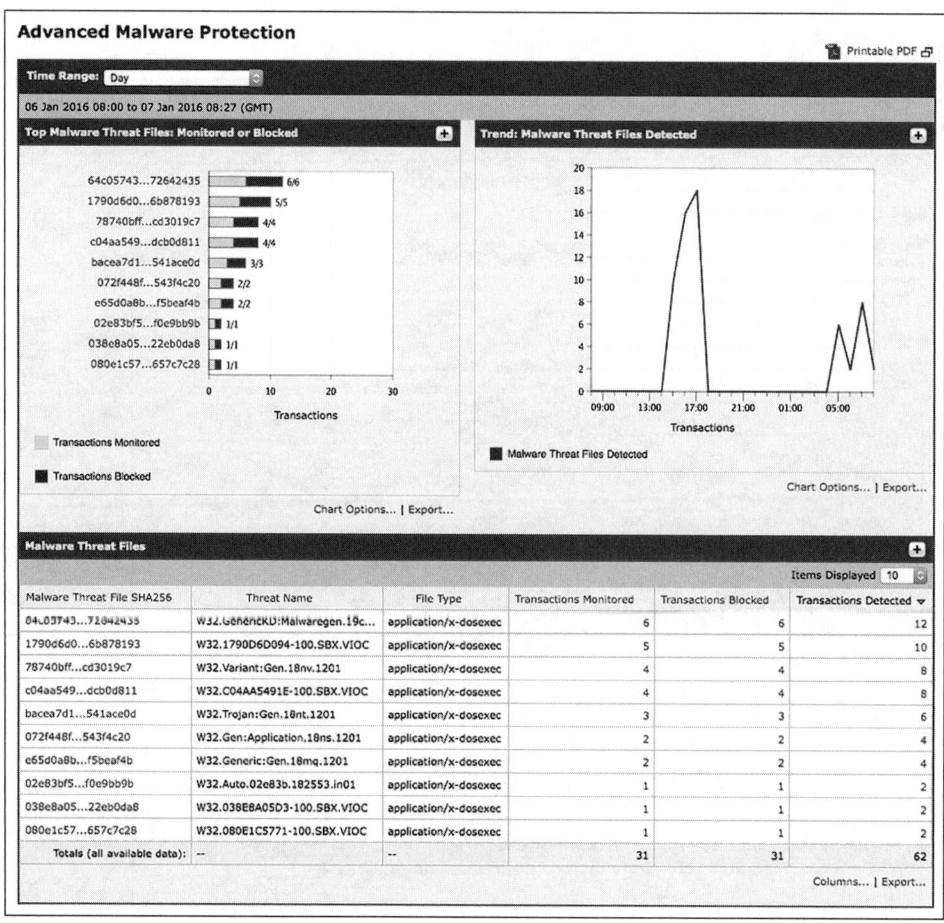

Figure 10-104 *AMP Report from ESA*

Figure 10-105 shows an example of an AMP report from ESA, called the File Analysis report. It allows you to search for a specific file hash at the top, and it shows the latest analysis in the middle and any pending files at the bottom.

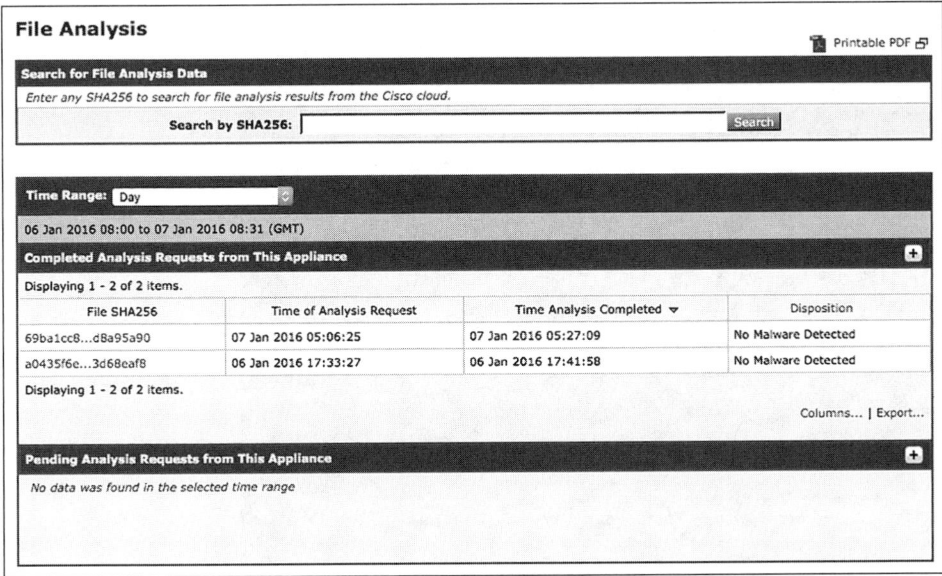

Figure 10-105 *AMP Report from WSA*

To determine whether a file was successfully sent to the cloud, you can use the File Analysis report. You can also use the **tail** CLI command and then select option 2, for the **amp_logs**, as shown in Figure 10-106.

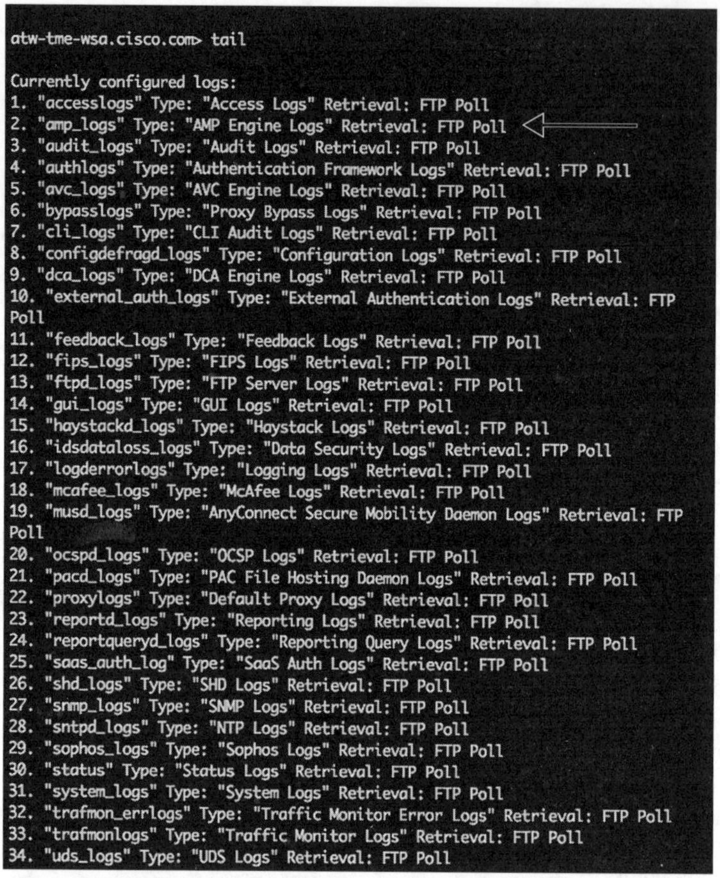

```
atw-tme-wsa.cisco.com> tail

Currently configured logs:
1. "accesslogs" Type: "Access Logs" Retrieval: FTP Poll
2. "amp_logs" Type: "AMP Engine Logs" Retrieval: FTP Poll
3. "audit_logs" Type: "Audit Logs" Retrieval: FTP Poll
4. "authlogs" Type: "Authentication Framework Logs" Retrieval: FTP Poll
5. "avc_logs" Type: "AVC Engine Logs" Retrieval: FTP Poll
6. "bypasslogs" Type: "Proxy Bypass Logs" Retrieval: FTP Poll
7. "cli_logs" Type: "CLI Audit Logs" Retrieval: FTP Poll
8. "configdefragd_logs" Type: "Configuration Logs" Retrieval: FTP Poll
9. "dca_logs" Type: "DCA Engine Logs" Retrieval: FTP Poll
10. "external_auth_logs" Type: "External Authentication Logs" Retrieval: FTP
Poll
11. "feedback_logs" Type: "Feedback Logs" Retrieval: FTP Poll
12. "fips_logs" Type: "FIPS Logs" Retrieval: FTP Poll
13. "ftpd_logs" Type: "FTP Server Logs" Retrieval: FTP Poll
14. "gui_logs" Type: "GUI Logs" Retrieval: FTP Poll
15. "haystackd_logs" Type: "Haystack Logs" Retrieval: FTP Poll
16. "idsdataloss_logs" Type: "Data Security Logs" Retrieval: FTP Poll
17. "logderrorlogs" Type: "Logging Logs" Retrieval: FTP Poll
18. "mcafee_logs" Type: "McAfee Logs" Retrieval: FTP Poll
19. "musd_logs" Type: "AnyConnect Secure Mobility Daemon Logs" Retrieval: FTP
Poll
20. "ocspd_logs" Type: "OCSP Logs" Retrieval: FTP Poll
21. "pacd_logs" Type: "PAC File Hosting Daemon Logs" Retrieval: FTP Poll
22. "proxylogs" Type: "Default Proxy Logs" Retrieval: FTP Poll
23. "reportd_logs" Type: "Reporting Logs" Retrieval: FTP Poll
24. "reportqueryd_logs" Type: "Reporting Query Logs" Retrieval: FTP Poll
25. "saas_auth_log" Type: "SaaS Auth Logs" Retrieval: FTP Poll
26. "shd_logs" Type: "SHD Logs" Retrieval: FTP Poll
27. "snmp_logs" Type: "SNMP Logs" Retrieval: FTP Poll
28. "sntpd_logs" Type: "NTP Logs" Retrieval: FTP Poll
29. "sophos_logs" Type: "Sophos Logs" Retrieval: FTP Poll
30. "status" Type: "Status Logs" Retrieval: FTP Poll
31. "system_logs" Type: "System Logs" Retrieval: FTP Poll
32. "trafmon_errlogs" Type: "Traffic Monitor Error Logs" Retrieval: FTP Poll
33. "trafmonlogs" Type: "Traffic Monitor Logs" Retrieval: FTP Poll
34. "uds_logs" Type: "UDS Logs" Retrieval: FTP Poll
```

Figure 10-106 *tail amp_logs*

Summary

In this chapter, you have learned all about the role of the AMP cloud for performing file disposition checks. You have examined the intelligence that feeds the AMP cloud and how AMP looks at security, using a prevention framework and a retrospection framework. You learned about the differences between public and private clouds and completed an installation of a private cloud instance.

Index

Symbols

Numbers

A

B

C

D

F

I

K

L

M

N

O

P

Q

R

S

T

U

V

W-X-Y

Z